A Buddhist Kaleidoscope:
Essays on the Lotus Sutra

A Buddhist Kaleidoscope: Essays on the Lotus Sutra

edited by
Gene Reeves

with a foreword by
Nichiko Niwano

KOSEI PUBLISHING CO. • *Tokyo*

The publication of this book was made possible by a grant from the Chūō Academic Research Institute, affiliated with Risshō Kōsei-kai, to commemorate the thirtieth anniversary of the founding of the institute.

Cover design by NOBU. The text of this book is set in a computer version of Palatino with a computer version of Optima for display.

First English edition, 2002

Published by Kōsei Publishing Co., 2-7-1 Wada, Suginami-ku, Tokyo 166-8535, Japan. Copyright © 2002 by Kōsei Publishing Co.; all rights reserved. Printed in Japan. ISBN 4-333-01918-4

Contents

Foreword

It is a great pleasure to introduce this volume of selected essays first presented by their authors at the International Conferences on the Lotus Sutra sponsored by Risshō Kōsei-kai.

These conferences originated from an idea proposed by Dr. Gene Reeves, former head of the Meadville/Lombard Theological School affiliated with the University of Chicago, who has long been fascinated by the Lotus Sutra. They have been organized by Dr. Reeves and Dr. Michio Shinozaki, until recently dean of Risshō Kōsei-kai's Gakurin Seminary. Rev. Nikkyō Niwano, the late founder of Risshō Kōsei-kai, dedicated his every effort to securing world peace through interreligious cooperation. He was firmly convinced that the wishes of the gods and the Buddha for human salvation were at root alike so that people of different religions would be able to open their hearts to one another and speak together frankly and with tolerance about what they believed.

Around 1980, he and the late Professor Yoshirō Tamura became increasingly aware that the Great Vehicle teachings of the Lotus Sutra were much less well-known in the West in comparison with such other strains of Buddhism as Zen, Tibetan, and Pali. With that in mind, it was proposed that interest in and understanding of the sutra could be deepened by inviting to Japan those among leading theologians and Buddhist scholars who were concerned with Buddhist-Christian dialogue.

Subsequently it was suggested that it would be a good idea if Risshō Kōsei-kai were to invite the North American Theological Encounter Group, which for many years was known to be interested in such dialogue, to discuss the possibility of conducting research on the subject of the Lotus Sutra. A study meeting by the group was held in Hawaii in 1980, organized by Professor Masao Abe, formerly of Kyoto University, and Professor John B. Cobb, Jr., of the School of Theology at Claremont, California. Entirely by coincidence, it happened that it became known after the study meeting had started that it had received financial support from the Niwano Peace Foundation, which is affiliated with Risshō Kōsei-kai.

The first International Conference on the Lotus Sutra was held in 1994. Annual conferences have been held since then and I am grateful to all who have participated in them. I have been able to meet and speak with many of them following the conferences and have been heartened by the challenging views and questions they have expressed. These have helped to cast fresh new light on our understanding of the Lotus Sutra.

As many readers will know, Risshō Kōsei-kai is based on the teachings of the Threefold Lotus Sutra. The encounter with the sutra by the founder, who passed away in 1999, confirmed for him the true Dharma of Śākyamuni Buddha. The sutra teaches of the One Vehicle by which all living beings are equally assured of attaining buddhahood. This is achieved through bodhisattva practice, creating the ideal world in which the lives of all are sustained by the help they provide each other.

The life of the bodhisattva has been compared to the lotus plant, which produces a blossom of exquisite beauty even though its roots are sunk in mud. The bodhisattvas, described by the Lotus Sutra as springing out of the earth, have been entrusted by the Buddha with the mission of extending the Great Dharma of truth and purity to all within this *sahā* world, the realm of actual suffering. They share the sufferings of people and sympathize with their pain, accepting the problems of the world as their own as they persevere in their practice. These nameless bodhisattvas are ourselves.

The law of transience that the Buddha taught applies to all living beings. The process of constant change is unending within the great life-force of which we are all a part. To recognize the law of transience is to become truly aware of the eternal life-force. To awaken to the truth of the One Vehicle also is to become aware that all things are interdependent and are sustained by this great eternal life-force. That is our faith, and it is our deepest wish that the Dharma and this wisdom will spread throughout the world.

I earnestly hope and pray that these selected essays originating from the Lotus Sutra conferences will provide the opportunity to acknowledge the profound significance of the sutra and that they will serve to encourage further research into its history and contents.

Nichikō Niwano
President, Risshō Kōsei-kai

Introduction

Gene Reeves

In July of 1994 a series of small international conferences was initiated at Risshō Kōsei-kai's Bandai-sō retreat facility on Mount Bandai, overlooking Lake Inawashiro in northeastern Japan. The first of these conferences, whose success led to their becoming a series, was actually the last of a series of meetings of the North American Theological Encounter group, which had been started earlier by Masao Abe and John Cobb, and continues to this day in a somewhat different form. Except for the first, which had a somewhat different format, all of the Bandai-sō conferences held to date have involved about fourteen invited participants meeting for about three days in a relaxed atmosphere. Since papers were written and distributed prior to the conference, conference time was devoted to discussion of issues raised or suggested by the papers.

The main purpose of these conferences has been to advance understanding of the Lotus Sutra among scholars teaching Buddhism or interacting with Buddhism in some other way. Thus, from the beginning, not only Buddhist scholars but Christian theologians and others have participated as well. My hope was, and is, that the Lotus Sutra would become as much a part of what one means by "Buddhism" in the West as it has in East Asia. At the same time, I thought it would be worthwhile for scholars who were not already familiar with it to be introduced, at least in a very cursory way, to Risshō Kōsei-kai, which is certainly one of the most successful of modern Buddhist organizations, and one which understands itself to be based on the teachings of the Lotus Sutra. It too, I believe, should be part of our frame of reference when we think and speak of "Buddhism" today.

Each of the conferences has had a different theme, and participants have been free to contribute to the conversation as they saw fit, occasionally by avoiding the designated theme altogether! For these reasons, contributions to the conferences, though more or less focused on the Lotus Sutra, have been quite diverse, diverse both with respect to subject matter and diverse with respect to approach. The essays in this book, for the most part selected from conference papers, are, therefore, truly a kaleidoscope, reflecting a good bit of that diversity. Some are primarily theological, some historical, some quite general, some focused more narrowly, some more scholarly, some written for a more general audience. Perhaps due to our choice of themes for the conferences, which was also I think a reflection of the concerns found in the sutra itself, a substantial number of these contributions are concerned with ethics and with social ethics.

Thus there is nothing necessary about the order in which these essays appear in this book. There is a certain progression, from more general concerns to historical concerns to contemporary concerns about ethics and society. But often even the more introductory or historical pieces at least point to, and sometimes are directed toward, contemporary concerns. This means that this book could just as well be read from back to front, from the last essay to the first, or in any other order which suits the interests of a reader. A kaleidoscope, after all, does not have a fixed pattern. For that reason, each essay has been kept as an independent unit, resulting in some repetition. A reader will, for example, be told the dates of Nichiren many times.

Most of the papers included in this volume have previously appeared in Risshō Kōsei-kai's magazine *Dharma World*, sometimes in an earlier guise. A few others have previously appeared in other publications, and that too is indicated in the publication data at the end of the book. Three of the papers included in this volume appeared earlier in *Dharma World* but were not written for one of the conferences. Since we were assembling here a diverse set of writings about the Lotus Sutra, most of which had been published in *Dharma World*, it seemed appropriate, in the interest of making them available to a wider range of readers, to include a few other articles from *Dharma World* even though they had no direct connection with the conferences.

Some of these essays have been written primarily for other Buddhist scholars, others are more popular in intent. From some points of view this will give a certain unevenness to the volume. My hope is that readers will appreciate the fact that the essays were not originally intended as parts of an integrated book, and find the resulting diversity to be an enriching reflection of their origins.

The Lotus Sutra is a large book, one which includes a diversity of literary forms, teachings, foci, and suggestions for interpretation. In this volume an additional kind of diversity will be apparent. I have not attempted to enforce uniform use of translated terms related to the Lotus Sutra, Buddhism, Japanese history and culture, and so on. That is not only because the English translations of the Lotus Sutra, the main source from which the authors quote, differ among themselves, but also because use of these translated terms varies according to the thinking and preferences of individual authors.

Use of diacritical marks for all Indic and Japanese words has, however, been standardized, except for terms, such as Buddha, dharma, bodhisattva, Mahayana, nirvana, and stupa, which have come into wide use in English. The following is a rough approximation of pronunciation: The long *ā* is pronounced like a in car; *ī* is pronounced like the e in me; *ū* is like oo in tool; and the *ō* sounds like the o in horn. For *ē*, the e in end should be prolonged. The letters *ś* and *ṣ* are like the English sh, *ñ* like nya, and *ṛ* like ri. The consonants *ḍ, ṃ, ṇ, ṅ,* and *ṭ* are not significantly different from the same letters without the diacritical marks.

Risshō Kōsei-kai was founded in 1938 by Nikkyō Niwano and Myōkō Naganuma. Naganuma died in 1957, Niwano on October 4, 1999, as this book was being planned. On November 15, he would have turned 93. Niwano did not have much of a formal education and spent his early adult years in the extremely turbulent times preceding and during the Second World War. Yet he displayed not only a kind of organizational genius, aesthetic skills, and an enormously charismatic personality, he was also a self-trained scholar who read very widely and wrote a very large number of books, several of which are quite scholarly. When I first met Niwano at the University of Chicago in 1983, the thing that impressed me most about him was his deep respect for scholarship, as reflected in his own extensive knowledge of Buddhist history and thought. It seemed fitting, therefore, that a sample of his work, previously published in *Dharma World,* begin this volume. The first chapter is, then, a translation of the first four sections of Niwano's ten-volume commentary on the Lotus Sutra, which is gradually being published in English in *Dharma World* but is not yet available in translation as a book.

While Niwano's commentary is scholarly in many ways, it also prominently displays his religious understanding of the Lotus Sutra centered on universal buddha-nature and the universal or "Original" Buddha. The pages included here constitute a very brief survey of the history of Buddhism and the Lotus Sutra in India, China and, especially, Japan. After describing the relation of the Lotus Sutra to the Sutra of Innumerable Meanings and the Sutra of Meditation on the Bodhisattva Universal Virtue and the traditional distinction between the Law of Appearance and the Law of Origin, Niwano discusses the origins of Mahayana Buddhism in the First and Second Councils and the legendary split of Buddhism into Hinayana and Mahayana divisions, the composition of the Lotus Sutra as a Mahayana text and its spread throughout India and transmission to China, especially its translation into Chinese by Kumārajīva, its interpretation by Chih-i, the sixth-century founder of T'ien-t'ai Buddhism, and its subsequent propagation by Tan-jan. Niwano provides more extensive coverage of the Lotus Sutra's influence on virtually all of the main figures in the history of Buddhism in Japan, along the way making some interesting doctrinal claims, such as the identity of the "Eternal Original Buddha" of the Lotus Sutra with Amida Buddha of Pure Land Buddhism, along with the idea that the spirit of the Lotus Sutra is the core of *nembutsu* practice. Niwano displays an exceptionally generous interpretation of the Lotus Sutra, an interpretation which has made it possible for Risshō Kōsei-kai to have a very positive and active approach to interfaith cooperation.

Niwano's historical introduction is followed by four other essays, each of which introduces the Lotus Sutra in different ways. The first is a very brief piece by Paul Swanson pointing to the "multiple meanings" of the Lotus Sutra, the variety of ways in which it has and can be understood, for the Lotus Sutra is not merely a set of characters on pages but also the Buddha Dharma itself. In the sutra's emphasis on the potential buddhahood, the potential goodness of all things, we might find, Swanson claims, an approach to contemporary issues such as the environmental crisis.

David Chappell attempts to show how the use of language, of diverse images, of a variety of heroic figures, etc. helps the reader to see it as a religious text, encouraging us to listen to it for growth, enabling us to grow into something beautiful for ourselves and for others. He emphasizes the interpersonal nature of the sutra, especially the ways in which its images and stories have an inclusive appeal, eliciting a different sermon for all who hear it, as its meaning and efficacy depend on the appropriation by the hearer. He stresses that the sutra expresses "organic" truth, a truth which is interactive and "dialogical."

Taitetsu Unno emphasizes the importance of "somatic realization," embodying the Lotus Sutra in everyday life, in the way in which one conducts one's life. He shows how such an emphasis is not only in the Lotus Sutra itself, but can also be found prominently in the thought and life of Kenji Miyazawa. Willa Jane Tanabe also stresses the somatic nature of the sutra, exploring associations expressed in Buddhist art between the Lotus Sutra, stupas, relics, and especially the body of the Buddha.

The next four essays are both theological and dialogical, reflecting the fact that many participants in the Lotus Sutra conferences have been Christian theologians, principally of course theologians interested in interfaith dialogue. John Berthrong, who is a Confucian scholar as well as a theologian, reflects on what it means for scholars to find themselves "in a situation of multiple religious participation," insisting that learning from other traditions need not mean giving up participating in depth in one's own tradition nor an irresponsible relativism in which commitment to the search for truth is abandoned. Berthrong uses insights from the Neo-Confucian philosophy of Chu Hsi for comparing the parable of the magic city in the Lotus Sutra with the Book of Revelation in the Bible.

Schubert Ogden's theological reflection is on the question: "How is it possible to affirm the validity of one's own religious tradition as a Christian while allowing for the possible validity of the other's religious tradition as well?" His conclusion is that this is possible only if Christians have an understanding of Christ as representing, rather than constituting, the truth about reality, much like the Lotus Sutra's understanding of Śākyamuni Buddha as representing a truth already present in every living being.

Michael Fuss attempts to show that it is in mission, known in the Lotus Sutra as *upāya*, that Buddhism and Christianity have common ground. Just as missionary activity continues the incarnation of Christ, *upāya* is the "self-expression of the Dharma in its universal compassion." Mission and *upāya* are "as gifts flowing freely from the dynamism of the ultimate Reality."

Malcolm David Eckel seeks to imaginatively place himself "in the situation of the 'preacher,' or *dharma-bhāṇaka*," in chapter 10 of the Lotus Sutra. He calls attention to the importance of words in both Christianity and the Lotus Sutra, particularly to the emotional power invested in words by this sutra. It says, for example, that any bodhisattva who hears a single stanza or word of this sutra and rejoices in it with a single thought will achieve supreme enlightenment. He explores some ways in which, in both traditions, words are food, both given and received, there is emphasis on unity in the face on diversity, and transformative power is embedded in images and metaphor. His is an exploration, informed naturally by Christian sensibility, of the meanings and power of grace and faith embedded in the Lotus Sutra, and therefore in the preacher/teacher of the Lotus Sutra.

These more theological essays are followed by a set which might broadly be termed "philosophical," reflections on various aspects of the teachings of the Lotus Sutra. John Mayer attempts to show how the Lotus Sutra provides a way of overcoming many of the debates and divisions which characterize contemporary Western philosophy. The sutra, for example, lets us understand "plurality and diversity through the parable of the herbs," but behind the diversity of meanings and realities is the ultimate reality of the buddha-nature. But the buddha-nature is nothing but the practice of compassion and "Buddhahood . . . is the continuous and temporal praxis of compassion."

Both J. Douglas Wolfe and Michael Pye are concerned about the understanding of time in the Lotus Sutra. Wolfe believes that the structure of the universe presented in chapter 16 of the Lotus Sutra "bears an uncanny resemblance to the modern scientific view." There, Śākyamuni Buddha "speaks of time and space as equivalent and inseparable values in calculations on the cosmic scale," in some sense prefiguring the views of Albert Einstein. Since the idea of the immeasurable life of the Buddha arose early in the devotional history of Mahayana Buddhism, Pye looks at the functions of "immeasurability" in a number of Mahayana sutras and finds that this term functions primarily to indicate being empty of characteristics. It "is part of a general discourse which seeks to indicate the ineffability of the true nature of things by disrupting conventional terminology." Thus, the so-called "eternal" Buddha of the Lotus Sutra is not eternal in the conventional and ontological Western sense, though some Asian Buddhists may take it that way. Rather the idea functions to help people overcome their ordinary ways of conceiving and thinking.

In "The Lotus Sutra as Radically World-affirming," I attempt to systematically examine the stories of supernatural events in the Lotus Sutra in order to show that its use of cosmology is not at all to offer a scientific or rational description of the cosmos but rather to enhance the stature of the interconnected realities of Śākyamuni Buddha, the Lotus Sutra itself, and this world, this *sahā* world in which suffering has to be endured. A prime purpose of the Lotus Sutra, I claim, is encouraging people to the bodhisattva practice of helping the living in this world. An important part of the strategy for accomplishing that is to firmly associate this world with the Buddha, and with the Buddha who preaches the Lotus Sutra, Śākyamuni.

The next set of essays are primarily historical studies. Jamie Hubbard's contribution is a close analysis of two contrasting senses of time found in the tradition and in the Lotus Sutra. One sees time as a cycle of cosmically recurring series of events; the other as linear and historical. Hubbard shows that a linear sense of time is intimately connected in the Lotus Sutra, not with the disappearance of the dharma, but with the importance of preaching and hearing the dharma, especially in such a period. Here the primary use of the "decline motif" is for the preacher of the sutra to preserve and spread its message. And this became a more pressing matter for those such as Nichiren who took the decline of the dharma to be primarily an exhortation to spread the Lotus Sutra, an activity to which Nichiren devoted his entire life. But for Nichiren the imperative to the bodhisattva to preach the true dharma in the latter age had social and political dimensions as well as religious ones. And this way of understanding the sutra would lead to Nichiren-based movements in the twentieth century being involved in social activism and international peace activities.

Hubbard's essay is followed by Lucia Dolce's extended study of the quite different treatment of the relation between the historical Śākyamuni Buddha and the universal Śākyamuni Buddha found in the thought of T'ien-t'ai Chih-i on the one hand and Nichiren on the other, the former making use of a threefold Buddha theory which allows for the existence of many buddhas, the latter having a theory in which all buddhas are reduced to Śākyamuni Buddha as the one true Buddha. This enabled Nichiren to understand this *sahā* world as the original Buddha land and the only possible paradise. For Nichiren, buddhahood "becomes a reality *of* history, not just *in* history," and this gives a powerful social dimension to Nichiren Buddhism.

Though it is not the central focus of her paper, Susan Mattis presents a thesis similar to John Mayer's, claiming that Chih-i's view of the phenomenal world, as dependent on a linguistic-conceptual system but not solely determined by it, suggests a middle ground that may avoid the weaknesses of the two extreme views that have dominated Western philosophy. The central concern of the paper is an attempt to clarify Chih-i's understanding of ultimate truth based on the Lotus Sutra by establishing the extent to which his understanding diverges from the conception of ultimate truth which Nāgārjuna derived from the Prajñāpāramitā-sūtras. What she shows is that, while both Nāgārjuna and Chih-i affirm that there is no distinction between the realm of ultimate truth and the realm of dependent origination, Chih-i, identifying the Buddha of the Lotus Sutra as the buddha-nature inherent in all things, affirms the reality of things as dependent existents. Whereas for Nāgārjuna, "emptiness" ultimately indicates the absence of a ground of cognition independent of the sociolinguistic system, for Chih-i, "emptiness" indicates the true nature of phenomenal existents which arise interdependently. This identity of ultimate truth and conventional reality is for Chih-i a central teaching of the Lotus Sutra. In contrast with the emphasis on the illusory nature of the phenomenal realm in the Prajñāpāramitā-sūtras, the Lotus Sutra celebrates the reality of the conventonal world with a profusion of concrete images.

Jacqueline Stone focuses on the social dimensions of the teachings of Nichiren, showing in considerable detail how Nichiren's exclusive faith in the Lotus Sutra, his idea that faith in the Lotus is the only path by which the present world could be transfigured as the Buddha-land, led him to affirm the precedence of Lotus Sutra faith over filial piety, loyalty to one's social superiors, and obedience to national rulers. Thus Nichiren "opened a ground for resistance to conventional social authority," which, while not a rejection of social and political authority, nevertheless did enable both Nichiren himself and the tradition which he founded to have a religious basis for criticizing and resisting social and political authorities at least at times, something relatively rare in the history of Buddhism but similar in important respects to contemporary efforts to establish a "socially engaged" Buddhism.

If Chih-i and Nichiren are the two most outstanding interpreters of the Lotus Sutra in more distant history, perhaps it can be said that the foremost interpreter of the Lotus Sutra in modern times is the poet, storyteller and scientist Kenji Miyazawa, one who interpreted the Lotus Sutra not in scholarly commentaries but in his life and work and is known by virtually everyone in Japan. Much of his short life was devoted to helping poor farmers, resulting in his being known as "Kenji *bosatsu*" for embodying the teachings of the Lotus Sutra in his life. Miyazawa's life and work are the focus of Steve Odin's contribution, especially their connection with the Lotus Sutra and Tendai and Nichiren teachings. Odin surveys several of Miyazawa's poems and stories to show the decisive influence on his life of the Lotus Sutra. He shows how, among other things, Miyazawa's theme of oneness with nature reflects the concept of nature found in the Lotus Sutra and in Tendai and Nichiren Buddhism, particularly the doctrine of "*eshō funi* or 'oneness of life and its environment,' which is itself an aspect of the more generic principle of *ichinen sanzen*—three thousand worlds in each thought-instant." Miyazawa's *Night of the Galactic Railway*, a standard fantasy tale read in Japanese elementary schools, said to be the first science fiction tale in modern Japanese literature, was turned into a popular animated film and used in various *manga* comic books. It is especially revealing of Miyazawa's understanding of Nichiren's mandala, with the title of the Lotus Sutra inscribed on it, as a vehicle for connecting readers to the reality of "fourth-dimensional space," the imaginative world of fantasy and therefore spiritual world, just as Nichiren understood it to reveal the unity of the individual and the universe.

Finally, Alexander Ignatovich discusses Leo Tolstoy's interest in Buddhism. Though there is no evidence that Tolstoy ever read any of the Lotus Sutra, Ignatovich suggests some areas of fruitful comparison of Tolstoys's ideas and those in the sutra, especially the theme in the Lotus Sutra of the presence of the buddha-nature in all living beings and Tolstoy's belief that "God's Kingdom is within you."

The next four essays have to do with the relation of Buddhism and society in the Lotus Sutra. Ruben Habito considers the place of the Lotus

Sutra in the development of Buddha-body theory, surveying its main lines of development and showing how ideas of the Buddha in the Lotus Sutra contributed to that development, and are connected with ethical practice. Much of what is taught about the Buddha in the Lotus Sutra is not unique to it, but "what makes the Lotus Sutra stand out . . . is the way it weaves these various elements to present a grand and compelling picture of the continuing dynamic activity of the Buddha, in a way that invites the devoted reader of the sutra to enter into this very activity itself, as one's response to the reading of the sutra." The Lotus Sutra, Habito shows, played a significant role in the development of Buddha-body theory by connecting the notion of the Buddha of immeasurable life with the notion of skillful means, portraying the Buddha's life as a dynamic, ceaseless, and compassionate activity, by presenting the different buddhas of the universe as emanations of the one Śākyamuni, thus paving the way for further speculation on the *saṃbhogakāya*, presenting it not only as enjoying the fruits of enlightenment but also as activity for the benefit of others, and by continuing a tradition of identifying the Buddha with the Dharma, implicitly affirming use of the notion of *dharma-kāya*. Just as the Lotus Sutra is integrative in many other ways, the practice it advocates is one which overcomes the separation of self-benefit and other-benefit. What one does for others brings benefit to oneself, and the benefit one receives from such activity benefits others. It is a realization of the fruit of enlightenment. Thus, the Lotus Sutra "grounds a kind of praxis that can be characterized in contemporary terms as a socially engaged Buddhism."

Masahiro Shimoda seeks to explain why the Lotus Sutra has been an inspiration for social movements in Japan. The central idea here is that, as shown especially in the two Mahāparinirvāṇa-sūtras, the Buddha was regarded as eternal or transhistorical from the beginnings of Buddhism. The Lotus Sutra merely reopens or presents anew the history of Buddhism by presenting Śākyamuni Buddha as both a historical and a history-transcending reality. The Buddha was, of course, closely related to truth, to the dharma. It is the dharma attained by the Buddha which distinguishes him from others. But the dharma which is beyond history has to be substantianted or embodied in history. Thus the Lotus Sutra superimposes the historical reality of Śākyamuni Buddha onto a concept of the Buddha as eternal. While in ancient India, given Buddhism's social location in the renunciation of family and worldly life, there was little interest among Buddhists in social life, in Japan the Lotus Sutra has repeatedly been given a social dimension. Social movements based on the Lotus Sutra have been rooted in the fundamental idea of the sutra that "the truth in the form of [the] Buddha's words should be repeatedly brought into the present situation by a preacher by skillful means," and proponents of the sutra have sought the origin of the truth by reciting the sutra and then returned to present historical reality by involving themselves in some kind of social movement.

Riccardo Venturini's brief essay is focused on the Lotus Sutra's emphasis on bodhisattva practice, calling attention to what he regards as contemporary examples of "collective bodhisattvas," understood not merely as a spiritual force but as a basis for social movements. And, like Odin, Venturini connects bodhisattva practice with the Tendai doctrine of *ichinen sanzen*, as such practice reflects the way in which a fragment of reality is also a totality, making this world of misery and conflict also the "tranquil realm of the Buddha."

Harold Kasimow, also emphasizing the place of the bodhisattva in its teachings, sees the Lotus Sutra as "A Buddhist Path to Mending the World." He takes issue with understandings of Buddhism found in writings of R. C. Zaehner, and more recently in statements of Pope John Paul II, for seeing Buddhism as negative, pessimistic, and unconcerned with social transformation. Kasimow holds that the Lotus Sutra is a call to both personal and social change. Its teaching that all human beings have a buddha-nature leads to its teaching that bodhisattvas vow to save all human beings, not separating their own individual enlightenment from that of others.

The next three essays are concerned with the ethics of the Lotus Sutra. Peggy Morgan considers the ethics of the sutra from a variety of angles, including that of being Christian and that of being a woman. The discussion is focused on three ethical issues: the validity of factual claims, the morality of skillful means, and the place of women in Buddhism. The relation of stories to factual claims is an ethical issue in the sense that "If people have been and are being told that this sutra was preached on the Vulture's Peak during his lifetime by the Buddha Śākyamuni and they then find out that there is good reason for questioning that this is historically the case, there might well follow a crisis of confidence in the integrity of the whole tradition. . . ." Morgan concludes that Mahayana sutras such as the Lotus avoid this problem by setting a scene in which the Buddha is still present, so the origins of a sutra are not restricted to the time of the historical Śākyamuni. Against charges that skillful means is overly permissive, Morgan claims that such a problem does not arise because this kind of ethic is available only to great bodhisattvas and buddhas, implicitly denying the claims of several other contributors to this volume who see skillful means as an ethical tool for all. Morgan also considers the question of Buddhism and women in the Lotus Sutra, including not only the story of the Nāga princess and referring to Miriam Levering's discussion of Prajāpatī and Yaśodharā, but also seeing the Kannon of chapter 25, where seven of the thirty-three forms of Kannon are female, as affirming that "enlightened nature belongs to women as well as men."

Damien Keown develops the thesis that the Lotus Sutra, to the degree that it has any ethics at all, is paternalistic. The text, he claims, does not deny the use of falsehood, but teaches that falsehood is justifiable. And the justification is always paternalistic—some person of greater wisdom and with good motive knows what should be done. Making use of a distinction between "strong" and "weak" paternalism, in which weak paternalism limits the right to intervene to cases where conduct is either substantially nonvoluntary or temporary intervention is necessary to establish whether it is fully voluntary, while strong paternalism insists that autonomy may be overridden even when the individual is competent and has made informed and voluntary choices, Keown concludes that the paternalism of the Lotus Sutra is of the "weak" variety. But the sutra is not, Keown claims, much concerned with ethics at all. The idea of skillful means, though it may be stretched into a teaching about the practice of bodhisattvas, which it becomes in the Vimalakīrti Sutra, has to do in the Lotus Sutra mainly with communicating the Dharma. The significance of the Lotus Sutra, accordingly, lies not in an ethical theory, but in "its bold claim that all teachings are provisional and ultimately to be dismantled."

In contrast with Keown, I try to show how, even in the Lotus Sutra, the idea of skillful means provides a kind of utilitarian ethics in which the consequences of acts are the most important determinant of their ethical merit. The teaching of skillful means, as an ethical doctrine, has as its central tenet the idea that one should not do what is expedient but rather what is good, the good being what will actually help someone else, what is, therefore, most appropriate. Skillful means are used primordially by the Buddhas and bodhisattvas, but in the Lotus Sutra, everyone is to some degree a Buddha and a bodhisattva, thus making the practice of skillful means relevant to all. The resulting ethics can be termed "bodhisattva practice" or "the bodhisattva-way," a way of using intelligence and compassion to determine fallibly what is appropriate in any given situation. In the Lotus Sutra, the notion of skillful means is both a description of what Buddhism is, or what Buddhist practice primarily is, and a prescription for what our lives should become. The Lotus Sutra, accordingly, is a prescription of a medicine or religious method for us—and, therefore, at once both extremely imaginative and extremely practical.

The final four essays are focused on more particular ethical issues:

Michio Shinozaki on the environmental crisis, Robert Florida on health care, and Lucinda Peach and Miriam Levering on gender issues.

In a sense making use of Hubbard's distinction between cyclical and linear views of time, Shinozaki wants to show that it is only by having a linear sense of time, in which history is important, in which human beings are not only part of nature but able to transcend their situation and transform it, that Buddhists can even approach contemporary environmental ethics. Like others in this book, it is in Nichiren, in Nichiren's "historical crisis consciousness" as shown especially in his idea of *mappō* and his use of five hermeneutical categories for determining ways of disseminating the teachings in the Lotus Sutra, that Shinozaki finds the most important Buddhist precedent for taking time and history seriously.

Robert Florida reviews the literature on Buddhist ethics and finds paternalism prevalent both generally and in the Lotus Sutra. While support can be found in such traditional social teachings for providing adequate health care for all people, an egalitarian sense of justice is not found in Buddhist traditional thought. Perhaps, Florida thinks, a Buddhist case for equitable distribution of health services could be built on Buddhist notions of compassion, friendship, and the the *noblesse oblige* expected of the ideal Buddhist monarch, all of which seem to be consistent with the teachings of the Lotus Sutra. The Lotus Sutra can be interpreted as no less than an extended sermon on how to live the bodhisattva path by using skillful means compassionately, thus embodying the four sublime states of "loving kindness for all sentient beings, compassion for the unhappiness of others, sympathetic joy for the happiness and good fortune of others, and equanimity." If a nation were to be governed according to these teachings, its health care system would be "a most excellent manifestation of Buddhist beneficence." A survey of references to medical practice in the Lotus Sutra leads to the conclusion that to be "true to the Buddhist tradition, any theoretical system of health care ethics must be based on wisdom and compassion, and all applications should manifest skillful means. The underlying principles of the Lotus Sutra are consistent with these, and the parables and references to medical matters offer some specific guidance."

Concerned broadly with the relevance of the Lotus Sutra to social responsibility, Lucinda Peach examines it in relation to issues of "gender justice." She examines a wide variety of references to women and females in the Lotus Sutra, especially the "prediction" narrative in which the Buddha's stepmother, Mahāprajāpatī, and his former wife, Yaśodharā, along with their followers are given prophecies of future enlightenment and the more famous story of the sudden enlightenment of the *nāga* princess. The gender-related images in the Lotus Sutra, she shows, are not all consistent with one another, or with the teaching that all the living equally have buddha-nature. Women are "apparently capable of full enlightenment, but are more closely tied to samsara than are men; they are present at the Buddha's teachings initially, yet are often absent, invisible, or ignored later. They are worthy of being instructed in the dharma by bodhisattvas, but are at the same time dangerous sources of sexual temptation." In the story of the *nāga* princess, Peach finds the sutra insisting on transformation into a male body as a prerequisite to full enlightenment, and thus weaker in its support of gender justice than some other Mahayana sutras, and much weaker than desirable. Still, while it fails to provide a clear affirmation of equality, the two narratives do support gender justice at least in a qualified way. The sutra's emphasis on the capacity of all, including women, for complete enlightenment, Peach claims, "is consistent with the principles of gender justice."

Miriam Levering asks the question: Is the Lotus Sutra good news for women? and concludes on a much more positive note than Peach. Because the sutra encourages women to become bodhisattvas and Dharma teachers who can share in the work of the Buddha, there is "ample reason for receiving the Lotus Sutra as 'good news,' not only for early Mahayanists, but also for people today." Levering has a different take on the story of the *nāga* princess. The princess is "one of very few characters in Mahayana Buddhist sutras who can be interpreted as 'realizing Buddhahood with this very body' or 'attaining Buddhahood in this very body' in the present moment of the text, in front of the reader or hearer, as it were." Central to Levering's understanding of the Lotus Sutra is the idea of the teacher of the Dharma. "To my mind, the most important good news that women receive in the story of the *nāga* princess's attainment of Buddhahood, if one reads the story in the context of the whole sutra, is that a female through hearing the sutra with her sharp roots attains very advanced bodhisattvahood and becomes a fully accomplished *dharma-bhāṇaka*, a preacher and teacher of the highest Dharma of the Buddha." Similarly, "In the context of the whole sutra it is of great significance for women that the Buddha in chapter 13 predicts for his aunt and foster mother, Mahāprajāpatī, and for his erstwhile wife, Yaśodharā, who are now nuns, that they will eventually become great teachers of [the] Dharma."

Closing this introduction, I would like to express deep and sincere gratitude to the staff of Risshō Kōsei-kai who have contributed to the success of the Bandai-sō conferences, especially those of the External Relations Section, the Chūō Academic Research Insitute, the Kōsei Publishing Company, and Bandai-sō. And it is especially fitting to extend a special note of thanks to Michio Shinozaki, who has participated in all of the conferences and has contributed to this volume. He has been my advisor and partner in organizing the Bandai-sō conferences and in much else over the past twelve years during which I have been privileged to live in Japan and have my work supported by Risshō Kōsei-kai.

1. Introductory

The Threefold Lotus Sutra:
An Introduction

Nikkyō Niwano

The Threefold Lotus Sutra consists of the Sutra of the Lotus Flower of the Wonderful Law (*Saddharmapuṇḍarīka-sūtra*) and two shorter related sutras, the Sutra of Innumerable Meanings and the Sutra of Meditation on the Bodhisattva Universal Virtue. For many centuries the three sutras, known collectively in China and Japan as the Threefold Lotus Sutra, have been highly esteemed not only as Buddhist scriptures but also as literature.

Long revered as "the king of all sutras," the Sutra of the Lotus Flower of the Wonderful Law, or Lotus Sutra, contains the essence of the teaching of Śākyamuni, the historical Buddha. Because of their close connection with the Lotus Sutra and their placement in relation to the central scripture, the Sutra of Innumerable Meanings is popularly known as the "opening sutra" to the Lotus Sutra, while the Sutra of Meditation on the Bodhisattva Universal Virtue is known as the "closing sutra."

The Buddha and the Lotus Sutra

Śākyamuni, or "Sage of the Śākyas," is the epithet by which the historical Buddha is best known today. According to accounts in the Buddhist scriptures, the founder of Buddhism was born to the king of the Śākyas, a small state in northeastern India, about twenty-five hundred years ago. Siddhārtha, as he was named (his family name was Gautama, another name by which the Buddha is often known), grew up surrounded by every comfort and was educated in the usual princely accomplishments of both art and arms. But as a young man he became keenly aware that all people, prince and pauper alike, are subject to the four sufferings of birth, aging, sickness, and death. The ephemeral pleasures of life lost all allure for him as he pondered the problem of suffering and its solution.

At the age of twenty-nine, he decided to renounce his princely status and become an ascetic in order to attain enlightenment[1] in the causes of human suffering and the way to overcome it. Leaving his wife and small son, he walked into the forest to begin his quest for truth.

Siddhārtha studied with a number of learned teachers, but none could satisfy him completely. He then practiced solitary austerities, but still the ultimate enlightenment eluded him. Finally, he seated himself beneath a *bodhi* tree and entered a deep meditative trance, during which he attained the supreme enlightenment that made him the Buddha, or "Enlightened One." He is said to have been thirty-five at the time.

For the next forty-five years Śākyamuni, as he was now known, traveled through north central India, teaching the roots of suffering and the way to eradicate them and thus liberate oneself from the cycle of birth and death. He gathered many disciples, who became the core of the Saṅgha, the community of believers. He died at the age of eighty, while traveling with some disciples. His last words to them were, "All phenomena are always changing. Endeavor to practice my teaching diligently."

Śākyamuni preached a great many teachings in his lifetime, so many that they are often spoken of as "the eighty-four thousand sermons." The scriptures, or sutras, recording and organizing these teachings number approximately seventeen hundred. Since ancient times the Lotus Sutra has been widely accepted as supreme among these sutras.

Why is this? There are several reasons, but the main one is that the Lotus Sutra incorporates the essential points of all the other sutras and is thus the very heart of Śākyamuni's teachings. The true nature of the universe and of human beings, how we should live and how we should relate to other people—the Lotus Sutra teaches us all there is to know about these things.

The most gratifying of the teachings of the Lotus Sutra are the elucidation of the truth that the Buddha is always with us, leading us, and of the principle of "the Reality of All Existence," which assures us that all human beings possess the buddha-nature, the potential for enlightenment, and that all can attain buddhahood if they strive to do so.

When we truly grasp the meaning of these teachings, we feel the sheer joy of life surge through us. This is not just joy at our personal existence but a great sense of purpose that wells up in us upon realization of our duty and ideal as human beings to make this world a land of everlasting peace. I believe that the Lotus Sutra is the supreme sutra because of the joy, sense of purpose, and energy that the truth it teaches arouses in us.

The Buddha preached the Sutra of Innumerable Meanings immediately before preaching the Lotus Sutra. In this sutra he explains the purpose of his many teachings over the past forty-odd years and the order in which he has preached them. He then announces that he has not yet revealed the truth in its entirety, though his teachings so far are all true and important, since all derive from the one truth. This is known as "the teaching of innumerable meanings."

Śākyamuni then proclaims that the one truth from which the teaching of innumerable meanings derives is "nonform," or "true form"; but because he does not discuss this concept in detail, it is difficult to grasp. However, the subject is taken up again in the Lotus Sutra, where it is discussed fully and at length. There the Buddha also makes clear that all the teachings he has preached so far are distilled in the truth preached in the Lotus Sutra, the central teaching of his lifetime.

The Sutra of Innumerable Meanings consists of three chapters, "Virtues," "Preaching," and "Ten Merits." Chapter 1, "Virtues," is regarded as the introductory part of the sutra. Chapter 2, "Preaching," is thought of as the main part and chapter 3, "Ten Merits," as the concluding part. Since this is a common method of analyzing the structure of the other two sutras of the Threefold Lotus Sutra, as well, let us explain it briefly.

The introductory part of a sutra is a general outline telling when and where the scripture was preached, who its audience was, and the reason it was taught. It is the gateway leading to the main part of the sutra, which contains the sutra's central meaning. The concluding part sets forth the merits that accrue to those who understand, believe, and practice what is taught in the main part. It instructs listeners to treasure the sutra and spread it throughout the world, and it also tells them that they will be protected by the buddhas if they do so.

The main part of the Sutra of Innumerable Meanings, chapter 2, "Preaching," consists of Śākyamuni's replies to the questions of the Bodhisattva-Mahāsattva Great Adornment. Only bodhisattvas whose practice was as advanced as that of Great Adornment could understand completely what the Buddha was saying here. That is why Śākyamuni decided to preach the Lotus Sutra after the Sutra of Innumerable Meanings. In the Lotus Sutra he explained the fundamental teaching of nonform (true form) from every angle so that everyone could understand it, elucidating the ultimate truth for all human beings for the first time.

Thus the Sutra of Innumerable Meanings is a transition from the "skillful means" of all earlier teachings to the ultimate truth of the Lotus Sutra.

The Lotus Sutra can be best understood after reading or listening to the Sutra of Innumerable Meanings, which is why the Sutra of Innumerable Meanings is called the opening sutra to the Lotus Sutra.

The Sutra of Innumerable Meanings was translated into Chinese in the late fifth century C.E. by Dharmajātayaṣas, an Indian monk who had gone to China. We do not know when it began to be read in conjunction with the Lotus Sutra, but Buddhist sources tell us that the great Chinese Buddhist teacher and exponent of the Lotus Sutra Chih-i (C.E. 538–97) read the two sutras together from his youth, so we know that it is a practice of long standing.

The Sutra of the Lotus Flower of the Wonderful Law

After preaching the Sutra of Innumerable Meanings the Buddha entered a state of contemplation, then began preaching the Sutra of the Lotus Flower of the Wonderful Law. This sutra consists of twenty-eight chapters. Several systems of dividing the Lotus Sutra in order to grasp its meaning have been suggested. The most appropriate, I believe, is a twofold division. First the entire sutra is divided into two parts: the first fourteen chapters make up the first part, the "Law of Appearance"; the rest of the sutra is the "Law of Origin." Each of these two major parts is then divided into introductory, main, and concluding parts.

The Law of Appearance refers to the teaching of the historical Buddha, who appeared in human form. The historical, or "appearing," Buddha is Śākyamuni, who was actually born into this world, attained buddhahood through his practice, and died at the age of eighty. The Law of Appearance can be summed up as Śākyamuni's personal testimony of his search for and attainment of enlightenment. He achieved the state of ideal humanity, awakening to the meaning and reality of the phenomena of the universe and of human beings and, based on that realization, the truth of how human beings should live and how they should relate to others. Śākyamuni also taught that our final goal is to reach buddhahood ourselves and firmly guaranteed that all can attain that goal if only they exert the necessary effort. In short, the Law of Appearance is the teaching that human beings must awaken to true wisdom and strive according to that wisdom.

Chapters 1 through 14 of the Lotus Sutra constitute the Law of Appearance, with chapter 1 serving as the introductory part, chapters 2 through 9 the main part, and chapters 10 through 14 the concluding part.

In the Law of Origin the Buddha reveals that he has been preaching to and enlightening living beings in every part of the universe from the infinite past. In other words, the Law of Origin reveals that the Buddha is, essentially, the great principle, or great life-force, that imparts life to everything in the universe. The Buddha in this sense is the "Original Buddha."

The Law of Origin calls us to awaken to the great truth that we are given life by the Original Buddha, the great principle of the universe. This awareness arises from wisdom, but is also a wonderful exaltation of the spirit that transcends wisdom. And when that happens, we experience vibrantly the great compassion of the Original Buddha.

Once we have experienced the Buddha's compassion, we realize that the highest virtue is to transmit that compassion to others. That is our true nature as human beings, as well as the most direct route to making the world a good and beautiful place to live. The Law of Origin, then, is the teaching of compassion.

The Law of Origin is contained in chapters 15 through 28 of the Lotus Sutra. The first half of chapter 15 is the introductory part. The main part starts with the second half of that chapter and continues through the first half of chapter 17. The remainder of the sutra is the concluding part.

The Sutra of Meditation on the Bodhisattva Universal Virtue

Śākyamuni preached the Sutra of Meditation on the Bodhisattva Universal Virtue in the Great Forest Monastery, situated on the outskirts of the city of Vaiśālī, after preaching the Lotus Sutra on Mount Gṛdhrakūṭa (Vulture Peak). It carries on from the last chapter of the Lotus Sutra, which concerns the Bodhisattva Universal Virtue, and also discusses this bodhisattva, but its true significance is that it teaches repentance as a practical method of applying the spirit of the Lotus Sutra in our lives.

We feel immensely encouraged when we study the Lotus Sutra, grasp the meaning of the Buddha's teachings, and realize that by practicing those teachings we can attain buddhahood. But when we return to daily life, we find ourselves besieged by worries and troubles. Myriad desires and evil thoughts arise in our hearts, threatening our new and hard-won courage. Though we may believe that we can attain buddhahood, unless we also know how to deal with emotional turmoil we are liable to succumb to delusion.

The Sutra of Meditation on the Bodhisattva Universal Virtue teaches the practice of repentance, which rids us of delusion. For this reason the Meditation Sutra or Repentance Sutra, as it is known, is inseparable from the Lotus Sutra. And because it is the sutra that we need to study as the conclusion of the Lotus Sutra, it is the closing sutra to the Lotus Sutra.

The Lotus Sutra in India

The Lotus Sutra indicates that Śākyamuni imparted the teachings it contains in the last eight years of his life. He delivered these teachings on Mount Gṛdhrakūṭa, or Vulture Peak, on the outskirts of Rājagṛha (the City of Royal Palaces), the capital of the northern Indian kingdom of Magadha. Together they made up Śākyamuni's last great sermon, preached in the foreknowledge that he would soon be leaving this world.

It is believed that the Lotus Sutra first appeared in written form five hundred to six hundred years after the death of the Buddha, or sometime during the first two centuries of the common era. In order to appreciate fully the value of the Lotus Sutra, it is important to know why the Lotus Sutra was put into written form at that time and how Shakyamuni's teachings were transmitted until then.

Śākyamuni was absolutely committed to freedom. The operation of his Order (the Saṅgha, or community of believers) was left to the individual initiatives of the members; Śākyamuni adopted the role not of a leader who ruled by wielding his authority but of one who guided and advised on the basis of his mastery of truth. Because of this, the various groups of followers in northern and central India organized themselves into self-governing bodies.

The same can be said of the doctrines of Buddhism. Śākyamuni did not dictate a standard set of doctrines to his followers. His teachings were not intended to be approached as a form of scholarly study. Their only purpose was to save people from suffering. As a result, Śākyamuni preached in many different ways, in accordance with his listeners' situations and capacities. At times he presented the ultimate truth in unvarnished form; at other times he preached the ideal human state; and at still other times he spoke in easily understood parables as he taught people how they should live.

Councils and Schisms

Because of Śākyamuni's method of instruction, his teachings are of extremely wide breadth and profound depth. During his lifetime it was impossible to organize these innumerable teachings into a neat, textbooklike system, and no doubt it never even occurred to anyone to do so.

Although Śākyamuni never attempted to standardize or systematize either his teachings or the operation of the Sangha, all his disciples and followers were unified under the influence of his unparalleled personal greatness. This unity continued for some time after his death. But inevitably, as time passed, this unity gradually weakened. Ironically and unfortunately, it was following a great council convened to standardize Śākyamuni's teachings that the first signs of a rupture among his followers became apparent.

This council was held in the rainy season of either the year of his death or the following year. Five hundred leading disciples gathered at the Cave of the Seven Leaves, outside Rājagṛha, where for three months they collected and organized the Buddha's teachings in what is known as the First Council, or the Rājagṛha Council.

At that time the teachings were not put into writing but were recited and checked for accuracy. When their accuracy was agreed upon, they were recited again in unison and memorized by all present. (The Sanskrit word for "council" is *saṃgīti*, which literally means "choral recitation" or "group recitation.")

The actual process was as follows. The disciple regarded as having remembered the greatest number of the Buddha's teachings in the most accurate form was given a special seat and, in response to the questions of the leader of the council, would begin his recital with the formula "Thus have I heard." He would then relate when, where, and in what circumstances he had heard the Buddha preach a particular sermon, after which he would repeat the sermon word for word. The other four hundred ninety-nine disciples would then compare the recited version with their own recollections, and when all present agreed unanimously on the accuracy of the sermon they would recite it in unison to fix it in their memory. Mahā-Kāśyapa was the council leader. Ānanda recited the teachings, or Dharma, while Upāli recited the precepts, or rules of monastic discipline (the *vināya*).

But an unexpected event occurred shortly after the council ended. One of the leading disciples, Purāṇa, had been on a long journey with many followers, spreading the teachings in Dakkhiṇāgiri, when he heard of Śākyamuni's death. When he finally made his way to Rājagṛha, the other disciples had just concluded their council.

After hearing the teachings that the council had agreed upon, Purāṇa assented to almost everything. He had one reservation, however. This had to do with the regulations concerning meals in the rules of monastic discipline. Śākyamuni had permitted disciples to acquire their own food, store food that had been received on begging rounds in the monastery, and prepare that food themselves. But the council had restored an ancient custom forbidding those activities. Purāṇa objected that this violated Śākyamuni's true intent.

Purāṇa and Mahā-Kāśyapa debated the issue, and their disagreement ended in a parting of the ways. Purāṇa declared that he would observe the Buddha's precepts as he had heard them, according to his own understanding, and left.

This seemingly minor incident was to lead eventually to the division of the Buddha's teachings into the two major branches of Buddhism known as Mahayana (the Great Vehicle) and Hinayana (the Small Vehicle). Mahā-Kāśyapa, the most venerable of the high-ranking monks, had always held that it was important to adhere strictly to every one of the Buddha's precepts. He can be called a representative of the formalist or conservative group among the Buddha's followers. Purāṇa, on the other hand, had dedicated himself to spreading the teachings. He believed that the spirit of the teachings was more important than the words in which they were couched: as long as one was true to that basic spirit, he maintained, one was free to choose the best means of expressing the spirit in action. In other words, he valued content over form, and can be called a representative of the progressive or liberal group in early Buddhism. These different ways of thinking just happened to surface in the issue of the monastic regulations concerning food.

For the next century the authority of the conservative group prevailed, and there were no notable incidents of strife. About a hundred years after the Buddha's death, however, a minor disagreement between the conservative and progressive groups led to the convening of the Second Council, at Vaiśālī. At this gathering all the representatives of the conservative group were learned and venerable elders, while most of the representatives of the progressive group were young monks. Once again the interpretations of the conservative group prevailed. But the younger monks could not bring themselves to accept this state of affairs and formed a separate group, which held its own meeting. That marked the first clear-cut division of Buddhists into two groups. The conservative group called itself the Way of the Elders, or Sthaviravāda (Theravāda in Pali), while the progressive group called itself the Great Assembly, or Mahāsaṃghika.

As the centuries passed, people's level of learning and culture and their lifestyle changed. The Way of the Elders, preserving as it did the ancient forms and precepts, inevitably fell behind the times. No longer perceived as relevant, it became a religion of monks that aimed solely at personal liberation. In fact, both the Sthaviravāda and the Mahāsaṃghika subdivided into many groups and lapsed into the scholastic study of Buddhism. As a result, their power to save people weakened.

Some people of the Mahāsaṃghika lineage, however, interpreted the spirit of Śākyamuni's teachings in a way that appealed strongly to the people of their time and proclaimed this to be the true teaching that would enable people to attain salvation. The Prajñā, or Wisdom, sutras formed the core of this new teaching. Many people were attracted to and joined this new group, and for about a hundred years its teachings spread widely.

The new group called its teaching the Great Vehicle, or Mahayana, and belittled the Buddhism of the older groups as the Small Vehicle, or Hinayana. But the older groups were not easily bested. They may have lost their power to guide the people, but the power of tradition was strong. They stood firm, criticizing the teachings of the new group as deviating from the Buddha's teachings, not being true Buddhism at all. This led to a bitter struggle between the old and new groups.

The differences of opinion between the two from the time of their initial emergence in the debate between Mahā-Kāśyapa and Purāṇa following the First Council to their clearer differentiation after the Second Council had not been especially rancorous. What a misfortune it was, then, that five to six centuries after the Buddha's death followers of the same Buddhist teachings should find themselves embroiled in such a bitter conflict.

It was around this time that the Lotus Sutra was put into writing. The purpose of recording the sutra sprang from a passionate commitment to broadening the perspective of both sides in the controversy, each so attached to its own point of view, and to redirecting their gaze to the single great Way of the Buddha's teachings.

Those who wrote down the Lotus Sutra wished to say to both groups: There is no Great Vehicle or Small Vehicle in Śākyamuni's teachings— there is only One Vehicle (Ekayāna); as disciples of the Buddha, you must stop quarreling over petty details and return to Śākyamuni's true intent, which is completely revealed in the great sermon he preached before his death. They proceeded to record that sermon as the Lotus Sutra. Here we see the great historical value of the Lotus Sutra. Of course, the value of its content is what determines its historical value.

The Transmission to China

Philosophies and movements that seek to embrace two ideologically and emotionally opposed groups and unite them are usually unsatisfactory compromises that are attacked by both sides. At first the Lotus Sutra was also subject to such attacks. But its wonderful message gradually earned for it the faith and support of many people, and in a short time it spread throughout India.

One reason for its wide acceptance was its literary appeal, for it was composed in a way that all could understand and that reached deep into their hearts. But while that literary style made a great impression at the time that the sutra was put into written form, its impact lessened as time passed and literary conventions changed; eventually it could no longer be understood without exegesis. Even the great Indian Mahayana scholar Nāgārjuna, who lived in the second or third century of the common era, not long after the Lotus Sutra was recorded, sighed at its profundity. These sorts of problems may have contributed to the fact that the Lotus Sutra did not become deeply rooted in India.

Even so, Nāgārjuna praised the Lotus Sutra, calling it a more valuable sutra than the Prajñā sutras to which he was devoted. And the first text the Indo-Scythian monk Dharmarakṣa (231–308?) chose to translate into Chinese when he went to China was the Lotus Sutra. So important did he consider its teaching that he retranslated the sutra in 286 under the title *Cheng-fa-hua-ching*. (This version is still extant.) When the great translator Kumārajīva (344–413), who had been studying in India, was about to return to his home country of Kucha, north of India, his teacher, Sūryasoma, bestowed upon him the Lotus Sutra as the most valuable, excellent teaching of the Buddha. From incidents such as these we can see that the great Buddhist masters were well aware of the importance of the Lotus Sutra.

The Chinese translation made by Kumārajīva, titled *Miao-fa-lien-hua-ching*, is universally regarded as the best translation. This is the version of the Lotus Sutra that was transmitted to Japan and is generally used there today. (There is a third extant Chinese translation, *T'ien p'in-miao-fa-lien-hua-ching*, made by Jñānagupta and Dharmagupta in 601.) Kumārajīva's father, Kumārāyāna, belonged to a prominent Indian family. He traveled to the land of Kucha, which lay between India and China, and married the younger sister of its king. Kumārajīva was born of that union. Buddhism was flourishing in Kucha, and at the age of seven Kumārajīva entered Buddhist orders with his mother. Later he traveled to India to study Mahayana Buddhism. His teacher, Sūryasoma, a prince of Yarkand, recognized his rare talent and character and bestowed the Lotus Sutra upon Kumārajīva before the disciple's return to Kucha, saying, "The sun of the Buddha has set in the west; its remaining radiance is about to reach the east. This sutra has a special connection with the northeast. Reverently propagate the sutra there." The words "a special connection with the northeast" were indeed prophetic, for in later ages it was in Japan, beyond China and also northeast of India, that the life of the Lotus Sutra truly blossomed.

In obedience to his teacher's injunction, Kumārajīva traveled to China to spread the teaching of the Lotus Sutra, but at that time China was racked by wars as kingdoms rose and fell, and he was unable to carry out his plan. Meanwhile, however, his fame spread, and finally, in 401, he was able to go to Ch'ang-an, the capital of the Later Ch'in kingdom, at the invitation of its ruler, Yao Hsing (393–415). By that time Kumārajīva was already in his late fifties. From then until his death at the age of sixty-nine he translated many sutras and was honored by the king as National Preceptor. Of course the Lotus Sutra was the most important of these.

T'ien-t'ai Chih-i

There were many errors in the earlier Chinese translations of the sutra, and Kumārajīva devoted himself to producing an accurate translation. In later ages, his translation of the Lotus Sutra was to become the core of Chinese Buddhism. After the founder of the T'ien-t'ai sect of Buddhism, Chih-i (538–97), known as "the little Śākyamuni," thoroughly studied the entire canon and proclaimed that this sutra alone expressed the Buddha's true intent, the Lotus Sutra enjoyed absolute preeminence in China.

Chih-i was born into a noble family in the kingdom of Liang. As a child he liked to visit temples and listen to the monks' lectures, and at the age of fifteen he decided to begin Buddhist practice. Three years later he entered Buddhist orders, and a mere five years later he had made such progress that there were no teachers in the vicinity to guide him. It was then that he heard of an eminent monk named Hui-ssu (515–77) living on Mount Ta-su. Chih-i decided to take his life in his hands and travel through the war-torn land to visit Hui-ssu. He arrived safely at Mount Ta-su and became Hui-ssu's disciple. Hui-ssu rejoiced at having encountered such a gifted pupil. He is said to have told Chih-i that long ago they had heard the Lotus Sutra together on Mount Gṛdhrakūṭa and that now their karmic paths had crossed again. As we review the subsequent history of the Lotus Sutra, we will realize just how significant that remark was.

After guiding Chih-i's practice for seven years, Hui-ssu told him he had nothing more to teach him and that he should now devote himself to propagating the Buddha's Way. Chih-i went to Chin-ling, the capital of the kingdom of Ch'en, and enthusiastically propagated the Mahayana teachings there. Chih-i possessed both great wisdom and great virtue, and he attracted a multitude of followers. Soon he was revered as a living buddha.

Eight years passed in this fashion. Yet Chih-i felt that he had still not attained enlightenment and that a final effort was needed to enable him to grasp the true message of the Buddha. He retired to a little hermitage on Mount T'ien-t'ai, where he embarked upon a life of intense contemplation, sometimes subsisting on nothing but roots and berries. The enlightenment that he attained in the course of this practice was the realization of the true message of the Lotus Sutra.

Using the insights of that enlightenment, he composed three great works: *Fa-hua-hsüan-i* (The Profound Meaning of the Lotus Sutra), *Fa-hua-wen-chü* (A Textual Commentary on the Lotus Sutra), and *Mo-ho-chih-kuan* (The Great Contemplation and Insight). It is no exaggeration to say that the composition of these remarkable works made the true worth of the Lotus Sutra comprehensible to people of all ages for the first time.

The *Fa-hua-hsüan-i* organizes and explains the doctrines presented in the Lotus Sutra. The *Fa-hua-wen-chü* selects important words and phrases from the Lotus Sutra and explains their significance and spirit. The *Mo-ho-chih-kuan* investigates, analyzes, and systematizes all the Buddhist teachings on the basis of the Lotus Sutra. As mentioned earlier, it was the literary style of the Lotus Sutra that made it so difficult for people of later ages to understand. Chih-i mastered the sutra's phraseology and carefully identified, elucidated, and organized all the sutra's teachings so that anyone could comprehend them. Thus it is Chih-i above all whom we must thank for clarifying the teachings of the Lotus Sutra and making them accessible to all. That is no doubt why he earned the epithet "the little Śākyamuni."

Chinese Sectarianism

Buddhism continued to flourish in China through the T'ang dynasty (618–907). But once again, as time passed various sects arose, each proclaiming itself superior to all others, which only confused ordinary people. As already noted, the Buddha's teachings are extremely numerous and broad in scope. Ordinary people could not hope to study them all. Nor would exhaustive study of the Buddha's diverse teachings lead automatically to salvation. Because of this, the venerable and eminent monks who were concerned with saving people often taught the Buddha's Way by choosing one sutra, or a portion of the rules of monastic discipline, or a particular philosophical treatise, telling the people of their time that if they only had faith in and practiced it they would be saved. These monks recommended a particular teaching on the basis of the religious experience they had attained through their own practice and after considering the times, the circumstances, and the capabilities of the people they were addressing. Each sect of Buddhism, then, was originally a valuable and living teaching.

The root meaning of the Chinese word for sect, *tsung*, is "basis" or "source." It does not signify the totality of a religion. A sect of Buddhism, then, is nothing more than a group of Buddhists who regard a certain text as the basis or source of the Buddha's teachings. The totality of Buddhism always transcends sectarian boundaries and is all-encompassing and equally true no matter what sect one belongs to. Despite this, after the death of a sect's founder, monks and lay followers of later generations lose sight of the founder's true message and come to think that their sect has a monopoly on the Buddha's Way. Unaware that their sect no longer meets the needs of the times, they remain convinced that its teachings are absolute and that no other teachings offer salvation. This is certainly an obstinate and foolish way to behave, but once we become subject to this way of thinking and acting we lose our objectivity and find it hard to realize what we are doing.

There were other reasons for the appearance of numerous sects of Buddhism in China. The Chinese people had a high regard for bureaucratic formalities, for one thing, and since people required government permission to enter Buddhist orders, organized sects were useful as a way of gaining official acceptance. The establishment of sects was also employed by the government to control the beliefs of the people by defining them along sectarian guidelines. These tendencies were introduced to Japan almost unchanged.

T'ang-dynasty China became rife with rival Buddhist sects. During that period a monk of Chih-i's lineage named Tan-jan (also known as Miao-lo; 711–82) studied all the Buddhist scriptures and concluded that although each sect had good points, it was the Lotus Sutra that revealed Śākyamuni's true message in its profoundest form. Thereupon he devoted himself to propagating that message. Thanks to Tan-jan's efforts the Lotus Sutra spread throughout China. Records show that when Saichō (767–822), the Japanese monk who transmitted the teachings of T'ien-t'ai to Japan, went to China to study, he met disciples of Tan-jan and was able to confirm his understanding of the T'ien-t'ai teachings with them. Those who follow the Lotus Sutra in China and Japan thus owe a debt of gratitude to Tan-jan, as well.

Religious Taoism, based on the teachings of Lao-tzu, a sage who probably lived in the fifth century before the common era, gained strength in China during the T'ang dynasty. Though Buddhism experienced a temporary revival during the Sung dynasty (960–1126), it gradually lost its vitality. From China it moved to Japan, where it blossomed anew.

The Lotus Sutra and Japanese Buddhism

The exact time of the transmission of Buddhism to Japan is unclear. One source states that in 538 King Syŏng-myŏng of the kingdom of Paekche, on the Korean peninsula, sent an image of the Buddha and sutra scrolls to the Japanese emperor Kimmei (538–71). (According to the *Nihon Shoki*, or "Chronicles of Japan," an eighth-century compilation of Japanese mythology and history, this took place in 552.) Yet there is evidence that Buddhism had been introduced to Japan long before that.

Thirty-nine years after the official date of the transmission of Buddhism to Japan, a copy of the Lotus Sutra was taken to Naniwa (present-day Osaka); and fifty-five years after the transmission, in the first year of the reign of Empress Suiko (593–628), Prince Shōtoku (574–622) was designated regent. It is with Shōtoku that the history of Japanese Buddhism really begins.

Shōtoku, a devout Buddhist, established many temples, including Shitennō-ji, in Naniwa. He also lectured on the Buddhist scriptures to court officials and, based on those lectures, composed commentaries on the Vimalakīrti Sutra, the Śrīmālā Sutra, and the Lotus Sutra. A manuscript of Shōtoku's commentary on the Lotus Sutra in his own hand, now in the Imperial Household Collection, is the oldest surviving example of Japanese writing.

In these commentaries Shōtoku declared his own belief in the supremacy of the Lotus Sutra. This was during the lifetime of Chih-i (538–97), but he was not yet known in Japan; his writings only reached Japan well over a century after Shōtoku composed his commentaries. It is highly significant, I think, that these two great contemporaries independently arrived at the same evaluation of the Lotus Sutra.

Shōtoku also wrote the famous Seventeen-Article Constitution. This document, based on the spirit of the Lotus Sutra, enunciated the concepts of national law and moral codes for the first time in Japan. It is no exaggeration to say that this represents the first flowering of civilization in Japan. We must never forget that the very dawn of Japanese civilization was infused with the spirit of the Lotus Sutra. From that time on, for almost fourteen hundred years, the spirit of the Lotus Sutra has pulsed in the hearts of the Japanese people and flowed through their veins.

In the twenty-nine years that Shōtoku served as regent, Buddhism became deeply rooted in the culture of Japan and the hearts of the Japanese people. After his death those roots continued to sink deeper and to spread until they reached every corner of the land.

Saichō and Kūkai

The next major development in the history of Japanese Buddhism occurred toward the end of the Nara period (710–94), when the great priest Saichō (767–822), who transmitted the T'ien-t'ai teachings to Japan and founded the Tendai sect there, appeared on the scene. Saichō was born in Shiga, in the province of Ōmi (present-day Shiga Prefecture). His father was a devout Buddhist, and from childhood Saichō enjoyed reading the sutras and paying his respects to Buddhist images. He entered Buddhist orders at the age of twelve and went to the center of Buddhism at the time, the city of Nara, where he devoted himself to practice. Being endowed with extraordinary abilities, he soon realized that he would not be able to approach the truth of the Buddha's teachings by the usual methods of Buddhist practice. At nineteen he retired deep into the recesses of Mount Hiei, near his place of birth, and threw himself into arduous solitary practice.

While studying various sutras and other Buddhist works, he became aware of the superiority of the T'ien-t'ai doctrines. No one had yet fully expounded these in Japan. After a difficult search he located copies of Chih-i's *Fa-hua-hsüan-i, Fa-hua-wen-chü,* and *Mo-ho-chih-kuan,* borrowed them, and read them. Deeply moved, he was convinced by his study of the T'ien-t'ai teachings that his own duty was to spread the Lotus Sutra.

Saichō established a temple called Ichijōshikan-in (later known as Komponchū-dō, the center of the Enryaku-ji temple complex) on Mount Hiei and made it his center for spreading the True Dharma, that is, the Lotus Sutra. His impressive learning and virtue earned him the trust of Emperor Kammu (781–806), who had moved the capital from Nara to Kyoto (then known as Heian-kyō) in 794, thus ushering in the long Heian period (794–1185). The emperor's favor led to a dramatic increase in Saichō's following, and the new Tendai sect flourished.

But the eminent priests of the Nara schools of Buddhism did not look kindly on Saicho's popularity. How uncomfortable it must have made them to see this young man of only thirty or so gaining strength and support—and that in a new place rather than the traditional center of Japanese Buddhism, the old capital of Nara. Their opposition gradually became more overt, finally taking the form of political action. People who felt that this antagonism should not be allowed to fester any longer obtained the court's permission for a debate between Saichō and representatives of the Nara schools on their positions and beliefs.

The debate was held at the temple Takaosan-ji (present-day Jingo-ji), in Kyoto, with Saichō facing more than ten leading Buddhist scholars of Nara. The entire party of Nara priests was won over by Saichō's exposition of the wonderful teachings of the Lotus Sutra and conceded defeat. The excellent character of the Nara priests is evinced by the fact that after returning to the old capital they had representatives of the seven Nara schools send a letter to the emperor declaring that they had been made to realize the great worth of the Lotus Sutra. Their respect for the truth and their ability to humble themselves and acknowledge their error are admirable indeed.

The Tendai sect did not depend solely on the Lotus Sutra, however. It also revered the Golden Light Sutra and the Sutra on the Benevolent Kings. These two scriptures are aimed at secular rulers; they describe the attributes of the virtuous monarch and teach that if the ruler governs in accordance with the Buddha's teachings, both the realm and the people will prosper. The emphasis on these two sutras indicates that Japanese Buddhism did not yet address the needs of the masses, but given the historical circumstances that was probably inevitable.

Saichō gained the trust of the court and the following of the common people, but he was not satisfied with this. Braving great perils, he later traveled to China to study and to climb Mount T'ien-t'ai to meet the disciples of Tan-jan and confirm his understanding of the T'ien-t'ai teachings. He also studied the Chenyen (Shingon in Japanese), or True Word, teachings of Esoteric Buddhism under the young Japanese priest Kūkai (774–835), who traveled to China on the same mission. This shows Saichō's greatness of spirit. Ordinarily, it would have been unheard of for a high-ranking priest to bring himself to study under a lower-ranked junior.

Saichō died at the age of fifty-five. After his death the court bestowed upon him the honorific title Dengyō-daishi, "Great Master Who Transmitted the Teachings." He was the second person in Japan, after Shōtoku, to devote himself to dissemination of the teachings of the Lotus Sutra.

Saichō's teachings continued to spread far and wide from the Tendai center at Enryaku-ji, on Mount Hiei. But in terms of secular power and influence, it was the Shingon sect, introduced to Japan by Kūkai (better known today by his posthumous title, Kōbō-daishi), that was preeminent in subsequent years. Kūkai, a man of great ability, gained renown not only for propagating Buddhism but also for his efforts to encourage all fields of study, culture, and industry. He traveled to the far corners of Japan and won the love and respect of the population as he taught them better methods of building bridges, dredging ponds, and using medicinal herbs.

Of course, it was only to be expected that Kūkai's great learning and virtue would also attract the respect and patronage of the court and nobility. Another reason for his popularity in high places was that the grand ceremonies characteristic of the Shingon sect suited the taste of the aristocracy. The favor of the upper classes thus shifted somewhat from the Tendai sect on Mount Hiei to the Shingon sect on Mount Kōya. If the clergy entrusted with guarding the lamp of the Dharma had been faithful to their task, this would have been no problem; but as time passed the Tendai leaders became concerned solely with their own narrow interests and with enhancing the worldly glory of Mount Hiei.

From the start, the Tendai sect had incorporated not only revealed, or exoteric, teachings, such as those of the Lotus Sutra, but also secret, or esoteric, teachings. Gradually the balance tipped in favor of the latter as the Tendai leadership pandered to the taste of the times. As if that were not enough, other problems erupted. Enryaku-ji became envious of the prosperity enjoyed by one of its subtemples, Mii-dera. Armed priests from Enryaku-ji attacked Mii-dera and put it to the torch. The spirit of Saichō was in total eclipse.

The same thing happened to the Shingon sect over the years, as Kūkai's teachings were neglected and forgotten. By the mid-Heian period, Japanese Buddhism in general had lost its purpose and had diverged greatly from the true essence of the Buddha's teaching. It was not merely religious institutions that had degenerated; believers' expectations of religion had diminished.

The Fujiwara clan dominated secular power. Peace prevailed, and the aristocrats composed poetry, played music, and enjoyed the game of love, giving themselves up almost entirely to lives of pleasure. The literary classics of the period, such as *The Tale of Genji* and *The Pillow Book* of Sei Shōnagon, contain vivid descriptions of that life. Even visiting temples was a type of amusement, with noblemen escorting gorgeously attired ladies to temples in ox-drawn carriages. Since the aristocrats were at the height of their power, the priests treated them most courteously, organizing banquets and joining in the revelry. All thoughts of preaching or listening to sermons were set aside; the priests' only concern was to win the favor of powerful courtiers and thus acquire higher rank and donations of temples and robes.

Public religious ceremonies were held only for practical benefits, such as protection from fires, earthquakes, and epidemics. Likewise, the purpose of most personal rites was to protect the clan from natural disasters and ensure its prosperity. Still worse, people prayed for misfortune to their enemies and death to their rivals in love. That the priests acquiesced, invoking such curses without a word of protest, shows how low Buddhism had sunk.

Another important feature of this period was total neglect of the needs of the masses. Only the aristocrats enjoyed lives of luxury; the lives of ordinary people were full of suffering. There were no public policies to protect or assist the people when famines or epidemics swept the land. In fact, the government continued to extract taxes from the commoners during such crises. Robbery, too, was rife. "Rashōmon," a short story by

Ryūnosuke Akutagawa (1892–1927) made into a film of the same name by Akira Kurosawa, graphically conveys the stark contrast between rich and poor and the unsettled mood of the times.

To further complicate matters, two warrior clans, the Minamoto (also known as the Genji) and the Taira (also called the Heike) became involved in rivalry between the imperial family and the Fujiwara clan. Kyoto became a battlefield, and the people were plunged into worse suffering than ever. Even if they had tried to turn to religion for succor, the temples and priests had become mere playthings of the upper classes, and the poor and lowly were not permitted to approach them. But the people's desire for salvation slowly swelled into a great, invisible tide sweeping over the land. The impetus toward a religious renaissance was gathering force.

The Rise of Nembutsu

Meanwhile, not all members of the aristocracy were content with their lives. As the Fujiwara clan continued its domination, factional considerations and rivalries began to play a more important role in personal success than ability, and corruption was rife. For every man who succeeded in gaining a place in the sun, many more were forced to remain in the shadows, their hopes dashed. These included men of great ability and integrity who had to reconcile themselves to life as underlings. Naturally, they questioned the way of the world or were afflicted by deep melancholy over their lot. And just as naturally, they sought something that would offer them support and comfort.

As this disquiet strengthened in both the upper and the lower classes, the teaching called *nembutsu*, or invoking the name of Amida Buddha, emerged, as if in natural response to the common need. This form of faith existed in both India and China, and it, too, was based on the spirit of the Lotus Sutra.

Amida is the Japanese name of the buddha called in Sanskrit Amitāyus, meaning infinite life, or Amitābha, meaning infinite light. That buddha is identical to the Eternal Original Buddha of the Lotus Sutra. The practice of *nembutsu* is the contemplation of taking refuge in that buddha. The eminent priests who spread *nembutsu* teaching, such as Genshin and Ryōnin, and those who further developed it, such as Hōnen and Shinran, had all studied the Tendai teachings on Mount Hiei, another indication that the spirit of the Lotus Sutra was at the core of *nembutsu* teaching.

The first person to propagate *nembutsu* in Japan was Kūya (903–72), a wandering priest. He went to Kyoto and stood on street corners, preaching in simple language. His message was that people should stop worrying about the troubles of this fleeting world and simply invoke Amida, who would save them unconditionally. Ordinary people, starved for spiritual sustenance, gladly flocked to this teaching. Later Kūya climbed Mount Hiei and studied the Mahayana scriptures again. Then he traveled through northern Japan spreading the *nembutsu* teaching, after which he returned to Kyoto, where he preached *nembutsu* to the townspeople until his death.

Genshin (942–1017) was born almost half a century after Kūya. He was deeply respected by the court and the aristocracy, but he did not let himself be swayed by that. He secluded himself in Yokawa, on Mount Hiei, and devoted himself to preaching and writing, which only served to heighten the respect in which he was held. Among his writings are the *Ichijō Yōketsu* (A Decisive Summary of the One Vehicle), which explains the Tendai doctrines, and the *Ōjō Yōshū* (The Essentials of Rebirth in the Pure Land), a work encouraging the practice of *nembutsu*. Owing to Genshin's efforts, the faith of the upper classes gradually moved in the right direction.

Ryōnin (1073–1132) taught *yūzū nembutsu*. The *yūzū*, or interpenetrating, *nembutsu* teaches that those who sincerely invoke Amida are given the strength of faith to reach out to others and save them. In the same way, the faith of others can save them. The faith of all people flows together in this way, interpenetrating until it becomes a great power to save all living beings. Through this wonderful teaching, *nembutsu* spread still further.

The next teacher of *nembutsu* was Hōnen (1133–1212), the founder of the Jōdo (Pure Land) sect. At the age of fifteen he ascended Mount Hiei to study the Tendai teachings. Then he went to Kurodani, another place on Mount Hiei, where he studied the Shingon teachings, and at the age of twenty-four he traveled to Nara and studied the doctrines of each of the schools there, thus attaining a broad knowledge of Buddhism.

The faith at which Hōnen arrived was the *senju*, or exclusive, *nembutsu*. We might say that Hōnen purified the *nembutsu* practice and faith in Amida. Up till then, those who had advocated *nembutsu* practice had preached the worship of not only Amida but other buddhas, as well. They had displayed great flexibility. Hōnen taught that relying exclusively on Amida and chanting *nembutsu* was the pure form of faith, and that only by this means would believers be saved. This exclusive form of faith had enormous power and attracted many followers of all classes, from the cloistered emperor Go-shirakawa and the regent Kujo Kanezane down to the overall population.

But the insistence that people could not be saved by worshiping any buddha other than Amida stirred the anger of priests of other sects of Buddhism, and they took advantage of the fact that some of Hōnen's disciples had transgressed the laws of the land to appeal to the court against him. As a result Hōnen was exiled to the province of Sanuki (present-day Kagawa Prefecture) in 1207. He was pardoned the same year, however, and in 1211 he was allowed to return to Kyoto, where he died early the following year.

Hōnen's teaching that neither learning nor rank was necessary for rebirth in the Pure Land, that the earnest recitation of *nembutsu* sufficed, was a most important development, since it offered salvation to ordinary men and women. It is no exaggeration to say that with Hōnen, Buddhism became a faith of the masses for the first time.

Shinran (1173–1262) entered religious life at Enryaku-ji in 1181, at about the age of eight. In 1201 he visited Hōnen in Kyoto and studied his teaching of *nembutsu*, finally becoming a disciple. At the time of Hōnen's exile, Shinran was banished to Echigo (present-day Niigata Prefecture). He was pardoned in 1211 but did not return to Kyoto. Instead he traveled to the eastern provinces of Japan, including Kōzuke (present-day Gumma Prefecture), Shimotsuke (Tochigi Prefecture), and Hitachi (Ibaraki Prefecture), where he attracted many followers. During this period he wrote *Kyōgyōshinshō* (Teaching, Practice, Faith, and Realization), thus founding the Jōdo Shinshū, or True Pure Land, sect. Around 1235 he returned to Kyoto, where he remained until his death. When Shinran became a disciple of Hōnen, he married, with his master's permission, becoming the first Japanese Buddhist priest to be openly married.

Shinran was a man of great warmth who, struggling with his own passions and wrenching personal experiences, fully developed *nembutsu* practice and made it still more accessible to ordinary people. His teaching differed from Hōnen's in an important respect. Hōnen urged people to chant the *nembutsu* unceasingly and implore Amida for rebirth in his Pure Land, whereas Shinran insisted that people are already saved through the absolute power of the Buddha and that when they realize this they cannot help chanting the *nembutsu* out of gratitude. This teaching of absolute salvation struck a deep chord in the hearts of the people, who were suffering from war and poverty. It comforted them and gave them hope for the future.

Rennyo (1415–99), a later propagator of the True Pure Land sect, brought Shinran's teaching to maturity by linking it with the practice of morality in daily life. The True Pure Land sect has long survived as one of the leading sects of lay Buddhism in Japan.

Zen Buddhism

In the period following the rule of the Heian court, through the time of the wars of the rival Minamoto and Taira warrior clans and into the thirteenth century, when the Hōjō clan grasped the reins of power, Zen Buddhism gained great popularity among the warrior class. Since warriors constantly confronted death, many subscribed to *nembutsu* teaching. But that teaching was rather passive. It is important to die at peace with oneself, but for warriors, the strength of mind to face the enemy in battle is just as important. And they have to cultivate spiritual strength in times of peace, as well. The *nembutsu* teaching did not offer the firm core of conviction, the strong, unmoving spirit, that warriors sought. This need contributed to the rise of Zen.

Zen (Ch'an in Chinese) Buddhism originated in China, when the Indian missionary priest Bodhidharma (fl. ca. 520), the founder of Ch'an Buddhism, selected the teachings from Śākyamuni's legacy that related to meditation and attaining liberation.

During the Heian period the Japanese priest Eisai (1141–1215) studied in China and introduced the Rinzai (Lin-chi in Chinese) sect of Zen to Japan in 1191; his great disciple Dōgen (1200–1253) took the teachings of the Sōtō (Ts'ao-tung in Chinese) sect to Japan in 1227. Both men had studied the Tendai teachings on Mount Hiei, and the writings of Dōgen in particular pulse with the spirit of the Lotus Sutra. The pervasive influence of Zen on Japanese culture is largely a legacy of the teachings of Dōgen, and Japanese Buddhism owes a great debt to him. It is a wonderful coincidence, I believe, that he died in the very year that Nichiren (1222–82) began to urge that all Buddhists return to the spirit of the Lotus Sutra.

Zen was a truly excellent way of life, but one that appealed mainly to priests and the intelligentsia; it remained somewhat removed from the daily life of the ordinary people. The *nembutsu* teaching, on the other hand, was deeply embedded in the hearts of the people, but its attitude toward life was passive, and it lacked the power to inspire them with the joy and purpose of life. Neither teaching encouraged the active desire to work with others to improve society and to build a better nation. Though individuals may find personal liberation, unless that evolves into a force to save society and humanity as a whole, ultimate salvation cannot be realized.

The Great Teacher Nichiren

It was Nichiren who directly addressed this problem. Zen, *nembutsu*, and Shingon were fine teachings in themselves, but each concentrated on a single aspect of the Buddha's message; none was comprehensive. These forms of Buddhism lacked the power to save people of all classes and to perfect society and the nation. How could this be achieved? Between his sixteenth and his thirty-second birthday, Nichiren devoted all his energies to pondering this question, making an exhaustive study of sutras on Mount Hiei, at Mii-dera, on Mount Kōya, and at Shitennō-ji. Finally he arrived at the conviction that the only way to achieve that goal was to disseminate the teachings of the Lotus Sutra.

On the twenty-eighth day of the fourth month of 1253, standing on the peak of Mount Kiyosumi, in present-day Chiba Prefecture, Nichiren proclaimed his vow to propagate the Lotus Sutra. At dawn that day Nichiren climbed to the mountaintop. Then, pressing his palms together and facing the direction of the sun rising over the Pacific Ocean, he intoned the words *"Namu Myōhō Renge-kyō"* in a sonorous voice. This was the first invocation of the *daimoku*.

The greatness of Nichiren's message cannot be overemphasized. He taught that true salvation is to be found in the practice of the teachings of the Lotus Sutra, and that the way to salvation should progress from understanding to faith and from faith to practice. Nichiren raised the theoretical aspects of the Buddha's teaching that Chih-i had clarified to their ultimate level through practice. And he took the lead in saving others, initiating a movement aimed at world reform. Due to Nichiren's efforts, the Lotus Sutra has been transmitted without interruption for over seven centuries, and we today have the opportunity to encounter its message.

But, as we have seen in other cases, Nichiren's true message was gradually lost or distorted. The first misinterpretation was to regard the *daimoku* as more important than the actual teachings of the Lotus Sutra. The Buddha's teachings were reduced to the simplistic idea that all one had to do to be saved was chant the formula *Namu Myōhō Renge-kyō*.

Namu is the Japanese pronunciation of the Sanskrit word *namas* (*namo* in Pali), which means "I take refuge in." This word may seem to be simply a rational statement, but it is not. It is, rather, the joyful cry of the soul in the instant that it leaps into the embrace of the Buddha, as it fuses with his teachings. *Namu* is the heart's spontaneous utterance of unconditional gratitude, of complete acceptance, as it gives itself completely to the Buddha and the Dharma. *Myōhō Renge-kyō* means "The Sutra of the Lotus Flower of the Wonderful Law." The meaning of *Namu Myōhō Renge-kyō*, then, is "How wonderful is the Lotus Sutra! I give my whole being to the true teaching of this sutra!" Nichiren's first recitation of the *daimoku* on the peak of Mount Kiyosumi was a proclamation of this profound emotion.

Above all, it is the teaching of the Lotus Sutra that is to be valued, together with the practice of that teaching. Those who chant *Namu Myōhō Renge-kyō* do so to implant firmly in their minds the commitment to receiving, keeping, and practicing the sutra. If people could be saved simply by chanting the *daimoku*, there would have been no need for Nichiren to bring a difficult text like the Lotus Sutra into the picture at all. There can be no question which is more valuable: to study the meaning of the Buddha's teachings and, following them, work toward creating a better life or simply to chant the title of a sutra.

The second misinterpretation of Nichiren's teaching concerns his emphasis, based on his careful consideration of the social circumstances of his time, on urgent measures to ensure the stability and peace of the nation in a religious sense. People of later times have misunderstood his intent, losing sight of the importance of individual salvation and focusing exclusively on social or national salvation. This in turn has been linked to nationalism and militarism, which are far removed from the Buddha's true message. Even today there are religious organizations whose primary goals are political rather than spiritual; they have made the same error.

The teaching of the Lotus Sutra is the teaching of human dignity, of human perfectibility, and of peace for all humankind. Let me repeat: What is truly valuable is the content of the Lotus Sutra, its spirit, and the actual practice of its teachings. By understanding, accepting, and practicing those teachings we can gradually approach a state of mind free from delusions while living ordinary lives in society. And when in addition we devote ourselves to one another's happiness, we not only improve ourselves but also make the world a better and more beautiful place in which to live. This is the ideal of those who practice the teachings of the Lotus Sutra.

Finally, some twenty-five hundred years after the Lotus Sutra was preached, the age has come when its true spirit is completely understood. This is also the age in which the goals of practice completely match the Buddha's true intent.

Now is the time for all of us to return to the truth of the Lotus Sutra's teachings and actively build a better tomorrow for ourselves, our families, and all humanity as we aspire toward the peace of the whole world.

Notes

1. In this essay *bodhi* is translated as "enlightenment" and "the Law" means the truth, the Dharma—the Buddha's teachings.

The Innumerable Meanings of the Lotus Sutra

Paul L. Swanson

The Lotus Sutra can be understood in many ways, or, to put it another way, the teachings of the Lotus Sutra are varied and multivalent. Actually, one of the most important of these many meanings of the Lotus Sutra is its very vagueness and that it presents itself as of "innumerable meanings." This potential—latent in its self-proclaimed "innumerable meanings"—provides the possibility for the Lotus Sutra to have meaning, not just in the past, but also specifically for the modern age.

Allow me to illustrate. In the introductory chapter we find Śākyamuni entering "the *samādhi* of the abode of immeasurable meanings." As if to put the electronic lasers and pyrotechnics of Disneyland to shame, flowers rain down from heaven and the Buddha emits a ray of light that illuminates uncountable universes. Then the Bodhisattva Mañjuśrī announces that the Buddha is about to preach the Lotus Sutra. However, the Buddha never does get around to preaching it. In short, an extravagant show is made to prepare for a sermon whose content is never exactly delineated.

What is this "Lotus Sutra" that is never preached? The content of the Lotus Sutra from chapter 2 on consists not so much in the Lotus Sutra itself, as in various praises for and instructions concerning the Lotus Sutra. The reason is that, in a broad sense, all of the Buddha-dharma is the Lotus Sutra, preached by the Buddha from the beginningless past. And if, in the words of the *Ta chih tu lun* (Treatise on the Sutra of the Perfection of Wisdom), the Buddha-dharma is not limited to the words of the sutras, but all good and beautiful words are the Buddha-dharma, then the same can be said of the Lotus Sutra.

The Lotus Sutra is of immeasurable meanings because it is equivalent to the Buddha-dharma. The Lotus Sutra in this sense is not limited to the extant text of twenty-eight chapters translated into Chinese so exquisitely by Kumārajīva (344–413), nor to the other versions of the text we know as the Lotus Sutra. All of the Buddha-dharma is the Lotus Sutra, and this is the basis for its incalculable potential. What we have as a text, the Lotus Sutra translated by Kumārajīva, testifies to the more universal Lotus Sutra that is of innumerable meanings, and the text points to and shares in this potential.

And in fact throughout history, from the profound and complex philosophy of the T'ien-t'ai master Chih-i (538–97) to the various religious experiences of those who had faith in the Lotus Sutra, to its various expressions and influence in the arts and literature, the Lotus Sutra has given birth to an immeasurable harvest of meanings in a wide array of fields.

This does not mean that the Lotus Sutra can mean anything we want it to, or that we can arbitrarily interpret it to our own liking. "Immeasurable" does not mean "anything" or "everything." It is important to know what the "Lotus Sutra" (in the limited, textual sense) says (and does not say), what it has meant (or not meant) to people in the past, how it has inspired (or not inspired) people, and what kinds of religious or other experiences it has led to.

On that basis we can more accurately and critically conclude what meaning the Lotus Sutra can have for our modern world. This is the duty of all religionists, whether Buddhist, Christian, or Muslim—to discover the meaning of their faith in their own social, historical, and cultural situation. For the Lotus Sutra adherent, it means the obligation to seek the meaning of the Lotus Sutra that is alive and meaningful for today. And precisely because the Lotus Sutra is of immeasurable meanings, it has the potential for providing meaning in our day.

Let me attempt a concrete example. Chapter 20 presents the story of Sadāparibhūta, the Bodhisattva Never Despise. This bodhisattva was so named because no matter who he saw or met, he would pay obeisance to them, in honor of their potential for buddhahood. He did not hold anyone in contempt. Is this not a model that has significant meaning in our day? If we would maintain this attitude toward all people, even to all living things, we would cease to be self-centeredly concerned only about our own well-being, or that of only our own families, or of only those of our own society, culture, or country. If we heard of an accident or disaster, we would be concerned not only about the Japanese, or the Americans, that were involved, but about each individual as a person.

To be aware of the potential Buddhahood—or in a more general sense, the potential goodness or value of all that surrounds us—is to be respectful of all that surrounds us. This attitude is a key to facing the environmental problems that are becoming increasingly severe in our day. If we cultivate this attitude, we can no longer be unconcerned about the ecology of places far away from our own environment. If we reach the point where we realize that we must respect and care for not only our own, but also the environment of people and places far away, then (for example) we will spontaneously stop buying items made from elephants' tusks and other endangered species, try to avoid wasteful use of products that require the destruction of tropical forests, cease using products that use destructive fluorocarbons, and attempt to lead a lifestyle that minimizes consumption and waste.

Who would have thought that the Lotus Sutra has anything to do with modern environmental issues? Yet this is but one example of the "immeasurable meanings" latent in the Lotus Sutra.

Organic Truth:
Personal Reflections on the Lotus Sutra

David W. Chappell

The Talmud wryly observes that "we don't see things as they are, but as we are." Keeping this witty remark in mind, I shall offer some views of the Lotus Sutra that have meaning to me, but which may claim little more authority than that. Indeed, among my colleagues the Lotus Sutra has the reputation of prompting and accommodating more different interpretations than any other Buddhist text. The text has been compared to the New Testament in size, and its East Asian version is arranged in twenty-eight chapters with prose and poetry interspersed. Nevertheless, the later chapters are so different from the earlier ones in style, approach, and content that many different messages have been found. Accordingly, I shall select a few themes that have special meaning to me, even though they may not fully represent the Lotus teachings.

Highest Dharma as Beyond Words

When introducing a recent set of articles on the Lotus Sutra, George and Willa Tanabe observed that the Lotus sermon that is the central topic of the Lotus Sutra is never taught.[1] This is not a new observation, and twenty-five years ago Shōzen Kumoi argued that no sermon was taught because the true Dharma is beyond words.

This claim that the truth is beyond words is a familiar theme in Buddhism, beginning with one of the oldest Buddhist texts, namely, the Suttanipāta, in chapter 5, verse 1076: "When a person has gone out [lit., home], then there is nothing by which you can measure him. That by which he can be talked about is no longer there for him; you cannot say that he does not exist. When all ways of being, all phenomena are removed, then all ways of description have also been removed."[2]

Even though the Dharma is beyond words, Professor Kumoi argues that the Buddha nevertheless must speak to help those who are eager and ready to listen. This was the argument made by the god Brahma to Gotama Buddha, according to older texts, and is the theme of the repeated questioning by Śāriputra in the Lotus Sutra. In addition, in the Lotus Sutra the Buddha must speak because the Buddhist listeners and independent practitioners (śrāvakas and pratyekabuddhas) needed to be told that they had not reached the highest truth and that they should not be satisfied with their level of attainment.[3] Accordingly, the attack by the Lotus Sutra on the śrāvaka and pratyekabuddha vehicles is an important reminder that the true Dharma always lies beyond any formulation or experience of it.

With this insight, it perhaps is understandable why the text does not contain the words of a "Lotus sermon" since the sutra assures us that the Dharma that is being preached is not to be limited to a particular formulation. What words could be adequate to express the meaning of true reality? Instead, meaning must always be related to the needs and capacities and situation of the hearer. By leaving the Lotus sermon unexpressed, the sutra makes the message of the Buddha open-ended and avoids idolatry. If the Lotus Sutra stated the ultimate Dharma in words, it would fall into the same error of the listeners and independent practitioners by absolutizing a particular, conditioned formulation or experience.

The Inner Lotus Sermon

My own view applauds these two points, namely, that the liberating Dharma is beyond words, and that those who feel their level of understanding and attainment is complete have stopped short of the full mystery of life. In addition, I would argue that the reason that the sermon is not and cannot be given in the Lotus Sutra is that the content of the sermon *necessarily involves the listener.* Accordingly, if there were any sermon recorded in the Lotus Sutra, it would be a sermon that had been heard and recorded by someone, and therefore would conform to the needs and capacities of that person. One of the repeated messages of the Lotus Sutra is that the Dharma is like rain that nourishes plants, grasses, and trees—it meets the needs of many, but each in its own way (chapter 5). The Dharma is responsive to our needs, but is flexible and not limited to one form.

Since the text argues that the Lotus sermon is an expression of the ultimate Dharma and many Buddhists affirm that they do hear the ultimate Dharma in the Lotus Sutra even though it is not written out, I would propose that it can be heard when someone is listening for a religious reason—such as searching for personal guidance and growth—in contrast to a detached study of the Lotus Sutra for some other purpose. Indeed, I would propose that reading scripture *seeking for personal guidance* may be a necessary requirement for reading any scripture as scripture, rather than studying scripture as prose or reciting it as poetry.[4]

The text itself favors subjective inquiry rather than detached study since it lacks clear organization or logic. A rational approach quickly becomes thwarted by the myriad secondary teachings and otherworldly descriptions. Chinese commentators developed two kinds of commentaries on the Lotus: one that commented line by line, and the other that expressed an "inner meaning" (*xuanyi*) or ultimate intent. For example, in the commentaries by Daosheng (ca. 360–434) and by Zhiyi (538–97), the focus is less on the text than on the Dharma, that is, on the underlying principle or the ultimate logos that was manifested through the whole text.[5] This emphasis on the ultimate that is conveyed through the text rather than just on the factual content accords with the hierarchy of medieval Christian exegesis that had four levels for reading scripture: (1) the historical, factual level, (2) the analogical level, (3) the moral level, and (4) the level of beatific vision. Accordingly, I agree that at the factual level there is no Lotus sermon in the text, but I would argue that at the analogical, moral, and beatific levels the Lotus Sutra has preached and continues to speak to the hearts of myriad religious practitioners.

Dharmic Shape-Shifting

In spite of the absence of a Lotus sermon, the Lotus Sutra continually leads the reader into an expectation that a sermon will be preached, and buddhas and bodhisattvas gather from the far corners of the universe in expectation to "hear what has never been heard before." One way to handle this dilemma is to suggest that the sermon will be preached to each of us individually if and when we approach the Lotus Sutra in devotion and trust and supplication. Because the Dharma is responsive and conforms to the needs of the listener, the Lotus sermon cannot be something that is given as an objective entity once and for all, and open to the scrutiny of all.

If one really wants to hear the Lotus sermon for oneself, then one must invoke the eternal Dharma, or the sutra, or the Buddha, and like Śāriputra ask for it to be preached to you. Based on the sutra, practitioners are invited to appeal to a variety of different figures, such as Guanyin (Skt., Avalokiteśvara), Mañjuśrī, Śākyamuni, the Eternal Buddha, the text itself, the eternal Dharma, and so on. I have not noticed any Zen-like emphasis on experiencing a "formless self" or "pure experience" or "emptiness" in the text. Rather, the text seems to delight in the diversity of the world in all its variety and transitoriness. Accordingly, practitioners are shown that many different figures may be vehicles for the Dharma or manifestations of the Dharma. Practitioners are invited to bring their particular needs, and to choose a particular form of the Dharma, of a buddha, bodhisattva, or text to petition, and to expect a concrete response in a mode that will be meaningful to the practitioner.

The text seems to assume that people relate to reality in different modes based on their different capacities and experiences. Christians have preferred familial imagery (Father, Son, and Mother), but this may not be suitable for everyone, and there are some who prefer a more impersonal term like Logos, or the Ground of Being. Whatever image is chosen, what is dominant in the Lotus is the process, namely, the Dharma is responsive and appropriate and nurtures growth. Instead of collapsing time and space into an eternal moment, an eternal and inclusive now, the text continually affirms the responsiveness of believers to the text or to the Buddha, and vice versa. In China and in my own experience, Guanyin has had special meaning as the focus of inquiry and the source of immediate help and reassurance.

I do not consider the imagery of the Lotus Sutra as objectively real, neither do I dismiss this imagery as merely metaphors for religious attitudes or as mental projections. When I invoke Guanyin I do not consider her to be just my imagination, but neither do I know what or who she is. I could just as well call out to the "benign indifference" of the universe, as Albert Camus has written, or to God through Christ as Paul recommended. While I feel more at home invoking Guanyin than Jesus, and prefer to see Jesus as a manifestation of Guanyin rather than the reverse, this is obviously a decision based on my own spiritual journey, not merely on some external differences. Although Guanyin represents a reality beyond myself, she is not wholly independent since her transforming presence is somehow related to and dependent upon my mind and experience for its power.

Just as I adopt some images from the Lotus Sutra as a means to relate to reality and to cope with life, I accept the claim made by other people that other parts of the Lotus are meaningful to them, even though these other forms or levels of reality expressed in the Lotus have proved inaccessible to me, so that the tasks for my religious life lie elsewhere. Nevertheless, the plethora of spiritual figures and images in the Lotus Sutra are important as background reminders to me not to reduce the whole of life to what I understand.

Many Buddhists have petitioned the sutra, or the Buddha, or Guanyin, and have testified to a saving response. Since the Dharma is responsive to local circumstances, as the Lotus Sutra tells us, and since different people articulate its meaning differently, the message that is received is often expressed in a fresh and creative way. (Hence the many diverse interpretations of the text.) This is how I interpret the refrain that the Lotus sermon is something that has "never has been heard before." While there are recurring patterns and qualities—such as being universally available, expressing compassion, promoting growth, and being nurtured by patience and calm—the Dharma's expression is ever fresh because it always is expressed relationally out of an interchange in which both "I" and "thou" are responsive, creative, and changing.

Buddhas as Active Gardeners

Everyone agrees that a central message of the Lotus Sutra is the announcement that all beings are called to the one vehicle, not the three vehicles: namely, they are called to attain buddhahood, and that anything less than that is inadequate. But what is special about the Lotus view of buddhahood? It is certainly not the list of the three-vehicle formulation since the three-vehicles list (of the *śrāvaka, pratyekabuddha,* and bodhisattva/buddha) is not unique to the Lotus Sutra, but can be found in very early Buddhist texts.[6]

It is important to note that there is also evidence to support the idea that the *pratyekabuddha* refers to someone who had attained an enlightenment equal to that of the Buddha, as the Aṅguttara-nikāya says: "Two, O mendicant monks, are the enlightened ones (buddhas). Which two? The Thus Gone One, worthy, properly and fully enlightened, and the individually enlightened (*pratyekabuddha*). These, to wit, O mendicant monks, are the two enlightened ones."[7]

What is even more fascinating is that these *pratyekabuddha*s have been found to emerge earlier than the Jain and Buddhist traditions, and to coexist with them.[8] For religious dialogue, it is important to note that Buddhism acknowledged the existence of enlightened people outside the Buddhist tradition. Nevertheless, Buddhist texts have also been critical of the *pratyekabuddha*s as lacking either the ability or inclination to transmit their enlightenment to others. This is sometimes expressed by saying that the difference between the *pratyekabuddha* and the Buddha-vehicle is that the former is enlightened by himself and for himself, whereas out of compassion for the world the buddha becomes a teacher to help others.

Also, there is some evidence to suggest that the *śrāvaka* and the buddha also share the same enlightenment and were equally called arhats.[9] The usual distinction between a buddha and a *śrāvaka* is based on the fact that it was a buddha who discovered the Dharma, whereas *śrāvaka*s only hear it and follow it.[10] Another important distinction can be added, especially in the light of the Lotus Sutra, that buddhas are also successful preachers, whereas *śrāvakas* have limited the truth to their own experience of it. Both *pratyekabuddhas* and *śrāvakas* share a similar failure: they both are unable to communicate and transmit the Dharma to others in different circumstances and with different abilities from their own.

The Lotus Sutra explicitly states in the doctrine of the three vehicles that all practitioners are subsumed into the one vehicle of buddhahood. This doctrine shows that religious truth always lies beyond any formulation or institutionalization of it. In addition, however, the Lotus Sutra shows that the Buddha-path means not just that everyone will receive buddhahood, but that buddhas and those on the Buddha-path must actively share it with others by adapting it to their needs and helping them to grow. Hence, the news that everyone can achieve buddhahood is both an opportunity for personal growth and a responsibility for the growth of others. This outreach of the Dharma in responsiveness to the uniqueness of others is one of the most outstanding features of buddhahood in the Lotus Sutra.

In summary, to this point we have seen that the Lotus Sutra especially embodies three things: (1) the transcendence of the Dharma taught by the Buddha in his Lotus sermon; (2) the opportunity and obligation of all beings to attain the highest Dharma equal to buddhahood; and (3) the responsibility that all beings will have in their role as buddhas (unlike the *pratyekabuddhas* and *śrāvakas*) to teach and save other beings in terms of their needs and capacities, as did Śākyamuni in the Lotus Sutra. Accordingly, the Dharma taught in the Lotus Sutra is not a verbal message, but a nonverbal action that is learned by watching and doing the Buddha's work of accommodating and nurturing others, of being an active gardener in helping the Dharma be planted and blossom for everyone.

The Extremes of the Lotus

Some have seen the Lotus Sutra as imperialistic in the sense that it criticizes other religious paths, specifically the ways of the *śrāvaka* and *pratyekabuddha* (the listener and the independent practitioner) in favor of the one way, the Buddha-vehicle (*buddhayāna*). At first glance the Lotus Sutra might even appear as a scripture for fundamentalists, whom I define as those who claim that there is only one saving truth, and that there is only one way to that truth, and that their way is it. There are many who have used the Lotus for text worship in a fundamentalist way who teach constant recitation of *"Namu Myōhō Renge-kyō"* (I put my faith in the Lotus Sutra) as an all-sufficient mantra to get what they want, and there are passages in the Lotus that support this practice. While simplistic, I must admit on reflection that there have been times of crisis in my life when I could only contain one thing, when I was reduced to or driven by only one thing. And so I can understand that some people some time can only handle one thing. Moreover, this is the approach of many Pure Land Buddhists, which they describe as the "white path" leading to Amida Buddha. For those at such a reduced level or in such a crisis, the Lotus offers "Namu Myōhō Renge-kyō" as a lifeline to grasp. The only way that I can accept this, however, is to place this fundamentalism inside the larger context of the Lotus, and to see it as a temporary expedient that is to be replaced by greater complexity as a person becomes stronger.

At the opposite extreme, balancing Lotus fundamentalism, is an abundance of material for those who revel in the complexity and grandeur and openness of life. A Nichiren bishop, Senchū Murano,[11] once said that this profusion of imagery in the Lotus Sutra resembled science fiction. The Lotus Sutra takes its readers into other worlds spread across huge expanses of time and space in which anything seems possible. For me, the incredible worlds painted in the text have little meaning, and instead of giving relief or hope or an enlarged perspective, they usually are intrusive, distracting, confusing, and unhelpful. Yet again on further reflection, I notice that the apocalyptic claims of the Gospels, or the theology of Paul, are no less confusing or surrealistic to me than these images, yet seem to have deep meaning for some people or to offer relief to others. Accordingly, as with Christian scripture, I have come to interpret them as metaphors for some experience of the transforming power and universality of the beyond, but do not take the descriptions as objectively real. I do not believe in the images as literally true, but I do not dismiss them as mere mental projections or dreams. They are just forms that are beyond what I can relate to.

The Lotus Sutra occasionally expresses the notion of emptiness as a minor topic,[12] but is expansive on the theme of upāya (compassionately responding to needs of others with temporary but useful actions). The Chinese Buddhist aphorism "The three realms are mind only" tells us that the world of life and death, the world of rebirth and fear, is a production of our own minds. This phrase is meant to show how our deluded thinking has created the conflicts we experience. However, this does not mean that the real world is created by our minds, only the false one. This understanding is sometimes illustrated by the case of a person who is dreaming that he is drowning in a raging river and can be saved either by finding a dream elephant to carry him to the shore or by waking up. Based on this view that our deluded thinking creates our dilemmas, when I read the parable of the magic city (chapter 7) I do not believe that the guide creates an objective city (or Pure Land). Rather, I see the action as taking place in relation to people's minds, where a temporary oasis is created until a person is strong enough to journey on. My view is that the Lotus miracles and magical devices are like the dream elephant—a temporary and helpful distinction that is real enough to help move people through a crisis and to prepare them for a later awakening.

The Highest Dharma as Inclusive

An important trait of the Lotus Sutra is the value of being inclusive. With the fires of Waco, Texas, still raging vividly in my memory, I realize that part of our task as religious thinkers is to find ways to connect with those driven into fundamentalism and isolationism—even as I recall the example of self-immolation in chapter 23 of the Lotus Sutra[13] that has been a model for numerous religious suicides in East Asia. Somehow this text has been able to encompass both fundamentalism and the fantastic within its extended time frame and within its context of critical awareness, stages of growth, compassion, responsiveness, maturity, and ultimate freedom. The Lotus Sutra recommends many practices that are usually rejected or condemned by conventional wisdom. This inclusion of such diverse practices may be seen as dangerous by some, but I value it and find few religious leaders in America who would be so open.

The Judas of early Buddhism is named Devadatta, and it is revealing that a late addition to the Lotus Sutra was a chapter on Devadatta. While usually cast as a troublemaker, he was seen by early Buddhism as too lazy, and then by later Buddhism as causing schisms by being too strict.[14] However, in the Lotus Sutra used in East Asia, Devadatta is proclaimed as the teacher of Śākyamuni Buddha, who says: "All because Devadatta was a good friend to me, I was able to become fully enlightened."[15] In addition, in the same chapter, Śākyamuni's practice is also surpassed by a young girl, the daughter of Dragon King Sāgara. We learn that for "immeasurable kalpas" Śākyamuni "carried out harsh and difficult practices, accumulating merit, piling up virtue, seeking the way of the bodhisattva without ever resting," so that "throughout the thousand-millionfold world, there is not a spot tiny as a mustard seed" where Śākyamuni did not "sacrifice his body and life for the sake of living beings."[16] Nevertheless, the dragon king's daughter attained enlightenment equal to his in the space of an instant. Even though the dragon king's daughter still had to become a male in the process of attaining buddhahood, for me this male prejudice is more than overcome by the overwhelming imagery of Guanyin as female in the East Asian Lotus tradition. Accordingly, what impresses me in this chapter is the role reversals whereby Śākyamuni is subordinated to Devadatta and the dragon king's daughter. This says to me that everyone and all people can and will and should be my teachers.

Even when the Lotus Sutra seems most exclusivistic and claims that only by the Buddha-vehicle will we attain liberation, in the next line we see this redefined in terms of "tactful teachings" which could include anything and everything—but under the Lotus perspective and at a time when it can be helpful to beings: "Only by the Buddha-vehicle will they [people] attain [real] extinction [of the three poisons]. There is no other vehicle except the tactful teachings of the Tathāgata."[17]

A startling example is the case of bodhisattvas who hide their true identity and appear as *śrāvaka*s and *pratyekabuddha*s "by numberless tactful methods."

> They show themselves possessed of human passions
> And seem to hold heretical views.
> Thus do my disciples
> Tactfully save all beings.[18]

Accordingly, we must "never despise" other beings, since they might be bodhisattvas in disguise, and certainly are destined to become buddhas (see chapter 20 on the Bodhisattva Sadāparibhūta, the Bodhisattva Never Despise).[19]

Although acknowledging the diverse ways of being religious—especially the three paths of the monastic *śrāvaka*, the independent *pratyekabuddha*, and the compassionate bodhisattva—the Lotus Sutra emphasizes that these are meaningful paths or phases of religious life, but that they are to be subsumed and completed in the ultimate attainment which is buddhahood itself. Accordingly, while affirming the value of all practices, the Lotus Sutra also evaluates and ranks such practices in terms of the highest attainment of universal buddhahood. This context means that all practices are not included equally and forever, but only conditionally and temporarily, and that all are finally judged by the measure of buddhahood to which we are all called.

The Highest Dharma as Manifest Dialogically in Response

For me the core message of the Lotus is the affirmation that a highest Dharma does exist and that it manifests to those who seek it or who need it according to their ability to understand and respond. According to Tiantai Zhiyi (538–97) this was expressed by the phrase *gan-ying daojiao,* meaning the communication of the eternal buddha-dharma in response to a person's need and request. Even though a person may not understand life or the Dharma, the Lotus gives the assurance that true reality (= the Eternal Buddha) is responsive to one's needs and assists a person and others to grow (as the rain assists different plants in chapter 5). This responsiveness becomes personified in chapters 24 and 25 by the diverse appearances of the Bodhisattvas Gadgadasvara and Guanyin, who are ready to meet the needs of believers. Since we have both faulty perception and a mistaken understanding about life, the responses of true reality to our needs sometimes take unusual forms, namely, well-intentioned and wise deception. For example, the promise of future pleasures may be needed to get little children out of a burning house (chapter 3), or the shock tactics of grief over the apparent death of their father may be needed to get irresponsible sons of a doctor to take their medicine (chapter 16); whereas for others a long period of preparation may be contrived before they are able to hear and respond (the poor son in chapter 4), and periodic rest and recreation may be needed for others before the journey is complete (the magic city, chapter 7).

What is also important to emphasize is that the oneness of the Eternal Buddha and the eternal flowering of the Dharma/lotus is manifest most often in the interpersonal arena, rather than in an introspective awareness of one's Formless Self (Hisamatsu or Lin-chi), or the overcoming of subject-object duality in a moment of pure experience (Nishida). While not denying these possibilities, the emphasis is much more on bringing the lotus into bloom in an interactive, interpersonal world in response to other beings with their needs and abilities.

Seiichi Yagi has proposed that the experience of religious awakening can take place in overcoming duality in at least three different but related spheres: (*a*) subject–object, (*b*) I–thou, (*c*) self–ego. I would propose that the main themes of the Lotus are mainly related to option (*b*). In contrast to the Perfection of Wisdom literature, the Lotus is not intent on asserting the unattainability or emptiness of any and all distinctions in the experience of emptiness, but of affirming that all vehicles are expedient means or helpful devices. Although this denies finality to any distinction, it does not deny their role as an expedient. Similarly, Chinese Tiantai used the idea of the Threefold Truth, which balanced emptiness with an awareness of the usefulness and presence of the three thousand worlds in a single moment of consciousness. Even though the fundamentalism, fantasies, and fanaticism of the Lotus Sutra are not to be substantialized as externally real and enduring, neither are they to be dismissed as empty or as merely internal and subjective dreams or projections. Rather, in the Tiantai tradition they can be seen as the result of reality manifesting itself in terms of the capacities and patterns of our minds—

being beyond and yet in our midst, being neither the same as nor different from (*buyi buyi*) our minds.[20]

Basically, the Lotus Sutra affirms the wisdom and the eternity of the Dharma ("Revelation of the Eternal Life of the Tathāgata," chapter 16), the inherent capacity of all people to receive it and to achieve eventual fulfillment (chapter 8), and the process of transmission that is in accord with the level, capacities, and growth process for each thing (chapter 5). In sum, within a vast vision of time and space, the Lotus affirms the capacities of all beings and affirms the goodness of all methods that are helpful. The ruling criterion is the growth and fulfillment of all beings. Accompanying this faith in the responsiveness of the Dharma (life) at its deepest levels and the confidence that it is good and intends growth, there is in turn an obligation: we, like the Dharma, are expected to be compassionate, responsive, and creative to help other beings grow.

The Highest Dharma Sponsors Growth

While mutual responsiveness and cooperative creativity are the major modes of action expressed by the Lotus for me, the major religious and ethical criterion is that of growth. The inclusiveness of the sutra teaches us that all things are to be nurtured, none are final or supreme, and that our vocation is both to grow and to help others to grow. Accordingly, the chief end of life is not to glorify God and enjoy him forever, but to grow and blossom, "to be all that we can be," so that we can become something beautiful for the world, and to help others do the same. Accordingly, the dominant model for me is the universal rain of the Dharma that nurtures different plants in different ways, a model that presents the world as a garden. As a consequence, religious actions are valued for their balance and nurturing quality within an organic view of life. Although diversity is celebrated, all activities are interdependent and adjustable, and no one path has permanency or authority. This makes Lotus Buddhism a very adaptable and protean religion.

Based on chapter 14, there is an emphasis on peaceful practices that include great discretion and restraint in social conduct, an abiding awareness of the emptiness of all things, and the avoidance of contempt for other teachers, scriptures, or religions. No discouragement should be given to people choosing other religious paths. "Also one should never engage in frivolous debate over the various doctrines or dispute or wrangle over them. With regard to all living beings one should think of them with great compassion."[21]

Nichiren, Risshō Kōsei-kai, Sōka Gakkai, Reiyūkai, and others inspired by the Lotus Sutra have been important examples of how Lotus Sutra

Buddhists are to be actively engaged in transforming society. Lotus Sutra Buddhists are not passive hearers of a finalized message, but their capacities and needs and goals help to shape the flowering of the Dharma here and now. Thus, they are both receivers and cocreators of the message and participate in the process of manifesting the Dharma. Accordingly, part of the task of our lives is to help creatively to realize the Dharma in each situation, and to bring it into being in our lives and in the lives of those who are in need and for a world in need.

Unlike the historical Jesus, the Lotus lacks a specific social agenda, or a historical expectation, or a list of commandments, or divine judgment. Since karma fulfills the role of moral judgment, and the Lotus claims to be potent even in a period of the decline of the Dharma, the main emphasis is not on an individual, group, or historical judgment, but on the individual as part of a cosmological process leading all beings toward ultimate buddhahood. Practitioners are to model themselves on the Dharma and should be compassionate and responsive to others, but the highly symbolic nature of the text, and the otherworldly imagery, does not connect them to specific social, economic, or political situations. By contrast, Jesus in the Christian Gospels advocates a social revolution.

The Lotus tradition is famous for its social and political activism in East Asia since the sutra itself gives vivid models of compassionate action. Although the Lotus lacks a program for social action, the text vividly shows bodhisattvas creating many expedient devices in the midst of a bewildering jumble of real but temporary distinctions that include and interpenetrate each other. Accordingly, to live in this world requires constant assimilation and evaluation because the distinctions, although real, are temporary and ever changing. Since practitioners must evaluate each situation themselves, they are called to constant participation, calmness, mindfulness, judgment, and creativity. This affirmation of our own capacities, roles, and duties in the work of Dharma-realization is one of the reasons that the Dharma blossoms are recurrently fresh.

On reflection, the tension between announcing that the Buddha is now about to preach the great Lotus sermon and the lack of an explicit Lotus sermon in the text may seem parallel to the tension felt by a Christian in experiencing that the kingdom is at hand while anticipating the kingdom that is to come. However, the text has many other sources of assurance that the Lotus sermon has already arrived: such as the announcement that all beings are destined for buddhahood, that all beings have the buddha-nature, that the Buddha only appeared to die but in fact is eternal, and that upholding this sutra will ensure great merit, salvation, and many worldly benefits. While full buddhahood may await a future time, today the vows have been made and fulfillment has been promised to numerous practitioners mentioned in the sutra. Although the goal has not been completed, the Lotus has been preached. Unlike the promise of heaven, or the hope of rebirth in the Pure Land in the next life, or the kingdom that is to come, the divine deeds have been done and the Dharma is fully available now. The only delay is in our own growth. Although the human readiness to achieve complete buddhahood may lie in the future, the supernatural resources of the Lotus Sutra and the Dharma and the Eternal Buddha are here now. As the story of the dragon king's daughter shows, the timing is up to us. No waiting for another is needed. We are already in an eternal summer.

This work of growth is what gives direction and meaning to our lives. Our role as bodhisattvas is to be both coreceivers and cocreators as we seek to manifest a Dharma in this organic and interdependent world that will be good and beautiful.

Organic Truth

Common complaints about the Lotus Sutra in the past have included the charge that the historical Buddha is a Docetic figure who only appears to be born in history (chapter 16), but is actually just conjured up as an expedient device to teach and lead us. That this is not an isolated theme in the Lotus can be seen by the story of the magic city (chapter 7) that is similarly conjured up to give pilgrims a rest so that they can regain their strength and vision in order to complete their journey to nirvana. Similarly, in chapter 10 we see the Buddha teaching Medicine King that if anyone is teaching the Lotus alone and unprotected, the Buddha will send an audience of monastics and laity, as well as protectors, whom he has "magically conjured." Of course, these examples of deception are compounded by the many "expedient messages" throughout the sutra, including the false promises given to children to prompt them to flee from a burning house, or a job offer given to a destitute son by a father who keeps his identity a secret, or a contrived situation to motivate the children of a doctor to take their medicine. In chapter 25 the sutra even personifies the Dharma in the figure of the Bodhisattva Guanyin, who promises to take any form that is needed in order to help people, and thirty-three different forms are listed as examples. The text is filled with magic and deception.

In the first section I argued that the Lotus sermon is not shown in the text because the ultimate Dharma is beyond words. In this last section I want to argue that the Dharma that is shown as words in the sutra, or that is embodied in its stories, or shown as the Buddha or as Guanyin, as fellow disciples or as detractors, as protectors or as enemies, as Buddhists or as Christians, is not to be taken at face value. The message of the Lotus Sutra that emerges for me is that Dharmic truth is relational, it is dialogical, and it is organic. It shows that messages from the Buddha are responsive to needs of people and conform to circumstances.

When reduced to objective truth and taken out of context, the Lotus teachings can be shown as deceptive or false or perhaps poetic license. However, I propose that this freedom to innovate and to transform truth derives from the I–thou context of the sutra: namely, the dynamic relationship between the Dharmic universe and the practitioner in which boundaries dissolve and the words or images that emerge transcend objective limits which are usually measured in isolation. The dialogical Lotus-truth transcends finitude, separation, and objective distinctions. It is more than pragmatic truth since its goal is not to get something done. Rather it is organic truth since it includes the capacities and needs of people, it is dynamically evolved through interaction, and its goal is the growth of beings into something beautiful for themselves and for others.

In the Lotus Sutra, truth is defined by what is helpful for growth, specifically religious growth, so objectivity in the text is sacrificed for the sake of seeing goodness and freedom where there was none before, so that everyone might blossom. But Buddhism for me always involves two truths, and each must be respected and given its proper weight.

Organic truth turns into harmful lies and real deception when the words are taken as literally true, and the magic is taken for objective reality. It is crucial that we recognize that the Dharma-truth celebrated in the Lotus Sutra is poetic, and that religious truth emerges in the overcoming of finitude and division. However, it always needs to be balanced by the truth of history and finitude, life and death. Lotus flowers cannot blossom alone in the sky, but only in the earth of local places and in response to local conditions. Each must be given its due: the truth that a real Gotama Śākyamuni Buddha did live and die must balance our awareness that an Eternal Buddha is still present for us. On the other hand, the Lotus Sutra reminds us that as the details and stresses of our own life consume and exhaust us, they also can provide enough dirt and water and sun to coax a lotus flower into bloom.

Notes

1. See the "Introduction" by George and Willa Tanabe, eds., *The Lotus Sutra in Japanese Culture* (Honolulu: University of Hawaii Press, 1989). George reports that he has had many people who disagree with him about this claim, but when he asks them what is the sermon of the Lotus Sutra they invariably re-

fer to different passages, such as the eternity of the Buddha, or the chapter on herbs, or the *upāya* chapter. (Private conversation, January 25, 1994.)

2. Shōzen Kumoi's comments are contained in Enichi Ōchō, ed., *Hokke shisō* (Kyoto: Heirakuji Shoten, 1969): 337, although the English translation is by A. Saddhatissa, tr., *The Sutta-nipāta* (London: Curzon Press, 1985), 123.

3. This statement echoes the "Protestant Principle" articulated by Paul Tillich that we must continually critique our understanding of the truth as too small in the name of the ultimate truth which lies beyond us.

4. Wilfred Cantwell Smith argues for scripture as a special genre of literature separate from prose and poetry. See his *What Is Scripture? A Comparative Approach* (Minneapolis: Fortress Press, 1993).

5. Tao-sheng's commentary *Miaofa lianhua jing yishu* interprets the main teaching in terms of the meanings of *li* (principles, truth, and path of the Buddha), even though *li* never appears as a word in the translation he was using. See Kim, Young-ho, *Tao-sheng's Commentary on the Lotus Sutra* (Albany: State University of New York Press, 1990). Also, Zhiyi wrote the very influential *Fahua xuanyi* (Inner Meaning of the Lotus Sutra) in which he spent two-thirds of the text expounding the meaning of the title! These two commentaries contrast with the *Fahua wenzhu* by Zhiyi and Guanding, which attempts a line-by-line exposition. See Swanson, Paul, *Foundations of T'ien-t'ai Philosophy* (Berkeley: Asian Humanities Press, 1989), which contains a translation of major portions of Zhiyi's commentary.

6. The three vehicles are found in the Mahāparinibbāna-sutta (a text which exists in Pali and in five other independent Chinese recensions) as part of a list of four kinds of practitioners, the last person being the "wheel-turning king." Also, in the Dakhina-vibhanga-sutta of the Majjhima-nikāya (a text surviving in Pali and in two other independent Chinese recensions) the three vehicles appear as the topmost of a list of fourteen practitioners.

7. Translated by Leon Hurvitz, "The Lotus Sutra in East Asia," *Monumenta Serica* 29 (1970–71), 716.

8. The argument that *pratyekabuddhas* were enlightened ascetics outside the cultus of the Buddhist community is made persuasively by Martin G. Wiltshire in his book *Ascetic Figures before and in Early Buddhism* (New York: Mouton de Gruyter, 1990).

9. For example, the Vināya passage that describes the Buddha preaching to his former five companions leading to their conversion, and concludes with the statement "there were then six arhats in the world," and the arhats are then designated buddhas, or enlightened ones.

10. *Taishō Daizōkyō* 2:19c; Khanda Saṃyutta-nikāya, No. 58.

11. Bishop Murano was one of the first to translate the Chinese version of the Lotus Sutra into English. See Murano, Senchū, tr., *The Lotus Sutra* (Tokyo: Nichiren Shū Headquarters, 1974). This remark about the imagery in the Lotus Sutra being like science fiction was made in a graduate seminar of mine at the University of Hawaii in the 1980s.

12. Such as in chapter 14. Burton Watson, tr., *The Lotus Sutra* (New York: Columbia University Press, 1993), 198, 200.

13. Watson, tr., *The Lotus Sutra*, 282.
14. See Hajime Nakamura, *Gotama Buddha* (Los Angeles: Buddhist Books International, 1977), 96.
15. Watson, tr., *The Lotus Sutra*, 184.
16. Ibid., 187.
17. Bunnō Katō, Yoshirō Tamura, and Kōjirō Miyasaka (with revisions by W. E. Soothill, Wilhelm Schiffer, and Pier P. Del Campana), *The Threefold Lotus Sutra* (Tokyo: Kōsei Publishing Co. and New York: Weatherhill, 1975), 162.
18. Ibid., 173.
19. A vivid example of anonymity by a modern Lotus group is the Donate a Meal Campaign in Japan sponsored by Risshō Kōsei-kai, which deliberately keeps a low profile in order to attract to this charitable activity for its own value people who might not participate if they knew it was being sponsored by a religious group.
20. This same distinction is used by Siming Zhili (960–1028) with regard to Amida Buddha and the Pure Land—it neither exists externally nor is it just imagined by the mind, but at one level it is different and at another level it is not. Although it is beyond the mind, we cannot discern its objective form because it is available only in terms of the mind.
21. Watson, tr., *The Lotus Sutra*, 204.

Somatic Realization of the Lotus Sutra

Taitetsu Unno

The Lotus Sutra, down through the centuries, has meant different things to different people in different cultures, but its unifying core is the somatic realization of its basic message: the negation of the delusory self and the embodying of wisdom and compassion. This is to be accomplished by the dedicated praxis of receiving and keeping the scripture through reading, reciting, expounding, and copying. These acts are not mere formalities or ritual acts but are intended to realize the teaching of the Lotus in one's own life, leading ultimately to compassionate action in the world. Its basic philosophy is summed up in the language of a contemporary exemplar of the Lotus teaching, Kenji Miyazawa (1896–1933), who once said, "Until the whole world attains happiness, there can be no individual happiness."[1]

I

A key term found throughout the Lotus Sutra is *ākāśa* or "space," which is not a constructed space but the unbounded space of spiritual vitality. *Ākāśa* involves a somatic realization, culminating in the liberation from all forms of human constructs and bondages. This is central to chapter 15 of the Lotus Sutra, entitled, "Welling Up out of the Earth."[2] When countless bodhisattvas volunteer to spread the teaching of the Lotus Sutra, the Buddha proclaims:

> Stop! Good men, there is no need for you to keep this scripture. What is the reason? My Sahā world-sphere itself has bodhisattva-mahāsattvas equal in number to the sands of sixty thousand Ganges rivers, each of whom has in turn a retinue equal in number to the

sands of sixty thousand Ganges rivers. After my extinction, these men shall be able to keep, read and recite, and broadly preach this scripture. . . .

These bodhisattvas all had bodies of golden hue, [displaying] the thirty-two marks and incalculable rays of light. They all had been under this Sahā world-sphere, in an open space belonging to this sphere.[3]

The English translation of *ākāśa* as "open space" may be misleading, for its basic definition is to be understood not spatially but spiritually.[4]

On the Sahā world-sphere's
Underside, in open space, they dwell.
Hard and firm of resolve and mindfulness,
Ever do they strive in their quest for wisdom,
Preaching a variety of fine dharmas,
Their hearts knowing no fear.[5]

The bodhisattvas who thus spring out from the space beneath this *sahā*-world join the Eternal Buddha, who also resides in *ākāśa*. Thus, this term clearly denotes a sphere of religious life in contrast to another term for space, *antarikṣa*, which may be called constructed space found in everyday usage, such as closet space, space bar, personal space, outer space, sacred space, as well as such words as spacing and spaced out. These are all human constructs in contrast to *ākāśa*, pregnant with religious significance, where the five basic practices are cultivated: 1) receiving and keeping the Lotus Sutra, 2) reading, 3) reciting, 4) expounding, and 5) copying the scripture.[6] Adherence to all these practices involves psychosomatic disciplines designed to accomplish the embodiment, the realization, of the Buddha Dharma.

Receiving and keeping the Lotus Sutra is the basis for realizing wisdom and compassion in daily life, and this is to be attained by upholding the four auxiliary practices. "Reading" cultivates knowledge of the scripture by repeated listening, reflecting, and absorbing the basic message. Traditionally, this is referred to as "reading with the body" (*shindoku*), whereby one's perception and ideas about the world are totally displaced by the contents of the Lotus Sutra. The accumulated sedimentation of the Buddha Dharma in one's body insures that its application to the problems of living becomes second nature. "Reciting" includes recitation from memory, but also chanting which comes from the depth of one's being. It thus becomes a total act of body and mind. "Expounding" means to preach and propagate the Lotus Sutra for the sake of all beings, intensifying the deepening of its basic message for one's own self-understanding, as well as that of others. "Copying" the scripture (*shakyō*) involves somatic involvement at every stage of the process, from rubbing inkstone, producing ink, using brush, writing on paper, and cleaning up to orderly rearrangement of the workplace. This requires one-pointed concentration of body and mind, such that the activity becomes what Merleau-Ponty calls the "habitual body."[7]

The successful somatic realization is described as the attainment of eight hundred virtues of the eye, twelve hundred virtues of the ear, eight hundred virtues of the nose, twelve hundred virtues of the tongue, eight hundred virtues of the body, and twelve hundred virtues of the mind. This is called the purification of the six faculties which means the elimination of defilements so that our senses can attain optimum functioning. Here again we see the integration of body and mind, so that countless impurities or "outflows" (*sāsrava*)—anger, hatred, jealousy, self-hate, arrogance, and so on—are purified.

The ideal teacher in the Lotus Sutra is one who embodies and manifests its message in his demeanor. According to chapter 10, "Preachers of the Dharma," the teacher must exemplify compassion, tender forbearance, and emptiness of all dharmas. In the words of the sutra,

> This good man or woman is to enter the room of the Thus Come One, don the cloak of the Thus Come One, sit on the throne of the Thus Come One, and only then preach this scripture broadly to the fourfold assembly. The room of the Thus Come One is the thought of great compassion toward all living beings. The cloak of the Thus Come One is the thought of tender forbearance and the bearing of insult with equanimity. The throne of the Thus Come One is the emptiness of all dharmas. It is only by dwelling securely among these that he or she can with unabating thought broadly preach this Scripture.[8]

Among the three—entering the room, donning the robe, and sitting on the throne of the Tathāgata—the second is crucial, for wearing the robe of a teacher means "acquiring the thought of tender forbearance and the bearing of insult with equanimity." This is true wisdom and compassion in its most vital and concrete form. The first, entering the room or great compassion, has to do with proper motivation; and the third, sitting on the throne, is the culmination of practice which is to see all things, including the self, as reality as it is, the manifestation of emptiness (*tattvasya-lakṣana*).

The definition of tender forbearance (*sauratya*) has multiple connotations—gentleness of heart, openness of mind, suppleness and lightness of body, ego-self without any hard edges. The physical manifestation of such a person appears as a gentle smile, centered stance, and relaxed shoulders. Ultimately, the religious life is not so much a matter of inner conviction or outward piety as it is of the way we conduct ourselves in life, whether walking, sitting, talking, eating, or sleeping.

A similar description of a Dharma preacher is also found in chapter 19, which is followed by chapter 20, "The Bodhisattva Never Disparaging (Sadāparibhūta)," as if to suggest a living model. It depicts the life of Sadāparibhūta, who embodies the spirit of the Lotus and constantly bows to everyone, to their inherent buddha-nature, never disparaging anyone. He bows to even those who abuse him and call him a "know-nothing bodhisattva."[9] Yet he never becomes discouraged and never disparages others, by virtue of which he attains purity of the mind and the faculties.

> You should know this: if a bhikṣu, bhikṣunī, upāsaka, or upāsikā holds to this Scripture of the Dharma Blossom, and if anyone with a foul mouth abuses or maligns him or her, then that latter person shall receive retribution for a great sin, such as was formerly described; while the merit gained by the former shall be as just mentioned, for his eyes, ears, nose, tongue, body, and mind shall be pure.[10]

The scripture then describes the power gained through such a purification. Having attained the purity of the six faculties, "he had acquired the power of great supernatural penetration, the eloquent power of the joy in preaching, and hearing what he had preached, all bowed down in belief and followed him."[11]

This extraordinary power has nothing to do with occult or extrasensory abilities. This is clear in the assertion reiterated that "with the pure ordinary eye engendered by father and mother a person shall hear and know everything," including the vast sweep of existence and all former and future lives. In fact, even if one has not attained this knowledge, one can know reality as it is:

> Though he [a person] shall not yet have attained knowledge without outflow, yet his mental faculty shall be as pure as this. Whatever intentions, or calculations, or speech this man has shall all match the Buddhadharma, none of it being out of keeping with true Reality. . . .[12]

The purification of the six faculties is thus available to any practitioner of the Lotus Sutra. One was Kenji Miyazawa, who exemplified the bodhisattva spirit of the Lotus Sutra, identifying with the plight of the poor and destitute peasants in northern Japan. He was brought up in a devout Jōdo Shinshū family, but he seems to have had disagreements with his father, who was a pious follower, and possibly with the Shinshū teaching itself. Regardless of his profession as a scientist, agronomist, storyteller, poet, and science fiction writer (to use a contemporary description), his devotion to the Lotus Sutra was total:

> Obeisance to the Lotus Sutra of Profound Dharma!
> My life—none other than the life of Profound Dharma.
> My death—none other than the death of Profound Dharma.
> From this human body to eventual Buddha body,
> I receive and keep the Lotus Sutra.[13]

Miyazawa attempted to put into practical action the life of Bodhisattva Never Disparaging of the Lotus Sutra, always concerned with the well-being of the impoverished peasants of northern Japan with whom he worked. His identification with the peasants is eloquently expressed in one of his most famous poems:

> Yielding neither to rain nor yielding to wind,
> Yielding neither to snow nor to summer heat,
> With a stout body like that,
> Without greed, never getting angry,
> Always smiling quietly. . . in everything,
> Not taking oneself into account.
>
> Looking, listening, understanding well and not forgetting. . . .
> If in the East there's a sick child, going and nursing him.
> If in the West there's a tired mother, going and carrying her bundle
> of rice,
> If in the South there's someone dying, going and saying you don't
> have to be afraid,
> If in the North there's a quarrel or a lawsuit, saying it's not worth it,
> stop it. . . .
> In drought, shedding tears,
> In a cold summer, pacing back and forth, lost.
> Called a good-for-nothing by everyone,
> Neither praised nor thought a pain,
> Someone like that
> Is what I want to be.[14]

Here Miyazawa is the "good-for-nothing" (*dekunobō*) who identifies with the "know-nothing bodhisattva," the Bodhisattva Never Disparaging of the Lotus Sutra. In both cases what was essential was *living* the Lotus teachings. This living can be the mastery of a single verse or a single sentence of the Lotus Sutra which would manifest the totality of the spiritual life. A single kind word, a simple gesture of compassion, is infinitely more meaningful than any conceptual understanding or discursive elaboration. This stress on what is truly valuable, as opposed to what we think is so, is found in other instances in the Lotus Sutra. Little value, for example, is placed on the *śarīra*, the remains of the Buddha, which is regarded as essential to the stupa. But the Lotus Sutra contends, "There is no need even to lodge śarīra in it. What is the reason? Within it there is already the whole body of the Thus Come One."[15]

II

The focus on the somatic in the religious life as taught in the Lotus Sutra is by no means unique to this scripture or this tradition. It is central to all schools of Buddhism whose ultimate goal is not so much the conceptualized notions of enlightenment, *satori*, or awakening, but how a person's psychosomatic realization is manifested in everyday life. As an illustration, I shall take two seemingly disparate expressions of Japanese Buddhism, Dōgen of Zen and Shinran of Shin Buddhism, contemporaries who lived in the thirteenth century. They both prescribe a method of religious discipline centered on the body. But it also has broader implications in the world of Japanese aesthetics and arts, covering an entire range of self-cultivation from the art of tea to the martial arts.

When Dōgen (1200–1253) repeats "dropping off body-mind; body-mind dropping off," it is total disengagement with all human constructs regarding the self or the body. The goal of his training collapses the process found in the Lotus Sutra—receiving, reading, reciting, expounding, and copying the scripture—into simple *shikan-taza* (just sitting) which is pursued not as a means but as the end itself. In order to achieve this the body is the primary locus of praxis, as made explicit by Dōgen, when he writes:

> Buddhist practice through the body is more difficult than practice through the mind. Intellectual comprehension in learning through the mind must be united to practice through our body. This unity is called *shinjintsunintai*—"the real body of man." *Shinjitsunintai* is the perception of "everyday mind" through the phenomenal world. If we harmonize the practice of enlightenment with our body the entire world will be seen in its true form.[16]

The total self-realization through *shikan-taza* becomes manifested in a supple body and mind (*shinshin-nyūnan*), suggesting lightness and gracefulness, gentleness and openness, centered movement and inexhaustible energy.

For his contemporary, Shinran (1173–1263), suppleness of body and mind is also the ultimate goal of *nembutsu* practice. This practice is not merely vocal repetition but the expression of the total being, involving deep awareness of the source of *nembutsu*, that is, the compassionate vow of Amida Buddha. Such a saying of *nembutsu* means a transformation of being made possible by the working of boundless compassion, specifically the Thirty-third Vow of Amida Buddha. This vow insures such a realization:

> May I not gain possession of perfect awakening if, once I have attained buddhahood, it is not the case that all kinds of living beings in the measureless, inconceivable world systems of all the buddhas in the ten regions of the universe, as their bodies are exposed to my radiant light, feel their body and mind become soft and pliant to a degree surpassing anything in the human or celestial realms.[17]

The transformation of the ego-self to an ego-free, pliant self is made possible by the working of the Primal Vow of Amida. Shinran's favorite metaphor for this transformation is found in his famous verses on ice and water:

> Through the benefit of the unhindered light,
> We realize shinjin of vast, majestic virtues,
> And the ice of our blind passions necessarily melts,
> Immediately becoming the water of enlightenment.

> Obstructions of karmic evil turn into virtues;
> It is like the relation of ice and water:
> The more the ice, the more the water;
> The more the obstructions, the more the virtues.[18]

That the hard, sharp edge of the ego-self is melted to become the water of enlightenment suggests that the ultimate goal of this tradition accords with the goal of attaining suppleness of body and mind. In fact, the Pure Land tradition always considered this central to the Buddhist tradition. Hence, Shinran quotes T'an-luan, the sixth-century Chinese Pure Land master, who writes: "Such bodhisattvas, by fulfilling the practice, in observing both the extensive and brief, of *śamatha* and *vipaśyanā*, attain the mind that is pliant and gentle."[19]

When we turn to the Japanese aesthetic and martial arts, we find the same focus on the body found in the training of *kata*, "form" or "mold," which originated in the mastery of the Noh dance and performance. This training involves three stages: physical, psychological, and spiritual. On the physical level the mastery of *kata* or "form" is the crux of the training.

A model is demonstrated by the teacher, and the burden of learning is on the student, who repeatedly observes and emulates the model until the *kata* is completely internalized. This results in a centered stance, ambidextrous movement, fluid performance, and supple body and mind.

In the process of this mastery, internal psychological changes occur. The monotonous repetition of *kata* practice tests the student's commitment, sincerity, willpower, emotional stability, and inner strength, but most importantly it reduces stubbornness, curbs willfulness, and eliminates bad habits of the body. With the investment in time and effort, psychophysical maturity takes place, ultimately leading to the complete mastery of *kata* which insures maximum performance, artistry, and power.

The highest achievement, however, is spiritual, which is the displacement of a rigid ego-self with a fluid, integrated self which can break free of *kata*, so that there appears spontaneously the unique flowering of talent, individual creativity, and uncanny resonance with reality.

III

The significance of the body in religious practice has been taken for granted, but it needs to be pursued and fully studied, so that its crucial place in spiritual and creative life can be secured. One of the first modern studies on this subject is found in a series of pioneering works by Yasuo Yuasa, who combines erudite knowledge of Western philosophy, Eastern religions, depth psychology, neurophysiology, and meditative practices.[20] In these works he divides consciousness into two basic parts: bright consciousness and dark consciousness.

Bright consciousness is capable of self-reflection, but it is disembodied. It is on the surface of consciousness, quick to respond and comprehend. Dark consciousness is something deeper, forming the base structure of consciousness. It is one with the body, heavy and slow. Conventional thinking is pursued by bright consciousness, unaware of dark consciousness which definitely affects the way we feel and think. The goal of somatic training is to bring to full awareness both forms of consciousness and see their interplay.

Thus, whether it is the purification of six faculties of the Lotus Sutra, the practice of *shikan-tanza*, the invocation of *nembutsu*, or the mastery of *kata*, the integration of bright and dark consciousness occurs of itself through somatic training. Then, what we believed is the active agent in bright consciousness turns out to be the passive agent of the working of dark consciousness brought to light through somatic training and discipline. Yuasa clarifies this as follows:

Generally speaking, meditative thinking first puts the body prior to the mind by letting the former comply with a set form. By setting up such an artificial situation, one realizes that the everyday understanding of the self is inauthentic. We are led to experience that the body, as the determination of the human subject, is an object that does not originally belong to the sovereignty of rational consciousness. Consequently, we recognize that it is the body that dominates the spirit, even in the everyday mode of self. Ordinarily, we simply forget this fact.[21]

In various works Yuasa proceeds to demonstrate the relationship between the surface structure of consciousness, which includes sensation and thinking centered in the cerebral cortex and connected to the limbs via the sensory-motor circuit, and the base structure of consciousness, involving feeling, connected to the autonomic nervous system. His analysis is much more complex, but it contributes to a better understanding of the somatic role in religious life that involves thinking, feeling, and sensation.

Notes

1. *Eureka*, Special Issue on Kenji Miyazawa (1993 reprint), 26
2. *Scripture of the Lotus Blossom of the Fine Dharma*, tr. Leon Hurvitz (New York: Columbia University Press, 1976)
3. Ibid., 225.
4. *Ākāśa* is also translated as "[infinite] space" in *The Threefold Lotus Sutra*, tr. Bunnō Katō, Yoshirō Tamura, and Kōjirō Miyasaka; and "element of ether" in *The Saddharma-puṇḍarīka*, tr. H. Kern (Sacred Books of the East, Vol XXI). For a helpful analysis of this term, see Kazuyoshi Kino's chapter on the Lotus Sutra in *Daijō bukkyō seiritsushiteki kenkyū* (Tokyo: Sanseidō, 1954), 323–34.
5. *Scripture of the Lotus Blossom*, 233.
6. The earlier portion of the Lotus Sutra, chapters 2–9, compiled probably before 50 C.E., mentions only three activities: receiving, reading-reciting, and explaining. Chapters 1 and 10–21, compiled around 100 C.E. emphasize the five practices. See Yoshirō Tamura, *Hokekyō*, Chūkō Shinsho, no. 196 (Tokyo: Chūō Kōron Sha, 1969), 44.
7. Yasuo Yuasa, *The Body: Toward an Eastern Mind-Body Theory* (Albany: State University of New York Press, 1987), 169.
8. *Scripture of the Lotus Blossom*, 180.
9. Ibid., 280.
10. Ibid., 279.
11. Ibid., 281.
12. Ibid., 276.

13. *Eureka*, 186.
14. *From the Country of the Eight Islands*, tr. Hiroaki Saitō and Burton Watson (Seattle: University of Washington Press, 1981), 505–6.
15. *Scripture of the Lotus Blossom*, 178.
16. *Shōbōgenzō: The Eye and Treasury of the True Law*, tr. Kōsen Nishiyama (Tokyo: Nakayama Shobō, 1976), Vol. I, 13.
17. *The Land of Bliss*, tr. Luis Gomez (Honolulu: University of Hawai'i Press and Kyoto: Higashi Honganji Shinshu Otani-ha, 1996), 169–70.
18. *The Collected Works of Shinran* (Kyoto: Jōdo Shinshū Nishi Hongwanji-ha, 1997), Volume I, 371.
19. Ibid., 167.
20. Among Yuasa's important works available in English are *The Body: Toward an Eastern Mind-Body Theory* and *The Body, Self-Cultivation, and Ki-Energy* (Albany: State University of New York Press, 1993).
21. *The Body*, 122.

Visual Piety and the Lotus Sutra in Japan

Willa Jane Tanabe

Multiple Meanings

The profuse visual references to the Lotus Sutra attest to its significance in East Asian Buddhism. There are transcriptions of the text itself, written in inks, stitched in silk threads, and scratched on stones; and there are illustrations of the scripture's stories, ideas, and deities, painted on scrolls and walls, sculpted in wood, and cast in bronze. However, the very diversity of artwork related to the sutra presents a hurdle in understanding the art because how we choose to sort or arrange the material will affect our analysis of it by privileging one set of contexts against another. In fact, religious art always works on multiple and synchronic levels. A painting or text can, for example, elucidate or narrate, but it can also call attention to itself as an object of sanctification, thus serving both as visual discourse and as an artifact of visual piety.

The multiple layers of meaning and function are especially apparent in the Lotus Sutra scrolls such as the copy of the *Fugen Bosatsu Kamboppon* chapter owned by the Yamato Bunkakan. The chapter is copied onto paper decorated with gold and silver foil and scattered gold and silver dust. Each row of ten characters is separated by silver ruled lines and each inked character is inscribed atop a multicolored lotus flower and encircled by a gold nimbus. While the expository function of the transcription is obvious, the scroll also exemplifies the devotional ideal of demonstrating one's adoration of the words of the Buddha by embellishing the transcription to produce a beauty of form to parallel the profundity of content. Furthermore, the treatment of each character as if it were a buddha also emphasizes the tenet espoused in the *Hosshi* chapter that

81

within the sutra "is the whole body of the Tathāgata."[1] This is a subject to which I will return later.

Similarly the frontispiece painting can transform the text into pictorial expositions of the content or can transfigure the text into images that particularize or contextualize the content in ways that emphasize the devotional nature of the image or object. The frontispiece to the *Fugen Bosatsu Kamboppon* chapter of the scroll at the Yamato Bunkakan manifests these dual tendencies and can be interpreted in several ways. The twenty-eighth chapter is brief and essentially declares that Fugen Bosatsu (Samantabhadra) will protect believers of the Lotus Sutra and will reveal himself to practitioners. The content of the chapter is rarely illustrated in frontispieces of works divided according to fascicle because the frontispieces to the eighth fascicle usually portray the more dramatic perils that confront humans from the *Kanzeon Bosatsu Fumombon* chapter or the magical feats of two princes from the *Myōshōgon Ō Honjihon* chapter, both of which are also in the eighth fascicle. For frontispieces in works divided according to chapter, it would be most appropriate to portray Fugen on the frontispiece to chapter 28. However, because transcriptions of the Lotus Sutra were often accompanied by *Bussetsu Kan Fugen Bosatsu Gyōhōkyō*, the closing sutra, whose frontispieces almost always display Fugen mounted on his elephant descending toward a lone practitioner, there may have been some reluctance to repeat the motif. The number of extant frontispieces devoted solely to this chapter are few and do not suggest a fixed pictorial interpretation other than representations of Fugen.[2]

The frontispiece from the Yamato Bunkakan scroll portrays a religious service conducted within a nobleman's residence. The limited number of guests and priests suggests that the ritual is not a complex one, such as a *hokke hakkō*, but rather an intimate service for family or close friends. The older priest who sits in front of a painting and holds what may be a censer in his hand is assisted by two other priests who sit behind lacquered tables and hold a decorated sutra. All have their mouths open in recitation of the scripture. Two young priests, their heads bowed and eyes closed, and four aristocrats, one man and three women, sit on the veranda. The nobleman holds a rosary and faces the interior while behind him sits a young girl facing the corner of the veranda. The other two women, wearing deeply-brimmed bamboo hats (*ichimegasa*), also face the interior of the room. One lifts the brim of her hat to rub her eyes while the other brings her sleeves to her eyes as if to wipe tears. The woman on the right appears to be the most important of the females because she is given more detail. Her robes, for example, are decorated in silver roundels and she wears a red strap (*kakeobi*) around her chest that signifies abstinence. Both this strap and the hats indicate that the women traveled to the service and that this is not their home.

What does this scene illustrate? If one looks at the content of the chapter, the scene could be understood as a general reference to the statement that Fugen will protect those who recite the sutra. We can speculate that the *honzon* within the scene is a painting of Fugen and the painter has merely set the scriptural promise of protection in a familiar setting and peopled it with his contemporaries. However, the details of the painting seem too specific to merely reflect a generalized exhortation to recite the text and some scholars have sought a more particular interpretation.[3] At least one scholar has suggested that this scroll might have been copied individually, not as part of a chapter per scroll set of twenty-eight as is generally thought, for the service of a court woman.[4] Certainly, the demeanor of the aristocrats and the activities of the priests suggest that this is a memorial service in which prayers and chanting by close friends are what the sponsors of the work wanted to emphasize. Indeed, the figures seem so individualized that scholars have suggested that the large central priest resembles Emperor Go-shirakawa, as seen in certain portraits. This theory is to some extent influenced by the fact that while the scroll has no date or inscription, it is accompanied by a later document that describes it as "a work in Go-shirakawa's own hand," and by another slip of paper that says it was "from the collection of Shirakawa-dera in Yamashiro no kuni." The Shirakawa area is well known for temples dating from the *insei* period, although this temple does not appear to correlate to any of the famous temples such as the Rokushō-ji.[5] While this theory is only one among several, and while frontispieces depicting recognizable historical figures are rare, the suggestion is tantalizing: the scene is of a memorial service for someone surrounding Go-shirakawa. Certainly most scholars date this work to the second half of the twelfth century, which permits this possibility.[6]

Other scholars have argued that we can understand the scene as a direct illustration of that portion of the chapter in which Śākyamuni, in response to Fugen's vow of protection, proclaims: "If there be any who receive and keep, read and recite . . . this Law-Flower Sutra, know that such are attending on Śākyamuni Buddha as if they were hearing this sutra from the Buddha's mouth."[7] The suggestion is made because the reciters face the copied text wherein the mutual identity of the Buddha and the text is emphasized by the treatment of each character as if it were an image of the Buddha. That is, the participants in the ritual are hearing the voice of the Buddha by reading the text.[8]

Taken as a whole, all of these various interpretations of the meaning of the frontispiece illustration point out the importance of both illustrating the text and performing acts of piety. The treatment of the copied text too expands its meaning to include doctrines not specifically mentioned in the *Fugen Bosatsu Kamboppon* chapter, that is, the idea of the mutual identity of the body of the Tathāgata and the sutra. In fact, the idea of the Lotus Sutra as the body of the Buddha and the treatment of the copied scrolls in manners similar to the treatment of relics is one of the characteristics of Lotus belief and practice, especially in the late Heian and Kamakura periods.

From Relics to Body

Relic worship in Japan goes back to the introduction of Buddhism from Korea. After its initial rejection, Buddhism was again sponsored by Soga no Umako, who tested the power of a relic he had been given by attempting to shatter it with a sledgehammer and by casting it into water "where it floated on the water or sank as one desired. In consequence of this, . . . [Umako and two others] held faith in Buddhism and practiced it unremittingly. . . . From this arose the beginning of Buddhism."[9] Nara and early Heian records often note the large number of relics brought back from China. In the late Nara period the priest Ganjin (arrived in Japan 754, d. 763) initiated an annual relic service (*shari-e*) at Tōshōdai-ji. In 860 Ennin initiated an annual relic service at Enryaku-ji and the *Sambō-ekotoba* makes special note that women, "who are forbidden access to Mount Hie, are apparently not satisfied with second-hand accounts."[10] Consequently, they attended relic services at Tōshōdai-ji and Hanayama monastery where "the offices of these services are assigned to ladies."[11] All of this shows the growing popularity of relics which were valued not only as manifestations of the presence of the Buddha but also for their apotropaic power and ability to secure blessings. Moreover, a recent dissertation argues that as they developed in popularity they also diversified in function, serving important political ends as well as religious ones. They not only became connected with individual funeral services but also were used in legitimacy rites for the state.[12] Thus the Heian court and religious establishments accepted relic services and worship as part of their regular ritual practice, although they had various purposes.

There were, from the very earliest Indian references to relics, at least two types: 1) bodily relics such as bone or ash (Jpn. *shinshari*), and 2) relics associated with the Buddha such as his robe or begging bowl (Jpn. *hōshari*). Included as part of the associative relics were the scriptures of the Buddha. Boucher points out that by the sixth or seventh century in

India, as reported by Yijing, Buddhists placed a dharma-relic verse within stupas.[13] Already in the Nara period, the Japanese used sutras and text in place of bodily relics. Prior to the formal establishment of the provincial temples and nunneries in 741, for example, Emperor Shōmu ordered 740 copies of the Lotus Sutra and the opening and closing sutras for installation in seven-story pagodas that were to be built throughout the country, and in the early Heian period Saichō (d. 822) built three *tahōtō* and placed within them one thousand copies of the Lotus Sutra.[14] Scriptures were also enshrined within miniature three-dimensional stupas. An early extant example of enshrining a text or verse within a stupa dates from 764–70 when Empress Shōtoku ordered one million miniature stupas containing *darani* for distribution to major temples. While Empress Shōtoku was inspired by the exhortation of the *Mujōkō-darani-kyō* to make such pagodas, clearly the use of text as associative relic was already accepted and continued to be used. One of the finest extant examples of a jeweled stupa intended to contain a Lotus Sutra dates from 1370 and is owned by Hompō-ji in Kyoto.[15] Many of the extant examples from the late Heian and Kamakura periods were recovered from sutra mounds in which the copied text (frequently the Lotus Sutra) was placed within bronze containers, sometimes in the shape of a stupa. The buried sutras are most frequently explained as expressions of Miroku (Maitreya) belief and concern the difficulty of preserving the teachings in the age of *mappō*, but inscriptions on the containers make clear that they also were produced at memorial services with the deceased intended as the recipients of the merit accrued by copying and preserving the sutras.

Besides being an object placed within stupas, the Lotus Sutra has also been inscribed onto stupas made of clay, wood, leaves, and paper. The many forms of these stupa-sutras were studied by the late Tsugio Miya, who noted that they combine two injunctions in the sutra itself: one for building stupas and the other for copying the sutra. The "clay stupa sutras" (*deitō-kyō*) were usually miniature clay stupas onto which one character was inscribed or molded. The "persimmon sutras" (*kaki-kyō*) and the "bamboo grass leaf stupas" (*sasa-hōtō*) were strips of wood frequently in the shape of stylized miniature stupas (*sotoba*) on which lines of characters from the sutra were copied. Literary records from the early twelfth century on often mention their use, the scale of which was sometimes staggering. An entry for 1140 in the *Sō Sainen konshi kinji kuyō mokuroku* describes the making of 69,384 *sotoba*, which is the number of characters contained in the Lotus Sutra and the opening and closing sutras. In addition to these sutras, the *Hannya shingyō* and the *Ninnō hannya-kyō* were copied onto *sotoba*, making in all 97,189 characters inscribed on as many *sotoba*. An entry for 1194 in *Sambutsujō shō* refers to eighteen copies of the

Lotus Sutra written on *sotoba*. These projects were notable for their scale, while examples of writing a single character of the Lotus Sutra within a stupa drawn on paper (*ichiji ichitō Hokekyō*) are often known for their beauty. Examples can be found in the works owned by Anrakujū-in in Kyoto, Homman-ji in Kyoto, Rinnō-ji in Tochigi, Togakushi Jinja in Nagano, and others. All of these were done for the making of merit or transfer of merit leading to blessings in this world or rebirth in the next, and were made by commoners as well as aristocrats.[16]

The most intimate connection between building stupas and copying sutras is seen in the *moji-tō*, in which characters are arranged in the shape of stupas. In this case the text is not placed within a stupa but becomes the stupa itself. The *moji-tō* are not unique to Japan, and the earliest example is probably the *Hannya shingyō* now owned by the British Museum (Stein 4289), which Miya dates to the late Tang or Five Dynasties period on the basis of its calligraphic style. The Chinese courtiers and literati continued to copy out *moji-tō* in later dynasties and also produced printed versions. A Korean example of the Lotus Sutra written in the form of a seven-story pagoda is now owned by Tō-ji in Kyoto. Thus there were many precedents from which the Japanese could take inspiration, but Japanese *moji-tō*, unlike those from the continent, include paintings around the stupa which illustrate the contents. Such works are called *hōtō* mandala and there are several Lotus Sutras among the extant examples in Japan. Those at the Danzan Jinja and Ryūhon-ji are the most famous because of Miya's research.[17]

We see here a variety of associations between the Lotus Sutra, stupas, relics, and the body of the Buddha. When the text of the sutra is placed atop a lotus flower or within a halo, it appears to be treated as the body of the Buddha; when it is placed within a stupa it appears to be treated as a relic. But what happens when the sutra becomes the stupa itself? In order to understand what it means for the sutra to become a stupa, we need to turn to the Lotus Sutra itself for its own understanding of the relationship between the two. At the beginning of this paper I referred to the passage in the Teacher of the Law (*Hosshi*) chapter in which the Buddha makes a remarkable distinction between relics and the body of the Buddha in relationship to stupas. Addressing the Medicine King, the Buddha explains that in all places where the Lotus Sutra is preached, read, recited, copied, or simply exists, a stupa should be built of seven jewels. "But there is no need to deposit relics [within it]. Wherefore? [Because] in it there is the whole body of the Tathāgata."[18] The difference between a relic and the body of the Buddha, then, is that a relic is only a part of but not the whole body of the Buddha. The point is repeated and emphasized in the next chapter, "Appearance of the Treasure Stupa"

(*Kenhōtōbon*). The treasure stupa does not contain a relic, which is the usual object enshrined in a stupa. Instead, the Buddha proclaims that "In this stupa there is the *whole body of the Tathāgata*."[19] This idea is repeated throughout the chapter, as in the climactic moment when Śākyamuni opened the door of the tower and the entire assembly "saw the Tathāgata Abundant Treasures . . . with his undissipated [unimpaired] body whole and as if he were in meditation."[20]

The difference between relics and body can be understood in a hierarchy or progression of meaning. The Lotus Sutra can be treated as a relic, but its distinctive character is seen in its identification with the body of the Buddha. As the body of the Buddha, the Lotus Sutra is not just the part that remains in the world after the rest of the Buddha is gone, but is the complete body itself. The question of what remains of the Buddha after he is gone is addressed in chapter 16, "Life Span of the Tathāgata," and the answer is that everything remains because the Buddha is never really gone. Not only is the sutra the whole, it is the eternal body of the Buddha. Since the Buddha is always present, he can be seen, and the sight of him also represents a culmination of a progression that takes place in religious practice. Added to the sight of the Buddha is another high point of practice: becoming the body of the Buddha.

Seeing and Becoming the Body

That a passage from chapter 16 is often recited at funerals is not surprising since that chapter asserts that the Buddha does not really die though he seems to disappear for a while. What he does is to pretend that he dies, and this is an expedient means to help people live moral lives. Morality, as we will see, is also rooted in a concern with the human body.

The passage reads as follows.

> . . . If the Buddha abides long in the world, men of little virtue who do not cultivate the roots of goodness and are [spiritually] poor and mean, greedily attached to the five desires, and are caught in the net of [wrong] reflection and false views—if they see the Tathāgata constantly present and not extinct, [they] will then become puffed up and lazy, and unable to conceive the idea that it is hard to meet [the Buddha] or a mind of reverence [for him].[21]

The constant presence of the Buddha will only breed neglect or even contempt arising from familiarity, and people will take the Buddha for granted, just as they do their parents who are still alive. The parable of the physician-father makes the point that his sick children will be shocked into taking their medicine if they believe that their father is dead, and such a fake death is duly arranged and has its predicted effect. Likewise, the Buddha must pretend to die, and the effects of such a faked death work well on the moral and religious life of his followers.

The first thing that happens when they see that he has passed into extinction is that they "worship my relics."[22] Here we see that the worship of relics is based on the perceived but mistaken notion that the Buddha is dead. Next, says the Buddha, they will yearn for the Buddha and "beget thirsting hearts of hope. . . . Wholeheartedly wishing to see the Buddha."[23] Only when they have become truly faithful and upright, gentle in intent, not even caring if their own lives be lost will the Buddha reappear in the world so that all of those who are gentle, peaceful, honest, and upright "will see me here in person."[24] The Buddha resorts to this expedient means to "cause living beings to gain entry into the unsurpassed way and quickly acquire the body of a Buddha."[25] The body of the Buddha and people's visual apprehension of it are primary religious objectives here, but the Buddha's constant presence would be too much of a good thing that would invite moral laxity and a demise in piety. However, even when the Buddha enters into temporary extinction, there must still be something that gives focus to visual piety, and that object is the relics of the Buddha. There is a kind of progression described here as the body of the Buddha goes into temporary extinction and is replaced by relics that foster a return of reverence, which allows the Buddha to reappear in bodily form, all so that living beings themselves can gain the body of the Buddha.

Visual deprivation as a means of promoting piety is also the basis of the *hibutsu*, the most famous of which are the Amida triad at Zenkō-ji and the Asakusa Kannon. But the invisibility cannot be too permanent, and there must be a replica or an unveiling every so often, once every thirty-three years, for instance, in the case of Kannon. William Bodiford has described such a *kaichō*, the lifting of the curtain to reveal the hidden image.[26] The interplay of visibility and invisibility is a powerful one, and we see its dynamics being deployed in chapter 16 of the Lotus Sutra.

The sutra makes it clear that one of the reasons why the Buddha absents himself as if he were dead is to provoke people to come to their moral senses. The seat of moral or immoral action is not just in the mind, but in the body as well. When our bodies perform actions, they are not simply carrying out commands issuing from the mind, but have their own integrity and responsibility. In many Buddhist analyses of sensory faculties, the mind is not given a privileged position of command over the other functions. Moral infractions are not to be blamed solely on wrong thoughts, bad intent, poor judgment, or a failure of courage, but on the eyes, mouth, nose, ears, and hands as well. Repentance therefore involves all of the sensory faculties, not just the mind and its resolutions or dissolutions.

The *Lotus Samādhi Repentance* (*Hokke sammai sengi*) attributed to Chih-i gives instructions on a basic Tendai repentance ritual. The setting is "the defiled and evil world five hundred years after the Tathāgata's extinction," when monks, nuns, and lay persons are joined by a host of others, including "those who wished to see the bodily form of the bodhisattva Samantabhadra, and those who wished to see all the manifest bodies of Śākyamuni and the Many Treasures Buddha from the Treasure Stupa."[27] This, of course, is a reference to chapter 11 of the Lotus Sutra in which the Treasure Stupa appears rising from the earth and containing the whole and complete body of the Many Treasures Buddha. Repeatedly the bodhisattvas convey to Śākyamuni their desire "to see this buddha's body."[28] The concern for seeing the body of the Buddha is sustained throughout the rest of the chapter.

Having described the multitude who wish to see buddhas and bodhisattvas, the *Hokke sammai sengi* goes on to give detailed instructions about performing the ritual, which takes three weeks to complete and is divided into ten parts: (1) purifying the place of practice, (2) purifying one's body, (3) making offerings for the three karmic acts, (4) giving reverence to the Three Treasures, (5) singing praises to the Three Treasures, (6) prostrating to the buddhas, (7) repenting one's sins, (8) practicing the way (of praising the buddhas), (9) chanting the Lotus Sutra, and (10) practicing proper visualization through *zazen* meditation. The lengthiest instructions are given for repentance, and each of the sensory faculties is taken up in turn with formulaic but detailed confessions of infractions committed by the eyes, ears, nose, tongue, body, and mind.[29] Moral rectification is accomplished through physical correction. And physical well-being is proof of moral and spiritual propriety. This idea is reflected especially in chapters 17 through 19 of the Lotus Sutra, which detail the benefits, many of which are physical, for those who uphold or teach the sutra. Such practitioners, for example, will never suffer mouth decay: "His teeth not be gapped, yellow, or black, Nor his lips thick, awry, or cracked, . . . His tongue neither dried up, black, nor shrunk; His nose high, long, and straight; His forehead broad, level, and upright; A joy for men to behold."[30] Such beliefs continue today. Affirming the inseparable connection between morality and the body in his exhortation to ordinary people in contemporary Japan, Kōshō Shimizutani, the chief abbot of Sensō-ji, the Asakusa Kannon Temple in Tokyo, speaks of repentance as an essential part of the process of realizing one's inherent buddha-nature, and cites the *Daijō honjō shinjikan gyō* to help make this point: "If you wash your dusty labors with the water of repentance, your own body will become a pure vessel."[31]

Upon completing all ten stages, not everyone will achieve the same results. Practitioners are divided into three groups according to their basic abilities, and each group is subdivided further into three levels. In the least capable group, those in the lowest level will have auspicious dreams, those in the middle level will see auspicious signs during *zazen* meditation, and those in the top level will experience joy and quiescence of mind and body. In the second group, those in the lowest level will attain *samādhi* in their meditation; those in the middle level will realize the subtleties of inhaling and exhaling, and establish connections with the wisdom and virtues of all the buddhas; and those in the top level will see the emptiness of things, which have no permanence and are neither born nor extinguished (*fushō fumetsu*). In the group of the most capable people, those in the lowest level will realize that their bodies and minds are like clouds, shadows, and dreams that have no reality. And what will the attainments be for those in the two highest levels? They will realize the most excellent of fruits, which surpasses even the realization of emptiness: *seeing* Samantabhadra and the *manifest bodies* (*funjin*) of Śākyamuni.[32]

The association between repentance and the body is, as we have seen, an intimate one and the place where such rites were conducted was the Lotus Samādhi Hall (*Hokke sammai dō*, also referred to as *Sammai-dō* or *Hokke-dō*). This hall also became connected with funeral rites. In his history of funeral practices in Japan, Noboru Haga points out that by the ninth century, the Buddhist influence in imperial funerary practices increased such that cremation became commonplace, and *sotoba*, stylized miniature stupas, were placed for the first time atop the burial mound for Emperor Daigo (r. 897–930). The next emperor for whom a *sotoba* was erected was Go-ichijō (r. 1016–36), and it was regarded as a *Sammai-dō*. In Emperor Horikawa's (r. 1086–7) case, his ashes were entombed at Ninnan-ji and the site was marked with the three-story stone pagoda within which were placed printed *darani* and a copy of the Lotus Sutra. The remains of Emperor Takakura (1168–80) were placed in a *Hokke-dō* as were the ashes of Emperor Go-horikawa (1221–32). While other kinds of entombment structures were used for deceased emperors (*gorin-no-tō*, for instance), Haga notes that the *Hokke sammai dō*, along with the *Tahōtō*, the Many Treasures Tower, were commonly used.[33] The *Hokke sammai dō* thus served also as a columbarium, a repository for the remains of the body.

Conclusion

Underlying the many ideas and teachings of the Lotus Sutra is the concern with and primacy of the body of the Buddha. It should not be surprising that the rituals and practices that developed in association with the propagation of the Lotus were also connected to occasions that required purification, repentance or commemoration of the body. It is fitting then that frontispieces, such as we have seen in the Yamato Bunkakan scroll, should also refer to such specific occasions, as well as illustrate passages of the text. Moreover, the mutual identification of the sutra with the eternal body of the Buddha encouraged glorification and adulation of the sutra as an icon, not a mere spiritual textbook. Thus it is also appropriate that the transcriptions of the text itself should incorporate ideas of the sutra as the body of the Buddha, as seen in the placement of the characters of the sutra atop lotus flowers as in the scroll at the Yamato Bunkakan, in the placement of the characters within stupas, or in their use as a structure to hold the body of the Buddha as seen in the *moji-tō*. Beautiful as these works are, they function primarily not as art but as objects of visual piety.

Notes

1. Bunnō Katō, Yoshirō Tamura, and Kōjirō Miyasaka, trans., *The Threefold Lotus Sutra* (New York: Weatherhill-Kōsei, 1975), 190.
2. The three extant frontispieces to this chapter in decorated scroll sets divided by chapter all display Fugen. They include frontispieces from the famous sets, Heike Nōkyō, Kunōji Hokekyō, and one now at Fujita Art Museum. Hirotoshi Sudō "Ichijirendai Hokekyō Kamboppon mikaeshi-e ni tsuite," *Yamato Bunka* 88 (September 1992), 11–21, esp. 14.
3. Yoshi Shirahata, "Ichijirendai Hokekyō Fugen Bosatsu Kamboppon to Ryōjin Hishō Kudenshū," *Yamato Bunka* 88 (September 1992), 1–10, esp. 7–8.
4. Sudō "Ichijirendai," *Yamato Bunka*, 17.
5. Sudō, "Ichijirendai," *Yamato Bunka*, 1, 20.
6. One example of a frontispiece depicting a historical figure is the frontispiece attached to the famous *ichiji ichijibutsu* scroll from the tenth century, owned by Zentsū-ji, which includes a portrait of Kūkai. See illustration in Nara Kokuritsu Hakubutsukan, eds., *Hokekyō no Bijutsu* (Nara: Nara Kokuritsu Hakubutsukan, 1979), 128.
7. *The Threefold Lotus Sutra*, 342.
8. Ibid.
9. W. G. Aston, tr., *Nihongi*, part 2 (London: George Allen & Unwin, 1956), 102.
10. Edward Kamens, trans., *The Three Jewels* (Ann Arbor: University of Michigan Press, 1988), 303.
11. Ibid.
12. Brian D. Ruppert, *Jewel in the Ashes: Buddha Relics and Power in Early Medieval Japan* (Unpublished Ph.D. dissertation, Princeton University).
13. Daniel Boucher, "Sūtra on the Merit of Bathing the Buddha," in Donald S. Lopez, Jr., ed., *Buddhism in Practice* (Princeton: Princeton University Press, 1995), 61.

14. Kenryō Kawakatsu, ed., *Tahōtō to Hokekyō shisō* (Tokyo: Tōkyōdō, 1984), 48–55.
15. See illustration in Nara Kokuritsu Hakubutsukan, ed., *Hokekyō no Bijutsu*, 142.
16. Tsugio Miya, *Kinji hōtō mandara* (Tokyo: Yoshikawa Kōbunkan, 1976), 1–3.
17. Miya, *Kinji hōtō mandara*, 4–7. See also Willa Tanabe, *Paintings of the Lotus Sutra* (Tokyo: Weatherhill, 1988), 102–8.
18. Italics added. *The Threefold Lotus Sutra*, 190.
19. Italics added. *Ibid.*, 196.
20. Ibid., 200.
21. Ibid., 252.
22. Ibid., 254.
23. Ibid., 254.
24. Burton Watson, *The Lotus Sutra* (New York: Columbia University Press, 1993), 231. "All see that I exist" is the translation from *The Threefold Lotus Sutra*, 255.
25. Watson, *The Lotus Sutra*, 232. The text uses the term *busshin*, that is Buddha body, but some translations remove the sense of physicality as in "To enter the Way supreme / And speedily accomplish their buddhahood." *The Threefold Lotus Sutra*, 256.
26. William Bodiford, "Soto Zen in a Japanese Town: Field Notes on a Once-Every-Thirty-Three-Years Kannon Festival," *Japanese Journal of Religious Studies*, Vol. 21, No. 1 (March 1994), 3–36.
27. T46:949b.
28. *The Threefold Lotus Sutra*, 197.
29. T45:952a–953b.
30. *The Threefold Lotus Sutra*, 273.
31. Kōshō Shimizutani, "Nemmatsu zuisō shiaku shūzen," *Sensō-ji*, No. 456 (December, 1997), 13.
32. T45:954c–955b.
33. Noboru Haga, *Sōgi no rekishi* (Tokyo: Yūzankaku, 1996), 53–54.

2. Theological Reflection and Dialogue

Considering the Lotus Sutra

John H. Berthrong

The question I have posed for myself is, How does a Christian scholar, greatly influenced by his exposure to various Confucian, Taoist, and Buddhist traditions and texts of East Asia, read and understand the Lotus Sutra? That I have been invited to consider this question, and that I do so from the perspective of a religious standpoint of diverse origins, speaks volumes about the modern religious world. The task of a religious intellectual, as I have learned from the Harvard Confucian, Tu Wei-ming, is to describe, explain, understand, and then commend one's tradition—or any tradition that comes to be part of one's religious world. Actually, any competent and honest scholar needs to be able to do at least the first three steps from description, to explanation, and then to understanding. It is finally the task of the religious scholar of a tradition then to take the final step of commending what has been described, understood, and explained as something worthy of our collective attention and appropriation.

The real hermeneutic trick these days, at least for those who admit that they live in a religiously plural world, is to decide just what tradition they belong to and which traditions have, in turn, contributed to one's own understanding of belonging to one's root tradition. For some this is an easy task. They believe themselves securely located within one of the great religious traditions of humankind, and even if they find other traditions worthy of respect, they do not perceive that these traditions have anything material to add to their root tradition. Other scholars find themselves in a messier situation; they discover that the boundaries of their spiritual world are more porous in the sense that, upon sincere reflection, they cannot deny that they are moved by what they read and experience in other faith traditions. In fact, as I have argued elsewhere, such scholars find themselves in a situation of "multiple religious participation."

One must hasten to add that multiple religious participation does not necessarily lead to syncretism or the thoughtless blending of traditions. The example of the Confucian tradition in China is illustrative of the situation. The Confucian tradition is a wonderfully protean creation of Chinese, Korean, Japanese, Vietnamese, and now even Western scholarly minds. There are great debates about the nature of the tradition. Is it a religion, a social philosophy, a political ideology, or a set of family rituals? Confucianism, which is merely the modern English term for all that went on under the general rubric of *ju-chia, ru-chiao,* or *tao-hsüeh* in East Asia, is not a creedal or doctrinal tradition. It even has a very fuzzy sociological organizational pattern that has changed from century to century as the tradition has developed in East Asia. But what does hold the Confucian Way together is a commitment on the part of all Confucians to the study and appropriation in their lives of the canon of the Confucian classics. One is a Confucian if one is moved by and participates in the study of the communally defined Confucian canon.[1] Of course, this is a minimalist functional definition of the membership in the Confucian Way. In terms of modern computer language, the hardware or basic operating system of the Confucian is constituted by the Confucian canon. Other programs and applications can be added, but the basic operating system is formed by its fundamental hardware and software.

Having briefly noted the irenic nature of Confucian self-definition, it is also important to note that the Confucians, like proponents of all great religious traditions, assumed that they were correct. Over the centuries Confucians have argued with Moists, Taoists, Legalists, Logicians, Yangists, Buddhists, Christians, and Marxists about the nature of truth. On the whole these debates and apologetics have been remarkably civilized in nature. There has been little overt religious persecution in traditional China even though Confucians have held their convictions about reality as strongly as any other religious community. The Confucian experience demonstrates that one can treat other traditions with interest and respect without giving up on questions of ultimate truth.

I believe that something similar happens when a modern Christian intellectual reads Confucian, Taoist, or Buddhist texts seriously. This does not mean that one becomes less of a Christian; in fact many scholars will speak eloquently of the fact that multiple religious participation enriches and transforms their understanding of their root tradition. However, the commitment to the root tradition does not waver. If the sense of participation and membership in one's root tradition begins to shift, then the honest person must seriously consider conversion. We ought to be in a position of being willing to convince and be convinced in interreligious dialogue.

Of course, in most cases the way an outsider will describe, explain, and then understand a tradition will be different from that of an insider. However, scholars have discovered that when they carefully attend to the study of a tradition with anything like an open mind, the distance between interpretations in these first three steps tends to narrow. While the methods and means by which this essentially descriptive task is carried out may vary, the community of scholars finds that it can understand and even appreciate the insights from beyond their own tradition. For instance, many Christian scholars have come to appreciate the Buddhist concept of *upāya*, skillful means, as a way to look at certain aspects of their own tradition, such as some of Jesus' teachings as recorded in the Gospels. Furthermore, W. C. Smith argues that until members of a tradition can recognize their tradition in another's description of it, the description is not really accurate as a corporate act of interpretation. Smith is quick to note that this does not mean that the outsider will use the same language or meaning patterns, but that adherents will still perceive an accurate rendition of what they believe and hold dear.

In terms of a religiously plural world, David Tracy has developed a model of the three audiences or styles of modern Christian theology in *The Analogical Imagination*. The first theological form is what he calls fundamental or foundational theology. This is a public and comparative form of theology and is most closely related to the philosophy of religion and natural theology; fundamental theology will also make use of material from other scholarly disciplines such as the psychology of religion and intellectual history, as well as the social sciences, in trying to understand the range of human religious activity. It does not warrant or privilege any one tradition or set of scriptures or creeds as normative for conversation. It is dialogical in the sense that the understandings and categories it uses must be agreed to by all involved in the conversation. It is the place where a great deal of interreligious dialogue takes place between and among members of religious traditions.

By its very nature, especially when it involves cross-cultural analysis, comparative theology as fundamental theology is a tricky business. While not all fundamental theology is comparative theology, it is hard to think of comparative theology that is not fundamental in Tracy's sense of foundational work. For instance, the very categories used to begin the conversation are always rooted in one linguistic, historical, philosophical, theological, and cultural tradition—in this case modern academic English of the modern and postmodern era. Fundamental theology is committed to the insight that there is no place of privilege and yet must start its conversation from some place. If the conversation were to begin in Chinese, Korean, or Japanese, the form and content of the conversation would be very different.

Take the very notion of religion itself. As many scholars have noted, this is a Western concept and it is often difficult to find the precise analogs for it in other cultures. Jordan Paper makes the point that if you ask modern Chinese about their religious membership the answer will often be confused from a Western point of view.[2] However, Paper points out that if you ask the same person, "Who do you sacrifice to?" then suddenly things become much clearer within the Chinese religious cosmos. Just knowing what question to ask about religion is not always easy. But it is only out of this kind of painstaking cross-cultural exchange that scholars will be able to generate a vocabulary suitable for foundational theology.

Tracy's second form is called systematic theology; this is a form of discourse that is built upon the reflection, analysis, and vocabulary of particular traditions. It is the kind of conversation that goes on within a tradition in terms of its own self-understanding and modes of discourse. As contrasted to fundamental theology, systematic theology precisely warrants and acknowledges its debt to a particular tradition, its scriptures and creeds. It is thought in service to particular communities of faith. It is also the place from which all the vocabulary of religion first flows because it is within traditions that ritual, practice, scripture, and dogma are generated. Because of human self-interest, people always tend to think that the way they see the world is the natural way. It has always struck me that many subtle Buddhist critiques of conventional thinking have been aimed at convincing the student not to take the inherited tradition as being in total conformity with the way the world really is. Most religions have a place of mystery, a place for faith that is beyond even the most subtle scholastic system. Within the confines of ultimate mystery, systematic theology expresses how we as a community of faith see the world and express this understanding as best we can with words, images, metaphors, icons, symbols, prayers, hymns, chants, and meditations.

The third form is praxis theology. This too is a public form of theology often linked to various issues of political theology, human rights, global ecology, or liberation and social justice and always is a form of theology that arises out of some practical or concrete situation of believers. Its methods seek to correct the faults of the present informed by a vision of what the Kingdom of God ought to be like. Praxis theology, therefore, can make use of, but not be bound by, the results or arguments of fundamental or systematic theology. However, because it is linked to liberation it is linked to the soteriological vision of fundamental and systematic theology.

On Reading the Metaphors

All great religious texts, the ones that traditions rightly esteem as scripture, are supple, suggestive, and serious works.[3] They are also multivalent in that they can suggest different things to different people in different times, and even now in entirely different religious traditions. One often wonders if there is anything like one core fiduciary reading of a text. In fact, it is probably the case that it is the faithful community that sets the norms for what a fiduciary reading of a text ought to be. For instance, the use that I make of the Lotus Sutra and the Revelation of Saint John will need to be judged as a religious act of exegesis by Buddhists and Christians as somehow reflecting what is in the text or what may be newly seen by means of reading the text in a different manner. It is the metaphor of the renewed creation that comes through following the bodhisattva path and the way of Christ that intrigues me.

Scriptures are also profoundly serious works. They are not written merely to provoke or amuse; they are written to enlighten, to call to repentance, and to show the person a way out of a predicament. While many scholars will not agree with John Hick's view that all religion deals in soteriology, I think that few would gainsay the fact that scriptures, when they become what Christians call the Living Word of God, do force their readers to confront the serious nature of their condition. Scripture can also turn us from untruth to the truth, from error to wisdom, from misconduct to correct living. From the Christian point of view, and certainly from the point of view of the book of the Bible I want to focus on, Revelation, this is deadly serious business. Much of the language and imagery of Revelation is calculated to make humankind face the fact that things do not always go well in the mundane world, and without a major renewal, can lead to our perdition. But that is not the whole message of Revelation. If damnation were all there is to tell, it would have been a sorry way to end the Christian canon. Nonetheless, the note of spiritual urgency does lead to a stressing of the uniqueness and exclusiveness of the path of Christ. Like a good doctor, to borrow from the Buddhist tradition, the author of Revelation wants to wake us up and to lead us onto the narrow path of salvation.

This leads to the question of exclusivism in religion. This is a pressing issue for contemporary Christian theology. In fact, it may be one of the most pressing issues that the Christian community faces today. While it has not always and everywhere been the case, it is probably a fair generalization that the Christian tradition has had an exclusive understanding of itself for most of its history. This makes a great deal of sense when we remember that the tradition began as a small and dismissed Jewish sect that had to struggle to find its own identity over against all the other larger and more powerful religions of the late Greco-Roman world. The texts of the New Testament bear witness to this need to protect the nascent community and to define it in exclusive terms. From the point of view of Christian systematic theology, this has always led to the tension between the universality of the offer of redemption in Christ and the particularity of the story of Jesus as the Christ.

One of the outcomes of this mode of exclusive thinking was to see the Christian faith as superior to all other forms of religious life in a militant way. However, I have come to believe that this is also a feature of all great religions even when they take a more charitable view of other religions.

Each religion really does believe that it knows the truth. The more inclusive or universalistic tradition will agree that other traditions do indeed also have the truth, and indeed may have a truth sufficient for the salvation or liberation of their followers. Nonetheless, even the most irenic and tolerant of traditions will make the point that they have something to offer that perhaps the other tradition does not have or has forgotten. No real religious tradition can give up entirely its claim to truth. Many Christians, somewhat to the consternation of many other Christians, are now at the point of thinking about making this kind of inclusive move within Christian systematic theology. If the Christian tradition as a whole does make this turn towards a more open, pluralist, inclusive, universalistic, and irenic view of the relationship of different religions to the Divine Reality it confesses to find in the life and teachings of Jesus as the Christ and as recorded in the Holy Bible, it may be as momentous for the Christian church as have been the various "turnings" of the Buddhist wheel.

The commitment of the Lotus Sutra to the bodhisattva path and Revelation's commitment to the reign of the Lamb of God will still remain, perhaps even reinforced by new insights. In fact, they must remain if the traditions are to stay faithful to the truth as they see it. It could be the case that even Tracy's way of illustrating the boundaries between fundamental and systematic theology reflects this potential sea change in Christian thought and praxis. Fundamental theology, with its openness to the world, already reflects a commitment to inclusive ways of thinking; systematic theology, even when and if it is informed by this change from an exclusive to an inclusive ethos, will still need to mediate these new insights through the language of the tradition. One of the most historically accurate things that can be said about any religious tradition is that it adorns its deposit of historical vocabulary and symbols with new meanings as it floats down the river of time. What will happen is that the bodhisattva and the Christ will take notice of each other and will be transformed. Bodhisattvas, if the Lotus is to be believed, are used to being transformed; such transformations have not been associated with the Christ, who is said to be unchanging from the beginning of days to the end of time and yet is made new at the coming of the Kingdom.

What Manner of Revealed Magic City Is This?

One of the first questions that springs to mind when a Christian first reads the Lotus Sutra is, what kind of text is this? It is demonstrably a sutra and not a philosophic treatise like the *Awakening of Faith* or one of the great commentaries of Chih-i or Kuei-feng Tsung-mi. In short, it does not present its teaching in a systematic form. The wonderful episodes that have endeared the Lotus to generations of East Asian Buddhists, such as the burning house, put us in a different religious world from the scholastic ruminations of Hua-yen or T'ien-t'ai thought. The wonderful and splendid images that float in front of our eyes, dazzle the mind, and open the heart remind the Christian reader, or at least this one, of the Revelation of Saint John, the last book of the Christian canon.[4] The image that comes to my mind when I let the Lotus Sutra speak to me is something like Revelation 21:5, "Then the One sitting on the throne spoke, 'Look, I am making the whole creation new.'" Perhaps this sense of newness is not what a Buddhist reader will get, but I cannot but think that there is something to this sense of renewal and refreshment when we contemplate the whole vast sweep of what the bodhisattva path truly means for all sentient beings. As is noted at the end of chapter 7, "The Magic City," the people are refreshed by their sojourn in the wonderful creation of the compassionate Buddha.

Of course, one of the first things that a Christian will recognize is the immense size of the Lotus Sutra when compared to the brevity of the New Testament as a whole, much less individual books such as Revelation. Parenthetically, this sense of brevity or compactness is almost always the sensation when Christians confront the world of Buddhist scripture—from the Christian point of view there is a vast sea of scripture that dwarfs anything in the Christian experience *qua* scripture. It is not that Christians do not have a great deal of literature, but historically, Christians have a restrained sense of the canon as scripture per se. Be this as it may, both the Lotus and New Testament are made up of many different parts. For heuristic purposes, and because of its imagery of the divine city, I will focus my attention on "The Magic City."

The reason for this is that both "The Magic City" and Revelation focus their attention and imagery on what can only be called divine palaces or cities. Frankly, alone in the New Testament canon does the vision of the Holy City of God in Revelation come close to the image of the palace in "The Magic City" in richness of detail and allegorical intent. Could one argue, for instance, that both cities function as *upāya* for their communities of faith? Or does it make any sense to think of *upāya* in the Christian context?

At the end of "The Magic City" the Buddha Universal Surpassing Wisdom reveals the true nature of the Magic City. In one sense the great and wonderful city is an illusion. But just because it is an illusion does not mean that it is unreal. Illusion, as religions and modern psychoanalysis have shown, can be as real as and often more real than what we embrace as the concrete facts and items of quotidian reality. On the Christian side, while the Christian does not say that the heavenly city is an illusion, it is certainly the realm of the great transformation, the dramatic moment when a person must choose life or death. The previous reality is an illusion if one is finally and decisively transformed by faith in Christ. One is driven to ask, if things are really made new, in a profound and complete sense, does not that imply, at least on one level, that what went before is or was an illusion because it did not represent the true reality of the human condition?

Another point that Buddhists will surely note is that not everyone makes it into the Kingdom, and this is very different from the joyous exit from the Magic City, wherein sentient beings find nirvana. Whatever else Revelation promises, it does not seem to include nirvana for all. This, of course, is the perennial question within the Christian tradition of the tension between the hope for universal salvation and the persistence of human perversity. One of the particular characteristics of the Christian tradition is that it has always embraced, in one way or another, the signs of religious crisis and expectation that marked its origin in the religiously tense world of late Greco-Roman antiquity. Christians can never quite escape their conviction that they are living in end times even if no one knows the day or hour of its revelation.

Therefore, one reading of Revelation influenced by the Lotus would be as an *upāya* designed not to let us too quickly forget how perverse human beings really are. No one has said it better than H. Richard Niebuhr when he remarked that much modern theology was too melioristic in that "a God without wrath brought men without sin into a Kingdom without judgment through the ministrations of Christ without a Cross." Niebuhr evidently thought that such a gospel would liberate no one; or that it would liberate so few that it did not deserve to be called a message of good news. Such a gospel would not be Christian if it did not meditate on the way of the cross, for without the cross there would be no Christian community. To paraphrase Alfred North Whitehead, Christ gave his life for the world, not a philosophic or even spiritual teaching. It has been the task of the Christian community to try to explain just what this sacrifice means in terms of human and divine wisdom.

While a Christian can appreciate the Buddhist point of seeking the liberation of all sentient beings, this is deservedly one of those points that remain contentious for Buddhist-Christian dialogue if we are honest and faithful to some of the main insights of both cumulative traditions.[5] The reach from the illusion of the Magic City to the new Kingdom may be too far to bridge at a single step. I will suggest that an insight from the Neo-Confucian philosophy of Chu Hsi (1130–1200) may help at this point. In East Asia the inclusion of a great Neo-Confucian thinker would not seem eccentric at all because of the great impact of Sung *tao-hsüeh* on all subsequent forms of East Asian intellectual and spiritual life. In East Asia interreligious dialogue always includes the recognition of more than two partners.

In fact, as Confucian-Christian dialogue begins to grow on its parallel course along with the more established Buddhist-Christian dialogue, it strikes me that without the Confucian voice, the dialogue is somehow incomplete when we review East Asian thought and praxis.[6] While it is true that each individual dialogue has characteristics of its own, there is also a need to cross-reference the bilateral dialogues in order to insure that the best form of communication goes on within any cultural area. So, for instance, there is an increasing awareness in Western interfaith dialogues that it is proper to have a three-way conversation of Jews, Christians, and Muslims if these traditions are to fully explore their common heritage as "people of the book" and to overcome some of the history of open hostility that has infected much of their joint history. My hypothesis is that there will need to be a three-way conversation of Buddhists, Confucians, and Christians in the modern world, especially if the Western Christian participants are going to fully understand the particular forms of East Asian religious history and contemporary discourse.

The particular Neo-Confucian concept chosen here to illustrate the usefulness of such a three-way dialogue is *ch'eng* as self-realization or actualization.[7] In the classical period of Confucian thought *ch'eng* is often translated as sincerity and is identified with such classics as the Great Learning and the Doctrine of the Mean.[8] While it is true that the word does mean sincerity, it denotes something much more active and inclusive in the Neo-Confucian scheme of things. It is not just a state or disposition of the will, though it is that of course. In Chu Hsi's reading of the term it connotes a process by which one seeks to embody the true principle of the person. What Chu Hsi is doing here, and this is what typically causes problems for Buddhists and Christians in their dialogues with the Neo-Confucians, is the characteristic Confucian penchant for what can only be called transcendent immanence. From the Confucian point of view both the Buddhists and Christians are correct about part of the truth even though neither of them fully embraces the full truth of the matter.[9] That is to say, from Chu's viewpoint, the Buddhists understand the immanence and universality of the Buddha-nature in every sentient being whereas the Christians understand the transcendent reference of the potential for immanent self-realization and how difficult the process actually is when human beings attempt to realize this fundamental nature. The trick, according to Chu, is to find the right balance between these poles of human nature. Of course, both Christians and Buddhists will find Chu's suggestions equally problematic from their own viewpoints.

One of the points that is made about the main themes of the Lotus Sutra is that it includes wisdom and compassion as essential elements of the message of the sutra. On the Christian side, one of the things that Revelation teaches is the theme of judgment and renewal. The Lotus Sutra's emphasis on wisdom and compassion also leads to the affirmation of the positive role of diversity within the cosmos. That is why the Lotus is so careful to make sure that it finds a place for all manner of beings and spiritual seekers. On the other hand, the Christian sense of judgment is closer to the notion of *ch'eng* in that one must will one thing alone in order to be on the path of purification. It seems to me that a work such as Revelation is asking a different question from what is heard in some parts of the Lotus. Revelation asks how a person must be focused in order to seek salvation. Just like Chu's notion of self-actualization being both a disposition and an action, so too the imitation of Christ is both a state of sanctification and also the process by which faith is infused into the person.

From the Neo-Confucian viewpoint, the Christian concern for resolve and radical judgment can be read as a form of self-cultivation, a call to an interior life of decision for Christ. This may be somewhat odd because Christianity, especially in its modern form, is taken as a paradigm for an extroverted tradition that does not always emphasize the interior life. The Buddhist tradition, on the other hand, especially in North America, is seen as the religion of meditation supreme. Of course, scholars of the two traditions know only too well how misguided such one-sided images are.

I am struck by what the Lotus Sutra could teach about the universal compassion of the divine reality if and when the Christian community decides to emphasize the universalism of its tradition. From the Buddhist point of view this will return us to the debate that raged in early medieval China about the same topic, i.e., are there any sentient beings without Buddha-nature? As everyone knows, and as the Lotus Sutra demonstrates, the Buddhist conclusion is emphatically that there is no one too wicked or clever to escape the compassion and wisdom of the Buddha. Actually, it is well within the scope of modern Christian theology to be able to come to grips with its inclusive and universal tendencies. The Lotus Sutra may help to nudge the Christians along this path. The Lotus may also help to illustrate that pluralism is something wonderful and not something to be feared. It will be for the Buddhists to say just what Revelation might contribute to the Dharma and Sangha.

But what kind of pluralism will this become? One of the favorite Christian ways of putting the issue is to talk about diversity-in-unity. But what is often not confessed is that the diversity is swallowed whole by the Western proclivity for unity and *nomos*. As many modern Confucian philosophers have noted, the Western dialectic is one of subordination rather than coordination. The Lotus here too suggests that diversity is real. Of course, the Confucians support such a notion. Will Christians learn this fact as well? Perhaps we will all have to wait till we have left our Magic City in order to find out the truth that will set us free.

Notes

1. It is important to note that the list of what constituted the Confucian canon itself has changed over the centuries. What began with the five classics now has grown to the final list of the thirteen classics.
2. See Jordan Paper, *The Spirits Are Drunk: Comparative Approaches to Chinese Religion.* (Albany: State University of New York Press, 1995).
3. Wilfred Cantwell Smith, *What Is Scripture? A Comparative Approach* (Minneapolis: Fortress Press, 1993) for an extended discussion of the nature of scripture in diverse traditions.
4. Of course, there are also many sections of the Hebrew Bible that also come to mind, such as the vision of the chariot of the Lord in the opening chapter of Ezekiel. However, for the purposes of this paper I will only deal with the specifically Christian part of the Bible.
5. However, one wonders how much longer this will be the case for the Christian tradition, at least in North America. I have come to believe that most North American Christians have become "universalists" in terms of the way this great debate was waged in the nineteenth century. This means that most modern Christians believe that God will find some way to save almost everyone.

The only exceptions would be paradigmatic figures of evil such as the devil. What really tends to divide North American Christians is not the question of universalism, though this is not often debated directly, but the question of "how" God will do this work. Saint Paul's great vision of the end of time wherein all creation will be reconciled to God is taken as the proof text for this universalistic sentiment. Liberals believe that God will do this because of God's divine love. The more conservative thinkers, remembering other parts of scripture, confess that they are not sure that they can intellectually say how or why God will save the reprobate sinner, but to believe otherwise would put boundaries around God's sovereign powers, and that would be impious. Most liberal Christians now believe that God does work in the other religions; here again conservative Christians are less sure that God works directly in the structures of the other communities of faith even though they are often willing to recognize that God does work in individuals if not whole communities.

6. This is obviously the case in East Asia, and more and more so now in the East Asian diaspora in the West. For instance, in terms of social ethics it is impossible to talk about East Asia without inducing Confucian and Buddhist insights. Furthermore, we know that Buddhism contributed to and stimulated the creation of the great Neo-Confucian systems from the T'ang right down to someone like Hsiung Shihli, considered to be one of the main founders of the New Confucian movement. In fact, Paul Varo Martinson, *A Theology of World Religions: Interpreting God, Self, and World in Semitic, Indian, and Chinese Thought* (Minneapolis: Augsburg Publishing House, 1987), points out that the East Asian religious experience is the most inclusive of all human religious communities. Not only is East Asia home to its own traditions—Confucianism, Taoism, Buddhism, Shinto, and various forms of popular religion—but also the major religions of South and West Asia such as Judaism, Islam, and Christianity.

7. See John H. Berthrong, "Master Chu's Self-Realization: The Role of Ch'eng," *Philosophy East & West*, 43, No. 1 (January 1993): 39–64, for discussion of the role of *ch'eng* in Chu's philosophic synthesis.

8. While *ch'eng* has always been a key Confucian ethical term, for our purposes it becomes even more important in the Sung period through the reflections of Chou Tun-i, Chang Tsai, and then Chu Hsi. It becomes one of Chu's favorite terms for describing not only the end of Confucian self-cultivation but also the process by which this end state can be achieved. What is important to note is that the end state is always just the beginning of yet another step in the process of becoming a sage. Strictly speaking, there is really no end state for the cultivation of Confucian virtue because every day brings new challenges and trials.

9. This is quite a normal move for most religious traditions. Even the most irenic traditions will grant that another tradition has part, though not all, of the truth. Only the true religion is held to embrace the whole truth, or at least as much of the truth as is humanly possible.

The Lotus Sutra and Interreligious Dialogue

Schubert M. Ogden

How is it possible to affirm the validity of one's own religious tradition as a Christian while allowing for the possible validity of the other's religious tradition as well?

My supposition in asking this question, the question of a Christian theology of interreligious dialogue, is that genuine dialogue of any kind is possible only on certain conditions and that one can enter into such dialogue only if one can somehow affirm the validity of one's own position without thereby denying that the other's position, also, can possibly be valid. This means that one ought never to take for granted that genuine interreligious dialogue is possible regardless of one's particular religious assertions. It is always possible that some such assertion should implicitly preclude genuine dialogue, since, if it is true, the other's religious tradition is *eo ipso* invalid and could not possibly be otherwise. Contrariwise, there is also always the possibility that one or more of the other's particular assertions should make genuine interreligious dialogue possible by implying that one's own religious tradition can be just as valid as it claims to be.

Such were my thoughts as I read the Lotus Sutra. I should like to think that the results of my reading, and thus the argument of this essay, can claim sufficient support in the text itself. But aware as I am of my preoccupation while reading the sutra, and of my still only very limited acquaintance with it, since it is accessible to me only in English translations, I want to allow for the possibility that its real teaching may be more or less different from what I take it to be. Therefore, I ask the reader to treat the conclusions for which I shall argue hypothetically: if, and only if, the Lotus Sutra teaches what I, following other commentators, take it to teach, does it have the significance for interreligious dialogue that I shall argue it has?

Chapter 2 of the Lotus Sutra states that buddhas appear in this world for "one great cause," that is, "to cause the beings to enter into the path of the Buddha's knowledge and insight." Therefore, "the Thus Come One [Tathāgata] by resort to the One Buddha Vehicle alone preaches the Dharma to the beings. There are no other vehicles, whether two or three."[1] Interpreters I have consulted hold that this "one way" (ekayāna), or "Buddha Way" (Buddhayāna), doctrine is a, if not the, principal teaching of the sutra. Thus Leon Hurvitz argues that of the two possible scriptures in the oldest layer of the sutra, one teaches that "there is only one Path to salvation, not three," while the other teaches that "the Buddha is not to be delimited in time or space, or indeed in any finite terms."[2] Similarly, Gene Reeves takes "the teaching of the Buddha-way" to be "one of the main or central teachings of the sutra," along with "the teaching of the eternal Buddha" and "the teaching of upāya (appropriate means)."[3] Consequently, I have no hesitation in following their readings, especially since my own attempts to come to terms with the text have led me to the same interpretation.

The more difficult question is just how this "one way" teaching is to be understood. How, exactly, is the one way, or the Buddha Way, related to the three ways from which it is also, at least verbally, distinguished, i.e., the follower-disciple's way (śrāvakayāna), the solitary attainer's way (pratyekabuddhayāna), and the awakening one's way (bodhisattvayāna)? Asked in terms of the parable in chapter 3, are the two ox-drawn carriages different, or are they the same? Are there four carriages, or are there only three? So far as I have been able to answer this question, it seems possible to argue that, in different senses, both are true, because, in one sense, the awakening one's way is one of three ways of entering the one Buddha Way, while, in another sense, it itself is that way, as neither of the other ways can be said to be. This is perhaps the same point made in a footnote to the Katō translation of the sutra in distinguishing between a "relative" and an "absolute" concept of the one Buddha Way.[4]

But be this as it may, and however one is to answer any of the questions about its central teaching, one thing seems clear: the Lotus Sutra is centrally concerned with the problem of religious plurality and seeks to solve this problem by teaching an ultimate religious unity. At the risk of anachronism, I should say that it does this along the lines more of what we today would probably think of as inclusivism than of pluralism. Although, in its view, the follower-disciple and the solitary attainer have both definitely entered upon the one Buddha Way, they can attain its final goal only by transcending what they already are and becoming something else—an awakening one who is destined to be fully awakened.

If we ask now why the sutra's teaching of the one way is plausible, if not convincing, the answer is yet another of its main or central teachings—namely, the teaching of *upāya*, which Reeves translates as "appropriate means," or, as I shall also say, following Hurvitz, "expedient devices." According to this teaching, the evident plurality of Buddhist ways is not denied or explained away but fully accepted. At the same time, the sutra's concern to teach an ultimate religious unity requires it to understand these plural ways as simply so many means or devices for effectively communicating the one Buddha Way to all the many beings in their actual plurality. Thus, as it actually exists in history, the one Buddha Way is represented only in the many Buddhist ways, all of which are legitimate to the extent that by their means the one Dharma can be taught to all and learned and practiced by each.

This in no way implies, however, that these different ways are in every respect equal. Although they are all alike expedient devices and, therefore, must all alike be distinguished from the end for which they are at most appropriate means, their respective relations to that end are not simply the same. On the contrary, as we noted above, the way of the awakening one, although in a sense distinct from this end, can also be said to be related to it in a sense in which neither of the other ways can. As one commentator explains it allegorically,

> [a] person who has entered this gate [sc. the follower-disciple's way and the solitary attainer's way] cannot enter the inner room of the Buddha-knowledge until he has first passed through the porch of the bodhisattva practice. At the same time, it cannot be said that the gate and the porch are not both included within the residence of the Buddha.[5]

The point, in any case, is that the teaching of appropriate means, or expedient devices, is itself essential to the core teaching of the one Buddha Way. There is good reason, then, for Reeves's characterization of it as one of the sutra's "major supporting teachings."[6]

The other such teaching that is particularly striking is the teaching in chapter 16 concerning the eternal and universal Buddha, who is effectively present and at work not only in this (*sahā*) world but in all worlds, past, present, and future. Far from being limited to the eighty years of one human career, the Buddha's life span is "incalculable," and he has ever taught and ever will teach, by one device or another, the one Dharma and the one Buddha Way to all living beings. Thus the Buddha says,

Since I attained Buddhahood,

. . . .

Ever have I been preaching Dharma, teaching and converting.
Countless millions of living beings
Have I caused to enter into the Buddha Path,
Since which time it has been incalculable kalpas.
For the beings' sake,
And as an expedient device, I make a show of nirvāṇa;
Yet in fact I do not pass into extinction,
But ever dwell here and preach Dharma.[7]

It is with good reason, then, that Michael Pye finds in the Lotus Sutra a unique application of the notion of *upāya*.

> [N]ot only is the teaching of the Buddha declared by this text to comprise a series of skillfully devised expedients, but the very appearance of the Buddha in this world is declared . . . to be a mere stratagem to draw beings to the Dharma. The actual Enlightenment is an event that took place, if it occurred in history at all, aeons ago. . . . Thus, in the *Lotus Sutra* it is not merely a question of particular teachings being regarded as secondary formulations. The very appearance of the Buddha, his setting the wheel of the Dharma in motion, and his winning of *nirvāṇa*, have a provisional, dialectical nature related to the needs of living beings in their diversity.[8]

Here, too, of course, one may well ask just how this teaching is to be understood. Does the text of the sutra itself warrant Nikkyō Niwano's claim that "[o]ur concept of the Buddha will be confused unless we understand the difference between the Tathāgata Śākyamuni as the historical Buddha and the Tathāgata Śākyamuni as the Original Buddha"?[9] And how apt is his suggestion that the relationship between "the Original Buddha" and "the appearing Buddha" can be easily understood by considering "the relationship between electric waves and television"?[10] However these and other questions should be answered, this much I take to be clear: the Lotus Sutra teaches that the truth about human existence explicitly represented by the man Śākyamuni is nothing less than the truth always already constituted by reality itself and, therefore, must be presented at least implicitly to each and every human being—and, in some way, to all living beings whatever.

No less clear, however, is its converse teaching that the truth always already constituted by reality itself, which must be at least implicitly presented to all living beings, is nothing other than the truth about human existence explicitly represented by the man Śākyamuni. In other words, the dharma taught by the historical Buddha not only represents the Dharma of the Original Buddha, but does so decisively—in such a way as to provide the formal norm for deciding the validity of any and all religious teachings. Niwano's interpretation, then, is entirely sound, that while "the Original Buddha is the Buddha who exists in every part of the universe from the infinite past to the infinite future, . . . only through the teachings of Śākyamuni, who appeared in this world in obedience to the truth of the Original Buddha, can we understand that truth."[11] This decisive significance of Śākyamuni also comes out in Niwano's other sentence already quoted, according to which it is none other than "the Tathāgata Śākyamuni" who is to be conceived not only as "the historical Buddha," but also as "the Original Buddha."

On my reading, then, the core teaching of the Lotus Sutra, or its essential message, can be summarized as follows: Notwithstanding the plurality of Buddhist ways, there is finally only the one Buddha Way that is more or less fully represented in each of them. Relative to this one way, all of the many ways are simply so many appropriate means, or expedient devices, whereby the Buddha takes account of the vast plurality of living beings, in their many different situations and with their many different needs. But more than this: even the decisive event of the Buddha's teaching in history is representative of the truth about human existence rather than constitutive of it. Consequently, in the final analysis, it, too, is but an appropriate means, or expedient device, for representing this truth, although, being the decisive such representation, it is at one and the same time constitutive of the one Buddha Way and of the many Buddhist ways that more or less adequately represent it.

Now, so far as I have been able to determine, the Lotus Sutra itself, as distinct from its interpreters and commentators, takes little or no account of religious plurality beyond that within Buddhism itself. At any rate, I have not found it saying anything very clear about whether or not the Dharma of the Original Buddha is, or can be, represented by non-Buddhists or whether or not those outside of the Buddhist tradition can already be, even as non-Buddhists, at least implicitly, or "anonymously," awakening ones. But even granting that the sutra's own concern with ultimate religious unity is effectively limited to unity among Buddhists, I still deem it worth asking whether its core teaching allows for or rather precludes genuine dialogue *between* religious traditions as well as within them. More specifically, could a Buddhist who asserted the sutra's essential message consistently enter into genuine interreligious dialogue with a Christian such as myself? Could she or he validly uphold the validity of all that the sutra centrally teaches without thereby denying that my tradition, also, can possibly be valid?

Before answering this question, I need to clarify an ambiguity in my use up to now of the term "validity" and its cognates. This I shall do by distinguishing two different forms or kinds of the thing to which the term may refer, which I shall speak of respectively as *"formal* validity" and *"substantial* validity." Given this distinction, one may say that a religious tradition, or any part thereof, is *substantially* valid if, or insofar as, it agrees in substance with any other valid religious tradition. Such a tradition can be *formally* valid, however, only if it is a tradition with which every other has to agree in substance if it is to be correctly affirmed to be substantially valid.

The claim typically made by a religious tradition is not merely that it is substantially valid when judged by some formally valid tradition other than itself, but rather that it itself *is* this formally valid tradition with which every other has to agree to be substantially valid. More precisely, then, the question I am asking is this: Could a Buddhist validly affirm the formal validity of the central teaching of the Lotus Sutra without thereby denying that my Christian tradition also can possibly be formally valid, in the way in which I as a Christian must affirm it to be?

The answer, I believe, is yes, assuming that the core teaching of the sutra is what I take it to be. The reason for this is that, according to this teaching, even the decisive event of the Buddha's appearance in history has a representative rather than a constitutive significance for realizing the truth about human existence. It in no way *constitutes* this truth, which is always already constituted by reality itself, but rather *represents* this truth, by making it present yet again, a second time, explicitly and, as I have said, decisively—in such a way as to constitute the Buddhist tradition, thereby providing the formal norm for deciding the validity of any and all religious teachings. Because it thus constitutes the Buddhist tradition, the event of the Buddha's appearance does indeed have a constitutive significance: everything specifically Buddhist is constituted by it, even as it, in turn, is more or less adequately represented by everything specifically Buddhist. But because even it does not constitute the truth about human existence, but rather represents this truth, affirmation of its decisive significance, and thus of the formal validity of the Buddhist tradition, does not preclude but, rather, allows for the possibility that I as a Christian may make a similar affirmation of the decisive significance of Jesus Christ and hence of the formal validity of the Christian tradition. Provided only that the truth about human existence represented by my Christianity is the same truth represented by Buddhism—but in no way constituted by Buddhism or even by the Buddha, but by reality itself—a Buddhist's affirmation of the formal validity of Buddhism can be completely consistent with my affirmation of Christianity as likewise formally valid.

Of course, only a Buddhist would have reason to affirm the decisive significance of Śākyamuni the Buddha and the formal validity of Buddhism, even as only I as a Christian would have reason to affirm the decisive significance of Jesus the Christ and the formal validity of Christianity. It lies in the nature of any religious tradition that only one representation can be decisive and thus constitutive of the tradition as such as the formal norm for deciding all questions of religious validity. For Buddhists that representation is the appearance in this world of Śākyamuni Buddha, just as for Christians it is the appearance in this same world of Christ Jesus. But this fact by itself in no way precludes the possibility that the claims to formal validity made or implied by both traditions may be valid claims. If the constitutive events of the respective traditions both have the kind of representative significance that the Lotus Sutra, for its part, clearly seems to assert of the appearance of the Buddha, there is no reason why adherents of the one may not validly affirm the formal validity of their own tradition even while allowing that adherents of the other may validly do the same.

The question that the Lotus Sutra puts to any of us who are Christians, however, is whether we, for our part, can appropriately understand the decisive significance of Jesus Christ to be the same kind of representative significance. I do not mean by this, I hasten to explain, whether we as Christians can appropriately understand Jesus in the same way in which Buddhists understand Śākyamuni, as the primary example of the enlightened life in which the truth about human existence is realized. To this question I am quite confident that the only answer would have to be negative.

But there is not merely this one way in which Jesus can be understood as representative of the truth about human existence, rather than as constitutive of it. Like those in many other religious traditions, Christians are accustomed to acknowledging not only *persons* who represent this truth for us by exemplifying it, such as prophets and teachers, sages and saints, but also *things* that are thus representative, such as word and sacraments. Moreover, Christians commonly allow that the whole authority of representative persons derives from the representative things they serve to mediate—whether the word they proclaim or teach or the sacraments they administer. It is not in the least surprising, then, that, beginning already in the New Testament, christologies have been developed in which Jesus is represented not simply as an exemplary holy person mediating some holy thing but as himself a holy thing—or, more exactly, as himself the primal source of *all* holy things. Thus for the author of the Fourth Gospel, for instance, Jesus is not simply the first and foremost preacher or teacher of the word, but is himself the word—which is to say, *the* Word by which all preachers or teachers are authorized to proclaim or teach. It is only another way of making the same point when Luther, following a distinction he learned from Augustine, lays down the christological rule that Jesus Christ is, first of all, a "sacrament" (*sacramentum*) and only then an "example" (*exemplum*). In other words, before we take Jesus to be the model for our own lives before God, we must take him to be the sign of God's own presence and power at work in our lives.

This is not the place to develop such a representativist christology or to argue for its appropriateness. The question here is only whether what Christians are bound to say about the decisive significance of Jesus Christ can be appropriately expressed by some kind of representativist christology, even if hardly by the usual, more familiar kind. If it can, then I as a Christian can assert what has to be asserted about Jesus Christ without thereby denying that the teaching of the Lotus Sutra concerning Śākyamuni Buddha can also be formally valid. But if, on the contrary, what is wanted is a constitutivist christology, because what must be asserted about Jesus Christ is not only that he decisively represents the truth about human existence, but also that he constitutes this truth, then, so far as I can see, I as a Christian cannot enter into genuine interreligious dialogue with Buddhism or with any other religious tradition. I cannot do so because the implication of my christological assertion is that no religious tradition other than my own could even possibly be formally valid in the way in which it claims to be.

Notes

1. Leon Hurvitz, trans., *Scripture of the Lotus Blossom of the Fine Dharma* (New York: Columbia University Press, 1976), 30.
2. Ibid., xvii–xviii.
3. Gene Reeves, "Outline of the Teachings of the Lotus Sutra" (paper prepared for the participants of the seventh meeting of the International Theological Encounter Group, Inawashiro, Japan, July 1994), 3.
4. Bunno Katō, *et al.*, trans., *The Threefold Lotus Sutra* (Tokyo: Kōsei Publishing Co., 1975), 60, n. 14.
5. Nikkyō Niwano, *Buddhism for Today: A Modern Interpretation of the Threefold Lotus Sutra* (Tokyo: Kōsei Publishing Co., 1976), 48.
6. Reeves, "Teachings of the Lotus Sutra," 3.
7. Hurvitz, *Lotus Blossom*, 242.
8. *The Encyclopedia of Religion*, s.v. "upāya."
9. Niwano, *Buddhism for Today*, 119.
10. Ibid., xxv–xxvi, 222–23.
11. Ibid., xxv–xxvi.

Upāya and Missio Dei:
Toward a Common Missiology

Michael A. Fuss

The liturgical invocation "In the name of the Father and of the Son and of the Holy Spirit" actualizes the very source of Christian mission, which draws its origin from the missionary mandate of Jesus: "Go therefore and make disciples of all nations, baptizing them in the name of the Father and of the Son and of the Holy Spirit" (Mt. 28:19). The very nature of God, one and at the same time trinitarian, is the motion of unbounded love that makes itself known in his dynamic action toward the world ("*ad extra*"). Mission, therefore, is a constitutive moment of the Christian idea of God, prior to the foundation of churches and communities; it is the expression of the most intimate Christian identity and is thus a theological rather than a territorial concept. It is strictly linked to God's own being. The trinitarian God in his divine fullness is mission, mutual exchange of love toward the other persons of the trinity and toward the world.

In a similar way Buddhism from its very origin is a missionary religion, too, as shown by the famous missionary mandate: "Go forth, O monks, for the blessing of the many folk, for the happiness of the many folk, out of compassion for the world, for the welfare, the blessing, the happiness of devas and men."[1] Impressive confirmation are the missionary activities throughout its long history, beginning from Emperor Aśoka, who made Buddhism a world religion by sending his messengers to regions like Sri Lanka and Burma, and as far as to the province of Epirus on the shores of the Mediterranean. One might even recall the more recent missionary attempts vigorously initiated at the World's Parliament of Religions in Chicago in 1893 with the participation of the Sinhalese monk Anagarika Dharmapala and a representative of the Zen tradition, Soyen Shaku, the latter accompanied by D. T. Suzuki. These events marked the beginning of the final passage of Buddhism into the Christian world after its subtle penetration of all the great cultures of Asia.

In this paper I will elaborate these two concepts of mission. My point is not just to speak of a numerical or geographical presence of either religion; I rather intend to disclose the deepest reason for the interaction of the two traditions by evaluating the doctrinal significance of the respective notions of "mission." This may open a perspective on a common missiology of Buddhists and Christians enabling them together to face the great challenges of our contemporary world.

Regarding Buddhism, the equivalent notion appears to be *upāya*, and it is my contention that in addition to the various proposed renderings like "tactfulness," "skillfulness," the overall meaning is precisely "mission" which, beyond a merely technical accuracy, would take into consideration the entire context of the usage of the term as well. Michael Pye has rightly pointed out that the whole of Buddhism "as a specific religion identifiable in human history, is a skilful means";[2] reading, therefore, *upāya* in a theological terminology would reflect its "missionary" nature both in view of the activities of bodhisattvas and, more fundamentally, in view of the dynamic self-communicating nature of the Dharma itself.[3]

Beyond pointing at close structural similarities between the two traditions, the common notion of "mission" will even support a comparative hermeneutics[4] in scriptural interpretation and foster practical awareness of each partner's deepest motives in their common witness to the world and to each other. Disclosing the missionary and *upāya* nature of each religious tradition implies, at the same time, recognizing a pluralism of cultures and a corresponding genuine pluralism in the expression of truth without, however, renouncing its essential oneness. Christian tradition conceives this diversity-in-unity as "interculturality,"[5] while the Buddhist tradition of the Lotus Sutra has elaborated the matching concepts of *upāya* for the diversity of the manifestations of the Dharma and the corresponding *ekayāna*, denoting the convergence of various vehicles into one way of salvation. Here the circular motion of both *upāya* and mission finds its completion: descending from the oneness of Reality and the divine impulse, it finds its perfection in making the entire earth a "pure land," void of clinging to itself, and thus integrating it again into the fullness of a pure relationship with the "All in All."

Upāya in Buddhism

The Sanskrit term *upāya* (Ch.: *fang-pien*, "method," "accommodation"; Jpn.: *hōben*, "means," "stratagem") etymologically derives from the root *i*, "to go," "to move," and expresses with the addition of the preposition *upā* the dynamic notion "to move under," "approaching."[6] Before its common translation as "means," "expedient," "stratagem,"[7] the term acquired thus a fundamental philosophical notion, analogous to "hypostasis," "substance," in Greek philosophical terminology, and discloses the enormous difference between the two modes of thinking. The Greek *hypostasis* derives from the composite *hypostasis*, which expresses a static concept of "staying under," "supporting." All Western philosophy has been based on this notion of "substance" as the ultimate basis of reality, while the same concept in Buddhist thinking is highly dynamic and cannot be expressed literally by any Western terminology. In searching for a possible analogy to other concepts of Greek thought, one might recall the symbolism of light as dynamic energy and adopt the term "epiphany," "radiance," or "lighting up," or even substitute the rather static "substance" with the dynamic "method," "way," in which the first principle and its achievement coincide. Such a "method," however, implies far more than a mere methodology of "the Buddha's skill in devising means to impress and convert people";[8] it is indeed an equivalent to Western ontology. M. Pye has thus defined *upāya* as "one of the fundamental principles of Buddhism as a working religion."[9]

In the Tantric tradition *upāya* is the creative energy of *prajñā* and *karuṇā*, which means the creative and revealing potency of the Dharma itself in its aspects of wisdom and compassion. The "union of *prajñā* with *upāya*, the male principle, produces great bliss (*mahāsukha*) which is the nondual quintessence of all entities."[10] *Upāya* remains specially related to *karuṇā*, the principle of compassion, and thus linked to the manifold appearances of Avalokiteśvara in the Lotus Sutra. It stands at the threshold of the manifestation of the One Reality in the phenomenal world of samsara. D. T. Suzuki remarks: "When Love worries itself over the destiny of the ignorant, Wisdom, so to speak, weaves a net of Skillful Means whereby to catch them up from the depths of the ocean called Birth-and-Death (samsara). By *upāya*, thus the oneness of reality wherein the Buddha's enlightened mind abides transforms itself into the manifoldness of particular existences."[11]

Upāya is here disclosed as the self-expression of the Dharma in its universal compassion that penetrates the whole of Reality; the missionary means of the Buddha are a secondary reflection of the essential nature of the Dharma. This nature is so purely transmitted in the Buddhist vision that its ontology becomes purely dynamic emptiness.

In a first approach to the encounter between Buddhism and Christianity, I wish to underline the common endeavor for enforcing the spiritual dimension of cultures. Today we do not any more need territorial wars between contrasting missionary mandates which only exhaust themselves in blind proselytizing and "hunting for souls." Following the Second Vatican Council the Church has stressed the need for a dialogical theology. In various ways the Council[12] understood its relations with other spiritual realities by the analogy of concentric circles that extend from an ecumenical brotherhood between Christian churches and denominations, through gradual relationships with the biblical and nonbiblical religions, and the dialogue with the realm of culture up to the contacts with those who sincerely follow the voice of their inner conscience.

The threatening signs of the times of a humankind that is rapidly going to lose its religious values in a growing climate of materialism and consumerism certainly do not advocate an exclusive proselytism, but rather a common witness toward life in its fullness. The present spiritual climate, and this seems valid at least for the transatlantic cultures of America and Europe, may be characterized by a polarity of two aspects of "mission": a widely diffused, often anonymous, receptivity of people in their search for authentic values and the explicit proclamation. Here again meet the two dimensions of Buddhist and Christian mission in terms of upāya: the rather passive disposition of unrest: "Come over and help us" (Acts 16:9); "So be it, World-Honored One; I desire joyfully to listen" (Lotus II, 59, 10); and the responding and inculturating, active announcement "Go into all the world and preach the gospel to the whole creation" (Mark 16:15); "Now I entrust it [the Dharma] to you. Do you wholeheartedly promulgate this Law [this Dharma] and make it increase and prosper far and wide" (Lotus[13] XXII, 301, 6f).

Missio Dei in Christianity

The Christian Church continues the mission of Christ. Jesus speaks to the Father: "I made known to them thy name, and I will make it known, that the love with which thou hast loved me may be in them, and I in them" (John 17:26). The interior mission of God, the trinitarian relationship of loving exchange between Father and Son in the Holy Spirit, leads toward an exterior activity, the communication of this same love to the whole created world, and leads further to the foundation of the Church as the mystical body of Christ that continues the divine mission. The Church as missionary agency is therefore essentially constituted within the mission of the Son, the fruit of his constant self-giving love to the Father; a highly dynamic relationship of which the Holy Spirit in whom this exchange takes place is the divine sign and seal.

In his ecumenical missiology Georg Vicedom places the foundations for Christian mission within the mystery of God's trinitarian dimension:

This is the ultimate mystery of mission from where it stems and from where it lives: God sends his Son, Father and Son are sending the Spirit. Thus he becomes not only the envoy, but the contents of this mission as well, without dissolving, however, the essential unity of the divine persons by this self-revealing trinity, for God acts wholly in every person of the godhead. . . . [The Church's] mandate is prefigured in the divine, her service is owed by the divine, meaning and contents of her activity are circumscribed by the *missio Dei*.[14]

Church and mission cannot be conceived as autonomous realities; they both owe their existence to their absolute relationship in the loving will of God: "The Church may speak of her mission only if she fulfills his [God's] intention of mission, because then it is embraced by the *missio Dei*."[15] Joseph Ratzinger quotes the paradoxical meaning of Jesus' saying in John 7:16, "My teaching is not mine, but his who sent me," to emphasize the total dependence of Jesus on the Father and to reveal this mutual relationship as the fundamental structure of every human being. He thus can affirm of Jesus Christ, as eternal "Son" of the "Father," that his nature is pure "mission":

If it is evident that the nature of Jesus as Christ is being in total openness, being 'from' and 'towards,' which nowhere clings to itself and nowhere stands in itself, then it is evident, too, that this nature is pure relationship (no substantiality) and as such pure relationship, pure union.[16]

The divine mission animates the Church, and the Church animates mission. A universal instrument of salvation, the Church is the epiphany of God among men, and her missionary activity continues the incarnation of Christ by her active engagement in authentic human development and her offering of salvation to all generations. Mission is the expression of such an essential relationship between God and the world by its dynamism of transforming the fallen material nature by the power of love in view of the eschatological reign of God where God is "all in everyone" (1 Cor. 12:6). The Holy Spirit manifests its activity from the moment the gospel of the resurrection begins to enter the world of peoples and religions. In the boldness of the witness of the Pentecostal community, "We hear, each of us in his own native language" (Acts 2:8), the liberating gift of the Holy Spirit, who transcends every human and cultural barrier, is realized in the mystery of proclamation and hearing, in the dynamics of receiving and putting into practice the gift of truth.

Inspired *Upāya* of the Buddha

To better understand this mystery of dynamic wisdom, it might be useful to compare once more the Buddha's *upāya* and the mission of the Holy
Spirit as gifts flowing freely from the dynamism of the ultimate Reality.
First of all, the two gifts of the Buddha's wisdom and compassion (*prajñā*
and *karuṇā*) have to be analyzed. On considering the manifold aspects of
the personality of the Buddha, Heinrich Dumoulin finds it problematic
to apply any of the given categories of comparative religion:

> The figure of the Buddha in its historical as well as its supernatural
> dimension constitutes the center of Buddhist practice of all schools.
> The aspects of his figure are too manifold to be condensed into one
> comprehensive theology. Neither could a religious category be
> named under which the Buddha could be listed. At least the Western
> science of religion cannot offer any given category for this purpose.
> The Buddha seems to form a special category, particular to the East,
> which in the complexity of its elements is open towards transcen-
> dence.[17]

Especially in view of a dialogue with Christianity, I want to propose
for the Buddha the category of the "Inspired One"; a term obviously in
contrast with the "incarnated" Jesus Christ, yet at the same time corresponding to his title "Awakened One" (Buddha). In the figure of the Buddha are blended in a unique way a human availability, matured during
the long period of his ascetic striving and culminating in the consciousness of an existential emptiness, and a sudden awareness of Reality, a
self-communication of the Dharma. These two moments culminate in the
Buddha's dynamic *upāya* toward his oral proclamation in the Buddhavacana, his preaching and later the canonical lore, out of the single motive of boundless compassion for all living beings. His message to the
world, the Dharma, is transcendental truth that operates by autonomous
inspiration in every human being, yet is mediated by the discourses or
scriptural canons of the Buddha. He becomes an indispensable mediator
of salvation (*upāyin*) who is able to propagate the ultimate Reality according to each being's perceptivity and lead them to the threshold from
where they can face the truth for themselves by their own experience:

> What they all entertain in their minds,
> All the ways they practice,
> How many kinds are their desires,
> And their former karmas, good and evil,
> The Buddha knows all these perfectly.[18]

I am the All Knowing, the All Seeing, the Knower of the Way, the Opener of the Way, the Preacher of the Way.[19]

While the "Awakened One" emphasizes the human efforts to pass over the threshold of illumination, the title "Inspired One" expresses this same mystery from the perspective of the dynamic Dharma that discloses itself to the Buddha and urges him to preach in human language by a variety of means. The "Inspired One" is more than a mystic, insofar as his private enjoyment of the highest bliss moves with inherent dynamism toward its salvific proclamation. He also is more than a prophet, as his message claims the totality of a new religious system, invites imitation of his own way, and finally leads to the deification of the founder. Yet the "Inspired One" is clearly distinct from a God "incarnate" as he never claims to embody the truth and grant salvation, but merely to show the way toward its achievement. These elements of the mediating function of the "Inspired One" are summarized in the following *gāthās*:

The Law-king . . .
Appears in this world;
According to the natures of all living beings,
He preaches the Law discriminately.
The Tathāgata is greatly to be honored
And profound in wisdom;
For long has he kept secret this essential [truth],
Not endeavoring hastily to declare it.
The wise, if they hear it,
Are able to believe and discern;
The ignorant doubt and turn away,
Losing it perpetually.[20]

Whereas the title "Awakened One" proceeds from the human realm and describes the release of human efforts by the perception of truth, the category of the "Inspired One" presupposes evidently an initial transcendental action on the human mind and finds its fulfillment in *upāya*. With a dynamism inherent in the Dharma itself, the vocational experience of the "Inspired One" moves toward its expression in the words of preaching and subsequently in scripture:

The voice of the Buddha is very precious,
Able to rid all creatures of distress.

Opportunely preaching the Law,
Faultless and inscrutable,
Which causes all to reach the wisdom throne.[21]

The entire composition of the Lotus Sutra evidences the transition from the "realm of trace" (*chi-men chiao-hua*) to the "realm of origin" (*pen-men chiao-hua*),[22] the "trace" Buddha being the historical, but provisional, Śākyamuni, while the real Buddha is only revealed in the second half of the sutra as the Buddha of unlimited duration. According to the T'ien-t'ai school, the historical Buddha is considered *upāya* of the *Dharma-kāya*. Moreover, the entire Lotus Sutra has been composed as a sacred drama, a mystery play,[23] around the emerging Mahāyāna doctrines; it actually has been performed as missionary *upāya* for the conversion of the multitudes. Its large diffusion and appraisal all over Asia may result from its poetical beauty, but much more from its plot, which elaborates the dramatic character of human life on the horizon of the boundless compassion of the ultimate Dharma. The entire life both of the Buddha and of every being is thus presented as *upāya*. The sutra attempts to render in human language the mystery of salvation and conjure before the eyes of the spectator the role he himself is to play in this eternal drama.

A Common Missiology

Overcoming by far the general notion of mission as the sometimes militant propagation of one's own faith, these considerations are an analysis of the foundation of mission in the realities of God and the Dharma and have thus disclosed a common ground for the propagation of each faith, which in the diversity of doctrinal contents is already aware of a fundamental convergence in essentials. Mission or *upāya* is not just a trick or attempt at persuasion; it is rather the humble cooperation of human agents with the compassionate dynamism of Reality. To a traditional understanding this may appear a paradoxical contradiction in terms. Hence it follows not that mission should be abandoned at all—it remains the first and ever-valid testimony of a personal faith commitment. On the contrary, mission can acknowledge a common source for Buddhism and Christianity and may thus contribute to greater harmony and understanding between religious traditions. Leaving aside the obvious doctrinal differences between the two traditions, the point is here to emphasize the climate of courageously acknowledging this common ground that will create the framework for such further dialogues in mutual confidence. Rooted in the basic experience of each religion, and thus touching their "meta-center,"[24] "mission" and "*upāya*" disclose the mystery of the trinitarian dimension as well as the self-revealing and compassionate dynamics inherent to the Dharma. In line with the affirmation of Msgr. P. Rossano, the late secretary of the Pontifical Council for Interreligious Dialogue, that we would be facing today the challenge of "increasing the weight of the spiritual element in the world,"[25] such a common ecumenism between Buddhists and Christians definitely marks the order of the day.

Such a common missiology finds its symbolic illustration even in the geographical location where Oriental and Occidental traditions meet. In the patriarchal basilica of Saint Sofia at Constantinople (Istanbul) faithful Christians (and Muslims) venerate the famous Byzantine mosaic of the "Seat of Wisdom," representing Mary with the child Jesus on the throne. The intimate exchange of giving and receiving love between a human mother and her divine child in the mosaic, and between mothers and children all over the world, represents the way of wisdom that is never embraced by mere human reason alone, but discloses a symbiotic oneness with a transcendental dynamism and creativity. From the subtle philosophical and theological considerations we return, at the end, to the ordinary routine of everyday life and to the common witness of Buddhists and Christians. The highest wisdom, the "Seat of Wisdom," cannot be found in academic circles of philosophers unless it is realized in everyday striving. Here the image of the Byzantine mother with her child becomes the icon of the deepest dimension of our human gatherings, our *hozas*, embraced by the virtue of creative *upāya* of compassion toward the life situations of our neighbors.

Again, the icons of the Buddha and Mary[26] disclose the basic human disposition toward the working of *upāya* through the openmindedness of persons who are empty of themselves. Christianity underlines this condition of *anattā* when it speaks of purity of heart as the indispensable condition to see God (Mt. 5:8). As the "mission" of the trinity, in the Christian tradition, entered into human history through the emptiness of Mary's "yes" to the plan of divine incarnation (*anattā* of the heart), *upāya* in the Buddhist tradition reaches its full self-realization in the purity of one's awakening to his original being (virginity of *citta*); from here *upāya* and mission become operative in human history and, like the creative Word, "do not return to God empty, but shall accomplish that which I purpose, and prosper in the thing for which I sent it" (Is. 55:11). Beyond all substantial differences between the two traditions that have to be faced in all sincerity and embraced by this climate of mutual trust, in this human openness appears the anthropological fundament on which alone a genuine dialogue seems possible and to which common witness has to be given in a world of growing self-centeredness. The paradoxical statement of Masao Abe, one of the great figures in Buddhist-Christian encounters, may therefore summarize the human foundation for a common missiology: "The positionless position, together with the boundless openness . . . can be properly realized only existentially, not merely logically or conceptually."[27]

Notes

1. *Mahāvagga* I. 11.1, in: tr., I. B. Horner. *The Book of the Discipline*, IV. London: Pali Text Society, 1982, 28.
2. M. Pye, *Skilful Means*. London: Duckworth, 1978, 5; 151, 161.
3. I would like to remark that M. Pye, op. cit. 14, envisages a more satisfactory translation of the term.
4. M. Pye. "Skilful Means and the Interpretation of Christianity," *Buddhist-Christian Studies* 10 (1990), 17–22; ed., M. Pye and R. Morgan. *The Cardinal Meaning. Essays in Comparative Hermeneutics*. The Hague: Mouton, 1973.
5. Following a conference by Card. J. Ratzinger, "Christ, the Faith and the Challenge of Cultures," Hong Kong, March 2–3, 1993. Already the diversity of the one message of Jesus according to the four gospels points to the constitutive theological pluralism within the New Testament.
6. M. Monier and Williams. *A Sanskrit-English Dictionary*. Oxford: Clarendon, 1979, 215.
7. Edited by T. W. Rhys Davids and W. Stede. *The Pali Society's Pali-English Dictionary*. London: Pali Text Society, 1979, 149.
8. *Upāya-kauśalya*, in: F. Edgerton. *Buddhist Hybrid Sanskrit Dictionary and Grammar*. New Haven, CT: 1953, 146.
9. *Skilful Means*, op. cit., 1; See the critique by J. H. Kamstra. "Skilful Means as a 'Germinative Principle,'" in *Numen* 27 (1980), 270–77.
10. N. N. Bhattacharyya. *A Glossary of Indian Religious Terms and Concepts*. Columbia, MI: South Asia Publ. 1990, 125, 161.
11. Translated by D. T. Suzuki. *The Lankavatara Sūtra*. London: Routledge & Kegan Paul, 1978 [reprinted], XIII.
12. Cfr. *Lumen gentium*, 16; *Gaudium et spes*, 40.
13. *The Threefold Lotus Sutra:* Innumerable Meanings, The Lotus Flower of the Wonderful Law, and Meditation on the Bodhisattva Universal Virtue. Translated by Bunnō Katō, et al., Tokyo: Kōsei Publishing Co. 1975.
14. G. Vicedom. *Missio Dei*. Munich: Kaiser 1958, 14: "Das letzte Mysterium der Mission, aus dem sie herauswächst und aus dem sie lebt, ist: Gott sendet seinen Sohn, Vater und Sohn senden den Geist. Damit macht er sich nicht nur um Gesand-ten, sondern zugleich zum Inhalt der Sendung, ohne daß durch diese Offenbarungstrinität die Wesensgleichheit der göttlichen Personen aufgelöst würde. Denn in jeder Person der Gottheit handelt Gott ganz. . . . Ihr Auftrag ist in dem göttlichen vorgebildet, ihr Dienst durch den göttlichen vorgegeben, Sinn und Inhalt der Arbeit von der Missio Dei her bestimmt."
15. G. Vicedom. op. cit., 13.
16. J. Ratzinger. *Einführung in das Christentum*. Munich: 1968, 146: "Wenn so deutlich wird, daß das Sein Jesu als des Christus ein gänzlich offenes Sein ist, ein Sein 'von-her' und 'auf-zu,' das nirgendwo an sich selber festhält und nirgendwo nur auf sich selber steht, dann ist zugleich deutlich, daß dieses Sein reine Beziehung ist (nicht Substantialität) und als reine Beziehung reine Einheit."; Cf. 149. The entire spectrum of meanings of *upāya*, even the notion as "stratagem," finds its equivalent in Christian proclamation as has been

shown by U. Mauch. *Der listige Jesus* [The Cunning Jesus]. Zurich: 1992, recalling the Japanese expression *uso mo hōben* (the end justifies the means).

17. H. Dumoulin. *Begegnung mit dem Buddhismus.* Freiburg-Basel and Vienna: 1978, 62f.
18. *Lotus Sutra,* op. cit., II, 62, 28f; cf. V, 126, 11ff.
19. Ibid., V, 127, 27ff.
20. Ibid., V, 129, 6ff.
21. Ibid., III, 78, 17f; 79, 19ff.
22. This interpretation has been accepted by Chih-i (538–97), the sixth patriarch of the T'ien-t'ai school, drawing a division of the sutra after chapter 14.
23. M. Fuss. *Buddhavacana and Dei Verbum.* Leiden: Brill, 1991, 193–96.
24. G. Rosenkranz. *Religionswissenschaft und Theologie.* Munich: 1964, 80: "Es ist eine Grunderkenntnis der modernen Religionswissenschaft, daß jede Religion inmitten ihres religionsgeschichtlichen Zusammenhanges ihr eigenes Metazentrum in sich trägt, das ihre historische Erscheinung durchwaltet und bestimmt. Das ihr aufgetragene Verstehen religiöser Phänomene bedarf der dauernden Bewegung, um in dies Innerste vorzudringen; wo dies nicht geschieht, kommt es zu einer folgenschweren Nivellierung in der Beurteilung religionsgeschichtlicher Parallelen und Konvergenzen." Cfr. the recent document *Dialogue and Proclamation,* published in 1991 by the Pontifical Council for Interreligious Dialogue, which mentions in no. 42 the deepest level of sharing one's religious experience.
25. P. Rossano. *I perché dell'uomo e le risposte delle grandi religioni.* Cinisello B.: Paoline, 1988, 15.
26. For a further elaboration of this analogy, see my "Buddha und Maria: Dynamische Leere als Ikone des Dialogs," in: *Studia Missionalia* 43 (1994), 211–44; M. Reis Habito. "The Bodhisattva Guanyin and the Virgin Mary," in: *Buddhist-Christian Studies* 13 (1993), 61–69; Yü, Chün-fang. "Guanyin: The Chinese Transformation of Avalokiteshvara," in: ed., M. Weidner. *Latter Days of the Law. Images of Chinese Buddhism 850–1850.* Honolulu: University of Hawaii Press, 1994, 151–81.
27. Masao Abe. "A Positionless Position," in: *World Faiths Encounter* no. 6 (1993), 69. London.

By the Power of the Buddha

Malcolm David Eckel

For if words are not things, they are living powers, by which the things of most importance to mankind are actuated, combined, and humanized.

—Samuel Taylor Coleridge

That there be things which flow out from a being and at the same time remain within it may sound surprising. Words are like that, amazing: they are uttered and yet they remain within us.

—Meister Eckhart

I have been asked to reflect on the words of the Lotus Sutra from a Christian perspective. I should say at the start that the apparent simplicity of this task makes me uneasy. In the end I can only speak from my own understanding, and my own approach to religious matters is as much informed by my study of Buddhism as it is by my identification with the Christian tradition. For me the two traditions are mapped very closely onto each other, and it would do violence to both to pull them apart. Instead of addressing the Lotus Sutra as if it were an object foreign to myself, I would prefer to place myself imaginatively in the situation of the "preacher," or *dharma-bhāṇaka*, in chapter 10 of the Lotus Sutra and respond to the text as if I were preparing to preach it. But I will imagine that I am going to preach it to a Christian congregation as a Christian preacher, with a Christian sense of curiosity about the relationship between text and Word and a Christian understanding of grace and salvation.

Words as Living Powers

William Empson has said that poetic words function as compacted doctrines.[1] In the exegesis of Christian scripture, this is only part of the truth. Doctrines themselves are compacted versions of *the* Word, and expositors of scripture have to do more than engage in doctrinal exegesis. They have to touch the points of tension in scriptural language where the Word presses against the language of ordinary discourse and yields a sense of divine energy or power, and they have to make this energy felt in the spoken word. Much has been said in Christian tradition about the power to nourish and inspire with the spoken word, but it could hardly be expressed more compactly than it was by Krister Stendahl in his ten commandments of biblical preaching: "You shall not read from the cookbook—serve the food."[2]

While this formulation of the relationship between words and the Word is thoroughly Christian, it is not inconsistent with the narrative style of the Lotus Sutra. The Lotus Sutra also is profoundly concerned with the act of preaching, in a way that seems almost magical to more pedestrian purveyors of the Word. At the beginning of the chapter entitled "The Preacher," the Buddha predicts that any bodhisattva who hears a single stanza or word of this sutra and rejoices in it with a single thought will achieve supreme enlightenment. In the next chapter, the preaching of the Lotus Sutra leads to one of the key events in the text, the miraculous manifestation of a stupa. From inside the stupa comes a voice of praise: "Well done, well done, Lord Śākyamuni. You have spoken well the discourse of the Lotus of the True Dharma."[3] This voice belongs to the Buddha Prabhūtaratna, who once made a vow that, whenever someone preaches the sutra, the stupa with his body will appear and applaud the preacher.

The kinship between Christian approaches to the preached Word and the verbal expression of the Lotus Sutra extends even to Krister Stendahl's carefully chosen metaphor of the Word as food.[4] At the beginning of chapter 6 of the Lotus Sutra, the chapter on the "prediction" *(vyākaraṇa)* of future awakening, a group of disciples asks the Buddha to predict their own destiny. They frame their request in the language of food.

O Worthy One, Great Hero, Lion of the Śākyas,
    Best of Men,
Have pity on us and speak the Buddha-Word.

You know what must befall us,
    O Best of Human Beings;

Sprinkle us with nectar
and make a prediction for each of us.

Someone who has survived a famine
and received good food,
May be told to wait
even when he has the food in his hands.

We have the same longing.
After investigating an inferior vehicle,
We are in a difficult time
and would like to receive the Buddha's knowledge.

The Perfect Buddha, the Great Sage
has not given us a prediction,
As if food had been put in our hands
and we could not eat.[5]

The disciples' request to "sprinkle us with nectar" clearly builds on the metaphor of the previous chapter on plants, where the Buddha is depicted as a great cloud that sprinkles the world with the rain of his teaching. But the request has other important lines of association as well. As Étienne Lamotte has pointed out in a note on "Perfumed Amṛta and the Sacred Meal,"[6] the term "nectar" (*amṛta*) also means "immortality" and is used frequently as a synonym of nirvana.[7] Unlike the "nectar" of Hindu mythology, the "nectar" of Buddhist texts is pictured as being sprinkled from above rather than being churned up from the depths of the sea, but the metaphor of the "descent" of the Dharma does provide a powerful Buddhist counterpart to the Hindu concept of the "descent" (*avatāra*) or "incarnation" of God.[8]

The layers of doctrine that are compacted in this metaphor do not stop with the Hindu doctrine of divine descent. It would be plausible to argue that the image of the rain in chapter 5 of the Lotus Sutra condenses all the essential doctrinal assertions of the text, precisely because the image itself is one of condensation and essence. The words of the chapter return again and again to the idea that the rain of the Dharma is one, and only the variations of the plants give the impression of varied effects. The Dharma has "one essence" (*ekarasa*), and the Buddha speaks only "one voice" (*ekasvara*), "one Dharma" (*ekadharma*), and "one Vehicle" (*ekayāna*).[9] With such a concern for the "essence" of the teaching, it is not surprising to find that chapter 5 is one of the richest chapters in presenting the language of Emptiness (the doctrine that there is no essence). The Sanskrit version of the chapter ends with three verses that tie together the doctrine of One Vehicle with the doctrine of Emptiness:

[He sees] all *dharma*s as the same,
 empty, and not diverse.
He does not see them,
 and he does not distinguish any *dharma*.

With great wisdom,
 he completely sees the Dharma Body.
There are not three vehicles;
 here there is only one vehicle.

All *dharma*s are the same; all are the same;
 they are always the same.
When someone knows this,
 he knows nirvana, immortality, and blessedness.[10]

For a Christian preacher the rhetorical associations of these ideas are particularly rich. To say that the Buddha's words are nectar recalls the book of Ezekiel (one of the richest of texts in the Hebrew Bible on the power of divine words). In a metaphorical sense, one can savor the image of God's command to Ezekiel that he eat the scroll on which God's words are written and take delight in the discovery that the scroll tastes as sweet as honey. The Gospel of John also speaks of the Word as food, and contains a similar concern for the idea of ascent and descent, a similar disposition toward unity in the face of diversity, and a similar movement between the pictorial language of metaphor and the language of doctrine. This Gospel also shows how the enunciation of scripture reflects the ritual life of a Christian community. Krister Stendahl's commandment to serve the food echoes and prepares for the ritual movement to the altar for the Eucharist, and the commandment itself can be treated as an admonition to bring the same ritual authenticity to the pulpit that a priest brings to the altar: the same sense of reverence and the same sense that one is not merely describing something but *doing* it. The key question for a preacher of the Lotus Sutra is whether the sutra also portrays the act of preaching in such a way that the sutra makes it possible for the preacher to step out of its pages and *do* it. To answer this question requires a closer look at the effect the sutra is said to have on its listeners. Is the sutra intended in some way to bring about a change in those who hear it? If so, is this change comparable to the change that Christians speak about as a "conversion"?

The Christian tradition is full of stories about the use of scripture to bring about a transformation in those who hear or read it. I doubt that it would be a great distortion of the tradition to say that one of the classic examples of such a transformation is an event recounted in the eighth chapter of Saint Augustine's *Confessions.*

> For I felt that I was still the captive of my sins, and in my misery I kept crying "How long shall I go on saying 'tomorrow, tomorrow'? Why not now? Why not make an end of my ugly sins at this moment?"
>
> I was asking myself these questions, weeping all the while with the most bitter sorrow in my heart, when all at once I heard the singsong voice of a child in a nearby house. Whether it was the voice of a boy or a girl I cannot say, but again and again it repeated the refrain "Take it and read, take it and read." At this I looked up, thinking hard whether there was any kind of game in which children used to chant words like these, but I could not remember ever hearing them before. I stemmed my flood of tears and stood up, telling myself that this could only be a divine command to open my book of Scripture and read the first passage on which my eyes should fall. For I had heard the story of Antony, and I remembered how he had happened to go into a church while the Gospel was being read and had taken it as a counsel addressed to himself when he heard the words: *Go home and sell all that belongs to you. Give it to the poor, and so the treasure you have shall be in heaven; then come back and follow me.* By this divine pronouncement he had at once been converted to you.
>
> So I hurried back to the place where Alypius was sitting, for when I stood up to move away I had put down the book containing Paul's epistles. I seized it and opened it; and in silence I read the first passage on which my eyes fell: *Not in revelling and drunkenness, not in lust and wantonness, not in quarrels and rivalries. Rather, arm yourselves with the Lord Jesus Christ; spend no more thought on nature and nature's appetites.* I had no wish to read more and no need to do so. For in an instant, as I came to the end of the sentence, it was as though the light of confidence flooded into my heart and all the darkness of doubt was dispelled.[11]

To say that this account of the conversion of Saint Augustine is an example of a Christian transformation is somewhat disingenuous, since it has served as a model for so many seemingly spontaneous experiences of conversion in later Christian history, just as it too was modeled on the conversion of another exemplary saint.

It is difficult for a Christian who has been shaped by the Augustinian tradition to read the Lotus Sutra and not be struck by similar narratives of conversion. When the Buddha speaks in the Lotus Sutra (and speaks the text of the Lotus Sutra itself), he does more than convey information: he elicits an emotional response that seems to mirror Augustine's own response to the words of scripture. An example is the response of the disciples to the prediction of the Buddha in Lotus Sutra chapter 9:

Then, when the disciples that were in training and those that were not had heard their own predictions directly from the Lord, they were happy, excited, satisfied, joyful, and full of delight and pleasure, and they spoke these verses to the Lord:

> We are satisfied, O Light of the World,
>   now that we have heard this prediction.
> We are as happy, O Lord,
>   as if we had been sprinkled with nectar.
> We have no doubt or uncertainty
>   that we will be the Best of Men.
> We are happy now
>   that we have heard this prediction.[12]

When this passage is read beside Augustine's claim that "the light of confidence flooded into my heart and all the darkness of doubt was dispelled," it almost seems as if they were following the same inner text. There is the same sense of excitement and joy and the same feeling of inner conviction that the lives of the disciples make sense in an entirely new way.

There is, of course, a large body of literature in Western languages about the psychology of conversion, and it would be far beyond the scope of this paper to attempt a complete account of the phenomenon of conversion in these two texts. But there are lines of connection that would be useful to a preacher who stands at the intersection of the two traditions. One connection is simply the emotional vividness and intensity of the event. In his classic account of conversion in *The Varieties of Religious Experience*, William James speaks first of emotional intensity, excitement, and engagement: "There may be great oscillation in the emotional interest, and the hot places may shift before one almost as rapidly as the sparks that run through burnt-up paper."[13] Augustine certainly burned with emotional energy at the moment of his conversion (although it would be more in keeping with the image of Augustine's tears to say that he was swept away by the flood of his emotions).[14] The string of near synonyms ("happy, excited, satisfied, joyful, full of delight and pleasure") that accompanies the key teaching events in the Lotus Sutra seems to convey the same sense of emotional intensity. I remember reading this formulaic list of synonyms when I was a student and thinking that it was nothing more than a distraction in my hunt for more serious points of doctrine, but for a preacher this list provides a crucial point of entry into the emotional logic of the text.

How is this emotional logic related to the text's doctrinal content? One way to address the relationship between emotion and doctrine is to ask what the disciples *know* when they feel this joy. James defines conversion as an experience "by which a self hitherto divided, and consciously wrong, inferior and unhappy, becomes unified and consciously right, superior and happy, in consequence of its firmer hold on religious realities."[15] Two clauses in this definition relate to an aspect of experience that might loosely be called "cognitive": there is a sense of movement from a divided to a unified self, and there is a greater grasp of reality. The notion of a unified "self" raises problems in a Buddhist context, of course, but it is not difficult to see both elements of this cognitive transformation in the disciples' response to the Buddha. Take, for example, the predictions that are described in chapter 8. The chapter begins with a prediction that a monk named Pūrṇa will become a glorious preacher of the Dharma, and it ends with the prediction that five hundred *arhats* will achieve buddhahood in regular succession. The *arhats* respond with a story about a man who, without his knowledge, has had a jewel sewn into his cloak. He wanders through a foreign country and struggles to obtain enough food to keep himself alive. Finally the friend who gave him the jewel finds him, and tells him to look into his cloak and use the jewel to buy food. This parable gives the impression at first of being another story about food, but it really is about knowledge. The man had everything he needed to keep himself alive but did not know it. He needed the friend to enlighten him about the riches that already were his.

In the case of the disciples, this enlightening knowledge consists of a vastly expanded vision of their own place in the career that leads to buddhahood. Instead of being content with an "inferior" path that leads only to nirvana, they suddenly see themselves as future buddhas, capable of bringing the same kind of powerful teaching to others. Most important of all (as the story of the hidden jewel makes clear), they already have begun, unbeknownst to themselves, to follow that path. This revised self-image involves an awareness of James's "unified self" in a sense that is different from the permanent "self" that Buddhist philosophers are accustomed to deny: it involves the sense that one has a crucial role to play in a vast historical process, and that elements of that role are already at play in one's own experience. This is the unity of a powerful and consistent narrative, not of a permanent and unchangeable being.

What is the jewel, then, that lies waiting to be revealed? The prose of chapter 8 is surprisingly reticent about identifying this important feature in the story, but the verses fill in the gap:

We were ignorant in the same way,
O Lord, about our previous vow,
Which the Lord had long given us in previous lives.[16]

The "previous vow" (*pūrva-praṇidhāna*) plays a crucial role in the religious environment out of which the Lotus Sutra and similar Mahayana texts arose.[17] The same word is used in chapter 11 to name the promise that the Buddha Prabhūtaratna made to manifest a great stupa whenever the Lotus Sutra is preached. It is used for the promise Dharmākara made to establish the Pure Land of Amitābha Buddha. And it names an important element in the ritual of bodhisattva practice in the Indian Mahayana. In this passage, the term might do nothing more than indicate that the disciples became aware at the moment of the Buddha's teaching that the Mahayana was something to which they had long aspired, but the use of the word "vow" also connects them by implication with the vows of some of the great buddhas of the Mahayana tradition. Much of the ironic richness of Augustine's *Confessions* comes from a similar ability to look back over the course of the author's life after the experience of conversion and see the movement of unconscious forces that give a completely new meaning to the narrative of the author's life.

For the preacher of scripture, however, the most striking similarity between the two types of conversion narrative may simply be the relationship between conversion and the words of a text. In Augustine's case the relationship has several layers. The immediate occasion for the change in Augustine's sense of self was the silent reading of a line from the Epistle to the Romans ("not in revelling and drunkenness"), but the words of this scriptural passage gained weight and power from a series of other textual voices. As Augustine wept with "the most bitter sorrow" in his heart, he heard a singsong voice that told him to "take it and read." The text explains that he heard these words as if they were simultaneously a divine command and an echo of the voice that Saint Antony heard pronouncing the words of a passage from the Gospel of Matthew. According to Athanasius's *Life of Antony*, the words from Matthew triggered Antony's decision to take up the life of a desert monk. Augustine interpreted the words of Paul as a similar catalyst for a new way of life. It is as if Augustine, even in a moment of the most intimate and direct experience, could not get textual voices out of his head—as if the account of his own conversion were being written as a book about a book (Athanasius's *Life of Antony*) about a book (the Gospel of Matthew).

The Lotus Sutra also gives the impression of being a book about a book, but in this case it is a book about itself. As Gregory Schopen has pointed out in an important article on the cult of the book in the early

Mahayana, the Lotus Sutra belongs to a category of texts that extol a form of book-centered piety.[18] To repeat, copy, and memorize the text is considered to be as powerful a means of generating merit as the worship of innumerable stupas; the place where the text is located is to be treated as a shrine (*caitya*); someone who preaches the sutra is thought of as performing the action of a buddha; the preaching results not only in a sense of emotional excitement but in a changed concept of the listener's life history; and the preaching of the text is pictured as being applauded by the miraculous manifestation of a buddha. The text has a clear vision of its own power and importance. But where is the place for a modern preacher?

Earlier I asked whether the sutra depicts the act of preaching in such a way that it also makes it possible for a preacher to do it. How would I enter into the text in the role of preacher? What is intriguing about the intertextuality in the conversion narratives in the *Confessions* and the Lotus Sutra is that it offers both a *description* of the relationship of this text with other texts and a *model* for the preacher's own leap beyond the text into the creation of a new text. It is as if the text of Augustine pauses in the midst of the narrative, turns to the reader, and asks: If Augustine did this with the text about Antony, and Antony did this with the text from Matthew, what are you going to do now with the text that sits in your hands? The Lotus Sutra pauses and asks: If this text became the new life-story of these great disciples and bodhisattvas, what is your story? What is your response? Questions like these are precisely the ones that get the preacher out of the cookbook and into the food. They bring power, directness, and life to the preacher's message.

If I were going to preach the Lotus Sutra to a Christian congregation and preach it with a sense of power, I would want to move beyond the question of verbal action (of doing things with words) to the question of power itself. Clearly the Lotus Sutra understands its own words to be imbued with power. But what is the nature of this "power"? In the shadow of the secular saints, Marx, Weber, and Foucault, one dares not use this word naively, but the role of the word in the religious setting of the Lotus Sutra is too important to avoid altogether. The word relates not only to the personal charisma of the preacher but to the power that the preacher attempts to make present from a source that may be very different from the preacher him- or herself. Does the Lotus Sutra help us illuminate the nature of its own power? The answer is yes. In Śākyamuni's explanation of Prabhūtaratna's promise, there is a word that, in the density of its meaning, comes as close to Empson's idea of a compacted doctrine as any in the text. The word is *adhiṣṭhāna*, a word that is translated by different authors as "vow," "wish," "resolution," "blessing," or "sustaining power."[19] Śākyamuni explains that when Prabhūtaratna arrived at the end of his career, at the moment of his *parinirvāṇa*, he made the following resolution (*adhiṣṭhāna*): "Let this stupa with my body appear in any world system where the discourse of the Lotus Sutra is revealed. When any Buddha preaches this discourse, may it stand above the assembly. And may the stupa applaud the Buddhas who teach the discourse of the Lotus Sutra."[20] It is by the power of *adhiṣṭhāna* that the stupa appears and Prabhūtaratna's voice sounds its praise for Śākyamuni's teaching.

The term *adhiṣṭhāna* is used again in the thirteenth chapter to explain why preachers of the Dharma should be honored and why the Dharma itself should be received with faith after the extinction (*parinirvāṇa*) of the Buddha: "Why [will its listeners be so pleased by this teaching]? O Mañjuśrī, this Dharma-teaching has been empowered (*adhiṣṭhita*) by all Buddhas. O Mañjuśrī, this Dharma-teaching has been eternally empowered (*nitya-adhiṣṭhita*) by the worthy Tathāgatas of the past, present, and future."[21] A similar combination of concepts occurs in chapter 15 on the "Life Span of the Tathāgata." The chapter begins with the Buddha exhorting the assembly of bodhisattvas to have faith (*abhiśraddadhadhvam*) in the truth of the Buddha's word. The bodhisattvas then say, "Speak, O Sugata, and we will have faith in what the Tathāgata says." The Buddha responds by saying, "Listen, O sons of good family, the force of my power (*adhiṣṭhāna-balādhānam*) is such that the world, with its gods, demons, and human beings, thinks that the Lord and Tathāgata Śākyamuni has now gone forth from the family of the Śākyas, gone to the seat of awakening in the great city of Gayā, and attained supreme awakening."[22]

These passages depict the function of *adhiṣṭhāna* as clearly as any in the Lotus Sutra. The word gains its force here and in other Buddhist literature from the perennial problem of the Buddha's absence. In the literature of the Abhidharma, the word *adhiṣṭhāna* is used to refer to the power that saints leave behind in their bones or relics: texts explain that when the saints are gone, *adhiṣṭhāna* remains and continues to bring about miraculous effects. In Mahayana tradition, where the question of the Buddha's absence is more complex, the word *adhiṣṭhāna* is still used in many texts (as in chapter 13 of the Lotus Sutra) to name a lingering power that affects events after the *parinirvāṇa* of the Buddha. In other settings (such as the passage just quoted from chapter 15 of the Lotus Sutra), however, the word breaks loose from its association with any particular buddha or period of time and refers simply to the power of the buddhas of any age. This makes it possible in Mahayana exegetical literature to say of Ānanda that he remembers the teaching of the Buddha *buddhādhiṣṭhānena* ("by the power of the Buddha") and for Sudhana, the young pilgrim at the end of *The Perfection of Wisdom in 8,000 Lines,* to say that it was the Buddha's *adhiṣṭhāna* that sustained him in moments of great difficulty. In the Perfection of Wisdom literature, the phrase "by the power of the Buddha" seems to express the same pervasive sense of humility, respect, and devotion that one would associate with the phrase *Inshallah* on the lips of a Muslim or "by the grace of God" on the lips of a Christian.

The passages from the thirteenth and fifteenth chapters of the Lotus Sutra also associate *adhiṣṭhāna* with the concept of "faith" (*śraddhā*) by arguing that listeners have faith in the Buddha's words precisely because the Buddha (or all the buddhas of the past, present, and future) has imbued them with power. "Faith" is a difficult concept in Buddhist literature from this period: at the same time it is quite simple and enormously complex. The term has an honorable history in Vedic literature, where it is used to name the attitude of trust that a person brings to a ritual act in order for it to be effective. This meaning carries over into Buddhist usage in the list of the five faculties (*indriya*). The five faculties lead from faith (*śraddhā*) to wisdom (*prajñā*) and suggest, quite naturally, that one needs to begin the practice of the Buddhist path with a sense of trust or confidence and then find that this confidence is verified by direct understanding. The trust necessary to begin the path is faith, and the understanding that concludes it is wisdom.

Faith never loses its role as a beginner's virtue in the Buddhist literature of India, but the texts of the early Mahayana develop a very different concept of what it means to *begin* the path, and this new understanding of the beginning of the path gives faith a weight and significance it did not have in earlier literature. In chapter 2 of the Lotus Sutra, where the assembly is purified of the proud monks, nuns, and lay disciples who are unprepared to be taught, faith is the characteristic that separates those who leave from those who remain.[23] This is faith in the simple sense of the confidence or trust necessary to receive a teaching. But we know from the chapters that predict the disciples' future careers that to hear and accept the teaching of the Lotus Sutra involves adopting a radically different sense of one's own identity. Those who have faith in the Lotus Sutra are not just beginners but are praised in terms that normally are reserved for advanced bodhisattvas.

> When this sūtra has been spoken,
>   any being who says, "I rejoice,"
> And receives it with honor,
>   you should consider irreversible.

> If that being has faith in this sūtra,
>   he has seen former Tathāgatas,

Has done them honor,
and he has heard this same Dharma.[24]

Faith in the Lotus Sutra may be a "beginning" in a technical sense, but it involves such a radical change in a disciple's sense of identity that the concept of "beginning" seems to dissolve. One sees oneself as part of an enormous process of salvation, much larger than a single life or world-system, and recognizes that one is, has been, and will be sustained in that process by the power of innumerable buddhas in the past, present, and future.

I suspect that you can see now where my argument is going. It is not uncommon for academic preachers to lull their audience to sleep with a long historical digression before they let the tired words of academic discourse yield to the power of the Word. When I imagine myself listening for the power of the Word in the Lotus Sutra, I tune my ears to the resonances in the relationship of *adhiṣṭhāna* and *śraddhā*, and what I hear is an echo of the relationship between the Christian words "grace" and "faith." The force of the word *adhiṣṭhāna* may arise initially from a concern for the Buddha's absence, but it represents a conviction that, whether the Buddha himself is absent or present, the Buddha's power is available whenever the mind turns with joy and faith toward the teaching that the Buddha left behind. You can imagine a Christian preacher leaning over the edge of the pulpit, looking the congregation in the eye, and saying that this power is present *here today* whenever we turn our hearts and minds toward the teaching of this great text.

Emptiness: The Place Where the Preacher Is Not

Kern's nineteenth-century translation of the Lotus Sutra contains a tantalizing passage about the accoutrements of the preacher:

> The wise man is always at ease, and in that state he preaches the law, seated on an elevated pulpit which has been prepared for him on a clean and pretty spot.

> He puts on a clean, nice, red robe, dyed with good colours, and a black woollen garment and a long undergarment;

> Having duly washed his feet and rubbed his head and face with smooth ointments, he ascends the pulpit, which is provided with a footbank and covered with pieces of fine cloth of various sorts, and sits down.[25]

There is a suggestion here of a venerable bishop, clothing himself in white, scarlet, and black, and gravely ascending the pulpit of an English cathedral. Unfortunately the suggestion is misleading, at least with regard to the pulpit. Kern translates the word *dharmāsana* more accurately elsewhere as "seat." But it would not be misleading to say that the Lotus Sutra is fascinated with the setting in which the sutra is placed or preached. The drama that surrounds the manifestation of the stupa in chapter 11 has to do with a respect for *place*. When Śākyamuni explains why Prabhūtaratna's stupa appears and applauds his own teaching of the Lotus Sutra, he says that Prabhūtaratna vowed that it would appear *wherever* the Lotus Sutra is preached. The locative force of this vow is repeated in the formula that Gregory Schopen drew attention to in his discussion of the cult of the book: any "spot of earth" (*pṛthivīpradeśa*) where the text is located "becomes a shrine" (*caityabhūta*). In chapter 20 this formula is expanded to include the assertion that any place where the sutra is revealed, taught, copied, pondered, preached, recited, or collected into a book is to be known as the seat of the Buddha's awakening (*bodhimaṇḍa*). This language of emplacement echoes a series of brief formulas about the preacher's seat in chapter 10:

After entering the Conqueror's resting place,
  putting on the robe,
And sitting on my seat,
  a scholar should fearlessly speak.

The strength of friendliness is the resting place,
  patience and kindness are the robe,
And Emptiness is my seat.
  When he has seated himself there, let him teach.[26]

What does it mean to say that Emptiness is the Buddha's seat? One way to approach a claim like this is to look at comparable passages in other Buddhist sutras. There is some help to be had from a passage in The Teaching of Vimalakīrti on the "seat of awakening" (*bodhimaṇḍa*).[27] Vimalakīrti's discourse identifies the seat of awakening with a long list of positive qualities, including "friendliness" (*maitrī*), which in this verse from the Lotus Sutra is identified as the "resting place" (*layana*) of the Buddha, and "patience and kindliness," which here are identified as the robe. The rhetorical strategy of identifying the external trappings of Indian ritual life with moral and cognitive states is common in Buddhist literature.[28] But there is a more important issue in this reference to Emptiness as the Buddha's seat than the spiritualizing of ritual acts. The most fundamental focal point of Buddhist devotion is the Buddha. But *where is* the Buddha, and what is there to be devoted to? The question is complicated enough in traditional accounts of the historical Buddha, when the Buddha is said to have deflected attention from his physical body to the body of his teaching (the Dharma Body), but it becomes much more complex as the tradition develops. The Dharma Body can be understood as the "body" of all "teachings" (*dharmas*) or as the body of all "qualities" (*dharmas*). If the word *dharma is* taken to mean "quality," the chief quality that constitutes a Buddha is the Buddha's knowledge, and the knowledge itself is indistinguishable from the truth or reality that the Buddha knows.[29]

This is one of the lines of speculation that lead to the identification of the Buddha with Emptiness: the defining feature of the Buddha is the Buddha's awareness, the Buddha's awareness is Emptiness, and the Buddha is equated with Emptiness. This process of identification is helped by a grammatical feature of the Sanskrit language in which a word that normally designates an object can be taken as referring to something that possesses that object. The word *bahuvrīhi*, for example, means "much rice," but is understood in Sanskrit grammar as referring to a person who possesses much rice. Indian commentators on Mahayana sutras do the same with the word Emptiness. They take it as referring either to Emptiness itself or to the *knowledge* of Emptiness. Of the two choices, the second often is preferred, because it takes an abstract concept and grounds it in a particular cognitive state.

Another line of speculation about the identity of the Buddha moves through the concept of the Dharma as teaching. The Buddha is identified with the Dharma, then the content of the Dharma is identified with Emptiness, and the Buddha is identified with Emptiness. No matter which line of speculation they follow, Mahayana philosophers conclude with a formula that appears to be as abstract and delocalized as any in the tradition: the Buddha is simply Emptiness. The irony in this formula, however, is that abstraction leads back to the language of location and place, in the sense that Emptiness leads back to an examination of things that are empty. The concept of Emptiness belongs to the Indian category of an "absence" (*abhāva*): it is an absence of one thing in another. Some Hindu schools treated absences as independent realities and argued that absences could be directly known.[30] Buddhist philosophers were unwilling to grant reality to such (non)entities, and developed an elaborate explanation of the way someone could perceive an absence by perceiving the *place* where a particular object is absent.[31] To perceive the absence of a book on a table, for example, would be to perceive the bare tabletop and nothing else. It follows from this line of argument that the perception of Emptiness, as the perception of an absence, is a perception of an empty place, and it is as important to know not only what needs to be left out when one sees things as empty but to know the nature of what remains.[32]

In my book on the Mahayana vision of the Buddha, I argue that this grammatical feature of the concept of Emptiness establishes a metaphorical continuity between the speculation of the philosophers and the practices of Buddhist worship. Emptiness may in a general sense be present everywhere, since everything is equally empty, but there are certain places where Emptiness has been known or is capable of being conveyed better than others. In a physical sense these might correspond to the great pilgrimage places in northern India where the Buddha is said to have been born, awakened, preached his first sermon, and passed away, and where pilgrimage texts suggest that even the most cold-blooded philosophers feel a certain shiver of recognition. In a traditional cognitive sense, they might correspond to the moment in the stream of a bodhisattva's consciousness when awakening occurs (the moment that is considered "the seat of awakening" in some Tibetan explanations of the bodhisattva path). In a more modern sense, they might correspond to the place in the depths of a person's own subjectivity where Emptiness is known and makes itself known to the subject. Keiji Nishitani describes this place with great metaphorical insight when he says:

> Only when the self breaks through the field of consciousness, the field of *beings*, and stands on the ground of nihility, is it able to achieve a subjectivity that can in no way be objectivized. This is the elemental realization that reaches deeper than self-consciousness. In standing subjectively on the field of nihility (I use the term 'stand' and refer to nihility as a "field," but in fact there is literally *no place* to stand), the self becomes itself in a more elemental sense.[33]

In all these cases, from the practice of Buddhist pilgrimage to the exploration of the depths of the individual subject, one confronts the meaning of the Buddha's understanding of Emptiness by confronting it in a place. While we do not know precisely what the Lotus Sutra means when it refers to the Buddha's "seat" (or Kern's "pulpit") as Emptiness, the preacher of the Lotus Sutra must also sit (or stand) in an empty place.

This is the place where I would feel as a Christian preacher that I had begun to put my feet on the ground in the text (with full acknowledgment of Nishitani's warning that even this text *literally* affords no place to stand). I would already have identified a metaphor of sustenance in the text that would allow me to think of the preaching process as serving food. I would have an image of conversion to work with as I began to imagine the effect of the text on its listeners. I would have related this concept of conversion to an underlying logic of faith, grace, and devotion. Finally, I would have touched the connection between the devotional logic of the text and its conception of ultimate reality as Emptiness. None of these formal pieces would necessarily appear in precisely this way in the preaching of the text. In fact, they would produce a rather wooden sermon if they did. But they would function as the framework within which the sermon would develop and take life. The one crucial question that would remain for me before I gave voice to the sermon would have to do with my own place in the logic of the text. How could I situate myself as a Christian preacher on the seat of Emptiness?

This question leads me back to Meister Eckhart (ca. 1260–ca. 1327), one of the great Christian inspirations for the Buddhist-Christian dialogue. Meister Eckhart is perhaps best known in the literature of the Buddhist-Christian dialogue for his exploration of the mystical awareness of God as Nothing. It certainly was this element in Eckhart's thinking that caught D. T. Suzuki's attention in the 1950s in his pioneering study of Christian and Buddhist mysticism.[34] But Eckhart also was a great preacher, and our knowledge of his theology is constructed largely from his sermons. The study of Eckhart has advanced quite substantially since the time of D. T. Suzuki, and it would exceed the limits of this essay to comment in detail about the relationship between his understanding of the God beyond God and Buddhist ideas of Emptiness.[35] But it is possible to take great inspiration as a preacher from his understanding of the power implicit in the enunciation of the Word and the relationship between the Word and silence.

Eckhart bases one of his Christmas sermons on a passage from The Wisdom of Solomon ("For while peaceful silence enwrapped all things, / And night in her own swiftness was in mid-course, / Thine all-powerful word leaped from heaven out of the royal throne"; 18:14–15) and begins the sermon itself with the following words:

> Here, in time, we are celebrating the eternal birth which God the Father bore and bears unceasingly in eternity, because the same birth is now born in time, in human nature. St. Augustine says: "What does it avail me that this birth is always happening, if it does not happen in me? That it should happen in me is what matters." We shall therefore speak of this birth, of how it may take place in us and be consummated in the virtuous soul, whenever God the Father speaks His eternal Word in the perfect soul.[36]

In Eckhart's words, and in the words of the text out of which he preaches, the challenge of the preacher is to sense the silence out of which the Word arises and to give it birth, not only in the world but in the preacher's own personality and in the personalities of the listeners. In other words, the preacher has to enact and embody the rising of the Word from silence.

For Eckhart this process would have had a literal counterpart in the way words arise from the silence that falls over a church when the preacher stands up to speak, but it also would have had a spiritual meaning. Eckhart speaks elsewhere of a poverty of spirit that empties the heart so that God is compelled to enter it.[37] It does not seem misleading to imagine that Eckhart the speaker would have engaged in a comparable process of emptying his own heart so that the Word could take life in the midst of his own words. In any case, this is the process that I would impose on myself when I entered the charmed space of the pulpit and gave voice to the teaching of the Lotus Sutra. I would center myself in the silence of the space around me, as I would situate myself in the empty space in the vault of the church, and I would allow the words to rise from the silent spaces of the heart.

It may seem odd to say that the solitary and seemingly egocentric act of preaching a sermon would require a spiritual poverty. But the experience of preaching has a dimension that recalls Eckhart's image of the birth of the Word. One reaches for a sense of spiritual transparency in which the preacher gets out of the way and lets the Word speak with a sense of spiritual transparency that may be very similar to what Eckhart had in mind when he used the word *Gelâzenheit* (modern German, *Gelassenheit*), "letting be." Schürmann explains that *Gelâzenheit* implies breaking the habit of possessing not only things but also oneself.[38] A preacher lets go of things in part by the specific discipline of weaving the preacher's own voice into the words of others (and vice versa) so that the preacher's voice functions as a device to allow others to speak. In this respect, the effacement of the ego in Eckhart's preaching is not dissimilar to the effacement of the author that is widely spoken about in contemporary literary criticism: in both cases the speaker or author dissolves in a force-field established by the voices of a powerful tradition.

Speaking as a voice in the force-field of contemporary religious theory, I could just as well have begun these remarks on the effacement of the preacher with a meditation on the opening lines of Michel Foucault's inaugural lecture at the Collège de France, a lecture in which Foucault enacts his elevation into the French scholarly pantheon by weaving his own voice into the interstices of another:

I would really like to have slipped imperceptibly into this lecture, as into all the others I shall be delivering, perhaps over the years ahead.

I would have preferred to be enveloped in words, borne way beyond all possible beginnings. At the moment of speaking, I would like to have perceived a nameless voice, long preceding me, leaving me merely to enmesh myself in it, taking up its cadence, and to lodge myself, when no one was looking, in its interstices as if it had paused for an instant, in suspense, to beckon me, while I stood in its path—a slender gap—the point of its possible disappearance.[39]

At the end of the lecture Foucault names the voice that echoed in the text of his own lecture, just as Eckhart named the voice of Augustine, and Augustine the story of Antony. In Foucault's case the voice belonged to Jean Hyppolyte, a teacher whom he had listened to for many hours in the same room and who was no longer present at that moment to hear him speak.

My intention in this study of the image of the preacher has been to lodge myself in the interstices of the words of the Lotus Sutra, the way Augustine lodged himself in the story of Antony, or Eckhart lodged himself in the words of Augustine, to sense the power of those words and to allow that power to speak through words of my own. If I were truly to make that power present (which I suspect remains still in the realm of the imagination), it would not be by my own power, but by the power of all the voices that echo in my own and by the *adhiṣṭhāna* of the Buddha.

Conclusion

In these notes for the construction of a sermon, I have attempted to follow a procedure that is comparable to the one I follow when I am preaching from a Christian text. To many preachers it will seem idiosyncratic, and to many scholars it will seem hopelessly "religious." I introduce it in part because the Lotus Sutra bears the marks of a preacher's text: it describes an act of preaching, and it provides a model to use in the act of preaching. I also introduce it in response to what I take to be one of the intentions of this group, namely, to promote a Buddhist-Christian dialogue between Christians and Buddhists, that is, between people who attend not only to the intellectual dimension of these two religious traditions but also to their enactment. But the truth is that we are not here simply as religious practitioners. We also are scholars, and as scholars we have the responsibility not merely to *do* religion but to stop and reflect on the significance of what we do. What then does this imaginative exercise in the preacher's art have to do with the larger project of the Buddhist-Christian dialogue?

First, it is meant to bring the devotional logic of Mahayana Buddhism to the top of the agenda, and in so doing to bring the rich, emotional world of Christian devotion to bear on the task of mutual understanding. I am as intrigued as any philosopher or theologian by the concepts of Emptiness, God, Christ, and the bodhisattva, but the most striking and unexpected thing I have learned from the actual practice of Buddhist-Christian dialogue came from a hymnal I read when I visited a Pure Land temple in Hawaii at the first major international conference on Buddhist-Christian dialogue. The line was: "Buddha loves me. This I know, for the sutras tell me so." The singsong rhythm of these words is so familiar to Christian audiences that it is impossible to speak them in a classroom and not be met with a smile. But the words posed a question that I struggled with for several years in conversations with Pure Land Buddhists and in the writing of my book on the Mahayana vision of the Buddha: What would it mean to love and be loved by Emptiness? Behind this question lay an even deeper one about the role of devotion in the development of the Buddhist tradition more generally. (I do not mean "devotion" in the narrow sense of the Indian term *bhakti*, although that term is worth pursuing, but devotion in the broad sense of love, respect, veneration, and faith for the Buddha and the Buddha's teaching.) Is devotion simply an epiphenomenon that is added onto the Buddhist tradition in order to make it palatable to an audience that cannot deal with the harsh realities of Emptiness? Or is it related in a fundamental way to the vision of Emptiness itself? I am convinced that the devotional aspect of the Mahayana is indeed fundamental and stems directly from the practical and conceptual requirement that Emptiness must be encountered in a place—a place that can serve as the focus for a full range of religious emotions, from awe and terror to affection and love. This aspect of Mahayana life and thought deserves more formal recognition than it has yet received.

While these comments have taken the form of notes for a sermon, I would be hesitant to preach them to a learned audience. They are meant to contribute to the process of dialogue and are offered in appreciation for the imaginative and emotional depths of the Mahayana tradition in general and for the Lotus Sutra in particular.

Notes

1. William Empson, *The Structure of Complex Words* (Ann Arbor: University of Michigan Press, 1967), 39.
2. To my knowledge, Bishop Stendahl's "Ten Commandments for Biblical Preaching" has not been published. I am working from a private copy dated March 1990.

3. *Sādhu sādhu bhagavan śākyamune / subhāṣitas te 'yaṃ saddharmapuṇḍarīko dharma-paryāyaḥ.* The Sanskrit text is quoted from *Saddharmapuṇḍarīkasūtra,* ed. P. L. Vaidya, Buddhist Sanskrit Texts Series, No. 6 (Darbhanga: Mithila Institute, 1960). The Vaidya edition is based on the text that functions as the *textus receptus in* Indological scholarship: H. Kern and B. Nanjio, eds., *Saddharma-puṇḍarīka,* Bibliotheca Buddhica 10 (St. Petersburg: Imprimerie de l'Académie Impériale des Sciences, 1912). The Kern and Nanjio edition is based on the Nepali recension. An earlier recension from Kashgar has recently been published but was unavailable for the preparation of this paper. Unless otherwise noted, the translations of the text of the Lotus Sutra are mine.

4. By saying that this is carefully chosen, I do not mean to suggest that Krister Stendahl invented this comparison. I have heard it quite independently from another preacher who began his career in a small town in Kentucky, and was told by one of his parishioners, "Well, preacher, you gave us a nice recipe, but you didn't bake any bread." The preacher was Walter G. Muelder, former dean of the Boston University School of Theology. The story was recounted in a matriculation sermon, September 23, 1993.

5. 6.10–14. The word *vibhojana* at the end of verse 6.11 is problematic. It probably is an editorial error for *vihbhājana* ("differentiation," "classification"). These verses raise the question of gender-specific language in the translation of Buddhist sutras. In this paper I will avoid gender-specific language in my own account of the bodhisattva path, but I will respect the text of the Lotus Sutra by leaving the gendered aspect of its own language intact.

6. Étienne Lamotte, *L'enseignement de Vimalakīrti* (Bibliothèque du Muséon 51. Louvain: Publications Universitaires, 1962), trans., *The Teaching of Vimalakīrti (Vimalakīrti-nirdeśa),* rendered into English by Sara Boin (London: Pali Text Society, 1976), 307–14.

7. As in Lotus Sutra 5.83.

8. The word *avatāra* is used with this implication in the titles of several important Indian Buddhist philosophical works, as I note in my discussion of the "descent" of the Dharma in Malcolm David Eckel, *To See the Buddha: A Philosopher's Quest for the Meaning of Emptiness* (San Francisco: HarperCollins, 1992).

9. 5.21, 35, 82.

10. 5.81–83.

11. Saint Augustine, *Confessions,* trans. R. S. Pine-Coffin (Harmondsworth, Middlesex: Penguin Books, 1961), 177–78.

12. 9.17–18 and preceding prose.

13. William James, *The Varieties of Religious Experience* (Harmondsworth, Middlesex: Penguin Books, 1982), 196.

14. The theme of the "bodhisattva's tears" makes a fascinating subject of study in the literary accounts of the bodhisattva path, as I note in *To See the Buddha,* ch. 7.

15. James, 189.

16. 8.42.

17. For a more extensive discussion of this important concept, see Eckel, *To See the Buddha,* 74–84.

18. Gregory Schopen, "The Phrase 'sa pṛthivīpradeśaś caitya-bhūto bhavet' in the

Vajracchedikā: Notes on the Cult of the Book in Mahāyāna," *Indo-Iranian Journal* 17 (1975): 147–81.

19. It is worth noting that this term *adhiṣṭhāna* is almost indistinguishable in many contexts from the word "vow" (*praṇidhāna*) that plays such an important role in the tradition of devotion to Amitābha Buddha. For more on this term and its connection with *adhiṣṭhāna*, see Eckel, *To See the Buddha*, 74–83.

20. Ch. 11 (Vaidya ed.: 149).

21. Ch. 13 (Vaidya ed.: 173).

22. Ch. 15 (Vaidya ed.: 189).

23. Those who remain are "established in the essence of faith" (*śraddhā-sāre pratiṣṭhitā*). Those who leave "have no faith" (*aśrāddhāḥ*).

24. 3.106–107

25. H. Kern, trans., *Saddharma-Puṇḍarīka or The Lotus of the True Law*, The Sacred Books of the East, vol. 21 (Oxford: Clarendon Press, 1884; reprint ed., New York: Dover Publications, 1963), 269.

26. 10.23–24.

27. Lamotte trans., 95–99.

28. A particularly elaborate example of this practice is found in the second chapter of Bhāvaviveka's *Madhyamakahṛdayakārikā*, translated by V. V. Gokhale, "The Second Chapter of Bhavya's *Madhyamakahṛdaya* (Taking the Vow of an Ascetic)," *Indo-Iranian Journal* 14 (1972): 40–45.

29. I have taken up several of the issues in this account of the relationship between the Buddha and Emptiness at greater length in my book *To See the Buddha*.

30. The name for this form of knowledge is *anupalabdhi* (noncognition). The most thorough English account of this doctrine in Hindu logic is B. K. Matilal, *The Navya-nyāya Doctrine of Negation: The Semantics and Ontology of Negative Statements in Navya-nyāya Philosophy*, Harvard Oriental Series, vol. 46 (Cambridge: Harvard University Press, 1968).

31. See, for example, F. Th. Stcherbatsky, *Buddhist Logic*, vol. 2 (Leningrad, 1930; reprint ed., New York: Dover Publications, 1962), 60–108.

32. Gadjin Nagao discusses an aspect of this issue in "What Remains in Śūnyatā: A Yogācāra Interpretation of Emptiness," in *Mahāyāna Buddhist Meditation: Theory and Practice*, ed. Minoru Kiyota (Honolulu: University of Hawaii Press, 1978), 65–82. I discuss the same issue in *To See the Buddha*, 65–72.

33. Keiji Nishitani, *Religion and Nothingness*, trans. Jan Van Bragt (Berkeley: University of California Press, 1982), 16–17.

34. D. T. Suzuki, *Mysticism Christian and Buddhist: The Eastern and Western Way* (1957; reprint ed., New York: Collier, 1962).

35. See, for example, Reiner Schürmann's comments on D. T. Suzuki in *Meister Eckhart: Mystic and Philosopher* (Bloomington: Indiana University Press, 1978). Part of the complexity of this question in present scholarship comes from the fact that we now know much more about the differences within the Buddhist tradition about the explanation and practice of the vision of Emptiness, as is evident in recent scholarship about Tibetan versions of the Mādhyamika tradition.

36. M. O'C. Walshe, trans., *Meister Eckhart: Sermons & Treatises*, vol. 1 (Longmead Shaftesbury, Dorset: Element Books, 1987), 1.
37. See the sermon "Blessed Are the Poor" in Schürmann, 214–20.
38. Schürmann, 16.
39. Michel Foucault, "The Discourse on Language" in *The Archaeology of Knowledge & The Discourse on Language*, trans. A. M. Sheridan Smith (New York: Pantheon, 1982), 215.

3. Philosophical Reflection

Reflections on the Threefold Lotus Sutra

John R. A. Mayer

The Threefold Lotus Sutra provides some very illuminating insights with respect to many of the debates and oppositions currently taking place in Western philosophy. The present paper represents reflections on how this Mahayana text is applicable to issues in contemporary philosophy.

One of the central debates in metaphysics and especially in ethical theory is the question of foundation. The position labelled "foundationalist" is the more traditional Western philosophical stance. It is tantamount to belief in a permanent universal truth from which norms can be deduced or inferred. Views or actions not based on this "foundation" are held to be simply erroneous and to be corrected. Post-moderns argue against foundationalism, maintaining that belief in a universal truth or an absolute norm inevitably leads the proponent to being committed, sincerely but arrogantly, to the notion that his or her own position is based on the "foundation" which makes it necessarily true, and any other position is either merely trivially different from his or her own, or else in error. Emmanuel Levinas has persuasively argued that belief in an absolute truth is a "closed" view, in contrast to an "open" one, leading to intolerance, a will to impose one's own commitments on unwilling others. Thus foundationalism is deeply related to violent notions such as imperialism, aggression, ethnicism, and racism, the recurrent features of the history of those who are committed to the notion of an absolute.

Levinas advocates an open universe in which radically diverse views are embraced by different people. It is diversity which makes an ethical claim on all of us. In Levinas's view, the proper ethical mode is to let the demands of the other take precedence even over our very deepest commitments; the mere fact that there are such others is the basis of rationally unharmonizable, incommensurable beliefs, claims, lifestyles, and values, each making a mute claim on us to sacrifice, compromise, hierarchically subject what is "our own" to the demands made by "the other." This leads to an "ethics without rules," since the very notion of "rules" is to overrule differences and not give sufficient recognition to the individuality and particularity of every context of decision-making. Thus "rules" are oppressive, and hence unethical.

The countercharge is that antifoundationalism is tantamount to an "anything goes" nihilism, a radical relativism, which demands tolerance even of oppression, exploitation, indifference, cruelty, wickedness, and abuse. Levinas's critics argue that a willing abdication from one's own commitments cannot be generally accepted, nor should it be idealized. A radically antifoundationalist view, while it discloses the dangers of foundationalism, must wallow in the simply unacceptable relativist position that Hitler and Mother Teresa were, as it happens, different in their respective commitments, and the fact that we might sympathize more with one rather than the other is irrelevant. Indeed, if we buy into Levinas's ethics, we might end up claiming that we should be obliging the Hitlers around us exactly because we share the commitments of the Mother Teresas.

So foundationalists and antifoundationalists both make persuasive arguments for our acceptance of their respective stances, each having something strongly persuasive about their own position and revealing something repugnant about the other. Each position implies unacceptable consequences. This leaves the reader-spectator stymied and adrift as regards the outcome of the "debate."

To further complicate matters, the foundationalist–antifoundationalist dispute is sequential to another deep division in moral–ethical theory in the West. This is the utilitarian–deontological controversy. The former, the utilitarian, asserts that humans are pleasure-seeking and pain-avoiding beings by nature, and that therefore what constitutes the ethically acceptable or preferred behavior is acting so as to produce the greatest pleasure for the greatest number. Human beings are unethical when they follow the demands of their own personal pleasures or pain-avoidances; they are ethical when they opt in accord with the greatest totality of consequential pleasures and pains, regarding themselves as only one of all those whom the actions may affect. Thus, to facilitate thinking in the context of ethical choice making, some utilitarian philosophers have attempted to devise calculi for arriving at the most moral of alternatives given particular options and situations.

In contrast, Kant, the principal spokesman for the deontological position, has argued against all such consequentialist approaches, maintaining that the ethical is determined by the will of the agent, rather than the consequences of the act, and that the good is the act performed from the motive of duty rather than either desire or inclination.

If one is left perplexed by these discussions and debates, the Threefold Lotus Sutra is of immense value for overcoming the foregoing quandaries. The title of the introductory sutra, the Sutra of Innumerable Meanings, gives a strong clue as to the direction of the resolution. The manifold diversity of the everyday world gives rise to countless ways of experiencing it, interpreting it, since experience makes accessible only a minute portion of the vast spatial and temporal diversity of the whole. Were the experiential disclosure largely to overlap in the case of two individual instances, the subjective inclinations and proclivities of the two individuals sharing similar experiences will result in interpreting them in quite different ways. The Sutra of the Lotus Flower of the Wonderful Law lets us understand this plurality and diversity through the parable of the herbs. It tells of the generous rain supplying the needs of diverse plants, be they grasses, herbs, flowers, shrubs, or mighty trees. The same rain nourishes them all, yet each grows according to its own particular nature. What is here presented is how diversity is produced from some underlying singular universal—the rain.

This seems to support the foundationalist position that behind the diversity of the many specific plants there is the unity of their source in the common nutrient, the rainwater. Thus the generosity of the sky in supplying water is the foundation of the richly diverse flora.

But to avoid the charge against the usual foundationalists, the Lotus Sutra also discusses how though there is a fundamental singular truth, a foundation to the universe, this truth is accessible only to the Buddha. Although all of us are lured and coaxed along the path to achieving Buddhahood, and, indeed, promised that it is within our essential possibilities, at the same time it is recognized that great discipline and compassion are required of us to go beyond our limited present stage of development. While the "foundation" is hinted at as the Void, and is characterized by the Ten Suchnesses, these are not readily assimilable concepts; indeed, they are not concepts at all; they imply the practice of compassion, the practice of self-sacrifice. It would be folly for those listening to the Buddha to think that they have a theoretical or conceptual grasp of the "foundation" of all.

To the contrary, what we can grasp is one or several of innumerable meanings. However, they are all meanings. Meanings of what? Meanings of the ultimate reality, of the Buddha-nature. However, any attempt to explicate what that is, is to present but one of its innumerable meanings. What we can grasp intellectually are meanings, not the ultimate reality. Only the Buddha can grasp the ultimately real, since Enlightenment is not the consequence but the precondition of such a power. The Buddha advises the bodhisattvas that every Law emerges, changes, settles, and vanishes every moment, instantly.[1]

It is obvious that such "impermanence" renders the Law beyond whatever it is that we call "knowing"; for our kind of knowledge requires that the known be bounded and stable enough to be what it is, to endure. For our kind of knowing is to know the known by its limitations, by its determinations which specify it to be this way rather than that. But whatever is such as to be accessible to this kind of knowledge is not the ultimately real. That, whose meanings the innumerable meanings qualify, cannot be presented; for whatever is capable of being presented, however true it may be, is just another meaning. That from which all the meanings derive is not itself another meaning; it is of an entirely different constitution, which is often presented in the text, only to be negated. As a propaedeutic we might be told of the Void, the Formless, the Absolute Nothingness, or the Ten Merits, but all these are but aids, stepladders for turning the wheel, useful devices, perhaps, but not to be clung to, investigated, analyzed, and especially not to be used as weapons against others who talk about God, or the Truth, or Suchness. All claims are to be transcended, the Void voided, the Truth abandoned as it becomes a Lie (Nietzsche), but the practice of compassion remains paramount. To be compassionate requires no doctrine. Compassion is not something one knows; it is something one does, and something one receives. The path to Enlightenment is compassion; and compassion rather than hostility and partiality is what is called for by the path to Enlightenment. The parable of the herbs is very clear in showing generosity or compassion for the thirst of the plants as the underlying "reality" of the diverse flourishing.

When in the Lotus Sutra we learn that the Buddha-nature is recognized in all, be they disciples such as Śāriputra, great bodhisattvas, relatives of the Buddha Śākyamuni such as Rāhula, or indeed villains such as Devadatta, we can see the universality of compassion, and generosity. These have to overcome hostility, revenge, and even judgement and justice. For all these require limits, contrasts, opposition, either–or thinking. And while we are not fully enlightened we are indeed in the clutches of contrast, thinking, judgement, preference, hierarchy. Enlightenment constitutes being beyond all this. How to be beyond it ? By always practising compassion, being mindful of the fact that less than full enlightenment is tantamount to suffering; to finding the impermanent unsatisfactory.

Be it in the parable of the magic city or the parable of the burning house, the suggestion is clear that skilful means are to be used for getting the willing cooperation of those whose despondency, disinterest, bad habits, or ignorance prevent them from doing what is ultimately for their own benefit. These parables fly in the face of some conventional modern claims, such as "the ends do not justify the means" and that knowing the good for the other when the other does not share that knowledge is "paternalism," and using deliberate deception in order to get the other to do what we think is best for that person is "manipulation." Thus the parables themselves are not instances of some absolute truth, but rather, persuasive devices, themselves to be abandoned once they have enabled us to behave compassionately. They, too, are merely skilful means to an end.

That this is a general practical approach is recognized in Mahayana traditions, in which it is claimed that the Buddha Śākyamuni taught different things at different times to different people, in each case saying what would be most beneficial for the advancement and enhancement of the audience. "I knew that the natures and desires of all living beings were not equal. As their natures and desires were not equal, I preached the Law variously. It was with tactful power that I preached the Law variously. In forty years and more, the truth has not been revealed yet."[2] Thus, the teachings of the Threefold Lotus Sutra are not the same as many of the other texts of the Pali canon or the Tripiṭaka, but they are held to be the most advanced by its devotees, because they are presented to a wonderful assemblage of the highest and greatest beings. In contrast to Tendai and Nichiren traditions, the Zen Buddhists focus on an unverbalized direct transmission of experience and wisdom, thus sidestepping the primacy of any of the formulated teachings; but because human beings are still human, the function of the sutras is replaced by *kōans* in the Zen communities.

It should be clear that there is a parallel between how the innumerable meanings are aspects of the self-same reality and how the individual differentiated beings all share in the Buddha-nature. This leads to the next difficulty. Is the Buddha-nature of each individual merely a potential, a seed, to be realized in some future time? Certainly that seems to be the intent of the promise to the individuals to whom Buddhahood is promised in the sutra. Alternatively, is each one already and eternally an aspect of the Buddha-nature, in which case realization is a change of attitude rather than a future-oriented project? Once again the answer to the problem lies buried not in who can make the best case for one or the other side of the dilemma; rather, the problem is in our way of looking at the matter, giving rise to two apparently disjointed alternatives: a case of either/or. The solution lies in seeing that though rationally the alternatives are disjointed, and make absolute alternative claims, the reality is such that both of these ways of seeing can be upheld, and neither is the whole truth. We are indeed all substantially at one with the Buddha; we have no individual selves. Really all of the multiplicity is a part of one and the same whole. Hence when we are compassionate, we fulfil our own nature and need. And yet to rest in the truth of the oneness of all Buddha-nature would leave us inactive, and untrue to our own nature. There is a task, a project, a goal that directs us. And that is the practice of the Law. By being on the bodhisattva path, offering the merits of our virtues to accrue to the benefit of all sentient beings, we practise the Law of what we are, and therewith become ourselves. It is the insistence of the either/or character of our question about whether we are either already Buddha-nature or we are to achieve that at some blessed moment when the bodhisattvas' task is done and all sentience stands ready to be enlightened. No, both claims are partially and simultaneously true; both are limited claims, and hence necessarily less than the whole truth. There are moments on our temporal horizon when we take one or the other as important and appropriate—but both are but skilful means for keeping the joy of our reality vivid.

This is but another Buddhist example of tactfulness and skilful means. When words help, words are offered. But these words are not the final goal; they are merely a means to get us unstuck if we are stuck in our path toward Buddhahood. The text teaches that when it is necessary, the Buddha will "deceive us into the truth," as Kierkegaard put it, just as in the parable of the magic city the tired pilgrims are lured toward their goal and dissuaded from giving up by the mysterious illusion of the proximity of a yet distant goal. Similarly, if we are to move beyond our habitual and limiting thoughts, perhaps potent new thoughts will affect our moving from our original stance. If a set of truth–claims helps us to move beyond our previous beliefs, the set has done its job. It does not, however, constitute a permanently satisfying and intelligible final answer. Once we are free from whatever delusion to which we were habituated, the tool of our liberation should be discarded rather than clung to. It was, after all, nothing more than a now spent tool. And so it is that tactfulness requires that what is spoken be effective rather than literally true.

Wisdom is exactly the power for skilful tactical action, that expresses effectively the compassion which respects the will of the many finite individuals, and involves the transformation of each into self-awareness as the Buddha-nature; self-awareness of the formless self. That we run around in puzzled conceptual circles: Why does one have to realize that which is already realized, and if all are the Buddha-nature, does it matter whether we are diligent or not? These are labyrinths of discursive reason. The Buddha mind is free of discursive reason, and has nonmediated, direct oneness with truth. And yet discursive reason, too, is but an aspect of the Buddha-nature.

Just as Hegel in the West has helped us see beyond the limiting laws of thought that Aristotle formulated as the conditions of rational thinking, the law of identity, that A = A; the law of noncontradiction, that nothing is both A and Not-A; and the law of excluded middle, that everything is either A or Not-A, so the Buddhist heritage is similarly a liberating one. Hegel shows that when one thinks about a seedling, a bud, the flower, and its fruit, there is a sense in which each is distinct and other than the other. But at the very same time they are all aspects of the one plant. The shoot anticipates the blossom; the flower is but the transformation of the blossom, and the fruit, the ripened flower, and the promise of the seed and the sprout. In some intuitive way we can here "understand" that the question should not be "Are they the same or different?" but rather that the very difference is involved in the sameness; each momentary unit portends the next moment, and is but the fulfillment of the previous one. The bud is and is not the flower; just as we are and are not the Buddha-nature. The flower is not some final goal that the bud seeks; it is but a next stage on an eternally continuous process; similarly, Buddhahood is not some eventual final achievement, it is the continuous and temporal praxis of compassion. This surely is the intent when in the sutra the audience are all considered bodhisattvas, when many would have deemed themselves mere *śrāvakas* or *pratyekabuddhas*.

Process implies time; time implies change; change implies goal or purpose; but the ultimately worthwhile goal or purpose is self-justifying, autotelic. Living compassionately is the Buddha-nature; and the compassionate being has his immediate objectives, activities. These activities both serve the needs of suffering sentiency and the needs of the bodhisattva. Perhaps ordinary people all need the transformative insight that Jean-Paul Sartre played on in his one-act play *Huis-clos* (No Exit). The setting of the play seems like an elegant hotel lobby, but we learn from the three characters found there that they believe this to be the reception area to hell. However, all are convinced that they were sent there by some mistake, and that they will eventually be redirected when the formalities of admission will commence. Gradually we the audience come to see that indeed the characters are in "bad faith," self-deceived if they think of themselves as paragons of virtue. However, it takes more time for the audience to realize that these persons are not in some receiving antechamber; they are in hell, and each causes it to be hell for herself or himself and the two others by their lack of sensitivity and lack of generosity.

Similarly, the Buddha-nature is not achieved in some indefinite future state; it is practiced in each instance of compassion and generosity. The bodhisattvas have Buddha-nature. The only "error" we make is that we think there needs to be some extinction, some "disappearance" when all other sentient beings achieve enlightenment. But that comes from our mistaken resentment of the transient and impermanent character of being; because we long for eternity and permanence, staticity and, in a sense, death. This is what makes the impermanent unsatisfactory, and hence *dukkha*. The Buddha teaches the overcoming of suffering through our own growing beyond the four unsatisfying ways of reacting to the complex manifold: clinging to the transitory good; resenting the transitory unpleasant; desiring the potential good; and fearing the potential bad. Since the "all" consists of the actual good and bad, and the potential good and bad, we suffer when we respond with clinging, resentment, desire, and fear. Were we to respond with joy and gratitude for the actual good, compassion, and resoluteness with respect to the actual bad, and simply abandon desire as well as fear, anticipating with hope, confidence, and serenity whatever emerges as the new, we will have attained enlightenment, and will be the full realization of our Buddha-nature. In the meanwhile, every moment so lived needs no redemption, and every moment lived with those unhealthful habits or *taṇhās* is but a transient moment, vanishing into the past, losing its significance, or possibly becomes an occasion for insight and self-transformation, in which case its negativity will have served a positive purpose. Thus these moments are redeemable. This is the sense in which a tragedy, once it is integrated and accepted, turns into a strength of character, and thus ceases to be tragic.

In conclusion, we see that the Threefold Lotus Sutra is an excellent text from which to learn that our disputes and debates, which set us against each other, and which call for arguments and judgements, are presupposing a kind of either/or logic which would have the truth as similar to a meaning, an opinion, a view. In terms of the first half of the Sutra of the Lotus Flower of the Wonderful Law we are exposed to the Law of Appearance, in terms of which we are not yet enlightened, but have within us each the potential to achieve Buddhahood. The second half, the Law of Origin, clearly asserts our fundamental unity with the Buddha. These two positions are not made to vie with one another for supremacy or correctness. They are equally promulgated by the Buddha, and each is independently intelligible. That which escapes our capacity to harmonize is left indeed as beyond our present ken, but nonetheless accessible to faith–discernment. Thus the thrust of the sutra is that the truth is quite different from meanings, opinions, and views, and is capable of sustaining many logically incommensurable and unharmonizable ones of these.

Speech and assertion are the pragmatics of turning the wheel, rather than the assertion of dogmatic verities. Commitment to one persuasive perspective sets us against one another, and blocks us from following the true Law, Compassion. Compassion when practised is our Buddha-nature, manifesting itself in bodhisattvic wisdom, serenity, power, and fulfillment. This is what the sutra persuades us to be loyal to. Ultimately, philosophy is not the art of rational argumentation; philosophy is the pursuit of wisdom, while argumentation is more a character defect than the substance of philosophy!

Notes

1. *The Threefold Lotus Sutra*. Bunnō Katō and others, translators (Tokyo: Kōsei, 1975) 12.
2. Ibid. 14

The Lotus Sutra and the Dimension of Time

J. Douglas Wolfe

Every culture based its first religion on what it saw in the sky. The cosmologies of the ancient Middle Eastern civilizations have come down to us in the names of the planets. Jupiter, Mars, Venus, and the others were the physical embodiments of Greco-Roman deities. Their motions and interactions were studied intently with a view to gaining an understanding of the cosmos and the place of humanity in it. The vastness and mystery of the heavens engendered stories of unknowable gods and heroes, and natural phenomena were ascribed to the whims of these denizens of the starry realm. Daily life must surely have been different in ages when ordinary people could see the gods simply by looking up.

The cosmologies of the ancients were inextricably tied to the religious views of the societies in which they flourished, and the same may be said of modern society. Scholars and men of religion alike point to a historical correspondence between the decline of religion and the advance of science in the Western world. Certainly we know too much about the physical universe to write off the cosmos beyond our daily experiences as the abode of ineffable divinity. Is there a religion which corresponds with the accomplishments of modern scientific inquiry? I believe that the Lotus Sutra points to a worldview which is consistent with the hard-won achievements of Western scholarship. In its sixteenth chapter, "Revelation of the [Eternal] Life of the Tathāgata," Śākyamuni reveals the vast time period since he attained Perfect Enlightenment. In order to make his message plain, he resorts to an analogy in which time and space are two inseparable aspects of a unified worldview. The structure of the universe he describes bears an uncanny resemblance to the modern scientific view.

Albert Einstein put the progress of cosmological science on a new footing when he published his two theories of relativity. Just before he began

161

his work, two scientists named Michelson and Morley had performed an experiment which showed that the speed of light is constant, regardless of the velocity of the light source or that of the observer. Einstein sought to place this apparent absolute value in perspective by working out a series of "thought experiments." He imagined what it would be like to travel through space on a beam of light. His inquiry, supported by extensive mathematical and theoretical work, led to a series of conclusions which seem wildly inconsistent with ordinary experience. For instance, if a spaceship could be accelerated to a speed close to that of light, an observer on Earth would see it increase in mass. A clock aboard the spaceship would appear to slow down. Yet passengers inside the spaceship would notice nothing unusual until they looked back to observe Earth. From their fast-moving point of view, they would see similar changes in the nature of time and matter back home.

The experience of the space travelers seems contrary to common sense, and Einstein says the universe we live in is filled with such apparent impossibilities. The reason the relativistic universe seems so strange is that its scale lies far outside the daily activities of human beings. Modern scientific calculation provides a means of dealing with very large numbers and distances. While we may be impressed by a mathematician's ability to speak in terms of light-years and billions of miles, that same scientist's activities in daily life are subject to the same constraints as any human's. When we can travel in cars or airplanes, or even in spacecraft to the moon and back, we operate at distances which correspond to the more familiar physics of Isaac Newton. Our experience of time is even more limited. We may travel in time in only one direction and at a fixed rate: forward, at one second per second. We will never experience the cosmos of Einstein's thought-experiments firsthand.

To understand Einstein's extraordinary view of reality, one must work within a framework which includes the three dimensions of everyday experience plus the fourth dimension of time. The seeming distortions of distance and time are examples of how we must think in four dimensions when discussing events on a cosmological scale. It is no longer sufficient to say that a certain event happened in a certain place and time. The modern physicist would say that the event began "here–now" and proceeded to "there–then." At the heart of Einstein's theory is the idea that there is no single, absolute starting point from which the universe may be accurately measured. Rather, one's perception of reality depends on one's frame of reference. A person on Earth will perceive the cosmos very differently from another traveling in a spaceship at a velocity near the speed of light. Yet both interpretations are valid within their respective frames of reference. Freeing his mind from the constraints of ordinary human experience, Einstein was able to formulate a model which brought previously inexpressible mysteries of the universe into the realm of modern mathematical computation.

Śākyamuni, in revealing the true nature of his enlightenment, uses another analogy in which a vast span of time is expressed in terms of huge distances. He speaks of time and space as equivalent and inseparable values in calculations on the cosmic scale. Between his first attainment of enlightenment and the present moment, "there have passed infinite, boundless hundreds of thousands of myriads of *koṭi*s of *nayuta*s of *kalpa*s." He asks his listeners to imagine the reduction of a great number of world-systems into atoms. Then he proposes traveling through space at great speed and dropping atoms one by one, each separated by a distance which could only be measured on an intergalactic scale. Then all the worlds visited, whether they received a grain of dust or not, are likewise pulverized. Śākyamuni says that the number of *kalpa*s that have passed since he first attained enlightenment exceed the total number of dust grains in the exercise by a vast span.

A *kalpa* is a time period close to a thousand lifetimes, and terms such as *koṭi*, *nayuta*, and *asaṃkhyeya* are Sanskrit expressions of very large numbers. These numbers are interpreted in various ways, and their translations require the use of modern exponential arithmetic, in which they are expressed as multiples of ten. An *asaṃkhyeya*, for instance, has been interpreted as equal to ten followed by fifty-nine zeroes. Although these numbers are very large, they are not the same as infinity. They are the sorts of numbers whose orders of magnitude are found in the modern scientist's measurements of cosmic times and distances.

In the Ceremony in the Air, Śākyamuni sets the stage for the revelation of the true nature of his enlightenment by removing his audience from the limited time–space of human experience. Before beginning his sermon, the Buddha made visible a great number of other worlds by means of a beam of light issuing from his forehead. Later all the beings present were physically lifted into a transcendent realm, far from the usual earthly frame of reference, which we would call outer space. The congregation of listeners was inconceivably large, described in the Sanskrit numbers of the time. The time required for the Buddha's sermon is also vast, expressed as a number of eons in the contemporary Sanskrit reckoning. Yet, to the participants, it seems to pass in a matter of hours. The congregation was introduced to the Buddha's realm, which includes perfect freedom of movement in both time and space, as the context for his most important teaching. Throughout the sermon, he spoke of his other existences in worlds unknown to his listeners, removed from Earth by vast spans of time and space.

Śākyamuni, in expounding the vast extent of his existence in time, chose the analogy of an imaginary trip through space. He operated in a frame of reference firmly grounded in a four-dimensional time–space continuum. The number of worlds described by the Buddha had no meaning to his human listeners; their experience only compassed a few small kingdoms in northern India. Only in the modern view of a universe filled with worlds orbiting stars, stars gathered into galaxies, galaxies gathered into clusters, and clusters of galaxies grouped into superclusters does the huge number of worlds mentioned by Śākyamuni begin to form a cohesive model. The idea of galaxies scattered throughout space was formulated early in the twentieth century, and evidence for the structure of galaxy superclusters has only been gathered in the last decade. Śākyamuni's seemingly impossible analogy is thus in agreement with the modern scientific model.

In the sixteenth chapter of the Lotus Sutra Śākyamuni describes the universe, and the span of his existence within it, as vast, yet finite. Although the myriad eons in his descriptions are far beyond ordinary human reckoning, he provides a way of counting them in his analogy of atoms and worlds.

Modern science tells us that the universe we live in is finite, yet unbounded. Measured in the four dimensions of time–space, it will seem to go on forever, but only because the speed of light cannot be exceeded. The travelers in Einstein's relativistic spaceship will never quite reach the speed of light. Time will slow down for them as they accelerate. They will never reach the "edge" of the universe. Śākyamuni reveals the true nature of the Eternal Buddha as transcending the limitations of space and time and encompassing existence as a whole. Thus the apparent mysteries revealed by the Buddha accord with what science has been able to achieve so far in its effort to understand the universe.

Mark Twain, commenting on Judeo-Christian belief, wrote, "Faith is when you believe in something even when you know it ain't so." Śākyamuni invited the bodhisattvas to whom he preached to "believe and discern the veracious words of the Tathāgata" to raise their consciousness to his high level. As modern science progresses to a more complete understanding of the universe, the profound perceptions of the Buddha are found to be in agreement with the results of humankind's irresistible curiosity.

The Length of Life of the Tathāgata

Michael Pye

For most modern Buddhists the Buddha himself, in some presentation or other, is the main focus of religious devotions. Such devotions vary considerably in function and style. At the same time, in the Buddhist world the question of precisely how one should regard the Buddha, or various buddhas, is not in itself a matter of great debate. Nevertheless, variations in the way in which the Buddha is viewed range quite widely. At the simplest, he is seen as a human being who provided an example to others, and who has long since passed away. Later devotion made much more of him. Taking on cosmic proportions in mythology and cosmology alike, the Buddha came to be regarded as higher than the gods (*devātideva*).

In Mahayana Buddhism the Buddha is understood somehow to epitomize the nature of the universe itself and as such to be present in all individual beings. Thus the status of the Buddha is not much different from the status assigned to God in the theistic traditions, even if the functions and the relation to the world are differently conceived.

Connected with these conceptual alternatives are the options in the respectful or worshipful attitude which Buddhists may hold toward the Buddha. At one end of the range is the idea that respect alone is his due, for the Buddha is no God to be worshiped but a human being who has shown others the "way" to enlightenment and nirvana. At the other extreme is the attitude which sees the Buddha in a specific form as the supreme focus of all reverence, and a source of assistance not only in the spiritual path but also in everyday difficulties.

In short, the Buddha is approached devotionally by many Buddhists in Asian countries more or less as God is approached, still today, by a significant number of people in Western countries. Even though prayers may be addressed to alternative buddhas or great bodhisattvas, it is widely

165

understood that these are alternative forms of the same basic principle of buddhahood which communicates spiritual power on the basis of deep insight.

This is summed up quite clearly in the distinctive Japanese word *go-honzon*, meaning literally "basic object of reverence," and perhaps more elegantly translatable as "central focus of reverence." Normally, every Buddhist temple has a "central focus of reverence." It might be a great bodhisattva such as Kannon-sama, or a buddha such as Yakushi Nyorai or Amida Nyorai. However, Śākyamuni Buddha (Shaka Nyorai), the historical Buddha, is also a common "central object of reverence."

Of course, the whole point of having a *go-honzon* is to focus the faith of the believer. The attitude of most Buddhist believers in Japan to the Buddha, under whatever name he is presented, is one of deepest respect and readiness to pay worship. One may ask, therefore, how such a devotional focus is related to the idea that the Buddha is essentially an exemplar, which apparently is how the Buddha was first understood by his followers.

As to the origins of this devotional conception, it is important to guard against misunderstandings about the development of Buddhist thought. There is certainly a case for thinking that in very early Buddhism the idea of the Buddha as a model for other people to follow was paramount. However, this did not remain the case for long.

It should by no means be thought that the development of the Buddha into a focus of cosmic significance, and hence deep religious devotion, was characteristic only of the Mahayana. It really began with the idea that the appearance of a buddha occurs at various times in the same manner, which is clearly documented in the Theravada Buddhist Canon. This idea had the effect of setting the historical Buddha in a mythical, cosmic perspective.

The teaching of the *Lokottaravādin* school as evidenced in the *Mahāvastu* is of interest in this regard. The *Mahāvastu* is a composite work, and the dating of its various parts is a complex problem in itself. Moreover, although its "buddhology" is quite elaborate, the teachings of the *Mahāvastu*, for various reasons, cannot be regarded as Mahayanist in character. Nevertheless, the idea that the Buddha, or a buddha, is a transcendental being who appears in our ordinary world in a contrived manner is a further twist to a view which was in general well established.

The further development of the devotional focus of Buddhism was accompanied by two important ideas which for their part are characteristic of the Mahayana. The first is that of the immeasurability of the life of the Buddha, to be further considered here, and the second is that of the three bodies of the Buddha. Contrary to the impression given in some publications, the idea of the three bodies of the Buddha arrived relatively late in the development of Mahayana Buddhism. Though a subject of interest in its own right, it does not need to be considered in the present context.

The idea of the immeasurability of the Buddha's life, however, arose during the formative period of Mahayana Buddhism, being found in the Shorter Perfection of Insight Sutra, the Lotus Sutra, and the Sutra on the Immeasurable Life of the Buddha (the Sukhāvatīvyūha Sutra), all of which are relatively early texts. To these may be added a very short chapter in the Avataṃsaka Sutra, and a rather important chapter in the text known as the Sutra of Golden Light.

As far as can be told, the latter was probably conceived somewhat later than the earliest Mahayana sutras, especially in its fuller form. But the chapter in question should certainly be considered along with other texts dealing with this subject, and has much in common with them. Interestingly, the Sutra of Golden Light also has a chapter on the "three bodies" of the Buddha which repays study. In this article a few important features of the treatment of "immeasurability" in these texts will be examined.

Immeasurability and Emptiness

First, it is extremely important to notice that a connection was made early on between the idea of immeasurability and emptiness.

In the Perfection of Insight [Wisdom] in Eight Thousand Lines (i.e., the Aṣṭasāhasrikā Prajñāpāramitā-sūtra), the disciple Subhūti asks the Buddha how a bodhisattva in training can recognize or "apperceive" the perfection of insight and is told that this is done through a series of thoughts which are "inclined toward all-knowledge."[1] Why so?

> Because all-knowledge is immeasurable and unlimited. What is immeasurable and unlimited, that is not form, or any other skandha. That is not attainment, or reunion, or getting there; not the path or its fruit; not cognition or consciousness; not genesis, or destruction, or production, or passing away, or stopping, or development, or annihilation. It has not been made by anything, it has not come from anywhere, it does not go to anywhere, it does not stand in any place or spot. On the contrary, it comes to be styled "immeasurable, unlimited." From the immeasurableness of space is the immeasurableness of all-knowledge.[2]

This passage shows us that the term "immeasurability" belongs to those which indicate the aspect of being without characteristics. It is not intended to make an ontological assertion. Rather, it is intended to indicate the aspect of "positionlessness," a term with which one may satisfactorily summarize the character of the Prajñāpāramitā and Mādhyamika schools.

A little farther on there is an extremely interesting passage. In the course of his dialogue with Subhūti, the Buddha (Bhagawan) declares that insofar as a bodhisattva "does not lack in perfect wisdom, to that extent he begets an immeasurable and incalculable heap of merit."[3] Incidentally, it would probably be less mystifying to translate this as "an immeasurable and incalculable amount of merit." Subhūti thereupon asks whether there is any difference between "immeasurable and incalculable." The answer runs: "It is 'immeasurable' because in it all measurements must cease. It is 'incalculable' because it exhausts all efforts to count it."[4]

It is evident from this that the two terms are close synonyms. Indeed the following exposition shows that they should not be distinguished in any way. "Immeasurability" is declared to be a synonym for "emptiness" and of "the signless" and "the wishless," but insofar as all dharmas are empty, all are inexhaustible and hence immeasurable. Yet at the same time, even words such as these are just "talk" and cannot be identified with the true nature of any dharmas, for "one cannot properly express the emptiness of all dharmas in words."[5]

In another extremely interesting passage, Subhūti asks about the meaning of the "great vehicle." "What is that great vehicle [upon which a bodhisattva rides]? . . . Who has set out in it? . . . Where will it stand?" The Buddha answers:

> "Great vehicle," that is a synonym of immeasurableness. "Immeasurable" means infinitude. By means of the perfections has a bodhisattva set out in it. From the triple world it will go forth. It has set out to where there is no objective support. It will be a bodhisattva, a great being, who will go forth, but he will not go forth to anywhere. Nor has anyone set out in it. It will not stand anywhere.

The Buddha continues in this vein, but we may skip the text to Subhūti's answer:

> The Lord speaks of the "great vehicle." Surpassing the world with its gods, men, and asuras, that vehicle will go forth. For it is the same as space, and exceedingly great. As in space, so in this vehicle there is room for immeasurable and incalculable beings. So is this the great vehicle of the bodhisattvas, the great beings. One cannot see its coming or going, and its abiding does not exist. Thus one cannot get at the beginning of this great vehicle, nor at its end, nor at its middle. But it is self-identical everywhere. Therefore one speaks of a "great vehicle."[6]

These ideas are extremely typical of the *prajñāpāramitā* literature and may be taken as part of the formative matrix in which the chapters on the immeasurability of the Buddha's life were conceived during the early phase of the development of Mahayana Buddhism. The key point to be learned from these passages is that "immeasurability" is part of a general discourse which seeks to indicate the ineffability of the true nature of things by disrupting conventional terminology. Whatever one can conceive of is part of the world as viewed by discriminating reason.

But the aim, in Mahayana Buddhism, is not to be entrapped by such discriminations. To avoid entrapment, the available terminology has to be used. But it is turned against itself. Thus a very large amount of merit is construed as being so large that it cannot be measured at all. And this in turn points to its "empty" nature, so that we arrive at the realization that a very large amount of merit is so immeasurably large that it is "no merit."

It is submitted here that such an understanding of the term "immeasurability" underlies the usage in other Mahayana works.

An example of how this works might be seen in chapter 26 of the Chinese version of the Avataṃsaka Sutra, which treats "the length of life of the Buddha" (or perhaps better "of the Buddhas"). In this chapter, which is very short, a list of ten Buddhas is adduced. According to this passage, one eon (which is a very long time) in the world of Śākyamuni is but one day and one night in the land of the Buddha Amitābha. This in turn is but one day and one night in the land of the Buddha Diamond, and so on throughout the whole list.

Although only ten are listed, which already amounts to a huge calculation, the list could be extended, it is said, to cover a million worlds. The bodhisattvas in these hugely extended worlds are therefore themselves "immeasurable" and "inexpressible." With this example we see how the play with huge numbers is carried through in order to lead beyond manageable concepts. Immeasurability is linked to inexpressibility, just as in the passages quoted earlier from the Perfection of Insight Sutra.

Immeasurability and Skillful Means in the Lotus Sutra

A crucial text for the discussion of this subject is, of course, chapter 15 of the Lotus Sutra, widely known as chapter 16 in the commonly used Chinese version produced by Kumārajīva. Since this text is in wide use today by millions of Buddhist practitioners, it is generally familiar and its contents need not be introduced in detail here. The important specific points to be noted are as follows.

First, the idea of immeasurability is presented in a manner which is completely continuous with the style of other Mahayana writings. For example, if an incredibly large number of worlds were ground down into dust and each grain of dust were carried one by one in an eastward direction and set down again, the number being calculated, how many might there be? Even if the number could be totted up, it has to be realized that the number of *kalpas* (ages) which have passed since the Buddha became a buddha is greater by far than the number of grains of dust which could possibly be counted.

Second, an important connection is made between the disclosure of the immeasurable length of the Buddha's life and the concept of skill in means or "skillful means." The apparent departure of the Buddha into a state of nirvana after a mere eighty years is a device to make the living beings take the matter seriously. This is further illustrated in the allegory of the physician's sons, who are only prepared to take medicine when they experience sorrow at the physician's feigned death.

Third, though the living beings require these various presentations, which are in themselves erroneous, the Buddha for his part is presented as seeing the threefold world (of past, present, and future) in its true character. For him there is no birth and death, no departing or arising, no reality or irreality. In other words, the Buddha sees things from a standpoint of nonduality or nondiscrimination.

While the first point, the graphic presentation of incredibly large numbers, establishes the connection between the Lotus Sutra and other texts such as the Avataṃsaka Sutra, the second and third points together set out a dialectic which is in principle the same as that of the Perfection of Insight Sutra cited earlier. The concept of "emptiness" is not emphasized and indeed occurs infrequently in the Lotus Sutra. However, the dialectic between provisional diversity and a final truth which transcends dualism and is inexpressible is closely parallel to that of the *Prajñāpāramitā* literature, the Teaching of Vimalakīrti, and indeed the Laṅkāvatāra Sutra.

There remain questions about the mode of presentation. These are strongly thematized in the Lotus Sutra itself, and not least in the chapter in question. Are the diverse teachings then false, once recognized as provisional? Indeed not, the argument runs, for they are to be understood in dialectical relationship (to use modern terminology) with the final truth, which itself is both one and inexpressible.

Looking beyond the questions raised directly in the text, we may also ask about the way in which the immeasurable length of life of the Tathāgata is presented in later Buddhist devotion. A readiness to recognize that the length of life of the Tathāgata transcends our comprehension has often led to a piety of its own. But does this piety always do justice to the profundity of the dialectic? This point will be reconsidered at the end of this article, after consideration of two more related texts.

Immeasurability in the Sutra of Golden Light

The presentation of the immeasurability of the duration of the Buddha's life in the Sutra of Golden Light (chapter 2) has very much in common with that of the Lotus Sutra. This fascinating sutra is not sufficiently well known today, although it appears to have been of considerable importance during the period when Buddhism was first introduced into Japan. One reason for this was the chapter entitled "Protection of the land by the four heavenly kings," which made Buddhism seem important to the state in a manner which the secular constitutions of today scarcely require. The very full Chinese version has thirty-one chapters which are all interesting in their own right.

In this full form, the text is surely later than the Lotus Sutra. This is indicated by the very existence of chapter 3 on "distinguishing the three bodies," which reflects a discussion postdating the composition of the Lotus Sutra. There is no corresponding chapter in the extant Sanskrit text. Parts of the sutra, however, may well be relatively old and its contents reflect themes which were current during the formative period of Mahayana Buddhism. Chapter 2, on "the length of life of the Tathāgata," belongs to these and is also to be found in the Sanskrit as chapter 2, though it is shorter there.

The starting point for the discussion of the length of life of the Buddha in this case is the questioning of a bodhisattva named Ruciraketu. Considering that Śākyamuni fulfilled the two conditions for leading a very long life, namely refraining from killing living beings and giving away food, how could it come about that he lived for a mere eighty years? As a result of these excellent thoughts entertained by Ruciraketu, his house was dramatically expanded to make room for the appearance of four cosmic buddhas, namely Akṣobhya in the east, Ratnaketu in the south, Amitāyus in the west, and Dundubhisvara in the north. This caused a dramatic appearance of great light and much music, flowers, and happiness, after which the four buddhas declared that Śākyamuni lived not for eighty years but longer than any known living being could possibly comprehend.

The length of the Buddha's life is then expressed as immeasurable by means of various analogies, such as the number of drops of water in the oceans, the number of particles in all the many Sumeru mountains of the various worlds, or the measurability of the sky. In the background of such statements a Brahmin full of reverence for the Buddha is depicted as asking for a tiny relic. He is confronted, however, with the view that there can in reality be no relics in that the buddhas are all inconceivable in their nature. Only as an expedient can relics have been deposited by them, for the benefit of living beings.

The various appearances of the Buddha are also to be understood in this way, and in particular the appearance of entering nirvana is carried through for their benefit, to aid their maturation. Clearly this line of thought is closely allied to that of chapter 15 (Chinese chapter 16) of the Lotus Sutra, and is quite consistent with it. Here too, the dialectic between the provisional, and sometimes amazing appearance of buddhas on the one hand and their reserved, ultimate nature as inconceivable and nondual on the other hand, is strongly set out with a wealth of metaphor and analogy.

Immeasurability and the Mythical Imagination

If the logic of "emptiness," sometimes referred to as the logic of identity, is fundamental to a full understanding of this way of thinking, so too is the mythical imagination, which is so often pressed into service. As a final example, the presentation of the Buddha Amitābha in the Sukhāvatī-vyūha Sutra may be briefly considered. It will be recalled that Amitābha (Amida in Japanese) Buddha is also known as Amitāyus, which refers not to an immeasurable "light" but to an immeasurable "life." He is known by this name in the Chinese writing known as the Sutra of Contemplation on the Buddha of Immeasurable Life (Jpn., *Kammuryōju-kyō*).

However, the concept of immeasurability is not discussed in this text, which shows that by the time the sutra was composed (probably in the early fifth century in central Asia or western China) the concept had become a recognized epithet rather than a subject needing to be set forth. Interestingly enough, the Sukhāvatīvyūha Sutra, the oldest of the three sutras given prominence by Pure Land Buddhists, is known in Sino-Japanese as Muryōju-kyō, that is "Sutra on the Immeasurable Life," meaning in this case the immeasurable life of the Buddha Amitābha. Much of this sutra is taken up with the elaboration of Amitābha's vows while still a bodhisattva and the description of the Pure Land of Amitābha in the cosmic west.

On the theme of immeasurability there is but one short passage. It comes in the context of a description of the astonishing light sent forth by this Buddha, lighting up innumerable Buddha-countries in all directions. In general, this is the same kind of mythological projection which is found at the beginning of the Lotus Sutra. As to the length of life, the Buddha Śākyamuni says to Ānanda: "The life of the Buddha of Immeasurable Life is extremely long. It is not possible to calculate it."[7] This is followed by a short passage which illustrates this incalculability in various ways. For example:

Even though all the beings of the ten quarters, having been born as human beings, having attained the ways of shravakas and pratyeka-buddhas, and all having assembled in one place, may sink into meditation, try to concentrate their powers of wisdom, calculate the length of his life for a period extending over a hundred thousand million *kalpas*, and try to know the length of his life, still is it not possible to know the limit.[8]

Other metaphorical problems follow, such as "This is like dividing a single hair into a hundred parts and wetting the one-hundredth part of such a hair, trying to draw up the inconceivable volume of water of a great ocean."[9] The text soon turns to other amazing features of the Pure Land itself, many of which reflect immeasurability, as in the endless multiplication of the seven jewels, or the huge height of the tree of enlightenment of the Buddha Amitābha (four million miles) or its huge circumference (fifty *yojanas* at the base). Like the passage adduced earlier from the Avataṃsaka Sutra, there is no explicit dialectic to be found here. At the same time it is clear that the sheer accumulation of numbers amounting to immeasurability is intended to bring release from small, fixed numbers. In this regard, the descriptions are continuous with those of the Lotus Sutra and the Sutra of Golden Light.

Buddhas Transcend Concepts of Time

It will be evident from the above that the idea of "immeasurability" or "incalculability" has been important in Mahayana Buddhism from an early time. Two Sanskrit terms are used to indicate this topic. One is *apramāṇa*, meaning "unlimited," and the other is *amita*, meaning "unmeasured" implying "immeasurability," as in the name of the mythical Buddha Amitābha. In the case of the Lotus Sutra, it is *pramāṇa* which figures in the title of chapter 15 (Chinese chapter 16).

Although these two words are not exactly the same, the fundamental point made whenever they occur in these texts is that the life of the Buddha is extremely long, so long that we cannot conceive it. In other words, the Buddha, or buddhas, are not only cosmically significant in terms of space, as is often set forth in the Mahayana sutras, but also in terms of time. They simply transcend our normal conceptions of duration.

On account of this transcendence of our normal concepts of time, the Buddha has sometimes been referred to in translated texts as "eternal," a word which in English recalls strongly the theistic understanding of God.

Presumably this is to make it easier for Western people to understand. It also reinforces the understanding that the Buddha, in this understanding of Mahayana Buddhism, is comparable as a focus of devotion to God in the Christian tradition. For not a few Buddhists, this is probably not far from being the case in practical devotion. But is it the underlying meaning of Buddhism, including Mahayana Buddhism?

Does "immeasurable" mean the same as "eternal"? In view of the apparent function of the idea of "immeasurability" in the group of texts considered above, the view taken here is that it does not mean the same as "eternal" in the context of theistic views of God, at least in their most common form. For one thing, the connection between the immeasurability of the length of life of a buddha and the concept of emptiness should be recalled.

Looking beyond the Perfection of Insight Sutra to the Lotus Sutra and the Sutra of Golden Light, we recall that here the main point lies in the dialectic between ordinary conceptions and inconceivable conceptions. The purpose of inconceivable conceptions is to help people get over ordinary conceptions. In these texts the idea of immeasurability is not intended to lead into positive metaphysics, even though, at a devotional level only, apparently metaphysical worlds may be imaginatively posited, as notably in Pure Land Buddhism. In Lotus Sutra Buddhism, the parable of the magic city in chapter 7 should certainly be adduced in the understanding of such projections.

Finally, it is interesting that the very long life of different, named buddhas, when denoted at all, is given as being of *varied* length. This was seen for example in the Avataṃsaka Sutra. Insofar as duration can be measured, it is variable. This assists us to avoid eternalism. In short, the idea of unlimited duration is a way of escaping specific length. That is all. We are not asked by these texts to entrap ourselves instead in the idea of unlimited duration. In Buddhist terms that would be worse than being caught in a span of exactly eighty years. It would be like being reborn among the long-lived gods: pleasant, but not conducive to nirvana.

Notes

1. Edward Conze, *The Perfection of Wisdom in Eight Thousand Lines & its verse summary* (Bolinas: Four Seasons Foundation, 1973), 191.
2. Ibid., 191.
3. Ibid., 211.
4. Ibid., 211.
5. Ibid., 211. The corresponding Chinese passages will be found in *Taisho Daizokyo*, VIII, 566.

6. Ibid., 91.
7. *The Shinshu Seiten*, 30.
8. Ibid., 30.
9. Ibid., 31.

The Lotus Sutra as Radically World-affirming

Gene Reeves

Introduction

In "Symbol and Yūgen: Shunzei's Use of Tendai Buddhism," William La-Fleur examines poetry which emerged in twelfth-century Japan under the influence of Tendai philosophy, and especially the Lotus Sutra. What he argues is that under the influence of Tendai's "ontological egalitarianism," in which "the abstract is no more and no less real than the concrete," medieval Japanese poets rejected all distinction between the sacred and profane in favor of a "strong reaffirmation of the phenomena of the empirical world." T'ien-t'ai Chih-i's understanding of leaving the empty and entering the provisional became, for the poets, a matter of rejecting allegory to turn to the immediacy of such things as trees and plants.[1]

Social responsibility, I take it, depends on some underlying sense of the value of this world. It can be contrasted both with a turn toward inwardness and a turn toward other worlds, either at the end of time or somehow above time. Such other worlds, inner and outer, are typically ideal worlds, worlds of pure selves, pure lands, or kingdoms of heaven construed to be both more valuable and more real than the everyday world of ordinary existence.

It may be an irony that a sutra which relates a variety of supernatural events and affirms a cosmic and universal Śākyamuni Buddha, one who is in every world and every time, does so not to reject the historical Śākyamuni or the temporal world, but precisely to affirm their supreme importance. And their importance lies in nothing more or less than that it is in this world that we, having been taught by the historical Buddha, are called to embody the life of the Buddha in our own acts and lives. This is why a part of the everyday liturgy of Risshō Kōsei-kai is the so-called *dōjō-kan:* "Know that this place is where the Buddha attained perfect enlightenment. In this and all places the buddhas accomplish perfect enlightenment. . . ."

There are, obviously, many ways to read a sutra, perhaps especially this sutra! I take it to be primarily a religious text, that is, a text whose primary aim is soteriological. Whatever polemical purposes it may have served in some now unknown part of India in some now unknown community of Buddhists, the text addresses itself to readers, and to the salvation of readers, in any time and place. Looking at the text in this way will not produce a uniformity of results, but can lead to a certain kind of vision of this text as primarily an ethical text, ethical not in the sense of offering a theory of morals, or in the sense of offering a set of commandments, but ethical in the sense of recommending a certain way of life, a way of life guided by a single overarching purpose.

That unifying purpose is nothing less than the salvation, the happiness, of the entire world, a purpose rooted symbolically in the Buddha's and bodhisattvas' vow to save all the living.

To that end, the sutra utilizes several closely related themes, especially *upāya* or appropriate means, the One Vehicle, buddha-nature, eternal Śākyamuni Buddha, and bodhisattva practice, all of which, in one way or another, affirm the importance of this world and the life in it of the reader.

The Dharma in Stories

The Lotus Sutra is, perhaps above all, a book of stories. It contains twenty-six or so stories used as teaching devices. It does not avoid teaching doctrine directly, but if we want to understand what the Lotus Sutra teaches we had better pay attention to its stories, and not merely to lines within them or to lines which explain them, but also to the overall thrust and function of those stories.

It is not incidental that the original Lotus Sutra probably began with the chapter on *upāya,* and then, in the next chapter told a story, the parable of the burning house, to illustrate and explain it. And this "Parable" chapter is immediately followed by the *adhimukti* chapter which is built around another story, the story of the rich father and the poor son. Actually, as we have it now, the whole sutra, or at least the first twenty-two chapters of it, is a story about a time when the Buddha was on the mountain called "Vulture Peak" and preached the Lotus Sutra.

Compared with abstract doctrine, stories are concrete. They embody teachings and, so to speak, give flesh to them in a way that abstract principles cannot. If we are to understand this sutra at all, we have to look closely at its stories. We may see that the extensive use of stories in the sutra is a kind of affirmation of the concrete. The stories, it says in effect, are at least as important an embodiment of the Dharma as any abstract statements. And what the stories are about are actions which embody the Dharma. It is in such action, which is understood in this sutra to be bodhisattva practice, that the Dharma is most concretely embodied and therefore most valuable and most real.

Stories of Supernatural Events

Several years ago, when I told my philosophy teacher, Charles Hartshorne, that I was working on the Lotus Sutra, he responded that he had not looked at it for many years but that what he remembered was that it had a lot of "miracle stories," something which he didn't like very much.

The entire setting of the Lotus Sutra is supernatural; from the first chapter to the last there is nothing in it which pretends to be historical. But, whereas in some other contexts miracle stories may have been used to assert the power in this world of some otherworldly power, their function in the Lotus Sutra is quite different. This is in part due, I think, to the fact that the whole setting of the sutra is supernatural story. In the Bible, for example, miracles take place in history, their telling occurs within a historical narrative. But in the Lotus Sutra, while there are brief references to historical events, the reader understands from the beginning that the miraculous events happen within a story. And such stories are devices, appropriate means, for teaching. They do not pretend to be accounts of history.

Since they are not accounts of history, it is important to look at how they do function, what purpose they serve. I think it can be shown that they function primarily to affirm the importance, the value and ultimate reality, of this world, and this is done in order to affirm the value and importance of the reader's life and practice as a bodhisattva. To show this, I want to look first at a few miracle stories.

The Jeweled Stupa and Representative Buddhas

Certainly one of the most interesting supernatural stories in the Lotus Sutra is the story of the stupa of Many Treasures Buddha in chapter 11. At the very beginning of the chapter, a huge, magnificently jeweled and highly decorated stupa rises up out of the ground and hangs in the air before Śākyamuni Buddha. Its fragrance spreads to the far corners of the world. The thirty-three gods rain flowers on it, while thousands of other gods and heavenly beings of all kinds make offerings of flowers, incense, necklaces, streamers, music, etc. in praise of this stupa.

From within the stupa came a loud voice praising Śākyamuni for preaching the Lotus Sutra. The assembled monks and nuns and lay people were both delighted and astonished. Seeing this, the Bodhisattva Great Eloquence[2] asked the Buddha why the stupa had emerged from the ground and a voice had come from it. The Buddha explained that a very long time ago in a very distant world to the East there lived a buddha named Many Treasures[3] who while still a bodhisattva promised that after he had passed away, if ever anyone preached the Lotus Sutra he would have his great stupa rise up before such a preacher as testimony to the truth of the sutra, and he would be able to hear the sutra preached directly and praise the one preaching it.

Great Eloquence said that the congregation would like to see the Buddha inside, and the Buddha explained that Many Treasures Buddha had also promised that if such an assembly wanted to see him, the buddha preaching the sutra would have to call to that place all of the buddhas of the ten directions—buddhas who are duplicates or representatives of Śākyamuni Buddha. The Bodhisattva Great Eloquence said that the whole assembly would like to see and pay respects to those buddhas as well. Then Śākyamuni Buddha emitted a ray of light from between his eyebrows which illumined all of those billions and billions of worlds, first in the East and then in all the other nine directions. The congregation could see the magnificence of those worlds, each with billions of bodhisattvas and a buddha preaching the Dharma.

Each of those buddhas announced his intention to go to see Śākyamuni Buddha and make offerings to the jeweled stupa. Instantly the *sahā* world was purified and suitably adorned for such a visit. Then all of those buddhas, each accompanied by a great many bodhisattvas, came to take a seat before the Buddha. But since there were not enough seats in the *sahā* world, even for the buddhas and bodhisattvas from just one of the ten directions, Śākyamuni Buddha had to purify billions and billions of worlds in the eight directions neighboring this *sahā* world and prepare them as well with lion seats under great jeweled trees, and when that was not enough he had to do the same thing with billions and billions of worlds neighboring the already greatly expanded *sahā* world, thus temporarily uniting them together as a single Buddha-world.

After they were seated, each of the buddhas sent an attendant to bring flowers to Śākyamuni Buddha, inquire about his condition, and express their desire to have the great stupa in the air opened. Then Śākyamuni went up in the air to the stupa, opened its door with the fingers of his right hand, and revealed to the congregation Many Treasures Buddha sitting with a still perfect body on the lion seat of the stupa. Many Treasures Buddha praised Śākyamuni for preaching the Lotus Sutra which he had come to hear, and the congregation celebrated by strewing heaps of flowers before the two buddhas. Then, invited by Many Treasures Buddha to do so, Śākyamuni joined him, so that the two were sitting side by side on the seat in the stupa. But then the others couldn not see very well and wanted to be raised up into the air also. Doing this, Śākyamuni Buddha expressed his desire to have others promise to protect and teach the Lotus Sutra after his extinction, even though preaching, writing, reading, and listening to the Lotus Sutra are extremely difficult, more difficult for example than walking around with the whole sky in one's hand or carrying the earth up to the heaven of Brahma on one's toenail!

This is a marvelous story, full of special imagery, cosmological in scope. But clearly such imagery is not so much for the purpose of explaining the nature of the cosmos as it is for extolling, first the Lotus Sutra, second Śākyamuni Buddha, and thirdly this *sahā* world.

Extolling the Lotus Sutra is both explicit in the chapter and implicit in the story. Many Treasures and the buddhas of the ten directions all come to the *sahā* world at least in part to hear the Lotus Sutra preached. In this way the stupa is subordinated to the preaching of the Dharma. I take this to mean that the construction and worship of stupas and the remains of the Buddha are not rejected but are relativized, made subordinate to the Dharma and in particular to the Dharma expressed in the Lotus Sutra.

Śākyamuni Buddha is praised for preaching the Lotus Sutra.[4] Not only all of the creatures of this world and the gods in the heavens of this world, but even all of the buddhas of all of the countless other worlds in every direction also praise and subordinate themselves to Śākyamuni Buddha. Especially by designating the buddhas of the ten directions as his representatives, he is given central importance in the entire cosmos.

The Chinese term here rendered as "representatives," but which might literally be rendered as "body parts," has been interpreted and translated in various ways. It may be a reflection of the belief that one of a buddha's supernatural powers is the ability to replicate himself. Exactly what is meant in the Lotus Sutra by the term is not clear. But one thing is very clear—all of these various buddhas, throughout the many, many worlds, are subordinate to Śākyamuni Buddha. Just how they are subordinate is not explained, no doubt because it is not important. What is important, given the priorities of the sutra, is the cosmic significance and superiority of Śākyamuni Buddha. Yet, at the same time, the reality or importance of those other buddhas is in no way denied.[5]

Śākyamuni Buddha is, of course, the buddha of the *sahā* world. Thus, by elevating the status of Śākyamuni Buddha to cosmic superiority over all others, the importance of this world is also stressed. Here we can see one of the main themes of the Lotus Sutra, evident in virtually all of its teachings—the importance of this world and of life in this world. In this story it is to the *sahā* world that the stupa of Many Treasures Buddha comes and it is the *sahā* world that is purified to receive all of the buddhas from other lands. The worlds of the other buddhas are described as wonderful in every way, but the buddhas leave those marvelous worlds in order to come to the *sahā* world and pay respects to its buddha.

In a sense, we may think that, since it is in it that the cosmic significance of Śākyamuni Buddha is revealed, praise for the sutra is always also praise for Śākyamuni Buddha. At the same time, because this is his world, praise for Śākyamuni Buddha is always also praise for this world.

The jeweled stupa in which the two buddhas sit is a kind of tower and the character has that meaning in Chinese. The image of such a tower, surrounded by the buddhas and bodhisattvas from all over the universe, is clearly an *axis mundi* image. Such images always, I suppose, give importance and power to the place where the axis is located, in this case to this world and its buddha.

The arrival of Many Treasures Buddha in his stupa and the image of him and Śākyamuni Buddha sitting side by side are very significant in another way. The sutra emphasizes the fact that the whole body of Many Treasures Buddha, not just his remains, is present in the stupa and that his voice emerges from it. But Many Treasures Buddha, we are told, had long ago passed into final nirvana. In this way the whole meaning of nirvana is called into question. And the sitting of the two buddhas side by side violates the assumption that there can only be one buddha in this world at a time.[6] This is one of the ways in which the Lotus Sutra teaches that stories of entering nirvana are teaching devices to get people to be more responsible for their own lives, a theme which is developed most explicitly in the story in chapter 7 of the guide who conjures up a city as a temporary resting place for some travelers who want to quit the journey.

This view of nirvana is also found in the parable of the physician and his sons. A wise and good doctor had many sons. One day, after the doctor left home on business, the sons drank some poison and were writhing on the ground when their father returned home. By that time, some of them had completely lost their minds, while others were not yet so seriously affected. Seeing the father returning, the sons were very happy and begged him to cure them. Consulting his books, the father prepared an appropriate medicine and urged his sons to take it. Those who had been least affected by the poison saw right away that the medicine was good for them, took it, and were immediately cured. Others, however, having already lost their minds, could not see that the medicine would help them. The father, realizing what was happening, decided to devise a way to reach them. He told them that he was getting old and would soon die, but was leaving the good medicine for them, with the recommendation that they take it. Then he went away again, and sent back a messenger with news that he had died. The sons, hearing that their father had died, felt lonely, deserted, and helpless, and their sadness caused them to come to their senses, whereupon they realized that the medicine was good for them, took it, and were completely cured. Hearing that they had recovered, the father returned home again.

In this parable, the physician-father of course represents the Buddha, and his supposed death is like the Buddha's entry into nirvana. In reality, in the view of the Lotus Sutra, the universal Buddha, the loving father of the world who is working to save all from suffering, has not and will not pass away. He pretends to pass away only in order to get people to be more responsible for their own lives. This is a good example of how the sutra takes what is a basically negative notion, nirvana, and turns it into a world-affirmative one.

The image of the two buddhas sitting side by side in the stupa has also been seen as a symbol of the mutual importance of the Dharma (Many Treasures Buddha) and the teacher of the Dharma (Śākyamuni Buddha), that is, of the idea that without a teacher the truth is dead.[7] While there may not be much in the text itself to support this idea of interpreting Many Treasures Buddha as a symbol of the Dharma, neither is there anything inconsistent with such an interpretation.

The idea in the story of the jeweled stupa that Śākyamuni Buddha creates a unified world out of many worlds is especially significant. The Lotus Sutra is an integrative sutra. Throughout, it emphasizes unity, oneness, integration, some kind of coming together. As the truth is ultimately one, i.e., without internal contradiction, so too the teachings of the Buddha who discovered the truth must be one. That is, finally there can be only one Buddha-way. But in the Lotus Sutra, the one does not destroy or denigrate the many. Though integrated, though the many become as one, they remain many. The cosmos only exists by virtue of the fact that it has worlds. Similarly, in the Lotus Sutra, the teaching, the Buddha Dharma, only exists by virtue of the many teachings. Neither right views nor right living can be a matter of replacing the many by the one.[8]

That the one who creates a single world out of many worlds is Śākyamuni Buddha is related to his being, as said earlier, both one and distributed throughout the cosmos. In other words, Śākyamuni Buddha can unify Buddhism and the cosmos, and therefore the life of the true hearer precisely because he himself is both one and many.

Bodhisattvas from Below

Elevation in importance of this world is nowhere more in evidence than in the story found in chapter 15 of the bodhisattvas who emerge from below the earth. The chapter begins with millions and millions of bodhisattvas who have come from other worlds asking Śākyamuni Buddha to allow them to preach the sutra in this world. But the Buddha promptly declined their offer on the ground that there are many, many bodhisattvas already in this world who can protect, read, recite, and teach the Lotus Sutra after his extinction. Whereupon the ground quaked all over the earth and a fantastically enormous number of bright, golden bodhisattvas and their attendants emerged from below the earth, where they had been living in empty space. They went to the two buddhas in the stupa in the sky, Many Treasures Buddha and Śākyamuni Buddha, paid respects to them, then to all the other buddhas on their lion seats on the ground, and then, after fifty small *kalpas* which seemed like only half a day, returned to the buddhas in the stupa in the sky, filling the skies over countless lands. These bodhisattvas were led by four great bodhisattvas—Superior Practice, Limitless Practice, Pure Practice, and Firm Practice,[9] who inquired about the health of Śākyamuni Buddha and received a favorable response from him.

Maitreya then asked the Buddha who these huge, magnificent bodhisattvas were that he had never seen before, and where they had come from, and who had taught the Dharma to them. Other bodhisattvas, those who had accompanied the buddhas from all of the other worlds, asked their buddhas the same question, and were told to listen to Śākyamuni Buddha's response to Maitreya. Then Śākyamuni explained that those countless bodhisattvas live in the empty space in the lower part of the *sahā* world, and that he himself has been teaching and leading them from the most remote past. But Maitreya protested that it had only been forty years since Śākyamuni was enlightened. How could it be possible that he had taught these innumerable bodhisattvas in such a short period of time? It is as impossible to believe, he says, as a twenty-five-year-old man claiming to have a hundred-year-old son!

Exactly what is meant by the empty space in the lower part of the *sahā* world below the earth is unclear. Probably it is simply the most convenient way to have this huge number of bodhisattvas be hidden, yet not be in the less than human regions within the earth, and not be among the heavenly deities, yet still be in the *sahā* world. In other words, both for the sake of the story and for the sake of the central message of the Lotus Sutra, it is important that these bodhisattvas be both hidden and of this world.

And we are asked to imagine that the numbers are staggering, both the number of bodhisattvas and the number of *kalpas* in which Śākyamuni Buddha has been teaching them. Clearly one purpose, perhaps the main one, of the story is to set up the "revelation" of the eternal life of the Buddha in chapter 16. How can so many bodhisattvas have been taught by Śākyamuni Buddha over such a long period of time? Because, even though everyone thinks he became enlightened not so long ago in Gayā, in fact it was a very long time ago. How long ago? Suppose someone took many billion universes each consisting of many billion worlds, ground them into fine dust, and went off to the east and, having passed through billions and billions of worlds, deposited a single particle of dust, and then repeated this until all of the dust was exhausted. Then suppose he gathered up all of the worlds, both those where a particle of dust had been deposited and those where none had been deposited, and ground all of those worlds into fine dust. The number of *kalpas* which have elapsed since Śākyamuni Buddha became enlightened is millions of billions times larger than the resulting number of dust particles.

Here there is an apparent contradiction—the sutra clearly insists that there is no time in which the Buddha is not present, but it also claims that he became a buddha. Chapter 16 answers Maitreya's question at the end of chapter 15 by teaching that Śākyamuni has been a buddha from the very remote past, but this does not explain how he both always is and yet became enlightened. What is involved here, I think, is that on the one hand, in order both to affirm this world and to identify the Buddha with the Dharma, the everlasting process which is the truth about the nature of things, it is important to have him be eternal or everlasting. Just as there is, and can be, no place from which the Buddha is completely absent, there is no time in which the Buddha is not present. On the other hand, the very meaning of "enlightenment" requires that it be a process, and thus requires that Śākyamuni Buddha *became* enlightened. In fact, in several places the Lotus Sutra teaches that Śākyamuni Buddha became enlightened only after countless *kalpas* of bodhisattva practice. Further, only if he became enlightened could Śākyamuni Buddha be a model for others or an encouragement for them to enter the Buddha-way. So an apparent contradiction remains unresolved.[10]

The sutra can be indifferent to such problems because they are soteriologically unimportant. Just as in chapter 24 when the Bodhisattva Wonderful Voice[11] expresses to the Buddha of his own land his desire to visit the *sahā* world to pay tribute to Śākyamuni Buddha, and that Buddha warns him that even though the *sahā* world is not smooth or clean and its buddha and bodhisattvas are short, he should not disparage or make little of that world or think that its buddha and bodhisattvas are inferior. In this story too the point is that the *sahā* world is not to be regarded as inferior. In other words, the real point here is an affirmation of the *sahā* world. It is, we are told, a world which should not look for help from other worlds because it does not need help from elsewhere.

Thus the use of miracle stories in the Lotus Sutra is exactly the opposite of what is so often the case. Instead of using stories of other worlds as a way of encouraging escape from or negligence toward this world, in the Lotus Sutra stories of other worlds are used to radically affirm the reality and importance of this world.

Flowers and Incense from Heaven

In chapter 16, the Buddha has made clear that he is alive at all times and, in this sense, universal or eternal. In chapter 17, having heard this, an incredibly large number of living beings, bodhisattvas, and bodhisattva-*mahāsattvas* receive various blessings, such as the ability to memorize everything heard, unlimited eloquence, power to turn the wheel of the Dharma, supreme enlightenment after eight, four, three, two or one rebirths, or the determination to achieve supreme enlightenment. In all, twelve different groups within the congregation assembled to hear the Buddha preach are mentioned here, each of them enormously large, and each having received various blessings as a consequence of hearing about the everlasting life of the Buddha.

In response to this joyous occasion, the gods in heaven(s) rained beautiful flowers and incense down on the innumerable buddhas of the ten directions who had assembled in the *sahā* world, on Śākyamuni Buddha and Many Treasures Buddha, then sitting together in the latter's magnificent stupa, and on the great bodhisattvas, and on the monks, nuns, laymen, and laywomen assembled there. Deep in the sky, wonderful sounding drums reverberated by themselves. The many Indras and Brahmas from the other Buddha-lands came. Then the gods rained all kinds of heavenly jewel-encrusted garments in all directions, and burned incense in burners which moved around the whole congregation by themselves. And above each of the buddhas assembled under the great jeweled trees, bodhisattvas bearing jeweled streamers and such, and singing with wonderful voices, lined up vertically, one on top of the other, all the way to the heaven of Brahma.

Clearly the events depicted here are both magical and cosmological in scope. The story involves countless worlds, buddhas, bodhisattvas, and wondrous events with flowers, sound, and incense—all in praise of the revelation, in the *sahā* world, of the good news of the Buddha's ever-presence.[12] Within the story it is, in a sense, important that there are many worlds in ten directions, and gods as well as buddhas, bodhisattvas, and humans. But, in another sense, how many directions there are, or how many different kinds of beings there are, has virtually no importance. In fact, here and I think only here, the text refers to nine directions, rather than the usual ten. What is important is that no matter how many directions there are, no matter how many worlds there are, and no matter how many kinds of living beings there are, all are delighted and transformed by and extol the ever-presence of the Buddha—the fact that none of them ever is or ever was or ever will be without the presence of the Buddha. The story uses a cosmological setting, but it does so for the purpose of proclaiming the significance and magnificence of Śākyamuni Buddha, the Buddha of the *sahā* world.

Bodhisattva Wonderful Voice

The image of illumination by light from the Buddha found initially in the first chapter is expressed again in chapter 24, which begins with the Buddha emitting light which illuminates other worlds. In this case, beams of light come both from the knob on top of the Buddha's head and from the tuft between his eyebrows. Here again the Buddha illuminated countless worlds to the East, but also a world beyond them where the Buddha known as Knowledge from the King of Constellations–Pure Flower[13] and the Bodhisattva Wonderful Voice lived. This bodhisattva, who was extremely large, beautiful, and radiant and who already had many great accomplishments, including attaining millions of different kinds of *samādhis*, when illumined by Śākyamuni Buddha expressed to the Buddha of his own land his desire to go to the *sahā* world to pay tribute to Śākyamuni Buddha and visit various bodhisattvas. The Buddha warned him that even though the *sahā* world is not smooth or clean, has both high and low places, and is full of dirt, and its buddha and bodhisattvas are puny, he should not disparage or make little of that world or think that its buddha and bodhisattvas are inferior. Then, through the power of his meditation, Wonderful Voice made eighty-four thousand gold and silver lotus flowers and other valuables appear not far from where Śākyamuni Buddha was sitting on Vulture Peak. Seeing them, Mañjuśrī asked Śākyamuni Buddha what they signified. When the Buddha explained that the flowers meant that the Bodhisattva Wonderful Voice, accompanied by eighty-four thousand other bodhisattvas, was coming to visit, to pay his respects to both Śākyamuni Buddha and the Lotus Sutra, Mañjuśrī wanted to see him and to know what Wonderful Voice had done to gain such great powers. Then the Buddha said that Many Treasures Buddha would summon the Bodhisattva Wonderful Voice.

Summoned to come to see Mañjuśrī by Many Treasures Buddha, this extremely tall and handsome bodhisattva, accompanied by eighty thousand other bodhisattvas, came to the *sahā* world on a flying platform of seven treasures, passing through all the worlds to the East, where the ground quaked in the six ways, flowers rained down from heaven, drums sounded in the heavens, and so on. Arriving at Vulture Peak, he descended from the platform, approached Śākyamuni Buddha, worshiped at his feet, presented him with a magnificent necklace, delivered various greetings and felicitations from the Buddha of his own land, and expressed a desire to see Many Treasures Buddha. Many Treasures Buddha, in turn, praised him for coming. Then the bodhisattva known as Excellent Flower[14] wanted to know what the Bodhisattva Wonderful Voice had done to merit such great powers.

Śākyamuni Buddha explained that once upon a time there was a buddha named King of the Sound of Thunder in the Clouds[15] in whose realm the Bodhisattva Wonderful Voice lived. Because he offered many kinds of beautiful music and eighty-four thousand jeweled bowls to the Buddha King of the Sound of Thunder in the Clouds, Wonderful Voice was reborn in the land of the Buddha Pure Flower and given great, supernatural powers. Thus, in previous lives the Bodhisattva Wonderful Voice had taken many different forms—including those of women and girls, animals, gods and other heavenly beings, buddhas, and so on—in order to expound the Lotus Sutra. He protects all living beings by taking whatever form—*śrāvaka*, *pratyekabuddha*, bodhisattva, buddha—is appropriate for teaching the Lotus Sutra to them.

When the Buddha taught this chapter, the eighty-four thousand bodhisattvas who had come with Wonderful Voice and numerous other bodhisattvas of the *sahā* world won the ability to transform themselves into other living beings. Then the Bodhisattva Wonderful Voice made offerings to Śākyamuni Buddha and to the stupa of Many Treasures Buddha, and returned home to report to the Buddha Pure Flower, again causing those lands to quake in six ways, flowers to rain down on them, and music to sound from their heavens.

Here again is expressed the idea that the *sahā* world, despite its obvious shortcomings, is something special, and that this is related to the presence in it of Śākyamuni Buddha. There may be other reasons for this, but I suppose that the great size and magnificence and accomplishments of the Bodhisattva Wonderful Voice contribute to the enhancement of the *sahā* world and Śākyamuni, since he comes to the *sahā* world to pay tribute to Śākyamuni Buddha.

In fact, there seems to be an implication here, and in other instances where bodhisattvas come from outside the *sahā* world to visit Śākyamuni

Buddha, that the *sahā* world is especially important because it is a more appropriate, that is, more difficult, place for bodhisattva practice. One of the repeated themes of the sutra is that one can and should learn from difficulties. Salvation, in this world, is not a matter of freedom from suffering and distress, but rather an ongoing process of overcoming evil by helping others. In this sutra, for example, Śākyamuni Buddha simply thanks Devadatta, well known elsewhere as the personification of evil, for being his teacher, and predicts that Devadatta too will become a buddha. In this sense, this world offers many opportunities for one to enter the Buddha-way through bodhisattva practice.

It is especially significant that here, toward the end of the Lotus Sutra, the Bodhisattva Wonderful Voice, a master so to speak of contemplation and *samādhis*, expresses his desire to praise not only Śākyamuni Buddha and the Lotus Sutra, but also a number of bodhisattvas. This is summed up nicely when Wonderful Voice expresses his desire to see Many Treasures Buddha and Many Treasures Buddha responds by praising him for "coming here in order to make offerings to Śākyamuni Buddha, listen to the Lotus Sutra, and see Mañjuśrī and the others." In this way contemplation is subordinated to or made servant to hearing the Dharma and doing bodhisattva practice in the *sahā* world. In a related way, it is said here that Wonderful Voice has the *samādhi* called "Manifesting All Kinds of Bodies," the power to take on any kind of form "for the sake of living beings." He has taken on numerous bodies, whatever form will result in salvation, in order to teach and save others.

The One and the Many

The second chapter, often called the key to understanding the first half of the sutra, teaches in some detail the doctrine of *upāya*, certainly one of the central teachings of the Lotus Sutra, and perhaps the most important. The chapter begins with the Buddha emerging from contemplation to explain to Śāriputra why it is that the wisdom of buddhas is so difficult, so nearly impossible, to comprehend. It is basically because, in order to save various living beings, all the buddhas have made use of an enormous variety of methods and teaching devices appropriate to different situations. Thus the three ways—the way of the *śrāvaka*, the way of the *pratyekabuddha*, and the way of the bodhisattva—are teaching devices to enable different kinds of people to enter the one Buddha way. Śāriputra, speaking on behalf both of himself and others, is perplexed, still does not understand, and repeatedly pleads with the Buddha to explain further. The Buddha twice refuses on the grounds that it would just further confuse things, but finally agrees to expound the full Dharma.

At this point, some five thousand monks, nuns, and lay people in the congregation, because they are so arrogant that they think they have already attained the highest possible wisdom and have no more to learn, get up from their seats, bow to the Buddha, and leave. The Buddha does not try to stop them, remarking that the congregation had thus been cleared of little needed twigs and leaves.

The Buddha then explained again that all the buddhas of the past, all the buddhas of the various worlds of the present, and all of the buddhas of the future resort to various literary and teaching methods, including a great variety of sutras, as required by the situation, all for the sake of leading people to the one Buddha-way. Such teachings, he insists, are neither empty nor false. In particular, the teaching of nirvana was invented for people not yet ready for the Great Vehicle in order to lead them to enter the Way by which they will become buddhas themselves. Included is a long list of practices, such as bowing to a Buddha image or making any offering to or entering a stupa, by which people have entered the Way toward buddhahood. All of this is in accord with the Buddha's ancient vow to lead all living beings to enlightenment, i.e., to lead them to become buddhas themselves.

With this, the Buddha announces that since buddhas very seldom appear in the world, he will now teach the One Vehicle, but only to bodhisattvas.

In chapter 3, Śāriputra, the leading *śrāvaka* and not normally regarded as a bodhisattva, feels like dancing for joy because he realizes the truth of the Dharma, that he too is destined to become a buddha and in that sense is, in fact, a bodhisattva. The Buddha further reassures him that this is indeed the case and explains that he will become the Buddha Flower Light[16] and describes that time and Buddha-land. This, in turn, causes all others in the assembly to rejoice and say that, after a first turning of the wheel of the Dharma at Vārāṇasī, the Buddha has now turned the wheel of the greatest Dharma.

Śāriputra, though encouraged by this assurance, on behalf of those devotees who do not yet understand once again beseeches the Buddha to explain why, if there are not three paths, he has so often preached them in the past. And this time the Buddha does so by means of the famous parable of the burning house.

A rich man's house, now in a bad state of disrepair and out of which there is only one narrow gate, catches on fire with his many children playing inside. Though he compassionately calls to them from outside, urging them to leave the burning house, they are too absorbed in their play to heed these warnings. So he tells them that if they come out quickly, outside the gate they will find sheep carts, deer carts, and bullock carts which he will give them to play with. Since such rare playthings are just what they wanted, the children rush outside, to the great joy of the father, and ask him for the promised carts. Instead, because he is rich and has many of them, he gives each of the children a much larger and fancier cart. The children, having received something they never could have expected, are overjoyed.

Then the Buddha interprets this parable for Śāriputra, explaining that he, the Buddha, is much like the father in the parable, attempting to save his children from the fires of birth, old age, disease, death, grief, sorrow, suffering, and so on, from which they cannot escape because they have many attachments. So he offers them the three vehicles as a way to get them through the gate, but rewards them in the end with the Great Vehicle. Just as the father cannot be accused of deceiving his children, the Buddha cannot be accused of deception for using appropriate means.

Parables are analogies, but never perfect ones. This parable provides an image of four separate vehicles. But if we follow the teaching of the sutra as a whole, the One Buddha Way is not an alternative to other ways; it includes them. A limitation of this parable is that it suggests that the diverse ways (the lesser carts) can be replaced by the One Way (the special cart). But the overall teaching of the sutra makes it plain that there are many paths within the Great Path, which integrates them, i.e., they are together because they are within the One Way. To understand the lesser ways as somehow being replaced by the One Way would entail rejecting the whole idea of the bodhisattva-way, which the sutra clearly does not do. In fact, the whole latter part of the sutra is a kind of extolling of the bodhisattva-way. Also, in the story itself, in running out of the burning house the children are pursuing the *śrāvaka, pratyekabuddha,* and bodhisattva ways. In terms of their ability to save, the three ways are essentially equal. They all work.

The parable is interpreted as saying that the world is like a burning house. But the idea of escaping from the world is not what the sutra teaches. Elsewhere it makes clear that we are to work in the world to save others. The point here, I think, is more that we are like children at play, not paying enough attention to the environment around us. Perhaps it is not the whole world that is in flames, but our playgrounds, the private worlds we create out of our attachments and out of our complacency. Thus, leaving the house is not escaping from the world but leaving behind our play-world, our attachments and illusions, or some of them, in order to enter a real world.

It is also relevant to note here that the father tells the children they can have what they most desire. He cannot simply force them out; he appeals to something already in them, something that will later come to be known as the "buddha-nature."

Sometimes the Buddha has to use appropriate devices in order to lead others to realize their potential. But this does not mean that any trick will do. The Buddha's devices are always appropriate—i.e., designed for the benefit of the recipient. The father thought about what would be appropriate for these particular children in this particular situation.

Even the very fancy cart which the father gives to the children is, after all, only a cart, a vehicle. All teachings and practices should be understood as devices, as possible ways of helping people. They should never be taken as final truths. But the fact that they can be and are used to save people means that they are very important truths, that is, sufficient to save people.

Thus in the Lotus Sutra, teaching is not teaching, or at least it is not Dharma teaching, unless someone is taught. In the first chapter heavenly flowers fall on both the Buddha and his listeners, indicating the equality of both. That idea is extended here in chapter 3 with the idea that the Buddha preaches only to bodhisattvas. The point is that to preach the Dharma is to be a bodhisattva—and to hear the Dharma is to be, to that degree, a bodhisattva. This is because really hearing is to take it into one's life, thus to practice it, thus to be a bodhisattva. Thus, it can be said that the buddhas come into the world only to transform people into bodhisattvas.

What the sutra condemns is not other people, and not the lesser vehicles, but arrogance—especially the arrogance of thinking one has arrived at the truth, at some final goal. Rather, we are called upon by this sutra to be "lifetime beginners," people who know they have much to learn and always will. The five thousand who walk out of the assembly in the second chapter are said to be like twigs and leaves and not really needed, but in chapter 8 they too are to be told that they will become buddhas.

Thus śrāvakas are also bodhisattvas. In every paradise, or paradise-like Buddha-land, there are countless śrāvakas, indicating that the śrāvaka-way is not to be rejected or discarded, but relativized, seen within a large context, which is the encompassing Buddha-way. Many śrāvakas, of course, do not know that they are bodhisattvas, but they are nonetheless. The Buddha says to the disciple Kāśyapa at the end of chapter 5:

What you are practicing
Is the bodhisattva-way.
As you gradually practice and learn,
Every one of you should become a Buddha.[17]

Buddha-nature

While the term "buddha-nature"[18] does not appear anywhere in the Lotus Sutra, the teaching of what would later be called buddha-nature runs through it like a cord, defining one of its central affirmations. It is a clear aim throughout the sutra to persuade the reader that every living being, including and most importantly the reader, has within a potential to become enlightened, to become a buddha.

One's buddha-nature is developed by following the Buddha-way, doing what buddhas have always done, bodhisattva practice. Central to the Lotus Sutra is the idea that Śākyamuni Buddha himself is, first of all, a bodhisattva. He has been doing bodhisattva practice, helping and leading others, for innumerable *kalpas,* and will continue to do so into the boundless future.

> Because all the living have various natures, various desires, various activities, various ideas and ways of making distinctions, and because I wanted to lead them to put down roots of goodness, I have used a variety of explanations, parables, and words and preach various teachings. Thus I have never for a moment neglected the Buddha's work.
>
> Thus it is, since I became Buddha a very long time has passed, a lifetime of unquantifiable *asaṃkhyeya kalpas,* of forever existing and never entering extinction. Good children, the lifetime which I have acquired pursuing the bodhisattva-way is not even finished yet, but will be twice the number of *kalpas* already passed.[19]

While it is very important that the Buddha and the *śrāvakas* are also in some sense bodhisattvas, it is even more important that you and I are bodhisattvas—called to grow in bodhisattvahood by leading others to realize that potential in themselves. To develop one's buddha-nature is to do bodhisattva practice, to follow the role model of the bodhisattvas.

Bodhisattvas as Role Models

I think there can be no question but what many, at least, of the stories about bodhisattvas are there to provide role models for human beings. They play a role in the ever-present tension between what already is and what is yet to be. To the extent that we have even lifted a single finger to point to the truth, we are already bodhisattvas. But how much more so those who faithfully follow the Lotus Sutra, that is, devote their lives to bodhisattva practice. And to encourage us in that direction there are stories of wonderful bodhisattvas.

Yes, people do pray to Kwan-yin for help, and Kwan-yin takes on whatever form is needed to be helpful. But while that story may present the hope of divine blessing, it is there primarily to show us what we should be. If Kwan-yin has a thousand arms with a thousand different skills with which to help others, we too need to develop a thousand skills with which to help others. This is the chief significance of the inclusion of the Kwan-yin chapter in the Lotus Sutra. It is there to encourage bodhisattva practice.

Appropriate Means: What Does It Mean to Be a Bodhisattva?

What, then, does it mean to be a bodhisattva? Basically, in the Lotus Sutra it means using appropriate means to help others. And that, finally, for the Lotus Sutra, is what Buddhism itself is. It is an enormous variety of means developed to help people live more fulfilling lives, which can be understood as lives lived in the light of their interdependence. This is what many of its stories are about: someone—a father-figure/buddha, or friend/buddha, or guide/buddha—helping someone else gain more responsibility for their own lives.

> Even if you search in all directions,
> There are no other vehicles,
> Except the appropriate means preached by the Buddha.[20]

Thus, the notion of appropriate means is at once both a description of what Buddhism is, or what Buddhist practice primarily is, and a prescription for what our lives should become. The Lotus Sutra, accordingly, is a prescription of a medicine or religious method for us—and, therefore, at once both extremely imaginative and extremely practical.

It is in this sense that appropriate means is an ethical teaching, a teaching about how we should behave in order to contribute to the good. It is prescriptive not in the sense of a precept or commandment, but in the sense of urging us, for the sake both of our own salvation and that of others, to be intelligent, imaginative, even clever, in finding ways to be helpful.

The Embodied Dharma

The Dharma can be found embodied in concrete teachings, including actions which are instructive, just as the Buddha can be found embodied— in Śākyamuni, and in you and me.

Thus Lotus Sutra Buddhism is radically world-affirming. This *sahā* (suffering) world is Śākyamuni Buddha's world. It is in this world that he is a bodhisattva and encourages us to be bodhisattvas. This world is our home, and it is the home of Śākyamuni Buddha precisely because he is embodied, not only as the historical Buddha, but as the buddha-nature in all things.

Thus, ordinary things, including ourselves and our neighbors, are not primarily to be seen as empty, though they are; not primarily to be seen as phenomenal, though they are; not primarily to be seen as illusions, though in one sense they are; not primarily to be seen as evil even though they may be in part. It is in *dharmas* (things/ "conventional" existence) that the Dharma is. It is in transient, changing things that the Buddha is. All things are, therefore, to be treated with insight and compassion and respect.

Use of the notion of emptiness (*śūnya* or *śūnyatā*) is not much in the Lotus Sutra. Of course, all things are empty. But undue emphasis on emptiness can too easily become a kind of nihilism in which nothing matters. In the Lotus Sutra everything matters.

The Buddha works to save all beings. Even poor Bodhisattva Never Dis-respectful,[21] who goes around telling everyone that they are to become buddhas, though initially not very successful eventually "converted a multitude of a thousand, ten thousand, millions, enabling them to live in the state of supreme enlightenment." And he later became the Buddha Śākyamuni!

Future-oriented

While the Lotus Sutra provides plenty of reason to be grateful to the past and thus was perhaps all too compatible with East Asian ancestor vener-ation, it is more adamant about the importance of bodhisattva practice as our contribution to the future.

The sutra is full of stories in which someone, usually a stand-in for the Buddha, tries to make things better for others in some way—a guide conjures up a rest facility so that his travelers will be able to continue their journey, a father-physician tricks his sons into taking an antidote for poison, another father entices his children out of their burning house by offering them rewards, still another father devises a way to gradually develop a sense of responsibility in his son.

In every case, appropriate action is a matter of being genuinely helpful toward others by somehow enabling them to be more responsible for their own lives and subsequently for the lives of others. Though Bud-dhist practice in East Asia has been concerned largely with the dead, the bodhisattva-way is primarily about the future and about future possibili-ties in the present.

Conclusion

What one finds in the Lotus Sutra, then, is a kind of cosmological/soteriological pattern in which supernatural stories enhance the Lotus Sutra itself, enhancing Śākyamuni Buddha, enhancing the *sahā* world, in order to encourage bodhisattva practice in the world, which is the Buddha-way to salvation. Bringing the cosmos and a variety of supernatural elements into the stories enhances the status of the sutra. The preaching of this sutra is something that is attended to not only by human beings but by all sorts of beings in innumerable or perhaps even an infinite number of places. This elevation of the status of the sutra in turn enhances the status of Śākyamuni Buddha, as he is the one who preaches the sutra. Throughout the sutra, buddhas and bodhisattvas come to this world to praise Śākyamuni Buddha for preaching the Lotus Sutra, which is here equivalent to the Dharma. And, since Śākyamuni Buddha is the Buddha of the *sahā* world, its status rises as well. It is to the *sahā* world that buddhas and bodhisattvas from other times and worlds come to praise Śākyamuni Buddha. And this, of course, elevates the status and importance of those who live in the *sahā* world—especially those who follow the teachings of Śākyamuni Buddha, take on responsibility for their own lives, and become practitioners of the bodhisattva-way, thus entering the Buddha-way which is their salvation. It says in effect that the lives of every single one of us living in this *sahā* world have cosmic significance. We can thereby be encouraged to pursue our own salvation, our own ends as buddhas, by practicing the way of the bodhisattva, by helping others.

Thus, for the Lotus Sutra, the whole cosmos in a sense, the whole virtually infinite number of worlds, larger than we can count or even imagine, this whole vast cosmic structure is related to us, is in a sense dependent on our choices and decisions in everyday life, as we are dependent on it. In this, as well as in other ways, the Lotus Sutra is radically world-affirming. But far from seeing this world as already perfected in some mystical way or to be accepted as it is, it affirms the world with all of its suffering as real and therefore as a place of bodhisattva practice.

References

LaFleur, William R. *The Karma of World: Buddhism and the Literary Arts in* 1983 *Medieval Japan*. Berkeley: University of California Press.

Hirakawa, Akira. *A History of Indian Buddhism: From Śākyamuni to Early* 1990 *Mahā-yāna*. Translated and Edited by Paul Groner. Honolulu: University of Hawaii Press.

Kloetzli, Randy. *Buddhist Cosmology.* Delhi: Motilal Banarsidass, 1983.

Lai, Whalen. "Why the Lotus Sutra?—On the Historic Significance of 1987 Tendai." *Japanese Journal of Religious Studies.* 14/2–3: 83–99.

La Vallée Poussin, Louis de. *L'Abhidharmakośa de Vasubandu.* 6 vols. Brussels: Mélanges Louis de chinois et bouddhiques. English trans. Leo Puden, 1971 *Abhidharma-kośabhāsyam.* Berkeley: Asian Humanities Press, 1988–89.

Niwano, Nikkyō. *Buddhism for Today: A Modern Interpretation of the Lotus Sutra.* Tokyo: Kōsei Publishing Co., 1976.

———. *A Guide to the Threefold Lotus Sutra.* Translated and adapted by Eugene Langston. Tokyo: Kōsei Publishing Co., 1981.

Pye, Michael. *Skilful Means: A concept in Mahayana Buddhism.* London: Duckworth, 1978.

Shioiri, Ryōdō. "The Meaning of the Formation and Structure of the *Lotus Sutra*," in *The Lotus Sutra in Japanese Culture,* edited by George J. Tanabe, Jr., and Willa Jane Tanabe. Honolulu: University of Hawaii Press, 1989.

Sadakata, Akira. *Buddhist Cosmology: Philosophy and Origins.* Tokyo: Kōsei Publishing Co., 1997.

Tamura, Yoshirō. "The Ideas of the Lotus Sutra," in *The Lotus Sutra in Japanese Culture,* edited by George J. Tanabe, Jr., and Willa Jane Tanabe. Honolulu: University of Hawaii Press, 1989.

Williams, Paul. *Mahāyāna Buddhism: The Doctrinal Foundations.* London: Routledge, 1989.

Notes

1. Chapter 4 of *The Karma of Worlds*
2. *Mahā-Pratibhāna* 大樂説
3. *Prabhūtaratna* 多寶
4. Though it is correct that the Lotus Sutra, in contrast with the *Prajñāpāramitā Sutras,* has the Buddha as a focus of faith, Whalen Lai's contention (86) that this is at the expense of having the Dharma as a focus of faith is unfounded. The Lotus Sutra does emphasize the importance of the Buddha, but never as distinct from the Dharma which he practices and teaches. It is no accident that the Lotus Sutra calls itself "*saddharma,*" or that what was originally the first chapter of the sutra is about appropriate means, which is both a teaching and a practice. What the Lotus Sutra does, in a variety of ways, is to hold the Buddha and the Dharma together as inseparable. The Dharma has no existence apart from being practiced and preached. But similarly, the Buddha only is the Buddha because he practices and preaches the Dharma. Thus the Tendai tradition saw the sutra as having two halves, the key to the first being the chapter on appropriate means, the key to the second being the chapter on the everlasting life of the Buddha.
5. It is important that Śākyamuni Buddha assembles the many buddhas. He does not "recall [them] into himself" as Lai has it (94). Recalling them into himself would suggest that the Lotus Sutra joins the *Prajñāpāramitā* tradition

in affirming the superior reality of the one over the many, something which the Lotus Sutra assiduously avoids in order to advocate the mutual reality of the one and the many. Nor does the Lotus Sutra say, as Kloetzli claims, that "the Buddha creates myriads of Tathāgatas . . . throughout the ten regions by means of his power of *adhiṣṭhāna* or self-multiplication." Nor are these many bodhisattvas, as he says, "understood to be illusory" (65). Nowhere does the sutra say or suggest such a thing.

6. It has been claimed (cf. Lai, 95) that the presence of the two buddhas together is an indication of a collapse of the distinction of past, present, and future into a single timelessness. But this is far from the perspective of the Lotus Sutra itself, which throughout relies heavily on an assumption that time is important and real. Even the appearance of Many Treasures Buddha in this story would lose most of its significance if there were no important difference between past and present. Kloetzli makes the admittedly speculative suggestion that all Buddhist cosmology falls into one of two categories—"those which accept time as the fundamental cosmological reality" and those "which accept space as the fundamental cosmological reality." The latter, he says, belong to the Mahayana and have their philosophical basis in the emptiness of the *dharmas* . . . as well as in the emptiness of the self" (135–36). But Lotus Sutra cosmology clearly does not fall into either of these strands. For it, both space and time are cosmologically, metaphysically, and religiously real and important.

7. Niwano (1976), 148.

8. This feature of the Lotus Sutra has not been well recognized, especially in English language literature. But one place where it is clearly described is in LaFleur. He writes, for example, "within the sutra there is an unmistakable philosophical move opposite to that in Plato's *Republic*, a move to affirm the complete reality of the world of concrete phenomena in spite of the fact that they are impermanent;" 87.

9. *Viśiṣṭacāritra* 上行, *Anantacāritra* 無辺行, *Viśuddacāritra* 淨行, and *Supratiṣṭhitacārita* 安立行

10. Lai is quite correct, therefore, in claiming that "the mystery in the Lotus Sutra is never actually phrased in terms of Śākyamuni being some docetic shadow of some eternal Wisdom. The mystery is rather that somehow the historical Buddha preaching the sūtra at Vulture Peak is at once the eternal Buddha preaching eternally this eternal sūtra at this . . . sacred mountain in India." (94)

11. *Gadgadasvara* 妙音

12. Niwano (1976) says that the fact of scattering flowers over everybody, as well as the Buddha, is an indication that those who hear the teachings are to be honored as much as those who teach (265).

13. *Kamaladalavimalanakṣatrarājasaṃkusumitābhijña* 淨華宿王智. Hereafter, termed "Pure Flower."

14. *Padmaśrī* 華德

15. *Meghadundubhisvararāja* 雲雷音王

16. *Padmaprabha* 華光

17. Cf. Watson, 106. The translation is my own. The reference to Watson's translation is for reference or comparison.

18. 佛性
19. Cf. Watson, 226–27.
20. Cf. Watson, 71. This is why I think Pye is quite correct in insisting that "'Buddhism' as a specific religion identifiable in human history, is a skilful means" (5). Or "Almost anything in the whole range of Buddhist teaching and practice can be described as *fang-pien* or skilful means" (36).
21. *Sadāparibhūta* 常不輕

A Tale of Two Times:
Preaching in the Latter Age of the Dharma

Jamie Hubbard

I. INTRODUCTION

A. Linear and Cyclical Time

Long-held assumptions dictate a fundamental difference between Western and Eastern notions of time and history: whereas the former are linear and finite, giving human history a particularistic reality and even urgency, the latter are cyclical and infinite, rendering human history, and hence human action—ethical action—within that history inconsequential. The Judaic messianic tradition and its Christian refiguration as eschatological promise/fulfillment are taken as superb examples of the linear orientation, premised as they are on one-time events that erupt into human history and change it (or end it) forever, teleologically and inevitably moving to a final perfection. This eschatological promise of final perfection is contrasted with a cyclical Indic cosmogony that renders the notion of a final end to world history meaningless, lost to the greater significance of cosmic repetition. In this vision there is no final end to history, no world *telos*, and, therefore, ultimately no progress at all.

We should note that it is the fate of humanity *qua* society that is seen to be at stake here, with the Western, linear vision of time functioning as a theodicy that, based upon the belief in a perfected and final future, engenders as well the specifics of a forward-moving and historically specific soteriology through which it may be or must be effected. More importantly for our purposes, however, is the ethical importance attached to human action in such a "one chance only" view of history, an emphasis that is lacking in a transcendent or existential view of time. Thomas Altizer, for example, has been one of the strongest advocates of the need for a historical reading of Judeo–Christian eschatology, for in a spiritualization of the revolutionary impulse of that view of time "Jesus is detached from history and viewed as an 'existential' Word" and thereby "faith ceases to be rebellion and becomes, instead, either escape or submission," whereas "genuine Christian existence must be directed to a rebellious attack upon the 'realities' of profane existence, and it is to just this attack that Jesus' ethical message calls the disciple."[1]

B. The Eternal Return

The Indic approach, on the other hand, as Heinrich Zimmer characterized it decades ago, is exactly individual and transcendent rather than social and historical, leading to a "fundamentally skeptical attitude toward social progress." He writes,

> This viewpoint [of world history] from on high is not to be shared by the chorus of actors, by the gods and demons, engrossed by their roles, but is achieved through the supreme aloofness of the ascetic renunciation of Śiva, and through his attitude of spiritual indifference. To reach this perfection of his, is, among men, a privilege reserved for single, outstanding individuals, saints, ascetics, and yogin, who transcend the Māyā of phenomenal existence by their own efforts; but the world-process as a whole is not meant for a gradual progress toward perfection. It is the peculiar glory of Western idealism, with Christianity broadening into progressive humanitarianism, to have conceived such a goal, and to foster an ardent faith which embarks again and again, after each setback, on its quest for collective perfection.[2]

Perhaps the most well-known proponent of this contrast has been Mircea Eliade, whose comparative studies of cosmogony and eschatology led to his elaboration of the "Eternal Return," a primitive view of time and history characterized by cyclical accounts of the countless beginnings and ends of world time. To these "countless beginnings and ends" he contrasts an "innovation of the first importance," the Judeo-Christian doctrine of a singular beginning, linear progression, and a triumphal endtime which represents the forsaking of "the circular Time of the Eternal Return [to] become a linear and irreversible Time. . . [that] also represents the triumph of a Sacred History."[3]

On first reading one is tempted to simply identify the many nineteenth-century and early twentieth-century Eurocentric constructions that inform this understanding, including an evolutionary or teleological view of history/humankind with Christianity as the developmental high point, a historical positivism or realism, and a somewhat facile Weberesque view of the "East" as embodying an otherworldy form of asceticism that precludes finding meaning or value in worldly participation and social development. Still, and in spite of the many alternative readings that have been offered of this generalization (e.g., the myth of eternal return breeds equanimity and optimism not resignation and despair, Judeo-Christian eschatological thinking has also "suffered" a transcendental inversion, the postmodern West is likewise freed from historical positivism and linear history, etc.), by and large the general scheme of linear time and world-historical *eschaton* versus a cyclic cosmos and transcendent, ahistorical salvation, with its various nuances, has been upheld.[4] Altizer, for example, one of the few Christian theologians to give Buddhist eschatological thinking serious and sympathetic consideration, concluded that even the Zen negation of "Buddhist transcendentalism . . . [that] fully parallels the radical Christian negation of transcendence" represents "a form of 'apocalypticism' in which nothing actually happens, in which there is neither world- nor self-transformation."[5] Similarly, the Buddhologist Roger Corless has written that,

> History is an academic discipline that has developed in the western hemisphere. The western hemisphere has been strongly influenced by the Abrahamic traditions (Judaism, Christianity, and Islam) and their conception of time as something created by God in and through which God manifests himself. On this view, time is meaningful. It has a beginning and an end, and the end is a goal, so that there is development, a progressive achievement of the goal. . . . History as a secular discipline has many of the features of the Abrahamic tradition's view of time . . . the assumption that time is meaningful and that development is real does not seem to have been given up by even the most radical critics of the philosophy of history. Buddhism, on the other hand, sees things as changing over time, but it does not see things as becoming more meaningful as they change. Change, for Buddhism, is a primary characteristic of cyclic existence (samsara), and history is just a lot of change. All that we can say about history, Buddhistically, is that as time goes on we get more of it."[6]

Buddhism is thus likewise seen to be concerned with individual liberation to a timeless truth in which sequential time is overshadowed by cyclical recurrence and the historical past by the predicted future appearance of the Buddha Maitreya, whose appearance is yet so many billions of eons in the future as to render it meaningless in terms of current events. Thus Buddhists, following the cyclical model and lacking a world-historical *eschaton*, are seen to define the end of all things not as a consummation of world history but rather as individual liberation from it, as with Zimmer's Śiva. Winston King, for example, sums up this attitude in comparison with the "world-shattering events" of Western eschatologies, noting that Buddhism

> points to the individual-existential situation as being more truly eschatological, i.e. as having to do with the *truly* ultimate [Nibbāna] . . . . Nibbāna was essentially non- or super-historical, available limitedly in even the worst ages. . . . It has *essentially* nothing to do with historical events but is human being face to face with Ultimate Ineffable Being, a state that fully and finally transcends historical and cosmic event, and individual life and death.[7]

C. Specific Time in Buddhist History

Leaving aside for the moment the validity of the overall generalization as well as the prescriptive evaluation of Zimmer and Eliade, we can of course find any number of traditions, persons, and historiographies within Buddhism that would seem to present, at the very least, minor counterpoints of concern for specific and social historicism to the overall theme of recurrence and individual transcendence, if not a fully world-historical *eschaton*. The *Kālacakra* ("Wheel of Time"), Jien's *Gukanshō*, the dispensationalism inherent in the "Three Turnings of the Wheel," the various Buddhist national narratives, and other examples may be cited in this regard. Another such counterpoint is the Buddhist tradition of the decline and/or demise of its own teaching, a tradition that is often considered to parallel Judeo-Christian eschatological thinking. Indeed, the stories that relate these traditions, most of which are patently *ex post facto* descriptions of actual events cast in the form of prophecies, evince a strong concern for specific history, linear timetables, the location of historical figures within those linear chronologies (usually as well a means of locating oneself within the same chronologies), and, most conspicuously, a great concern for the temporal relationship between the present time and the past time of the historical Buddha.

Unlike the cosmic and cyclical schemes of multiple, coexisting Buddhas the teaching of the decline of the dharma is concerned neither with recurring events nor with grand visions of eternity but with the declining fortunes of the unique teachings of a singular historical figure brought about not by the inevitable and relentless progress of the cosmos but by specific *and avoidable* human failings, and, most interestingly, human fail-ings of the Buddhist community. Rather than being dwarfed by the greater significance or ultimacy of the cosmic cycle, the individual's loca-tion in temporal relation to Śākyamuni, the Buddha of our historical time, thus takes on a special urgency. Hence too successively distant ages were seen to require different "dispensations" of the dharma so as to accord with the times of the practitioner, an idea fundamental to the Pure Land tradition and one which renders temporal change important indeed. Concluding her overview of the many Buddhist traditions of its own de-cline, for example, Jan Nattier argued that, at least in these traditions, "the question of 'what time it is' has mattered, and at times has mattered very much, to a substantial proportion of Buddhist believers."[8] Indeed, Nattier has argued that the overall context of the decline tradition is analogous to that which inspired the prophets of the Hebrew Bible, whose sharp social and religious critiques surely comprise one of the great sources of socioethical thinking.

D. The Decline of the Dharma in East Asian Buddhism

In East Asia, however, a curious change occurs: on the one hand, the a-historical, cosmological, and cyclical traditions of innumerable Buddhas of the past, present, and future give rise to the imperative for historical change found in the messianic and apocalyptic Maitreya movements.[9] On the other hand, the more historical traditions of decline are refigured in such a way that the decline is understood to be existential rather than historical, and essential or constitutive of human experience rather than acquired and hence avoidable or alterable. Thus, perhaps representing the culmination of this trend, Shinran wrote in the thirteenth century that the decline of the dharma was a matter of existential reality for living be-ings in the age of the true dharma as well as the age of decline, and, more recently, the Kyoto School philosopher Hajime Tanabe (1885–1962) dis-cussed the decline of the dharma in terms of a "constitutive evil" of hu-manity; both require the saving power of the *dharmakāya*, a timeless and transcendent truth represented, notably, by the Buddha of Immeasurable Life. Although this shift perhaps represents a return to what Winston King referred to as the "more truly eschatological" concern for the tran-scendence of the "individual-existential situation," a return to the "true" emphasis of the Buddhist tradition (similar to Zimmer's transcendent view of the Hindu tradition), it can also be seen as analogous to the tran-scendental inversion that Altizer has criticized in Christian eschatologi-cal thinking. If this is indeed the case, does this also validate the view of

Buddhism as, in the end, unconcerned with linear time and world-historical eschatologies, and, by extension, contributing to that oft-noted lack of social and ethical consciousness in the Buddhist, especially East Asian Buddhist, traditions? And where does the Lotus Sutra, conspicuous in its emphasis on the cosmic and infinite yet also giving rise to some of the more socially activist Buddhist traditions, fit into this scheme? I believe that the answer to this question lies in its equal emphasis on the decline of the teachings of the historical Buddha, an emphasis expressed as an imperative to preserve and spread those teachings, in short, the imperative to preach, an important but little-studied aspect of the Buddhist tradition.[10] In order to better understand these issues, let me briefly outline the origins of the decline tradition before turning to the way in which this tradition was incorporated into the Lotus Sutra.

II. THE TRUE DHARMA AND ITS DECLINE

A. Not the Transcendent Truth That Disappears

At many points within the Buddhist tradition we find a dynamic tension between the rhetoric of an unbounded, atemporal truth *(dharmatā)*, and the representation of that truth as the teachings of a historical person, and it is within the latter, that is, within Buddh-*ism*, the vicissitudes of the teachings in the world, that the tradition of the true dharma *(saddharma)* and its decline takes shape. Thus we should note from the very beginning that it was never the dharma conceived as the causal uniformity of all things *(dhammatā)* that was believed to decline or disappear. As is well known, that will remain the same whether the tathāgatas were to arise or not to arise.[11] Hui-yüan (523–92), for example, lamenting the lot of the Buddhist faith at the hands of Emperor Wu, states,

> This is the fate of our time . . . it is truly lamentable that we are unable to attend [the Buddha-dharma] at this time, but the truth of the Dharma cannot be vanquished! I ask that you virtuous ones please understand this and not be overly grieved.[12]

This is more important than has usually been recognized, for it directs our attention to the lived tradition of the teachings as the locus of the timeless, ahistorical truths that more often are the focus of doctrinal study. That is to say, rather than the essential truth of the dharma per se, it highlights the importance of the teachings, and the spirited rivalry over who maintains the correct teachings is at the core of both the production of the decline traditions as well as their later sectarian use.

B. Origins of *Saddharma*

1. *Nikāya* Buddhism

All religions that stem from the vision, charisma, and leadership authority of a historical founder face a turning point after he or she passes away and is no longer directly available to determine matters of doctrine and practice among the followers. Buddhism was no exception to this rule, particularly in light of the fact that Śākyamuni refused to appoint a successor, declaring instead that the dharma was to guide the community after his passing. Thus the years following Śākyamuni's passing saw any number of occasions on which questions of interpretation of the dharma arose, quickly leading to codified versions of institutional rules and teachings, and the tradition also preserves stories of the various councils and other means whereby the community sought to preserve those authoritative teachings. It is in this context of the time following the historical Buddha, then, that the question of preservation and interpretation becomes important, and it was quickly seen that, all other things considered, conservative literalism offered a formidable means of accurate preservation and propagation of the dharma. By "conservative literalism" I am referring to a resistance to change any portion of the accepted canon, including, as we shall see, the language and literary forms, as well as the content.

In addition to councils and other forms of canon-creation, one of the means whereby the early Buddhist community attempted to secure this conservative literalism was through the rhetoric of the decline or even disappearance of the *saddhamma* (Skt. *saddharma*), the "true dhamma" or the "good dhamma." Although *saddhamma* can simply mean a good or auspicious thing (as, for example, in the "seven *saddhamma*" of faith, shame, appreciation of consequence, learning the teachings, vigor, mindfulness, and wisdom), in the context of the decline tradition throughout the Pali literature it is used to indicate the teachings that must be safeguarded and which will be lost without due diligence. In other words, *saddhamma* is used to refer to the authoritative teachings (*pariyatti*) in contradistinction to misinterpretations, false attributions, misquotes, and other deviations from the proper and accurate transmission of the teaching, and it was argued that lack of attention to this proper transmission of the *saddhamma* would lead to its disappearance.

The *Aṅguttara-Nikāya*, for example, tells us that we must guard not only against those who would fabricate the word of the Buddha (*buddhavacana*) from whole cloth, that is, those who would claim, "as utterances of the Tathāgata, what he never said or uttered, and he who denies what was said or uttered by the Tathāgata," but also against the one "who proclaims as already explained a discourse which needs explanation (*neyyattha*), and he who proclaims as needing explanation a discourse already explained (*nītattha*)."[13] Another *sutta* from the *Aṅguttara-Nikāya* that shows a concern for even literal orthodoxy warns against "the wrong expression of the letter (of the text) and wrong interpretation of the meaning of it," which would lead to the "confusion and disappearance" of the true dhamma, for "if the letter be wrongly expressed, the interpretation of the meaning is also wrong." On the other hand, "if the letter be rightly expressed, the interpretation of the meaning is also right" which leads to the "establishment, the non-confusion, to the non-disappearance of true Dhamma."[14] Here we are clearly (and quite "literally") told that it is the *letter of the law* and not the spirit ("interpretation of the meaning") that is of central importance in the preservation of the dhamma.[15] The section on the confounding of the *saddhamma* from the *Aṅguttara-Nikāya* similarly warns that a careless attitude towards the hearing, mastering, contemplating, analyzing, and practicing the dhamma would lead to its disappearance.[16] The order—hearing and mastering first and undertaking practice last—clearly indicates the priority of orthodoxy relative to orthopraxy. It is somewhat ironic, of course, that, as in the writings of the New Testament, the concern for accurate transmission of the true teachings actually indicates the existence of differing interpretations, differing visions, and no doubt differing transmissions. Although there are other traditions, doctrinal deviation and dissension within the Sangha is by far the most conspicuous threat to the preservation of the *saddhamma* in the early texts; no doubt the teachings of the emerging Mahayana were among those new teachings and interpretations targeted by the rhetoric of decline.

2. Mahayana

Just as the *nikāya* rhetoric of the decline of the dharma was really an exhortation to preserve the dharma and never meant to indicate that the teachings were actually gone, the Mahayana appropriation of that rhetoric remains fundamentally a rhetoric of doctrinal legitimacy; it functions not, however, by arguing that the decline can be staved off by hewing to a conservative orthodoxy but rather by claiming that its own doctrines are not only superior in truth value but uniquely efficacious in the "latter days" (*paścimakāla*) after the passing of the Buddha.[17] The first step to the eventual use of the decline motif as legitimizing a new "dispensation" of the dharma was the Mahayana transformation of the terms of its deployment. That is, while the Mahayana continued the strategy of claiming a literal form of orthodoxy (*buddhavacana*) for their traditions and texts (for example, the story of Nāgārjuna's recovery of the *Perfection of Wisdom* texts), they also refigured the decline motif in such a way as to change its meaning from a time when the dharma would be gone or supplanted by false dharma to a time when its own superior dharma would not merely still be available, but, as proven precisely by its persistence, tested and certified in its superiority.

No doubt aware that the most common chronologies of decline described the time of their own activity and likely sensitive as well to the charge of creating "new" or "counterfeit" dharma, we find that one of the most prominent uses of the decline motif in the Mahayana is as a "proof metaphor" to stylistically indicate its own superior truth value in such a time. Self-conscious in its reaction to the conservative *nikāya* attempt to preserve the tradition, this strain is both highly specific ("*this* text is the *saddharma* and will be *uniquely* efficacious in such troubled times") at the same time it claims the high ground of the universal, hearkening more to the truth per se or *dharmatā* than its historical encapsulation; like the truth-body (*dharmakāya*) of the Buddha himself, the word of the Buddha is ever available to those who will but listen. The *Vajracchedikā*, for example, in speaking of "the future time, in the latter age, in the latter period, in the latter five hundred years, when the True Dharma is in the process of decay"[18] exhibits little concern with such a period as a historical time of declining capacity: "Even at that time, Subhūti, there will be bodhisattvas who are gifted with good conduct, gifted with virtuous qualities, gifted with wisdom, and who, when these words of the Sutra are being taught, will understand their truth."[19] The *Vajracchedikā* speaks of the "latter five hundred years, when the True Dharma is in the process of decay" only as an opportunity to contrast its own continued efficacy. It thereby coopted the *topoi* of the *nikāya* rhetoric, asserting its superiority based not simply on a claim to represent literal and historical orthodoxy (*buddhavacana*) but also on truth value and hence relevance even in a time of decay, a time for which the "Hinayana" had already prophesied their own lack of efficacy.[20]

III. TRANSCENDENT AND PARTICULAR TIME IN THE LOTUS

A. The Immeasurable Duration of the True Dharma

The functional origins of the term *saddhamma* were not lost on the redactors of the *Saddharmapuṇḍarīkasūtra*, a text which extols the most inclusive ideal of the Buddhist tradition at the same time that it is passionate in asserting its own status as the "true dharma" (*saddharma*) and "sole vehicle" (*ekayāna*). Similarly, the Lotus combines a distinctly cosmic and cyclical view of the universe with the same sort of specific and apologetic perspective found in the *Vajracchedikā*. The former outlook, that is, the perspective of the eternal return, is found in the many references to twenty minor *kalpas* of the true dharma followed by twenty intermediate *kalpas* of the semblance dharma, or forty *kalpas* of each, or thirty-two *kalpas* of each, etc. and, of course, in the central teaching of the immeasurable lifetime of the Buddha.[21]

> O Mahāsthāmaprāpta, the life-span of the Buddha Bhīṣmagarjita-svararāja was as kalpas equal to forty myriads of *koṭis* of *nayutas* of sands of the Ganges River. The true Dharma abided for kalpas equal to the number of particles in Jambudvīpa. The derivative Dharma abided for kalpas equal to the number of particles in the four continents. After having benefited the sentient beings, the Buddha entered *parinirvāṇa*. After the extinction of the true and derivative Dharmas, there appeared in this land another Buddha who was also called Bhīṣmagarjitasvararāja. . . . In this way there appeared two myriads of *koṭis* of Buddhas one after another, all of whom had the same name.[22]

Although not in the same place or even in the same context as its references to the two periods of the true dharma and the semblance dharma, like the *Vajracchedikā* the Lotus also speaks of the time "after the Tathāgata's final nirvana, in the latter age, the latter period, the latter five-hundred years, when the true dharma is in decay."[23] The Chinese translation by Kumārajīva even uses the term "*mo-fa*" or "final dharma," possibly the first occurrence of the term.[24]

Given the use of the two periods of the dharma and the presence of decline motif, many are tempted to see the Lotus Sutra as a primary source for the tripartite schema of decline that became so influential in Japan (that is, the three periods of the true dharma, semblance dharma, and final dharma). Although, as discussed below, I do think that it contributed greatly to the "hermeneutics of orthodoxy" that are so much a part of the decline traditions, we need to be very careful in assessing its contributions to the chronological orderings of decline. That is, its usage of the two periods of the dharma is more likely drawing on the cosmological traditions than the *topos* of decline, which explains why the settings in which the periods of the true dharma and the semblance dharma appear are so exaggerated (myriads of millions of *kalpas, kalpas* equal to the number of atoms in the continent of Jambudvīpa, etc.). Thus too the cyclical nature of these descriptions, in which, after the two periods of a Buddha's dharma, a Buddha of the same name will appear, as many as "twenty hundred thousand myriads of *koṭis* of Buddhas," of the same name.[25] Finally, and most telling, none of these cyclical descriptions are of the duration of the historical Buddha's dharma, whereas the instances of the decline motif are typically represented as the decline of Śākyamu-ni's dharma.[26]

Further, although the Lotus presents a clear two-period scheme in which the semblance dharma follows and is, at least chronologically, distinct from the period of *saddharma*, which is also chronologically distinct from the lifetime of the various tathāgatas (which, interestingly, adds up to "three periods of the dharma"), there is no sense here of a qualitative difference between the periods. The Lotus Sutra does not speak of the two periods in terms of decay or sequential loss of capacity; rather, as Nattier has shown, this use of the semblance dharma indicates precisely that period after the death of the Buddha when his teachings *were* available, hence "it refers to the real and ongoing presence of the *saddharma*."[27] But even this is not the real point of this *topos*: the two periods of the dharma as described in the Lotus Sutra are rather related to the grand cosmic drama of the Buddha's immeasurable lifetime, the basic theme of the sutra, and not the theme of decline.[28] In a manner typical of Indian rhetorical style, the Lotus bolsters this drama with incomprehensible numbers (such as "immeasurable, innumerable thousands of myriads of millions of *kalpas*"). Given that the periods of the true dharma and the semblance dharma (*saddharmapratirūpaka*) are not used in the same part of the text or same context with the "latter five hundred years" when the True Dharma is in decay (*saddharma-vipralopa*), it is not unreasonable to assume that we have two entirely different strands of the tradition coming together in the same text. Aside from the textual evidence that the two represent different *topoi*, there is also a rather glaring doctrinal inconsistency in the notion of a period of the destruction of the dharma following the Buddha's extinction or final nirvana, given the Lotus Sutra's insistence that his final nirvana was but a fiction and his lifetime in fact is immeasurable. We can thus conclude that the trope of the two periods represents the eternal return or the transcendent view, whereas the decline motif represents a concern for linear and unique history. What, then, is the practical thrust of that concern for linear and specific history?

B. The Destruction of the True Dharma: *Saddharma-vipralopa*

Although the Lotus never became a major source in the early Chinese development of the decline tradition, it *is* filled with reference to decay, the "latter five hundred years," and the like in the context of doctrinal persecution, concern for teaching and conversion, and a polemic assertiveness about its own message, and it is in this that I believe we can see the significance of its use of the decline motif. Of course, the most obvious example of this is the coopting of *saddharma* for the title of the text itself.[29]

That is, much like the *Vajracchedikā*, the Lotus uses the theme of the decline not in order to wail and bemoan the sad fate of the true dharma but
rather as an opportunity to assert the importance of the *hearkening* to true
dharma (albeit redefined), particularly in such a period. Thus, according
to the text, due to the power of the sutra itself there will still be those who
will gain innumerable merits and enter into nirvana if they but receive,
hold, preserve, and transmit it.[30] In this way, and as with the earlier traditions, the rhetoric of decline is deployed in the Lotus not to condemn
moral decay but rather to assert its own importance. Indeed, if we examine the specific instances in which this trope occurs, we find that virtually
all references that make use of the terms of the decline tradition (i.e., the
"age of decay," "evil age," "five defilements," "latter five hundred years,"
"latter age after Śākyamuni's *parinirvāṇa*," and the like) are accompanied
by some sort of declaration of the continued efficacy of the Lotus, a vow
to spread and teach it even in such a period, the abuse that its defenders
can expect to face in such a period, the merit that will accrue from teaching it, etc.[31] Broadly speaking this rhetorical context can be divided into
three types, though there is considerable overlap among them: 1) the
merit of preserving the Lotus Sutra in the latter age and the virtues of
those who do so; 2) how to preach the Lotus Sutra in the latter age; and
3) the faults of those who reject the Lotus Sutra in the latter age, typically
mixed with the merits of accepting it.[32] It is also interesting that those
portions of the Lotus generally thought to be the earliest (i.e., chapters
2–9) contain no references to the decline, which predominate in the middle layer, suggesting that the decline trope was added during the process
of expansion as a means of encouraging those who had come under fire
for preaching the original text. This fits in well with my thesis that the
central message of the decline trope is the preaching of the dharma, for
as Ryōdō Shioiri notes, the dominant theme of the middle layer of the
Lotus (where we find the majority of references to the decline) is to
"emphasize the command to propagate the Lotus Sutra in society as
opposed to the predictions given in [the earlier chapters of] the future
attainment of buddhahood by the disciples."[33] Let us look briefly at some
examples of each category, and then consider the effect that this had on
Nichiren, perhaps the most famous disciple of the Lotus Sutra and one
who certainly took seriously its message of decline and the attendant
need to preach its truth.

1. Virtues of preserving the *saddharma* in the latter, evil age[34]

> Know that anyone who preserves the Lotus Sutra
> Is an ambassador of the Buddha
> Who feels compassion for sentient beings.

Those who preserve the Lotus Sutra
Were born here in this world,
Withholding themselves from the pure land
Out of their compassion for sentient beings.
Know that such people are born
Where and when they will.
They are born in this evil age
To extensively expound the highest Dharma.
Such expounders of the Dharma should be revered
With offerings of divine flowers, perfumes,
Heavenly jeweled clothing and exquisite celestial jewels.
Those who preserve the sutra
In the evil age after my *parinirvāṇa*,
Should be paid homage with palms pressed together
Just as one pays homage to the Bhagavat.[35]

Bhagavat! If there are those who preserve this sutra in the corrupt and evil age of the latter five hundred years, I will protect them and rid them of their heavy cares, make them attain happiness and allow no one to strike at them through their weaknesses.[36]

2. Teaching the *saddharma* in the latter age[37]

After my passing into *parinirvāṇa*, during the latter five-hundred years, you must spread it far and wide on the Jambudvīpa Continent and not allow it to be destroyed . . . you should protect this sutra with your transcendent power. Why is this? Because this sutra is good medicine for the ills of the people on this Jambudvīpa Continent.[38]

3. Rejecting the *saddharma* in the latter age[39]

If in the latter age there is anyone
Who preserves this sutra,
I will dispatch him to the world of humans
To carry out the Tathāgata's task.
If throughout one entire kalpa
There is anyone with erring thoughts
Who always disparages the Buddha
With an angry complexion, the consequences of
His grave errors will be incalculable.
If there is anyone who speaks
A hostile word even for an instant
About those who recite and preserve this Lotus Sutra,
His fault will be even greater.[40]

In the evil age of the corrupt kalpa
There are many fearful things.
People possessed by evil spirits
Will scorn and slander us.
But we shall wear the armor of patience
Because we trust and revere the Buddha;
And we will persevere under these difficulties
In order to teach the sutra.[41]

Clearly, then, the primary use of the decline motif in the Lotus Sutra is to argue for the need to preserve and spread its message, that is, an exhortation to the preacher of the Lotus. The evil, latter age is not, of course, the only context in which upholding and teaching the Lotus Sutra is extolled—indeed, this is one of the major themes of the scripture. As I have earlier argued, "This reminds us that, together with Christianity and Islam, Buddhism is a missionary religion, and the role of the preacher as missionary [dharmabhāṇaka] is indeed forcefully argued throughout the Lotus Sutra. Thus, too, we should remember that . . . the primary function of upāya is discovered in the preaching activity of the bodhisattvas," that is to say, offering the gift of the dharma.[42] Given the earlier use of the decline motif to argue for a more conservative orthodoxy, its redeployment to justify the new dispensation of the Lotus must represent a deliberate strategy of accommodation.

IV. THE EVANGELIST NICHIREN

Nichiren was one who clearly embraced the import of the Lotus Sutra's combination of the rhetoric of decline with the mission and virtue of preaching the true dharma. That is, although the Lotus Sutra, as with Mahayana scriptures in general, may have appropriated the tradition of the decline in order to assert its own orthodoxy or truth value in such an age, for those like Nichiren who came to believe that they were actually living in the predicted age of the final dharma (as the latter age had come to be understood, Chin. mo-fa, Jpn. mappō), the issue was more pressing, and on this issue the Lotus is forceful: during the period of the final dharma the practical imperative is none other than that of the dharmabhāṇaka, the preacher of the dharma, specifically the preacher of the true dharma of the Lotus Sutra. For Nichiren, the logic was easy: the supreme practice of the Mahayana generally is that of the bodhisattva, and the supreme gift of the bodhisattva is the gift of the teachings, the

gift of the dharma. By Nichiren's time, however, there were many interpretations of the dharma contending for the place of *saddharma*. As Jacqueline Stone has put it, "Nichiren's search for a teaching valid in the
mappō era stemmed from a desire for objective truth. Contention among
rival Buddhist sects—exemplifying the *Ta-chi-ching's* prediction of an age
when 'quarrels and disputes will arise among the adherents to my teachings' . . . awoke in him a resolve to discover which, among the so-called
'eighty-thousand teachings,' represented the Buddha's true intention and
could benefit people in the last age. . . . Eventually he concluded that the
Lotus Sutra, and none other, represented the pinnacle of Śākyamuni's
teachings."[43]

Envisioning himself to be doing the work of Viśiṣṭacārita, leader of the
bodhisattvas that spring up from the earth to take charge of "extensively
teaching" the Lotus after Śākyamuni's final nirvana, Nichiren took per-
sonally the commission to propagate the Lotus during the latter days of
the dharma. In view of the historical specificity of the decline tradition, it
is also significant that Nichiren understood that it was because the bodhisattvas from under the earth had been personal disciples of Śākyamuni
in the past that he entrusted the propagation of the Lotus to them in the
latter age and turned down the request of the numerous other bodhisattvas.[44] So too his stress on the historical Buddha as the refuge for this
age rather than Amida or other cosmic Buddhas. His sense of the importance of the specific, linear time in the development of Buddhism is also
clearly seen in the *Senji Shō*, "The Selection on Time," in which he nar-
rates the history of Buddhism from Śākyamuni to his own day in the
context of the decline of the dharma. As he writes in the opening sentence, "One who wishes to study the teachings of Buddhism must first
learn to understand the time."[45] His conclusion, of course, is that in the
latter age of the final dharma the propagation of the Lotus Sutra was the
supreme path, albeit a difficult path. Nonetheless, and for Nichiren this
was the important message of the Lotus, to give the gift of the dharma
and establish sentient beings in truth is the ethical imperative at the core
of the true dharma, even if it means abuse and vilification:

> I am fully aware that if I do not speak out, I will be lacking in com-
> passion. I have considered which course to take in the light of the
> teachings of the Lotus and Nirvana sutras. If I remain silent, I may
> escape harm in this lifetime, but in my next life I will most certainly
> fall into the hell of incessant suffering. If I speak out, I am fully
> aware that I will have to contend with the three obstacles and the
> four devils. But of these two courses, surely the latter is the one to

choose. . . . Persons like myself who are of paltry strength might still be able to lift Mount Sumeru and toss it about; persons like myself who are lacking in spiritual powers might still shoulder a load of dry grass and yet remain unburned in the fire at the end of the kalpa of decline; and persons like myself who are without wisdom might still read and memorize as many sutras as there are sands in the Ganges. But such acts are not difficult, we are told, when compared to the difficulty of embracing even one phrase or verse of the Lotus Sutra in the Latter Day of the Law. Nevertheless, I vowed to summon up a powerful and unconquerable desire for the salvation of all beings, and never to falter in my efforts.[46]

For Nichiren, the advent of the latter age or the *final* dharma meant none other than a redoubled effort to disseminate the *true* dharma, and he saw this mission precisely as the ethic of the bodhisattva, the mandate to save all beings through the gift of the truth. In this, I believe, he was accurately reflecting the historical specificity of the decline motif, both in its original form as a polemic of orthodoxy and in the manner that it was employed within the Lotus Sutra as an injunction to preach the true dharma.

V. Conclusion

I have discussed the decline of the dharma in the Lotus Sutra as intimately related to what I consider to be one of the main themes of the Lotus, the propagation of the dharma and the missionary activity of the preacher of the dharma, the *dharmabhāṇaka*. I have also tried to give a more general context for this discussion by contrasting a linear sense of time fraught with unique historical meaning with a more cosmic cycle of eternally recurring events, and have touched briefly on the ethical import typically ascribed to each. In this context the decline of the dharma is seen to be an example of a linear "eschatology" in which great concern is given to the specific history of Śākyamuni's teachings and their continued existence in the world. In neither the early use of this tradition nor in its later Mahayana incarnation was it ever taught that the dharma was really gone, rather the decline was always used to exhort fidelity to a particular version of the true dharma. This theme is well represented in the Lotus Sutra, in which virtually every instance of the decline motif is accompanied by a reference to the true dharma, the merits of upholding and propagating it, how to teach it, or the dangers of ignoring or slandering it. In these instances the true dharma is not understood as transcendent truth but rather the specific truth of the Lotus Sutra.[47] The cosmic, cyclical scheme of numerous Buddhas existing in numerous worlds, appearing in countless and eternal succession, is also found in the Lotus, replete with reference to different periods of their dharma, and is thus often seen as related to the decline of the dharma, especially in the form of the three periods of the dharma (true, semblance, and final). However, the cyclical trope in which the two periods appear in the Lotus has been shown to be thematically and textually unrelated to the linear progression of the decline motif.

I have also suggested that Nichiren read the decline theme of the Lotus not in terms of this theme of eternal return, taking the point of the rhetoric of the decline of the dharma to be specific and historical, to be in fact an exhortation to the accurate preservation and transmission of the true dharma, and to that end he worked tirelessly throughout his life. Nichiren was, no doubt, an evangelist: a person whose profound encounter with the message of truth in the Lotus Sutra converted him to a messenger seeking to bring the good news to all humanity. This tradition, then, is one in which a transcendent approach to time is thoroughly mediated by a concern for unique and specific history and individuals. More generally we could perhaps also say that it is this more linear sense of time, closely tied to the declining fortunes of the teachings of a particular human being and the difficulties that await those who would disseminate his teachings, that inspired Nichiren to make the link between the troubles of the predicted last times, his evangelical mission to establish the true teachings, and the peace and prosperity of the nation (*risshō ankoku* 立正安國). That is to say that for Nichiren the ethical imperative of the bodhisattva in the latter age, the imperative to preach the true dharma, was linked to social concord as well. The vicissitudes of Nichiren's attempts to establish a peaceful nation are well known, as is the fact that in the early twenty-first century it is mostly Nichiren-based movements that lead Japanese Buddhist organizations in any sort of social activism and international peace activities—groups such as Risshō Kōsei-kai, Nipponzan Myōhō-ji, and Sōka Gakkai.[48] Finally, then, we could ask if this drive to social activism on the part of contemporary Nichiren-derived movements is in any part due to the fact that Nichiren himself drew his evangelical inspiration from the Lotus Sutra's sense of linear time and distance from the founder rather than the other sense of time equally found in the Lotus Sutra, a cosmic and cyclical sense of time, a time of "eternal return"? The answer to this question, however, must await another time.

Selected Bibliography

Altizer, Thomas. *Oriental Mysticism and Biblical Eschatology*. Philadelphia: The Westminster Press, 1961.

————. "Response to Winston L. King's 'Zen and the Death of God'" in *The Theology of Altizer: Critique and Response*. Philadelphia: The Westminster Press, 1970.

Corless, Roger. *The Vision of Buddhism*. New York: Paragon House, 1989.

Davidson, Ron. "Standards of Scriptural Authenticity" in Robert Buswell, *Chinese Buddhist Apocrypha*. Honolulu: University of Hawaii Press, 1990.

Eliade, Mircea. *Myth and Reality*. New York: Harper Torchbooks, 1963.

Hare, E. M., trans. *The Book of the Gradual Sayings (Aṅguttara-Nikāya)*, vol. III. London: Luzac & Company, 1952.

Hubbard, Jamie. "Buddhist-Buddhist Dialogue? The *Lotus Sutra* and the Polemic of Accommodation" in *Buddhist-Christian Studies* 15, 1995.

King, Winston. "Eschatology: Christian and Buddhist." *Religion* 16, 1986.

Kisala, Robert. "Japanese New Religions and the Concept of Peace" in *Research in the Social Scientific Study of Religion* 7, 1996.

Kubo, Tsugunari and Akira Yuyama, trans. *The Lotus Sutra*. Berkeley: The Numata Center for Buddhist Translation and Research, 1993.

Nattier, Jan. *Once Upon a Future Time*. Berkeley: Asian Humanities Press, 1991.

O'Leary, Stephen D. *Arguing the Apocalypse: A Theory of Millenial Rhetoric*. Oxford: Oxford University Press, 1994.

Stone, Jacqueline. "Seeking Enlightenment in the Last Age" in *The Eastern Buddhist* (New Series), vol. XVIII, no. 2, 1985.

Watson, Burton, et. al. *Selected Writings of Nichiren*. New York: Columbia University Press, 1990.

Woodward, F. L. trans. *The Book of the Kindred Sayings*, 5 vols. London: The Pali Text Society reprint, 1973.

Woodward F. L. trans. *The Book of the Gradual Sayings (Aṅguttara-Nikāya)*, vol. I. London: Luzac & Company, 1951.

Wogihara, U and Tsuchida C., eds. *Saddharmapuṇḍarīka-sūtra*. Tokyo: Sankibō Book Store, 1958.

Zimmer, Heinrich R. "The Hindu View of World History According to the Purāṇas" in *The Review of Religion*, vol. VI, no. 3 (March 1942), 1942.

Notes

1. Altizer 1961: 102, 110–11
2. Zimmer: 168
3. Eliade: 64–65
4. King: 177, 181; O'Leary: 29–30
5. Altizer 1970: 229–30
6. Corless: xix

7. King: 182

8. Nattier: 141

9. See, for example, Daniel L. Overmeyer, *Folk Buddhist Religion: Dissenting Sects in Late Traditional China* (Cambridge, MA: Harvard University Press, 1976) and Alan Sponberg and Helen Hardacre, eds. *Maitreya, The Future Buddha* (Cambridge, England: Cambridge University Press).

10. Recent articles that deal with this topic include Mahinda Deegalle, "Buddhist preaching and Sinhala Religious Rhetoric: Medieval Buddhist Methods to Popularize Theravāda" in *Numen*, vol. 44 (1997) and Andrew Olendzki, "Mission and Dialogue: A Paradox?" in *Buddhist-Christian Studies*, vol. 17 (1997).

11. Woodward 1973, vol. 2, Part II: 21

12. T #2060, 50.490c

13. Woodward 1973, vol. 1: 54. Cf. T #2, 592c–593a. Ron Davidson, in "Standards of Scriptural Authenticity" (*Chinese Buddhist Apocrypha* [Honolulu: University of Hawaii Press, 1990], 294–97), notes that the complementary attitude is that the dharma is more than the literal words of Śākyamuni Buddha, and encompasses all that spoken from the vantage point of the truth per se (*dharmatā*) or that conduces to its realization, including the teaching of previous Buddhas as well as his enlightened disciples. Still, the tendency has been to try to validate teaching by somehow or another giving it the legitimacy of the more literal meaning of Buddhavacana (McDermott, "Scripture as the Word of the Buddha," *Numen*, 31 [July 1984], 30–31; see also Davidson, 303–05).

14. Woodward 1951, vol. 1: 53

15. The countervailing attitude is found in the Buddha's well-known injunction *against* formalizing the language of the dharma, preferring instead, for example, regional dialects (Davidson: 292–93).

16. Hare, vol. III: 132. See also Hare: 180–81, 239–40; Woodward 1951, vol. IV: 49–50.

17. It might be more accurate to say that the Mahayana texts, perhaps self-consciously, include a move to argue their legitimacy not only upon their literal claim to the status of *buddhavacana* but also upon their claim to better represent truth (*dharmatā*) per se.

18. See also Nattier's discussion of the Sanskrit and Chinese variants of this phrase: 33–37, 91–94, 106, n. 111; other texts of the *Prajñāpāramīta* corpus which use substanially the same formula include *The Large Sutra on Perfect Wisdom* (trans. E. Conze, Berkeley: University of California Press, 1975), 328 (minus the reference to "the latter five-hundred years") and the *Suvikrāntavikrāmi-Paripṛcchā Prajñāpāramītā-Sūtra* (ed. by Ryūshō Hikata, Kyoto: Rinsen Book Co., 1983), 124 (Chinese translation 565 by Upaśānya, T #231, 8.231b).

19. Nattier: 31, 57

20. The *Pratyutpannabuddhasaṃmukhāvasthitasamādhi-sūtra* even claims that it will disappear *until* the latter period of decay (Harrison, *The Samādhi of Direct Encounter* [Tokyo: The International Institute for Buddhist Studies, 1990], 96 ff).

21. E.g., T #262, 9.20c, 21a, 21c, 29c, *passim*.

22. Kubo and Yuyama: 278

23. Skt: *tathāgatasya parinirvṛtasya paścime kāle paścime samaye paścimāyāṃ pañcāśatyāṃ saddharma-vipralope vartamāna*, from *Saddharmapuṇḍarīka-sūtra*, edited by U. Wogihara and C. Tsuchida (Tokyo: Sankibō Book Store, 1958), 241.

24. T #262, 9.37c.

25. E.g., T #262, 9.50c.

26. Nattier: 85–86

27. Nattier: 86

28. Even in China it seems that the settings and descriptions of the two periods in the Lotus are much too far beyond a sense of history to inculcate any sense of historical or social foreboding, as the Lotus is not mentioned in the standard lists and encyclopedias of decline texts such as the *Fa yüan chu lin*, which lists over fifteen references to the decline but makes no mention of the Lotus (T #2122, 53.1005 ff).

29. Hubbard 1995: 124–25

30. E.g., T #262, 9.10b (chapter 2), 31a (chapter 10), 38c (chapter 14), etc. See Nattier, "The *Candragarbha-sūtra* in Central and East Asia" (Ph.D. thesis, Harvard University, 1988), Appendix 2 for a complete list of all references to the "latter age" in the various versions of the Lotus.

31. Similarly, in the *Mahāparinirvāṇa-sūtra* use of a seven-hundred year timetable of decay, "Though certain moral failings (especially on the part of the monks) are mentioned, issues of doctrine are given greater attention" (Nattier, 39).

32. I am indebted to Jan Nattier for pointing this out to me.

33. Shioiri, Ryōdō, "The Meaning of the Formation and Structure of the *Lotus Sutra*" in George J. Tanabe, Jr. and Willa Jane Tanabe, eds. *The Lotus Sutra in Japanese Culture* (Honolulu: University of Hawaii Press, 1989), 31.

34. For further examples of the virtue of preserving the true dharma, see also T #262, 9.31a (chapter 10), 34a (chapter 11), 37a (chapter 14), 37c–38a (chapter 14), 38b (chapter 14), 39c (chapter 14), 46a (chapter 17), 51b (chapter 20), 54b (chapter 23), 61b (chapter 28), and 62a (chapter 28).

35. T #262, 9. 31a (chapter 10); This and the following quotations from the Lotus Sutra are adapted from Kubo and Yuyama: 171–72

36. T #262, 9.61a (chapter 28); Kubo and Yuyama: 336

37. For further examples of the exhortation to spread the true dharma in the latter age, see also T #262, 9.37b (chapter 14), 37c (chapter 14), 38b (chapter 14), 38c (chapter 14), 39a (chapter 14), and 51b (chapter 20).

38. T #262, 9.54c (chapter 23); Kubo and Yuyama: 301

39. For further examples of the retribution for rejection of the Lotus Sutra in the latter age, see also T #262, 9.10b (chapter 2), 36b (chapter 13), 36c (chapter 13), and 62a (chapter 28).

40. T #262, 9.31a–31b (chapter 10); Kubo and Yuyama: 172

41. T #262, 9.36c (chapter 13); Kubo and Yuyama: 203

42. Hubbard 1995: 127

43. Stone, 44

44. Watson: 174

45. Watson: 183

46. Watson: 79

47. The same specificity of the Lotus is seen in its use of *upāya*, in which the Lotus itself is never considered as *upāya*, but rather as the unsurpassed truth; this is quite different from the more thoroughgoing use of *upāya* in, for example, the *Vimalakīrti-sūtra*, in which the doctrine of nonduality renders all utterances of the Buddhas equally provisional and equally *upāya*; ultimately, of course, this leads to the "thunderous silence of Vimalakīrti" as the only possible "statement" of nonduality; cf. Hubbard 1995: 124.

48. For a study of the relationship between the ideas of peace, individual moral cultivation, and national mission in Japanese new religious movements, see Kisala 1996.

Between Duration and Eternity: Hermeneutics of the 'Ancient Buddha' of the Lotus Sutra in Chih-i and Nichiren

Lucia Dolce

The nature of the Buddha of the Lotus Sutra has been extensively discussed in the long history of exegesis of this scripture. One of the issues that have been debated is whether the Śākyamuni represented in the Lotus Sutra is the historical Buddha who preached this scripture at the end of his life, or an ever-existent, universal Buddha who encompasses in himself the other Buddhas of the universe. This question has generated divergent theories, which have shaped the understanding of the meaning of the entire text and affected the *Weltanschauung* of those who put their trust in this sutra.

This paper explores some aspects of the problem as it was defined within the T'ien-t'ai/Tendai Lotus tradition. It focuses on two figures in this tradition, belonging to different ages and countries: Chih-i and Nichiren. Chih-i (538–97) is regarded as the *de facto* founder of Chinese T'ien-t'ai. His commentaries on the Lotus Sutra, especially the line-by-line exegesis *Fa-hua wen-chu*, and his explanation of the meaning of the sutra as expressed in the characters which form its title, *Fa-hua hsuan-i*, are essential sources for the study of the Lotus Sutra. Nichiren (1222–82) was the originator of one of the schools of medieval Japanese Buddhism, which is now named after him, but which he himself called the "Lotus School." He developed Chih-i's thought, conferring on the Lotus Sutra an absolute value and creating a religious practice exclusively focused on this sutra. In its turn, Nichiren's thought would influence the interpretations of modern Buddhist denominations based on the Lotus Sutra, like Risshō Kōsei-kai.

My analysis concentrates on the sixteenth chapter of the Lotus Sutra, "The Long Life of the Tathāgatha," which is regarded as the core of the second half of the scripture,[1] the so-called "section of the origin."[2]

According to this bipartition, the first half, or "section of the trace,"[3] of which the second chapter of the sutra, "Skillful Means," is representative, deals with the activity of the historical Buddha in this world and his soteriological activity with regard to sentient beings. The second half, by contrast, is centered on the world of an "original" Buddha[4] and on the way he attained buddhahood, and hence addresses the issue of the true nature of the Buddha. The flowering of a philosophy centered on the "section of the origin" was one of the most interesting developments in the hermeneutics of the Lotus Sutra. Nichiren, in particular, regarded the Buddha described in this part as embodying the fundamental reality presented by the Lotus Sutra, and the enlightenment depicted in the sixteenth chapter as crucial to the understanding of the relation between the Buddha and humanity. I shall investigate the reading that Chih-i and Nichiren give in their works of the past existence of this Buddha and of his relation to the three temporal realms (past, present, and future) and to other Buddhas of the Buddhist pantheon.

A Problem of Temporal Categories

The sixteenth chapter of the Lotus Sutra presents Śākyamuni as a Buddha who enjoys an infinite life span :

> Thus it is, since I became Buddha in the very far distant past,[5] [that my] lifetime is of infinite *asaṃkhyeya kalpas*, forever existing and immortal.[6] . . . The lifetime which I attained by pursuing the bodhisattva-way is not even yet accomplished but will still be twice the previous number [of *kalpas*].[7]

The existence of the Buddha appears to have a duration which stretches "infinitely" in the past and in the future. However, this infinity is expressed in terms of time, posing a logical contradiction which affects the classification of this Buddha as eternal.

Why in the Lotus Sutra is the attribute of "far distant"[8] given to Śākyamuni, the historical Buddha who appeared in India in the sixth century B.C.E.? The Lotus Sutra is perhaps the only scripture which discusses the past of Śākyamuni in these terms. In China some of its early commentators inferred an idea of eternity from the uncountable number of *kalpas* expressing the distance between the present of Śākyamuni and his past. Yet, other interpreters reckoned this past to retain a temporal dimension, and for this reason considered the Lotus Sutra inferior to scriptures such as the Nirvana Sutra, where the idea of the eternal existence of everything sanctioned the eternity of the historical Śākyamuni as well.[9] With Chih-i, and in Japan even more emphatically with Nichiren, we find a positive evaluation of the assertion of the Lotus Sutra that the historical Buddha attained buddhahood in a remote past. It should be asked, however, whether this assessment led to a metaphysical justification of the historical Buddha as a manifestation (one of the many) of an absolute Buddha and also how the nature of Śākyamuni Buddha before his recent enlightenment attained under the bodhi tree was understood. The issue is the conflict between the historicity and physicality of the Śākyamuni who attained buddhahod in a certain place at a certain time and a universal Śākyamuni able to represent the essence of buddhahood.

The spatial dimension in which the sutra places Śākyamuni also reflects this ambivalence. The scripture says that Śākyamuni lives forever on Vulture Peak, and in his other abodes as well; that for an uncountable time Śākyamuni has been preaching in this *sahā* world, and yet that his teaching has benefited not only the beings of this world, but also those of other worlds.[10] At the same time, the text speaks of other Buddhas, who teach through expedients and whose teachings are all true. The sutra does not explicitly declare whether the omnipresence of Śākyamuni Buddha in the universe symbolizes the existence of one single Buddha, or whether this "original" Buddha comprehends all other Buddhas of the universe. The question thus remains open.

Chi-i's Interpretation: A Threefold Buddha

Chih-i's exegesis of the sixteenth chapter of the Lotus Sutra in his *Fa-hua wen-chu* contains a criticism of previous interpretations of the meaning of "distant past," and a discussion of different categorizations of the Tathāgata: the twofold Buddha-body and the threefold Buddha-body, the Buddha of the origin, and the Buddha of the trace.[11] Here I will examine how Chih-i applies the theory of the threefold Buddha-body to the Buddha of the Lotus Sutra.[12] The scripture does not mention the different bodies of the Buddha but Chih-i employs existent theories of Buddha-bodies to illustrate the meaning of the text and, at the same time, to present his solution to the conflict between a noumenal and a phenomenal Buddha.

The three bodies the Buddha is endowed with are the dharma body, the recompense body *(saṃbhoga-kāya)*, and the transformation body *(nirmāṇā-kāya)*.[13] Chih-i explains the nature of each of these three bodies and the way in which their enlightenment is displayed, supporting his arguments with passages from chapter 16.

The dharma body is defined as a principle "without causes and without results,[14] whether there is a Buddha or no Buddha,[15] . . . everywhere present but without difference, without movement and yet coming forth [i.e., enlightened]."[16] Chih-i infers this from the sentence in the Lotus

Sutra: "There is neither birth nor death, or going away or coming forth; neither living nor dead, neither reality nor unreality; neither thus nor otherwise."[17] The dharma body is therefore a *principle* which reveals the perfect suchness[18] without distinctions. Its enlightenment is the unchangeable, pure-by-nature *tathāgata-garbha* (that is, the buddha-nature), which allows the Tathāgata to "know and see the aspect of the triple world as it is, in its real nature."[19] Since the dharma body is in accord with the principle of suchness, both its nature and its appearance are eternally as they are, whether it is manifested or not as a Buddha; therefore it is not relevant whether it is measurable or not, that is, whether it has duration or not.[20] In another commentary on the Lotus Sutra, Chih-i refers the phrase "neither thus nor otherwise" to the Middle Way, which in Tendai philosophy is synonymous with the real truth.[21]

The recompense body has its scriptural evidence in the passage which proclaims: "The power of my wisdom is such, the light of my wisdom shines infinitely, my life is of countless kalpas, from long-cultivated karma obtained."[22] Chih-i explains that wisdom (the Buddha-eyes) is the foundation of this aspect of the Tathāgata: it is through wisdom that the Tathāgata attains buddhahood, it is wisdom that allows the recompense body to partake of the ultimate reality.[23] As we shall see, here the emphasis is on the practice which leads to buddhahood.

The third body, the *nirmāṇā-kāya*, is characterized by ever-changing form and colors, and by its continuous appearing in the world. This is the meaning of the passages in the sutra ". . . whether I show myself or others, my deeds or other's,"[24] and ". . . revealing myself extinct and not extinct."[25] The *nirmāṇā-kāya* appears in numerous lives and numerous extinctions, is endowed with names which are never the same, and has different ages (the Buddha gives different accounts of the duration of his life).[26] The Tathāgata in this aspect attains enlightenment in a particular place, as shown by the scriptural assertion that "Śākyamuni Buddha left the palace of the Śākyas and entered the place of enlightenment, not far from the city of Gayā."[27] The life of the *nirmāṇā-kāya* is affected by the principle of causation.[28] Being bound to causality, this body is measurable; hence it typifies Śākyamuni as a Buddha restricted in both temporal and spatial terms. Yet, Chih-i underlines the idea that, because finite impermanence cannot be the principle that informs the existence of a Buddha, the transformation body can be seen as partaking in the immeasurable if one does not speak of its activity.[29]

According to Chih-i, in fact, the three bodies are both permanent and impermanent, and are all three inherent in the Buddha of the Lotus Sutra: "One body is three bodies; it is not one, it is not different."[30] Chih-i here employs the point of view of the "perfect teaching"[31] and applies the principle of "one is three," which characterizes this type of teaching, to the three Tathāgatas, thus introducing a perspective quite different from that of earlier interpretations. He calls the virtue of being neither one nor three a "secret" or "mysterious"[32] quality and presents it as peculiar to the Buddha of the Lotus Sutra, which other scriptures do not reveal.[33] He denies that the three bodies are either in a horizontal, that is, equal, relation (referring to their innate merits[34]) or in a vertical, that is, hierarchical, relation (referring to the merits derived from practice[35]). [36]

This integration notwithstanding, Chih-i eventually puts the accent on one of the three bodies:

> This chapter reveals the three bodies. If they are differentiated in a vertical sense, the true one is the recompense body. The wisdom of the recompense body, being one with what is above and in accord with what is below, encompasses the three bodies. . . . The text says 'In the very far distant past since I became Buddha, I have benefited human beings in the three worlds.' What is enlightened is the dharma body, what causes enlightenment is the recompense body. Because the dharma [body] and the recompense [body] become one, things may receive benefits. . . . Thus, the correct meaning [of the scriptural passage] is to postulate the virtues of the Buddha in his recompense body.[37]

This is perhaps the most interesting feature of Chih-i's theory of the three bodies. The *saṃbhoga-kāya* represents a Buddha who has a beginning, and thus is finite before attaining enlightenment, but who becomes immeasurable, infinite, after his awakening. It exemplifies a Buddha who encompasses in himself both historical existence and universal principle: not an absolute Tathāgata who assumes for some time a phenomenal form and then goes back to his true nature, but a Tathāgata who is, at the same time, his true nature and his temporal manifestation.

Why does Chih-i put the emphasis on this body, regarding it as the correct interpretation of the Śākyamuni of the Lotus Sutra? I think that the *saṃbhoga-kāya* represents Chih-i's response to the question of the relation between temporality and eternity. For Chih-i the reality hypostasized by the Lotus Sutra is not a type of monistic oneness, unchanging and substantial, but is an interdependent unity, the nature of which is best conveyed by the expression "one yet many, many yet one." It is, we may perhaps say, an organic unity, created by the reconciliation of duality. The interaction of the bodies of the Buddha in the *saṃbhoga-kāya* is one example of this reality. By emphasizing the recompense body, which emblematizes the enlightenment the Buddha achieved through practice and the activity he performs preaching, Chih-i also presents buddhahood as a process, which has by definition a location in time and place. Emphasis on the *saṃbhoga-kāya*, however, leaves open the question of the type of eternity presented in the Lotus Sutra, since this Buddha-body has a beginning in time.

One Universal Buddha?

Does Chih-i's theory of the threefold body endorse the idea of one single Buddha for all ages? Śākyamuni is the Buddha of the present (e.g., the moment in which the Lotus is preached) because of the enlightenment he attained in the far distant past and the merits he accumulated in long years of practice after that "original" time. But what is his nature in the period between that first enlightenment and the present?

According to Chih-i, the time between his original attainment of buddhahood and the "transformation" of the Buddha as Śākyamuni does not have the same characteristics as the "original time." In this temporal interval, Śākyamuni was a bodhisattva who practiced under various teachers, such as the Buddha Universal Wisdom or the Buddha Burning Light described in other chapters of the Lotus Sutra. These Buddhas of the past are for Chih-i distinct from Śākyamuni, and he even criticizes some opinions in favour of an identification of the Buddha Burning Light with Śākyamuni, which seem to have been current at his time.[38] Explaining the passage of the Lotus that says: "During that time I have spoken about the Buddha Burning Light and others, and talked of his entering into *nirvana*,"[39] Chih-i remarks that if we identify Burning Light with Śākyamuni, we eliminate the cause of Śākyamuni's present buddhahood: Śākyamuni, in fact, is born as a Buddha thanks to the many religious practices he performed under the instruction of Burning Light. The enlightenment that took place in the original time seems therefore to be, in Chih-i's interpretation, only one of the causes which allows Śākyamuni to be a Buddha now, only the seed[40] of his buddhahood. I will return to this point.

One may here suggest that Chih-i regarded Śākyamuni as the Buddha of only one of the three temporal worlds. In fact, in his annotations to chapter 16 of the Lotus Sutra one also finds that the three Buddha-bodies are identified with three different figures of the Buddhist pantheon: "The Tathāgata of the dharma body is called Vairocana, translated with Omnipresent; the Tathāgata of the recompense body is called 'Rocana,' translated with Pure and Perfect; the Tathāgata of the transformation body is called Śākyamuni, translated as the 'One Who Has Realized Enlightenment Once.'"[41] Chih-i tries not to assign separated existences to these

Buddhas. Appealing to various canonical sources, among which the Sutra of Meditation on the Bodhisattva Universal Virtue (the capping scripture of the Threefold Lotus Sutra), he reiterates: "When Śākyamuni Buddha is called Vairocana, that is only another name, it is not a different substance."[42] The length of this paper does not allow an investigation of the meaning of such a Buddha, who does not belong to the iconography of the Lotus Sutra proper. It needs to be underlined, however, that Chih-i does not necessarily connect the three bodies with Śākyamuni. Moreover, within the iconography of the Lotus scripture, one finds other instances of their identification with different Buddhas: Prabhūtaratna as the dharma body, Śākyamuni as the recompense body, and Śākyamuni's emanation bodies[43] as the transformation body.

Therefore it is debatable whether Chih-i ever conceived the idea of one single Buddha, or found it meaningful. There is, in fact, a fundamental difference between the doctrine that "the three bodies are one body" and the idea that "all buddhas are one Buddha only" (issaibutsu ichibutsu)[44], which would later be put forward in Japanese Tendai. Chih-i acknowledged, and justified, the existence of other Buddhas, and did not eventually reduce them to Śākyamuni Buddha (they are not Śākyamuni's upāya). In the last analysis, Chih-i regarded Śākyamuni only as the most important Buddha of the Lotus Sutra and only as the Buddha of the present world. He claimed that the three bodies all reveal the "origin," but he never qualified this original time as *the* absolute time. His "origin" is just the archetypal movement, the attainment of buddhahood.

Between Chih-i and Nichiren

Discussion of the nature of the Śākyamuni of the Lotus Sutra continued in the T'ien-t'ai/Tendai tradition after Chih-i. In Japan, a gradual shift of emphasis occurred in the interpretation of Chih-i's thought. Already in works of the founder of the school, Saichō (767–822), one may detect a certain tendency toward the elimination of the temporality of Śākyamuni and the theorization of a Buddha whose three bodies are all "uncreated."[45] After Saichō the stress is definitely on the dharma-kāya, and the absolute nature of Śākyamuni is often formulated through an identification, explicit or not, with Mahāvairocana, the Tathāgata of esoteric Buddhism, whom the relevant texts present as an absolute Buddha always existent as such.[46] In the medieval period various commentaries on the Lotus Sutra produced in the Tendai school would regard the Śākyamuni of the far distant past as a threefold body enlightened as it is, and the innumerable kalpas of his far distant past (numerous as "five hundred

230 PHILOSOPHICAL REFLECTION

grains of dust" in the sutra) as a metaphor, an example of conventional explanation.[47] The danger of such a reading of the scripture would be to overlook the importance of practice as the means through which Buddhahood is attained, which is a central issue in the sutra.[48]

Nichiren's Interpretation: One Single Buddha

Nichiren's interpretation of the Śākyamuni of the Lotus Sutra, although it took as its point of departure Chih-i's theories, was definitively influenced by various hermeneutical patterns that developed in the Japanese exegetical tradition of the Lotus Sutra, and by Nichiren's personal experience of the reality disclosed in the scripture.

Nichiren reread the entire sutra focusing on the "section of the origin." From this perspective, he constructed an image of Śākyamuni Buddha as the only true Buddha of all Buddhist systems, and eventually produced an interpretation of the Lotus Sutra very different from that of Chih-i. In Nichiren's writings we find a sort of dilation of the chapters constituting the second half of the Lotus Sutra, especially the end of chapter 15 and chapter 16, which Nichiren judges to be almost exclusively representative of the meaning of the entire scripture. This corresponds to the dilation of the temporal dimension expressed in those chapters, that is, the distant past in which Śākyamuni obtained his original enlightenment. Nichiren absolutizes this original moment and makes it the only significant time, and relates it to the existence of humanity in a certain time and place.

He writes:

> The true attainment of buddhahood in the far distant past is the original ground[49] of all the Buddhas. To use a metaphor, if the vast sea is the true enlightenment in the past, the fishes and birds are the thousand two hundred and more Venerables. Had the enlightenment in the past not occurred, the thousand two hundred and more Venerables would be without roots like duckweed. . . .[50]

> When the past [of Śākyamuni] and [his] eternal abiding are disclosed, all Buddhas become Śākyamuni's emanations. At the time of the earlier sutras and of the first part of the Lotus Sutra, the various Buddhas performed each practice and each discipline side by side with Śākyamuni. . . . Now it is manifest that the various Buddhas [of other sutras] all are followers[51] of Śākyamuni. . . . When the Buddha is the Buddha of the far distant past, even the great bodhisattvas of the "trace section" and the great bodhisattvas of other realms are disciples of the Lord of the Doctrine Śākyamuni.[52]

In chapter 15 of the sutra, Śākyamuni's emanations materialize, having been asked to gather from the ten directions.[53] Chih-i had already suggested that the emanation-bodies of Śākyamuni prove that he had not attained enlightenment only forty years before preaching the Lotus Sutra, otherwise there could not have been so many kalpa-old beings who had received instruction from him.[54] However, Chih-i did not invest Śākyamuni's emanations with a universal significance, probably because he did not regard Śākyamuni as the only true Buddha of the universe. Nichiren's declaration that all Buddhas enlightened in the past are emanations of Śākyamuni is of a different nature: it challenges the equality of all Buddhas and, furthermore, operates as a reduction which unifies all Buddhas, not only those appearing in the Lotus Sutra, but also those appearing in other scriptures of the Buddhist canon. It should be noted that this "absolutization" of Śākyamuni, although reminiscent of the idea that "all Buddhas are just one single Buddha" developed by esoteric Tendai in Japan, does not proceed by equating Śākyamuni with another Buddha already defined as universal, like Vairocana, but rather by including all Buddhas (Vairocana, too) in the person of Śākyamuni.

Nichiren discusses at length how all Buddhas are enlightened because of their relation to Śākyamuni Buddha.

If we consider the stage of results,[55] the many Tathāgatas are Buddhas of a past ten kalpas, one hundred kalpas or a thousand kalpas long. Lord Śākyamuni is a Buddha who has [attained] the complete result[56] of subtle awakening[57] as many kalpas ago as five hundred particles of dust. The various Buddhas of the ten directions such as the Tathāgata Vairocana, the Tathāgata Amitābhā and the Tathāgata Bhaiṣajyaguru are followers of our original teacher, the Lord Śākyamuni. One moon in the sky floats in the water as ten-thousand [moons]. . . . This Buddha Abundant Treasures, too, is a follower of the Lord Śākyamuni of the chapter "The Long Life of the Tathāgata."[58]

An Infinite Transformation Body

How does Nichiren, from this conception of the nature of the Buddha of the Lotus Sutra, develop Chih-i's theory of the threefold-body with its stress on the saṃbhoga-kāya?

Nichiren classifies all the Buddhas of sutras other than the Lotus and the Śākyamuni described in the first section and in the last six chapters of the second section of the Lotus scripture as temporal bodies, or "Buddhas of the Hinayana."[59] Only the Śākyamuni who reveals his enlightenment in the past embodies the true Mahayana Buddha. To indicate the infiniteness of this Buddha, Nichiren uses the expression "without beginning and without end,"[60] which properly belonged to a context related to Mahāvairocana Buddha and signified an existence not subject to temporal limitations. This expression suggests that Nichiren attributes an eternal nature to Śākyamuni, and at first seems to imply that he envisages a *dharma-kāya* as the only ground of any reality. But Nichiren develops this infiniteness in a different direction.

Nichiren emphasizes that the Lotus Sutra is the only scripture where not only the dharma body, but also the recompense body, and the transformation body are presented as "infinite": "When other Mahayana sutras speak of 'without beginning and without end,' they refer to the *dharma-kāya* only, not to the three bodies."[61] Nichiren does not regard the distant past represented by the five hundred *kalpas* as a metaphorical image, but as a concrete reality identifying an active original body, a "Buddha who in the far distant past has truly manifested himself, has truly practiced, and has truly actualized his enlightenment."[62] Consequently, the meaning that Nichiren attributes to Śākyamuni is not symbolized either by a transcendental body whose existence is set in a world other than ours or by the recompense body of which Chih-i spoke.[63] This "without beginning without end" of the temporal body is most difficult to believe, Nichiren repeatedly suggests, but the infiniteness of the *nirmāṇā-kāya* is the crucial evidence that the Buddha has always abided in this world and that his soteriological activity has been constant since the original time.

Thus Nichiren resolves the conflict between the mundane and the ultimate by creating an all-encompassing Śākyamuni Buddha, who maintains characteristics of the historical Śākyamuni (the activity of preaching) and at the same time is endowed with attributes of the *dharma-kāya* (infinite existence). In this way, the dharma world itself comes to be conceived as the phenomenal reality which actualizes the ultimate truth. Borrowing from Tendai terminology, Nichiren calls this reality "a concretely accomplished 'three thousand worlds in one single thought.'"[64]

One Buddha-land

According to Nichiren, in the second section of the Lotus Sutra Śākyamuni speaks of this *sahā* world as the *original land*, a pure Buddha realm compared to which the other lands of the ten directions are mere conventional worlds.[65] In Chih-i's exegesis the "original land" is the land in which the original Buddha attained enlightenment, therefore the realm of only one type of Buddha. This "*sahā* world of the original time" contrasts with the *sahā* world where human beings live, which retains the characteristics of a "trace-land." For Nichiren, on the contrary, there is only one *sahā* world. Vulture Peak, the place where the Lotus Sutra is taught, represents both this world of ours and the most perfect world, the only possible "paradise." There is no other reality, neither for humanity, nor for the Buddha. Whereas Chih-i apparently believed in the Western paradise of Amitābha and hoped to reach it after his death,[66] Nichiren considered the assembly on Vulture Peak a symbol of those who, having received the teachings of the Lotus Sutra, are able to transform our *sahā* world into a "resplendent land."[67]

In Nichiren's hermeneutics the original land thus equals the human world. Since the world where humans live is also the original world in which the Buddha attained buddhahood, phenomenal reality becomes the ground of the most complete enlightenment, which opens to ultimate reality. This enlightenment of the Buddha in the remote past justifies the buddhahood of all beings of this world: Nichiren insists that the *śrāvakas* and *pratyekabuddhas* who are promised enlightenment in the first section of the Lotus Sutra could never in fact attain it if the original enlightenment of the Buddha described in chapter 16 had not occurred.[68]

For Nichiren, the revelation of the original Buddha which takes place in the sixteenth chapter has two meanings: that of a theory of the nature of the Buddha, and that of a speculation on the situation of humankind. Śākyamuni's "original causes and original results"[69] become the turning point which allows postulating the contemporaneity of human beings to the Buddha. Human beings, in their spatial and temporal limitations, share the temporality of Śākyamuni in this world. Nichiren uses a theory elaborated by Chih-i according to which the past of Śākyamuni is reflected in the past of his disciples. This is the tie established, in the original time, between Śākyamuni and those who listen to the sutra or are willing to accept it. From here Nichiren draws the certainty of buddhahood for human beings:

> We living beings of this land are since as many *kalpas* ago as five hundred particles of dust Śākyamuni's beloved children[70]. . . . [The relation] between a Buddha with ties[71] and the living beings [bound] by karmic ties[72] can be compared to [the reflection of] the moon in the sky floating on clear water. A Buddha without ties in relation to sentient beings is like a deaf man listening for the sound of thunder or a blind man turning to sun and moon.[73]

The presentation of the relationship Buddha–humanity in terms of father and son also deserves attention. The term "the Buddha's children" appears often in the sutra to indicate the Buddha's disciples, bodhisattvas, and all those who practice according to the teaching of the Buddha. They are called "children born of the Buddha's mouth."[74] Nichiren underlines that only a Buddha coming from this *sahā* world can be considered father of the beings living in this world. Other Buddhas who abide in different parts of the universe are not qualified because they do not have this bond, thus their existence is almost irrelevant for people, or at best an *upāya*.

The Buddha-Seed

The Lotus Sutra does not discuss a universal buddha-nature but often speaks of a universal buddha-seed. Chih-i re-uses the image of the seed to formulate a temporal succession in the process of enlightenment, which reflects also the way the Buddha acts: the seed is first sown, then left to sprout and grow, and finally the plant ripens. As mentioned earlier, in Chih-i's exegesis of the enlightenment of Śākyamuni the time between the sowing (the original enlightenment of Śākyamuni) and the ripening (the recent enlightenment of Śākyamuni) is an *upāya*, because the deeds Śākyamuni performs during this period are according to teachings other than the Lotus Sutra. The Lotus Sutra represents the world of the original enlightenment of Śākyamuni and that of his present enlightenment. The world in between is denoted by the other sutras Śākyamuni preached during his lifetime according to people's capacity.

In Nichiren's interpretation the *upāya* no longer has a function, the seed becomes equivalent to enlightenment,[75] and the planting of the seed[76] amounts to the attainment of buddhahood.[77] The temporal interval between the primordial time and the present of Śākyamuni loses significance, and so does the difference between the original time and original land and the present of human beings. The Lotus Sutra is the buddha-seed planted in people, the only means to realize the human potential for buddhahood. At any moment this scripture is read and diffused, the seed of buddhahood is again planted in everybody who chooses to listen and keep it, and the primordial relation with the Buddha is reestablished. If nobody "uses" the sutra, the seed disappears and no one is aware of their tie with the Buddha.

The seed is thus the necessary and sufficient cause of buddhahood. Yet, compared with the idea of buddha-nature, unchangeable by definition, the seed gives the idea of something belonging to the phenomenal world, subject to disappearance. "If people do not believe in this sutra and vilify it, then they cut off all the buddha-seeds in the world," the sutra says.[78] It is thus necessary to sow the seed again. If buddha-seeds occur "according to circumstances and conditioned cause," as suggested in the Lotus Sutra itself, both the infinite action of the Buddha and one's own activity are necessary. The image of the seed also conveys a more indi-

vidual nuance than the universality of the buddha-nature: "Human beings defiled by evil encounter the bodhisattvas of the *honmon*, and the
buddha-seeds are planted."[80]

The World of the *Honmon*

The accent on the world of enlightenment represented by chapter 16 of
the Lotus Sutra seems at first to concentrate on the Buddha and on the
nature of buddhahood. Yet, the exegesis elaborated within the T'ien-t'ai/
Tendai tradition develops a religious view which, in various ways, addresses the position of humanity: a true Buddha cannot exist without human beings (because it is from among humans that a Buddha emerges)
and human beings cannot exist without a Buddha (because the Buddha
represents the essence of humanity).

Nichiren asserts that the Buddha-world is the only reality and at the
same time restores the historical perspective as the only context in which
the dimension of the absolute open to human beings is concretized. The
Buddha's enlightenment, that is, "the merits acquired by Śākyamuni
through his practice,"[81] is epitomized in the five characters of the title of
the Lotus Sutra. Therefore, if someone "receives and keeps" the sutra and
obtains access to its meaning through the recitation of the title, they will
be endowed with these merits. "The Śākyamuni of subtle enlightenment is
our blood and our flesh. The merits of his practice, are they not our
bones and marrow?," Nichiren writes.[82] Buddhahood becomes a reality *of*
history, not just *in* history. Nichiren's emphasis is not on the absolute per
se, but on the relative which has to change to become absolute. A shift
occurs from the three worlds of universal time (past–present–future) to
the actual historical moment, and this gives a social dimension to Nichiren Buddhism. The endowment with the Buddha-world, however, is the
exclusive prerogative of the "practitioner of the Lotus": "One who keeps
the sutra is endowed with the Buddha-bodies and performs Buddha's
acts."[83] The emphasis on a concrete realization of original time leads to
the interpretation of the truth represented by the discourse of the Lotus
Sutra as a truth which does not exist beyond the confines of history.

References

Abbreviations

CDZ   *Chishō Daishi zenshū*, 4 vols. In *Dai Nihon bukkyō zensho*, 150 vols. Bussho Kankōkai, ed. Tokyo: Bussho Kankōkai, 1912–22.

DDZ   *Dengyō Daishi zenshū*, 5 vols. Hieisan Senshūin, ed. Tokyo: Sekai Seiten Kankō Kyōkai, 1989.

T   *Taishō shinshū daizōkyō*, 100 vols. Takakusu Junjirō, et al., eds. Tokyo: Daizō-kyōkai, 1924–35.

Teihon   *Showa teihon Nichiren shōnin ibun*, 4 vols. Risshō Daigaku Nichiren Kyōgaku Kenkyūjo, ed. Minobu: Minobusan Kuonji, 1988 (enl. ed.).

Threefold   *The Threefold Lotus Sutra*. Katō Bunnō, Tamura Yoshirō, et al., trans. Tokyo: Kōsei Publishing, 1975.

Primary sources

Chih-i. *Fa-hua hsuan-i* (Full title: *Miao-fa lien-hua ching hsuan-i*). T no. 1716, 33:681–815. *Fa-hua wen-chu*, (Full title: *Miao-fa lien-hua ching wen-chu*). T no. 1718, 34:1–151. Japanese translation: *Hokke mongu*, in *Kokuyaku issaikyō-kyōshobu 2*, Daitō shuppansha zōhan, 1993 (rev. ed.).

Enchin. *Hokkerongi*, CDZ 1

Kuan p'u-hsien p'u-sa hsing-fa ching. Translated by Dharmamitra. T no., 9:389–94.

Miao-fa lien-hua ching. Translated by Kumārajīva. T no. 262, 9:1–62

Nichiren. *Hokke shingon shōretsuji*, Teihon 1:302–10. *Hokke shuyōshō*, Teihon 1:810–18. *Ichidai goji keizu*, Teihon 3:2333–43. *Kaimokushō*, Teihon 1:535–609. *Kanjin-honzonshō* (full title: *Nyorai metsugo gogohyakusaishi kanjin honzonshō*), Teihon 1:702–21. *Shōjō shōbutsu yōmon*, Teihon 3:2319–23. *Shōmitsubō gosho*, Teihon 1:820–27. *Sōya nyūdō dono garigosho*, Teihon 1:895–12.

Secondary sources

Andō, Toshio. *Tendaigaku—konpon shisō to sono tenkai*. Kyoto: Heirakuji Shoten, 1968.

Asai, Endō. *Jōko nihon tendai honmon shisōshi*. Kyoto: Heirakuji Shoten, 1973.

Kitagawa, Zenchō. "Nichiren shōnin ni okeru 'Juryōbon no butsu' ni tsuite," *Osaki gakuhō* 129:94–118.

Sakamoto, Yukio. "Chugoku ni okeru Hokekyō kenkyūshi no kenkyū." In *Hoke-kyō no chūgokuteki tenkai*, Yukio Sakamoto, ed. Kyoto: Heirakuji Shoten, 1972, 3–41.

Satō, Tetsuei. *Tendai daishi no kenkyū*, Tokyo: Hyakkaen, 1961.

Tamura, Yoshirō. "Nihon tendai no jikanron." In *Hokke bukkyō no buddaron to shujōron*, Hōyō Watanabe, ed. Kyoto: Heirakuji Shoten, 1985, 215–40.

Tamura, Yoshirō. *Hongaku shisō ron*. Tokyo: Shunjūsha, 1990.

Watanabe, Hōyō. "Nichiren shōnin no busshōron." In *Hokke bukkyō no buddaron to shujōron*, Hōyō Watanabe, ed. Kyoto: Heirakuji Shoten, 1985, 401–23.

Notes

1. The division of the sutra in two parts is one of the ways in which the text was divided by its interpreters in order to clarify its doctrines.
2. 本門
3. 迹門
4. 本佛
5. 久遠
6. 常住不滅
7. *Miao-fa lien-hua ching* (Jpn: *Myōhōrengekyō*) T 9:42c. The English translation is from *The Threefold Lotus Sutra* (hereafter *Threefold*), 251–52.
8. 久遠
9. Early Chinese interpretations are known from the account that Chih-i and Chi-tsang, another great commentator on the Lotus, give in their works. For an outline of the major issues involved in the discusssion, see, for instance, Yoshirō Tamura, "Nihon tendai no jikanron," 215–22, where the Lotus Sutra is compared to other scriptures following the arguments used by Chinese exegetes to explicate the question of this distant past.
10. T 9:43b-c; *Threefold*, 254–55.
11. *Fa-hua wen-chu*, second part of fascicle 9, T no. 1718, 34:127a–135a. See also the Japanese translation in *Kokuyaku issaikyō-kyōshobu* 2:419–48 (hereafter *Hokke mongu*).
12. For a brief dicussion of the different positions before Chih-i, see Yukio Sakamoto, "Chūgoku ni okeru Hokekyō kenkyūshi no kenkyū," 18–23.
13. 法身, 報身 and 応身, This theory is a development of the idea of two bodies of the Buddha, which distinguishes between a true body (真) that is motionless and a transformation body (応) that, endowed with wisdom, appears in the world and realizes enlightenment.
14. 非因非果
15. 有仏無仏
16. T 34:128a.
17. T 9:42c; *Threefold*, 251.
18. 圓如
19. T 9:42c; cf. *Threefold*, 251.
20. T 34:128b.
21. Cf. *Fa-hua hsuan-i*, T 33:704c: "The chapter of 'The Life of the Tathāgata' says: 'No suchness and no difference.' This is the Middle Way. 'Suchness' corresponds to the true reality, 'difference' corresponds to the mundane."
22. T 9:43c; *Threefold*, 256, slightly changed.
23. T 34:128b-c.
24. T 34:128a and 128b. Cf. T 9:42c; *Threefold*, 251.
25. T 9:43b; *Threefold*, 254.
26. Cf. T 9:42c; *Threefold*, 251.
27. T 34:128b. Cf. T 9:42b; *Threefold*, 250, slightly changed.
28. 縁理
29. T 34:128c.

30. T 34:129a.
31. 円教
32. 秘 or 密
33. T 34:129c: "When we say 'one body is the three bodies,' this is secret 秘; when we say 'the three bodies are one body,' this is mysterious 密."
34. 性徳
35. 修徳
36. Toshio Andō notes that to deny both a horizontal and a vertical relation among the three bodies does not mean to overlook their differences, which in terms of aspect (相) and function (用) do remain. However, since Chih-i understands the three bodies within the context of the perfect teaching, which is informed by the principle of encompassment of the nature (shōgu 性具), eventually the nature of the three bodies comes to be identical; therefore, each can contain the other. Toshio Andō, Tendaigaku—konpon shisō to sono tenkai, 157–60.
37. T 34:129a (simplified).
38. Cf. T 34:130a-b.
39. T 9:42b-c; Threefold, 251.
40. 種
41. T 34:128a. Vairocana and Rocana are in fact two renderings of the name of the Buddha of the Avataṃsaka sūtra, Vairocana.
42. Cf. Kuan p'u-hsien p'u-sa hsing-fa ching (Jpn: Kanfugen bosatsu gyōhō kyō) T 9:392c; Threefold, 362.
43. 分身
44. 三身即一身 and 一切佛一佛
45. This is actually a hotly debated point of Saichō's doctrine, and some scholars question whether Saichō actually did assert the idea of "the three uncreated bodies" (musa sanshin). Cf. Shugokokkaishō, DDZ 2:567, where the expression appears; cf. also Chūmuryōgikyō, DDZ 3:581. For a discussion of the sources, see Endō Asai, Jōko nihon tendai honmon shisōshi, 111–18.
46. An example is offered by Enchin's Hokkerongi, a commentary on the Lotus Sutra which, although usually considered to follow traditional Tendai interpretation closely, is certainly influenced by esoteric patterns, as this statement proves: "The threefold body of the perfect teaching (engyō 円教) is discussed as three centering on the dharma [body]". Hokkerongi, CDZ 1:256a. For a discussion of Enchin's position, see Endō Asai, Jōko nihon tendai honmon shisōshi, 536–37.
47. 仮説
48. For a discussion of the various questions presented by the late Heian and medieval interpretations, known as hongaku shisō, see, for instance, Yoshirō Tamura, Hongaku shisō ron.
49. 本地
50. Shōmitsubō gosho, Teihon 1:824.
51. 眷属
52. Kaimokushō, Teihon 1:576-7. "Followers" here indicates those who have received Śākyamuni's teachings.

53. For this reason Nichiren regards this chapter as an introduction to chapter 16. Cf. *Kaimokushō, Teihon* 1:572.
54. Cf. *Fa-hua hsuan-i*, T 33:798b, where Chih-i says that, because Śākyamuni had numerous emanations, it was understood that he must have attained enlightenment in the far distant past. Nichiren quotes the passage in his *Kaimokushō, Teihon* 1:572.
55. 果位
56. 果満
57. 妙覚
58. *Hokke shuyōshō, Teihon* 1:812.
59. Cf. *Shōjō shōbutsu yōmon, Teihon* 3:2319.
60. 無始無終
61. *Hokke shingon shōretsuji, Teihon* 1:308 (simplified). Cf. also *Kaimokushō, Teihon* 1:552.
62. 久遠実成実修実証ノ仏 Cf. *Ichidai goji keizu*, Teihon 3:2342.
63. This is my opinion. However, contemporary interpretations of the Nichiren denominations incline toward the characterization of Nichiren's Buddha as recompense body. Cf., for instance, Zenchō Kitagawa, "Nichiren shōnin ni okeru 'Juryōbon no butsu' ni tsuite."
64. *ji ichinen sanzen* 事一念三千
65. Cf. *Kaimokushō, Teihon* 1:576.
66. Cf. Tetsuei Satō, *Tendai daishi no kenkyū*, 556–59.
67. 寂光土
68. Cf. *Kaimokushō, Teihon* 1:552.
69. 本因本果
70. 愛子
71. 有縁
72. 結縁
73. *Hokke shuyōshō, Teihon* 1:812.
74. T9:6c; *Threefold*, 56. Nichiren calls the practitioner of the Lotus a son of the Buddha. Cf. *Nichimyō shōnin gosho,Teihon* 1:645.
75. 種即脱
76. 下種
77. For an outline of the idea of buddha-seed in Nichiren's writings, see, for instance, Hōyō Watanabe, "Nichiren shōnin no busshōron."
78. T 9:15b; *Threefold*, 103 (chapter "A Parable").
79. Cf. T 9:9b; *Threefold*, 70 (chapter "Skillful Means").
80. *Sōya nyūdō dono garigosho, Teihon* 1:904.
81. 因行果得
82. *Kanjinhonzonshō, Teihon* 1:711.
83. *Kanjinhonzonshō, Teihon* 1:7.

Chih-i and the Subtle Dharma of the Lotus Sutra: Emptiness or Buddha-nature?

Susan Mattis

In the second chapter of the Lotus Sutra the Buddha arises from *samādhi* and, addressing the gathered assembly, delivers a brief panegyric in praise of the ultimate Dharma, the truth that all Buddhas have realized. After repeated requests by the disciple Śāriputra, the Buddha promises that he will expound this "profound and subtle Dharma" for the benefit of all living beings.[1] His promise is followed by a series of parables demonstrating that all those who place their faith in this supreme teaching will attain Buddhahood. In the sutra, however, one finds very little explicit discussion of what is known in the Buddhist tradition as "ultimate truth" (*paramārtha satya*).

Most of the Lotus Sutra is occupied with elaborate descriptions of the benefits of embracing its teaching and with exhortations to "accept and uphold, read, recite, copy, and teach" it. Where explicit doctrinal statements are made, they are difficult to interpret. They appear in the context of a mythical discourse that is more suited to inspiring religious feeling and devotion than to providing a cognitive understanding of ultimate truth. Further, the few theoretical assertions in the sutra appear to derive from diverse and possibly conflicting Buddhist traditions. The sutra even casts doubt on the Buddha's ability to preach the Dharma, declaring that this Dharma is "inexpressible" and can only be understood "by a Buddha." (p. 29) The lack of a theoretical exposition of doctrine has left the sutra's exegetes largely responsible for determinate conceptions of the ultimate Dharma it claims to possess.

Perhaps more than any other individual, Chih-i (538–97), the founder of the Chinese T'ien-t'ai school of Buddhism, influenced the East Asian Buddhist tradition's understanding of the sutra. Chih-i's corpus provides a conceptual articulation of the Dharma, but it possesses its own ambiguities and has become the subject of divergent interpretations. This article proposes a reading of Chih-i's exposition of the ultimate truth that resolves some of its ambiguities and clarifies how Chih-i accommodates the diverse aspects of the discourse of the sutra.

Chih-i's philosophical views incorporate ideas from several of the traditions of Buddhism transmitted to China from India, but the single most important influence on his thought was the teaching of Nāgārjuna, the prominent Indian Buddhist master who systematized the doctrines of the *Prajñāpāramitā* (Perfection of Wisdom) sutras and founded the Mādhyamika school of Buddhism. To clarify Chih-i's understanding of ultimate truth, it is necessary to establish the extent to which his teaching diverges from the conception of ultimate truth Nāgārjuna derived from the *Prajñāpāramitā* sutras. Prior contemporary studies of the relation between Chih-i and Nāgārjuna have taken one of two positions: either that the two teachers' conceptions of the ultimate truth are identical or that Chih-i goes beyond Nāgārjuna's conception by introducing the notion of a "pure mind" that transcends Nāgārjuna's "two truths" of emptiness and conventional existence.[2]

This writer rejects both of these interpretations and develops a third position, occupying something of a middle ground between them. Chih-i does not conceive of the ultimate truth as an absolute "pure mind," but his philosophy differs significantly from the Mādhyamika in regard to the ontological status accorded to the "conventional truth." This reading of Chih-i's exposition of ultimate truth situates his vision of the Dharma of the Lotus Sutra within the context of other Buddhist traditions and within contemporary concerns of Western philosophy.

Emptiness and the Buddha of the Lotus Sutra

The fundamental question regarding the Lotus Sutra's vision of ultimate truth is its relation to the essential teaching of the *Prajñāpāramitā* sutras, the doctrine of emptiness (*śūnyāta*). While the sutra does not expound the principle of emptiness at great length, it refers to emptiness on several occasions, and many of its principles and teachings appear to presuppose the concept of emptiness. One of the most extensive direct references to it appears in chapter 5:

> Those grasses and trees, shrubs and forests, and medicinal herbs do not know themselves whether their nature is superior, intermediate or inferior; but the Thus Come One knows this Dharma of a single mark and a single flavor, namely, the mark of deliverance, the mark of disenchantment, the mark of extinction, the mark of ultimate nir-

vāṇa of eternally quiescent nirvāṇa, finally reducing itself to Emptiness. (p. 103)

In this passage the sutra declares that despite their apparent diversity, the ultimate truth of all beings is the single mark of emptiness. Later, in chapter 10, the sutra further expounds that it is through the realization of this emptiness of the *dharmas* that one gains entrance into Buddhahood:

The room of the Thus Come One is the thought of great compassion toward all living beings. The cloak of the Thus Come One is the thought of tender forbearance and the bearing of insult with equanimity. The throne of the Thus Come One is the emptiness of all dharmas. It is only by dwelling securely among these that he or she can with unabating thought broadly preach this Scripture of the Dharma Blossom to the bodhisattvas and the fourfold assembly. (p. 180)

In addition to statements such as these directly referring to emptiness, passages which proclaim a singular ultimate truth of all *dharmas* or which deny any distinction between the phenomenal realm and ultimate truth may be viewed as expressions of this doctrine. Thus, a passage in chapter 2 which states that the "reality" of all aspects of all *dharmas* is their "suchness" (*tathatā*) appears to be a reference to the emptiness of the *dharmas*:

Concerning the prime, rare and hard-to-understand dharmas, which the Buddha has perfected, only a Buddha and a Buddha can exhaust their reality, namely, the suchness of the dharmas, the suchness of their marks, the suchness of their nature, the suchness of their substance, the suchness of their powers, the suchness of their functions, the suchness of their causes, the suchness of their conditions, the suchness of their effects, the suchness of their retributions, and the absolute identity of their beginning and end. (pp. 22–23)[3]

In chapter 16 the Lotus Sutra asserts the identity of the world of samsara, the cycle of birth and death, and the realm of the Buddha, a central theme of the exposition of emptiness in the *Prajñāpāramitā* sutras. Using vivid language the Lotus Sutra explains that the transient phenomenal world, which to the unenlightened is a place of torment, is itself the "pure land" of the Buddha:

When the beings see the kalpa ending
And being consumed by a great fire,
This land of mine is perfectly safe,
Ever full of gods and men;
In it are gardens and groves, halls and towers,
Variously adorned with gems,

As well as jeweled trees with many blossoms and fruits,
Wherein the beings play and amuse themselves;
. . . .
My Pure Land is not destroyed,
Yet the multitude, seeing it consumed with flame,
Are worried, and fear the torment of pain;
The likes of these are everywhere. (p. 243)

Another motif of the Lotus Sutra that associates it with the tradition's expositions of emptiness is the distinction made between the revelation of
the Buddha Dharma in this sutra and the "expedient devices" the
Buddha has previously used to lead practitioners to this truth. The Lotus
Sutra is famous (or infamous) for denouncing the doctrines taught to the
śrāvakas (voice-hearers) as "expedient devices" intended only to prepare
the practitioner to grasp the truth revealed in the sutra. In one passage,
the "nirvāṇa" taught to the voice-hearers is repudiated explicitly on the
grounds of the emptiness of all *dharmas:*

Though I preach nirvāṇa,
This is no true extinction.
The dharmas from their very origin
Are themselves eternally characterized by the marks
of quiet extinction. (p. 37)

Unquestionably the Lotus Sutra accepts the Mahayana teaching of
emptiness as an important expression of the Buddha's ultimate Dharma.
On the other hand, two factors discourage a facile identification of the
sutra's teaching on ultimate truth with "emptiness" as conceived in the
Prajñāpāramitā sutras: the complete absence of a systematic exposition of
the doctrine of emptiness and the Lotus Sutra's extraordinary depiction
of the Buddha. There is a considerable difference between the treatment
of the Buddha in the *prajñāpāramitā* tradition and in the Lotus Sutra. In
the *Prajñāpāramitā* sutras a distinction is made between the physical
body of the Buddha (*rūpa-kāya*) and the *dharma-kāya*. *Dharma-kāya* in the
Aṣṭasāhasrikā Prajñāpāramitā Sūtra has three meanings: the teachings of
the Buddha, the ultimate truth revealed in those teachings, and the Buddha's realization of that truth, that is, the Buddha's pure mental *dharmas*
cognizing ultimate truth.[4] The *prajñāpāramitā* tradition disparages the
idea of devotion to the *rūpa-kāya*, e.g., the practice of worshiping stupas
containing relics of the Buddha, and directs its praises to the *dharma-kāya*.
Generally this means that the unchanging, impersonal truth, emptiness,
is the only correct "object" of veneration.

The Lotus Sutra, on the other hand, focuses on veneration of the Buddha and of the sutra itself. The Buddha of the Lotus Sutra, however, is not simply the human being, Śākyamuni, who lived at a certain point in history, practiced meditation, and attained enlightenment at the age of thirty-five. The Buddha of this sutra is a supramundane Buddha who has acquired mystical powers and a limitless future existence, and is ceaselessly working for the salvation of all beings. Śākyamuni of the Lotus Sutra emits rays of light from his pores that illuminate "all the worlds of the ten directions" (p. 286) and has the power to create innumerable "emanations" or "replicas" of himself that fill the universe preaching the law. (pp. 185–87) In chapter 16, the historical Buddha, Śākyamuni, reveals for the first time his true identity, announcing that he became a Buddha not under the *bodhi* tree in India some forty years ago, but "hundreds of thousands of myriads of millions of *nayutas* of *kalpas*" previous to this and that he has remained in the world since, leading others to their liberation. (p. 237)

Scholars dispute what the framers of the Lotus Sutra intended by this image of the Buddha. The fundamental question is whether the Buddha of the Lotus Sutra is to be understood as an individual who, on attaining Buddhahood long ago, acquired supernatural powers and an indefinitely long future life span, or is to be viewed as the imaginative symbolic representation of ultimate truth, perhaps conceived as a cosmic Buddha or a pervasive principle of Buddhahood in the universe. The central issue in the dispute over the ontological status of the Buddha is the question of his life span. If Śākyamuni represents ultimate truth, presumably he (it) would be eternal. According to the Lotus Sutra the Buddha's future life span is infinite; the Buddha will not become extinct, that is, he will not enter into *parinirvāṇa* but will always remain in the world preaching the Dharma. (p. 242) The sutra, however, portrays Śākyamuni as having become a Buddha at a specific time in the remote past. The passage in which Śākyamuni reveals his true identity states that he has been a Buddha for "millions of *nayutas* of *kalpas*," a very long time indeed, but still a finite length of time; later in the same chapter the Buddha refers to his longevity as "gained after cultivation of long practice," indicating again that he was not always enlightened. (p. 244)

These ambiguities notwithstanding, in China the Buddha of the Lotus Sutra was traditionally understood as a representation of the eternal *dharma-kāya*, his unimaginably long life span being seen as a metaphor for the "beginningless" truth realized by the Buddha.[5] From this standpoint, the mythic images of Śākyamuni's pores emitting light that pervades the universe and of his body splitting into innumerable forms that fill the ten directions are metaphorical representations of the pervasive and unchanging ultimate truth and its salvific function. When Śākyamuni of the

Lotus Sutra is understood as the *dharma-kāya*, and the *dharma-kāya* or ultimate truth is identified as emptiness, the difference between the Lotus Sutra and the *Prajñāpāramitā* sutras appears to be one of style, not substance. As a representation of the *dharma-kāya*, however, the concrete and dynamic image of the supramundane Śākyamuni may suggest a somewhat different conception of ultimate truth than that found in the *Prajñāpāramitā* sutras.

Chih-i's interpretation of the Buddha of the Lotus Sutra is complex and multifarious. He is best known for his explication of the Buddha as a "triple-bodied Buddha" that is at once the historical individual Śākyamuni (the *nirmāṇa-kāya*), a being of supernatural powers acquired through eons of bodhisattva practice (the *saṃbhoga-kāya*), and the eternal *dharma-kāya*. In other contexts he views the sutra's fantastic descriptions of the Buddha's being and powers as a representation of the state of realization attained through Buddhist practice.[6] For our purposes what is most important is Chih-i's interpretation of Śākyamuni as a representation of the *dharma-kāya* or ultimate truth. Considering the Buddha as an expression of ultimate truth, Chih-i further identifies the Buddha of the Lotus Sutra as the inherent Buddha-nature (Chin., *fo-hsing*). He vigorously repudiates an earlier interpreter who denied that the Lotus Sutra teaches the Buddha-nature. "How," he asks rhetorically, "can [Fa-yün] say that [the Lotus Sutra teaches] a finite Buddha when [the Lotus Sutra says] that [the Buddha's life] previously exceeded [in length of years the number of] the sands of the Ganges River, and his next life is twice the above number." Later in the same work he declares explicitly that the Buddha's essence is "the inherently pure mind, the Buddha-nature and the direct cause for Buddhahood."[7]

In Chih-i's view there can be no doubt that the ultimate truth revealed in the Lotus Sutra is the inherent Buddha-nature. Chih-i felt that the Lotus Sutra surpasses all others in its articulation, demonstration, and explanation of the promise that all sentient beings can become Buddhas. The doctrine of universal Buddhahood is proclaimed in the second chapter, where Śākyamuni explains that instead of three "vehicles," or ultimate goals for three different kinds of beings, the *śrāvakas, pratyekabuddhas,* and bodhisattvas, there is only one goal, Buddhahood, for all. The sutra also demonstrates the universality of Buddhahood by depicting the dragon king's daughter (possessing the disadvantages of being both female and a reptile) instantaneously attaining enlightenment, and by predicting the future enlightenment of the Buddha's cousin, Devadatta, who had committed the most heinous evils—attempting to kill the Buddha and to disrupt the Buddhist Saṅgha. Chih-i believed that only a doctrine of universal Buddha-nature could justify the sutra's unqualified promise that all sentient beings can become Buddhas. The sutra's visionary representation of the identity of the Buddha Śākyamuni with all reality may therefore be taken as a revelation of the Buddha-nature inherent in all things.

Although widely accepted in the East Asian Buddhist tradition, from the standpoint of modern scholarship this identification of the ultimate truth of the Lotus Sutra with the Buddha-nature is controversial. The sutra never mentions the Buddha-nature, and the concept of it derives from sutras of the *tathāgata-garbha* tradition that appeared later than the Lotus Sutra. For this reason, several modern commentators have argued that in interpreting the Lotus Sutra as affirming an inherent Buddha-nature, Chih-i is interpolating ideas from the *tathāgata-garbha* tradition which have no warrant in the sutra. According to the *Tathāgata-garbha* sutras and treatises, all sentient beings inherently possess, as the intrinsic nature of their own minds, the *tathāgata-garbha*. Literally, *tathāgata-garbha* means the embryo or womb (*garbha*) of the Buddha, one who has "thus come" (*tathāgata*) from the truth. The *tathāgata-garbha* is the Buddha's pure consciousness of ultimate truth, an undifferentiated, empty awareness devoid of conceptuality and its objects. In some sutras this "pure mind" is conceived as a substratum, which while remaining intrinsically pure and undifferentiated appears under the influence of defilements as the realm of samsara. Though free of delusive conceptual constructions, it is not entirely lacking in characteristics; the *tathāgata-garbha* is portrayed alternately as a store (or "womb") which possesses the qualities of fully achieved Buddhahood and needs only to be uncovered, and as an inchoate "seed" of Buddhahood which must be cultivated and developed. In either case, the message of the *Tathāgata-garbha* sutras is that all sentient beings possess a permanent pure consciousness or Buddha-nature that enables them to become Buddhas.

The concept of Buddha-nature in the *tathāgata-garbha* tradition is difficult to reconcile with the Lotus Sutra's affirmation of the truth of emptiness. As developed in the *Prajñāpāramitā* sutras and the Mādhyamika tradition, the doctrine of emptiness asserts that there is nothing, either phenomenal or transcendent, that exists independently and possesses self-essence. In the Mādhyamika tradition the Buddha-nature taught in the *tathāgata-garbha* tradition was viewed as a provisional teaching for those not yet prepared to grasp the truth of emptiness. While it is true that most Mahayana schools, including the Mādhyamika, assimilated the term Buddha-nature to refer to that which makes the attainment of Buddhahood possible, the term acquired different meanings in accordance with the diverse theoretical views of the Buddhist schools. The Mādhyamikas identified emptiness as the Buddha-nature or "cause" of Buddhahood because the wisdom attained by contemplating the emptiness of all things leads to full Buddha-hood. Emptiness may also be regarded as the cause of enlightenment because the absence of an inherent nature in things ensures that the mind can always change from a state of delusion to enlightenment.

In spite of the textual and theoretical difficulties with the concept of Buddha-nature, Chih-i insists that the Buddha of the Lotus Sutra represents the inherent Buddha-nature and uses the term *tathāgata-garbha* in his treatises and lectures to denote ultimate truth.[8] He even goes so far as to describe the ultimate truth as "eternal, blissful, selfhood and pure," adopting a famous phrase from the *tathāgata-garbha* tradition's Mahā-parinirvāṇa Sutra.[9] It therefore is not surprising that many scholars believe Chih-i explicitly rejects Nāgārjuna's view of the ultimate truth as "emptiness" and posits that the ultimate truth revealed in the Lotus Sutra is a real, absolute "pure mind" at once transcendent to and immanent within the phenomena. If this is Chih-i's intent, the references in the sutra to emptiness must be taken as merely provisional or partial expressions of the truth that is more fully expressed through the image of the eternal and all-pervading Śākyamuni.

The following analysis of Chih-i's theoretical exposition of ultimate truth will show that this is a misunderstanding of Chih-i's use of the Buddha-nature terminology. Chih-i assimilated the terminology of the *tathāgata-garbha* tradition to distinguish his conception of ultimate truth from the emptiness of the Mādhyamika school, but he did accept the *tathāgata-garbha* tradition's notion of a transcendent pure mind. To clarify how Chih-i appropriates and modifies Nāgārjuna's conception of ultimate truth we will first take a brief overview of the Mādhyamika position.

Chih-i's Appropriation of Mādhyamika

In Sanskrit the term *śūnyāta* (emptiness) is used to indicate the absence of something; in the Mahayana tradition it indicates specifically that no cognized being possesses a "self-essence" (*svabhāva*), an identifying characteristic or mark that belongs to the object independent of its relation to any other object. Emptiness is a correlate of the fundamental principle of the Buddhist religion, the doctrine of dependent origination (*pratītya-sam-utpāda*). In Buddhist thought in general no distinction is made between the conditions of a thing's existence and the conditions of our cognition of the thing; to be, something must be cognized as a being. This means that the Buddhist doctrine of dependent origination encompasses both what might be distinguished in the West as the relativity of our conceptual cognition and the causal or ontological dependence of the cognized object. A thing is equally a merely "conditioned" existent by virtue of its being cognized relative to other concepts and by virtue of its causal dependence. It is not difficult to see that if the principle of dependent origination holds for all cognized entities, nothing possesses a self-essence. Emptiness therefore simply expresses the truth of the realm of dependent origination, and there is no ontological distinction between the realm of ultimate truth (emptiness) and the realm of conventional truth, the world of ordinary cognition.

In the Mādhyamika tradition what is relatively cognized is known as a *prajñapti-upādāya*, a "designation" that is "dependent" or "based upon" something else.[10] Through the arguments of the Mūla-madhyamaka-kārikās, Nāgārjuna demonstrates that all cognized beings are "dependently designated," that is, cognized through concepts that are meaningful only through their relation to other concepts. Thus Nāgārjuna establishes that the range of what originates dependently is coextensive with the range of what is dependently designated. Since the cognition of all objects is dependent on the mental acts that form relative concepts, from the Buddhist viewpoint the objects of ordinary cognition "exist" only in virtue of these mental acts of discrimination and synthesis.

Further, the fact that all cognition is dependent on conceptual construction means that the conceptual activity that constitutes the referents of ordinary cognition is not founded on anything intuited directly, independent of conceptual activity. From the absence of an independently cognized ground for conceptual construction, Nāgārjuna draws a radical conclusion about the ontological status of the world of ordinary cognition: It is the intentional correlate of conceptual activity that is determined solely by the conventions of a sociolinguistic system.[11] Conceptual activity constructs referents which serve as the ground for other conceptually constructed referents in an ultimately ungrounded matrix of merely relative existence.

As elucidated by Nāgārjuna, "emptiness," the absence of an independently existent mark or characteristic, implies the absence of a ground of cognitions independent of the sociolinguistic system and is equivalent to the merely conventional (*saṃvṛti*) existence of all phenomenal beings. It follows that the ultimate truth of the realm of dependent origination may be expressed by the simultaneous affirmation of the "two truths" of emptiness and merely conventional or "dependently designated" existence.

Nāgārjuna's refutation of the objective ground of conceptual construction applies to every conceptual cognition of the phenomenal realm, including even the cognition of "dependent origination," understood as signifying the interdependent existence of phenomenal entities. The objective reality of the ontological principle of dependent origination falls with the repudiation of the objective reality of the phenomenal existents themselves: It would make no sense at all to speak of an objectively established dependent origination where there are no "objectively real" things to be causally related to one another. The understanding of phenomenal things as conditioned and impermanent is ultimately as groundless as the illusion of something permanent and independent.

The "truth" (if we can call it that) that Nāgārjuna proves in the Mūla-madhyamaka-kārikās is that our concepts never apprehend an ontological truth, they give no knowledge of the nature of things as they objectively exist, independent of our conceptual acts. As Nāgārjuna says, "No dharma anywhere has been taught by the Buddha of anything."[12]

As a Mahayanist and follower of Nāgārjuna, Chih-i accepts the basic principles of the Mādhyamika exposition of emptiness. He affirms that all cognized beings are dependently originating and "empty" of self-essence. He also recognizes the validity of Nāgārjuna's demonstration that all things that originate dependently are "dependently designated." However, in one important respect Chih-i's conception of ultimate truth diverges from that of the Mādhyamika school: Through careful use of terminology, Chih-i distinguishes his conception of the "dependently designated" existence of phenomenal entities from that of Nāgārjuna.

In Kumārajīva's translation of the Mūla-madhyamaka-kārikās, the Sanskrit prajñapti-upādayā (dependent designation) is translated by the Chinese term chia-ming, which has the same basic epistemological connotations as the Sanskrit original. It indicates that the "name" (ming) of a concept of an object is established "provisionally" (chia), that is, relative to the cognition of other objects. However, as Ng Yu-kwan has pointed out, Chih-i drops the "name" (ming) of "provisional name," creating a new locution, "the provisional," which can refer equally to the "relative" or "dependent" existence of the object as to the relativity of its designation.[13] This minor revision in terminology reflects a significant change in understanding of the ontological status of the realm of dependent origination. It suggests that for Chih-i the objects of ordinary cognition are not merely "dependent designations," that is, not merely the correlates of a conceptual activity determined solely by the conventions of a sociolinguistic system. Rather than merely dependent "names," they are dependent existents.

But what does Chih-i's affirmation of the (conditioned) existence of the dependently designated phenomena mean? Chih-i consistently maintains that all phenomena exist dependent on the conceptualizing mind. On the other hand, Chih-i informs us that this mind is also empty and arises dependent on its object.[14] At one level what Chih-i is saying can be understood as simply descriptive of the intentionality of consciousness. Every thought, every conceptual act, is a consciousness of something, something within a realm of interdependent entities. The empty, mutually dependent existence of conceptual consciousness and the object means that any attempt to discover an independent essence of either will always end in failure; nowhere does there arise an identifiable phenomenon that is pure consciousness, separated from what it is consciousness of, or that is the object "in itself," independent of the conceptual activity that apprehends it.

In addition, however, Chih-i's insistence on the mutual interdependence of conceptualizing thought and cognized objects appears to entail a critique of Nāgārjuna's characterization of cognized objects as the objective correlates of a merely "conventional" conceptual activity. By emphasizing that conceptualizing thought is conditioned by its object, Chih-i makes it known that conceptualizing thought is not a self-generating activity that arbitrarily posits its own objectivities. Rather, the "object" and "thought" must be understood as equiprimordial and mutually conditioning—the objective correlate determines the conceptual activity as much as conceptual activity determines the objective correlate.

But what is this "object" that conditions thought activity? Since the Buddhist is always only concerned with the phenomenal realm, that is, with what "is" for consciousness, the "object" cannot refer to a "thing in itself" that causally determines consciousness. The only plausible answer is that Chih-i is suggesting that there is a perceptual dimension of experience which is in some way determinative of conceptualizing acts. Thus, while the perceptual object never appears as a pure given independent of conceptualization, both the perceptual and conceptual aspects of objects must be acknowledged and understood as equiprimordial and mutually conditioning. Understanding Chih-i's assertion that the mind is conditioned by the object in this way, we can see the legitimacy of his repudiation of the Mādhyamika view that conceptual activity is determined by merely conventional sociolinguistic practices: In Chih-i's view, the practice of linguistic-conceptual activity is conditioned by the perceptual dimension of experience as much as conceptualization conditions what we perceive.

Nāgārjuna and Chih-i concur that there are no independently intuited objective referents, but while Nāgārjuna infers from this that the objects of phenomenal cognition are conventionally established, Chih-i suggests that there are causal determinants of conceptual-linguistic construction. Either position is plausible, and probably neither is provable. Nāgārjuna may have reasoned that if nothing appears to consciousness independent of conceptualizing acts, there is no way of knowing that cognitions are grounded in anything that is not posited by the cognizing mind. Concerned with the epistemological problem of finding an independent ground for our cognitions, he equates the impossibility of knowing that there is such a ground with its nonexistence.

Chih-i, on the other hand, does not let the impossibility, in principle, of a pure perceptual givenness deter him from accepting the more natural proposition that such a preconceptual dimension of experience is in some way manifest in, and determinative of, cognitions. Chih-i is simply not concerned with the epistemological issues of Nāgārjuna and does not feel that our inability to prove that our cognitions are determined by a perceptual dimension must force us to assert that they are conventional constructs, a function of arbitrary sociolinguistic practices.

The distinction between Nāgārjuna's view of the ontological status of phenomenal existents as "dependent designations" and Chih-i's interpretation of them as "dependent existents" signifies an important difference in their conceptions of the correlative term "emptiness." For Nāgārjuna, "emptiness" ultimately indicates the absence of a ground of cognition independent of the sociolinguistic system. To say that emptiness is the truth of the realm of dependent origination does not characterize the "being" of what arises dependently, but simply asserts that our cognition of the realm of dependent origination has no objective ground.

Chih-i, on the other hand, understands emptiness—the absence of independently existing essences—as the true aspect or true nature (*shih-hsiang*) of phenomenal existents that arise dependent on a plurality of conditions. For the Mādhyamika, emptiness is an epistemological truth, the realization that cognized objects are relatively established and lack objective ground. For Chih-i, emptiness is an ontological truth, the realization of the truth of phenomenal entities which, though temporary and conditioned by concepts, are not merely the constructs of thought.

In spite of these important distinctions, what Chih-i and Nāgārjuna share in common should not be underestimated. Both unqualifiedly affirm that there is no distinction between the realm of ultimate truth and the realm of dependent origination. As Nāgārjuna states in the Mūla-madhyamaka-kārikās, "There is nothing whatever which differentiates the existence-in-flux (samsara) from *nirvāṇa*; / And there is nothing whatever which differentiates *nirvāṇa* from existence-in-flux."[15] Chih-i also maintains that the "Middle Path" or ultimate truth is not a transcendent reality but simply the realm of dependent origination, realized as empty and dependently existent. In *The Great Calming and Contemplation* he states this unequivocally: "The dharma-nature and totality of dharmas are not two, not separate. . . . The dharmas of the ordinary are themselves the dharma of ultimate reality."[16]

For Chih-i as for Nāgārjuna there is no reality or truth to be realized beyond the play of the ephemeral, conditioned elements of the realm of dependent origination; the ultimate, middle truth is nothing other than the realization of the true aspect of the phenomenal realm, that is, its empty, conditioned existence. This identity of ultimate truth and phenomena is for Chih-i the central and unequivocal teaching of the Lotus Sutra, the message embodied in the image of the Buddha pervading all realms of existence.

Chih-i and the Language of Tathāgata-garbha

Chih-i expresses his conception of the ultimate truth of phenomenal entities as the simultaneous affirmation of "three truths": That which originates dependent on causes and conditions is (1) empty (k'ung), (2) provisionally (i.e., dependently) existent (chia), and (3) the middle way (chung).[17] The simultaneous affirmation of emptiness and dependent existence is obviously in accord with Mādhyamika philosophy. The assertion of the third, middle truth, however, has reinforced the view that Chih-i introduces to his conception of the ultimate truth notions from the tathāgata-garbha tradition. While some interpreters believe that the third, middle, truth is nothing more than the explicit affirmation of the identity of the truth of emptiness and the truth of provisional existence, others hold that the middle truth is a reference to the real, absolute pure mind of the tathāgata-garbha tradition.

Indeed, Chih-i's characterizations of the ultimate truth are ambiguous and often appear to affirm monistic conceptions like that found in the Tathāgata-garbha sutras. In addition to defining ultimate truth as the simultaneous affirmation of emptiness and dependent existence,[18] he defines it on some occasions as the negation of both emptiness and dependent existence and on others as the simultaneous affirmation and negation of emptiness and dependent existence.[19] The impression created by these descriptions of an absolute reality transcending the realm of empty, dependently originating phenomena is further reinforced by Chih-i's consistent use of the term tathāgata-garbha to refer to the ultimate truth.

Nonetheless, the central importance in Chih-i's thought of the identity of all phenomena with ultimate truth militates against the idea that Chih-i understands the ultimate truth as a pure mind. When ultimate truth is conceived as a pure consciousness, in itself devoid of conceptuality and its objects, there is a fundamental dichotomy between the ultimate truth and the phenomenal realm. Even when, as in the Hua-yen tradition, the pure consciousness is understood as the ground for the appearance of the phenomenal realm, a true oneness of the phenomena and ultimate truth is not obtained; the phenomena are one with ultimate truth only insofar as phenomenal particularity is transcended and one discovers the unitary pure consciousness within all.[20]

Chih-i's use of descriptions of ultimate truth that suggest a transcendence of "both emptiness and dependent arising" can be better accounted for with reference to the discrepancy between our concepts of "emptiness" and "dependent existence" and the ultimate nonconceptual cognition of the truth of the realm of dependent origination.[21] Chih-i enlists as alternative definitions for the ultimate truth the apophatic expression "neither existence nor emptiness" and the paradoxical "both existence and emptiness and neither existence nor emptiness" to reinforce our awareness that even the concepts of emptiness and dependent existence cannot perfectly represent the ultimate truth. The fact that we must transcend even the concepts of existence and emptiness to attain the fullest apprehension of the truth does not indicate that the truth itself transcends phenomenal existence.

Similarly, the use of the term *tathāgata-garbha* to designate ultimate truth should not be interpreted in isolation from the whole tenor of Chih-i's thought. As we have seen, for Chih-i ultimate truth is the true aspect of the phenomenal entities that are affirmed as real, although temporary and conditioned, existents. It is possible that Chih-i designates ultimate reality as *tathāgata-garbha* to distinguish his positive conception of the ultimate truth as the "true aspect" of phenomenal existents from the merely negative epistemological emptiness of Nāgārjuna. Far from positing an ultimate truth beyond the phenomenal realm, the term *tathāgata-garbha* should be understood as the strongest possible assertion that the realm of dependent origination is itself the ultimate truth.

In his teachings on meditative practices, Chih-i explains that by contemplating a "single moment of thought" (*i-nien*) one can realize the ultimate truth.[22] A famous passage in *The Great Calming and Contemplation* explains that the contemplation of the ultimate truth of the single instant of thought reveals that it "contains" or "encompasses" (*chü*) all "three thousand" of the categories of dharmas in Chih-i's complicated analysis and classification of the elements of phenomenal existence.

> Now one mind comprises ten *dharma*-spheres, but each *dharma*-sphere also comprises ten *dharma*-spheres. One sphere comprises thirty kinds of worlds, hence a hundred *dharma*-spheres comprise three thousand kinds of worlds. These three thousand are contained in a fleeting moment of consciousness. Where there is no mind, that is the end of the matter, but, when a mustard-seed's quantity of mind comes into being, in and of itself it contains the three thousand.[23]

During the tenth century a heated debate centering on this passage's interpretation arose between two groups of T'ien-t'ai followers, the "home-mountain" (*shan-chia*) group—which eventually retained the claim to orthodoxy—and the "off-mountain" (*shan-wai*) group.[24] The "off-mountain" group equated the "single instant of thought" with the "pure consciousness" that, according to certain sutras of the *tathāgata-garbha* tradition, is the intrinsic nature of mind and is the ultimate truth or "suchness" of both mind and all phenomena. According to this reading of the passage, Chih-i asserts that all *dharmas* are "one" with the mind or "encompassed" by the mind because the intrinsic nature of all *dharmas* is the undifferentiated, empty "pure awareness." The *dharmas* are seen to be "unified" or "one" when meditation on the mind reveals that the particularity and diversity of phenomena are false constructs and only the intrinsic nature of pure consciousness is "real."

As indicated above, the "off-mountain" group's interpretation creates an untenable distinction between the phenomena and ultimate truth. The "home-mountain" group, led by Ssu-ming Chih-li (960–1028), remained consistent with Chih-i's thought by interpreting the "instant of thought" in the above passage as any transient, conditioned moment of phenomenal consciousness. Chih-li further held that this encompassing of all reality is the ultimate truth not only of a moment of consciousness, but of every phenomenal existent. Stevenson writes that "Chih-li gravitated toward a theory of 'encompassment [of totality] within particulate features themselves' (*hsiang-chü*), such that in each and every mark, 'all marks manifest simultaneously in perfect repleteness' (*hsiang hsiang wan-ran*)."[25] Although Chih-i only referred explicitly to the mind as encompassing all phenomena, this further extrapolation is justified by the identity of all phenomena with ultimate truth. In the *Profound Meaning of the Lotus Sutra* Chih-i reminds his audience that the "mind" in no way differs from all other *dharmas* and is singled out as the object of contemplation only because it is closest to us. (p.197)

Every *dharma*, contemplated in its ultimate truth, reveals itself as pervading all phenomena. Most significantly, the ordinary moment of consciousness encompasses all *dharmas:* "All one can say is that the mind is all *dharmas* and that all *dharmas* are the mind."[26] We are now in a better position to understand how the image of Śākyamuni in the Lotus Sutra represents the ultimate truth of the phenomenal realm, the Buddha-nature. From Chih-i's standpoint, the depiction of the all-pervading Śākyamuni does not figure a "pure" consciousness that is devoid of conceptuality and its objects and simultaneously the ground of phenomenal existence; it is rather an image of the "true aspect" of the phenomena themselves, the ordinary *dharmas* that are at once empty and provisionally existent, each encompassing the totality and therefore both "one" and "many." This ultimate truth of the phenomenal realm is the "Middle Way" that Chih-i refers to as the resplendent realm of the Buddha which is "eternal, blissful, selfhood and pure." The ultimate truth may be identified as the cause of Buddhahood or the Buddha-nature (*tathāgata-garbha*) because it is the identity of one's own mind with this truth which makes the real-ization of the truth and the attainment of Buddhahood possible. However, it must be stressed that the Buddha-nature for Chih-i is not the transcendent pure mind of the *Tathāgata-garbha* sutras, but simply the "true aspect" of the moment of ordinary consciousness and of all phe-nomena.

Conclusion

In Chih-i's view, the ultimate truth revealed in the Lotus Sutra differs significantly from the teaching of emptiness as elucidated by Nāgārjuna and the Mādhyamika school. The difference Chih-i establishes, however, is not the result of an imposition on the Lotus Sutra of notions of a pure consciousness. Chih-i finds the sutra in complete agreement with the Mādhyamikas in their identification of ultimate truth with the phenome-nal realm. The difference between Chih-i's conception of the ultimate truth of the Lotus Sutra and Nāgārjuna's teaching of emptiness lies in a much more subtle divergence of views in regard to the status of phenom-enal existence.

From Chih-i's standpoint, the dependence of all phenomenal entities on thought construction, affirmed throughout the Mahayana tradition, does not entail that they are established solely by sociolinguistic conven-tions and that their "truth" is only their groundlessness, their mere con-ventionality. Chih-i affirms that the phenomenal entities do provisionally (dependently) exist; simultaneously empty and dependently arising, their interpenetrating existence is a positive phenomenon, a reality that while not independent of conceptual activity is not merely the groundless cor-relate of conceptual acts. Chih-i's affirmation of phenomenal existence is intimated by the Lotus Sutra's elaborate descriptions of the wonder of the Buddha realm. This realm of the Buddha, filled with gardens of jewel trees, magnificent towers and halls, incense and music, is not a pure land beyond this world but the realm of phenomenal existence itself seen in its truth. In contrast to the *Prajñāpāramitā* sutras, which emphasize the il-lusory nature of the phenomenal realm, the Lotus Sutra celebrates its "true aspect" with a profusion of concrete images.

Chih-i's exposition of the truth revealed in the Lotus Sutra situates the sutra at the center of contemporary concerns of Western philosophy. For most of its history, the Western tradition has been characterized by the quest for an objective truth. Even after Kant's "Copernican Revolution" dashed the hope for knowledge of the world as it is "in itself," the quest remained essentially unchanged: if we could not know the external world objectively, at least we could possess the truth of our own subjectivity and its manner of constructing our experience. Underlying this quest for truth is a particular view of language that has dominated Western thought since the time of the ancient Greeks.

According to this view, the meaning of a word lies in its reference to an object, to something perceived in the world, or perhaps to a purely ideal object intuited by the mind. This theory presupposes that we first observe the world and find in it diverse objects; we then put like objects into classes and form concepts that refer to the whole class, finally giving our concept a phonetic sign or name. Nietzsche was one of the first Western thinkers to seriously question this view of language. He explored the ways in which language structures how we think and suggested that our concepts and grammatical forms determine what kinds of "things" we will believe to exist. Following Nietzsche, in the twentieth century structuralist and poststructuralist philosophers have brought to prominence the idea that our linguistic conceptual system is a conventional social construct in which each element is defined by its "difference" from other elements. Instead of thought and language reflecting existents, the "existents" we cognize are a function of the concepts defined by our linguistic system. Thus twentieth-century postmodern thought has embraced a theory of language that is diametrically opposed to the beliefs of the preceding philosophical tradition.

As many people have noticed, in reversing its earlier understanding of language, Western philosophy has converged with Buddhist thought, which has always emphasized the role of language in the construction of experience. In particular, scholars have observed the similarities between Mādhyamika philosophy and twentieth-century linguistic philosophy and poststructuralism. This movement within the Western tradition, however, is not without its critics. Perhaps in asserting that meaning is solely a function of the linguistic system, contemporary Western thinkers have overcompensated for the naive belief that language merely expresses what is first apprehended by the mind. Chih-i's view of the phenomenal world, as dependent on a relatively constructed linguistic-conceptual system but not solely determined by it, suggests a middle ground that may avoid the weaknesses of the two extreme views that have dominated Western thought so far.

Notes

1. All quotations from the Lotus Sutra are from Leon Hurvitz, trans., *Scripture of the Lotus Blossom of the Fine Dharma* (New York: Columbia University Press, 1976).

2. Paul Swanson argues forcefully for the former view in *Foundations of T'ien-t'ai Philosophy* (Berkeley: Asian Humanities Press, 1989); Ng Yu-kwan provides a defense of the latter position in *T'ien-t'ai Buddhism and Early Mādhyamika* (Honolulu: University of Hawaii Press, 1993).

3. Kumārajīva's translation may not correspond to the Sanskrit texts. See Hurvitz, *Scripture of the Lotus Blossom of the Fine Dharma*, 349–50, for a discussion of this passage. (In the T'ien-t'ai tradition this passage is cited as a reference to the threefold truth of emptiness, provisional existence, and the middle way).

4. Paul Williams, *Mahāyāna Buddhism* (London: Routledge, 1989), 173.

5. There were exceptions to this view. Fa-yün, is a notable example.

6. See Jacqueline Stone, "Mystical Interpretations of the *Lotus Sūtra* in the Thought of Nichiren" in *Epoché* 14 (1986):50–52.

7. Chih-i, *The Profound Meaning of the Lotus Sutra* [*Fa hua hsüan i*], translated in Swanson, *Foundations of T'ien-t'ai Philosophy*, 170, 190.

8. For instance, Chih-i writes, "Whether we speak of sense faculty or sense object, both are the *dharmadhātu*, both ultimate emptiness, both the *tathāgatagarbha*, and both the middle way." See Chih-i, *The Great Calming and Contemplation* [*Mo-ho chih-kuan*], trans. Neal Donner and Daniel B. Stevenson (Honolulu: University of Hawaii Press, 1993), 194.

9. Chih-i, *Profound Meaning*, 192.

10. See verse 24:18 of the *Mūla-madhyamaka-kārikās* for Nāgārjuna's use of this term. Translated in Frederick J. Streng, *Emptiness, A Study in Religious Meaning* (Nashville: Abingdon Press, 1967), 213.

11. There are varying interpretations of Nāgārjuna's exposition of emptiness in the *Mūla-madhyamaka-kārikās*. Among Westerners who have interpreted Nāgārjuna's arguments are Chris Gudmunsen (*Wittgenstein and Buddhism* [London: The Macmillan Press, 1977]), Frederick Streng (*Emptiness*), Waldo Ives ("Nāgārjuna and Analytic Philosophy," in *Philosophy East and West* 25 [July 1975]:281–90), Nathan Katz ("Nāgārjuna and Wittgenstein on Error," in *Buddhist and Western Philosophy*, ed. Nathan Katz [New Delhi: Sterling Press, 1981]), C. W. Huntington (*The Emptiness of Emptiness: An Introduction to Early Indian Mādhyamika* [Honolulu: University of Hawaii Press, 1989]).

12. Verse 25:24 of the *Mūla-madhyamaka-kārikās*, in Streng, *Emptiness*, 217.

13. Ng Yu-Kwan, *T'ien-t'ai Buddhism and Early Mādhyamika*, 131.

14. Chih-i, *Profound Meaning*, 198.

15. Verse 25:19 of the *Mūla-madhyamaka-kārikās*, in Streng, *Emptiness*, 217.

16. Chih-i, *The Great Calming and Contemplation*, 166. This is more poetically expressed in the famous phrase, "There is not a single sight nor smell that is not the middle way." Although often attributed to Chih-i, this expression is found in Kuan-ting's introduction to *The Great Calming and Contemplation*. See Donner and Stevenson, 113.

17. Paul Swanson (*Foundations of T'ien-t'ai Philosophy*, 123) points out that there is little direct discussion of the threefold truth concept in Chih-i's writing, although it is implicit throughout Chih-i's thought and works. For explicit references to the concept, see Chih-i, *The Great Calming and Contemplation*, 176–78 and Chih-i, *On the Four Teachings* [*Ssu chiao i, chüan* 1 & 2], trans. Robert F.

Rhodes. *Shin Buddhist Comprehensive Research Institute Annual Memoirs* 3 & 4:118.

18. Chih-i, *Profound Meaning*, 201.

19. Chih-i, *The Great Calming and Contemplation*, 172.

20. Chan-jan, the important eighth-century restorer of the T'ien-t'ai school, made a similar argument against the view that Chih-i posits a pure consciousness. See Chan Chi-wah's dissertation *Chih-li (960–1028) and the Formation of Orthodoxy in the Sung T'ien-t'ai Tradition of Buddhism* (Ann Arbor: University Microfilms, 1993), 62. For Chan-jan's interpretation of Chih-i, see also Linda Penkower, *T'ien-t'ai during the T'ang dynasty: Chan-jan and the Sinification of Buddhism* (Ann Arbor: University Microfilms, 1993).

21. Chih-i discusses at length the necessity of transcending conceptual thought to realize the ultimate truth in *The Profound Meaning of the Lotus Sutra*, 202–04.

22. In the first volume of *The Great Calming and Contemplation*, Chih-i refers to the meditation on the true nature of a thought in the midst of all activities as the "*samādhi* of maintaining wakeful awareness of thought." It is also called the "neither-walking-nor-sitting *samādhi*." See 262–304.

23. Translated in Leon Hurvitz, *Chih-i (538–97): An Introduction to the Life and Ideas of a Chinese Buddhist Monk*, in *Mélanges Chinois et Bouddhiques*, Vol. 12, 1960–62, 311–12.

24. For a discussion of this dispute, see Chan Chi-wah, *Chih-li (960–1028)*. See also Stevenson's essay, "The *Mo-ho chih-kuan* and T'ien-t'ai Tradition," in Chih-i, *The Great Calming and Contemplation*, 84–96.

25. Stevenson, "The *Mo-ho chih-kuan* and T'ien-t'ai Tradition," in Chih-i, *The Great Calming and Contemplation*, 89.

26. Chih-i, *The Great Calming and Contemplation*. Translated in Hurvitz, *Chih-i (538–97)*, 311.

When Disobedience Is Filial and Resistance Is Loyal: The Lotus Sutra and Social Obligations in the Medieval Nichiren Tradition

Jacqueline I. Stone

The social dimensions of Lotus Sutra–related faith and practice in Japan have for the most part been embedded in larger Buddhist traditions of action for the sake of others. In premodern times, these included giving alms, to cultivate compassion and relieve the sufferings of the poor, as well as "building bridges and digging wells," traditional activities of *hijiri* or itinerant monks that both exemplified the bodhisattva ethos of helping others and benefited specific communities. Lotus Sutra devotion also overlapped the social aspects of Buddhist thaumaturgy and ritual performance. The Lotus, along with other scriptures, was traditionally recited and lectured on for the peace and prosperity of the country and was also used in memorial prayers for the dead—prayers believed not only to repay the sponsor's obligation to deceased relatives by leading them to enlightenment, but to protect the society of the living from the malign activities of vengeful ghosts.

The twentieth century saw the rise of "socially engaged Buddhism." Informed by modern insights into the constructed nature of human institutions, socially engaged Buddhism redefines delusion and suffering not merely as an individual matter, but as built into and perpetuated by the very structure of social institutions. Engaged Buddhists often regard the effort to reform social institutions along more egalitarian lines as an indispensable component of Buddhist liberative practice. In modern Japan, the civil resistance displayed by Nihonzan Myōhōji in the antinuclear cause, as well as the peace movements and refugee relief work sponsored by Risshō Kōsei-kai and Sōka Gakkai, both NGO affiliates of the United Nations, may be broadly considered as Lotus Sutra–related forms of socially engaged Buddhism. In these cases, too, faith in the Lotus Sutra has been assimilated to larger concepts of Buddhist social responsibility.

In the tradition of Nichiren Buddhism, however, we find the Lotus Sutra linked to a view of social responsibility that is distinctive. Nichiren (1222–82) numbers among the founders of the so-called "new Buddhist" movements of Japan's Kamakura period (1185–1333). He is known for his exclusivistic doctrine that upholds faith in the Lotus Sutra alone and denies the soteriological efficacy of other Buddhist forms. Now in the degenerate, Final Dharma age (*mappō*), he taught, embracing faith in the Lotus Sutra and chanting its *daimoku* or title, *Namu Myōhō Renge-kyō*, is the sole vehicle of liberation. Moreover, because the practitioner as subject and his or her objective, the outer world, are from a Mahayana standpoint nondual, upholding faith in the Lotus Sutra was in Nichiren's view not only a matter of personal salvation but also, in modern terms, the practitioner's "social responsibility." This essay aims at clarifying this social dimension of Nichiren's teaching. It first examines the world view and doctrinal foundations upon which he defined exclusive faith in the Lotus as the only socially responsible stance for a Buddhist to adopt. It then explores how exclusive commitment to the Lotus Sutra was related to Nichiren's view of individual obligations within the framework of *bushi* (warrior) society in medieval Japan, from which Nichiren drew most of his followers. Lastly, it considers how the medieval Nichiren Buddhist tradition viewed the practitioner's obligations toward the country, as seen through its distinctive practice of "admonishing the state."

World View and Doctrinal Foundations

Like many people of medieval Japan, Nichiren accepted the idea of an indivisible unity between the microcosm of the individual and the macrocosm of the greater universe. Within this unity, human ritual and moral actions were believed directly to affect the outer world. This premise underlay belief in the efficacy of esoteric rites performed for timely rainfall or good harvests, or the attribution of natural disasters such as drought or floods to human wrongdoing. In the influential Tendai Buddhist tradition from which Nichiren emerged, the moral unity of the individual and the world was schematized in terms of the "nonduality of dependent and primary [karmic] recompense" (*eshō funi*). In other words, the individual's karma or actions—thoughts, words, and deeds—were thought to bear culumative fruit in two simultaneous and interconnected modes: as the collection of physical and mental aggregates that form individual living beings, and as those individuals' outer circumstances or container world. Thus the living subject and his or her objective world were held to be fundamentally inseparable—a relationship that Nichiren likened to that of a body and its shadow.[1] Moreover, because all phenomena are from a Mahayana standpoint without independent substance, the ten realms of existence from hell to Buddhahood were said to interpenetrate, each of the ten realms encompassing the others within itself. Thus for one who achieves awakening, the present world is the Buddha's pure land. For Nichiren, the inherence of the pure land in the present world was not merely a matter of philosophical or contemplative insight; when individuals realized enlightenment, he taught, their world would be materially transformed:

> When all people throughout the land enter the one Buddha vehicle and the Wonderful Dharma [of the Lotus] alone flourishes, because the people all chant *Namu Myōhō Renge-kyō* as one, the wind will not thrash the branches nor the rain fall hard enough to break clods. The age will become like the reigns of [the Chinese sage kings] Yao and Shun. In the present life, inauspicious calamities will be banished, and people will obtain the art of longevity. When the principle becomes manifest that both persons and dharmas "neither age nor die," then each of you, behold! There can be no doubt of the sutra's promise of "peace and security in the present world."[2]

This passage points to both continuities and breaks between Nichiren's teaching and broader, contemporaneous currents of Buddhist thought. Teachings about the nonduality of this world and the Buddha's pure land, expressed in such terminology as "the *sahā* world is the land of ever-tranquil light (*shaba soku jakkōdo*)" or "worldly truth embodies ultimate reality (*zokutai nishin*)," formed a standard doctrinal feature of both Tendai and Shingon esoteric Buddhist traditions. Similarly, belief in the apotropaic powers of the Buddha-Dharma to ensure harmony with nature and prosperity in the social sphere also was a common assumption underlying the sponsorship of esoteric rites for nation protection (*chingo kokka*). Nichiren's distinctive reading of these ideas derived from his "single-practice" stance: The ideal Buddha-land could be realized in this world, but only by exclusive faith in the Lotus Sutra.

Like other figures prominent in the new Kamakura Buddhist movements, Nichiren took the advent of the *mappō* era as a mandate to abandon traditional Buddhist stances allowing for a plurality of practices according to the differing capacities and inclinations of individuals and to instead embrace an ethos of "exclusive choice" of a single practice, claimed to be universally valid, which was thereby invested with absolute status.

The first person to make this move had been Hōnen (1133–1212), founder of the Japanese Jōdo or Pure Land sect, who taught that now in the evil age of the Final Dharma, men and women can no longer reach salvation through their own efforts but only by entrusting themselves to the compassionate power of the original vow of the Buddha Amida of the western pure land and repeating the *nembutsu*, or invocation of Amida's name. Nichiren objected both to Hōnen's extreme emphasis on "Other-power" and the locating of salvation in another world after death, but he too espoused the notion of a single, universally feasible practice: faith in the Lotus Sutra and the chanting of its *daimoku*. Nichiren upheld Tendai understanding of the Lotus as the supreme and final teaching of Śākyamuni Buddha, unique in promising Buddhahood to all. The sutra's title, in his view, encompassed in itself all Buddhist teachings and the seed of Buddhahood, reserved by the Buddha for the evil age of *mappō* when people would need it most.

Nichiren's Tendai contemporaries, too, held the Lotus Sutra to be all-inclusive, but generally took this to mean that, properly understood, any practice, such as chanting Amida Buddha's name or invoking the Bodhisattva Kannon, could be considered practice of the Lotus Sutra. Nichiren decried this interpretation as a confusion of the true and the provisional and rejected all other, "pre–Lotus Sutra" teachings as no longer suited to the present time of *mappō*. Like medicine that stands too long on the shelf and becomes poisonous, these other teachings and the practices based upon them were, in his view, not only soteriologically useless but positively harmful. For Nichiren, to willfully set aside or ignore the Lotus in favor of other, "lesser" teachings amounted to "slander of the Dharma" and would pull the practitioner down into the lower realms of rebirth.

He therefore taught his followers that one should not only embrace faith in the Lotus Sutra oneself, but spread that faith to others, assertively rebuking adherence to other, provisional teachings. This is known as *shakubuku*, the "harsh method" of propagating the Dharma by actively challenging "wrong views." Nichiren saw *shakubuku* as compassionate action that would enable others to form a connection with the Lotus Sutra and save them from both misfortune in this world and rebirth in the evil realms.

In practice, his criticism of other Buddhist forms brought down on Nichiren and his followers the anger of both religious and worldly authorities; he himself was twice exiled and once nearly beheaded, while some among his followers had their lands confiscated or were imprisoned. Yet Nichiren concluded that this opposition represented an opportunity to purify himself of his own slanders against the Dharma committed in past lifetimes. And in light of the Lotus Sutra's own statements that its devotees in an evil age after the Buddha's nirvana will meet with enmity, the hostility he encountered confirmed to him the validity of his position. He and his disciples accordingly came to valorize meeting persecution for the Dharma's sake (*hōnan*) as a proof of one's faith and a guarantee of one's future Buddhahood. This transcendent, soteriological side of *shakubuku* practice was at the same time inextricably intertwined with notions of responsibility to society and country. We have seen that Nichiren saw faith in the Lotus as the sole path by which the present world could be transfigured as the Buddha-land. Conversely, he regarded both the natural disasters and political upheavals of his day as directly attributable to the failure of his contemporaries to recognize the unique truth of the Lotus and embrace it exclusively. Over the course of his career he would come to interpret every significant event of his age in this light: The defeat of the Taira clan by the Minamoto in 1185 and the rise of *bushi* power, resulting in the establishment of the *bakufu* or warrior government in Kamakura; the retired Emperor Gotoba's defeat in his attempt to overthrow the Kamakura *bakufu* in the Jōkyū Uprising of 1221; and the Mongol invasion attempts launched against Japan in 1274 and 1281 for him all stemmed from rejection of the Lotus Sutra in favor of provisional teachings. In his famous treatise *Risshō ankoku ron* (Establishing the correct [Dharma] and bringing peace to the country), submitted in 1260 as a memorial or admonition to the retired shogunal regent, Hōjō Tokiyori, Nichiren blamed recent disasters—earthquakes, epidemics, and famines—on the spread of the exclusive *nembutsu* teaching of Hōnen, who had urged people to "close, discard, ignore and abandon" all teachings other than the Pure Land sutras as too profound for the limited capacity of beings of the Final Dharma age.

> When the perverse is preferred and the true forgotten, won't the benevolent deities be angered? When the perfect [teaching] is rejected in favor of those that are incomplete, won't evil demons seize the advantage? Rather than perform ten thousand prayer rituals, it would be better to prohibit this one evil![3]

In his later years, as Nichiren's position of exclusive devotion to the Lotus grew increasingly refined and focused, Zen, the *vinaya* revival movements, and both Shingon and Tendai esoteric traditions joined the *nembutsu* as targets of his criticism.

In sum, Nichiren shared with his contemporaries the assumption that human action, especially ritual action, affects the greater cosmos. He also embraced widespread strands of Buddhist thought, articulated especially within the Tendai school, about the inherence of the pure land in the present world. What was different in his case was the exclusive stance. Because, in his view, only the Lotus Sutra leads to enlightenment in the

Final Dharma age, it was not enough to embrace it oneself; one had also to teach others. And because the self and the outer world are nondual, the fact of individuals privately embracing or rejecting the Lotus Sutra had public consequences; thus *shakubuku*, the repudiation of provisional teachings, was both a religious and a social responsibility.

The Lotus Sutra and Filial Piety

Now let us consider how this social dimension of Nichiren's teaching affected his and his community's understanding of the practitioner's obligations in social relationships, specifically, the obligations of filial piety and loyalty. Since the Lotus was for Nichiren the only true teaching, all religious and worldly values had of necessity to be subsumed within it. In his major treatise *Kaimoku shō* (Opening the eyes), Nichiren argues that faith in the Lotus Sutra represents the highest form of filial piety:

> Filial piety as the Confucians teach it is limited to this life. Because they provide no means to help one's parents in future lifetimes, the saints and sages of these outer teachings are such in name only. The heterodox paths [of India] are cognizant of past and future [lifetimes] but [likewise] provide no path by which to help one's parents [in future lifetimes]. It is the Buddhist path that enables one to help one's parents in their next life; thus its saints and sages merit the name. However, in the various sutras and schools of the Hinayana and Mahayana preached before the Lotus Sutra, it is difficult to attain the Way, even for oneself. How much more, to enable one's father and mother to do so! Now in the case of the Lotus Sutra, the [promise of] Buddhahood for mothers was revealed with the teaching that women [such as the Nāga princess] can become Buddhas, and the [promise of Buddhahood] for fathers was revealed with the teaching that evil men such as Devadatta can become Buddhas. This sutra represents the "classic of filial piety" of the inner scriptures.[4]

The notion that Buddhism embodied a superior form of filial piety, in that its promised benefits extend beyond this life, was by no means new. It represented an ongoing attempt on the part of Buddhist monastics to defend their celibate and world-renouncing institution in Indic or East Asian societies, where performing caste duties or carrying on the ancestral line were considered primary social obligations. Hence the appearance of sutras addressing this theme, such as the *Mo-ye ching*, which says that, after attaining Buddhahood, Śākyamuni at once ascended to the *trāyastriṃśa* heaven to preach the Dharma to his mother, or the *Hsin-ti kuan ching*, often cited by Nichiren as stating, "Abandoning one's obligations and entering the Unconditioned is called the true repayment of obligations." What distinguishes Nichiren's view is the linking of filial piety to exclusive faith in the Lotus Sutra, representing the Lotus as embodying the only true way of filial piety by virtue of its promise of universal Buddhahood. This raises the question of what would happen if a practitioner's exclusive commitment to the Lotus Sutra—Nichiren's definition of true filiality—were to conflict with his or her parents' wishes, which conventional understanding demands that filial children must obey. Nichiren is quite explicit on this point:

> In any matter, one who goes against his father and mother or who refuses to follow the ruler is deemed unfilial and incurs Heaven's punishment. However, should they become enemies of the Lotus Sutra, then disregarding the will of one's parents or ruler is filial conduct and repays one's obligation to the country.[5]

This statement is significant in that Nichiren's exclusive devotion to the Lotus Sutra opens up a religiously mandated ground for resistance to conventional social authority. This stance was to have repercussions for individuals within his community in his own lifetime and for the Nichiren Buddhist institution in the centuries after his death. Based on the evidence of Nichiren's letters, let us look at two cases among his early followers of individual devotees caught in a conflict between loyalty to parents or other immediate authority figures and faith in the Lotus Sutra.[6]

Ikegami Emon-no-tayū-no-sakan Munenaka was a warrior of Musashi Province. He and his younger brother (whom the Nichiren tradition names Munenaga) were early converts to Nichiren's teachings. Details concerning him are scarce; his family may have been direct vassals (*go-kenin*) of the Hōjō clan, who ruled the Kamakura *bakufu* as regents to the shogun. There is also a tradition that Munenaka served the *bakufu's* Department of Works (*saji bugyō*). Munenaka's father (according to tradition, named Yasumitsu) was a lay patron of the prominent monk Ryōkan-bō Ninshō (1217–1303), a disciple of Eison (1201–90), a leader in the *vinaya* revival movement, and inheritor of Eison's Saidai-ji precept lineage. Ninshō was also valued by *bakufu* officials for his thaumaturgical powers as an esoteric ritual specialist. Nichiren, however, wrote that Ninshō and his followers were hostile to him and blamed Ninshō's machinations for his exile to Sado Island from 1271 to 1274 and the attendant persecution of his followers in Kamakura. Inevitably, perhaps, friction developed between father and sons over their differing religious commitments.

Around 1275 or 1276, Munenaka's father disowned him on account of his persistent refusal to abandon his allegiance to Nichiren. In warrior families of the time, a father's authority was virtually absolute and his right to disinherit his children was supported by law. Disinheritance carried severe social and ecomomic consequences. Nichiren, then living in reclusion on Mount Minobu in Kai Province, wrote to the two brothers and their wives instructing them how to approach the situation. First, he states unambiguously that the claims of the Lotus Sutra must transcend the claims of parents:

> The Lotus Sutra is the eye of all Buddhas. It is the original teacher of the Lord Śākyamuni himself. One who discards even a single character or dot of it commits an offense greater than killing his father and mother a thousand or ten thousand times over or drawing blood from the bodies of the Buddhas of the ten directions. . . . In general, one should obey one's parents, but on the path of Buddhahood, not obeying them [when they oppose the Lotus] is surely the basis of filial piety.[7]

Second, Nichiren urges the brothers to see their conflict with their father in broader, soteriological terms as a specific instance of the struggle between delusion and the aspiration for enlightenment. Theirs, he suggests, is not an isolated case but part of a larger cosmic pattern, in which all who embrace the Lotus may be expected to meet great obstacles in their efforts to escape samsara and achieve Buddhahood:

> This world is the domain of the devil king of the sixth heaven. Since time without beginning, all living beings have been his vassals. Within the six paths, he has not only built the prisons of the twenty-five realms to contain them, but made wives and children into shackles and parents and lords into nets that stretch across the skies. . . . He will enter the bodies of wives and children to deceive husbands and parents, or possess the ruler of the country to threaten practitioners of the Lotus Sutra, or enter fathers and mothers to harrass filial children.[8]

The assertion that parents and rulers can function as demonic influences obstructing Buddhist practice radically relativizes the social claims of family and clan loyalty.

Third, having shown the brothers' conflict with their father to be part of a larger, cosmic drama, Nichiren undercuts the opposition between the two sides by constructing a narrative in which both father and sons are caught in the same causal chain: Their father now opposes their faith in the Lotus out of delusion, while they themselves must undergo this trial as the karmic effect of their own, similar deluded opposition to the Lotus in prior lifetimes:

In the past, we opposed practitioners of the true Dharma. Now we have instead come to embrace it ourselves, but because of the offense of having hindered others [in their practice] in the past, we should by rights fall into a great hell in the future. However, because the merit of practicing the true Dharma in this life is powerful, the great sufferings of the future are summoned [into the present] and encountered in lessened form. . . . To eradicate the offenses of slander against the Dharma committed in the past, you are now oppressed by parents with false views and live under a ruler who hates practitioners of the Lotus. . . . Never doubt but that you slandered the Dharma in past lifetimes. If you doubt it, you will not be able to endure the minor sufferings of this life, and if you should yield to your father's admonitions and abandon the Lotus Sutra against your intention, then not only will you yourselves fall into hell, but your mother and father will fall into the great Avīcī hell as well.[9]

In this narrative, the practitioner experiences the effects of Dharma slander from the past while his persecutor perpetuates it in the present. In Nichiren's reading, however, the one with faith in the Lotus Sutra can utilize the opportunity to purify himself of past offenses, and, by upholding it whatever the cost in worldly terms, liberate both himself and his persecutor. This view shifts agency from the father to the sons, who, in social terms, are the subordinate parties in the relationship and have the lesser authority.

Lastly, Nichiren urges upon the brothers a perspective from which all worldly vicissitudes are relativized: "No matter what misfortune may befall you, regard it as a dream and think only of the Lotus Sutra."[10]

Munenaka's father apparently relented and reinstated him once but then disinherited him again in 1277. Throughout this family ordeal, Munenaka seems never to have faltered; it is probable that he had left his father's house and was staying with his mother's family.[11] His father's rather drastic decision to disinherit him was made possible by the presence of the younger brother, who could perhaps be persuaded where the elder brother could not. This younger brother, known by his military title Hyōe-no-sakan, apparently wavered for a time, influenced perhaps by more conventional understandings of the loyalty due to a parent or by the unexpected opportunity to supplant Munenaka as his father's heir. This time, Nichiren's admonitions focused on the vacillating younger brother:

Emon-no-tayū-no-sakan [Munenaka] has again been disowned by your father. As I said to your wife, this was certain to happen. I told her that since you are unreliable, she had better be resolved. . . .

Since you consider only immediate matters, you will probably follow your father, and deluded people will praise your conduct . . . [But] if you follow your father, an enemy of the Lotus Sutra, and abandon your brother, a practitioner of the One Vehicle, is that being filial? . . . If you curry favor [with your father] for the sake of a trivial inheritance and fall into the evil paths on account of your faintheartedness, don't blame me! . . . If by a hundred- or thousand-to-one chance you should decide to heed my advice, then confront your father and declare: "Because you are my father, I should obey you in all things, but because you have become an enemy of the Lotus Sutra, if I obey you in this, I would be unfilial. Therefore I will abandon you and follow my brother. If you cast him off, know that you cast me off as well."[12]

Nichiren goes on to quote the Nirvana Sutra to the effect that the number of parents one has had in successive lifetimes cannot be counted, not even if one were to cut up all the plants and trees in the world to make tallies. From this he concludes,

It is easy to obtain parents, but hard to meet the Lotus Sutra. Now, if you reject the words of a father, who is easy to come by, and stand by [your brother,] a friend of the Lotus Sutra, which is difficult to meet, then not only will you yourself achieve Buddhahood, but you will also lead [to Buddhahood] the father whom you rejected.[13]

This, Nichiren goes on to suggest, would parallel the example of Śākyamuni himself, who went against his father's will in abandoning his position as crown prince but went on to achieve enlightenment, becoming the Buddha and leading his parents to enlightenment as well.

This particular story had a happy ending. The younger brother decided to stand by the elder, and their father relented in the face of their joint resolve. Not long after, he, too, became Nichiren's follower. From his letters, we can see how Nichiren's exclusivistic approach to faith in the Lotus Sutra transformed his understanding of the received social ethic of filial piety. Obligations to one's parents are relativized by the higher claim of the Lotus Sutra. Nevertheless, this is a transfiguring, not a rejection, of filial piety. It is only at the conventional, social level that defying parents for the sutra's sake can be understood as unfilial; viewed from the premise of causality operating over past, present, and future lifetimes, such resistance is redefined as a more authentic form of loyalty and social responsibility. As historian Yutaka Takagi has pointed out, Nichiren's teaching transcends worldly ethics, but, at the same time, based on the premise of faith in the Lotus Sutra, reinforces them.[14]

The Lotus Sutra and Feudal Loyalty

"Loyalty," wrote Nichiren, "is filial piety extended beyond the family."[15] In the *bushi* society to which most of his followers belonged, the relationship between a warrior in service and his immediate lord followed a model structurally similar to that of the family. How Nichiren saw exclusive commitment to the Lotus Sutra as affecting the obligations of this relationship may be seen from a series of letters he wrote to one Shijō Nakatsukasa Saburōzaemon-no-jō Yorimoto (d. 1296, also known as Shijō Kingo). Like Ikegami Munenaka, Yorimoto was an early lay convert to Nichiren's teaching. He was a vassal to Lord Ema Mitsutoki—and later, to Mitsutoki's son, Chikatoki—of the Nagoe branch of the ruling Hōjō clan. The bond between the Shijō and the Nagoe was a close one: Yorimoto's father had also served Mitsutoki, even accompanying him into exile to Izu Province in 1246 when Mitsutoki came under suspicion of plotting a rebellion. In turn, Mitsutoki had protected Yorimoto from the persecution aimed at Nichiren's followers in the wake of Nichiren's exile to Sado in 1271.

From the evidence of about forty extant letters, Yorimoto seems to have been particularly close to Nichiren. By Nichiren's own account, when he came near to being beheaded by *bakufu* authorities in 1271, Yorimoto accompanied him to the execution grounds, determined to commit *seppuku* and follow him in death.[16] He also sent supplies to Nichiren while the latter was in exile on Sado and even contrived to visit him there. Yorimoto had some knowledge of medicine and treated Nichiren during the illness that plagued him in his last years. Nichiren also named Yorimoto's children.

However, as a warrior in service to the Hōjō who had twice ordered Nichiren's exile, it was perhaps inevitable that Yorimoto's religious commitments would come into conflict with his social obligations. Yorimoto made at least one explicit though unsuccessful attempt to persuade Lord Ema to embrace Nichiren's teaching. A 1274 letter from Nichiren commends him for this act:

> Although your mind is one with mine, your person is in service elsewhere [i.e., to a vassal of the ruler, who opposes Nichiren]. Thus it would seem difficult for you to escape the sin of complicity [in slander of the Dharma]. But you have most admirably informed your lord about this teaching and recommended it to him. Even if he doesn't heed you now, you yourself have escaped offense. From now on, you had better be circumspect in what you say.[17]

Circumspection does not seem to have come easily for Yorimoto, a quick-tempered man. Whether for this or other reasons, by 1276, friction seems to have developed between him and the head of the Nagoe clan. Judging from Nichiren's letters, Yorimoto was thinking of leaving his lord's service, a course of action that Nichiren opposed as disloyal to the very man whose material support had, however unintentionally, allowed Yorimoto to fulfill his social and religious obligations:

> Whose aid kept me from starving to death in the province of Sado, and allows me to keep reciting the Lotus Sutra [here in reclusion] in the mountains? Yours alone. And as for what makes your assistance possible, it is due to the lay monk [Ema Mitsutoki]. . . . It is also because of his favor to you that you are able to care for your parents. No matter what may happen, should you abandon such a man? If he rejects you repeatedly, then there is nothing to be done, but you must not reject him, not even if it costs your life.[18]

The tension grew worse, however, exacerbated by ugly reports made to the lord by Yorimoto's fellow retainers, with whom he had come into conflict for unknown reasons. Then in the summer of 1277, a Tendai monk named Ryūzō-bō, newly arrived from the Tendai center on Mount Hiei near the imperial capital, was preaching in Kamakura. Sanmi-bō, a scholar-monk who was Nichiren's disciple, went to hear him preach and asked Yorimoto to accompany him. By Nichiren's account, after the sermon Sanmi-bō engaged Ryūzō-bō in debate and scathingly demolished his doctrinal interpretations before the assembled audience. Others, however, reported to Lord Ema that Yorimoto and his warriors had burst in wearing arms and disrupted the proceedings. In addition, the humiliated Ryūzō-bō enjoyed the support of the monk Ninshō, for whom Ema—like the father of Ikegami Munenaka—entertained deep respect. Angered, Lord Ema (at this point, probably the son, Chikatoki) sent Yorimoto a letter demanding that he write a pledge of loyalty, renouncing his exclusive faith in the Lotus Sutra and his allegiance to Nichiren.[19] Yorimoto forwarded the letter to Nichiren at Mount Minobu along with one of his own, describing the affair and expressing his refusal to comply with his lord's demands. In response, Nichiren wrote, in the persona of Yorimoto, an elaborate defense, declaring Yorimoto's loyalty to Chikatoki but construed in a very different sense than what the lord was demanding. In this long document—the *Yorimoto chinjō*—Nichiren has Yorimoto explain why the highest expression of a warrior's loyalty to his lord is not unquestioning obedience but faith in the Lotus Sutra:

> In the same letter you [Chikatoki] say: "To obey one's lord or parents, whether they are right or wrong, is exemplary behavior, ap-

proved by the Buddhas and *kami* and in accord with worldly virtue. Because this is the most important of important matters, I [Nichiren, in the persona of Yorimoto] will not venture to give my own view but will cite original texts. The Classic of Filial Piety says, "A son must reprove his father, and a minister must reprove his sovereign." Cheng Hsüan comments, "When a sovereign or father behaves unjustly and his minister or son does not admonish him, that will lead to the country's ruin or the family's destruction." The *Hsin-hsü* says, "One who does not admonish a ruler's tyranny is not a loyal retainer. One who does not speak from fear of death is not a man of courage.". . . I can only grieve to see my lord, to whom I am so deeply indebted, deceived by teachers of an evil Dharma and about to fall into the evil paths.[20]

The text goes on to liken Ema Chikatoki to King Ajātaśatru, who took the depraved Devadatta, the Buddha's enemy, as his teacher, and Yorimoto, to the minister Jīvaka, a devout Buddhist who admonished Ajātaśatru. "The great king disapproved of his minister's devotion to the Buddha, much as you are displeased with me." But perhaps, it continues, just as Jīvaka ultimately converted Ajātaśatru to Buddhism, Yorimoto will save Chikatoki in the end. In view of Yorimoto's and his father's past service to the Nagoe and the family's past favor to him, Nichiren has him say, "How could I now think of you distantly? I will follow you even to the next life, and if I attain Buddhahood, I will save my lord as well."[21]

Chikatoki was not persuaded, and the situation deteriorated as Yorimoto fell further out of favor. Shortly after, Chikatoki confiscated Yorimoto's estates, and other retainers of the clan plotted against his life. Yet Nichiren continued to admonish him not to leave Chikatoki's service. At the same time, as he had with the brothers Ikegami, he urged Yoritomo to keep before him a perspective relativizing the successes and failures of this world: "A whole lifetime is like a dream. One cannot count on to-morrow. Even should you become the most miserable of beggars, don't dishonor the Lotus Sutra."[22] The next year, Chikatoki fell ill and found himself obliged to call on Yorimoto's skills as a physician. Soon the samurai was restored to favor and new lands were granted to him.

Nichiren's letters to Ikegami Munenaka and Shijō Yorimoto show how he redefined the social obligations of filial piety and loyalty through the lens of exclusive faith in the Lotus Sutra. His advice in the two cases reveals a common structure. Loyalty to the Lotus takes precedence over loyalty to parents and lords; where the demands of worldly authority conflict with the demands of the practitioner's faith, he or she must defy the former and uphold the latter. To this extent, Nichiren opened a ground for resistance to conventional social authority. This is not a denial of worldly loyalty or filial piety; rather, these social obligations, while refigured by commitment to the Lotus, are also reaffirmed in its light. However, Nichiren's exclusive faith in the Lotus refigures social obligations in a way that inverts hierarchy, according the greater agency to the person in the weaker or subordinate position in the social relationship of parent and child, or lord and vassal. The same principle would no doubt apply in other, hierarchially constructed social obligations, such as those of husband and wife. To a female follower, Nichiren once wrote, "No matter what sort of man you may marry, you must not follow him if he is an enemy of the Lotus Sutra."[23] Ultimate moral authority is shown to derive, not from socially determined relationships, but from faith in the Lotus Sutra.

"Admonishing the State"

The conflicts experienced by Ikegami Munenaka with his father and by Shijō Yoritomo with his lord were representative of the early stages of Nichiren's community, when virtually all followers were converts. After Nichiren's death, as his tradition became institutionalized, the Hokkeshū (as Nichiren Buddhism was then called) was in many cases the hereditary religious affiliation of entire families. Thus it grew less common for an individual believer to experience conflict with parents or other close social superiors over the issue of faith in the Lotus Sutra.

Where the potential for such conflict remained, however, was in the relationship of the Hokkeshū itself, or of its individual lineages, to persons in the highest positions of political authority. Nichiren had clearly established that loyalty to the Lotus Sutra should take precedence over loyalty to one's sovereign. "Having been born in the ruler's domain, I may have to follow him with my body," he wrote, "but I don't have to follow him with my mind."[24] More precisely, exclusive commitment to the Lotus Sutra—even if the ruler should oppose it—was in his view the highest form of loyalty to the country, for only faith in the Lotus could transform the present world into the Buddha-land. In this way, Nichiren's notion of the practitioner's obligation to the country paralleled that of obligations to parents and feudal lords. It was institutionalized in the practice of *kokka kangyō*, literally "admonishing and enlightening the state," a practice unique to the Nichiren tradition.

The practice of "admonishing the state" was initiated by Nichiren himself, who is considered to have done so on three occasions. The first time was in 1260, when he submitted his memorial or treatise of remonstration, the *Risshō ankoku ron,* to Hōjō Tokiyori, urging that other teachings—specifically Hōnen's exclusive *nembutsu*—be set aside in favor of the Lotus Sutra in order to stem the calamities then ravaging the country. In light of various scriptural passages about the disasters that afflict a country where the true Dharma is ignored or slighted, Nichiren also predicted that, were his advice ignored, two further disasters, internal strife and foreign invasion, would occur. A rebellion within the Hōjō clan in 1272 and the Mongol invasion attempts of 1274 and 1281 seemed to bear out his words. Elsewhere, Nichiren wrote that the suffering he witnessed in the wake of a great earthquake in 1257 and epidemics in 1259 prompted him to search the Buddhist scriptures for an explanation of the cause of, and solution to, these troubles. As we have seen, he concluded that the cause lay in "slander of the Dharma," which he interpreted as rejection of the Lotus Sutra. Because people had abandoned the true Dharma, the protective deities had abandoned the country. "In the end, there was no choice but to compile a treatise of remonstration, which I called *Risshō ankoku ron.* . . . I did this solely to repay the debt I owe to the country *(kokudo)."*[25]

Nichiren's second act of *kokka kangyō* occurred just prior to his arrest on the twelfth of the ninth month in 1271, when he was summoned before Hei (Taira) no Yoritsuna, deputy chief of the Bureau of Retainers *(samurai dokoro)* to answer for his criticism of the teachings upheld by prominent monks. "What I have said was out of concern for this country. If you wish to maintain peace in the realm, then summon those monks and hear them [debate] in your presence. Otherwise, if you punish me unreasonably on their behalf, the country will regret it later. In punishing me, you reject the Buddha's envoy."[26]

The third time was in the spring of 1274, when he was released from his sentence of exile to Sado Island, returned to Kamakura, and was again summoned before Hei no Yoritsuna to advise on how to cope with the impending Mongol invasion. Nichiren's response—to abandon official patronage for all other forms of Buddhism and rely solely on the Lotus Sutra—was not a course that the *bakufu* was either inclined or able to implement. Following this encounter, Nichiren went into reclusion on Mount Minobu, citing the *Li-chi* (Book of Rites) to the effect that one who admonishes the ruler three times and is not heeded should withdraw.

"Admonishing the state" was for Nichiren an act of proselytizing, of rebuking Dharma slander, and of discharging loyalty to the "country" or society at large, based on the premise that the enlightenment of the Lotus Sutra was not purely subjective but would positively transform the land. This form of action was continued, even institutionalized, by Nichiren's later followers, in the spirit of attempting to complete what he had initiated: the establishment of the Buddha-land in Japan through the spread of faith in the Lotus Sutra.

"Admonishing the state" generally took the form of submitting *mōshijō* (letters of admonition) to the ruler—the emperor or more frequently the shogun—or to his local representatives. *Mōshijō* typically restated the message of Nichiren's *Risshō ankoku ron*, emphasizing the difference be-tween the provisional teachings and the Lotus Sutra and urging that sup-port be withdrawn from all other forms of Buddhism and given to the Hokkeshū alone. Sometimes they requested sponsorship of a public de-bate with monks of other sects in order to demonstrate the superiority of the Lotus Sutra—an opportunity that Nichiren had sought in vain through-out his life. Often a copy of the *Risshō ankoku ron* itself was appended, or less frequently, a work of the writer's own composition conveying a simi-lar message. Copies of *mōshijō* survive written by five of Nichiren's six leading immediate disciples, and *kokka kangyō* was also practiced enthu-siastically by the third generation of Hokkeshū clerics. Examples include Niidakyō Ajari Nichimoku (1260–1333) of the Fuji lineage based in Suruga, veteran of many debates and memorializings, who died at age seventy-four en route to Kyoto to admonish the newly reinstalled Emperor Godaigo.[27] Jōgyōin Nichiyō (1298–1374) of the Nakayama lineage in Shimōsa also journeyed to Kyoto in 1334 to present a letter of admoni-tion to Godaigo, requesting imperial sponsorship for a debate between the Hokkeshū and other sects. On presenting his letter, he was arrested and imprisoned for three days, giving him much satisfaction at having suffered persecution, even briefly, for the Lotus Sutra's sake.[28]

The majority of *kokka kangyō*, however, occurred in the Muromachi pe-riod (1333–1573), the age of Ashikaga rule. Of the more than forty extant *mōshijō* dated between 1285 and 1596, most are concentrated during this time.[29] Among Hokkeshū branches in eastern Japan, going up to Kyoto to "admonish the state" came to be considered almost obligatory for any monk holding the position of chief abbot (*kanzu* or *betsuzu*) of the head temple of a lineage, in effect confirming him as a true Dharma heir to Nichiren, one who carried on the founder's work. Special respect ac-crued to those like Nichiyō who encountered hostility from the authori-ties as a result.

The Ashikaga shoguns were generally ready to allow Hokkeshū monks opportunities to preach and establish temples in Kyoto. However, as the country's de facto rulers, they had constantly to balance rival fac-tions, including powerful daimyo and influential temple-shrine complexes, which were major landholders and political forces in their own right. It would have been impossible—assuming that any of the Ashikaga were sufficiently sympathetic—to endorse one form of Buddhism exclusively.

Thus repeated memorializing was sometimes forbidden. Since Nichiren had set a precedent by making three admonitions, Hokkeshū clerics determined to follow his example, thereby deliberately placing themselves in conflict with the authorities, and were occasionally punished. "Admonishing the state" could also be a source of tension, not only externally, between the Hokkeshū and government officials, but internally, between the tradition's radical and conservative factions.[30] In the process of institutionalizing, well-established Hokkeshū temples had found it expedient to modify Nichiren's strict exclusivism in the interests of accomodating their wealthy and aristocratic patrons. Despite the fact that *kokka kangyō* was impeccably orthodox, abbots of such temples often feared that extreme or repeated acts of admonition might anger the authorities and thus jeopardize their hard-won gains.

Accordingly, the most enthusiastic and persistent *kokka kangyō* practitioners tended to be monks who had broken away from more established Hokkeshū lineages to found new ones. Genmyō Ajari Nichijū (1314–92), who left the Nakayama lineage to establish his own school, criticized the Nakayama abbot, saying, "In the end, he never appealed to the emperor, nor even adressed admonitions to [officials] in the east, spending his life in vain,"[31] thus suggesting the importance attached to *kokka kangyō* practice as conferring legitimization. Nichijū, founder of the Kyoto-based Myōmanji or Kenpon Hokke lineage, was a veteran of many *kangyō* who had memorialized the chancellor (*kanpaku*) Nijō Morotsugu, the shogunal deputy (*kanrei*) Shiba Yoshimasa, and other officials in Kyoto and Kamakura on multiple occasions.[32] In 1391, he admonished the shogun Ashikaga Yoshimitsu twice and was warned not to do so again. Seven years later, his disciples Nichinin and Nichijitsu memorialized Yoshimitsu again, and, according to the records of their lineage, were arrested and tortured. Another famous example is Kuonjō-in Nisshin (1407–88), who at one point was ousted from his own, Nakayama, lineage for his unrelenting purist stance that offended leading patrons. Nisshin preached throughout the country, established thirty temples, and memorialized high officials on eight occasions. Nisshin's defiance of the shogun Yoshinori's warnings against repeated acts of admonition and his fortitude under torture in prison are celebrated in the Edo-period *Record of the virtuous deeds of Saint Nisshin.*[33]

The actions of these devoted remonstrators reflect their conviction in Nichiren's teaching that one should declare the unique truth of the Lotus Sutra, even at the risk of one's life, and that meeting persecution for the sutra's sake demonstrates the validity of one's faith and acts as a guarantee of future Buddhahood. Though sometimes opposed by more moderate factions within the Hokkeshū, their stance accorded with Nichiren's example; consequently they enjoyed tremendous popularity among lay followers and were celebrated in the tradition's hagiographies. They also kept alive Nichiren's teaching of a religious and moral ground that transcends worldly authority and that accorded to those who "admonished the state" a status higher than the officials who persecuted them.

At the same time, while establishing one's Dharma credentials, *kokka kangyō* was also deemed an act on behalf of the country and society. Based as they were on the premise that natural disasters and social harmony reflect errors in religion, such admonitions on the part of Hokkeshū prelates were put forward most frequently during times of social disturbance. An example can be found in another veteran remonstrator, Shinnyo-in Nichijū (1406–86), contemporary with Nisshin, who composed a work of admonition titled *Collection on the Wonderful Dharma and the governance of the realm*,[34] which he is said to have presented to the shogun Yoshimasa in person in 1465.[35] Its introduction (*meyasu*) makes clear the inextricable relationship that Nichijū and others of the tradition perceived among exclusive commitment to the Lotus Sutra, readiness to give one's life for its propagation, and loyalty to the country:

> The Sutra of the Lotus Blossom of the Wonderful Dharma is cherished by the Buddhas and is the Dharma that nourishes the *kami*. It is the innermost secret and esoteric method for bringing peace to the realm and security within the four seas, for quelling disasters and subduing foreign enemies. The sutra promises "peace and security in this world and birth in a good place in the next". . . . However, the doctrines espoused by the various sects are deluded with respect to [the distinction between] provisional and true teachings, like confusing the sovereign with commoners; they deviate from our connection to the Buddha, like forgetting the relationship of parent and child. . . . If I failed to admonish this, I would be guilty of disloyalty to the country. . . . I do this solely for the sake of the Buddha-Dharma, for the sake of the ruler's law, and more broadly, for the sake of all living beings. I ask that you investigate this matter, and, if what I say proves unfounded, that you will at once put an end to my life.[36]

Nichijū's time was one of political instability, as powerful daimyo increasingly threatened Ashikaga rule. In addition, over the preceding few years, several provinces had experienced widespread drought as well as flooding from storms, resulting in poor harvests and consequent famine. In 1461, an epidemic increased the death toll, and displaced persons streamed into the capital. Like Nichiren two hundred years before him, Nichijū saw the problem as fundamentally a religious one, and its solution in conversion to the Lotus Sutra. Like other practitioners of *kokka kangyō*, in his own eyes, this insight gave him the authority, indeed the obligation, to admonish the country's ruler.

Conclusion

Understandings of the Lotus Sutra such as those found in medieval Tendai Buddhism that allowed for a plurality of practices tended not to generate social conflict, since virtually any form of practice could in theory be defined as practice of the Lotus. It was the exclusive nature of Nichiren's faith in the Lotus that potentially pitted child against parent, vassal against lord, and religious institution against worldly rule. At the same time, in a way that more inclusive readings of the Lotus could not, it explicitly established a source of moral authority transcending that of the social hierarchy—in the family, clan, or nation. However, it was not a simple denial of social obligations in the name of a transcendent reality, but a refiguring of them in such a way that the practitioner's religious and social responsibilities were ultimately identified.

After Nichiren's death, his exclusive approach to faith in the Lotus was not always easy to institutionalize, and at times the mainstream of the tradition adopted a more accomodating stance. Nevertheless, it remained as a resource within the tradition, capable of being revived at critical junctures. One example was the *fuju fuse* ("neither receiving nor giving") movement of the late sixteenth century and early seventeenth century within the Nichiren tradition that condemned as a form of Dharma slander the acceptance of alms from non-believers in the sutra or the performance of religious services for them, regardless of their social status or political power. The *fuju fuse* movement offered sustained resistance to growing *bakufu* control of religion and was eventually banned, its adherents being martyred, exiled, or driven underground.[37] Or, in the twentieth century, during the Pacific War, at a time when the majority of Buddhist institutions of both Nichirenshū and other sects were actively supporting militant imperialism, one can point to individual Nichiren followers who risked their lives to uphold Nichiren's exclusivistic stance in defiance of state control of religion. These included several leaders of the small Nichiren denomination Honmon Hokkeshū who were arrested and imprisoned for statements in doctrinal publications subordinating the Japanese deities, Amaterasu and Hachiman, to the eternal Buddha of the Lotus Sutra, and Tsunesaburō Makiguchi (1871–1944), founder of the Sōka Kyōiku Gakkai, precursor to today's Sōka Gakkai, who was arrested and died in prison, having refused to have his followers enshrine in their homes the obligatory *kamifuda* or amulets of the imperial Ise shrine, as mandated by government order.[38] Neither the *fuju fuse* martyrs nor those

Nichiren Buddhists imprisoned during the Pacific War for opposition to goverment religious policy can in any way be said to represent the majority of Nichiren adherents of their times, nor can their resistance be deemed historically "successful" in the sense of altering the course of events. But they kept alive Nichren's teaching that worldly authority can, and on occasion must, be defied in the name of the Dharma.

This teaching did not develop into a secular critique of social authority or a modern view of social responsibility. From a contemporary perspective, it seems relentlessly and naively monocausal to locate the source of all social problems in "slander of the Dharma" and to find their solution in exclusive faith in the Lotus Sutra. In a pluralistic age, religious exclusivism is often looked upon as socially irresponsible, because of its potential to aggravate conflict in an already divided world. Nichren's exclusivistic stance in particular conflicts with deeply cherished presuppostions, often Western in origin, about Buddhism as a religion of "tolerance." Nevertheless, it is significant in having established an explicitly religious basis from which social authority could be critiqued and resisted—something rather rare in the history of Japanese Buddhism.

(Unless otherwise noted, all translations from the Japanese are by the author.)

Notes

1. *Zuisō gosho, Shōwa teihon Nichiren Shōnin ibun* (hereafter STN) 1:873.
2. *Nyosetsu shugyō shō,* STN 1:733.
3. *Risshō ankoku ron,* STN 1:217.
4. STN 1:590.
5. *Ōshajō no koto,* STN 1:917.
6. The following discussion is indebted in part to Yutaka Takagi, *Nichiren to sono montei* (Tokyo: Kōbundō, 1965), 221–53
7. *Kyōdai shō,* STN 1:920–21, 928.
8. *Kyōdai shō,* STN 1:922, 923.
9. *Kyōdai shō,* STN 1:924–25.
10. *Kyōdai shō,* STN 1:933
11. Yutaka Takagi, *Nichiren to sono montei,* 229, n. 15.
12. *Hyōe-no-sakan-dono gohenji,* STN 2:1402–3.
13. *Hyōe-no-sakan-dono gohenji,* STN 2:1405.
14. *Nichiren to sono montei,* 232.
15. *Hōmon mōsarubekiyō no koto,* STN 1:443.
16. *Shijō Kingo-dono goshōsoku,* STN 1:505.
17. *Shukun ni nyū shi hōmon men yodōzai ji,* STN 1:834.
18. *Shijō Kingo Shakabutsu kuyō ji,* STN 2:1187.
19. Although the evidence is not altogether clear, Takagi argues convincingly that

the head of the Nagoe clan at this time, with whom Yorimoto came into direct conflict, was probably not Mitsutoki but his son Chikatoki (*Nichiren to sono montei*, 250, n. 2).

20. *Yorimoto chinjō*, STN 2:1355–56.
21. *Yorimoto chinjō*, STN 2:1358.
22. *Shijō Kingo-dono gohenji*, STN 2:1362.
23. *Oto gozen goshōsoku*, STN 2:1100.
24. *Senji shō*, STN 2:1053.
25. *Ankoku ron gokan yurai*, STN 1:422.
26. *Shuju onfurumai gosho*, STN 2:962–63.
27. Nichiko Hori, ed., *Fuji shūgaku yōshū* 5:34.
28. *Ikki shoshū zengon kiroku*, *Nichirenshū shūgaku zensho* (hereafter NSZ) 1:447.
29. Hōyō Watanabe, *Nichirenshū shingyō ron no kenkyū* (Tokyo: Kokusai Bunka Shinkōkai, 1976), 135–40.
30. See my "Rebuking the Enemies of the *Lotus*: Nichirenist Exclusivism in Historical Perspective," *Japanese Journal of Religious Studies* 21/2–3 (1994): 231–59.
31. Cited in Takashi Nakao, *Nisshin: Sono kōdō to shisō* (Tokyo: Hyōronsha, 1981), 64.
32. For the activities of Genmyō Nichijū and his disciples, see Risshō Daigaku Nichiren Kyōgaku Kenkyūjo, ed., *Nichiren kyōdan zenshi* 1 (hereafter *Zenshi*) (Kyoto: Heirakuji Shoten, 1984), 214–27, and *Nichiun ki* (*Monto koji*), NSZ 5:62–94.
33. *Nisshin Shōnin tokugyō ki*. On Nisshin's activities, see, for example, Takashi Nakao, *Nisshin: Sono kōdō to shisō*; *Zenshi*, 262–71; and Jacqueline Stone, "Priest Nisshin's Ordeals," in George J. Tanabe, Jr., ed., *Religions of Japan in Practice* (Princeton: Princeton University Press, 1999), 384–97.
34. *Myōhō jise shū*
35. On Nichijū's activities, see *Zenshi*, 271–73.
36. *Myōhō jise shū narabi ni dōshimatsu kiroku*, NSZ 19:206.
37. On the *fuju fuse* movement, see, for example, Eishū Miyazaki, *Fuju fuse ha no genryū to tenkai* (Kyoto: Heirakuji Shoten, 1969), and Jeffrey Hunter, "The *Fuju fuse* controversy in Nichiren Buddhism: The debate between Busshōin Nichiō and Jakushōin Nichiken," Ph.D. dissertation, University of Wisconsin at Madison, 1989.
38. On the imprisonment of Honmon Hokkeshū leaders, see William P. Woodard, "The Wartime Persecution of Nichiren Buddhism," *Transactions of the Asiatic Society of Japan*, third series, vol. 7 (1959), and Shigemoto Tokoro, *Kindai shakai to Nichiren-shugi* (Tokyo: Hyōronsha, 1973), 202–06. On Makiguchi, see *Fuji shūgaku yōshū* 9:428–48.

The Lotus Sutra in the Writings of Kenji Miyazawa

Steve Odin

Kenji Miyazawa (1896–1933) is now regarded as one of modern Japan's foremost poets, as well as the beloved author of children's stories that are still popular. Some people even consider his 1927 story *Ginga tetsudō no yoru* ("Night of the Galactic Railway"), first translated in 1987 as *Night Train to the Stars*, to be the country's first modern science fiction tale. In recent years it has served as the basis for a hit animated film and as the inspiration for a number of *manga* comic books.

As explained by Toshiko Toriyama,[1] Miyazawa's pedagogical ideas stemming from his years as a high school teacher gave rise to a new philosophy of education calling for an overall integration of body and mind and a close association with nature. This also led to the recent establishment of alternative educational institutions known as Kenji's schools (*Kenji no gakkō*), first in Nagano Prefecture and now elsewhere in Japan as well. After resigning from his teaching position in 1926, Miyazawa took up farming, whereupon he became known throughout the Tōhoku area of northern Japan as "Kenji *bosatsu*," or Kenji the bodhisattva, dedicated to helping the poor farmers of his native Iwate Prefecture improve their crop yields with his knowledge of agricultural science.

One of the most strikingly original characteristics of Miyazawa's literary efforts is his attempt to forge a synthesis of religion and science, insofar as they use innovative poetic images combining Buddhist religious concepts with scientific-technological metaphors. Miyazawa's literary imagination typically rises toward the heavens, both the spiritual heaven of the afterlife described in Buddhist cosmology and the starry heavens studied by astronomers, then descends back again to transform everyday life into a buddha-world, with a cosmic vision that sees the whole galaxy in each part.

From biographical accounts it is known that Miyazawa converted to Nichirenism upon first reading the Lotus Sutra in 1915, then joined a Nichiren Buddhist society, installed the sacred mandala of Nichiren Buddhism in his home, took up the daily practice of studying, chanting, and transcribing the Lotus Sutra, propagated the teachings of Nichirenism in the streets, edited a volume of Nichiren's writings, and had free copies of the Lotus Sutra distributed upon his death. He lived as a lay Buddhist practicing self-denial, celibacy, vegetarianism, and renunciation of material values. At the same time he was known for his ecstatic communion with nature and the cosmos, which he expressed through writing poetry and fiction, as well as through music and painting. Furthermore, Miyazawa incorporated various images, concepts, and themes derived from the Lotus Sutra into his literary works.

Miyazawa's Stories and Skillful Means

Miyazawa's life, thought, and writings were all greatly influenced by the Lotus Sutra. J. T. Rimer puts it this way: "Miyazawa's commitments to Buddhist belief caused him to place the Lotus Sutra . . . at the center of his meditations. The metaphysical underpinnings provided by this great sacred text run like a thread through his sensibility as expressed in his poetry."[2]

Or, in the words of author and translator John Bester: "Clearly, the main debt in Miyazawa's moral outlook is to Buddhism. He was, in fact, a serious student of the Buddhist scriptures. Some of his stories ('A Stem of Lilies') are explicitly Buddhist fables, while others incorporate colorful images from the sutras, especially the Lotus Sutra."[3]

The underlying function of Miyazawa's works can be explained in terms of chapter 2 of the Lotus Sutra, "Tactfulness," a title that can also be translated as "skillful means." It is through skillful means (upāya) that the Buddha tactfully adjusted his manifold provisional teachings to the different capacities and levels of understanding of his followers. It can be said that Miyazawa employs symbolic images of the literary imagination as upāya to open the reader's vision to the expansive, interpenetrating, multidimensional cosmos of the Lotus Sutra. His utilization of stories as upāya is rooted in the very method of the Lotus Sutra itself, which at one level functions as an imaginative literary work containing stories, fables, and parables used as expedient devices to communicate Buddhist teachings as adjusted to all levels of understanding.

"A Stem of Lilies" is a brief children's story representing one of Miyazawa's more explicit Buddhist tales, using imagery reminiscent of the Lotus Sutra. In this tale the people in a small kingdom prepare for a visit by the Buddha, and as they await his coming, suddenly a brilliant golden light rises like a rainbow over the forest and beyond the river where the Buddha is about to appear, and all prostrate themselves in reverence. The narrator concludes, "All of this happened, I am sure, somewhere, two hundred million years or so ago." This is immediately reminiscent of chapter 1 of the Lotus Sutra, in which the Buddha illuminates the world with a ray of light. It also recalls chapter 16, "Revelation of the [Eternal] Life of the Tathāgata," wherein it is disclosed that Śākyamuni did not become the Buddha in India twenty-five hundred years ago, but in fact has an eternal life span and was enlightened countless hundreds of millions of years ago in the infinite *kalpas* of time without end.

Miyazawa's tales are often in the form of fables to communicate Buddhist moral teachings derived from the Lotus Sutra. Generally, Miyazawa's stories express a Mahayana Buddhist ethics of "compassion," inspired by the Lotus Sutra bodhisattva ideal of universal compassion, salvation, and happiness for all living beings. Because of Miyazawa's belief in the Buddhist ethics of compassion and the moral law of karma functioning as the principle of "cause and effect," he refused to kill or harm any living creature and for this reason became a strict vegetarian, a theme he takes up in "The Vegetarian Festival."[4] In his chilling tale "The Restaurant of Many Orders,"[5] Miyazawa brings to light and underscores the cruelty of those who take sadistic pleasure in hunting animals for sport. Through a clever plot twist, there is a reversal in which the bloodthirsty hunters suddenly find themselves at a restaurant for animals of the forest—and the hunters are now the gourmet human dishes listed on the menu. Miyazawa's own struggle with the inherent pain of existence wherein all living things must kill and themselves be killed, as well as his aspiration to transcend the need to kill in order to live, is expressed in "The Nighthawk Star." In this tale a nighthawk is so troubled by his need to eat insects to live and terror of himself being eaten by larger predators that he decides to ascend and immolate himself in the burning phosphorous of a glowing star, and the nighthawk star continued to burn with a translucent blue light forever.[6]

Like his poetry, Miyazawa's children's stories reveal his profound communion with nature. Indeed, in the original preface to an anthology of children's stories Miyazawa tells his readers: "All of the stories . . . were given to me by the rainbow or by the moonlight, in the forests, the fields, or along the railroad tracks. . . ."[7] Miyazawa's recurrent theme of oneness with nature reflects the general concept of nature found in the Lotus Sutra and the Lotus Sutra tradition of Tendai and Nichiren Buddhism. Chapter 5 of the Lotus Sutra propounds that the grasses, trees, shrubs, and medicinal herbs of the forest are all equal in that they all have the mark of eternally quiescent nirvana and are ultimately reducible to "emptiness." Similarly, chapter 2 of the sutra proclaims the "suchness" of all dharmas. In the Japanese Tendai teaching of "original enlightenment," later assimilated into Nichiren Buddhism, these passages from the Lotus Sutra came to be understood as "grasses and trees can attain buddhahood," or in an even more radical formulation, as "mountains and rivers, grasses and trees, can attain buddhahood."

Another central idea in the Tendai and Nichiren Buddhist concept of nature rooted in the Lotus Sutra which enters into the literary imagination of Miyazawa is the doctrine of *eshō funi* (oneness of life and its environment), which is itself an aspect of the more generic principle of *ichinen san-zen* (three thousand realms in one thought). Miyazawa's many children's stories focusing on unity with nature function as an *upāya* for imparting the Tendai and Nichiren Buddhist philosophy of original enlightenment rooted in the Lotus Sutra, whereby even mountains and rivers, grasses and trees, all have the buddha-nature. The deep communion with nature in Miyazawa's stories is a skillful means by which to teach the principle of "oneness of life and its environment." Oneness with nature, the interdependence of phenomena, and recognition of the emptiness, voidness, and suchness of dharmas, along with the intrinsic buddha-nature, original enlightenment, or potentiality for buddhahood in all events, together establish the philosophical basis for his Mahayana Buddhist ethics of universal compassion, salvation, and happiness of all life.

Miyazawa's most popular children's tale undoubtedly is "Night Train to the Stars," in which he draws on images, concepts, and ideals from Japan's Lotus Sutra tradition. While all of this is developed under the subterfuge of recounting a simple children's story, the tale nonetheless contains religious, moral, and philosophical themes that can be appreciated by any reader. To use the language of the sutra itself, it can be said that for Miyazawa, "Night Train to the Stars," like his other children's stories, functions as an expedient device for spreading the teachings of the Lotus Sutra to people of all ages.

Miyazawa's Basic Inspiration

As shown by Junsaku Bundō, the sutra was the fundamental inspiration for everything in Miyazawa's life.[8] His passionate engagement with Nichiren Buddhism, based on the teachings of the sutra, has also been emphasized by Naotarō Kudō: "Miyazawa sought the education of his soul in the Nichiren sect of Mahayana Buddhism. . . . He began his lifelong custom of transcribing parts of the Sutra every day, believing that this act of piety would foster spiritual fellowship in the community."[9]

Kudō adds: "Miyazawa was so absorbed in the Nichiren sect that . . . he apprenticed himself to Chigaku Tanaka (1861–1929), the then-famous preacher and leader of the Nichiren sect called the 'Pillar of the State' [Kokuchūkai]. Miyazawa led a strenuous life preaching the tenets of Nichirenism."[10]

As proclaimed in chapter 19 of the sutra, "The Merits of the Preacher," a boundless stock of accumulated merit based on the law of karma, or the principle of "cause and effect," is acquired by those receiving, keeping, reading, reciting, preaching, interpreting, explaining, copying, and transcribing even one line from the Lotus Sutra. It therefore is easy to see how Miyazawa's daily religious practice of transcribing passages from the sutra came to merge with his other daily practice of writing poems and children's stories.

Donald Keene mentions Miyazawa's sudden conversion after reading the Lotus Sutra for the first time: "His parents were devout believers in Jōdo [Pure Land] Buddhism, but after a reading of the Lotus Sutra in 1915, which made him tremble with joy, he became converted to Nichiren Buddhism. It has been said that he lived his entire life in accordance with the spirit of this sutra, which he kept with him always."[11]

Several years after his dramatic conversion, Miyazawa edited an anthology of selected writings by Nichiren (1222–82). Keene relates an event that occurred in the period between Miyazawa's conversion and his subsequent joining of a Nichiren Buddhist society. According to Miyazawa's own notebooks, several volumes of Nichiren's writings once fell off a bookshelf and hit him on the head. Miyazawa took this to be a "miracle," a divine revelation that he should become more actively involved with the dissemination of Nichiren's teachings, and he thereupon left for Tokyo to join Tanaka's Pillar of the State Society. It was at this time, around 1921, that he became engaged in missionary work for the society.

Miyazawa continued his practice of transcribing the Lotus Sutra even on his deathbed. He made a final request to his father that one thousand copies of the sutra be printed and distributed with a note saying that the purpose of his life's work was only to spread the teaching of the Lotus Sutra.[12]

From 1921 to 1925, Miyazawa taught high school at Hanamaki Agricultural School. Through his dedication to helping the poor farmers of Iwate Prefecture increase their crop yields, he attempted to embody the Lotus Sutra ideal of a self-emptying compassionate bodhisattva through his own moral conduct, while at the same time giving poetic expression to this concept through his writing.

The poem known by the first line as "Ame ni mo makezu" (Unyielding in the Rain) was entered in Miyazawa's notebook on November 3, 1931. Actually more like a prayer than a poem, it was in fact to become Miyazawa's most popular, inspirational, and often-quoted poem in Japan.[13]

Unyielding in the rain
Unyielding in the wind
Unyielding in the summer heat and snow
He has a strong body
Devoid of greed
Never angry
Always quietly smiling
He eats a little brown rice a day
Miso and a few vegetables
In everything
He never considers himself
He carefully observes and understands
And never forgets
He lives in a small thatched-roof hut
In a field in the shadows of a pine tree grove
If there is a sick child in the east
He goes to care for him
If there is a tired mother in the west
He goes to carry bundles of rice
If there is a person near death in the south
He goes to say "Don't be afraid"
If in the north there is a dispute or lawsuit
He demands that they stop their triviality
Tears flow at the time of a drought
He walks about shaken in a cold summer
Everyone calls him a fool
He is not praised by anyone
And nobody troubles him
That is the kind of person
I want to become.[14]

It is significant that in his notebook for this poem Miyazawa sketches versions of the mandala, or *go-honzon*, used for practice in Nichiren Buddhism.[15]

The centrality of the sutra in Miyazawa's life is perhaps best expressed in a poem he wrote from his sickbed at the age of thirty-three. Although he recovered and lived for several more years, until his death from tuberculosis at the age of thirty-seven, the verse was composed with the existential intensity of a death poem:

I will die soon
Today or perhaps tomorrow.
I ponder anew what I am, but the Law . . .
Whether I die and return to the void,
Or whether I feel myself
In the end, I am nothing once again,
Only one Law operates here.
This original Law has been called the Lotus Sutra . . .
And the countless buddhas, too, are the Law.
And the original Law of the many buddhas
  is the Lotus Sutra.
I will obey the Lotus Sutra of the Supreme Law.
To live is the Supreme Law,
To die is the Supreme Law,
From now unto eternity, I hold fast to the Law.[16]

A Galactic Journey

"Night of the Galactic Railway" is enjoyed by adults and children alike as a fantasy about a young boy named Giovanni and his friend Campanella, who ride an intergalactic train through space while having various adventures and meeting unusual characters. Yet in the final passages it becomes clear that Giovanni and his friend Campanella, the latter having drowned in an accident, are in fact on a celestial railroad for departed souls journeying to the afterlife. Indeed, the tale can be characterized as a near-death experience for Giovanni, who has a special ticket allowing him to sojourn to the heavenly realms of the "fourth dimension" and then return to earthly existence in the "third dimension." In her introduction to another English-language version published as *Night of the Milky Way Railway*, Sarah M. Strong emphasizes that in the guise of a simple children's fantasy the story is actually about a near-death experience, a story of the afterlife told in terms of a Buddhist cosmology projected onto the heavens.[17]

Strong points out that in mythology, the Milky Way often was depicted as the path that the souls of the dead travel from this world to the realm of the afterlife. In his story Miyazawa invents his own imaginary Festival of the Milky Way, along with a galactic journey to the other world by the Silver River of the Milky Way, with occasional references to the two traditional Japanese festivals of Tanabata and Obon. The former is the summer star festival celebrating the legendary annual meeting of the cowherd star (Altair) and the weaver maid star (Vega), who were able to meet only on the seventh night of the seventh lunar month. Among the best known celebrations of Tanabata in Japan are those in Sendai, in the Tōhoku region where Miyazawa lived, on July 7 and in Hiratsuka on August 7.

According to the traditional calendar, the Obon festival is celebrated during the nine days following Tanabata, when people welcome back the spirits of their dead ancestors who are then sent off again to the other world. The festival features the tradition described by Miyazawa of "lantern floating." His image compares the earthly river dotted with floating spirit lamps with the heavenly river of the Milky Way spreading across the sky, both functioning as pathways of souls to the other world. Campanella falls into this river during the festival and drowns, thereby coming to board the galactic dream train to the stars.

The *Go-honzon* and "Giovanni's Ticket"

The key section of Miyazawa's tale is the ninth and final chapter, "Giovanni's Ticket." In this section the two young boys are somehow riding a dreamlike night train through the expanse of space when the train conductor asks all passengers for their tickets. Campanella, like the other passengers, has a small gray one-way ticket. Giovanni, however, pulls out a large folded sheet of paper with mysterious black characters written down the center. On examining this ticket the conductor is astonished and inquires: "Did you obtain this [ticket] from three-dimensional space, sir?" The bird-catcher, another passenger, then exclaims:

> Wow, this is really valuable! This ticket will even allow you to go up to the real Heaven. Not just Heaven, it is a pass that enables you to travel anywhere you want. If you have this, of course, you should be capable of traveling anywhere on this Galactic Railway of the imperfect fourth-dimension of fantasy.[18]

While Campanella and the other passengers use their one-way tickets to reach the heavenly realm of departed souls, Giovanni alone possesses a magical round-trip pass that enables him to freely travel from the "third-dimensional space" (*sanji kūkan*) of the ordinary physical world to anywhere in "fourth-dimensional space" (*yoji kūkan*) of the spiritual world, the realm which Miyazawa refers to as the "fourth dimension of fantasy" (*gensō daiyoji*). This notion of the "fourth dimension," or "fourth-dimensional space," also described as the "fourth dimension of fantasy," is yet another example of Miyazawa's characteristic style of using novel poetic images which fuse traditional Buddhist concepts with modern scientific notions, in this case, the "fourth dimension" described by Buddhist cosmology, the new physics and modern art.

What is this extraordinary railway ticket that enables one to enter the afterlife in the spiritual fantasy realm of dreamlike consciousness in fourth-dimensional space, and then return to the ordinary physical realm of waking consciousness in three-dimensional space? According to some scholars, in Japan and in the West, Giovanni's ticket is the *go-honzon* (principal object of worship), or mandala of Nichiren Buddhism, with a calligraphic inscription of the *daimoku* (*Namu Myōhō Renge-kyō*) down the center.[19]

In her introduction to *Night of the Milky Way Railway*, Strong also discusses this identification of Giovanni's ticket with the mandala of Nichiren Buddhism:

A *mandala* is generally thought of as a diagram, a schema representing the real or ideal universe. In the Nichiren sect, *mandala* refers not to a pictorial diagram but to a schema composed of words. At the center of the Nichiren *mandala* (the *daihonzon*) are the characters of the Nichiren *mantra* (*Namu Myōhō Renge Kyō*) written in the startling, bold hand of the founder of the sect. When Kenji became a member of the Kokuchūkai as a young man, he was sent a copy of this sacred *mandala*. He had it mounted to make a small hanging scroll and he installed it with considerable ceremony in his own home.[20]

She asserts that according to various Japanese scholars "the Nichiren *mandala* was at the back of Kenji's mind when he wrote the key chapter of *Night of the Milky Way Railway*, titled 'Giovonni's ticket'," with its mysterious calligraphic ideograms inscribed down the center of the scroll.

This identification is given further support when considered in relation to the use of the *daimoku* in some of Miyazawa's other works. Critic Takao Hagiwara points out that some of Miyazawa's poems end with the *daimoku*, sometimes in the original Sanskrit. Hagiwara says that the recurrent onomatopoeia of Miyazawa's poems has much to do with the incantatory effects of the Lotus Sutra he chanted. He adds that in such verses Miyazawa has the *daimoku* placed in parentheses and indented so as to be "marked off" from the rest of the poem, creating incongruities and gaps in the texture of his style, thereby revealing the "other realm," the fourth-dimensional reality of the afterlife.[21]

The Milky Way as a Vacuum

One important section of "Night of the Galactic Railway" connects the scientific concept of a vacuum with the Buddhist idea of empty space. Miyazawa uses the Japanese term *shinkū*, meaning "true space" or "true emptiness." The character designating "space" (*kū*) also functions as the standardized character for the Buddhist concept of *śūnyatā*, "emptiness" or "voidness." Thus, as is characteristic of Miyazawa's writing in general, he employs a poetic image to combine scientific concepts with Buddhist religious images from the Lotus Sutra.

In Nichiren's interpretation of the sutra, this identity between emptiness and conventionally designated phenomena is expressed in terms of the Tendai Buddhist philosophical doctrine of the three truths, namely, the middle truth (*chūtai*) which posits the equivalence of conventional truth (*ketai*) and the truth of emptiness (*kūtai*). Hence, it is of considerable interest to examine how the Tendai doctrine of three truths is expressed through the literary imagination of Miyazawa.

In his 1983 book *Modern Japanese Poets and the Nature of Literature*, Makoto Ueda sees "Night of the Galactic Railway" as imaginatively expressing the Buddhist idea of the nonsubstantial self as "impermanence," a flux of transitory events rapidly blinking on and off like an electric lamp on alternating current:

"Giovanni saw that he and his thoughts along with the train, the scholar, the Milky Way, and all else, glowed brightly, faded out, glowed again, faded again, and when one of the lights glowed there spread out the whole wide world with all its history, but when it faded there was nothing but empty darkness. The blinking grew faster and faster, until everything was back as before."

Ueda holds that Giovanni's technological metaphor of an AC lamp expresses a Buddhist cosmological view of reality as an impermanent flux of momentary events flashing in and out of existence, wherein the nonsubstantial self and all dharmas glow in brilliant radiance, then fade to darkness, oscillating back and forth, thus establishing an equivalence between emptiness and phenomena.

Ueda continues, "In faster and faster alternation, he [Miyazawa] sees both the fundamental emptiness underlying all phenomena and the transitory existence of himself and all the world fuse into samsara, the stream of appearances comprising repeated births and deaths that is reality as we ordinarily know it. . . . Giovanni's vision reveals the unity of the phenomenal world and empty darkness in the ongoing process of constant transformation or change."[22]

Hence, in terms of the Tendai philosophical doctrine of "three truths" expounded by Nichiren Buddhism based on the Lotus Sutra, Giovanni's vision of the self and all dharmas incessantly blinking on and off, like an AC electric lamp, is itself a literary depiction of reality as an equivalence of conventional phenomena (*ketai*) and the void of empty darkness (*kūtai*) in the truth of the middle way (*chūtai*).

The Pillar of the Weather Wheel

The brief yet suggestive fifth chapter, "The Pillar of the Weather Wheel" (*Tenki-rin no hashira*), of Miyazawa's "Night of the Galactic Railway" has elicited a great deal of interpretation. In Japan, dharma-wheels (*hōrin*) were sometimes placed on pillars at Buddhist temples so the faithful could spin them by pushing a handle while walking in a circle. By turning the prayer wheel once around the central post, one could in only a few moments erase bad karmic effects while adding the incalculable benefits and stock of good merits accumulated by one who reads, chants, preaches, transcribes, or translates the Lotus Sutra from beginning to end. The karmic benefit achieved by turning a dharma-wheel is thus equivalent to that acquired by circumambulating a Buddhist stupa.

Masanobu Yoshimi argues that Miyazawa's wheel is in fact the dharma-wheel, holding that there is a parallel between his weather wheel and Tantric Buddhist prayer wheels.[23] Strong points out that "Not all temples had these wheels, but in Kenji's day the Shōanji in his hometown of Hanamaki did. This dharma wheel was first erected in the 1860s. . . . As a child and young man Kenji would have been familiar with the original wheel and post."[24] Bun'ichi Saitō says this mysterious wheel can be specifically traced to an image in the Lotus Sutra, what is referred to in chapter 11 as the resplendent "seven-jeweled stupa."[25]

It should be emphasized that for votaries of the Lotus Sutra in Japan, the scripture is valued not only for its cognitive meanings or its evocative imagery, but even more so for its incantatory effects as a *dhāraṇī* spell. One of the most important features of Nichiren Buddhist practice is the use of the *daimoku* as a mantra for eradicating karma, realizing original enlightenment and awakening to innate buddha-nature. The Tantric Buddhist practice of spinning the Dharma-wheel used to accelerate the accumulation of merit is brought to its ultimate conclusion by the teachings of the Nichiren sect, whereby one can achieve the incalculable benefits of reciting the whole Lotus Sutra by only chanting the *daimoku*.

The "Galaxy Within"

In the fifth volume of *Mo-ho chih-kuan* (Great Calmness and Insight), Chih-i (538–97), the founder of T'ien-t'ai Buddhism in China, claims that hidden in the depths of the Lotus Sutra is to be found the ultimate Buddhist principle of *ichinen sanzen* (three thousand realms in each thought-instant).[26] Nichiren quotes from this volume at the beginning of his treatise *Kanjin honzon shō* (The True Object of Worship) to clarify how the *go-honzon*, or mandala of the Lotus Sutra, has the structure of "three thousand realms in each thought-instant," as generated from the "mutual containment of ten worlds":

The mind at each moment is endowed with the Ten Worlds. At the same time, each of the Ten Worlds is endowed with all the others, so that one mind actually possesses one hundred worlds. Each of these worlds in turn possesses thirty realms, which means that in the one hundred worlds there are three thousand realms. The three thousand realms of existence are all possessed by the mind in a single moment . . . if there is the slightest bit of mind, it contains all the three thousand realms.[27]

In "The Ideas of the *Lotus Sutra*," Yoshirō Tamura, one of Japan's foremost scholars of the Lotus Sutra, elucidates Miyazawa's literary images and concepts in relation to the cosmological dimensions of the sutra, as well as to its interpretation by Chih-i and Nichiren.

Chih-i systematized the teaching of the "three thousand realms in one mind," and the Japanese priest Nichiren . . . depicted the ten realms of being in the form of a mandala. The teaching of the "Three thousand realms in one mind" explains that the realm of the microcosm (one mind) and the realm of the macrocosm (three thousand realms) are interdependent and one in their true state, forming a harmonious whole under the wonderful law as the one vehicle. The mandala of the ten realms of being illustrates diagramatically the existences of various beings in the universe under the wonderful law as the one vehicle. One modern-day believer in the *Lotus Sutra*, Miyazawa Kenji . . . , made the following appeal in his *Nōmin geijutsu gairon kōyō* (Introduction to the Farmer's Art):

First of all,
Let us become sparkling, minute bits of dust
And scatter in all directions in the sky.

He urged a commitment of self to the infinite universe through the *Lotus Sutra*.[28]

In Miyazawa's writings, the Tendai Buddhist formula of *ichinen sanzen* is expressed through the poetic vision of enlightenment as a cosmic consciousness of the "galaxy within." In his 1926 essay "An Introduction to the Farmer's Art," he writes:

The happiness of the individual cannot be attained without first realizing the happiness of the whole world.

The concept of self will gradually evolve from the individual to include the group, society, and finally the universe.

Is this not the same path as that followed and taught by the saints of old?

The new age will be found where the world becomes one consciousness and a single, living entity.

To live strongly and truly is to live in awareness of the galaxy within you and to respond to it.

Let us seek true happiness for the whole world; the search itself is the path.[29]

Miyazawa's imaginative depiction of Buddhist enlightenment as expanded awareness of a "galaxy within" and its relation to the bodhisattva ideal of universal compassion, salvation, and happiness for all life, is fully encapsulated in these lines. This theme is also an epiphany at the conclusion of "Night of the Galactic Railway" when Giovanni declares to Campanella that from this point on: "Surely, I am also going to search for the real happiness of everyone!"[30]

Notes

1. *Kenji's School: Ideal Education for All*, trans. Cathy Hirano, (Tokyo: IFLC, 1997).

2. J. Thomas Rimer, *A Reader's Guide to Japanese Literature*, (Tokyo, Kōdansha International, 1999) 145–46

3. Miyazawa, *Matasaburo the Wind Imp*, trans. John Bester, (Tokyo: Kōdansha, 1972) xi.

4. "Begitarian taisai" in *Miyazawa Kenji zenshū*, 10 vols., (Tokyo: Chikuma Shobō, 1986), vol. 6, 445–51. Hereafter MKZ.

5. "Chūmon no ōi ryōriten," MKZ, vol. 6, 40–51.

6. "Yodaka no hoshi," MKZ, vol. 5, 83–92.

7. *Chūmon no ōi ryōriten* (The Restaurant of Many Orders), MKZ, vol. 8, 15.

8. *Miyazawa Kenji no bungaku to Hokekyō* (The literature of Kenji Miyazawa and the Lotus Sutra), (Tokyo: Mizu Shobō, 1993).

9. "On the Poet Miyazawa Kenji," *Japan Quarterly*, (July-September, 1991) 333.

10. Ibid., 334.

11. *Dawn to the West: A History of Japanese Literature, Vol. 4*, (New York: Columbia University Press, 1999) 284.

12. Ibid., 284.

13. Shuntarō Tanikawa called "Ame ni mo makezu" the "noblest" Japanese poem of modern times. See Miyazawa, *A Future of Ice: Poems and Stories of a Japanese Buddhist: Miyazawa Kenji*, translated by Hiroaki Satō, (San Francisco: North Point Press, 1989) xiii.

14. The translation is my own. The original can be found in MKZ, vol. 3, 469–71.

15. See "Ame ni mo makezu techō" in MKZ, vol. 10, 35–84 & 78–80.
16. Toshiko Toriyama, *Kenji's School: Ideal Education for All*, trans. Cathy Hirano, (Tokyo: IFLC, 1997) 40.
17. *Night of the Milky Way Railway*, trans. Sarah M. Strong, (Armonk, New York: M. E. Sharpe, Inc., 1991).
18. MKZ, vol. 7, 268.
19. This identification of the ticket with the *go-honzon* of Nichiren Buddhism was first made by Yasuo Irisawa and Taijirō Amazawa in their jointly authored *Tōgi—"Ginga tetsudō no yoru" to wa nani ka* (A debate—What is "Night Train to the Stars"?), (Tokyo: Kōdansha, 1979).
20. *Night of the Milky Way Railway*, 103
21. "Innocence and the Other World: The Tales of Miyazawa Kenji," *Monumenta Nipponica: Studies in Japanese Culture*, Vol. 47, No. 2. (Summer 1992) 246–48.
22. Makoto Ueda, *Modern Japanese Poets and the Nature of Literature*, (Stanford: Stanford University Press, 1983) 185–86.
23. Masanobu Yoshimi, *Miyazawa Kenji no dōtei* (Kenji Miyazawa's Journey), (Tokyo: Yaedake Sobō, 1982).
24. *Night of the Milky Way Railway*, 93.
25. "Tenki-rin no hashira: kagayaku bakari no shippō no tō setsu" (The pillar of the weather wheel: The "resplendent seven-jeweled stupa" theory), *Taiyō* 50 (Summer 1985) 21.
26. Yasuji Kirimura, *Outline of Buddhism*, (Tokyo: Nichiren Shoshū,1989) 97.
27. *Selected Writings of Nichiren*, trans. Burton Watson et al., (New York: Columbia University Press, 1990) 150.
28. "The Ideas of the *Lotus Sutra*,"in *The Lotus Sutra in Japanese Culture*, George J. Tanabe and Willa J. Tanabe eds., (Honolulu: The University of Hawaii Press, 1989) 42.
29. MKZ, vol. 10, 18.
30. *Ginga tetsudō no yoru*, 2nd Edition, Foa Bunko, (Tokyo: Iwasaki Shoten, 1996) 197.

Echoes of the Lotus Sutra in Tolstoy's Philosophy

Alexander Ignatovich

It is well known that the great Russian writer Leo Tolstoy (1828–1910), author of *War and Peace* and *Anna Karenina,* was also a dedicated moral thinker and Christian reformer, especially in his later years. Less appreciated is that his personal philosophy was closely related to the basic teachings of the Sutra of the Lotus Flower of the Wonderful Law.

After undergoing a personal spiritual crisis in the late 1870s, Tolstoy devoted the greatest part of his time and energy to a dedicated quest for the meaning of life. He left us some 164 essays and articles, most of them devoted to ethical and social issues, and which also raised profound religious and philosophical questions. Among the best-known writings he produced in the 1880s and 1890s were *A Confession* (1882), which described his crisis and subsequent moral suffering, *A Short Exposition of the Gospels* (1881), *The Kingdom of God Is within You* (1893), and *The Christian Teaching* (1894–96).

The author was born into a noble family and was a practicing member of the Russian Orthodox church. Beyond any doubt, the Christian ideal was the underlying basis for his continuing philosophical reflections on human nature. Ultimately he reached the conclusion that Christian beliefs as formalized by the leading denominations were fallacious, and this caused him to reject the authority of the Orthodox church, resulting in his excommunication.

Tolstoy had long had an interest in other religious-philosophical teachings. As a young man he had wanted to learn more about the faiths of India and China. It probably would be an exaggeration to say that non-Christian beliefs influenced the development of his outlook on the world. Nevertheless, his views on some important issues, questions related to the universal elements of human nature in particular, were sometimes surprisingly similar to the interpretations offered by other religions. Thus a comparison of Tolstoy's concept of "human nature" with the interpretation of the same subject in the Lotus Sutra is of considerable interest because that sutra and such others as the body of Prajñāpāramitā sutras encompassing all versions of different lengths of collected *prajñāpāramitā* scriptures, the Nirvana Sutra of the Mahayana canon, and some parts of the Flower Garland Sutra are early sutras of the so-called new Buddhism that began to develop on the eve of the Common Era. Its followers called it Mahayana (Great Vehicle), in contrast to the "old" Buddhism, which they termed Hinayana (Small or Lesser Vehicle). In time, of course, the Lotus Sutra became the best-known and most influential sutra in East Asian Buddhism.

Tolstoy's interest in Buddhism was of long duration. He referred to the Buddha many times in his later works and once wrote specifically about him. On February 18, 1910, in the last year of his life, he completed the introduction for an article by P. Boulanger about the Buddha and they were published together as a pamphlet. Tolstoy read Buddhist texts until the end of his life—in translation, of course—and they appear to have made a great impression on him.

In his personal library could be found such books as *Buddhism: Studies and Materials* by the prominent Russian Buddhologist Ivan P. Minayev, published in St. Petersburg in 1887, and a collection of Hinayana sutras translated by Nikolay I. Gerasimov from English into Russian and published in Moscow a year later. In these works the most important Hinayana texts from the *Tipiṭaka* were included. The many notations Tolstoy made on the pages indicate his interest in them.

Tolstoy's library also contained the following: Bhikku Nyanatiloka, *The Word of the Buddha*, Rangoon, 1907; Subhadra Bikschu, *Buddhistischer Katechismus zur Einfuehrung in die Lehre des Buddha Gotamo*, Leipzig, 1908; P. Carus, *The Gospel of Buddha, According to Old Records*, Chicago, 1895, and by the same author, *Nirvana: A Story of Buddhist Philosophy*, Chicago, 1896 (the latter was translated into Russian by Boulanger and published in Moscow in 1901).

Tolstoy apparently knew nineteenth-century Buddhological works rather well. Also among his books were influential titles on Buddhism by the German authority H. Oldenberg and by T. Rhys Davids, a renowned British Buddhologist, whose books were published in Russian. Nevertheless, almost all that he knew concerned Hinayana Buddhism. His knowledge of Mahayana Buddhism was minimal, largely because of the level of European and American Buddhological studies at that time.

This determined his view of the religion and his understanding of its essence, which he expressed in full measure in *A Confession*, where he wrote about Buddhism more directly than in his other works. In particular, he recounted there the story of young Prince Siddhārtha, the future Śākyamuni Buddha, seeing for the first time a very old person, a seriously ill person, and the body of a dead person. Tolstoy concludes: "Śākyamuni could find no comfort in life and decided that life itself is the greatest evil. He directed all the forces of his being to liberating himself and other [living beings] from the suffering of the cycle of birth and death, and to achieving this liberation in such a way that the cycle would be annihilated forever and never repeated. Many sources of Indian wisdom tell of this."

This estimation of Buddhism as especially pessimistic was more or less typical of Tolstoy and can be found in practically everything he wrote about it. Yet his general estimation of it was positive, probably because he was impressed by its belief in liberation from suffering. In *What I Believe* Tolstoy emphasized that the essence of Buddhism consists in "the teaching of how everyone can be saved from the evils of life." In addition, he stressed in his treatise *The Christian Teaching* that the greatest thinkers in human history, including Śākyamuni, had realized the contradiction between "human life with its demand for the good and its continuation on the one hand, and the inevitability of death and suffering on the other."

Two translations of the Lotus Sutra, both from the Sanskrit, were published in European languages in Tolstoy's lifetime. One was by Eugene Burnouf in French and the other by H. Kern in English. Neither was in Tolstoy's library so it is not known if he knew of them. He probably was aware of the existence of the Lotus Sutra, however, because he did own an English-language book by Lafcadio Hearn, *Gleanings in Buddhafields: Studies of Hand and Soul in the Far East* (1897), although some of its pages remained uncut. Hearn opened chapter 4 with a quotation from the Lotus Sutra in words that he italicized: "*There shall not remain even one particle of dust that does not enter into Buddhahood.*" There is no way of knowing, however, if Tolstoy read it.

The resemblance of opinions about human nature reached by the great Russian writer, as well as of his ethical philosophy, to ideas conveyed in the Lotus Sutra resulted from his own reflections. Tolstoy's conclusions about humanity and his concept of "God's kingdom within you" have something in common with the words of the sutra, although they were based on completely different initial premises. For example, Tolstoy accepted the Christian idea of the Creation without reservation although it is alien to all streams of Buddhism.

Śākyamuni declared in the Lotus Sutra three fundamental truths of

Mahayana Buddhism: the possibility for every living being to become a buddha, the eternal life of the Buddha (this affirmation anticipated the development of the doctrine of the Three Bodies of the Buddha which is of extreme importance to Mahayana Buddhism), and the existence of bodhisattvas, perfect human beings who have realized their primordial Buddha-nature and are trying to fully bring about deeds aimed at liberating living beings from their sufferings.

According to the classic T'ien-t'ai division, the Lotus Sutra has two parts: "the realm of trace"—sermons by Śākyamuni before he declared his eternity (the first half of the sutra, chapters 1–14)—and "the realm of origin"—sermons by Śākyamuni after he declared his eternity (the second half of the sutra, chapters 15–28).

A distinctive theme of the Lotus Sutra, of course, lies in its declaration of the presence of the Buddha-nature in all living beings. For that reason, chapter 12, "Devadatta," and chapter 20, "The Bodhisattva Never Despise," are of special interest in connection with Tolstoy's belief that "God's kingdom is within you" and his insistence on nonviolence. He tried to show that the happiness of human beings (in the truest meaning of the word) depends on our inner potential and is conditioned by human nature, which is similar to ideas in the Lotus Sutra.

The underlying theme of most of Tolstoy's religious-philosophical writings after 1881 was his assertion of the inherent power of Mind, or "rational consciousness," in human beings. This is reminiscent of the Buddhist concept of prajñā, or wisdom. The "indivisible spiritual and immortal being" of which he wrote in What I Believe is functionally identical to the human beings who realize their Buddha-nature. In that work he also wrote: "But Mind that illuminates our life and makes us change our deeds is not illusion and that is why it is impossible to deny it in any way."

Tolstoy sympathetically cited in his Weekly Readings: The Essence of Christian Teaching the words of the Russian religious thinker Fyodor Strakhov: "God and I are one, said the Teacher, but if you consider my body to be God you are wrong. If you consider to be God my nonbodily being which is separate from other beings you also are wrong. You will not be wrong only when you understand within you my true 'I' which is one with God and is one in all people. In order to understand this 'I' it is necessary to let yourself grow as a man." So we see that Tolstoy's idea about the inherent essence of God (or, using his words, "Mind" and "rational consciousness") indeed has something in common with the inherent Buddha-nature described in the Buddha's sermons, and perhaps in the clearest way in the Lotus Sutra.

Tolstoy also asserted that the realization of their true "nature" by human beings pushes them to do good. He wrote about this in The Christian

Teaching. Here too we can find a resemblance between Tolstoy's views and the Lotus Sutra, where revelation of a human being's true "nature" (that is, the Buddha-nature) presupposes the fulfillment of good deeds.

It is well known that the teaching of not resisting evil with violence and the principle of loving one's enemies played a major role in Tolstoy's ethical philosophy. He considered these the most important guideposts for human life. A comparative analysis of his religious-philosophical writings from the latter part of his life demonstrates the similarity of the views of the great Russian writer with those of the Lotus Sutra. It must be stressed, however, that it is not a question of the influence of Mahayana Buddhism on Tolstoy, which he may only have known slightly. Despite his conflict with the Russian Orthodox church, he always considered himself a Christian, and possibly more orthodox than the official church. Yet the closeness of Tolstoy's understanding of the human "nature" conveyed by the Lotus Sutra is beyond dispute.

4. Buddhism and Society

Buddha-body Theory and the Lotus Sutra: Implications for Praxis

Ruben L. F. Habito

Our task in this paper is to consider the place of the Saddharma-puṇḍarīka-sūtra (the Lotus Sutra) in the development of Buddha-body theory in the history of Buddhist thought. The first section will present a rough sketch of the main lines of development of Buddha-body theory up to the formation of two kinds of *trikāya* doctrine. The second section will highlight the view of the Buddha in the Lotus Sutra and note the elements that may have played a role in this development. The concluding section will offer reflections on the significance of this Buddha-view in the Lotus Sutra for Buddhist praxis past and present.

Buddha-body Theory in Historical Perspective

The Mahāparinibbāna-suttanta relates how Śākyamuni, foreseeing his impending demise, addressed his disciples on how they should comport themselves after his departure:

> Therefore, Ānanda, in this world, make yourselves unto a lamp, do not take refuge in any but yourselves; make the teaching [*dhamma*] unto a lamp, do not take refuge in anything but the teaching.[1]

This injunction, however, did not prevent the disciples, in their devotion toward their departed teacher, from cultivating practices of veneration toward the relics of his physical existence. The teaching [*dhamma*] was indeed enshrined as a point of refuge, but parallel with this, the teacher [the Buddha] was also so enshrined. Evidence from Pali scriptures indicates that an earlier version of the formula for refuge placed the Buddha on parallel with the *dhamma* as object of refuge, suggesting that the third element, the sangha, was a later addition.[2]

It is because the Buddha had realized the truth (*dhamma*) that he was able to teach it (*Bhagavā dhammaṁ deseti*). This close association between the teacher (Buddha) and the teaching (*dhamma*) is a characteristic note that can be discerned in Pali scriptures in general.

> [Listen,] Vakkali, one who sees the *dhamma* thus sees me. One who sees me thus sees the *dhamma*. Indeed, Vakkali, seeing the *dhamma*, one sees me, and seeing me, one sees the *dhamma*.[3]

This association between the Buddha and the Dhamma lies in the background of the usage of a key term in Buddha-body theory, that is, the term *dharmakāya*. This term, which took on metaphysical nuances in later periods, originally meant "the collection of teachings," that is, whereby one may be able to identify and locate the presence of the teacher even after the latter's entry into nirvana.

A passage in the renowned Milinda-pañho (The Questions of [King] Menander) exhibits this usage:

> In this manner, O Great King, the Blessed One has extinguished all delusive passions, and has entered into that final state of extinction. The Blessed One, having thus entered this state of extinction, is not manifested, saying 'He is here,' or 'He is there.'
>
> However, O Great King, the Blessed One is manifested by virtue of the collection of teachings [*dhamma-kāyena*]. For indeed, O Great King, the *dhamma* is that which has been taught by the Blessed One.[4]

This is basically the same use that we find in the early *Prajñāpāramitā* literature of the term *dharmakāya*, to mean "the body of teachings." In this context, we now find a distinction being made between this *dharmakāya*, the body of teachings (including the prescriptions for disciplined life, or *sīla*, meditative practice, or *samādhi*, and the study of the teachings which brings wisdom, or *prajñā*) taught and left by the Blessed One to the disciples on the one hand, and the *rūpakāya*, or that body of form and shape that once walked the earth on the other, of which there are still physical relics that are venerated by the disciples in public places.

In the Eight Thousand-Line Prajñāpāramitā (Wisdom) sutra, for example, we find the following word of caution addressed to the disciples:

> Indeed, the Tathāgata is not to be seen in the body of form and shape [*na rūpakāyato drastavyaḥ*]. For the bodies of the teachings [*dharmakāyāḥ*]—these are Tathāgatas.[5]

This is also echoed in the well-quoted verse from the Vajracchedikā-prajñāpāramitā-sūtra, or Diamond Wisdom Sutra.

Those who try to see me in form and shape,
Those who try to hear me with sounds and voices,
These are striving in mistaken directions,
These people will not be able to see me.

Buddhas are to be seen as the dharma.

Indeed, the Teachers are the body of dharma [*dharmakāya*]
And the way things are [*dharmatā*] is not to be known.
This [indeed] is not knowable.[6]

Needless to say, in Wisdom literature the summit of the Dharma is no other than *prajñāpāramitā*, or the perfection of wisdom itself, based on the realization of *śūnyatā*.

This distinction between the "body of Dharma" and the "body of form and shape," gave rise to a "two-body" theory, wherein the former is emphasized as the locus wherein the true Buddha can be seen, with the concomitant devaluing of the latter as a mistaken or misguided direction to turn in the search for enlightenment. In other words, this "two-body theory" distinguishing the *dharmakāya* from the *rūpakāya*, which implies the former as the true place to look for the Buddha rather than the latter, most likely arose among those engaged in the practice of the Six Perfections (*pāramitās*) leading to the realization of *śūnyatā*, to distinguish themselves from the devotees whose practice was centered on the veneration of the Buddha's relics.

From the first century B.C.E. onwards, parallel to the movement that led to the composition of the Wisdom sutras expounding the practice of the Six Perfections, there was a surge in popular devotion to various savior figures, themselves Awakened Ones, who had taken vows to assist all sentient beings and liberate them from their sufferings—Amitābha (Amitāyus), Bhaiṣajyarāja (Medicine King), Akṣobhya, among others. It was most probably also during this time that the main chapters of the Lotus Sutra, presenting Śākyamuni as the Tathāgata of Immeasurable Life, were composed.[7]

Corollary with these devotional movements, speculation concerning the status of an Awakened One continued, and notions of "Buddhas of the Past" and "Buddhas of the Ten Directions" or of different realms became part of common discourse. It was the question of the status of the great savior buddhas who were the objects of devotion in these popular movements that later gave the impetus for the formulation of a threefold Buddha-body (*trikāya*) theory in Mahayana treatises.

One of the noted treatises that expounds on the *trikāya* theory is the Mahāyāna-sūtrālaṃkāra, a fourth-century composition. Here the three bodies are presented as follows:

Concerning the distinctions of the Buddha-body: . . . The one of self-nature [*svābhāvika*], the enjoyment body [*saṃbhogyaḥ kāya*] and the one of transformation [*nair-mānika*]—

These are the distinctions in the bodies of the buddhas.
The first is the ground [*āsraya*] of the [other] two.

These are the three kinds of bodies of the buddhas. The one of self-nature is *dharmakāya*, characterized by the revolution of the ground (*āsraya-parāvṛtti-lakṣanaḥ*).

The entirety of the bodies of the buddhas
Is to be known in these three bodies.
The Ground, the [body for] Self-[benefit], and the [body for] Other-benefit—
These are revealed in these three bodies.[8]

Here the first body is understood as the ground of the other two, and is characterized by the "revolution of the ground"—a technical term which indicates a transformative experience wherein a delusive state of mind is abandoned and the wisdom of nondiscrimination begins to function: the wisdom that has realized *śūnyatā*. In short, the ground that makes a buddha a buddha is none other than the realization of this wisdom of *śūnyatā*. The "fruit" of this realization is the manifestation of the second, "enjoyment body," characterized as that which receives self-benefit in this transformative experience of enlightenment. And out of the same ground of enlightenment, i.e., the first body, is the (third) "body of transformation"—that which is manifested for the benefit of other beings, guiding them and assisting them on their own way to enlightenment. This third body, with different manifestations throughout history, is the outflow of compassion that is grounded in the wisdom of enlightenment.

The Ratnagotra-vibhāga Mahāyānottaratantra-śāstra is another influential treatise that presents the threefold-body theory, but in a different form.

This [buddhahood] manifests itself in the variety of the three bodies: the body of self-nature, and others, represented by qualities of Profundity, Magnificence, and Magnanimity, respectively.

Here, the Body of Self-nature of the Buddha is to be known as having five characteristics,
And is endowed with five kinds of properties.
It is uncreated, indivisible, devoid of two extremes,
Liberated from the three obstructions of defilement, ignorance, and distraction. . . .

[The enjoyment body], enjoying the Truth [*dharma*] in various forms,
Manifests the Truth of its very nature.
Being a natural outflow of compassion,
It works unceasingly for the sake of sentient beings. . . .

[The body of transformation] knowing the world,
Perceiving the world fully, filled with Great Compassion
Manifests itself in various transformations, without being separated
from the body of Truth [*dharmakāya*].

Self-benefit and that of others
[Characterizes] the Body of the Highest Truth [*para-mārtha-kāyaḥ*]
And the phenomenal [*saṃvṛti*] bodies grounded upon it.[9]

Here we notice a difference from the account of the Mahāyāna-sūtrā-lamkāra in the description of the relatedness of the three to one another. In the Mahāyāna-sūtrālaṃkāra, the first body is the "ground," the second receives (literally, "enjoys") the self-benefit (*svārtha*) of enlightenment, and the third works for the benefit of others (*parārtha*) out of compassion. In the Ratnagotra-vibhāga Mahāyānottaratantra-śāstra, the first body is described as receiving the self-benefit of enlightenment, and the two (phenomenal) bodies, in their different spheres of activity, function toward the benefit of others, using all kinds of excellent appropriate means, out of boundless compassion, without being separated from its ground, i.e., the *dharmakāya*.[10]

This may at first glance seem to be a minor difference, but a consideration of the implications leads to an understanding of two different views of buddhahood and the praxis leading to its realization. There are many aspects to examine in detail regarding this crucial difference between the Mahāyāna-sūtrālaṃkāra and the Ratnagotra-vibhāga Mahāyānottara-tantra-śāstra in their accounts of the threefold Buddha-body, but we can summarize these in the following manner:

The Mahāyāna-sūtrālaṃkāra presents a *trikāya* theory that we can describe as "ascending," whereas the Ratnagotra-vibhāga Mahāyānottara-tantra-śāstra *trikāya* theory is "descending."

Ascent can be understood as an activity or movement from this world to the world yonder, or from this human personal existence to the impersonal *dharmadhātu*, the world of *dharmatā*. Descent is the reverse; it is revival and affirmation of humanity, or personality in human existence.[11]

The focus of the ascent is the realization of wisdom, whereas the focus of descent is the activity flowing from compassion. The Mahāyāna-sūtrā-lamkāra, as a treatise expounding the view of the Yogācāra school, presents its Buddha-body theory in the context of the practice of this school, that is, the (ascending) practice centered on yogic meditation leading to enlightenment. The fruit of this practice is thus enjoyed by the second body. The third (transformation) body is manifested to assist other beings in taking the (ascending) path.

The Ratnagotra-vibhāga Mahāyānottaratantra-śāstra on the other hand, expounding the *Tathāgata-garbha* doctrine, or the teaching summarized in the statement that "all sentient beings are endowed with the capacity for buddhahood," presents its *trikāya* theory from this perspective, that is, from the presupposition that all beings are already in possession of that which they are meant to realize (enlightenment), and need only to open their eyes to this very reality. The activity of the Buddha (called *Tathāgata-dharmakāya* in the Ratnagotra-vibhāga Mahāyānottaratantra-śāstra), as one who looks at the phenomenal world from the standpoint of the summit, is to "descend" from this summit and, out of compassion, manifest one's presence in the triple world, to enable sentient beings to open their eyes and realize in what their true "nature" consists.[12]

Thus, self-benefit that belongs to the first body (of self-nature) is turned around toward the benefit of others, and the second (enjoyment) as well as the third (transformation) body are both presented as working in this regard each in its own sphere: the Great Savior Buddhas continue their activity of compassion (as Amitābha, leading sentient beings to the Pure Land; Bhaiṣajyarāja, working toward the healing of beings, etc.); and earthly manifestations (beginning with, but not confined to, the historical Śākyamuni) help beings by their skillful means (*upāya-kauśalya*) toward the realization of their true nature as originally enlightened.

It is this latter theory, presenting a unified picture of an All-Wise and All-Compassionate Buddha manifested in different bodies, who employs various skillful means throughout the different historical eras and in different realms, that came to be most influential in Tibet, China, Korea, and Japan, in terms of the way it served as a backdrop of Buddhist faith and practice that ran across sectarian lines.

The Buddha Mahāvairocana, the centerpiece of the Esoteric tradition, illuminating all beings with its all-pervading wisdom and preaching the Dharma universally in different modes and forms, can be noted as a developed form of this Buddha-view.[13]

Let us now examine some aspects of the Buddha-view of the Lotus Sutra.

The View of the Buddha in the Lotus Sutra

It has been noted by scholars that key elements in the Buddha-view of the Lotus Sutra can be found in other texts written before or around the same time, indicating that these elements were therefore by no means original to the Lotus Sutra. For example, the spatial and temporal extension of the dimensions of the life of the Tathāgata, a keynote theme of the Lotus Sutra, is a notion that can be found in other sources, including the *Mahāvastu*, the Pali *nikāyas*, and treatises of the various sectarian groups that were active around the beginning of the Common Era or before.[14]

The presentation of the Buddha as savior is likewise not unique to the Lotus Sutra, noting that Amitābha, Bhaiṣajyarāja, and others were also understood as exercising a similar role toward all sentient beings. Further, the identification of Buddha with the Dharma, presented on several levels,[15] is a point in continuity with views also reflected in Pali sources.

What makes the Lotus Sutra stand out, however, is the way it weaves these various elements to present a grand and compelling picture of the continuing dynamic activity of the Buddha, in a way that invites the devoted reader of the sutra to enter into this very activity itself, as one's response to the reading of the sutra.

Let us pick out some salient elements.

First, regarding the immeasurable life span of the Tathāgata, it has been pointed out that the originality of the Lotus Sutra is not so much in expounding this notion as such, a notion which, as noted above, is also found in other (non-Mahayana) writings, as in its presentation of this unlimited life span as the backdrop for its teaching on various kinds of skillful means (*upāya*) employed by the Tathāgata to lead ordinary beings to awakening.[16]

The narration of the parable of the burning house (chapter 3) and of the parable of the wayward son (chapter 4), the illustration of the Tathāgata's compassion likened to rainwater which is showered upon different kinds of herbs, grasses, trees (chapter 5), the depiction of the Tathāgata as like a good physician with many children who pretends to go away to bring his children to their senses (chapter 16), and so on, all come together to present a coherent picture of the one Tathāgata engaged in dynamic activity on behalf of all sentient beings of many shapes and forms and of various dispositions.

Another salient feature in the Lotus Sutra worth mention at this juncture is the understanding of sentient beings as the children of the Tathāgata. This notion is one that played a significant role in the later development of the *Tathāgata-garbha* doctrine.[17]

The innumerable buddhas who have emanated from the one Tathā-gata, preaching the Dharma in all the worlds in all directions, and now depicted as coming together to return to one place again to hear the word of the Tathāgata (chapter 11, "Beholding the Precious Stupa"), is another aspect to note. This indicates a way of regarding the different buddhas (objects of devotion of different groups) as ultimately springing from one and the same source.

In all this, the grounding of such activity in the realization of śūnyatā is not blurred from the horizon.

> The Tathāgata knows and sees the character of the triple world as it really is [yathābhūtaṁ]: there is neither birth nor death, or going away or coming forth; neither living nor dead; neither reality nor unreality; neither thus nor otherwise.[18]

Needless to say, this description echoes the various expositions of śūnyatā in the Prajñāpāramitā literature. In other words, it is the realization of śūnyatā that is the fulcrum around which the compassionate activity of the Tathāgata revolves.

We see in the Lotus Sutra an attempt to find a point of integration of the important notions connected with the different devotional and meditative practices engaged in by Buddhist followers of the time.[19] The message of the One Vehicle (ekayāna) integrating the three ways of the hearers, solitary ascetics, and the bodhisattva, needless to say, is at the centerpiece of the whole Lotus Sutra. The Lotus Sutra can also be seen as presenting an integrative view of two main streams in the Mahayana movement—the stream of popular devotion to the buddhas of the different realms (buddha-centered practice), and the stream represented by the Wisdom literature, with its emphasis on the realization of śūnyatā as the fount of all wisdom and compassion (Dharma-centered practice)—presenting these as compatible in the context of the One Vehicle (ekayāna).

It will be recalled that in the latter stream, there was a marked emphasis on the pursuit of the Dharma, with the implied or expressed denigration of the popular devotional practice directed toward the physical relics of the Buddha, manifested in the veneration of stupas. The Lotus Sutra, though leaning toward the devotional side with its accounts of the veneration of relics and its positive valuation of stupa worship, finds middle ground on this point. In the latter part of the sutra, especially the chapters "Beholding the Precious Stupa" ("Stūpa-saṁ-darśana," chapter 11) and "The Merits of the Preacher" ("Dharmabhāṇaka-anusaṁsā," chapter 19), the main concern centers on the preservation of the True Dharma and its proper transmission to later generations after the "extinction" of Śākyamuni Buddha, especially in times of persecution. Thus, statements made in the sutra about the particular merits of propagating the sutra and of preaching this wondrous Dharma (*saddharma*) to others highlight this emphasis on the Dharma itself. In other words, this whole emphasis echoes the theme found in Pali and other sources: "One who sees the Dharma, sees me."

In this connection, there is one passage in the Sanskrit version (not found in Kumārajīva's translation) wherein the term *dharmakāya* appears.

All things are equal, are empty, devoid of characteristics:
Whoever does not desire any of these things, and who sees things without making distinctions,

That is a Great Wise One, who sees the body of Dharma in its entirety [*dharmakāyaṁ aśeṣataḥ*]
[And sees that] there are not three vehicles, there is this only one vehicle indeed.

All things are equal, all are the same, always the same.
One who knows thus, knows nirvana, deathlessness, beatitude.[20]

As it does not appear in Kumārajīva's translation, it is surmised that this was a later addition, and hence the passage is problematic. But we may simply take it as it is, as a passage from an extant Sanskrit version, and note that its use of the term *dharmakāya* reflects the earlier sense of "collection of teachings," and does not contain any suggestion of the later-developed meaning in the context of the threefold Buddha-body theory.

There seems to be no other appearance of the term *dharmakāya* in the Lotus Sutra. Thus it would be an anachronism to use this term (in the sense of the later-developed *trikāya* theory) to refer to the Tathāgata portrayed in the sutra. What is clear, however, is that the nuance from the wider tradition identifying the Buddha with the Dharma, and vice versa, figures as prominently in the Lotus Sutra as well.[21] And from this perspective, the appellation *dharmakāya* as applied to the Buddha can be seen as implicitly affirmed in the Lotus Sutra, within a spectrum of meaning continuous with previous Buddhist tradition. The description of the ceaseless compassionate activity of the Tathāgata that is a hallmark of the Lotus Sutra then, can be noted as one significant stage on the way to the later-developed notion, although there is no *explicit* reference connecting the term *dharmakāya* to this view of the Buddha in the Lotus Sutra as yet.

In sum, the Lotus Sutra played a significant role in the development of Buddha-body theory in the following manner. First, it connected the notion of the Buddha of immeasurable life (already found in other texts) with the notion of skillful means, portraying a dynamic and ceaseless activity of the Buddha as grounded in compassion. Second, it presented the different buddhas of the different realms as emanations of the one Tathā-gata identified with Śākyamuni, as one attempt at unifying the different buddhas who are objects of devotion by different groups in different quarters, under one coherent framework. This is a contribution in the direction of understanding the connectedness among the various buddhas venerated by different groups at the time. Thus, in this context it also paved the way for further speculation on the *saṃbhogakāya*, presenting it as not only exercising the function of self-benefit (*svārtha*) as "enjoying" the fruits of enlightenment, but likewise of activity toward the benefit of others (*parārtha*) as a natural outflow of that enlightenment. The depiction of the multitudes of buddhas, emanations of the one Tathāgata, as preaching the Dharma in various realms, is seen in this context. And third, the Lotus Sutra received and carried on the tradition regarding the identification of Buddha with the Dharma in its own particular way. With this it also *implicitly* affirms the use of *dharmakāya* to point to the Buddha, leaving the way open for further developments in the notion that would more explicitly refer to the Tathāgata as full of wisdom and in ceaseless activity on behalf of all sentient beings, as in the Tathāgata-Dharmakāya of the Ratnagotra-vibhāga Mahāyānottaratantra-śāstra.

Implications for Praxis

A consideration of the difference in the Buddha-body theories of the Mahā-yāna-sūtrālaṃkāra and the Ratnagotra-vibhāga Mahāyānottaratantra-śāstra as described above would highlight some implications of the Buddha-view of the Lotus Sutra for ongoing Buddhist praxis.

The focus of the *trikāya* theory of the Mahāyāna-sūtrālaṃkāra is on the *saṃbhogakāya* as enjoying the fruits of enlightenment (self-benefit). This focus is connected with prescriptions of practice understood as an ascending path toward enlightenment that would enable such "enjoyment": the practice of the Six Perfections, with emphasis on meditative trance (*samādhi*) leading to wisdom (*prajñā*), as elaborated in the Yogacāra school. It is upon reaching the summit of this ascent, that is, the realization of enlightenment described as "the revolution of the ground" (*āśraya-parāvṛtti*), that one can make the "descent" and begin to work for the benefit of others.

In contrast, the *trikāya* theory of the Ratnagotra-vibhāga Mahāyānot-taratantra-śāstra does not focus so much on one or another of the three, but expounds the three as aspects of the one integral *Tathāgata-Dharmakāya*. In this framework, practice for self-benefit, i.e., toward enlightenment (ascribed to the first body) naturally flows into the practice for other-benefit, that is, the ceaseless activity to lead all beings to this enlightenment (ascribed to the other two bodies). This Buddha-body view thus calls for a mode of praxis in a "descending" direction, that is, with an emphasis on placing oneself at the service of the Tathāgata's ceaseless activity for the benefit of others based on compassion.

Needless to say, it is this descending mode of practice that comes out most prominently and is emphasized in the Lotus Sutra. Grounded in faith-discernment (*adhimukti*) in the Tathāgata as portrayed throughout the sutra, that is, as full of compassion and working unceasingly and on all fronts on behalf of living beings, the reader is given encouragement and empowerment to participate in this action based on compassion, reassured of the merit therein. The kinds of activity described include (but are not limited to) receiving and keeping this sutra, reading or reciting or expounding or copying it (chapter 19, "Dharmabhāṇaka"). The exposition of the merit of these actions pertaining to the preservation and propagation of the Dharma as expounded in this sutra assures the attainment of self-benefit as one engages in action oriented for other-benefit.

In short, the praxis that comes out of the teaching of the Lotus Sutra, true to the integrative spirit of this sutra, is one that cuts through the separation between self-benefit and other-benefit. What one does for others connected with proclaiming and preaching the compassionate wisdom of the Tathāgata as taught in this sutra, reaps benefit for oneself, and vice versa, the benefit one receives in such activity by its very nature benefits others.

This is a very apt description of the path of the bodhisattva who seeks enlightenment not just for oneself, but precisely for and on behalf of all sentient beings. The engagement in the various tasks of assisting sentient beings of all kinds and forms, in all places and circumstances, toward alleviating their suffering and removing various obstacles to enlightenment, is itself the realization of the fruit of this enlightenment. In other words, the Buddha-view of the Lotus Sutra grounds a kind of praxis that can be characterized in contemporary terms as a socially engaged Buddhism.

The history of transmission and reception of this sutra, and its abiding influence in different cultures of East Asia, are a testimony to the actuality of "self-benefit-*qua*-other-benefit" that this sutra proclaims.[22] The activity of the adherents of this sutra in different parts of the world today can be seen likewise as the confirmation of the self-fulfilling nature of its prophetic words.

316 BUDDHISM AND SOCIETY

References

Habito, Ruben. "Busshin-ron no Tenkai" (The Development of Buddha-body Theories), *Shūkyō Kenkyū* 237 (1978): 111–31. "On Dharmakāya as Ultimate Reality—Prolegomenon for Buddhist Christian Dialogue," *Japanese Journal of Religious Studies* 12 (1985): 233–52. "The Trikāya Doctrine in Buddhism," *Buddhist Christian Studies* 6 (1986): 53–62. "Mikkyō ni okeru Hosshinkan no Haikei" (Backgrounds of Views on Dharma-kāya in Esoteric Buddhism), *Indogaku-Bukkyōgaku Kenkyū* 36 (1987): 141–48.

Hirakawa, Akira. *Shoki-Daijōbukkyo no Kenkyū.* Tokyo: Shunjūsha, 1968.

———. *Shoki-Daijō to Hokke-shisō.* Tokyo: Shunjūsha, 1989.

Katō, Bunnō, and Yoshirō Tamura, et al., *The Threefold Lotus Sutra.* New York: Weatherhill; Tokyo: Kōsei Publishing Co., 1975.

Nagao, Gadjin. *Mādhyamika and Yogācāra—A Study of Mahāyāna Philosophies.* Ed. by L. S. Kawamura. Albany: State University of New York Press, 1991.

Pye, Michael. "The Lotus Sutra and the Essence of Mahāyāna," *Buddhist Spirituality: Indian, Southeast Asian, Tibetan, and Early Chinese.* World Spirituality: An Encyclopedic History of the Religious Quest, vol. 8. New York: Crossroad, 1993.

Reeves, Gene. "Outline of the Teachings of the Lotus Sutra," Paper distributed for the first International Conference on the Lotus Sutra, 1994.

Suguro, Shinjō. "Hokkekyō no Budda-ron" (Buddha-view in the Lotus Sutra), in Hōyō Watanabe, ed., *Hokke-Bukkyō no Budda-ron to Shujōron* (Concepts of Buddha and Sentient Beings Based on the Lotus Sutra). Kyoto: Heirakuji Shoten, 1985, 61–110.

Takasaki, Jikidō. *Nyoraizō-shisō no Keisei* (The Formation of Tathāgata-garbha Doctrine). Tokyo: Shunjūsha, 1974.

Tamaki, Kōshirō. "Hokke-Bukkyō ni okeru Budda-ron no Mondai" (The Problem of the Buddha-view in the Lotus Sutra), in Hōyō Watanabe, ed., *Hokke-bukkyō no Budda-ron to Shujōron* (op. cit.), 3–59.

Tamura, Yoshirō. *Hokekyō* (The Lotus Sutra). Tokyo: Chūkō-shinsho, no. 196. Chūō Kōron Sha, 1969.

Tanabe, George Jr., and Willa Jane Tanabe. *The Lotus Sutra in Japanese Culture.* Honolulu: University of Hawaii Press, 1989.

Teramoto, Enga, and Yūshi Hiramatsu, eds. *Zō-kan-wa San-yaku Ibushū-rin-ron* (Tibetan-Chinese-Japanese Triple Translation of the Treatise on the Wheel of the Differing Sects). Tokyo: Kokusho Kankōkai, 1974.

Notes

1. *Dīgha Nikāya*, *II*, 99–101. Translations of passages from *Dīgha Nikāya*, *Astasahāsrika-Prajñāpāramitā*, *Mahāyāna-sūtrālaṃkāra*, *Ratnagotra-vibhāga Mahā-yānottaratantra-śāstra*, and *Samyutta-Nikāya* are my own. For Lotus Sutra texts, Yukio Sakamoto and Hiroshi Iwamoto, eds., *Hokekyō*, 3 vols., Tokyo: Iwanami Bunko, 1962–67, and P. L. Vaidya's Sanskrit edition, *Saddharmapuṇḍarīka*

Sūtra, Darbhanga: The Mithila Institute, 1960, and the English translation by Bunnō Katō, Yoshirō Tamura, et al., *The Threefold Lotus Sutra*, New York: Weatherhill; Tokyo: Kosei Publishing Co., 1975, were consulted.

2. *Samyutta-Nikāya, I.,* 30; *Dīgha Nikāya, II,* 208, 211, 221, 227.

3. *Samyutta-Nikāya, III,* 120.

4. *Milinda-pañho,* 73.

5. *Astasahāsrika-Prajñāpāramitā,* 513, 1.15–16.

6. *Vajracchedikā-prajñāpāramitā-sūtra,* 56–57.

7. Hirakawa, 1968, 1989.

8. *Mahāyāna-sūtrālaṃkāra, IX,* 60, 65.

9. *Ratnagotra-vibhāga Mahāyānottaratantra-śāstra II,* 43, 44, 49, 53; *III,* 1.

10. *Ratnagotra-vibhāga Mahāyānottaratantra-śāstra IV,* 1–88.

11. Nagao, 1991, 201.

12. Habito, 1978, 1985, 1986.

13. Habito, 1987.

14. Teramoto and Hiramatsu, eds., 1974; Tamaki, 1985, among others; Pye, 1993.

15. Suguro, 1985.

16. See Pye, 1993, 172–73.

17. Takasaki, 1974.

18. Katō et al., 1975, 251.

19. Tamura, 1969; see Reeves, 1994.

20. V:81-83; Vaidya, 1960, 96.

21. See Suguro, 1985.

22. See Tamura, 1969, 121–98; also Tanabe and Tanabe, 1989.

How Has the Lotus Sutra Created Social Movements?: The Relationship of the Lotus Sutra to the *Mahāparinirvāṇa-sūtra*

Masahiro Shimoda

Introduction

No one can survey even a small part of the history of Indian Buddhism without being surprised at the remarkable number of manuscripts of the Lotus Sutra found in various areas in Asia, ranging in age from the seventh century C.E. to nearly modern times.[1] In the world of Indian Buddhism among the manuscripts discovered to date, these manuscripts are the largest in number, far more numerous than the second largest. One must be struck again by the fact that the sutra has initiated an equally surprising number of social movements throughout the history of Buddhism in Japan.[2]

The former suggests that the sutra gained distinguished popularity in the world of Mahayana Buddhism. The latter, on the other hand, not only shows great interest by the Japanese in the sutra but at the same time hints at the way in which the sutra has generally been accepted in different societies: the sutra would come alive again to people in a new situation in a renewed appearance with its substance unchanged.

These two seemingly irrelevant things—the repeated effort of copying the sutra by hand, a monotonous activity done throughout the ages in India, and the frequent appearances in Japanese history of new social activities based theoretically on the sutra, involving in contrast renewed experiences—seem to provide an important context in which to find a hidden structure of the theory of the Lotus Sutra.

But how is it possible to relate these two ostensibly unaffiliated or even antithetical facts? I am fully aware that some of my colleagues in the field of Buddhist studies may be unwilling to accept this kind of viewpoint because these two facts apparently do not share enough historical situation in common to be examined in a comparative study.

Nevertheless, this paper will make an attempt to do this from the perspective that the Lotus Sutra has a fundamental structure from which a worldwide range of cultural manifestations could emerge beyond the respective cultural restrictions. In this sense, this paper might well be regarded as taking an idealistic rather than a historical approach to the Lotus Sutra.

Interpretation of Śākyamuni Buddha's *Parinirvāṇa*

First, I would like to draw attention to the fact that the Lotus Sutra, as the first and second chapters of the sutra clearly show, intends to reopen the history of Buddhism, presenting Śākyamuni Buddha not as a historical but as a history-transcending reality.

The Lotus Sutra begins by overlapping the present situation of the sutra with that of ancient times when the historical Śākyamuni Buddha decided to give his first sermon after being persuaded out of his strong reluctance to preach by the god Brahma. This seems to be possible only if it was supposed by the compilers of the Lotus Sutra that the Buddha was never extinguished at the time of his *parinirvāṇa* at Kuśinagarī.

This reasoning may well bring our attention to a group of sutras known under the name of the *Mahāparinirvāṇa-sūtra*, which mainly discuss the issue of the Buddha's existence after entering *parinirvāṇa*.

The *Mahāparinirvāṇa-sūtra* in Hinayana

There are two versions of the sutras known under the name of the *Mahāparinirvāṇa-sūtra*, belonging to Hinayana and Mahayana traditions respectively. The former is available in Sanskrit, Chinese, and Tibetan versions, both in the form of an independent sutra and in the form of incorporated sutras in several schools' *vinaya* and *sutta piṭakas*. Without doubt, it predates to the compilation of the Lotus Sutra.

This Hinayana version of the sutra has drawn a great deal of attention from modern scholars in Buddhist studies because it provides a lot of information regarding Śākyamuni Buddha's last moments in this world. Most scholars, of whom Ernst Waldschmidt and Andre Bareau are representative, tried to discover a nucleus of the sutra by positing the idea that it was compiled based on certain kinds of historical facts and then gradually enlarged in the direction of greatly enhancing the Buddha's image.[3]

For this sutra, this theory about a compilation process may well be right on the whole, but it is not necessarily satisfactory. When this argument is carried so far as to say that the *Mahāparinirvāṇa-sūtra* (MPS) was compiled originally with the intention of conveying the facts of Śākyamuni Buddha's death, we can no longer agree.[4]

A closer historical and philological study of this sutra by the present author has shown that the nucleus of this sutra contains two miracles which took place at the time of Śākyamuni Buddha's death: one is the miracle of the Buddha's entering into the highest stage of meditation (*samādhi*) at the very moment of passing from this world, and the other is that of the Buddha's body (*śarīra*) or relics (*śarīras*) being protected from the cremation fire.

The former, which of course cannot be a descriptive account and instead must be an interpretation of the Buddha by the compilers, tries to show that the Buddha was not extinguished even after his *parinirvāṇa* but is still existing in some invisible form named *parinirvāṇadhātu*. The latter suggests that the Buddha's remains, which in fact symbolize the Buddha's eternal reality in later Indian Buddhism, will never decay. Both have the intention of imparting to us the eternal Śākyamuni Buddha in a form different from that at the time he was alive.

The Buddha's Existence
as a Necessary Condition for Producing a Sutra

It might be good for us to be reminded here that any sutra, whether it belongs to Hinayana or Mahayana, could exist only if the revealer, the Buddha, existed. A formula placed at the beginning of all the sutras contains a phrase, such as *"ekaṃ samayam* (Skt., *ekasmin samaye) bhagavān . . . viharati sma"* (Thus have I heard. At one time the Lord was staying at), ensuring the Buddha's existence. The Buddha's existence is one of the most important necessary conditions enabling a sutra to come into existence.[5]

Things are the same in the case of the MPS insofar as it is a sutra. If this sutra in its core had only the intention of declaring the Buddha's death, which necessarily leads to the Buddha's nonexistence in the present, the MPS would inevitably face a sharp contradiction with the rest of the sutras, by attempting to deprive all the sutras their most fundamental and vital element. The MPS would not have been composed if this conflict, which can be expected to arise from the subject of the Buddha's death, had not been successfully overcome in some manner.

The event of Gotama Buddha's death must have been modified so as to meet a necessary requirement of all sutras: that is, that the Buddha must always exist in some way. The MPS managed to clear this problem up by verifying the Buddha's eternity in the two different ways seen above.

The *Mahāparinirvāṇa-sūtra* in Mahayana[6]

According to common understanding, the two sutras with the same title *Mahāparinirvāṇa-sūtra*, one belonging to Hinayana and the other to Mahayana, are said to have no relation to each other. In fact, however, these two sutras are at least properly to be placed in the same editorial line.

The main subject, which is firmly shared by these two groups of sutras, is the eternal reality of the Buddha. It would be good to briefly sketch an outline of the Mahayana *Mahāparinirvāṇa-sūtra* for the special purpose of understanding that the Buddha's essence has been regarded as eternal throughout the history of both Mahayana and Hinayana traditions.

The Mahayana *Mahāparinirvāṇa-sūtra* (MMPS) contains three layers that disclose the process in which the sutra was progressively composed. The cardinal point shown in the first layer is almost the same as that in the core of the MPS. It claims that the Buddha is beyond this material world (*asaṃskṛta*) and exists eternally.

The second layer sheds the same light on the Buddha as the first stage, but in another way, by introducing the concept of "*lokanuvartanā*." The idea of *lokanuvartanā*, as will be explained below, essentially serves to remove substantial meaning from a variety of events in the life of the Buddha. If we accept this concept, the event of the Buddha's passing away into nirvana related in many Mahayana sutras, including the Lotus Sutra, is to be regarded as an illusion displayed by the Buddha for the benefit of sentient beings. The Buddha is thus taken to be eternal and beyond all historical expressions.

The third layer demonstrates the teaching that all sentient beings have the Buddha-nature (*asti buddhadhātuḥ sarvasattveṣu*). This idea can be seen as an internalization of the Buddha's reality in sentient beings, especially the reality represented in the Buddha's relics (*buddhadhātu*) as an eternal Buddha.

All the three stages of the MMPS, together with the core of the MPS, refer to the eternity of the Buddha though they deal with the theme of the Buddha's *parinirvāṇa*. This betrays the intrinsic principle on which all sutras could be produced: the principle that the Buddha must be eternal. With this taken into account, it is clear that both groups of sutras, Hinayana and Mahayana, can be placed in one and the same current of thought—that having to do with the Buddha's omnipresence, a current which might have been running since his nirvana.

PERSONIFICATION OF THE TRUTH IN THE HISTORY OF BUDDHISM

The Buddha Within and Beyond History

One of the most distinguishing characteristics of Buddhism when compared with the Vedic religions lies in the fact that Buddhism has a human being as its founder. In Brahmanism, all the sacred texts called *śruti* have to be revealed by gods and handed down to human beings. In other words, the Vedic tradition claims that the origin of religious texts cannot be substantiated in history. Buddhism, on the other hand, has its starting point at a specified time in history, that is, at the time of the Buddha's first discourse on the dharma. The Buddhist sacred texts are not merely beyond history, they must be embodied in history.[7]

However, we should here be careful not to ignore the fact that the existence of the Buddha was regarded as eternal, as we have seen in the good examples shown in both Hinayana and Mahayana *Mahāparinirvāṇa-sūtras*. This means that Buddhist sacred texts which are revealed by the essentially eternal Buddha are in a sense considered to be beyond history. The Buddha and his discourses are thus characterized by the two incompatible aspects of being both within and beyond history.

The word "Buddha," awakened [one], can have a complete meaning only when properly supplemented by words such as "from delusion to truth." "Buddha" must be closely related to truth, to the dharma. It is not Śākyamuni Buddha's superior ability as a human being but the truth, the dharma itself, attained by the Buddha that distinguishes the Buddha from other people. This truth, the dharma, is not of course confined to a specific history.

In explaining legends about the Buddha, modern scholars tend to surmise without much reason that the Buddha was looked on as a human being at the beginning and gradually deified in the course of time, culminating in the many Buddhas shown in various kinds of Mahayana sutras. This assumption does not, however, conform to the historical evidence. As far as hagiographic materials go, the Buddha has been seen from the outset as a reality both within and beyond history. We cannot restore a part of Śākyamuni Buddha's biography without using Buddhist records which are tinged more or less with deified, exalted characteristics of the Buddha.

Taking these factors into consideration, we can say that, when seen from the perspective of Buddhists living in ancient India, the truth, the dharma, which is beyond history, must be substantiated, or incarnated if you like, in the historical dimension by Śākyamuni Buddha. Current understanding by modern scholarship of the "deification of the Buddha" is far from satisfactory with respect of the intimate interrelationship between the Buddha and the dharma.

Buddha's Personification in Iconography

Ancient Buddhists' understanding of the Buddha as a superhuman being can also be evidenced in the world of Buddhist iconography. It is widely known that there are no Buddha statues or images found from the early periods of Buddhist art. The Buddha is always represented in some way other than by his own image, such as his seat, footprint, a bodhi tree, a dharma wheel, a stupa, and so on. Artists at that time and place did have anthropomorphic ways of expression, as many human and humanlike creatures, including the Buddha's disciples, were shown in Buddhist art. But ancient Indian artists consciously abstained from representing Śākyamuni Buddha in a human form.

In the first century C.E., after several centuries of the Buddha's absence from art, Buddha images appeared almost simultaneously and independently in two regions, Gandhāra and Mathūla, which were separated by too great a distance to have been in communication with each other. This is the first evidence of the appearance of personified images of Śākyamuni Buddha in the world of iconography. One must be surprised that it took more than four or five centuries for Buddhist India to represent Śākyamuni Buddha in an anthropomorphic image.

This fact testifies to a trend in ancient India in which the Buddha was gradually personified, not deified, in the course of time.

The Concept of "Lokanuvartanā"[8]

The idea *lokanuvartanā*, which literally means "[the Buddha's behaving] in conformity with this-world appearances," had a great influence, especially on Mahayana Buddhism. This compound word is used in many sutras belonging to the Mahāsāṃghika school as a predicate whose subject is all of Śākyamuni Buddha's behavior from his birth to "entering into *parinirvāṇa*." This concept of *lokanuvartanā* must have been produced in a current of devaluing the Buddha's historical actions and more highly than ever esteeming the Buddha's existence beyond history.

Lokanuvartanā has much to do with another key concept of Mahayana Buddhism, "*śūnya[tā]*, [every thing] being devoid of substantiality."

These two terms are synonymous in meaning while having different usage: *śūnyatā* is applied in rather philosophical materials to all the phenomena, while *lokanuvartanā* is confined to more or less literary texts such as the Buddha's hagiography and used to qualify the Buddha's behavior. Nevertheless, they have in common the meaning that something important can be liberated from a particular historical context.

The idea of *lokanuvartanā*, as already mentioned in explaining the case of the Mahayana *Mahāparinirvāṇa-sūtra*, serves first of all to emphasize the Buddha's eternal reality beyond historical restrictions.

However, we should not miss the crucial point that this idea at the same time enables the eternal Buddha to appear repeatedly in this historical world, as the Buddha's behavior is essentially to be exhibited "in conformity with the world." The Buddha's action must be substantiated in this-worldly history, as was demonstrated in his hagiography as an ideal example by Śākyamuni Buddha.

"Lokanuvartanā" thus encompasses two opposed meanings regarding Buddha's existence, eternal and historical, and can be said to be one of the most representative concepts in Indian Buddhism. This idea must have had a decisive influence on keeping the sutra tradition as one in which sutras continued to be produced.[9]

ORIGIN OF SOCIAL ACTIVITIES IN THE LOTUS SUTRA

Revelation of a Hidden Origin in a Historical World[10]

As mentioned above, the Lotus Sutra has the intention of superimposing the historical reality, Śākyamuni Buddha, onto the concept of the eternal Buddha. The construction of the first and second chapters of the Lotus Sutra has been designed basically to overlap with the story of Śākyamuni Buddha's first sermon.

Almost all the legends about the Buddha corroborate both Gotama's great hesitation in expressing the truth which he himself discovered and the god Brahma's encouragement of Gotama Buddha to make the truth public. This brings to light a conflict between truth and its teller which seems to have pervaded ancient Vedic society. In Vedic religion truth cannot be discovered by a human being and in this sense cannot be materialized in history.

According to Buddhists in India, in contrast, truth was revealed by Gotama Buddha. This understanding of truth cannot help but violate the intrinsic principle of the Vedic traditional idea of truth. In this respect, the Buddha's hesitation and especially the god Brahma's persuasion can be regarded as an important attempt by Buddhists at first to evade this possible conflict and then to modify the traditional way the truth can manifest itself. The hidden origin of truth can be manifested in a historical world by the birth of the Buddha in this world.

The Lotus Sutra's Reinterpretation of the Buddha's Hesitation to Preach

The Buddha in the Lotus Sutra begins delivering his discourse after having been entreated thrice by his disciple. This is without doubt a new interpretation by the Lotus Sutra of the existing legend about the Buddha's hesitation before the first sermon. In the common legends, the persuader is the god Brahma, while it is Śākyamuni Buddha's great disciple Śāriputra in the case of the Lotus Sutra. Śākyamuni Buddha is to the god Brahma what the Buddha in the Lotus Sutra is to the disciple Śāriputra. The common legend of Gotama Buddha presupposes as its context the previous history of Vedic religion. The Lotus Sutra, on the other hand, has its own Buddhist historical tradition as a background of its discourse.

When compared with the role which the legend about the Buddha's hesitation before the first sermon took in the history of Buddhist tradition, it becomes evident that the Lotus Sutra uses the same plot for the purpose of melding Gotama Buddha into the Buddha in the Lotus Sutra. This restatement of the story first of all enables Gotama Buddha to be liberated from the historical limitations which Buddhist tradition may have imposed in the course of time, and then makes it possible for the Buddha in the Lotus Sutra to be as real as Gotama Buddha.

This could be done only within a structure which shows the Buddhists' way of understanding how truth should appear: truth with a hidden origin can be revealed by a specific person in history.

Dharmabhāṇaka as Truth in Person

This intention disclosed in the Lotus Sutra is in fact developed by a human narrator known as a dharmabhāṇaka. As mentioned in the previous paragraph, the truth, which can be expressed only in the Buddha's words, must be embodied in a historical world by a specific person. The dharmabhāṇaka is a person who works for this purpose. He can be said to be a man of truth or a personified truth.

This means in turn that the Buddha or Tathāgata in the Lotus Sutra is, when seen from a this-worldly dimension, no other than the narrator dharmabhāṇaka himself who mediates the Buddha's words.

The integrity of both elements, truth and its teller, is all the more difficult to separate in the world of orality.[11] There was no text available in the form of a book independent of the narrator. The first page of the text begins at the time one starts delivering the discourse and the last page is turned when the teaching ends. Even though we admit by logic that the real truth exists in words and not in the personality of the narrator, these two factors must be practically identical in the world of oral transmission in which ancient India remained for a long time, even after introducing a writing system.

Disclosure of the Sutra Tradition in Mahayana Buddhism

Nevertheless, we should be heedful of the fact that these two factors, truth and its teller, are not exactly one and the same. The narrator must constantly remain as an interlocutor between the truth and the hearers. He always goes back to the origin of the truth and brings and opens it in front of the hearers in this present world.

This performance was based on the intrinsic principle of revealing truth in the Buddhist world which we have frequently mentioned: the truth must be manifest by being substantiated in history by a mediator. On this understanding, with the additional help of the influential concept of *lokanuvartanā*, the Mahayana sutras could continue to be produced.

The truth here is not regarded as something static; it has to be repeatedly revived and made dynamic. It cannot be completely the same in appearance as it was at the time of Gotama Buddha's preaching, but should be properly modified so as to fit the always changing situation.

An Analogy Between a Text and a Society

India and China

After taking a long way around of viewing the history of the Indian sutra tradition, we have at last reached the point of discussing the main issue of this paper, that is how it has been possible for the Lotus Sutra to induce social movements in Japanese history. We cannot deal with this subject in adequate detail, but will point out rather briefly the main points as a framework for further study.

Special attention should be paid to the fact that religious texts generally functioned as providers of social theory in ancient India. Vedic literature was taken as normative not merely for religion but for social life as well. Religious life and social life were closely interrelated.

Things are the same in principle in the case of Buddhism. But as compared to Vedic religion, Buddhism in ancient India generally showed far less interest in social life. It is one of the peculiar characteristics of Buddhism, unlike Brahmanism, that social activity and religious life were separated by means of renunciation.

Buddhism, at least theoretically, had no rites of passage and provided no ritual services for lay people. Indian Buddhists sought to overstep the bounds of the *jāti-varṇa* (caste) system by ignoring the holy relationship between religion and society established by Vedic tradition. That is why Indian Buddhism had little ability to modify Indian society.

This was also true of China for a different reason. In China, for a long time up to at least the middle of the Tang Dynasty, Buddhism was inclined to confine itself to academic societies composed of a limited number of the elite. The Lotus Sutra was ranked at the highest position in the exegetical works of orthodox Chinese Buddhism, but was not given much opportunity to work positively for social purposes. Uprooted from the ground of society, Buddhism in India and China began to disappear from the horizon of the world.

Japan as a Conclusion of the History of the Lotus Sutra

Only Japan seems to have succeeded in providing the Lotus Sutra with a favorable context in society in which the sutra could fairly freely manifest the potential within it. In Japanese history, the Lotus Sutra has been repeatedly projected onto the social dimension, beyond the terminological limitations, usually difficult to get rid of, which historically different societies, such as ancient India and modern Japan, almost inevitably try to impose.

Social movements grounded on the discourses of the Lotus Sutra are rooted in a fundamental idea of the sutra: the truth in the form of the Buddha's words should be repeatedly brought into the present situation by a preacher by skillful means (*upāya-kauśalya*). As has been reiterated so often, the truth handed down to us by the Lotus Sutra must be substantiated by evidence in present history. Accordingly, proponents of the Lotus Sutra have to go to the origin of the truth by reciting the sutra and return to present reality by involving themselves in some kind of social activity.

In India and countries around it, this seems to have been done almost entirely by the activity of copying Lotus Sutra manuscripts without developing social activities. In this case, repeating the performance of going to the origin of the truth and returning to the present time was consistently confined to the text itself.

In Japan, on the other hand, the Lotus Sutra and a given society have created a large and inseparable context which should be construed by a narrator of the sutra. For Japanese Buddhists, the origin of the truth is incarnated in the words of the Lotus Sutra, and they should be verified in the present historical world. This world is not merely a negative obstacle to be stepped over as was the case in ancient India, but an important screen on which sacred words must be projected.

In a sense, Buddhist history can be said to begin at the time when Śākyamuni Buddha entered into *parinirvāṇa*. This must have been an irreconcilable experience for all Buddhists because it was at first an event which cut completely the only line of communication between the truth and the present world. At the same time this must have made them fully realize for the first time that the truth and its teller can be two different things, as the truth revealed by Gotama Buddha remained even after his nirvana. It seems no accidental thing that Nichiren had a high regard for the Mahayana *Mahāparinirvāṇa-sūtra*.

Truth once obtained cannot be handed down to the next generation without being substantiated in a given situation, just as was done by Gotama Buddha. This can be accomplished only if a mediator himself is a Buddha.

Notes

1. Shōkō Watanabe claims that the Gilgit manuscripts must be dated to the seventh century. If his assumption is accepted as it is, these would be the oldest manuscripts of the Lotus Sutra found to date. Shōkō Watanabe (ed.), *Saddharmapuṇḍarīka Manuscripts in Gilgit*, 2 vols., Tokyo: The Reiyūkai, 1972–75). However, Professor Hirofumi Toda at Tokushima University, one of the most eminent authorities in this field, has suggested to me in private communication that this date might be earlier. Examples of another kind of manuscript, which have a different Gilgit writing style, have been found in the Schøyen Collections and identified as a part of the Lotus Sutra by Professor Kazunobu Matsuda. These are probably older than those edited by Watanabe. (松田和信 Kazunobu Matsuda, ノルウェーのスコイエン・コレクションと梵文法華経断簡 の発見 "New Sanskrit Fragments of the Saddharmapuṇḍarīka-sūtra in the Schøyen Collection, Norway—A Preliminary Report," 東洋学術研究 *The Journal of Oriental Studies* #38-1, 1999. 5, 4–19)

2. When we view the whole history of Japanese Buddhism from ancient to modern times, especially focusing on the subject of benevolent or welfare services in the prewar period, it is definitely an exaggeration to say that Buddhist social movements have been created largely, not to mention exclusively, on the basis of the Lotus Sutra. (See 吉田久一 Kyūichi Yoshida, 日本近代仏教社会史 研究 *Nihon Kindai Bukkyō Shakaishi Kenkyū* [A study of the social history of Japanese Buddhism in modern times], 2 vols., 吉田久一著作集 *Yoshida Kyūichi Chosakushū*, #5, #6, Tokyo: Kawashima Shoten, 1991. 11. This work is very

helpful in providing almost exhaustive historical materials and studies with regard to Buddhist social movements in modern Japan). Those who initiated social activities with pious faith in the Lotus Sutra seem to have been more or less involved in political movements. This must have a close relation with Nichiren's attitude of trying to modify this world accompanied by a strong consciousness of himself as a bodhisattva, a messenger who is sent from a true world for the purpose of realizing an ideal in this world. After World War II, however, a new movement has emerged from new religions, such as Risshō Kōsei-kai, that show a good deal of sympathy for social benevolence regardless of political stances.

3. Andre Bareau, *Recherche sur la biographie du buddha dans les Sūtrapiṭaka et les Vinayapiṭaka anciens ii: Les dernièrs mois, les parinirvāṇa et les funeralles, tome 1,* Publications de L'École Francais d'Étrême-Orient #77, Paris, 1970; tome 2, 1971; "La composition et les étapes de la formation progressive du Mahāparinirvāṇa- sūtra ancien," *Bulletin de l'École Francais d'Étrême-Orient #66,* Paris, 45–103. Ernst Waldschmidt, "Beiträge zur Textgeschichte des Mahāparinirvāṇasūtra," *Nachrichten der Academie der Wissenschaften in Göttingen* (NAWG), 1939, S. 55- 94; *Die Überlieferung vom Lebensende des Buddha, eine vergleichende Analyse des Mahāparinirvāṇasūtra und seiner Textentsprechungen,* erster Teil, 1944, zweiter Teil 1948, Göttingen; "Wunderkrafte des Buddha, eine Episode im Sanskrit- text des Mahāparinirvāṇasūtra," *NAWG (Von Ceylon bis Turfan,* 1967, 120ff.); *Das Mahāparinirvāṇasūtra, Text in Sanskrit und Tibetischen Entsprechung im Vinaya der Mulasarvāstivādins,* Teil 1-3, Berlin, 1950–51. For other works re- garding the MPS, see 下田正弘 Masahiro Shimoda, 涅槃経の研究：大乗経典 の研究方法試論 *Nehangyō no Kenkyū: Daijōkyōten no Kenkyū Hōhō Shiron* (A Study of the *Mahāparinirvāṇasūtra*: with a focus on the methodology of the study of *mahayāna sūtras),* Tokyo: Shunjūsha 1997. Several manuscripts of the *hīnayāna* MPS were newly discovered among the Schøyen Collections, which reportedly belong to a different lineage from any lineage of manuscripts which had been found to date. See Matsuda op.cit., 10–11.

4. With regard to the compilation process of the MPS and for a detailed discus- sion of these issues, see Shimoda, op.cit., 62–75.

5. Cf. Shimoda, op. cit., 65–67; Gream MacQueen, "Inspired speech in early Mahāyāna Buddhism 1," *Religion* #11, 1981, 303–09; ibid. 2, *Religion* #12, 1982, 49–65.

6. Ibid.

7. Cf. 下田正弘 Masahiro Shimoda, ブッダと真理：「ブッダの神格化」を問い直す "Budda to Shinri: Budda no Shinkakuka o Toinaosu" (Buddha and the truth: questioning the concept of deification of the Buddha); ブッダ：大いなる旅路 "Budda, Ōinaru Tabiji" (Buddha's great journey), NHK Shuppan (Japan Broadcast Publishing Co., Ltd.), 1998. 6, 169–14; ブッダの神格化という概念の 再検討 "Budda no Shinkakuka to iu Gainen no Saikentō" (Reconsideration of the concept of "deification of Gotama the Buddha" underlying modern Bud- dhist studies,) 宗教研究 *Shūkyō Kenkyū,* #319, 1999. 5, 271–72.

8. 高原信一 Shin'ichi Takahara, Mahāvastu にみられる福徳論 "Mahāvastu ni Mirareru Fukutokuron" (A theory of merit accumulation in the Mahāvastu),

福岡大学35周年記念人文学論集 *Fukuoka Daigaku 35 Shūnen Kinen Jinbungaku Ronshū*, Fukuoka, 1969, 177–141 (L). Paul Harrison, "Sanskrit fragments of a Lokottaravādin tradition," L. A. Hercus, et al. (eds.), *Indological and Buddhist Studies, Volume in honor of professor J. W. de Jong on his sixtieth birthday*, Canberra, 1982, 211–43; "Some reflections on the personality of the Buddha," 大谷学報 *The Ōtani Gakuhō*, #74-4, 1995, 1–19 (L).

9. The following are materials which refer to the idea of *lokanuvartanā*; 1. *Mahā-vastu*, i.167.15–170.10, en 3 vols, E. Senart (ed.), Paris 1882, 1890, 1897; 2. *Niraupamyastava*, G. Tucci, (ed.), 309–25, "Two hymns of the Catuḥ-stava of Nagārjuna," *Journal of the Royal Asiatic Society*, 1932; 3. *Prasannapadā*, L. de La Valle Pousin (ed.), *Mūlamadhyamakakārikās* (*Madhyamikasūtras*) *de Nagārjuna avec le Prasannapadā Commentaire de Candrakīrti* , Bibliotheca Buddhica iv, St. Peters-burg, 1903–13, 548.5–9; 4. *Madhyamakāvatāra*, Poussin (ed.), *Madhyamakāvatāra par Candrakīrti: Traduction Tibetaine*, Bibliotheca Buddhica ix, St. Petersburg, 1912, 134.1-135.12; 5. *sTon nyid bdun cu pa'i grel pa*, Peking ed. #5628, Vol. 99, 309b8-310a1; 362a3-4; 6. *Mahāparinirvāṇasūtra* (*Mahāyāna*), Peking ed. #788, Vol. 31, Mdo Tu 61b-66b3; 7. *Lalitavistara*, S. Lefmann (ed.), 1902, 119.7, 238.3, 392.8; 8. 佛説内蔵百宝経 *Fo shuo nei zang bai bao jing*, Taishō Shinshū Daizō-kyō, Vol. xvii, No. 807, 751b–753c; Corresponding Tibetan versions: *Derge Mdo Tsa* 303a6–308a7, *Peking Mdo, Mu* 304b2–309a6.

10. Concerning the Buddha's hesitation to preach the first sermon, there are so many studies that it is difficult to enumerate them exhaustively. But almost all scholars have taken the hesitation as a mere performance by the Buddha to induce the God Brahmā to verify the authenticity of Buddhism in Vedic India. This understanding may not be completely off the mark, but is insufficient when brought into the light of the controversial relationship underlying the relation between truth and specific history in India. I am preparing another more detailed paper on this topic, which will appear in a coming issue of the *Journal of the Chūō Academic Research Institute*. For a good analysis from the viewpoint of the historical development of this topic, see 坂本 (後藤) 純子 Junko Gotō Sakamoto, 梵天勧請の原形 "Bonten Kanjō no Genkei" (The Proto-type of the Story: "Brahmā's Request") in *Indogaku Bukkyōgaku Kenkyū*, #41–1, 1993.12, (67)–(72).

11. Walter J. Ong, *Orality and Literacy: The Technologizing of the Word*, London/New York: Routledge, 1982.

A Buddha Teaches Only Bodhisattvas

Riccardo Venturini

The Lotus Sutra not only is one of the most widely diffused and venerated Buddhist sutras in East Asia, as a universal and nonsectarian scripture, but also has been recognised by Saichō (767–822), Dōgen (1200–53), Nichiren (1222–82), and other prominent Buddhists as the expression of the Buddha's highest teachings. It is important, therefore, for anyone in the West striving for a deep understanding of the Dharma to apply himself or herself to this text, which is rich not only in philosophic truths but also in poetic expressions.

If we want to know what the Lotus Sutra has to offer for people of today, who are more and more involved in problems on a global scale, we must highlight the nature of the listeners to whom the Buddha taught the Dharma. The Buddha said that he taught only bodhisattvas, because only they in the purity of their faith could understand him, and to them he entrusted the task of being apostles of the Dharma. Who, then, are the bodhisattvas? Do we want to be one of them or do we lack the motivation?

When, through the mysterious concurrence of external and internal causes, the individual directs all his energies toward the Buddha, and the Buddha turns to that person, there occurs the awakening of the mind that aspires to enlightenment (*bodhicitta*) and to follow the Way of the Buddha and the path of spiritual discipline (*bodhicitta-utpāda*). It is the moment of "conversion" or great resolution, in which the bodhisattva, sustained by faith in enlightenment, takes great vows and is ready to set out on the path, to begin the journey of *pāramitā* practice.

In the Lotus Sutra the Buddha affirms that he employed nirvana (in its meaning of extinction, cessation, emptiness in a negative sense) as a didactic method to save people blinded by ignorance and dominated by the thirst for existence:

For this reason . . .
I set up a tactful way for them,
Proclaiming the Way to end sufferings,
Revealing it through nirvana.
Though I proclaim nirvana,
Yet it is not real extinction.
All existence, from the beginning,
Is ever of the nirvana nature."[1]

It is important for Westerners, who have had a distorted and negative view of the Buddhist concepts of void and nirvana, to reflect on these words. Void, in fact, being emptied itself, becomes fullness. This changing and impermanent world in which we live is itself the real world. Any difference between nirvana and samsara vanishes; and the same nirvana, which as a "designation" is also empty and unreal, becomes alive and concrete in the realisation of life's indivisibility, in the collapse of self-centeredness and in the awareness of the interrelatedness of all things.

Bodhisattvas, then, do not live as ascetics in the desert of their spiritual pride, insensitive to the sufferings of unenlightened beings. The plight of those who suffer misery and delusion stirs their hearts and spurs them to compassionate acts, to which they subordinate their quest for their own enlightenment, having already chosen lives of absolute nondualism. Far from enjoying a separate happiness, bodhisattvas feel a "vicarious suffering," with others and in the place of others. They do not therefore "renounce" nirvana, but emancipate themselves from the pursuit of a false aim, living the true nirvana in a "return" to the everyday world.

The Buddha in his wisdom can affirm that the world is already saved and pure. As the Lotus Sutra says, "Tranquil is this realm of mine." Nonetheless, in his compassion, since the world is full of beings who groan amid miseries of every kind, the logic of love draws him to reveal the Dharma to people devoid of wisdom and full of attachments:

The Triple World is not safe,
Just as the burning house,
Full of all kinds of sufferings,
Was greatly to be feared.
Ever there are the distresses of birth,
Old age, disease, and death;

.   .   .   .

Now this triple world
All is my domain;
The living beings in it
All are my sons.

But now this place
Abounds with distresses;
And I alone
Am able to save and protect them.[2]

For this reason the buddhas appear in the world:

Because the buddhas, the world-honored ones, desire to cause all living beings to open [their eyes] to the Buddha-knowledge so that they may gain the pure [mind], [therefore] they appear in the world; because they desire to show all living beings the Buddha-knowledge, they appear in the world; because they desire to cause all living beings to apprehend the Buddha-knowledge, they appear in the world; because they desire to cause all living beings to enter the way of the Buddha-knowledge, they appear in the world.[3]

For this reason Śākyamuni, the Eternal Buddha, says he is committed, for a time without end, to bodhisattva practice.

Along with the "treasures" of the Buddha and the Dharma, we must never forget the third treasure, the Sangha, or community of bodhisattvas. In a country like Japan, thanks to the generosity and sacrifices of many, there are movements that realize what I would call "the collective bodhisattva," which can operate in the world not only as a spiritual force, but also with the potential and authority of mass movements. The presence of a "collective bodhisattva" is a great blessing that nurtures the faith even of people far away, who are aware of this living and fraternal force at work.

Taking others' suffering on oneself and purifying it without allowing oneself to be contaminated is the mission of the bodhisattva, who clears a world polluted by ignorance and selfishness. As Saichō, the founder of Japan's Tendai sect, said, "To take evil upon oneself and to give good to others, and to forget about oneself and to work for the benefit of all, is the ultimate in compassion."[4]

Not discriminating between friends and enemies, tending not to have "personal" needs, appreciating all beings and all situations, bodhisattvas never pause in their constant, merciful practice (nondualism in action), always treat others as they would like to be treated, and are always ready to help others to overcome their misery.

Faced with war, hunger, human rights violations, today the "collective bodhisattva" can carry out a marvelous program of "collective mercy" that is unconditional, requiring no reward. It is through their function of taking on and conveying the suffering of sentient beings to a vaster Will that bodhisattvas do their harmonizing and purifying work. They know also that their mission is not to eliminate what is evil and negative from the world, but in their passion for the relative, they work for harmony not as a goal but as a method, sharing the destiny of humankind.

The maximum commitment to serving others, united to awareness of the limits of every action, represents the dynamic realization of the Middle Path. Each limited and concrete action can certainly redeem just a fragment of the world, but through the prayer/meditation also a fragment becomes totality (*ichinen sanzen*). In this way, liberation is not put off to a utopian future, and suffering is not related to an inevitable karma or to the logic of economics or power. To the eyes of the Buddha and in the hand and heart of the Sangha, we are bound together by warm links of solidarity and loving kindness.

In other words, Buddhist liberation consists of the union of suffering and salvation. Redemption is not obtained through a sacrifice offered to a divinity which, with its intervention, "mends" the world, destroying what we qualify as negative and as a source of suffering. Redemption is found in overcoming conflict and opposition, and in the creation of a more subtle harmony between order and disorder. This is a path that doesn't involve nonsuffering, but the nonsuffering-of-suffering; a path which, we could say according to French writer Marguerite Yourcenar, if it doesn't make us mad with joy, at least it make us wise with pain.

That is why we can affirm that this world, full of misery and conflict, is, nonetheless, the tranquil realm of the Buddha.

Notes

1. Bunnō Katō, Yoshirō Tamura, et al., *The Threefold Lotus Sutra*, Tokyo: Kōsei Publishing Co., 1975, 66.
2. Bunnō Katō, Yoshirō Tamura, et al., 98.
3. Bunnō Katō, Yoshirō Tamura, et al., 59.
4. J. Stevens, *The Marathon Monks of Mount Hiei*, London: Rider, 1988, 41.

A Buddhist Path to Mending the World

Harold Kasimow

Winston King, the noted American pioneer of Buddhist studies, has argued that the Buddhist tradition is deeply preoccupied with personal salvation, but not at all concerned with transforming society. I would like to explore this widespread vision of the Buddhist tradition, with special emphasis on the views of Pope John Paul II. Later I examine whether the Lotus Sutra is concerned only with the individual or with both the individual and society.

Writing on Theravada Buddhism, King states that "one of the features of the study of Buddhism most frustrating to the Western mind is the effort necessary to discover a social philosophy within it. . . . To tell the truth, the Buddha had little, either of concern for society as such or of firm conviction of its possible improvability."[1] According to King, this lack of interest in improving society is explained by the fact that by the time of the Buddha there was a great deal of dissatisfaction with the world and a complete turning away from it and all its pain.

Robert Charles Zaehner (1913–74), the late Spalding Professor of Eastern Religions and Ethics at Oxford University, claimed that Hindus, Jains, and Buddhists held an extremely pessimistic view of this world: "And so the main preoccupation of all three religions was to become the search for a way of escape from this samsaric world into something that is beyond the passage of time—the Nirvana of the Buddhists, the Brahman-Atman of the Hindus."[2]

Zaehner is very critical of any form of mysticism that negates the world, which is precisely how he views the Hindu and Buddhist mystics.

'Classical' Hinduism and Buddhism are both essentially religions of escape, and there is no doubt that they make a powerful appeal to a certain type of mind, to all, indeed, who have lost their sense of purpose, for they consider that 'ordinary life is hopelessly unsatisfactory, exposed to constant pain and grief, and in any case quite futile.' Such religions, though a useful antidote to the prevalent materialism, would seem to be ultimately unsatisfactory psychologically because they deprive human existence as we know it of all meaning.[3]

This vision of the Buddhist tradition supports the position of Max Weber, the eminent sociologist of religion, who claimed that for Buddhism "salvation is an absolutely personal performance of the self-reliant individual. No one, and particularly no social community, can help him. The specific asocial character of genuine mysticism is here carried to its maximum."[4]

The view held by Zaehner and Weber is shared by Pope John Paul II in his evaluation of the Buddhist tradition. John Paul II, who taught at a university in Poland for a number of years, is a sophisticated theologian and the world's most influential spiritual leader. Although he is not an expert on Buddhism, his statements on the Buddhist tradition deserve careful consideration.

John Paul II on the Buddhist Tradition

The following two quotations from th Holy Father's best-selling 1994 book *Crossing the Threshold of Hope* capture his main assumptions about Buddhism:

The 'enlightenment' experienced by [the] Buddha comes down to the conviction that the world is bad, that it is the source of evil and of suffering for man.[5]

Buddhism is in large measure an *'atheistic' system*. We do not free ourselves from evil through the good which comes from God; we liberate ourselves only through detachment from the world, which is bad. The fullness of such a detachment is not union with God, but what is called nirvana, a state of perfect indifference with regard to the world. *To save oneself* means, above all, to free oneself from evil by becoming *indifferent to the world, which is the source of evil*. This is the culmination of the spiritual process.[6]

Because I believe that John Paul wishes to see an honest and open encounter between Roman Catholicism and the other religions of the world, I am surprised by his portrayal of Buddhism. It seems to me to be in the spirit of nineteenth- and early twentieth-century writings on Buddhism by Christian missionaries. Buddhists throughout the world have been deeply offended by the pope's negative description of their tradition, and in January 1995, when John Paul visited Sri Lanka, the local Catholic bishops reportedly made a public apology, insisting that the pope had not meant to hurt the feelings of Buddhists.[7]

I do not think that the idea that Buddhism is atheistic, that it is not preoccupied with the idea of a supreme being, is upsetting to all Buddhists. On the contrary, many Buddhists argue that the idea of God is an attachment from which we must free ourselves. They argue that the Buddha did not believe in a theistic concept of God. It is a false idea that has brought serious problems for humanity.

Truly problematic for Buddhists are the pope's claims that "according to Buddhism the world is bad, that it is the source of evil and suffering for man" and that nirvana is "a state of perfect indifference with regard to the world." According to Buddhism, the world in itself is not bad. The source of our suffering is our own desires, our thirst, greed, and clinging to a permanent self, which is an illusion. When we free ourselves from the false notion of a permanent self, then this earth can become for us a paradise.

It appears to me that Pope John Paul II, like many other Western students of Buddhism, gets stuck on the first of the Four Noble Truths. This does teach that life is suffering. Therefore, the pope concludes that Buddhism is pessimistic. However, he does not pay sufficient attention to the fact that the Noble Truths go on to tell us that we can overcome suffering by extinguishing the greed which causes the suffering in the first place.

Nirvana is not, as the pope claims, "a state of perfect indifference with regard to the world." Rather, it is seeing the world with new, awakened eyes. Through the process of meditation, we can totally transform the way we see the world. After attaining nirvana, the Buddha did not leave the world, but devoted the next forty-five years to teaching humanity how to be joyful by becoming more fully present in the world. Millions of Buddhists would bear witness that the Buddha's compassionate heart helped them to attain joy in this very life.

I cannot agree with Pope John Paul II and other Western scholars, such as Zaehner, who claim that Buddhism is preoccupied only with personal salvation and not with the transformation of society. My understanding is that the aim of Buddhism is not only to perfect character, but also to beautify the entire universe. As the British scholar of Buddhism Trevor Ling stated:

For Buddhism is not, as so many Westerners have imagined, a private cult of escape from the real world. The word 'imagined' is used deliberately because such a view of Buddhism can proceed only from the exercise of the imagination, not from knowledge of the Buddha's teaching, or of the nature of the Buddhist community, the *Sangha*, or from Buddhist history. To speak of Buddhism as something concerned with the private salvation of the individual soul is to ignore entirely the basic Buddhist repudiation of the notion of the individual soul. The teaching of the Buddha was not concerned with the private destiny of the individual, but with something much wider, the whole realm of sentient being, the whole of consciousness. This inevitably entailed a concern with social and political matters, and these receive a large share of attention in the teaching of the Buddha as it is represented in the Pali texts.[8]

A moving statement by the young Western Buddhist priest Maura O'Halloran, written shortly before she died, speaks directly to this controversial issue:

I'd be embarrassed to tell anyone, it sounds so wishy-washy, but now I have maybe 50 or 60 years (who knows?) of time, of a life, open, blank, ready to offer. I want to live it for other people. What else is there to do with it? Not that I expect to change the world or even a blade of grass, but it's as if to give myself is all I can do, as the flowers have no choice but to blossom. . . . So I must go deeper and deeper and work hard, no longer for me but for everyone I can help. . . . Thus, I should also work politically, work to make people's surroundings that much more tolerable, work for a society that fosters more spiritual, more human, values. A society for people, not profits.[9]

Does she seem like a person who negates the world? I do not think so. I do not believe that Pope John Paul II intended to anger the Buddhist world. Buddhism is an extremely complex and diverse religious tradition, and it seems that the pope's knowledge of it is based predominantly on Christian interpretations rather than on Buddhist sources.

John Paul II is the most influential supporter of interfaith dialogue so desperately needed in today's world, and thus I can only hope that he will carefully reconsider his view of Buddhism, a tradition which so many Roman Catholics and other non-Buddhists have found to be spiritually enriching to their lives.[10]

A Path to Individual and Social Healing and Transformation

The Lotus Sutra is the most influential sutra for East Asian Buddhists.

Scholars of Buddhism speak of it as the bible of Mahayana Buddhism. The sutra itself claims that it is the most excellent teaching that leads to supreme, perfect enlightenment. The central issue that I now raise is whether the Lotus Sutra is only concerned with personal transformation or whether it also has a call within it to remake society. My contention is that it is a call to both personal and social change and can therefore serve as a rich source for transforming society in the twenty-first century. Many of the key concepts of the Lotus Sutra are found in the moving parables throughout the text. Two of the central concepts developed in it are the idea of one vehicle and the doctrine of skillful means.

In the second chapter of the sutra, the Buddha explains to Sariputra, one of his principal disciples, that there is only one vehicle, not three, through which all human beings become buddhas. He explains that the vehicles of the *śrāvaka* and *pratyekabuddha* do not lead to perfect enlightenment. These two paths are presented only as devices to encourage people to enter the one true path, the path of the bodhisattva. The devices are needed because most people are not sufficiently mature to receive the final message found in the Lotus Sutra.

These two central concepts are illustrated in the first parable in the sutra, the parable of the burning house. It is retold by Leon Hurvitz in the introduction to his translation of the sutra:

> A rich man had a very large house. The house had only one entrance, and the timber of which it was made had dried out thoroughly over the years. One day the house caught fire, and the rich man's many children, heedless of the fire, continued to play in the house. Their father called to them from outside that the house was afire and that they would perish in the flames if they did not come out. The children, not knowing the meaning of 'fire' and 'perish,' continued to play as before. The man called out once more, 'Come out, children, and I will give you ox-drawn carriages, goat-drawn carriages, and deer-drawn carriages!' Tempted by the desire for new playthings, the children left the burning house, only to find a single great ox-drawn carriage awaiting them.[11]

Just as the father devised a scheme of three different carts in order to save the children, but only gave them one cart, the Buddha, using skillful means, speaks of three paths to salvation, when in fact there is only one true path, the path of the bodhisattva.

The critical point to consider is what distinguishes the *śrāvaka* and *pratyekabuddha* from the bodhisattva. In order to answer this question, I will briefly consider how the bodhisattva is characterized in Mahayana

Buddhism. The major characteristic of bodhisattvas is their great love and compassion for all human beings. Robert Thurman calls bodhisattvas "Buddhist messiahs."[12] Although there are major differences between the concepts of the messiah and the bodhisattva, there are also essential affinities.

According to Jewish tradition, the messiah comes to destroy evil and to bring peace, justice, and righteousness to the entire planet. The classical Jewish view of the messiah is "the prophetic hope for the end of this age, in which a strong redeemer, by his power and his spirit, will bring complete redemption, political and spiritual, to the people of Israel, and along with this, earthly bliss and moral perfection to the entire human race."[13] Earthly bliss and moral perfection are precisely what the bodhisattvas aim to bring about.

The Lotus Sutra teaches that all human beings possess buddha-nature. Bodhisattvas, therefore, make a vow to save all human beings. They do not separate their own enlightenment from that of other beings. That is the meaning of compassion (*karuṇā*). For the bodhisattvas, there is no wisdom (*prajñā*) without compassion. A bodhisattva will not rest until all people are saved. And because all people have the buddha-nature, they all will eventually attain liberation.

It seems to me that the *śrāvaka*, a term applied to the arhat of Theravada Buddhism, and the *pratyekabuddha* are not following a path that leads to perfect enlightenment because they are not devoted to saving all other human beings. From the perspective of the Lotus Sutra, these paths are monastic and escapist because they do not show sufficient concern for society. The Lotus Sutra speaks of the arhats and *pratyekabuddhas* as "extremely conceited" because they erroneously think that they have already attained nirvana. They are, in the words of the sutra, "obsessed by utmost arrogance."[14] It is clear that they have not attained full enlightenment. Enlightenment would not only free them from conceit and arrogance, but also would involve them in devoting all their energies to mending the world, which is the key characteristic of a truly enlightened being, a bodhisattva.

Unlike the classical Jewish prophet, who according to Abraham Joshua Heschel is considered "a madman by his contemporaries" because of his intense indignation against injustice in society,[15] the way of the bodhisattva is different, but he is equally committed to bringing about social justice. The way of the bodhisattva reminds me of a statement by Rabbi Bunam, a great Hassidic teacher, who thought that "our sages say: 'Seek peace in your own place.' You cannot find peace anywhere save in your own self. In the psalm we read: 'There is no peace in my bones because of my sin.' When a man has made peace within himself, he will be able to make peace in the whole world."[16]

It is clear that bodhisattvas, who postpone their own enlightenment, want to bring healing to both the individual and society, but they do this by using skillful means to heal every individual they encounter.

Religions Offer Different Paths

The religious traditions of the world offer different paths that lead to individual healing and social transformation. As we become more deeply immersed in a religious tradition, we find that there are in fact different paths within each tradition. Within Hinduism, for example, the path of knowledge is different from the path of love. There are also numerous paths within the Hindu tradition. This diversity of paths is true for all religious traditions. Even a brief exploration of how Western scholars of the comparative study of religion have compared and contrasted the Abrahamic religions with Asian religions will help us understand why many people in the West believe that Asian religions, especially Buddhism, with its strong monastic stream, are lacking in social responsibility.

Zaehner presented a typical Western view on this issue. He saw a radical difference between the Abrahamic religions that originated near the river Jordan and the Asian religions that were nourished by the Ganges. For him, the religions of India were mystical and otherworldly, with an emphasis on the individual. The religions of the Near East were prophetic and this-worldly and focused primarily on the community. Zaehner claimed that the message of the mystic "is renunciation of the world in order to partake in an internal order," whereas the message of the prophets was "the dealings of the eternal with this world of space and time."

The Asian path of the mystics makes no demands on human beings, as compared with the prophets, who are constantly making demands of the people and who, in Zaehner's words, are "extremely uncomfortable people."[17] The Asian mystics, according to Zaehner, are not committed to the world of space and time; they tend to ignore the suffering of humanity. Their major preoccupation is to attain nirvana and leave the senseless suffering forever: "Salvation means salvation *from* the world, not salvation and sanctification *of* the world."[18]

In contrast to the mystical religions of India, Zaehner found that prophetic religions are deeply concerned with the everyday. This concern is captured by the prophet Amos: "But let justice well up as waters, and righteousness as a mighty stream" (Amos 5:24). What may seem to most of us a minor injustice is a catastrophe from a prophetic perspective. The prophets single out kings and priests and especially the rich who oppress the poor, those who, in the words of Amos,

> . . . sell the righteous for silver
> And the needy for a pair of shoes—
> They that trample the head of the poor
> into the dust of the earth. (Amos 2:6, 7)

The classical prophets are passionate and articulate champions of human rights in pursuit of peace and justice for all.

Zaehner, who was a convert to Roman Catholicism, further claimed that although Christianity belongs to the family of the Abrahamic religions, it is radically different from both Judaism and Islam. The difference is due to the fact that Christianity "introduced into a monotheistic system an idea that is wholly foreign to it, namely, the incarnation of God in the person of Jesus Christ."[19]

If I understand Zaehner correctly, he seems to be saying that Christ brings a balance to Christianity between the mystical and prophetic streams. Therefore, Zaehner concluded, "the only religion that has from the very beginning been both communal and individual is Christianity: its dual purpose is to build up the body of Christ on earth and to seek out the kingdom of God within you."[20] This makes Christianity unique and superior to other religious traditions. Zaehner became convinced that Christ is the fulfillment of all religions.

Zaehner was aware of the bodhisattva ideal to save all humanity, which conflicts with his view of the Asian mystic. He explained that Mahayana Buddhism, particularly in such texts as the Lotus Sutra, with its idea of faith in the Buddha and the concept of Buddha-nature, is moving closer to Catholic Christianity. He claimed that in the Lotus Sutra "the final aim is not Nirvana . . . but the discovery of the Buddha-nature within one—eternal wisdom and unfailing compassion."[21] Zaehner concluded: "The really significant development in Japanese religion is not Zen but the emergence of Neo-Nichirenism in the form of Soka Gakkai . . . due, one supposes, to its communal activity and political and social commitment."[22]

Zaehner was one of the most original thinkers in the comparative study of religion. However, I am dubious about many of his ideas, such as that among the Abrahamic religions only Christianity has a rich mystical tradition. That is most certainly not accurate. Both Judaism and Islam have a strong mystical dimension.

With regard to the Buddhist tradition, I find his view of the bodhisattva very problematic:

> The Bodhisattva ideal is perhaps the most grandiose that the Indian mind has ever conceived; and it finds its fulfillment as nowhere else in the figure of the Crucified. But whereas the Bodhisattvas are mythical beings thought out by man in his desperate longing that

such beings might exist, Christ is the true Bodhisattva, God made Man, suffering with man, and crucified by man and for man that He might release him—not indeed from the suffering of this world, but from the burden of sin that causes that suffering. "When his tremendous task is accomplished and his vow fulfilled, the Bodhisattva, like the countless souls he has helped out of this world of suffering, himself disappears without name or trace into the 'emptiness' of Nirvana.[23]

By stating that the bodhisattva "disappears without name or trace," Zaehner was attempting to defend his thesis that Buddhism is essentially otherworldly and not concerned with the community. I would contend that the parables in the Lotus Sutra do not support such a view. For me the parable of the burning house certainly shows the concern of the Buddha for all human beings. The parable of the physician's sons, however, will make it clear that the disappearance of the Buddha is not a real disappearance.

I therefore will conclude with this parable as retold by Hurvitz:

A physician who had been away from home a long time returned to find his sons suffering from an ailment. He prescribed for them an appropriate medicine, which certain of them took but which others, mad from poison, refused. Those who took it were immediately cured, while the others continued to languish in their malady. The physician accordingly went away and circulated the rumor that he had died. This shocked the ailing sons back to their senses, after which they too took their father's medicine and were cured. When he heard of this, the father made his appearance again.[24]

In this parable, the Buddha, with his great compassion for all humanity, employs skillful means and tells his sons that he is leaving, but in fact the Buddha is present and continues to work for the benefit of the world.

All religious traditions have an important role to play in mending the world. We can heal the world in more than one way. We need the prophets of the West and the "magnificent messiahs" of the East. Bodhisattvas and Buddhas of the Lotus Sutra who make the vow to save all sentient beings and who teach that all human beings should be treated as if they were our mother can all serve as beautiful models for people who strive for personal transformation and the healing of the entire world community.

The Declaration on a Global Ethic, which was signed in September 1993 by leading religious teachers of the world who met at the Parliament of the World's Religions in Chicago, declares that "Earth cannot be changed for the better unless the consciousness of individuals is changed first."[25] This declaration, which was signed not only by Buddhists, but also by Jews, Christians, and Muslims, is in the spirit of Buddhism. The unique ways of the bodhisattva and the prophet are both working to mend the world. To bring about redemption we need both of these paths.

Notes

1. Winston King, *In the Hope of Nibbāna* (LaSalle, Ill.: Open Court, 1964), 176–77.
2. R. C. Zaehner, *Hinduism* (London: Oxford University Press, 1962), 67.
3. R. C. Zaehner, "Conclusion," in *The Concise Encyclopedia of Living Faiths*, ed. R. C. Zaehner (Boston: Beacon Press, 1959), 415. The quote within this quote is taken from the article "Buddhism: The Mahayana" by Edward Conze printed in the same volume, 301.
4. Max Weber, *The Religion of India: The Sociology of Hinduism and Buddhism* (Glencoe, IL.: Free Press, 1958), 213.
5. Pope John Paul II, *Crossing the Threshold of Hope* (New York: Knopf, 1994), 85.
6. Ibid., 86. Italics in the original.
7. Tad Szulc, *Pope John Paul II: The Biography* (New York: Scribner, 1995), 467.
8. Trevor Ling, *The Buddha: Buddhist Civilization in India and Ceylon* (New York: Scribner, 1973), 122.
9. Maura O'Halloran, *Pure Heart, Enlightened Mind: The Zen Journal and Letters of Maura "Soshin" O'Halloran* (Boston: Charles E. Tuttle Co., 1994), 233.
10. This section is based in part on my article "John Paul II and Interreligious Dialogue: An Overview" in *John Paul II and Interreligious Dialogue*, ed. Byron Sherwin and Harold Kasimow (Maryknoll, New York: Orbis, 1999). This book contains the pope's core writings on Buddhism, Islam, and Judaism and responses to him by prominent Buddhist, Muslim, and Jewish scholars.
11. "Preface," in *Scripture of the Lotus Blossom of the Fine Dharma*, trans. Leon Hurvitz (New York: Columbia University Press, 1976), xi.
12. Robert A. F. Thurman, "The Buddhist Messiahs: The Magnificent Deeds of the Bodhisattvas," in *The Christ and the Bodhisattva*, ed. Donald S. Lopez, Jr., and Steven C. Rockefeller (Albany: State University of New York Press, 1987), 65.
13. Joseph Klausner, *The Messianic Idea in Israel: From Its Beginning to the Completion of the Mishnah*, trans. W. F. Stinespring (New York: Macmillan, 1955), 9.
14. *The Threefold Lotus Sutra*, trans. Bunnō Katō, Yoshirō Tamura, and Kōjirō Miyasaka (Tokyo: Kosei Publishing Co., 1975), 62.
15. Abraham Joshua Heschel, *The Prophets* (New York: The Burning Bush Press, 1962), 18.
16. Quoted in Martin Buber, *Tales of the Hasidim: The Later Masters* (New York: Schocken, 1948), 264.
17. R. C. Zaehner, *The Comparison of Religions* (Boston: Beacon Press, 1958), 26.
18. R. C. Zaehner, "Religious Truth," in *Truth and Dialogue in World Religions: Con-*

flicting Truth-Claims, ed. John Hick (Philadelphia: The Westminster Press, 1974), 10.

19. R. C. Zaehner, *Hindu and Muslim Mysticism* (New York: Schocken Books, 1969), 2.

20. Zaehner, "Religious Truth," 17.

21. Ibid., 15.

22. Ibid., 17.

23. Zaehner, *Comparison of Religions*, 187.

24. Hurvitz, xiv.

25. *A Global Ethic: The Declaration of the Parliament of the World's Religions*, ed. Hans Küng and Karl-Josef Kuschel (New York: Continuum, 1993), 15.

5. The Lotus Sutra and Buddhist Ethics

Ethics and the Lotus Sutra

Peggy Morgan

Introduction

My approach to the study of the Lotus Sutra and to the subject of the
Lotus Sutra and ethics is from the perspective of a Western woman with
a Christian background and as an academic who teaches in the field of
religious studies. The methods contributing to this field of study are various and include history, sociology, philology and textual interpretation,
anthropology, and philosophy. For me, one of the most important of the
many approaches that are both possible and stimulating within the field
of religious studies is phenomenology of religion. The central emphasis
of phenomenology of religion as an accumulation of conventions is the
understanding of religious traditions as far as is possible from the points
of view of those who believe in and belong to them.[1] The challenge of
studying in this way is to make the subject of study speak with its own
authentic voice. This naturally involves working closely with members
of religious traditions and the necessity of bringing to the material sympathetic imagination and a bridging of worldviews. In the light of this
style of study and interpretation it was particularly interesting and important that the first draft of this paper was presented at a conference or-
ganised by one of the Buddhist movements, Risshō Kōsei-kai, for which
the Lotus Sutra is the central devotional and teaching text.

The theme "Ethics and the Lotus Sutra" can be placed quite naturally
against the background of my recent writing on ethics[2] and its choice is
undoubtedly linked to the considerable interest being generated by the
debates about values going on worldwide at the moment and the questions being raised about the global nature of ethics.[3] I have included in my
interpretation of the title not only some of the teaching within the sutra

which has bearing on ethics in some way, but also wider issues such as the sutra's claims about its own source and use. I have also drawn out different types of themes that relate to ethics and worked with them in different ways. The discussion was based both on my own reading of the text and on the need to take account of Buddhist voices and perspectives.

From the point of view of Buddhists from the T'ien'tai (Tendai) and Nichiren sects the Lotus Sutra is a central scripture. Dr. Michio Shinozaki has pointed out that Risshō Kōsei-kai tends to identify itself with the Buddhism of the Lotus Sutra, rather than being a Nichiren-affiliated school.[4] In the preface to his *A Guide to the Threefold Lotus Sutra*, the late Nikkyō Niwano, founder of Risshō Kōsei-kai, sees it as "a valuable and practical spiritual guide for living in these troubled times."[5] Rev. Niwano makes two further points to illustrate his comment and these link with my general theme. First, he says that the Lotus Sutra teaches that people can change for the better, and second, that it teaches that all beings are equal.[6] He traces its impact from the time of Kumārajīva's translation of the text from Sanskrit into Chinese to its introduction by Shōtoku Taishi into Japan and Saichō's teaching of it at Enryaku-ji on Mount Hiei, a place that was to influence so many great teachers, such as Shinran, Dōgen, and Nichiren himself. Paul Williams, a Buddhist scholar from the U.K. who is also a practising Buddhist within the Tibetan dGe lugs pa tradition, says, "For many East Asian Buddhists since early times the Lotus Sutra is the nearest Buddhist equivalent to a bible—one revealed work containing the final truth, itself sufficient for salvation."[7]

Historical Claims as an Issue in Ethics

The request that I received to contribute something on ethics and the Lotus Sutra for the Third International Conference asked me to be "more theological than historical." There are some problems for me in this. I do not find the term "theological" an appropriate one to use when dealing with Buddhist material, because Ultimate Reality in Buddhism is not articulated as a personal God (*theos* in Greek). This is a perception that I am anxious to keep to the forefront as someone who wants to work phenomenologically. But I do, on the other hand, find ethical issues can arise from debate about historical issues. What follows is a case in point.

The authority of Buddhist sutras has traditionally rested on their being Buddha *vac* or Buddha *vacana*, the word of the Buddha, and this has usually been understood as the word of the historical Buddha Śākyamuni. The Lotus Sutra presents itself as the teaching of Śākyamuni Buddha, dwelling in the city of King's Home (*Rājagṛha*), on Vulture's Peak or Mount of the Numinous Eagle (*Gṛdhrakūṭa*), surrounded by many *arhats* and bodhisattvas and emitting a white light from the circle of hair on his forehead. The white light is seen as a portent and "It is because he wishes all the living beings to be able to hear and know the Dharma [teaching/truth], difficult of belief for all the worlds, that he displays this portent."[8]

That this is understood as claiming a literal root in the life of the historical Buddha can be illustrated by the struggle of a Tibetan student studying at Indiana University when he first read the Lotus Sutra. "As a devoted Buddhist, he accepted the verdict of his tradition that all Mahayana scriptures (including this very peculiar sutra) were the word of the Buddha Śākyamuni. But at the same time it seemed quite clear to him that the Lotus Sutra conflicted with everything that he, as a Mahayana Buddhist monk, had been taught and said, 'I can't believe that the Buddha would say such things.'"[9]

The setting is a mixture of historically linked and mythological description which raises real questions about the origins and authority of the sutra. Its emergence on the stage of history is described by Williams in the following way.

> The earliest Chinese translation was made by Dharmarakṣa in 286 C.E. (revised in 290 C.E.). The version which conquered East Asia, however, and therefore by far the most significant version given the *sūtra*'s importance in East Asian Buddhism, was the Lotus translated by Kumārajīva and his team of translators in 406. . . . Kumārajīva's *Lotus Sūtra* consists of twenty-eight chapters. It is not a homogeneous work. Japanese scholars, who have carried out extensive study of the *Lotus Sūtra*, are inclined to see the oldest part of the text as having been composed between the first century B.C.E. and the first century C.E. (Chapters one to nine, plus Chapter seventeen). Most of the text had appeared by the end of the second century.[10]

To support his statements, Williams quotes two Japanese scholars and one Western scholar.[11] The literal link of the Lotus Sutra with the historical Buddha Śākyamuni is thus questioned in historical scholarship, including that done by Buddhist scholars, along with that of other great Mahayana sutras. For many historically minded people this tension can present a crisis of confidence and the raising of what is an ethical question about making claims for the sutra's origin that are not "true," which tends in this context to mean historically accurate. If people have been and are being told that this sutra was preached on Vulture Peak during his lifetime by the Buddha Śākyamuni and they then find out that there is good reason for questioning that this is historically the case, there might well follow a crisis of confidence in the integrity of the whole tradition of the teaching and the authority figures who have handed on that tradition.

This sounds harsh as I have stated it, but I think it is a realistic presentation of the challenge involved. It is a challenge that has been experienced by many Christians as a result of historical critical work on the Christian Bible during the last century or more and is therefore a familiar one to Westerners coming into Buddhist scholarship. There is an imaginative exploration of the challenge in the life of one man in the nineteenth-century novel by Mrs. Humphrey Ward entitled *Robert Elsmere*.[12] But the challenge should not be seen as one that comes to the material and to eastern Buddhists from the outside culturally and solely as part of a package of post-enlightenment Western thought. The distinguished Japanese thinker Tominaga Nakamoto (1715–46 C.E.) also questioned Śākyamuni Buddha's authorship of the Mahayana sutras and says:

> The scholars of later generations vainly say that all the teachings came directly from the golden mouth of the Buddha and were intimately transmitted by those who heard him frequently.[13]

Tominaga seems to have been the first writer "systematically to question the assumption that the Mahayana sutras, or indeed others, were transmitted directly from the Buddha himself. He did this by the critical, historical method of juxtaposing innumerable variations in the various texts and illustrating how these arose in order for some point to be made over against another school."[14] He did this entirely independently of Western scholarship. He states that:

> We can tell that for long after the Buddha's decease there was no fixed exposition among his followers and there were no writings upon which one could depend. Everybody renewed the teaching according to their opinions and passed it on orally.[15]

> Many of the sūtras were compiled by people five hundred years after the Buddha, so they contain many words from these five hundred years.[16]

This kind of challenge made on the basis of historical investigations and claims about historical truth needs to be taken seriously within as well as outside religions, if scholars and members of traditions are to communicate with each other. But, being more phenomenological, so does the style of language being used by a tradition in the claims that it makes, and with it the possibility that different kinds of truth claims are being made.

One of the best investigations and analyses of the issue of the claims of sutras to be the word of the Buddha, to my knowledge, is that presented in two articles in the journal *Religion* in 1981 and 1982 by Graeme MacQueen. His investigation uses the evidence of the tradition itself to build a coherent picture. He notes that at the time of the Mahayana sutras' emergence, traditionalists in the Buddhist community called attention to the fact that these were not literally the word of the Buddha as it was collected in the Pali canon and that they were therefore spurious. MacQueen investigates what the Pali canon itself takes as the authority behind a sutra and finds a significant number of sutras there also that are spoken by other than the Buddha but which are included for one of three main reasons: because the Buddha approved of what was said by a disciple, because he invites and gives someone permission to teach, and because he affirms a person's wisdom and ability, so by implication approves what they teach. These are all seen as Buddha *vacana* in some way. All of these, though, assume the existence of the historical Buddha to validate them. But MacQueen also describes a purely functional understanding of Buddha *vacana* (the word of the Buddha) and that is described in the Pali canon itself.

> The doctrines, Upāli, of which you may know: 'These doctrines lead one not to complete weariness (of the world), nor to dispassion, nor to ending, nor to calm, nor to knowledge, nor to the awakening, nor to the cool (nibbana)'—regard them definitely as not Dhamma, not the discipline, nor the word of the Teacher. But the doctrines of which you may know. 'These doctrines lead me to complete weariness, dispassion, ending, calm, knowledge, the awakening, the cool'—regard them unreservedly as Dhamma, discipline, the word of the Teacher.[17]

Mahayana sutras such as the Lotus do not rest, however, on this kind of principle alone. They set a scene in which the Buddha is still present so their origins are not restricted to the time of his historical birth as Śākyamuni. MacQueen's understanding that this is not a fraudulent claim rests on an appreciation of the Mahayana belief that the Buddha had never gone away and is still present, though only the faithful are aware of this. There is a completely new emphasis and understanding of the Buddha as more than an enlightened teacher in history. Of course Mahayana Buddhists may claim that it is not discontinuous with the understanding within the Pali canon, though it is not the understanding developed in Theravada Buddhism. The mythological setting of the giving of the teaching in the Lotus and other sutras sets them against this background and there is in the text a *dharma-bhāṇaka*, an inspired speaker who is the channel and messenger. Williams gives an example from the *Pratyutpanna sūtra* of this being attained through meditation practice.

> While remaining in this very world-system that bodhisattva sees the Lord, the Tathāgata Amitāyus; and conceiving himself to be in that world-system he also hears the Dharma. Having heard their

exposition he accepts, masters and retains those Dharmas. He wor-
ships, venerates, honours and reveres the Lord . . . Amitāyus. After
he has emerged from that *samādhi* [meditative absorption] that bodhisattva also expounds widely to others those Dharmas as he has
heard, retained and mastered them.[18]

In the case of the Lotus Sutra we can add to MacQueen's exploration
the general understanding that derives from the sutra itself that teaching
is a device and that things taught have only an interim truth, a truth that
is useful if it takes people along the path towards enlightenment. This fits
in with the quotation from the *Aṅguttara nikāya*, given above. The whole
tone of the scripture is quite different from any intent to claim historical
validity. It is mythological, poetical and full of imaginative narrative
(stories, parables) intended to produce insight and wisdom, not factual
knowledge.

In the Lotus, the Buddha is no longer regarded as a mere mortal but
as a sublime being with supernatural powers who preaches in a
mythological paradise surrounded by thousands upon thousands of
followers.[19]

Michio Shinozaki has stated the situation for Buddhists in the following way:

From the perspective of religious experience, the Buddha will appear
together with us on the Divine Vulture Peak when we are upright
and gentle and wish to see the Buddha. The Divine Vulture Peak is
the sacred place where the Lotus was expounded by Śākyamuni
Buddha. Such a place can be everywhere for religious people. When
people seek to meet the Buddha, wherever they are, it is the place for
'uniting' between the Buddha and the people in their vision.[20]

Historical context is only one device used in Buddhism. The historical
Buddha himself was an *upāya kauśalya*, a skillful means for helping beings. The real source of the teaching is beyond a historical figure.

The Ethics of Skillful Means

I shall now move on from the ethical issues involved in the claims for the
sutra's origins and a phenomenological insight into this issue from a
Buddhist point of view to the general theme of ethics and the Lotus
Sutra. When beginning my investigations I looked in the indexes of various books on Buddhist ethics to see what connections others had made
on this theme.[21] I was surprised to find no substantial references to the

Lotus Sutra in them. When I looked under skillful means (*upāya kauśalya*), however, I found some significant material. Damien Keown, for example, talks about "the apparently transmoral doctrine of Skilful Means."[22] The entry on *upāya kauśalya* in the Bowker-edited *Dictionary of World Religions*, from which an earlier quotation is taken, says that the only way to bring the ignorant and deluded onto the path of liberation involves a certain degree of duplicity, such as telling lies, but that the Buddha is exonerated from all blame since his only motivation is compassionate care for all beings.[23] Both of these references seem to indicate that at first sight the overtones of the term *upāya kauśalya*, the sutra's key teaching, are ethically questionable.

Pye presents a chart with the pre-Buddhist, post-Buddhist and Buddhist meanings of the Sanskrit, Chinese, and Japanese terms for the concept *upāya kauśalya* which he translates as "skilful means."[24] In a later chapter, he presents a discussion of the range of meanings of the word *hōben*, usually used to translate *upāya kauśalya* in modern Japanese. Pye gives this a lot of attention in chapter 8 of his book and quotes Founder Niwano's attempt to overcome the sense of "expediency" in the derivation and root of the term which might be linked with the idea of a trick or lie. He quotes:

> If we look up the character *hō* of *hōben* in a dictionary we find that it means "dead square" . . . and thus also "correct". . . . *Ben* means "measure". . . . Therefore the term *hōben* means "correct measure". . . . Originally it meant a teaching device which exactly fits the person and the circumstances.[25]

The place of the concept of *upāya kauśalya* within the Buddhist tradition certainly affirms and demands a definitive interpretation. Skillful means, as well as morality, is on the Mahayana list of the ten *pāramitās* (perfections) of which there are six on the Theravāda list. Keown highlights that this focus is twofold wisdom/insight (*prajñā*) and skillful means (*upāya kauśalya*). He quotes the *Vimalakīrti nirdeśa sūtra*, which presents the perfection of wisdom (*prajñā pāramitā*) as the mother and skillfulness in means (*upāya kauśalya*) as the father of the bodhisattvas.[26] He sees the two as so interdependent that the absence of one results in bondage rather than liberation. So, for example, the *Vimalakīrti sūtra* (1V. 16ff.) says in relation to *upāya kauśalya*:

> When a Bodhisattva rejects false views, the invasion of the passions, residual tendencies, affection and aversion, and transfers to perfect enlightenment the good roots he has cultivated without producing pride, these are skillful means acquired through wisdom and it is deliverance.[27]

Both Williams and Keown give examples from Mahayana sutras other than the Lotus Sutra of what Keown calls "radical ethical conclusions."[28] Williams points out that "all is subordinated to the overriding concern of a truly compassionate motivation accompanied by wisdom. All is relative."[29] Keown puts it this way: "Mahayana sources allow varying degrees of latitude to a *bodhisattva* when performing his [*sic*] saving work."[30]

The examples he gives are not from the Lotus Sutra itself, but as illustrations of what is perhaps the Lotus Sutra's central doctrine; they are important as examples of the ethical issues inherent in its stand.

> The Lord has taught that what is forbidden may be performed by one who perceives with the eye of knowledge a special benefit for beings therein. . . . The forgoing exemption does not apply to everyone, only to cases of the exercise of compassion in its highest degree by one who is of a compassionate nature, who is without a selfish motive, solely concerned with the interests of others and totally dedicated to this ideal.[31]

The examples he quotes of what he calls "permissive attitudes," he indicates, were the focus of considerable heart searching. Williams introduces modern examples as well as those from the classical texts. The examples he includes are the story of how in a previous life the Buddha killed a man and that this was the only way to prevent the man from killing five hundred other people and spending a very long time in hell realms. He exercised compassion both towards those who were about to be killed and towards the potential murderer. How this relates to the central Buddhist teaching that *karmic* consequences are the fruits of intention is not explored at this point. But this kind of story, Williams says, has provided the basis for violence by Tibetan monks trying to defend the Dharma against Chinese Communist invaders.[32]

What needs to be borne in mind when considering these examples is that *upāya* is an attribute of those already perfect in ethics and insight, it is the seventh stage (*bhūmi*) of the bodhisattva path. This means that *upāya* is not presented as a normative path for all to follow but as something manifest in the activities of Buddhas and great bodhisattvas. Their true domain is mythical and cosmic, hence the setting of the opening of the Lotus Sutra. The language to communicate their skill-in-means and compassion is one that engages not so much with our inclination and powers of imitation but with our imagination. It is highly symbolic and communicated by stories and descriptions of ingenuity not by history or moral paradigms. It has what a Tibetan Buddhist friend of mine calls the "wow" quality. "Just imagine that people could be that skillful, that compassionate!" is what she described as the typical effect of these kinds of stories and examples on Mahayana Buddhists.

In seeing *upāya kauśalya* as the symbolic affirmation of the importance of *karuṇā* (compassion), Keown makes a link with situation ethics, as expounded by Joseph Fletcher.[33] Just as situation ethics for the Christian affirms an ethic rooted in the principle and practice of love (*agape*), which is the one thing that is intrinsically good, so:

> An *upāya*-inspired ethic would break free of the code of laws passed on through tradition and approach the situation of ethical decision-making not empty-handed but armed with a revised scale of values in which compassion (*karuṇā*) is predominant.[34]

> As more and more emphasis is placed upon the welfare of others as the sole end, the means employed to achieve it are questioned less and less. The *bodhisattva* who is motivated by *karuṇā* will seek the well-being of his fellow creatures and choose that course of action which has best consequences irrespective of moral norms which might prohibit it. It is, of course, assumed that the act will promote the well-being of others, and this is where *prajñā* plays its part. . . .[35]

The area obviously related to this, the centrality of which is mentioned earlier, is the emphasis in Buddhism on motivation, on intention as that which bears *karmic* fruit. It is the *cetanā*, the motivation that determines the moral quality of an act: intention rooted not in greed, hatred, and ignorance but in generosity or liberality, loving-kindness, compassion or benevolence, and wisdom or understanding. It may be the case, as the above example of the man with murderous intent seems to indicate, that a bodhisattva's intention can override the *karmic* fruits of others' intentions. But any emphasis on intention is also challenged by a query about consistency. Does not the Lotus Sutra suggest that even if you drop a flower offering accidently, it will still be effective? It is also challenged by the fact that skillful means are judged by their effectiveness. If an action or a teaching works, then it is seen to be skillful. But the same action, for example of deceiving someone, if not effective might seem to be the word or action of an unenlightened person and therefore fall into the category of an unethical word and deed.

Turning to the Text

I now want to look in more detail at parts of the text of the Lotus Sutra and the teachings it communicates as they relate to ethics. Translations of the sutra are readily available. I am most familiar with that by Hurvitz,[36] from which the following quotations are taken, but will cross-refer to other texts as appropriate.

The Buddha sees everything; the usual *karmic* consequences of actions (p. 6), the actions of giving and of reverence, but most importantly "he wishes all living beings to be able to hear and know the Dharma" (p. 12) and precipitates "a Dharma-rain that shall satisfy the seekers of the Path" (p. 21). For Buddhists as well as the general reader, the main point about this cosmic setting is the extraordinariness of the Buddha's nature and therefore the extraordinariness of the knowledge and wisdom that can claim to teach all living beings. This again is something to be wondered at and not something that Buddhists can claim for themselves. The beginning of the second chapter confirms this point. "The Buddha's wisdom is profound and incalculable . . . hard to understand" and "the Thus Come One's knowledge and insight are broad and great, profound and recondite, without measure and without obstruction" (p. 22). "I and the Buddhas of the ten directions are the only ones who can know these things" (p. 23), which statement is followed by a list of very distinguished types of followers who "still could not know it" (p. 25). So:

> The Buddha, by the power of expedient devices,
> Demonstrates the teaching of the three vehicles.
> The living beings, attached to this object and that,
> He attracts and thus enables to extricate themselves (p. 25).

Śāriputra asks "whether this is the ultimate Dharma or whether it is [merely] a path to tread [toward that Dharma]" (p. 27). The Buddha, as in the seminal story in the Pali canon of his encounter with Brahma Sahampati after his enlightenment, is reluctant to teach further until asked three times and then confirms what the Kosei translation calls "tactfulness."[37] This extraordinary cosmic setting, combined with the confidence that "means" and the fulfillment of an innate potential are available for all beings to tread the path to enlightenment, even the evil Devadatta, suggests the balance for readers of humility and gratitude combined with personal self-respect and confidence, which are both spiritual and ethical values that the tradition then seeks to develop into action.

The Story of Belief and Understanding

There are many stories in the Lotus Sutra, sometimes called parables, which illustrate aspects of its teaching. One of these stories, in chapter 4, has been called by some, The Parable of the Prodigal Son, thus echoing the title of a Christian story in the New Testament. Both stories teach about a son who leaves home, forsakes his father, and after a time becomes destitute. In the Christian story, the destitute son remembers his home and decides to go back and ask his father's forgiveness. The father welcomes him home with open arms, despite his behavior, and forgives him, asking his brother to make a family feast to celebrate his return. Father in the Christian story is an image used for God, who is thus seen as loving and forgiving to the sinner who returns and asks for forgiveness for his behavior. Teaching about the love and forgiveness of God is central to Christianity and illustrated par excellence by the story of the incarnation itself: the entering of God into human flesh to share the human predicament and help humanity "from within," with all the suffering that this involves. This teaching of the self-emptying (*kenosis* in Greek) of God in the form of Jesus Christ is most classically articulated in Paul's letter to the Philippians, chapter two. In that letter, it is obvious that this self-emptying of God is not only the instrument of human redemption but the central ethical paradigm of Christian teaching. God is the protagonist. He does not wait for any human initiative, because that could not effect the salvation that is necessary. This powerful theology and the example that it suggests have motivated Christians through the ages to enter lovingly into the situation of others in a spirit of self-renunciation.

But to my mind, this radical ethic is not captured and sustained at all deeply in the Christian story of the Prodigal Son, where the emphasis is on the need for the sinner to repent and ask God for forgiveness with the confidence that God as a loving father will welcome him home. It is a story that emphasizes that we have to initiate a return to God for salvation to be effective.

On the other hand, the Buddhist story of the son who left home and became destitute has always seemed to me to have something in it of the radical ethic of the Christian teaching of the self-emptying love of God in the incarnation. It is not, of course, being presented in the same framework of ideas as the Christian teaching, which is an obvious problem for any systematic comparative worldview analysis. In the Buddhist story, the father is the cosmic Buddha, portrayed at the beginning of the sutra amidst the host of cosmic bodhisattvas. In another famous story in the Lotus Sutra, this Buddha-father uses skillful means to rescue his children from a burning house, which is an image of *saṃsāra*, with its fires of greed, hatred, and ignorance. To return to the story of the father whose son has left home, I have always found this Buddhist narrative a more satisfying illustration of the self-emptying, incarnational paradigm of Christianity than the New Testament parable of the Prodigal Son, to which it is often compared. The father in the Buddhist story takes the initiative, because we are told the son has completely forgotten who he is and what is his inheritance. It is the father who goes in search of his destitute son and who has to disguise himself, leave behind his wealth, and sink to the son's level to make contact. The contact that he makes has to be adapted to his son's mental state and destitution, and the father only gradually and skillfully nurtures him back to a situation where he can let him know who he is and that he is the heir to great wealth, which is the Buddha-nature.

This emphasis on adaptation, even disguise, as a skillful means is fully in keeping not only with the Buddha's teaching but with the bodhisattva path. The needs of beings are various, and in chapter 25 there is the description of the ways that the bodhisattva "who observes the sounds of the world," which is the translation of the name of Avalokiteśvara, and Kuan-shih-yin, takes thirty-three forms in order to help beings. This chapter of the sutra has circulated separately as a sutra in its own right and is linked with the thirty-three station pilgrimage sites and links us to my next theme.

The Lotus Sutra and the Place of Women in Buddhism

The debate about the place of women in the Buddhist traditions is now well-established, thanks to the theoretical and practical work of women such as Thailand's Chatsumarn Kabilsingh, who heads the International Asssociation of Buddhist Women, and Rita Gross, whose seminal work, *Buddhism After Patriarchy*, bridges so many issues.[38]

Westerners who are not used to the conventions of Buddhist art often react to the rounded forms of the images of Buddhas and bodhisattvas and, in the case of bodhisattvas, to their jewelled robes, with comments about their feminine appearance. It can be suggested that this sense of ambiguity is entirely appropriate since the true nature of an enlightened being is beyond sexuality, beyond the characteristics of male and female. But it can also be seen as helpful to women within the Buddhist tradition that the bodhisattva Kuan-shih-yin (also Kwan-yin, Kanzeon, and Kannon) is imaged as the female form of the male Avalokiteśvara, the Lord who looks down on the sufferings of the world.[39] This affirms that the enlightened nature belongs to women as well as men, those in female as well as male forms. This is certainly illustrated in the Pali canon in the named examples of those women who became enlightened at the time of Gotama Buddha.

Chapter 25 of the Lotus Sutra is a central section and is used as a text in its own right. The transformations which it recounts of the one who hears the cries of the world into thirty-three forms, seven of which are female, has a practical outreach in the thirty-three site pilgrim routes in Japan with their different images of Kannon. These and other images, such as the huge, free-standing figures of Kannon in Japan, introduce popular practices and a powerful visual dimension to set alongside the text.[40]

In chapter 12 of the Lotus Sutra, which focuses on the story of Devadatta, the bodhisattva Wisdom Accumulation asks Mañjuśrī whether there are any beings who, putting this scripture into practice, might speedily gain Buddhahood. Mañjuśrī suggests the daughter of the Nāga (dragon or serpent) King Sagara, who is barely eight years old. When Mañjuśrī's description of her attainments is questioned, she suddenly appears and recounts them for herself. At this point Śāriputra says:

> You say that in no long time you shall attain the unexcelled Way. This is hard to believe. What is the reason? A woman's body is filthy, it is not a Dharma-receptacle. How can you attain unexcelled bodhi? . . . Also a woman's body even then has five obstacles. It cannot become first a Brahmā god king, second the god Śakra, third King Māra, fourth the sage-king turning the Wheel, fifth a Buddha-body. How can the body of a woman speedily attain Buddhahood?[41]

Her response to his question is to turn into a man! This causes considerable confusion and in other versions of similiar stories in other Mahayana sutras, the questioner is turned into a woman. We are left with the queries "What are these external forms that we judge so important? How do they relate to enlightenment?" These questions are central for the Buddhist and are ones to which there is a confident answer that physical forms are illusory and insubstantial compared with the potential for enlightenment that is within all sentient beings.

Miriam Levering has also highlighted the prediction of Buddhahood made by Śākyamuni to his aunt and stepmother Prajāpatī and his former wife, Yaśodharā, who are described as nuns in the assembly of chapter one of the Lotus Sutra. In chapter 13, it is predicted that these two women will in future attain Buddhahood and the Buddha says, "I will say that in ages to come, amid the Dharmas of sixty-eight thousands of millions of Buddhas, you will be a great teacher of the Dharma, and the six thousand nuns, some still learning, some already sufficiently learned, will accompany you as teachers of the Dharma."

Levering also refers to other Mahayana texts where the power to create bodies is one of the powers of a bodhisattva, allowing us to "read the story of the *nāga* princess as one of a female advanced bodhisattva simply exercising her *ṛddhī-bala* [powers] in creating a transformation in what she already knows to be insubstantial, as the goddess [Devi] in the *Vimalakīrti-nirdeśa sūtra* does."[42]

Conclusion

What this paper has sought to introduce and reflect upon is not only some important ethical issues that emerge in any consideration of this important text, the Lotus Sutra, but also the many different ways in which this and other questions can be approached in the study of religions. Demonstrably an area or dimension of a religion such as ethics is inextricably related to the other dimensions of religious life such as narratives, doctrines, experience, rituals, and even the visual arts. It is also inextricably linked with the distinctive interpretations of the religious communities whose text it is, as well as scholarly dialogue where questions and insights may be a part of the environment within which traditions themselves skillfully adapt and change.

Notes

1. For an exploration of the roots of phenomenology of religion, see E. Sharpe, *Comparative Religion*. 2nd. ed. Duckworth, 1975: chapter 10.
2. A full length study can be found in J. Cox, P. Morgan and C. Lawton, *Ethical Issues in Six Religious Traditions*. EUP, 1996.
3. See H. Küng & K-J. Kuschel. *A Global Ethic: The Declaration of the Parliament of the World's Religion*. SCM, 1992; M. Braybrooke, *Stepping Stones to a Global Ethic*. SCM, 1992 and H. Küng, *Yes to A Global Ethic*. SCM, 1996.
4. M. Shinozaki, "The Buddhist Three Treasures in the Thought of the Lotus Sutra." Paper presented at the Third International Conference on the Lotus Sutra, Bandai-sō, Japan, July 1997: 3.
5. Nikkyō Niwano, *A Guide to the Threefold Lotus Sutra*. Kosei Publishing Co., 1981: 7.
6. Ibid., 10.
7. P. Williams, *Mahāyāna Buddhism*. RKP, 1989: 141.
8. L. Hurvitz, *Scripture of the Lotus Blossom of the Fine Dharma*. Columbia University Press, 1976: 12; N. Niwano, op. cit.: 12.
9. J. Nattier, "The Lotus Sūtra: Good News for Whom?" Paper presented at the Third International Conference on the Lotus Sutra, July 1997: 2.
10. Williams, op. cit.: 142.
11. H. Nakamura, *Indian Buddhism*, Hirakata: Kansai University of Foreign Studies, 1980; K. Fujita, "Pure Land Buddhism and the Lotus Sutra," in É. Lamotte, *Indianisme et Bouddhisme: Mélanges offerts à Mgr Étienne Lamotte*, Louvain: Université Catholique de Louvain, 1980; M. Pye, *Skilful Means*, London: Duckworth, 1978.
12. H. Ward, *Robert Elsmere*. 1888. Oxford University Press reprint, 1987.
13. Tominaga Nakamoto, *Emerging from Meditation*. M. Pye, tr., Duckworth, 1990: 4 and 81ff.

14. Ibid., Introduction: 5.
15. Ibid., 83.
16. Ibid., 86.
17. *Aṅguttara nikāya* quoted by MacQueen.
18. Williams, op. cit., 30, quoting from P. Harrison, *Journal of Indian Philosophy*, 1978: 9: 35–57.
19. J. Bowker, *The Oxford Dictionary of Religions*. Oxford University Press, 1997: 587.
20. Shinozaki, op. cit., 16.
21. There is now a solid body of writing in the field of Buddhist ethics. Examples are: H. Saddhatissa, *Buddhist Ethics*. George Allen & Unwin, 1970; D. Keown, *The Nature of Buddhist Ethics*. Macmillan, 1992; D. Keown, *Buddhism and Bio-ethics*. Macmillan, 1995; D. Keown, ed. *Buddhism and Abortion*. Macmillan, 1998.
22. Keown, *The Nature of Buddhist Ethics*, op. cit., 129.
23. Bowker, ed., op. cit., 1008.
24. Pye, op. cit., 17.
25. N. Niwano, *Hokkekyō no Atarashii Kaishaku* 法華経の新しい解釈 (A New Commentary on The Lotus Sutra). Kōsei Publishing Co., 1966, 96, quoted in Pye, op. cit., 148.
26. Keown, 1992: 131.
27. Quoted in Keown, op. cit., 132.
28. Ibid., 150.
29. Williams, op. cit., 144.
30. Keown, op.cit., 151.
31. Ibid., 151.
32. Williams, op. cit., 145.
33. J. Fletcher, *Situation Ethics*. SCM, 1966.
34. Keown, 1992., 188.
35. Ibid., 189.
36. L. Hurvitz, op. cit.
37. *The Threefold Lotus Sutra*. Translated by Bunnō Katō and others, Kōsei Publishing Co., 1975: chapter 2: 51.
38. Some examples of the now extensive literature are: C. Kabilsingh, *Thai Women in Buddhism*. Parallax Press, 1991; R. Gross, *Buddhism After Patriarchy*. State University of New York Press, 1993 with extensive biblographies; D. Paul, *Women in Buddhism*. Asian Humanities Press, 1979; K. Tsomo & L. Sakhyadhita: *Daughters of the Buddha*. Snow Lion, 1988; M. Batchelor, *Walking on Lotus Flowers*. Thorsons, 1996; C. A. F. Rhys Davids & K. R. Norman, *Poems of Early Buddhist Nuns*. Pali Text Society, 1989.
39. See *Buddhist Paintings*. Kōsei Publishing Co., 1981. A magnificent volume of paintings by Ryūsen Miyahara, with text by Mosaku Ishida, Takashi Hamada, Yasushi Murashige, and Shigeru Matsubara.
40. M. Palmer, J. Ramsey, & M-H. Kwok, *Kuan Yin*. Thorsons, 1995, gives a full account of the stories and practices surrounding this figure. Some of the pilgrim sites have a set of thirty-three images in one place, so that in visiting a

single temple a pilgrim can have visited all thirty-three temples on a pilgrim route. For an illustration of one of the huge figures of Kannon, see H. Bechert and R. Gombrich, *The World of Buddhism.* Thames and Hudson, 1984: 179.
41. Hurvitz, op. cit., 200–1
42. Points from M. Levering's paper, "Is the Lotus Sutra 'Good News' For Women?" delivered at the Third International Conference on the Lotus Sutra, B. Watson, 191–92, L. Hurvitz, op. cit., 203.

Paternalism in the Lotus Sutra

Damien Keown

"I looked up and saw God . . . and I knew he wanted me to lie."

—*The Herbal Bed*

In two places in the Lotus Sutra the question is explicitly asked whether the deception involved in the use of skillful means is immoral. In both cases the question is raised at the end of a parable in which a surrogate for the Buddha perpetrates a deception. The first time is in the parable of the burning house which occurs in the third chapter of the sutra. The second is in the parable of the physician who travels abroad which occurs in chapter 16. The parable of the burning house is so well known it hardly needs repetition, but I will quote below the summary provided by Michael Pye:

> A wealthy old man has a great house with only one door. The house is in a decrepit state, and a fire breaks out, threatening to engulf all the man's children who are absorbed in play within the house. The old man calls them in vain, then resorts in desperation to skillful means (*fang pien*). Knowing the kinds of things which they all like, he calls out that there are goat-carts, deer-carts and bullock carts waiting for them outside the door. Upon this they all come scrambling out of the house and are saved from the flames. The three kinds of carts are nowhere to be seen, but instead the old man gives to each one a still more splendid chariot, beautifully ornate and drawn by a white bullock .[1]

In the following paragraph Pye explains how the question of lying arises:

367

The question is then raised, by way of comment on the story, as to whether the old man was guilty of a falsehood. "Śāriputra's answer to this is that he was not, but it is not only this judgment which is interesting but also its justification. The emphasis is put not on the fact that the children received a better vehicle than intended, which might after all be taken to cover their failure to receive the specific kinds which were originally promised. Rather, the discrepancy is justified by the fulfillment of the old man's intention to bring them out from the flames. Even if they had not received any carts at all it would have been inappropriate to speak of a falsehood, because the original thought of the old man was: "I will get my children to escape by a skillful means."[2]

For convenience I will also quote Pye's summary of the second parable, that of the physician:

A physician is traveling abroad, and in the meantime his sons drink some poisonous medicines and become delirious. When he returns he prepares good medicine for them. The ones who take the good medicine recover, but the others have quite lost their senses and refuse to take the good medicine. The father reflects, and decides upon a skillful means to make them take it. He warns them that he is very old and approaching death, then leaves for another country from where he sends a messenger back to report that he has died. The sons are overcome with grief, come to their senses and take the medicine which he had prepared. Hearing this the father returns and they are united. Immediately following the story the question is raised as to whether the physician in this case was guilty of a falsehood, and the answer returned is that he was not. Then the Buddha declares: "I am also like this. Since I became a Buddha . . . for the sake of all the living I have declared by my power of skillful means that I must enter nirvana, and yet no one can rightly say that I have perpetrated a falsehood."[3]

Merely to raise the question of whether the Buddha lied is revolutionary in the context of earlier ethical norms. Lies are not the sort of thing one normally associates with a Buddha, and what prompts the question is surely the clear awareness of the redactors of the text of the tension between skillful means and traditional morality. Buddhism prohibits lying and deception under various of its moral codes, most notably in the fourth of the Five Precepts. The Buddha in the Pali canon never lies to anyone. He tells us himself "A *Tathāgata* . . . is pure in conduct whether of act, or speech, or thought. There is no misdeed of any kind concerning which he must take care lest another should come to know of it."[4] He says that he detests evil conduct in body, word, and thought.[5] Buddhaghosa says of him that he always speaks the truth.[6] *Arhats* as a class are said to be incapable of breaking the precepts such as those against killing, stealing, lying or having sexual intercourse.[7] On the contrary, Buddhas are traditionally identified with truth and truthfulness and the Pali canon puts a premium on accuracy, clarity and fidelity. In the light of this to intimate that the Buddha might be guilty of deception is verging on heresy.

As noted above, the Lotus Sutra responds to the charge of lying with a denial. In the case of the old man, as noted above, it responds by claiming that the Buddha was not guilty of a falsehood because of his intention, which was "I will get my children to escape by a skillful means." And in the case of the physician, although the justification offered is less explicit, it would appear to be of the same kind, namely that the intention was to save the lives of the ailing sons.

In the case of the burning house, the sutra's answer to the charge of lying seems unsatisfactory. If we understand lying to mean the deliberate communication of an untruth with the intention that others may be deceived, it seems indisputable that the old man lied. After all, did he not tell the children—knowing very well that it was not the case—that there were three different kinds of carts waiting for them outside the house? While his motive might have been a benevolent one, his intention (that to which he directed his will in the execution of his plan) was certainly to deceive. And in the case of the second example, how can it be that the physician is not guilty of a falsehood when he himself sent a message saying he was dead? It is hard to imagine how he could have been confused about the facts in this case! Once again, while his motive was the benevolent one of saving his children, his intention was indubitably that his children should be deceived. How, then, can the sutra maintain that the old man and the physician were not guilty of a falsehood?

I think we must understand the text as claiming not that there was no falsehood in these and the other cases, but that the falsehood was justifiable. The justification offered—that in each case some wise person acting with a good motive "knew best" what should be done—may be characterized as paternalistic. Ethically such conduct seems ultimately grounded by the principle of beneficence. In Western medical ethics the principle of beneficence has been accorded a primary place,[8] and has traditionally been interpreted to mean that it is justifiable in certain circumstances for a physician to do whatever in his judgment was in the best interests of the patient, even if this meant manipulating the truth. The justification for this turns on the fact that the physician has a deeper knowledge and understanding of the patient's condition than he himself has, and is committed to the patient's welfare and well-being. In the words of Beauchamp and Childress:

> When the analogy of the father is used to illuminate the role of professionals or the state in health care, it presupposes two features of the paternal role: that the father acts beneficently (i.e. in accord with his conception of the interests of his children) and that he makes all or at least some of the decisions relating to his children's welfare rather than letting them make those decisions. In professional relationships the argument is that a professional has superior training, knowledge, and insight and is in an authoritative position to determine what is in the patient's best interests. In short, from this perspective, a professional is like a parent when dealing with independent and often ignorant and fearful patients.[9]

Throughout the Lotus Sutra, the justification offered for the use of skillful means seems similar to that in paternalistic medicine. It is the case in the two examples cited from the Lotus Sutra (one of which specifically includes a physician) and in other of the parables in the text, such as the son who did not know himself in chapter 4, the magic city in chapter 7, or the Buddha's life span in chapter 16. In all these cases one of the parties is wiser or more knowledgeable and has privileged access to knowledge or information not held by the other. The wiser party, such as the old man in the burning house, the physician or the guide, also seeks from a beneficent motive to manipulate the truth with the aim of furthering the well-being of the other party.

The traditional model of benevolent paternalism in medicine just described has increasingly been challenged in the last thirty years, and may be said to be in large-scale retreat before a new approach to medical ethics which emphasizes the autonomy of patients rather than the authority of medical personnel. At the heart of the debate is the conflict between two principles. The first, beneficence, we have already discussed. The second is autonomy. Beneficence lends authority to healthcare professionals to do what they deem in the patient's best interests, while autonomy places the primary responsibility for decision-making in the hands of the patient. The view that when these two principles conflict autonomy should be given priority is now widely regarded as the norm. The following extract from the President's Commission for the Study of Ethical Problems in Medicine and Biomedical and Behavioral Research is a typical statement of this position:

> The primary goal of health care in general is to maximize each pa-

tient's well-being. However, merely acting in a patient's best interests without recognizing the individual as the pivotal decision maker would fail to respect each person's interest in self-determination. . . . When the conflicts that arise between a competent patient's self-determination and his or her apparent well-being remain unresolved after adequate deliberation, a competent patient's self-determination is and usually should be given greater weight than other people's views on that individual's well-being. . . . Respect for the self-determination of competent patients is of special importance. . . . The patient should have the final authority to decide.[10]

The problem of paternalism in a medical context arises from the fact that the physician's assessment of the situation may differ from that of the patient. Patients may be distressed, depressed, under the influence of drugs and medication, and not competent to make decisions which are fully rational in light of all the relevant circumstances. Other patients may be competent but choose treatment or other options which seem to the physician to be unsatisfactory or even harmful. The problem for the physician is whether to allow the scales to tip in favor of autonomy and respect the patient's choices however unreasonable they may seem, or to weight them in favor of beneficence which may lead to paternalistic intervention.

The concept of paternalism has been analyzed more widely in political philosophy than it has in ethics. As a justification for the restriction of individual liberty by paternalistic political regimes it has been attacked by both Kant and Mill, although neither considered it explicitly in the more complex contexts where it seems justifiable by appeal to beneficence. The Oxford English Dictionary dates the term to the 1880s and gives the root meaning as:

. . . the principle and practice of paternal administration; government as by a father; the claim or attempt to supply the needs or to regulate the life of a nation or community in the same way a father does those of his children.

Beauchamp and Childress offer a shorter definition of paternalism as: "the overriding of a person's wishes or intentional actions for beneficent reasons."[11] The issue of truth-telling comes up in many cases involving paternalism, typically in the form of deception, lying, or non-disclosure of information.

When is paternalism justified? Although Mill opposed paternalism he considered that it was justifiable on some occasions to intervene temporarily in a person's freely chosen actions. He argued that there are cases where a person may be unaware of the dangers involved in the course of action they have embarked upon or may be temporarily unable to understand the true nature of their situation. In his view it would be justifiable to restrain such a person temporarily in order to warn them of the risks they faced, but thereafter they should be released and allowed to make their own choice as to whether to continue on the chosen course or not.

Developing this idea some contemporary writers take the view that paternalism is justified only with the consent of the party to be restrained, whether this is express or implied. They argue that because at times we may all be tempted to engage in rash or dangerous conduct it is reasonable to regard the state as having an implied devolved authority to intervene to protect citizens against themselves. For example, by restricting the freedom of citizens to engage in duelling, the state protects them against the consequences of temporary hot-headed behavior when they feel themselves slighted. But what of the case of mentally deranged persons who are a danger to themselves and others but who do not wish to be confined? Theorists such as Rawls and Dworkin justify their confinement by a "but for" theory of consent, which holds that paternalistic intervention is justified since the person would consent but for their compromised condition. Others, such as Beauchamp and Childress, justify paternalism not through consent but solely by beneficence. They write:

> Our thesis is that beneficence alone is the justification of paternalism, just as it is of parental actions that override the preferences of children. We do not interfere in the lives of our children because we believe that they will subsequently consent or would rationally approve. We interfere because we think the intervention gives them a better life, whether they know it or not.[12]

This reference to children brings us back to the Lotus Sutra, which would appear to share the justification for paternalism just offered. It is getting the children out of the house that justifies the actions of the old man, not their consent. Indeed, it seems pointless to ask for their consent for they are not competent to give it being "attached . . . to their games, . . . unaware, ignorant, unperturbed, unafraid."[13] In most of the parables, indeed, those who are the beneficiaries of skillful means (although in some of the more extreme cases to be mentioned below perhaps we should call them the "victims") are repeatedly portrayed as incompetent to make fully autonomous choices.

Opponents of paternalism would argue that such paternalistic intervention cannot be justified because it involves a violation of individual rights and unduly restricts free choice. They argue that paternalism is unacceptable because authority resides rightfully not in the manipulator but in the individual whose life is manipulated. Antipaternalists argue in general that autonomy should be respected and that unless there are compelling reasons individuals should be free to proceed as they wish.

Much depends, of course, on the facts of each case and the competence of the individual concerned to make autonomous choices. In this connection Joel Feinberg makes a useful distinction between "strong" and "weak" paternalism.[14] Weak paternalism limits the right to intervene to those cases where conduct is either "substantially nonvoluntary" (that is to say, nonautonomous), or when temporary intervention is necessary to establish whether it is fully voluntary. In other words, it requires that the individual's mental or emotional capacities be compromised in some degree, for example by illness or serious depression. Preventing someone under the influence of LSD from attempting to fly from a high balcony would be an example of weak paternalism. In cases of this kind there is no real conflict between beneficence and autonomy since the individual in question is often temporarily non-autonomous.

Strong paternalism, on the other hand, insists that autonomy may be overridden even when the individual is competent and has made substantially informed and voluntary choices. Strong paternalism does not invoke notions of compromised ability or the temporary loss of autonomy. Strong paternalism can be seen in cases such as forcibly administering blood transfusions to Jehovah's Witnesses or force-feeding prisoners on hunger strike.

What kind of paternalism do we see at work in the parables in the Lotus Sutra? It would seem to be weak paternalism. Those who are deceived in the parables are depicted as in some respect temporarily compromised with respect to their autonomy. The children are engrossed in their toys and unaware of the very real danger of the fire; the sons of the physician are dying and in need of a cure; the travelers in the wilderness are tired and distressed, and so forth. Furthermore, the deception is a temporary one and the truth is revealed once the danger is past. The parables in the Lotus Sutra, then, are all cases of weak paternalism justified by beneficence and which involve no serious threat to the principle of autonomy.

How accurately these parables reflect the underlying truth of the situation they purport to represent is, of course, quite another topic. Whether the Buddha's early followers can really be likened to deluded children or not is debatable, but it is not a question I can enter into here. When discussing parables it would be unwise to press the analysis of the content too far. If we did, we might begin to raise other questions which might lead us to view the old man in a different light. For instance, why did the old man, who is described as "of incalculable wealth, owning many fields and houses, as well as servants," let his house fall into such a chronic state of disrepair? Is he not indirectly to blame for the near tragedy by allowing his house to become a fire hazard? Was he too mean to spend his money on appropriate fire precautions or just a foolish old man who failed to maintain his property adequately? Apart from the state of the house, why did he permit such serious overcrowding in allowing up to five hundred people inside at one time? Perhaps there is a wider social critique intended and the story wishes to point an accusing finger at the social workers and civil authorities for failing to address the chronic overcrowding and rehouse the family? Finally, there is no mention of the old man's wife; should we see here a covert reference to the particular problems of single parents?

Humor aside, it would clearly be a mistake to press questions of this kind too far, since at some point the parable, like an analogy, begins to break down and a too literalistic treatment will yield increasingly diminishing returns. The central concern of the Lotus Sutra, after all, is not ethics but the notion of skillful means, and for the remainder of this essay I would like to discuss some of the nuances of this term and explain why I think one particular development in the idea is misguided.

I think we can distinguish four separate senses of skillful means in Buddhist sources, the first of which is seen in early Buddhism. According to the Pali canon, after his own awakening the Buddha reflected on how difficult it would be to communicate his experience and at first inclined away from a teaching career (the story is retold in a more dramatic form in chapter two of the Lotus Sutra). Once he resolved to teach, however, the Buddha excelled as a skillful teacher, elucidating his doctrines using anecdotes, parables, metaphor, imagery, and symbolism, or as the texts have it, teaching "in many a way and in many a figure." This, it seems, is the germ of the idea of skillful means; as Michael Pye puts it concisely, "there is a problem about communicating *Dhamma* to anybody."[15] Central to the notion of skillful means is the dialectic of the "relationship between the articulated form and the inexpressible goal."[16] As Pye tells us, there is no evidence that the Buddha ever used the terminology of skillful means to characterize his teachings. The term "skillful means" occurs only rarely and incidentally in the Pali canon, only once, for example, in the whole of the *Dīgha Nikāya,* and only then in as a bare item in a list in the *Saṅgīti Suttanta.* Nevertheless, there appears to be a matrix of ideas common to both early Buddhism and the Lotus Sutra. When the Buddha teaches Brahmins, for example, he borrows and adapts the concepts of Brahmanism. In the *Tevijja-sutta* he is asked by two young Brahmins how to achieve union with Brahma. He criticizes those who speculate about Brahma without having seen him face to face, and then teaches the practice of the *Brahma Vihāras*. Similarly, when asked by Soṇadaṇḍa how to worship the six directions the Buddha gives this ancient Brahmanic ritual a new ethical spin by relating it to social obligations and family life. What we are seeing here is the practice of skillful means before anyone had invented a special name for it. As Pye puts it: Although the term *upāya* is anachronistic here, strictly speaking, the way of thought which it represents surely is not."[17]

The second phase in the development of the concept is found in the Lotus Sutra, which crystallizes and makes explicit the notion of skillful means understood as a methodology for the transmission of the Dharma. The underlying question the text addresses is how to express the inexpressible, or how to communicate a profound experience—namely enlightenment—in a soteriologically effective way. There are no radically new doctrines in the Lotus Sutra, and its significance lies instead in its bold claim that all teachings are provisional and ultimately to be dismantled.

The Lotus Sutra also constitutes a pivotal phase in the further development of the concept of skillful means leading to its ethicization in the third but particularly the fourth and final phase. I should make clear that what I am referring to here are not historical developments but logical or conceptual ones, which might have occurred in a range of literary sources in no clear chronological order. What I think we see in certain of the metaphors in the Lotus Sutra is an ambiguity and perhaps the beginning of a slide from skillful means as a teaching device to skillful means as a principle of ethics for bodhisattvas. In the Lotus Sutra, skillful means is a teaching about the nature of the Teaching. However, in the *Vimalakīrti sūtra*—which will serve as an example of the third aspect of the concept—skillful means is also about practice, as something done by bodhisattvas in the course of their daily lives. It governs a bodhisattva's mode of relating to other people, and as such begins to lead them into ethically grey areas. Vimalakīrti, for example, dissembles and pretends to be ill. He visits brothels, drinking houses, gambling dens, and converses with harem girls. Although in his capacity as a layman, Vimalakīrti breaks no precepts, his conduct could be described from the perspective of early Buddhism as sailing close to the wind.

In the fourth phase the line skirted by Vimalakīrti is crossed, and we move out of a grey area into one which in terms of traditional moral norms is unambiguously wrong. Here we find bodhisattvas intentionally breaking the precepts, not just the lesser and minor ones but several of the most serious ones. Examples of things which, according to certain texts, bodhisattvas are allowed to do include killing, stealing, having sexual intercourse, and lying. In these contexts skillful means functions as a kind of trump card which overrides the requirements of ordinary morality and supposedly allows the bodhisattva to transgress with impunity. The *Bodhisattva-bhūmi*, for example, explicitly permits breaches of the first four precepts in certain circumstances in the course of the exercise of skillful means by a bodhisattva, and clearly wishes to develop skillful means into a principle of normative ethics.[18] An even earlier text, the *Upāyakauśalya sūtra*,[19] recounts an episode when the Buddha as the captain of a ship in a previous life killed a bandit in order to save the lives of 500 merchants.[20] Special categories of permitted offenses find their way into a number of Mahayana sources. The most recent I have come across is in the sixteenth century Nyingma treatise on moral conduct entitled *Ascertaining the Three Vows*, published recently by Wisdom.[21] Although for the most part a standard text on vinaya and bodhisattva virtues, this work digresses at one point to claim that the ten evil paths of action (*daśakuśalāḥ-karmapatāḥ*) may be performed by one of pure intention who seeks to benefit sentient beings.

Rarely is an attempt made to offer a serious defense for claims of this kind, and as an ethical theory I think it faces serious problems. Notions of this kind have surfaced from time to time in the Christian tradition but have always been rejected by the mainstream in favor of the view of Saint Paul that "evil must not be done that good may come of it" (Rom 3:8). I do not intend to offer a critique of this inchoate Buddhist ethical theory here but to link up this fourth aspect of the concept of skillful means with my earlier discussion of paternalism in the Lotus Sutra. To do this, let me quote what the Tibetan text just cited says about the third precept:

> It is permitted to commit adultery if a woman or man is suffering tremendously from desire and claiming they will surely die if they do not have such sexual contact. In order to temporarily alleviate their suffering and ultimately lead them to the path of virtue, adultery is permitted as an act of compassion.[22]

The scenario envisaged here verges on the farcical. A bodhisattva confronted with such a request might do better to remind the other party that no one ever died from not having sex, and recommend a cold shower as the most appropriate remedy for the complaint in question. Instead, this precept seems to want to turn bodhisattvas into "hookers for Buddha," with all the deception and manipulation that entails. At this point beneficence has run riot and autonomy is paid scant heed. Rather than respecting the autonomy of the other party, a bodhisattva is encouraged to manipulate his or her new friend sexually and emotionally on the grounds that "a bodhisattva always knows best." There are alternative and probably more constructive ways to deal with the situation described, such as encouraging the person afflicted by desire to sublimate the sexual energy into constructive channels or to use this as an opportunity to practice self-control. If the parties are married it might be a good opportunity for marriage counseling. Rather than explore these options, however, the bodhisattva is encouraged to resort to a devious manipulation which is paternalistic in that it discourages individuals from taking responsibility for themselves and denies them the opportunity to grow up by making their own mistakes and learning from them.

The logical outcome of the evolution of skillful means in this direction is to turn Buddhism into a religion of reincarnating nannies constantly looking for new noses to wipe. To employ a medical analogy once again, bodhisattvas are being encouraged to treat the symptoms rather then the cause of the disease. The causes of suffering are craving and ignorance, but it seems that bodhisattvas are being encouraged in these texts to act as if all that mattered was the alleviation of the symptoms. Suffering, however, is not always pointless, and can often lead to personal growth and spiritual maturity. For these texts, however, pain is the ultimate evil, and accordingly the role of the bodhisattva is to be a social worker who infantilizes his or her clients, running hither and thither with Kleenex and Band-Aids to soothe every ache, pain, and tantrum.

To sum up, I have identified four aspects of skillful means in Buddhist sources. The first refers to the Buddha's personal skill as a teacher and involves no dissembling or deception of any kind. The second aspect is the one we see in the parables in the Lotus Sutra, such as that of the burning house. The text is concerned mainly with the nature and status of the Dharma as a vehicle for communicating the truth, and only addresses ethical questions obliquely, as when it asks and answers in the negative the question whether the Buddha told a lie in chapter two. We see there the germ of the idea of how skillful means could be stretched beyond a concern about teaching the Dharma to a practice engaged in by bodhisattvas. The parables in the Lotus Sutra embody a form of paternalism which may be described as 'weak' insofar as the balance between beneficence and autonomy has not tipped too far in favor of the former. The third aspect of skillful means is seen in the *Vimalakīrti sūtra* where it becomes an aspect of a bodhisattva's conduct, in other words something a bodhisattva does. The fourth and final development is seen in those sources which explicitly authorize the breaking of precepts by bodhisattvas. At this point the concept has become misshapen by being stretched far beyond its original context. Happily, this final development in the evolution of skillful means does not appear to have attained wide acceptance in the Mahayana.[23]

Notes

1. Michael Pye, *Skilful Means: A Concept in Mahayana Buddhism*. London: Duckworth, 1978: 37.
2. Ibid: 37 f.
3. Ibid: 57.
4. Dīgha-Nikāya: iii. 217.
5. Vinaya: iii. 3.
6. Dīgha-Nikāya-Aṭṭhakathā: i. 914.
7. Dīgha-Nikāya: iii. 235; d. iii. 133.
8. In the Hippocratic work *Epidemics*, it is expressed in the form "As to disease make a habit of two things—to help, or at least to do no harm." Quoted in Tom L. Beauchamp and James F. Childress, *Principles of Biomedical Ethics*, third ed. Oxford: Oxford University Press, 1989: 209.
9. Ibid: 212 f.
10. Ibid: 210.
11. Ibid: 214.
12. Ibid: 216 f.
13. Leon Hurvitz, *Scripture of the Lotus Blossom of the Fine Dharma (The Lotus Sūtra)*. New York: Columbia University Press, 1976: 58.
14. Joel Feinberg, "Legal Paternalism." *Canadian Journal of Philosophy* 1 (1971): 105–24.
15. Pye, *Skilful Means*: 123.
16. Ibid: 124.
17. Ibid: 128.
18. See the discussion of this text in chapter six: Damien Keown, *The Nature of Buddhist Ethics*. London: Macmillan, 1992.
19. Tatz states, "Its composition may date from the first century B.C." *The Skill in Means (Upāyakauśalya) Sūtra*. Trans. Mark Tatz. Delhi: Motilal Banarsidass, 1994: 1.
20. The story is narrated in Tatz (1994: 73 ff).
21. Ngari Panchen and Wangyi Gyalpo, *Perfect Conduct: Ascertaining the Three Vows*. Boston: Wisdom Publications, 1996.
22. Ibid: 96.
23. Tatz disagrees, suggesting "The higher ethic wrought by skill in means affects the whole of the Bodhisattva path" (1994: 16). A lot depends, of course, on what one understands by a "bodhisattva." Is it any follower of the Mahayana, or a highly evolved enlightened being? Since the *Upāyakauśalya sūtra* ends by expressly forbidding its novel interpretation of *upāya* to be communicated even to independent Buddhas (Tatz 1994: 87), it would seem to be reserved for those closer to the end of the path than the beginning.

Appropriate Means as the Ethics of the Lotus Sutra

Gene Reeves

In this paper I claim that *upāya* or *hōben* in the Lotus Sutra, contrary to how it has often been translated and understood, is an ethical doctrine, the central tenet of which is that one should not do what is expedient but rather what is good, the good being what will actually help someone else, the doing of which is also known as bodhisattva practice. Further, the doctrine of *hōben* is relativistic. No doctrine, teaching, set of words, mode of practice, etc. can claim absoluteness or finality, as all occur within and are relative to some concrete situation. But some things, doing the right thing in the right situation, can be efficacious, sufficient for salvation.

As for use of "expedients" in translations of *upāya* or *hōben*, in the Lotus Sutra translations Hurvitz uses "expedient devices," Murano "expedients," and Watson "expedient means." In the earlier translation from Sanskrit, Kern used "skillfulness" for the most part, including in the title for the second chapter, but in a footnote he equates this with "able management, diplomacy, *upāya-kauśalya*," and then goes on to say that "Upāya means an expedient," followed by some other silly things (p. 30). Other authorities can be cited. In *Outlines of Mahayana Buddhism* (1907), D. T. Suzuki says, "The term *upāya* literally means expediency," (p. 64) and later, talking about the Lotus Sutra, says that the term "is very difficult to translate into English but literally means 'way,' 'method,' or 'strategy'" (p. 261 footnote) and then, in another footnote, says that *upāya* means "expedient," "stratagem," "device" or "craft" (p. 298). Other, more recent authorities can be cited. Franklin Edgerton's *Buddhist Hybrid Sanskrit Dictionary* (1953) gives "skill in expedients" for *upāya-kauśalya*. Peter N. Gregory, in the glossary of the recent *Inquiry into the Origin of Humanity* gives "expedient means" for *upāya*, and in the entry for the Lotus Sutra says that it is noted for "its teaching of expedient means" (p. 218). It should be clear that the use of "expedient" and its variants for the Lotus Sutra's *upāya* and *hōben* is well established.

What is wrong with "expedient"? Briefly, it is deeply rooted in an ethical frame of reference which is about as diametrically opposed to the ethical perspective of the Lotus Sutra as one can get. The *Random House Unabridged Dictionary* has as its second definition of "expedient": "conducive to advantage or interest, as opposed to right." Moreover, "expediency" is defined as "a regard for what is polite or advantageous rather than what is right or just; a sense of self-interest." Though one could argue that this term does not *have* to carry such freight, the fact of the matter is that it is deeply embedded in a biblical ethics which is essentially deontological because it is rooted in notions of divine commandment and human obedience. In John 11:49–50, for example, we find:

> And one of them, named Caiaphas, being the high priest that year, said to them, "You know nothing at all. Nor do you consider that it is expedient for us, that one man should die for the people, and not that the whole nation perish.

And in several places, in the King James version at least, Saint Paul uses the term "expedient" to mean "profitable" to oneself. The Bible, of course, has had a major impact on what terms mean in English.

Thus, a very basic meaning of "expedient" is an act which is done in spite of principle in order to benefit oneself. It is rooted in an ethics and in a vision of reality in which there is a radical, unbridgeable gap between principles and self-interest. Though they may be internalized, principles are given, by God or Nature, or the metaphysical structure of reality. Principles are lawlike, and thus their disobedience requires just punishment. To do the expedient thing is to ignore or go against what is right in order to gain some selfish benefit.

But this is exactly what, according to the Lotus Sutra, *hōben* cannot be. It is part of the very definition of *hōben* in the Lotus Sutra that it is always for the benefit of someone else. Not in this sutra, or in any other that I know of, is there even a single example of *hōben* in which the doer forsakes some principle for his or her own benefit.

Of course, within a Buddhist utilitarian and teleological ethics the good done for someone else may also benefit the doer. In Christianity one finds notions of an ideal of completely selfless love, *agapé*. To some extent such notions are related to Greek ideas of God as being so perfect and complete that he cannot possibly want or need anything. But from most Buddhist perspectives, certainly from the perspective of the Lotus Sutra, this is a false ideal. In the story of the rich father and poor son, for example, the Buddha-substitute, the rich father, feels that his own life is incomplete so long as the son is away from him.

> "If I could only get my son back and entrust my wealth to him," he thought, "how contented and happy I would be, with no more anxiety!"[1]

So there are at least two things wrong with "expedient" as a translation of *hōben*. On the one hand, use of it presupposes a contrast with principle (law, divine command, etc.) which is not generally applicable in East Asian Buddhism, and on the other hand, it carries negative connotations of action for one's own benefit which are incompatible with the whole thrust of the Louts Sutra.[2]

"Expedient" is not, of course, the only translation of *hōben*. The most extensive, and in my opinion best, study of *upāya* is Michael Pye's *Skilful Means*. But even Pye, after conducting a nearly exhaustive study of the terms *upāya*, *upāya-kauśalya*, and *fang pien*, and defending "skilful means" as the best translation for these terms, says, "Of course translations of Mahayana texts in Buddhist Hybrid Sanskrit may want to follow the vocabulary more closely and use simply 'means' or 'expedient' for *upāya*."[3]

I have no problem with "skillful means" as a translation of *upāya/hōben*. It might even be the best overall translation for Buddhist texts in general. But I am not persuaded that it is the best possible way to understand the meaning and thrust of the term *hōben* of the Lotus Sutra.

Hōben as Skillful and Appropriate

It is true that in all of the stories in which *hōben* is demonstrated, some skill is involved, sometimes even a special skill. The best illustration of a special skill being involved is a story, from which the chapter gets its title, about a physician who goes to the Himalayas to collect four special herbs to use in special ways in order to cure a man who has been blind from birth. It is interesting that this story is not included in the Chinese version[4] of the Lotus Sutra.

Skill is involved in most of these stories. But what kind of skill? A father gets his children out of a burning house by promising them a reward.[5] Another father gets his children to take an antidote for poison by pretending to be dead. Still another father guides his unambitious son toward greater and greater responsibility. A tour guide conjures up a phantom city in order to give people a needed resting place during a hard journey. A man sews a jewel into the garment of his poor friend. A very powerful king holds back an extraordinarily precious and unique jewel which he kept in the topknot of his hair until he sees a soldier of great merit. None of these acts is especially skillful. They are clever, perhaps, but not especially skillful, at least in the sense of requiring some special skill.[6] And while some of the characters performing these acts are stand-ins for the Buddha, it is not at all evident that all are. Some think, as does Michael Pye, that it is of prime significance that buddhas use skillful means. And, indeed, it is very often the case in Lotus Sutra stories that it is the Buddha or Buddha stand-in who uses appropriate means. But I do not think teaching us about buddhas is what is primary for the Lotus Sutra. Rather, bodhisattva practice and therefore the practice of appropriate means is intended primarily for us, the readers. Remember too that the chief example of a doctrine which is a skillful means is the doctrine or story of the Buddha's entry into nirvana—and it is a doctrine or story which, from the perspective of the Lotus Sutra, has misled lots of people into thinking that the Buddha is no more.

What we are told repeatedly in the sutra is not that these acts are skillful, though they may be, but that they are appropriate, appropriate to the condition of the hearers. It is because people are different and their situations are different that the buddhas, as the rain nourishes the great variety of plants according to their different needs, feed the Dharma according to what is needed. One could argue, of course, that knowing that an appropriate thing is needed and being able to perceive the situation well enough to figure out an appropriate action is itself skillful. And so it is. But it is nevertheless the case that what is emphasized is not so much the skill as it is the appropriateness. This is why I think "appropriate means" is the best translation for *hōben* in the Lotus Sutra.

What is it that makes something appropriate? At the end of the story of the burning house, the Buddha asks Śāriputra whether the father has lied or not, and Śāriputra responds that the father had not lied, and would not have lied had he given the children even very tiny carriages. Why? Simply because the device worked. The children got out of the house in time to save their lives.

Two things are relevant here: the device worked, and it worked at saving lives.

Hōben as Practical

Apparently, some people think that Buddhist ethics is primarily a matter of what is inside oneself; that it is primarily a matter of consciousness and compassion. But there is hardly a hint of this in the Lotus Sutra. The ideal, in the Lotus Sutra too, is a combination of wisdom or insight, compassion, and practice. The entrance to the Great Sacred Hall at the headquarters of Risshō Kōsei-kai in Tokyo, for example, is dominated by huge pictures of three bodhisattvas: Mañjuśrī, Maitreya, and Samanta-bhadra, representing wisdom, compassion, and practice, and the three parts of the Lotus Sutra in which these three are thought to be promi-nent. In the Lotus Sutra itself and in Lotus teaching, the three are interde-pendent and perhaps in one sense equally important. It can, for example, be said that practice can lead to enhanced wisdom and compassion. But it is clear that the flow has to be primarily the other way, toward practice as a consequence of wisdom and compassion. Thus, in contemporary jar-gon, the Lotus Sutra is very results-oriented. Of course, it is important that the father of the children in the burning house and the father of the poor son are concerned about their offspring and want to save them, and it is important that they are smart enough to figure out a way to save them, but it is most important that they are successful in saving the chil-dren.

The story of Devadatta is very instructive here. Its message is that even our enemies, regardless of their intentions, can be bodhisattvas for us if we regard them as such. In this sutra, Devadatta, the embodiment of evil in so much Buddhist literature outside of the Lotus Sutra, is thanked by the Buddha for being helpful. "Thanks to my good friend Devadatta, I was able to develop fully the six *pāramitās*, with pity, compassion, joy, equanimity," etc. The Buddha learned from his experiences with Devadatta, making Devadatta a bodhisattva, but we are not told that this was in any way a function of what Devadatta himself intended. Good intentions may be good in their own right, but they are not what is all important or even most important in a bodhisattva. What is more im-portant is effectiveness, effectiveness in leading others to the Buddha-way, and thus to their salvation.

It is their "only" salvation because outside of the Buddha-way there is, and can be, no other way. If an act is salvific it is good, and if it is good it is bodhisattva practice, and if it is bodhisattva practice it is included in the Buddha-way. Whatever else it is, the Buddha-way is good and in-cludes everything good, that is, everything that leads to salvation.

To say that an act has good consequences is not, however, to say that it is necessarily good in every respect. An act of good consequences may stem from evil motives. The consequence does not make the motive good. The fact that Devadatta became a bodhisattva for the Buddha does not mean that Devadatta's motives are thereby somehow transformed from evil to good. The Lotus Sutra does emphasize consequences and the practice of the bodhisattva-way for the purpose of saving living beings. But it also makes repeated reference to the importance of planting good roots—supporting the view that good deeds tend to lead to good ends. In this sense the ethics of the Lotus Sutra is not purely teleological.

Salvation as the Buddha-way

There is ample ambiguity in the Lotus Sutra about the nature of salvation. We are told that the Buddha has vowed to save all the living. The nature of that state, variously termed buddhahood, supreme enlightenment, etc., is not unambiguously clear, however. But if we look at the stories which present themselves as being about salvation, the matter is not, or at least not always,[7] so complicated. Lives are saved. In some cases they are saved from fire or poison, literally from death. In other cases, they are saved from a mean existence, from poverty and from an attitude which is complacent about poverty. In all cases, what is involved is a failure to achieve one's potential to be a bodhisattva and a buddha.

What does it mean to be a buddha?

There are obviously many ways of reading the Lotus Sutra, including, I suppose, several legitimate ways, by which I mean ways reasonably consistent with or based upon the text itself. Without trying to argue for such an interpretation here, I will simply share with you that I see the text as being primarily soteriological. That is, I think its main purpose is not to teach Buddhist doctrines or refute other interpretations or forms of Buddhism, but to incline the reader's heart, and especially behavior, in a certain way. There are, for example, numberless claims in the sutra to the effect that everyone, be they poor, not very bright, female, even evil, absolutely everyone without exception is destined to become a buddha. I take it that this is not just a proto-buddha-nature doctrine, though it is that, and not just a metaphysical assumption, though it does express an underlying metaphysics. What is intended primarily, I think, is that you and I understand that we can become Buddha-like because we have that capacity already within us simply by virtue of being alive. This capacity or potential is in everyone. It does not have to be earned and it cannot be taken away. But it does need to be developed.

The Buddha-way as Bodhisattva Practice

The way in which you and I can develop our buddha-nature is by following the Buddha-way, doing what buddhas have always done, namely, following the way of bodhisattva practice. It is absolutely central to the Lotus Sutra, I think, that Śākyamuni Buddha is, first of all, a bodhisattva. We are told that he has been doing bodhisattva practice, helping and leading others, for innumerable *kalpas*. Whenever the enormously long life of the Buddha is described, it is not meditation that he has been doing, at least not primarily, but teaching and leading and changing others, thus turning them into bodhisattvas.

Because all the living have various natures, various desires, various activities, various ideas and ways of making distinctions, and because I wanted to lead them to put down roots of goodness, I have used a variety of explanations, parables, and words and preach various teachings. Thus I have never for a moment neglected the Buddha's work.

Thus it is, since I became Buddha a very long time has passed, a lifetime of unquantifiable *asaṃkhyeya kalpas*, of forever existing and never entering extinction. Good children, the lifetime which I have acquired pursuing the bodhisattva-way is not even finished yet, but will be twice the number of *kalpas* already passed. [8]

But the Buddha and those with the title of bodhisattva are not the only bodhisattvas. *Śrāvakas* are also bodhisattvas. That is why there are plenty of them in every paradise, or paradiselike Buddha-land described in the Lotus Sutra. Most *śrāvakas*, of course, don't know they are bodhisattvas, but they are nonetheless.

What you are practicing
[the Buddha says to the disciple Kāśyapa]
Is the bodhisattva-way.
As you gradually practice and learn,
Every one of you should become a buddha.[9]

And, of course, most importantly, you and I are bodhisattvas. No matter how tiny our understanding or merit, no matter how trivial our practice, we are, to some extent, perhaps tiny, already bodhisattvas. And we are called to grow in bodhisattvahood by leading others to realize that potential in themselves.

This is why, I think, so many stories about bodhisattvas are taken up in the latter part of the Lotus Sutra, no doubt added later. These stories round out, so to speak, the teaching of *hōben* with which the sutra begins. The term *hōben* is used very little in these chapters because by the time we get to them we should understand that *hōben* is what bodhisattvas do.

In the Lotus Sutra it is not, as in some texts, just advanced or seventh-stage bodhisattvas who use *hōben*. Though there are frequent references to the stage of nonregression in the Lotus Sutra, there are none at all to the ten-stage bodhisattva doctrine found, for example, in the Avataṃsaka Sutra.

While the doctrine of *hōben* is primarily what makes Lotus Sutra ethics teleological, the understanding of bodhisattva practice as doing the work of the Buddha to save all the living is also teleological. If a bodhisattva was only trying to improve his or her own character as an end in itself, he or she would not be a bodhisattva, as the very meaning of "bodhisattva" in the Lotus Sutra is one who effectively contributes to the salvation of others. Certainly that practice should be guided by rules and principles, but it must finally be judged by the results.

Bodhisattvas as Role Models

I think there can be no question but what many, at least, of the stories about bodhisattvas are there to provide role models for human beings. They play a role in the ever-present tension between what already is and what is yet to be. To the extent that we have even lifted a single finger to point to the truth, we are already bodhisattvas. But how much more so those who faithfully follow the Lotus Sutra, that is, devote their lives to bodhisattva practice. And to encourage us in that direction there are stories of wonderful bodhisattvas.

Yes, people do pray to Kwan-yin for help, and Kwan-yin takes on whatever form is needed to be helpful. But while that story may present the hope of divine blessing, it is there primarily to show us what we should be. If Kwan-yin has a thousand arms with a thousand different skills with which to help others, we too need to develop a thousand skills with which to help others.

Bodhisattva Ethics

What, then, does it mean to be a bodhisattva? Basically, in the Lotus Sutra it means using appropriate means to help others. And that finally, for the Lotus Sutra, is what Buddhism itself is. It is an enormous variety of means developed to help people live more fulfilling lives, which can be understood as lives lived in the light of their interdependence. This is what most of the stories are about: someone—father-figure/buddha, or friend/buddha, or guide/buddha—helping someone else gain more responsibility for their own lives.

> Even if you search in all directions,
> There are no other vehicles,
> Except the appropriate means preached by the Buddha.[10]

Thus, the notion of appropriate means is at once both a description of what Buddhism is, or what Buddhist practice primarily is, and a prescription for what our lives should become. The Lotus Sutra, accordingly, is a prescription of a medicine or religious method for us—and, therefore, at once both extremely imaginative and extremely practical.

It is in this sense that appropriate means is an ethical teaching, a teaching about how we should behave in order to contribute to the good. It is prescriptive not in the sense of a precept or commandment, but in the sense of urging us, for the sake of both our own salvation and that of others, to be intelligent, imaginative, even clever in finding ways to be helpful.

Hōben as Provisional

Ways of being helpful are not, at least not primarily, grounded in principles. The Lotus Sutra has very little to say about precepts, though it does not reject them and in chapter 14 (Carefree Practice) the Buddha provides four sets of prescriptions which bodhisattvas should follow, one having to do primarily with outward behavior, one with speech, one with attitudes, and one with intentions. But these are to be understood, I think, not as commandments but more like counsel or rules of thumb. Principles, at least in the strongest sense, are eternal, God-given, or at least implanted permanently in the nature of things. The hōben of the Lotus Sutra, in contrast, are provisional. Once used, they may no longer be useful, precisely because they were appropriate for some concrete situation. The children will not return to the burning house to be saved again. Once his sons have drunk the antidote to the poison, their father need not again tell them that he has died. This is because these stories involve discoveries, made rapidly or gradually. And once something has been seen or discovered, it cannot be unseen or undiscovered, though it might, of course, be rediscovered or be discovered again independently. So the means by which it is discovered is always provisional, viable in some point in time. Once the father has guided his son to maturity, he can die in peace, no longer needed. Once a raft has been used to cross over to the other shore, we no longer need the raft and we would be seriously burdened by trying to take it with us over land.[11]

In such provisionality there is a scriptural basis, not so much for a critique of the tradition, but for the continuing development, the continued flowering of the Dharma. And this is why the Lotus Sutra provided an important basis for the transformation of Buddhism in a Chinese context. From the perspective of the Lotus Sutra the transformation of Avalokiteśvara into Kwan-yin is not a corruption of Buddhism but a flowering.

The story of the conjured city is very instructive here. It is about nirvana, certainly one of the central doctrines of traditional Buddhism. And what does this story say about nirvana? Basically it says that the teaching of nirvana was a teaching device to enable people to get a bit of rest before continuing on the Buddha-way, like an elegant rest area on a highway. The Buddha didn't go away into some extinction. There is no place and no time where the Buddha is not, or where he is not becoming enlightened. The Buddha's entry into nirvana, we are told, is part of a story, used to get people to be more responsible for working out their own salvation.

The Lotus Sutra tells us in many places that it is new, that people who hear and receive it gain something unprecedented, something they never had before. But the teaching of appropriate means is not so much a new teaching as it is a new way of understanding all Buddhist teachings. Notice that the Lotus Sutra does not propose throwing away the term "nirvana" or the story of the Buddha's nirvana. Rather it puts nirvana in a new light. It relativizes it, making it subordinate to the larger purpose of becoming a buddha, i.e., of doing bodhisattva practice.

The Embodied Dharma

As I understand *hōben* in the Lotus Sutra, it would be a serious mistake to think that *hōben* are lesser teachings which can now be replaced by some higher teaching.[12] All appropriate and effective teachings are *hōben*, in endless variety. There is, of course, a larger purpose which they serve; they are, after all, means not ends; but the encompassing purpose or truth which they serve is not another teaching. It is a Dharma that can only be found embodied in concrete teachings, including actions which are instructive, just as the Buddha can only be found embodied—in Śākyamuni, and in you and me.

One of the ways, I think, in which the Lotus Sutra and its teaching of *hōben* is ethical is by being radically world-affirming. By this I mean simply that it is this *sahā* world which is Śākyamuni Buddha's world. It is in this world that he is a bodhisattva and encourages us to be bodhisattvas.[13] This world is our home, and it is the home of Śākyamuni Buddha, precisely because he is embodied, not only as the historical Buddha, but as the buddha-nature in all things. Thus, things, ordinary things, including ourselves and our neighbors, are not primarily to be seen as empty, though they are; not primarily to be seen as phenomenal, though they are; not primarily to be seen as illusions, though in one sense they are; not primarily to be seen as evil even though they may be in part. It is in *dharmas* (things/"conventional" existence) that the Dharma is. It is in transient, changing things that the Buddha is.[14] They are, therefore, to be treated with as much insight and compassion and respect as we can muster.

It is perhaps something of an irony that the sutra which affirms a cosmic Śākyamuni Buddha, one who is in every world and every time, does so not to reject the historical Śākyamuni or the temporal world, but precisely to affirm their supreme importance.[15] And their importance is nothing more or less than that this world is where we, having been taught by the historical Buddha, are called to embody the life of the Buddha in our acts and lives. This is why a part of the everyday liturgy of Risshō Kōsei-kai is the *dōjō-kan*: "Know that this place is where the Buddha attained perfect enlightenment. In this and all places the buddhas accomplish perfect enlightenment. . . ."[16]

It is relevant in this connection to notice that there is not much use of the notion of emptiness (*śūnya* or *śūnyatā*) in the Lotus Sutra. Of course, all things are empty. But it is because they are empty that there is space, so to speak, for the development of one's buddha-nature. If things were substantial, they could not truly grow or change. But because they are without substantiality, they can be influenced by and have influence on others. Undue emphasis on emptiness is rejected because it can easily become a kind of nihilism in which nothing matters. In the Lotus Sutra everything matters. The Buddha works to save all beings. Even the poor Bodhisattva Never Disrespectful, who goes around telling everyone that they are to become buddhas, though initially not very successful, eventually "converted a multitude of a thousand, ten thousand, millions, enabling them to live in the state of supreme enlightenment."[17] And this is to say nothing of the fact that he later became the Buddha Śākyamuni!

In one sense, I suppose, the Lotus Sutra does not provide an ethics at all. It does not tell us what to do in any particular situation. It suggests that if we devote ourselves to bodhisattva practice; take refuge as appropriate in the Buddha, the Dharma, and the Sangha; thus entering the Buddha-way; we will find resources within ourselves and in others for dealing creatively with our ethical issues, for working, for example, for world peace, for a better society, for greater cooperation among peoples of different cultural and religious traditions. The sutra does not say that this way will ever be easy. But it does claim that in it is to be found great joy.

Notes

1. Cf. Watson, 82. Here and elsewhere in this paper quotations from the Lotus Sutra are my own translations, based primarily on Yukio Sakamoto and Yutaka Iwamoto, *Hokekyō*, 3 vols. (Iwanami, 1989). For convenience, page references are given to *The Lotus Sutra*, translated by Burton Watson (Columbia University Press, 1993).
2. Unfortunately, for my purposes at least, both the Chinese *fang pien* and the Japanese *hōben* can have, especially outside of Buddhism, connotations of convenient for oneself. Perhaps that is a source of the "expedient" translations.

3. Michael Pye, *Skilful Means: A Concept in Mahayana Buddhism.* (London: Duckworth, 1978), 14. There would be ample justification for translating *upāya* as "means," in which case *upāya-kauśalya* would be something like "skill in means." But, while this distinction apparently is important in the Sanskrit text, there is no comparable distinction in Kumārajīva's translation into Chinese.

4. While everyone says that there are other translations from Sanskrit to Chinese, especially that of Dharmarakṣa, I have never actually seen one or compared one with the translation of Kumārajīva, on which, so far as I know, all Japanese versions and all English translations are based, save Kern's. In any case, the influence of Kumārajīva's translation has been so pervasive in East Asia that, from a historical point of view, it is the basic locus of what we call the Lotus Sutra. So far as I am concerned, Kumārajīva's translation is *the* Chinese version, i.e., the only Chinese version we need be concerned about.

5. It is not exactly pertinent here, but I do want to point out that, while there are stories in the Lotus Sutra where it can fairly be said that deception is advocated as *hōben*, this is not the case in the story of the burning house, which is the prime example of *hōben*, the story the Buddha uses to explain *hōben*. Usually, I think, misunderstanding is simply a matter of not paying enough attention to what the text actually says. For example, in an unpublished paper, one scholar says that the father broke his promise by only giving the children one vehicle after promising them three, and that this is because he only had one vehicle to give. Of course, the text plainly says that he gave them much more than he had promised because he realized that his wealth was so great he could afford to be more generous. And though the text is not entirely unambiguous on this, the easiest way to read it is that he gave each of them a great vehicle. It clearly does say that the father has countless numbers of such great vehicles. Michael Pye even retells the story in such a way that the father lies by telling the children that the carts they want are waiting for them outside when in fact they are nowhere to be seen (op. cit., 37). The text, on the other hand, does not say that there were no small carriages. Rather, the overjoyed father, reflecting on his great wealth, thinks it would be unfair to give the children small and inferior carts. Someone else, I'm not sure who, to support his view that the story advocates deception, once argued that if I, as a university dean, were to offer him a position for $40,000 and then, after he arrived, told him that since we had just received a large grant and would pay him $140,000 instead, I would be guilty of deception! On any fair reading of the text itself, there are no grounds for saying that this story advocates deception.

6. There are, of course, plenty of stories in the later chapters in which special, even magical, skills are required: assembled buddhas display their divine powers by extending their tongues up to the heaven of Brahma and emitting a magnificent, many-colored light which illuminated the entire universe from the pores of their bodies; the Bodhisattva Medicine King rides a platform of seven treasures into the sky to pay tribute to the Buddha who was living there; Gadgadasvara (Wonderful-Voice) Bodhisattva made eighty-four thousand gold and silver lotus flowers and other valuables appear not far from where Śākyamuni Buddha was sitting on Mount Gṛdhrakūta and later went

to the *sahā* world on a flying platform of seven treasures; the sons of King Śubhavyūha (Wonderfully Adorned) use a variety of wonders in the sky in order to purify their father's mind and enable him to understand the Dharma and practice the Buddha-way; the Bodhisattva Samantabhadra rides around in the sky on his six-tusked white elephant to protect anyone who keeps the sutra in the five hundred years after the Buddha's extinction.

7. One complication for my interpretation is the very important story of the Nāga princess in chapter 12. Except for the fact that she has been an excellent teacher and "carried out all of the practices of a bodhisattva in an instant," there is not much hint of her being a bodhisattva. It's precisely for this reason that the Bodhisattva Accumulated Wisdom (Prajñākūṭa) has great trouble accepting the girl as a candidate for buddhahood.

8. Cf. Watson, 226–27.

9. Cf. Watson, 106.

10. Cf. Watson, 71. This is why I think Pye is quite correct in insisting that "'Buddhism,' as a specific religion identifiable in human history, is a skilful means." Op. cit., 5. Or "Almost anything in the whole range of Buddhist teaching and practice can be described as *fang-pien* or skilful means." Op. cit., 36

11. But it is never the case, as Pye claims, that we are told to turn around and destroy the raft. "The idea [of skillful means] entails that every item of Buddhist communication has incorporated within it the requirement that it should eventually be dismantled." Op. cit., 130.

12. I am well aware of the fact that many have read the Lotus Sutra through the eyes of Nāgārjuna. It seems quite clear that T'ien-t'ai Chih-i did this to some extent. (See Paul L. Swanson, *Foundations of T'ien-T'ai Philosophy: The Flowering of the Two Truths Theory in Chinese Buddhism*, Asian Humanities Press, 1989.) It is also the case that there are a few, but only a few, passages in the Lotus Sutra which can be cited to support such a reading. Though this is not the place to argue for it, I think there is an abundance of evidence, taking the sutra as a whole, that its view is much more pluralistic than this. In its view there are many, many truths, all of which serve, more or less well or badly, the one purpose of leading people to salvation. But that one purpose is not another truth, not a different kind of truth, and certainly not a higher form of truth. Its superiority lies solely in its great inclusiveness, not as some kind of higher truth or reality, but as the Dharma which is always and everywhere embodied in many concrete teachings, practices, and acts. So far as I can tell, Nāgārjuna virtually never uses the term *upāya*. For him there are two kinds of truth: relative truth (*saṃvṛti-satya*) on the one hand and ultimate truth (*paramārtha-satya*) on the other. The Chinese equivalent of this ultimate truth, *chen ti* (*shintai* in Japanese pronunciation), does not appear anywere in the Lotus Sutra, I think.

13. Elsewhere I have tried to show that the Lotus Sutra is almost entirely indifferent to cosmololgy as such, but uses traditional Buddhist cosmology to elevate Śākyamuni Buddha to cosmic status and making him central to the entire cosmos, which in turn elevates the status of his *sahā* world that is the world in which we, along with all of his bodhisattvas, are called upon to do his work

of saving the living. Thus, in this sutra, even cosmology serves a soteriological and, in that sense, ethical purpose. Our acts are cosmic in scope because they are in the world of the Śākyamuni Buddha who is cosmically influential.

One wonders whether it was the Lotus Sutra which Kenneth Inada had in mind when he wrote: "Be it said once and for all that Buddhist philosophy cannot admit or submit to any ideas with cosmic dimensions. If such were ever the case, then it would be . . . [a] certain outlandish and corrupted form of Buddhism which in all eventuality would have little or no real meaning for those who earnestly pursue the true basic doctrines." (*Nāgārjuna*, Sri Satguru Publications, 1993, 11)

14. Though he fails to understand why "emptiness" does not have a prominent role in the Lotus Sutra, this kind of affirmation of the concrete is well described by William LaFleur in a discussion of medieval Japanese poets in "Symbol and Yūgen: Shunzei's Use of Tendai Buddhism" in *The Karma of Words: Buddhism and the Literary Arts in Medieval Japan* (University of California Press, 1983). This can also be seen very clearly in the storyteller and poet Kenji Miyazawa. See, for example, *A Future of Ice: Poems and Stories of a Japanese Buddhist: Miyazawa Kenji,* translated by Hiroaki Sato (North Point Press, 1989).

15. Part of what world affirmation involves in the Lotus Sutra is, as Nichiren correctly saw, what we might call "taking time and history seriously." See "The Selection of the Time" in *The Major Writings of Nichiren Daishonin,* Vol. 3 (Nichiren Shōshū International Center, 1985) 79ff. or in *Selected Writings of Nichiren,* Philip B. Yampolsky, ed. (Columbia University Press, 1990), 181ff.

16. *Kyōden: Sutra Readings* (Risshō Kōsei-kai, 1994) 9.

17. Cf. Watson, 268.

6. Particular Issues

A Buddhist Approach to the Ecological Crisis: The Historical Consciousness in Nichiren

Michio T. Shinozaki

Introduction

In this paper, my intention is not to present a Buddhist view of the modern ecological crisis, but rather to find the possibility of a new Buddhist approach to the ecological crisis, one which is not naturalistic, but rather involves a historical consciousness of the crisis.

In terms of the relationship between humans, nature, and history, there are at least two Buddhist approaches to thinking about the ecological crisis. One is to claim that the ecological crisis was caused by anthropocentric ways of thinking and acting deeply rooted in the Judeo-Christian tradition's understanding of nature: humans are encouraged to dominate nature. Thus, some Buddhists believe that a Buddhist approach can offer a remedy for solving the ecological crisis. The solution can be found, they say, in the Buddhist understanding of the relationship between nature and humans. This remedy is shared by the so-called Oriental religions in general, in that humans become aware of an original oneness with nature. It is a kind of naturalism which admires the beauty of nature and is animistic. Nature is the ideal, in the process of eternal return, and humans are part of this rhythm. This approach basically involves the correction of the separation of nature and humans by affirming the anti-Westernizing notions of animism and polytheism or pantheism against absolute monotheism.

The idea of ecological crisis presupposes the Judeo-Christian view of linear and irreversible development to the end (*telos*) of time. In contrast, in one Buddhist view of history there is a cyclic movement of history in which historical events are part of natural phenomenal change. Even

395

though it is purposeless, humans are a part of this cosmological and phenomenal movement. Such a view lacks the historicality of human beings
and events and the idea of development. There is an absence of historical
consciousness.

The other Buddhist approach is based on historical consciousness from a
Buddhist perspective. Even though they appreciate the cosmological view
of the eternal return in cosmic time, historical consciousness is deeply embedded in modern Buddhists. If Buddhists recover Nichiren's awareness
of history, they will become more effective in communicating Buddhist
faith to modern people. In order to think about the modern ecological
crisis, we have to examine what modern ways of thinking presuppose.
Gordon Kaufman and others claim that the notions of science and ecological crisis clearly presuppose a unidirectional movement of time.[1] In
this sense, Buddhists need to scrutinize and reassess the Buddhist view
of the cyclic movement of history in its relation to the ecological crisis. In
order to do this, we find a Buddhist notion of "the unidirectional movement of time," or more specifically, of "historicocultural development"
in the thought of Nichiren (1222–82), the Kamakura period founder of
the Nichiren sect.

1. THE NATURALISTIC APPROACH TO THE ECOLOGICAL CRISIS

Some Buddhists think that one of the most important notions of ecological consciousness is the affirmation of eternal return. There are several
reasons for this. Modern technological advancement has created a lot of
so-called dead (polluted) materials which resist the natural cycle-recycle
process. And modern science and technology never cease, constantly
moving forward, and not necessarily with a goal (*telos*). Thus, naturalists
think that humans are part of a nature which has the characteristic of
eternal return. This idea of eternal return is the opposite of viewing time
as a linear process with a definite beginning and end, as in the traditional
Judeo-Christian understanding of history.

Let me introduce some Buddhist interpretations of history which are
related to consciousness of ecology and evolution.

By assimilating Nieztsche's notion of the eternal return of the same,
Takeshi Umehara maintains that one of the most important characteristics of Japanese culture is the recognition of all living beings as the same
and of their eternal cycling between life and death.

One of the most famous and beloved poets, Bashō, made his home
traveling in Japan. His travel account, the *Oku no Hosomichi* (The Narrow
Road to the Deep North), begins:

The months and days are the travellers of eternity. The years that come and go are also voyagers. Those who float away their lives on boats or who grow old leading horses are forever journeying, and their home is wherever their travels take them.[2]

This poem shows the eternal cyclic nature of life and death for all living beings.

Japanese religious tradition has seen *shizen* (nature) as the "rhythm" of the great life of nature, not in the sense of the regularity of law, but rather as in transience. Yet, according to Umehara, this rhythm is seen as an eternal cycling between life and death for all living beings. Bashō sees that humans are the same as the sun (days) and the moon (months), grass and trees, in such a way that they continue to travel a life of life and death.[3]

A fundamental Buddhist view of the world is that everything in this universe is interrelated and changing. The Buddhist vision affirms that all existence, including human and nonhuman, animate and inanimate, is inevitably and mutually related or dependent. In Japanese Tendai Original Enlightenment Thought this came to be understood as *sansen sōmoku shikkai jōbutsu* (mountains and rivers, grasses and trees, have the buddha-nature). Not only human and other living beings, but all beings, sentient and nonsentient, have the buddha-nature. Among them there is no division. They are authentically the same.

And there is the idea of incessant cycling between this world and the other world, sometimes referred to as the afterlife. There is a continuity between this world and the other world. This eternal return of life and death is also seen in the food chain, and in material circulation in nature. Umehara's point, I think, is that rediscovery of the importance of the eternal return of life and death is for the sake of the coexistence of humans and nature.

Takurō Kishine interprets the Buddhist idea of transmigration from the perspective of a cosmological view in the context of the ecology issue. Transmigration can be understood as a cyclical system of material and energy. The nonorganic environment, which is the ecological system of nonliving beings, is the world of death. On the other hand, the organic environment, which is the system of living beings, is the world of life. Within this system of living beings are humans, animals, plants, and microorganisms. A cyclical system between material and energy can be seen in relation to the world of life and the world of death (the system of nonliving beings).[4] Therefore, the ecological system is a transmigration between the worlds of life and of death. It is the rhythm of life and death.

The Lotus Sutra can be interpreted in this naturalistic way. Within this approach, human desires must be restricted and controlled, and even purified. With few desires and/or purified desires, humans can become attuned to the rhythm of nature. The five precepts point to the right control of human desires. The first four, not-killing, not-stealing, not-committing-adultery, and not-telling-lies, signify respectively control of violence, economy, sex, and knowledge, the four different kinds of eros. And the final precept, not-using-intoxicants, signifies the root of the other four, control of narcissistic self-assertion (self-toxication).[5] This narcissistic self-assertion can be understood as a human-centered "will to grow" continually through scientific and technological exploitation of nature and other living beings. Thus, in order to regulate the human "will to grow," humans keep their desires quiet and minimized. Another phrase from the Lotus Sutra—"the six organs of the body are purified and free from any attachment"—also indicates the control of human desires. Chapter 28 says, "Such will be content with few desires and able to do the works of [the Bodhisattva] Universal Virtue."[6] This encourages people to control human desires and to reduce them.

1.2. A Possibility of Poetic Power

Let us critically evaluate this naturalistic approach. First of all, such a "no-thinking" approach does not think about ecological crisis. I will quote one such criticism by Shirō Matsumoto.

> Let us not forget, either, that the ecological movements of today were not generated by Eastern naturalism. They were initiated by Westerners, and founded on the traditions of rationalism and respect for human rights. It is simply not logically possible to derive the environmental movement and environmental ethics from an Eastern naturalism expressed in such phrases as "mountains, rivers, plants, and trees are all enlightened." Such "naturalism" leads nowhere but to the "natural state of doing nothing." It does not direct us to think or actively to seek remedies to our problems. In order to acknowledge the "wrongs" brought about by destruction of the natural world and to right these wrongs by changing our way of living, we need to think and to act. But it is this very thinking and acting that is totally rejected in the "no-thinking" and "no-action" of Eastern naturalist philosophy.[7]

With the same line of argument Professor Masao Abe is critical of the lack of approach to modern scientific and historicocultural problems in Zen's nondualistic thinking, which has the danger of falling into a "not thinking." He says, "That Zen today lacks the clue to cope with the problems of modern science, as well as individual, social, and international ethical questions, etc., may be thought partially to be based on this [nondualistic thinking]."[8]

There is at least one way in which nondualistic thinking may have the power to impact ecological problems in this scientific and technological world. Heidegger sees that technological and scientific thinking as a "calculative thinking" has the structure of the will to power. This thinking cannot provide the fundamental ground for human existence, so this thinking is groundless in the sense that it cannot ground itself. In other words, within a certain frame of reference or area in which this thinking is made secure, it can be "calculative." In this process of being secure within certain domains, science and technology never stop, but continue to advance without a purpose. Our way of thinking in this modern world is always and already embedded in this "calculative thinking," so even if we have to construct a new approach to the ecological crisis we cannot escape from this "calculative thinking" which is inseparably embedded in the concatenation of this dualistic, technological, scientific thinking.

The serious issue is whether possibilities can be found for religious and ethical thinking under the domination of calculative thinking, that is, under the domination of dualistic, technological, scientific thinking. In this context, the power of nondualistic thinking, which can be symbolized by poetic thinking and acting, is plausible. Such nondualistic thinking may not be useful thinking, but it may be provocative, and meaningful for the existence for humans. When we look at the powers of poets, artists, and religious saints, they can be seen as the forest dwellers of the modern technological world. They can heal the nihilism created by the scientific and technological worldview, a world in which we can no longer see any goals of technological advancement.

1.3. Buddhist Cosmology and Lack of Historical Awareness

Now let us return to the critique of Buddhist naturalism. Both Abe and Matsumoto criticize Buddhist naturalism, but they do not offer any constructive ideas for developing ecological movements or ethics. In the face of the ecological crisis, certainly Buddhist naturalistic and nonself thinking is limited. If Japanese Buddhists are satisfied simply with a proposal that if humans can recover the oneness of nature and humans, then the ecological crisis we are facing now can be solved, it is reasonable to surmise that they are naive and do not think through to the essence and the reality of science and technology in this modern world. Japanese Buddhists should also realize that Japan is one of the most highly industrialized nations and is suffering as a result of the ecological crisis. They cannot be blind to the fact that they are deeply and inevitably situated in this modern technological world.

In the Buddhist naturalistic understanding of it, history is a cosmological rather than a historicocultural process. Buddhist cosmological history involves a cyclical process of increase and decrease within the universe. "The universe, with its multiple worlds and variety of living beings, eternally repeats a cycle of fourfold change," such as long periods of dissolution, nothingness, creation, and duration.[9] This is understandable if we look at cosmological time, which goes beyond the time of individuals and human life on this planet. Yet, in relation to ecological problems which humans have created in human history, it is neither useful nor creative. Buddhist naturalists ignore the historicocultural process of humans. It is commonly said that Buddhists have not taken the historicocultural world seriously into account, especially with respect to the present world of science and technology. Theravada Buddhism has a tendency to move away from worldly things and Mahayana Buddhism, especially Zen, focuses on enlightenment, avoiding the dualistic world, the world in which we humans face an ecological crisis.

Buddhist cosmology can be understood scientifically, but we have to know that after scientific cosmology was accepted among the people, Buddhists claimed that science and Buddhism were not contradictory. But modern science and technology have not emerged in the Buddhist tradition. Instead of thinking about the realities of the technological world, many New Age Buddhists are naively proud of the compatibility of science and technology with the Buddhist Dharma. For example, Akira Sadakata concludes his book, *Buddhist Cosmology*, talking about the relation of Buddhist cosmology to modern scientific ideas:

> There are a surprising number of similarities between Buddhist Cosmology and modern science. We have seen how Buddhism regards the world as a plurality, coming into being and then disintegrating over a long period of time, a process which continues infinitely into the past and the future. Numbers concerning space and time increase in geometric ratio, and the field of vision concerning the universe, in terms of the very small and the very large, expands virtually to infinity. If we remove the graphic, the dogmatic, and the mythological from the expressions of Buddhist cosmologists, we are left with a series of concepts that resemble in no small way the conclusions of modern science. We may include here ideas such as the solar and galactic systems, the birth and extinction of nebulae, the birth of the heavenly bodies from cosmic dust, and the concept of thousands

and billions of light years. If we translate the words of two thousand years ago into our modern tongue, it becomes apparent that Buddhist and modern cosmology are not all that far apart.[10]

In this sense, Buddhist cosmology and science are not contradictory. "Buddhist cosmology skillfully combines the scientific and the religious, unremittingly concerned with the nature of human suffering and deliverance from that suffering."[11] From the soteriological point of view, human existence in reality means that humans suffer from the cyclical change of the universe and can be saved in two ways: one is that humans can be liberated from this cycle of suffering by transcending it; the other is that they are originally part of this universe and can return to its rhythms.

From a reflective point of view, we can say that Buddhists found ideas similar to their own in science and scientific cosmology, but we have to acknowledge the fact that modern science and technology did not emerge from Buddhist teachings or Oriental philosophy. At the same time, naive views of the similarities prevent Buddhists from seeing the demonic power of science and technology and from examining critically the essence of science and technology.

2. Construction of Historicocultural Evolution in Buddhism

2.1. The Human Position in the Ecological Order

Shirō Matsumoto criticizes Buddhist naturalism for its affirmation of the continuity of human and other beings.

> I am not blind to the current movements across the globe to protect nature and animals from the environmentally disastrous work of human hands. I, too, recognize the need to raise ecological consciousness, but with one obvious proviso: "It is worse to kill human beings than to kill nature or animals."[12]

In Buddhism, humans are part of all living beings (*shujō*) and, as mentioned earlier, the idea that mountains and rivers, grasses and trees have the buddha-nature signifies that there is a continuity among humans, other living beings, and nature. It is a philosophy of symbiosis or coexistence. If we understand humans as biological beings, it is difficult to find a complete separation between humans and other animals, especially given the advancement of gene analysis through molecular biology.

Humans are distinctive in the religious sense that they can become enlightened, and save other beings to ensure their enlightenment. In the understanding of the Tendai doctrine of ten realms, a human being has the possibility of being reborn in six lower realms, and of transcending the six and entering one of the four other realms of hearer, cause-knower, bodhisattva, and buddha.

In cosmological perspective humans are part of the universe, but at the same time are uniquely distinctive living beings aware of the ten realms. In this Tendai understanding, humans are not merely living beings, but also self-aware beings who have the power to transcend their situated circumstances. This does not mean that the life of a human being is more important than that of an animal, but humans are especially unique among other living beings in the sense that they can at least ponder such questions and take responsibility for their own salvation (enlightenment) and for that of other living beings.

2. 2. Historical Awareness

There is an issue concerning the position of humans in the ecological order. It is obvious that if humans (or similar animals with self-consciousness) did not exist on this planet, no one could destroy so many other lives or pollute this earth through the use of science and technology. On the one hand, as biological beings humans are not superior to other living beings, though they are distinctive in their awareness that their own and other living beings' existence totally depends on the ecological balance of this planet Earth. Only humans are capable of having such an ecological awareness.

I want to show that from a Buddhist perspective humans are not only part of nature, but can transcend their historical situation and deliberately transform it significantly. In other words, humans are distinctively and decisively shaped by historical situations. This means on the one hand that they are always and already situated in a history, and on the other hand that they can orient themselves to shape it through reflecting on the past, present, and future. In order for Buddhists to consider the ecological crisis in the modern world, humans must be seen as not merely products of natural evolution, but also as products of historical and cultural evolution and able to transcend such historical and cultural situatedness. In order to show this, I have to consider the evolutionary-developmental view of time, which the modern cosmological and biological sciences presuppose, in the Buddhist tradition. Without such consideration, Buddhists cannot think about how they can tackle the ecological crisis which we are now facing. I want to show a perspective found in the Lotus Sutra faith tradition, and especially in Nichiren, in which humans have a historicocultural awareness.

3. A New interpretation of Dependent Origination

3.1. Dependent Origination as a Process of Evolution

We have to find a way to consider a Buddhist view of history through reinterpreting the notion of dependent origination. The Buddhist Dharma, dependent origination, can be seen in terms of the process of evolution. This notion is also expressed in the doctrine of the twelve-linked chain of dependent origination.

The twelve-linked chain of dependent origination deals with human existence and the reality of human life and other living beings. There are many theories explaining the various relationships among the links of the twelve-linked chain, but one of the more popular explanations is found in Abhidharma Buddhism. It takes a developmental perspective such that the twelve links represent cause and effect in the three periods of past, present, and future of human beings. This view shows dependent origination as a process of human development.

Through reinterpretation of the twelve-linked chain of dependent origination, some Buddhists try to understand human beings as having developed through an evolutionary process from the unicellular microorganism of some billions of years ago.[13] This way of understanding represents one of the varieties of causality in the Sarvāstivādin interpretation of the twelve-linked chain of dependent origination. Kōgen Mizuno says that the Sarvāstivādins saw the twelve-linked chain as including four kinds of causation:

> The first is instantaneous (*kṣaṇika*) causality, in which the twelve links occur simultaneously and causality is a simultaneous and logical relationship. In the second, consecutive (*sāmabandhika*) causality, the twelve links, as psychophysical phenomena, change and develop moment by moment. The mental and physical actions of an individual's daily life are in accordance with this. The third is periodic (*āvasthika*) causality, that is, cause and effect in the three periods, in which the twelve links are dependent states in the past, present, future. This is simply the traditional interpretation. . . . The final type, infinitely successive (*prākarṣika*) causality, point out that the connections among the twelve links are not confined to the three time periods (of an existence) but extend infinitely into the past and the future.[14]

Thus, this doctrine of the twelve-linked chain of dependent origination can explain certain developments of humans and other living beings, eventuating in unprecedented development caused by *karmic* force. There are two aspects: one is the cyclical process of life and death, which is the repetition of the same pattern of life and death, but at the same time each living being is unique and new species emerge one after another in an evolutionary process on the basis of previous *karma* and present action.

In addition, even though authentic interpretation of the twelve-linked chain of origination lies in "instantaneous causality" in the moment of enlightenment, we can rediscover and reevaluate highly the final type, "infinitely successive causality," which is understandable to the modern historical mind in the secular world.

3.2. Toward Renewal of the Historicocultural Aspect of Humanity

Kōgen Mizuno brings up the important and original implications of the doctrine of dependent origination, saying that this doctrine has to do with human existence, and other phenomena of the universe, and also that its main concern is the concrete resolution of problems of human life. This doctrine is significant because it provides a coherent and meaningful account of human existence and the universe on a phenomenal level and of how humans can have a meaningful life through suffering, pleasure, delusion, and enlightenment within such a universe, society, and in their own lives.

> Our present existence is made up not only of the sum total of our own past experiences—arising from character, ethics, politics, economics, culture, and the arts—but also of our close connections, both spatial and temporal, with the world around us.[15]

Thus, our present existence serves as an important shaper in determining our future and has a crucial influence on our surroundings. We humans are unique in the sense that we have an awareness of dependent origination in the spatial and temporal dimensions, along with responsibility for human existence and the surrounding environment. If we do not cope with present ecological issues in the age of science and technology, we are violating the Buddhist principle of dependent origination.

4. NICHIREN'S HISTORICAL CONSCIOUSNESS

I want to propose that Nichiren's idea of *mappō* lies in his historical crisis consciousness, which presupposes a unidirectional movement of time. The concept of *mappō* involves a kind of Buddhist eschatology. This historical crisis consciousness can be significant for a Buddhist approach to ecological crisis in the modern world, which also presupposes the unidirectional movement of time.

Underlying Nichiren's faith there is always his awareness of historical time. The first line of one of his five great works, *Senji-shō* (The Selection of the Time), says, "To study the Buddha-Dharma one should first of all learn about time."[16] Nichiren called himself "the true follower (practitioner) of the Lotus Sutra in the age of *mappō*." Through facing crises, he was attracted to the teaching of *mappō* in the sutras. His was a historical crisis consciousness.

4.1. *Mappō* and the Lotus Sutra

I will briefly discuss *mappō shisō* (the idea of degeneration of the Dharma),[17] especially in relation to the Lotus Sutra. I want to show that such thinking emerged out of historical reality and historical consciousness.

The origin of this idea of the degeneration of the Dharma can be traced back to India. It was derived partly from internal corruption in the Sangha, and partly from external threats from social, political, and religious powers that could lead to the degeneration of the true Dharma and its practice. The Sanskrit term for *mappō* is *saddharma-vipralopa*. In Indian Buddhism the idea of *mappō* is found in the *Sūryagarbha* (*Daihōdō nichizōkyō*) and the *Candragarbha* (*Daihōdō gatsuzōkyō*). These views were incorporated into the *Mahāyānâ-bhismaya sūtra* (*Daijō-dōshōkyō*).

Such ideas were developed in China. Hui-ssu (515–77) of the T'ien-ta'i school developed this idea and assigned definite dates to the three periods after Śākyamuni Buddha's death: the *shōbō* (the true Dharma), the *zōbō* (the imitative or semblance Dharma), and the *mappō* (the last Dharma). The first period is the period when Buddhist teachings, practices, and enlightenment all exist. In the second period the teaching is practiced, but enlightenment is no longer possible. In the last period only teachings are alive, but practices and enlightenment no longer exist. There are four different kinds of views concerning the duration of the first and second periods. They consist of combinations of five hundred years and one thousand years. The period of the *mappō* is regarded as lasting ten thousand years after the second period.[18]

In the Lotus Sutra the theory of the true Dharma and the imitative Dharma was combined with the theory of *kōmetsu* (the extinction of *kalpas*). After each of various buddhas died, there were the *kalpas* of the true Dharma and of the imitative Dharma. The Lotus Sutra says,

After that buddha's extinction [Flower Light Buddha]

> The Righteous Law will abide in the world
> For thirty-two minor kalpas
> Widely saving living creatures.
> At the expiration of the Righteous Law,
> The Counterfeit Law [will abide] for thirty-two [minor kalpas]. (Three-fold, p. 83)[19]

The term "*mappō*" can be found in chapter 14 of the Lotus Sutra. According to Ryūjō Yamada, this was Kumārajīva's translation of the Sanskrit term "*saddharma-vipralopa*" (the extinction and destruction of the true Dharma).[20]

Many phrases referring to *mappō* can be found in the Lotus Sutra.

> After the extinction of the Tathāgata, in [the period of] the Decline of the Law, he who desires to preach this sutra should abide in the pleasant ministry [of speech]. (Threefold, p. 226)

> The bodhisattva-mahāsattva who, in the corrupt ages to come, when the Law is about to perish, receives and keeps, reads and recites this sutra, does not cherish an envious and deceitful mind. . . . (Threefold, p. 228)

The Lotus Sutra as a whole has the idea of the *mappō*, but does not clearly systematize the three periods of the true Dharma, the imitative Dharma, and the *mappō*. The time of the dissemination of the Dharma (or of this sutra itself) can be designated as being in an evil (or corrupted) age of the degeneration of the Dharma.

According to Zuiei Itō's "Nichiren Shonin no Rekishi Ishiki [Saint Nichiren's consciousness of history]," we can witness the strong fever of *mappō* consciousness in the Lotus Sutra because the True (or Wonderful) Dharma (*saddharma*) which this sutra advocates is contrasted with the imitative Dharma, and is contrasted as well with the extinction and destruction of the Dharma. Therefore, the view of Buddhist history expressed in the Lotus Sutra is established from a future-oriented consciousness in which the *telos* in this history is to establish the true Dharma which was originally expounded in the period of the true Dharma.[21]

Itō suspects that this view of Buddhist history was formed through reflecting on the historical reality in which Buddhists experienced a crisis from the maligning of the Dharma, something which precipitated other crises. In other words, this sutra itself was edited by a group who concerned themselves with embracing the true Dharma in a historical context, such as praying for the happiness of the people in this world in a period of corruption. The Indian way of thinking inherently lacked any concrete historical concern, so this sutra too does not concern itself with chronology.

In Japan in the late Heian period all the suffering arising from political and social instability and natural disasters adversely affected the minds of the people to the extent that the scenes describing hell in Genshin's *Ōjōyōshū* appealed to them. A kind of *mappō* mood captured the period. The people felt that the *mappō* age had really arrived.

4.2. Nichiren and *Mappō* Thought

In this section I want to show that Nichiren's idea of *mappō* is based on a linear view of history and that he also reflected on the historical reality of his time through hermeneutical interpretation. His understanding of *mappō* is not pessimistic, but rather a challenge to change this world instead of seeking self-realization in the inner world. His attitude is not naturalistic, but rather a challenge to transform the historical reality of this world.

According to Shigemoto Tokoro, there are three historical backgrounds to Nichiren's view of *mappō*: Buddhist history, natural history, and social history.[22]

Buddhist history refers to the time frame of the *mappō* in the history of Buddhism before the Kamakura period. Natural history refers to the various kinds of extraordinary natural disasters and catastrophes that occurred during the Kamakura period. Social history refers to the various kinds of social disturbances and instability of that era, such as the internal divisions within the Kamakura regime, and the crises over the survival of the Japanese from the Mongol raids of 1274 and 1281. Nichiren was concerned with this world, but society was full of distress and the people were suffering from natural disasters, calamities, and social instability precipitated by political struggles and wars. He wanted to establish the true Dharma of the Lotus Sutra in order to respond to such crises. With such motivation, he wrote the *Risshō Ankoku Ron* (Establishment of the True Dharma for the Protection of the Country) and presented it to the government, proclaiming that if the true Dharma, that is the unification of Buddhism based on the Lotus Sutra, is firmly established, then the country could be made secure and the people attain happiness.

Thus, his crisis consciousness of the *mappō* originally derived from these three elements. In addition, another important factor was his experience with persecution, which was brought on by his exclusivistic faith in the Lotus Sutra along with his criticism of other sects, especially the Pure Land practice of *nembutsu*.[23]

Nichiren used the Daijikkyō in his analysis of the five periods of the degeneration of the Dharma. In *Senji Shō* (The Selection of the Time) he says,

> In the *Daijuku* Sutra [Daijikkyō], Shakyamuni Buddha, the World-Honored One, addresses Bodhisattva Gatsuzō and predicts the future. Thus he says that the first five hundred years after his passing will be the age of attaining liberation, and the next five hundred years, the age of meditation (making one thousand years). The next five hundred years will be the age of reading, reciting, and listening and, the next five hundred years, the age of building temples and stupas (making two thousand years). Concerning the next five hundred years after that, he says, "Quarrels and disputes will arise among the adherents to my teachings, and the Pure Law will become obscured and lost.
>
> These five five-hundred-year periods, which total twenty-five hundred years, are delineated in different ways by different people.[24]

Thus, Nichiren adopted these five five-hundred-year periods from the Daijikkyō. This theory signifies a decline of human capacity in some sense, but it may be interpreted differently; that is, as signifying the process of secularization, i.e., the transformation from the monastic to the secular world.

The first and the second five-hundred years, for attaining liberation and practicing meditation respectively, are referred to as the age of morality and spirituality, corresponding to the true Dharma. The practice of the monastic tradition is fully implemented. The third five-hundred years of reading, reciting, and listening implies an age of learning, emphasizing the faculties of the analytical mind. This period is an interim between secluded monastic life and the secular world. The fourth five-hundred years of building temples and stupas implies a materialistic and aesthetic age. It is the period of secular power supporting the monastic tradition. The third and the fourth periods together correspond to the imitative Dharma. The fifth five-hundred-year period implies an age of ideological competition emphasizing the values of theoretical reason along with expression of self-centered desires, resulting in a loss of morals and religion. It is a period of complete secularization. Thus, this theory as a view of history is a kind of eschatology beginning from the golden age of the true Dharma and ending with the end of the Dharma, but its hidden aim is to inspire the crisis consciousness of the extinction of the true Dharma and give rise to restoration of the true Dharma.

Nichiren made an effort to find evidence that his present day was "two hundred years into the *mappō*," or "two thousand and two hundred years after the extinction of the Buddha," by referring to several sutras and Chinese historical writings.[25] While paying close attention to the interpretation of the periods by the Meditation Master Tao-ch'o of China, Nichiren read the Lotus Sutra as a prophetic writing to predict the future, declaring,

> There is no doubt that our present age corresponds to the fifth five-hundred-year period described in the *Daijuku* Sutra, when "the Pure Law will become obscured and lost." But that which is to come after "the Pure Law has become obscured and lost" is the Great Pure Law of Namu-myoho-renge-kyo, and the heart and core of the Lotus Sutra.[26]

Nichiren tried to prove that this declaration of his present age was the fifth five-hundred-year period by citing the Daijikkyō and the Lotus Sutra. He wrote,

> The seventh volume of the Lotus Sutra says, "In the fifth five hundred years after my death, widely declare and spread [the Lotus Sutra] and never allow its flow to cease." This indicates that "widely declaring and spreading [the Lotus Sutra]" will be accomplished in the time after "the Pure Law becomes obscured and lost," as the *Daijuku* Sutra puts it.
>
> Again, the sixth volume speaks of "one who is able to uphold this sutra in the evil age of the Latter Day of the Law," and the fifth volume talks of "the latter age when the Law is on the point of disappearing." The fourth volume states, "Since hatred and jealousy toward this sutra abound even during the lifetime of the Buddha, how much worse will it be in the world after his passing?" And the fifth volume says, "The people will be full of hostility, and find it extremely difficult to believe." And the seventh volume, speaking of the fifth five-hundred-year period which is the age of conflict, says, "Do not allow the devil, the devil's people, or the deities, dragons, yakṣas, kumbhāṇḍas, or their kind to seize the advantage."
>
> The *Daijuku* Sutra says, "Quarrels and disputes will arise among the adherents to my teachings." And the fifth volume of the Lotus Sutra similarly says, "There will be monks in that evil age," "Or there will be forest-dwelling monks," and, "Demons will take possession of others."[27]

Through interpreting historical reality with the mirror of the sutras, Nichiren was able to grasp that his present time was within the the *mappō*. It was a time for disseminating the Lotus Sutra which had been anticipated and prophesied by the Buddha for the sake of the people in this *mappō*.

Based on his interpretations of the sutras, especially the Lotus Sutra, Nichiren took historical reality seriously, with a crisis consciousness of his own historical situation. His mission of awareness of the bodhisattva is firmly rooted in his understanding of the historical reality of "the present now."

Here, I do not intend to discuss his methods of calculating such historical dates. It is objectively not correct, but the important point is that his understanding of history is unidirectional; the three temporal worlds of past, present and future are real. Through reading the sutras wholeheartedly, he interpreted his present historical reality with his crisis consciousness and found his mission to change this secular world on the basis of his faith in the Lotus Sutra.

5. NICHIREN'S HERMENEUTICAL APPROACH: HISTORICOCULTURAL ELEMENTS

Nichiren took understanding his current situation seriously. It consists of five hermeneutical categories (*gokō*) for determining ways of disseminating the teachings in the Lotus Sutra. This is extensively developed in his essay, *Kyōkijikoku Shō* (The Teaching, Capacity, Time and Country).[28]

Nichiren's advice in *Risshō Anraku Ron*[29] to the Kamakura government was ignored. Instead he was exiled to Izu at the age of forty-one. Gradually he began to develop a way of understanding sutras within the context of his historical situation. This is referred to as the "Five Categories for Propagation," (or of "meaning" or "understanding") which are norms of interpretation—the teaching, the hearers, the age, the country, and the sequence of propagation.[30] These "Five Categories" are found in the *Kyōkijikoku Shō*[31] and in the *Kenhōbō Shō*.[32]

Nichiren paid special attention to the following passage, which helped him develop the five categories expressed in the *Kyōkijikoku Shō*.

After the Tathāgata is extinct [such a one],
Knowing [this] sutra that the Buddha has taught,
[Together with] its reasoning and process,
Shall expound it according to its true meaning.
Just as the light of the sun and moon
Can dispel the darkness,
So this man, working in the world,
Can dispel the gloom of the living
And cause numberless bodhisattvas
Finally to abide in the One-vehicle. (Threefold, p. 300)

The phrase, "After the Tathāgata is extinct [such a one]," indicates time, i.e., the time of the *mappō*. The phrase, "Knowing [this] sutra that the Buddha has taught," means "teaching." The phrase, "[Together with] its reasoning and process, / Shall expound it according to its true meaning" shows that the sutra intends to speak within the context of historical process and reasoning. This means that the historicocultural elements of the sutras and of the land and the people have to be taken seriously. And the last part is, "Just as the light of the sun and moon / Can dispel the darkness, / So this man, working in the world, / Can dispel the gloom of the living / And cause numberless bodhisattvas / Finally to abide in the One-vehicle." According to the Nichiren sect, Nichiren considered this phrase to fully express the mission of the Bodhisattva Supreme Conduct—who sprang out of the earth.

The first of these five hermeneutical categories is teaching (*kyō*). It is the teaching of the sutra itself. The second is capacity (*ki*), that is the capacity of the hearers toward whom any teaching is directed. The Lotus Sutra was taught for the lowest common denominator of people in the *mappō* period.

The third category is time (*ji*). Even with the true teaching and the appropriate people to hear it, unless the time is right, it cannot be disseminated successfully. The right time, the true teaching, and the capacity of people are all important. Through interpreting sutras Nichiren concluded that the present moment was in the *mappō* when it was the right time for disseminating the Lotus Sutra for the full realization of the salvation of all people.

Nichiren has another view of time. As seen in his sublime and religious expressions, the notion of time is similar to "the eternal now." It is expressed in his main treatise, *Kanjin Honzon Shō* (The True Object of Worship). The following passage is widely acknowledged as the core of Nichiren's thought.

> The *saha* world Shakyamuni revealed in the *Juryō* chapter is the eternal pure land, impervious to the three calamities and the four cycles of change. In this world the Buddha is eternal, transcending birth and death, and his disciples are also eternal. This is the three thousand worlds or the three realms of existence within our own lives.[33]

This shows that the unity of this *sahā*-world and the eternal pure land coincides with the very moment of uniting historical time and eternity. Yet, even though he had such religious experiences, his dominant understanding of time is chronological.

The fourth category is country (*koku*). Japan was especially suitable for the dissemination of the Lotus Sutra. For Nichiren, the concept of country did not necessarily mean a political state only, but also the land or the earth as a natural environment.[34]

The fifth category of interpretation is sequence of propagation (*jo*). It is important to know a reasonable order or process for propagating the true teaching. For example, the popularity of provisional Mahayana Buddhism, he thought, was a preparatory path to true Mahayana Buddhism.

Now let us look at how Nichiren took the historicocultural aspects seriously.

> Question: When is the time for the preaching of the Hinayana sutras and the provisional sutras, and when is the time for the preaching of the Lotus Sutra?
>
> Answer: Even bodhisattvas, from those in the ten stages of faith to those on the verge of full enlightenment, find it difficult to judge matters concerning time and capacity. How then can ordinary beings such as ourselves be able to judge such matters?
>
> Question: Is there no way to determine them?
>
> Answer: Let us borrow the eye of the Buddha to consider this question of time and capacity. Let us use the sun of the Buddha to illuminate the nation. [35]

He tried to consider the historicocultural aspects, i.e., time and capacity of the people by the "Buddha's eye" which can perceive all things in the past, present, and future and the "Buddha's sun" which signifies the illumination of the darkness of this world.

6. NICHIREN'S APPROACH TO ECOLOGICAL CRISIS

Let us reinterpret these categories in relation to the modern ecological crisis.[35] The first category, *kyō*, signifies knowing the true teaching. This means the kind of teachings that can save all the living beings facing the ecological crisis in the *mappō*. In the face of the ecological crisis we need to try to find what kind of teachings can save this earth and all living beings. Teachings here may include humanistic and scientific studies which find ways to tackle and solve this ecological crisis. Chapter 19 of the Lotus Sutra says, "And that which he preaches, according to its several meanings, will not be contrary to the truth. If he refers to popular classics, maxims for ruling the world, means of livelihood, and so forth, all will coincide with the True Law" (Threefold, p. 286). Nikkyō Niwano interprets this quotation as follows:

> The phrase "popular classics" means books to guide human life other than religious works, such as works on ethics or philosophy. Indeed, this phrase is not limited to books but also includes the Buddha's teachings as preached through speech. The phrase "maxims for rul-

ing the world" refers to teachings concerning such matters as politics, economics, and law. The phrase "means of livelihood" refers to discussing with and guiding others who are in industry, such as agriculture, manufacturing and commerce.[37]

This quotation implies that the ways of understanding practical and secular concerns of those who have deep and sincere faith in the true Dharma will naturally coincide with the true Dharma. It also implies those who have faith in the Dharma must concern themselves with the so-called sciences. In this context, Buddhists must be concerned with ecological issues and with the kind of political, economic, and social principles that can save living beings from suffering. They must concern themselves with such global issues and learn about them.

Why do we have to concern ourselves with this world? In chapter 16, the Lotus Sutra says that the transhistorical Śākyamuni Buddha, the Eternal Buddha, has "constantly been preaching and teaching in this world, and also leading and benefiting all living beings in other places," in the countless domains. In the same chapter the Buddha says, "The lifetime which I attained by pursuing the bodhisattva-way is not even yet accomplished." This means that within this present time, the everlasting buddha is helping and saving in the historical reality of this world by appearing in it, and preaching the Dharma. The Buddha concerns himself with this world through practicing the Dharma.

Śākyamuni Buddha himself has already practiced the bodhisattva way by teaching innumerable bodhisattvas. His everlasting life is one of practicing the bodhisattva way. In chapter 16, the Lotus Sutra says,[38]

> Ever making this my thought:
> How shall I cause all the living
> To enter the Way supreme
> And speedily accomplish their buddhahood?

Like Nichiren, we can read this message in relation to our present historical situation. The eternal life of the Buddha is revealed in concrete and practical activities of the bodhisattva way in this world. In the process of concrete bodhisattva practices, the Eternal Buddha keeps them in mind, and watches over all the living and leads them toward buddhahood. The members of Risshō Kōsei-kai believe that wherever or whenever we practice bodhisattva ways, the Buddha appears and is there teaching the Dharma.[39] We can see the Buddha's response to those who practice the bodhisattva way in this world. In this sense, the bodhisattvas who are actively engaged in ecological issues can receive inspiration from the dynamism of the eternal life, amidst their bodhisattva activities.

The second category, *ki*, signifies knowing the level of understanding of people in this modern age. In order to understand the capacity of humans in this age, the notion of the Evil Ages of the Five Decays (*gojoku akusei*) needs to be reinterpreted.

In chapter 2, the Lotus Sutra says, "The buddhas appear in the evil ages of the five decays—the decay of the kalpa, decay through tribulations, decay of all living beings, decay of views, and decay of lifetime." The decay of the *kalpa* is the decay that comes from a long lapse of time, such as during wars, natural disasters, pestilence, etc. This notion affirms the long historical process of decaying in such a way that evils arise and are accumulated. Second, the decay through tribulations refers to the rise of desires and consequently of evil acts. Third, decay of all living beings signifies a condition in which all living beings become mentally and physically weak. It is especially true that people with a modern lifestyle are becoming weaker in the six organs of the body. For example, it is difficult for us to distinguish traditional and safe vegetables from artificial and polluted ones by sight, taste, touch, and so on.

Decay of views refers to ideological disputes. Wrong views flourish. Fifth, the decay of lifetime means that the span of life is shortened. In Japan longevity has increased, but the quality of life has declined. Not only in Japan but also in other highly industrialized societies "life" is reduced to matter and death, and therefore life as a whole is concealed from human eyes. The vitality of life is decreasing because modern humans cannot see, hear, smell, touch, sense, and think of the dynamism of "life." Toshiko Toriyama says that modern civilization deprives humans of their capacity to act on their feet on this earth through hearing the voices within their own bodies. While listening to one's own body, one can feel the vitality of one's life and hear the voice of nature.[39] Thus, the present is the Evil Age of the Five Decays, an age in which people are attached to their illusions.[41]

In the face of the ecological crisis what kind of consciousness can people have? How far can they be expected to be aware of the ecological crisis under the technological and scientific domination that pervades their everyday lives? With this crisis, what kind of hope can humans have?

The third category, *ji*, signifies knowing the right time. At present we are facing an ecological crisis. In the twenty-first century, during the course of our global age, what kind of ecological problems will we face? In order to find some possible solutions to the ecological crisis, we have to understand how science and technology developed and how they are likely to affect living beings on this planet in the future.

The fourth category, country, signifies knowing the situation in which we live. Nichiren saw the great earthquake of the Shōka era and the great comet of the Bun'ei era as omens of the appearance of the Bodhisattva Supreme Conduct and paid close attention to the Mongolian incursions and other political disturbances as well. The notion of country implies natural, political, and economic phenomena such as these occurring in the land.

The Lotus Sutra affirms this world, saying

> Now this triple world
> All is my domain;
> The living beings in it
> All are my children.
> But now this place
> Abounds with distresses;
> And I alone
> Am able to save and protect them.[42]

Just as parents love their children, the Buddha always shows his compassion for all living beings in this world. The significance of this quotation is that it is not in some other world, but in this world that the Buddha's salvation will be fulfilled.

In chapter 7 there is a story that under the Buddha Universal Surpassing Wisdom sixteen bodhisattvas attained perfect enlightenment and each became buddhas with respective realms. Fifteen of the sixteen bodhisattvas became buddhas in other lands. "The sixteenth is I myself, Śākyamuni Buddha, who has accomplished Perfect Enlightenment in the *sahā*-domain [*shaba-kokudo*]," (Threefold, p. 161). This means that Śākyamuni Buddha is the great teacher of this *sahā*-world, but it also implies that this planet Earth is important because it is on this planet that Śākyamuni Buddha first appeared in history.

In the Lotus Sutra we can find something similar to the Christian notion of stewardship of the earth. Niwano comments on the event in chapter 15 of the Lotus Sutra where the Buddha refused the offer of help from the many bodhisattvas coming from other lands and entrusted this *sahā*-world to the many bodhisattvas who sprang out of the earth. This means that "the world in which we live should be purified and made peaceful through our own efforts as dwellers in the world."[43]

Thus, Śākyamuni Buddha and the bodhisattvas are associated with this world. The Lotus Sutra says, "These bodhisattvas have all been dwelling in the world of empty space underneath the *sahā*-world."[44] It is obvious that the Lotus Sutra concerns itself with this world, including the land or the earth. The lotus flower is rooted in the muddy earth.

There is a notion that this world is the Buddha's domain which should be pure, and that bodhisattvas work to make it pure. This implies implicitly that the bodhisattvas' work is associated with ecology. The following is found in the Lotus Sutra:

> The domain of that buddha
> Will be peerless in pure splendor,
> . . . . (Threefold, p. 139)
>
> His [Buddha] land will be pure
> . . . .
> Bodhisattvas and śrāvakas,
> . . . .
> Will adorn his [Buddha] domain. (Threefold, p. 141–42)

We can interpret the purity of the Buddha land as an ecological planet Earth because this world is the Buddha's domain and should be the Buddha's land in the future.

Understanding our ecological crisis means knowing the earth on which we live. It is the global and borderless society which is just like a burning house in the parable of the burning house in chapter 3 of the Lotus Sutra, suffering from fear of pollution, nuclear bombs, and narrow and exclusive nationalism. In this *sahā*-world humans are entrusted by the Buddha to be his coworkers for the sake of realizing purity in this *sahā*-world.

The fifth category, sequence, signifies knowing what the most important priorities are among the many principles in order to save planet Earth. The concept of sequence signifies rethinking the ideas and principles which have emerged in the tradition and finding priority in the events. If we follow Nichiren's use of three categories of evidence, we have to take events in this present world seriously, and find their underlying meaning presented by the Buddha in order for people to become enlightened and the world to become peaceful.

CONCLUSION

Buddhist approaches to the modern ecological crisis depend on a Buddhist understanding of history. The naturalistic approach is based on the cyclical movement of time. In this understanding humans are a part of nature. If they are attuned to the natural rhythm, i.e., the eternal return of the same, they can escape from the modern ecological crisis. This is a quite universal concept and a most acceptable position in Buddhism.

The other approach, i.e., the historicocultural approach, depends on the unidirectional movement of time. Humans are not merely a part of nature, but biohistorical beings believed to have the power to create and maintain the ecological balance necessary for the survival of all living beings. I think that "taking time seriously," i.e., thinking and acting in this historical reality, is one way to tackle the enormity of the ecological crisis. In this context, the Lotus Sutra is concerned with this world and with historical time, i.e., with *mappō* consciousness. Nichiren's crisis consciousness of the *mappō* reveals his view of history to be one in which his present time is in the *mappō* within the unidirectional movement of history. His mission as the Bodhisattva Supreme Conduct is based on his understanding of the historical reality of "the present now."

I have discussed the way in which Nichiren understood his present situation from a historicocultural perspective. This is found in his theory of the five hermeneutical categories. I pointed to a possibile way of dealing with ecological crisis. Through recovering Nichiren's sense of the Lotus Sutra, Buddhists in the Lotus Sutra tradition can have a foundation from which to deal with the modern ecological crisis created by humans in human history.

Notes

1. Gordon Kaufman, "An Afterthought," at the 1998 International Buddhist-Christian Theological Encounter (Indianapolis), April 28, 1998, unpublished.
2. Donald Keene, *Japanese Literature: An Introduction for Western Readers* (New York: Grove Press Inc., 1955), 12–13.
3. Takeshi Umehara, *Mori no Shiso ga Jinrui o Sukū* [Thinking about Forests Can Save the Human Race] (Tokyo: Shōgakukan, 1991), 204–6.
4. Takurō Kishine, *Bunmei-ron* [Essay on Civilization] (Tokyo: Tōyō Keizai Shinpōsha), 145–48.
5. Tōru Kunō, "Epirōgu: Shinri Gakusha no Koromo o Kita Senkyōshi—Rogers" [Epilogue: Rogers as a Missionary Dressed as a Psychologist], in *Rojazu o Yomu* [Reading Karl Rogers] by Tōru Kunō, Yasuhiro Suetake, and others (Tokyo: Iwasaki Gakujutsu-sha, 1997), 202–3.
6. Nikkyō Niwano, *Buddhism for Today: A Modern Interpretation of the Threefold Lotus Sutra* (New York: Weatherhill, 1961), 416.
7. Shirō Matsumoto, "The Lotus Sutra and Japanese Culture," in *Pruning the Bodhi Tree: the Storm over Critical Buddhism,* Jamie Hubbard and Paul Swanson, eds. (Honolulu: University of Hawaii Press, 1997), 402–3.
8. Hans Waldenfels, *Absolute Nothingness: Foundations for a Buddhist-Christian Dialogue,* J. W. Heisig, trans. (New York: Paulist Press, 1980), 96.
9. Akira Sadakata, *Buddhist Cosmology: Philosophy and Origins* (Tokyo: Kōsei Publishing Co., 1997), 181–83.
10. Ibid.

11. Ibid.

12. "The Lotus Sutra and Japanese Culture," 402–3.

13. Nikkyō Niwano, *The Lotus Sutra: Life and Soul of Buddhism* (Tokyo: Kōsei Publishing Co., 1970), 198–211.

14. Kōgen Mizuno, *Essentials of Buddhism* (Tokyo: Kōsei Publishing Co., 1996), 145–46.

15. Ibid., 139.

16. My translation. Cf. Nichiren, *Selected Writings of Nichiren*, trans. Burton Watson and others, ed. Philip B. Yampolsky (New York: Columbia University Press, 1990), 183.

17. I owe this idea to Daigan and Alicia Matsunaga, *Foundation of Japanese Buddhism*, vol. 1 (Los Angeles: Buddhist Books International, 1974), 218–23.

18. "Shozōmatsu," *Japanese-English Buddhist Dictionary: Revised Edition* (Tokyo: Daitō Shuppan-sha, 1991), 332. "Shozōmatsu," in *A Dictionary of Japanese Buddhist Terms*, Hisao Inagaki, ed. (Kyoto: Nagata Bunshōdō, 1984), 323.

19. References to "Threefold" are to *The Threefold Lotus Sutra*, Bunnō Katō, Yoshirō Tamura, and Kōjirō Miyasaka, trans. (Tokyo: Kōsei Publishing Co., 1975).

20. Takao Maruyama, "Kichizō no Sanjisetsu to Go-gohyaku-sai Setsu" [Chits'ang's Theory of the Three Periods and the Five Hundred Years After], in *Hokke Bunka Kenkyū* (1975), p.70.

21. Zuiei Itō, *Nichiren Seishin no Gendai* [Nichiren's Spirit for Today] (Tokyo: Daizō Shuppan, 1989), 229.

22. Shigemoto Tokoro, *Nichiren no Shisō to Kamakura Bukkyō* [Nichiren's Thought and Kamakura Buddhism] (Tokyo: Toyama-bō, 1965), 311.

23. In 1261 at the age of 40, he was exiled to Izu Island, and in 1271 to Sado Island. He frequently experienced persecution.

24. *Selected Writings of Nichiren*, 186–88.

25. *Nichiren no Shisō to Kamakura Bukkyō*, 317.

26. *Selected Writings of Nichiren*, 187.

27. Ibid., 188.

28. "The Teaching, Capacity, Time and Country," in *The Major Writings of Nichiren Daishonin*, Vol. 4 (Tokyo: Nichiren Shōshū International Center, 1986), 7–21.

29. "Risshō Ankoku Ron" [Establishment of the True Dharma for the Protection of the Country], in *The Major Writings of Nichiren Daishonin*, Vol. 2, Revised (Tokyo: Nichiren Shōshū International Center, 1995), 3–46.

30. In "The Teaching, Capacity, Time and Country" the fifth category is clearly the sequence of teaching or propagation. But Nichiren also says there that one who takes these five categories into account can be a true teacher. The Nichiren tradition often uses the "teacher" rather than "sequence" as the fifth category. See Asai Endo, "Gogi-han no Keiseikatei no Kōsatsu" [Essay on the Formation of Gogi] in *Nichiren Shōnin Kyōgaku no Tankyū* [A Study of Saint Nichiren's Teachings] (Tokyo: Sankibo Busshorin, 1997), 3–28.

31. "The Teaching, Capacity, Time and Country," 7–21.

32. "Admonitions against Slander," in *The Major Writings of Nichiren Daishonin*, Vol. 1 (Tokyo: Nichiren Shōshū International Center, 1979), 163–68.

33. *Selected Writings of Nichiren*, 166.

34. *Nichiren no Shisō to Kamakura Bukkyō*, 340.
35. *Selected Writings of Nichiren*, 186–88.
36. This section was written under the influence of Zuiei Itō's *Nichiren Seishin no Gendai.*
37. *Buddhism for Today*, 301–2.
38. *The Threefold Lotus Sutra*, op. cit., 256.
39. Ibid., 19. The Sutra of Innumerable Meanings says, "This sutra originally comes from the abode of all buddhas, leaves for the aspiration of all the living to buddhahood, and stays at the place where all the bodhisattvas practice."
40. Toshiko Toriyama, *Inochi ni Fureru* [Touching Life] (Tokyo: Tarō Jirō-sha, 1985), 106–7.
41. *Buddhism for Today*, 49–50.
42. This paragraph is called "the preaching of the Three Merits of Shakyamuni Buddha: (1) his merit as lord, because the triple world is his possession or domain; (2) his merit as leader or teacher, because he alone saves all living creatures: and (3) his merit as father, because all are his sons [children]." [Threefold, footnote 98–9]. Nichiren praised this paragraph and Shakyamuni Buddha for these three merits.
43. *Buddhism for Today*, 177.
44. *The Lotus Sutra*, trans. by Burton Watson (New York: Columbia University Press, 1993), 219.

The Lotus Sutra and Health Care Ethics

Robert E. Florida

In the last several years there has been an increase of interest in the field of Buddhist ethics, particularly health care ethics. In this paper I will review the medical implications found in the Lotus Sutra. I will first discuss some general ethical principles that apply in health care with reference to the Lotus Sutra, and then go on to specific references in the sutra to medicine.

Buddhist Medical Ethical Principles

In traditional Buddhist societies, medical ethics, as a systematic formulation of principles and their application to cases, has not been a major concern. That is not to say that Buddhists have ever ignored illness and health care. On the contrary, the metaphor of the Buddha as the supreme physician, who cures the ills of the world and of the individual sufferer, is ancient and major in the Dharma.[1] Furthermore, caring for the sick both within and without the monastic order has been understood as an excellent way to manifest such primary virtues as compassion and friendship.

Nonetheless, it is only recently that there have been attempts to work out systems of health care ethics in Buddhist contexts.[2] One of the latest and most ambitious is *Buddhism and Bioethics* by Damien Keown.[3] His general theoretical approach is based mainly on Theravada primary texts, and centres Buddhist ethics on three "basic goods": life, knowledge (*prajñā*), and friendship.[4] These three values inform the next lower level, the level of precepts or ethical rules. Precepts in turn guide decision-making in specific ethical situations.

Respect for life (*ahiṃsā*), the first of the "basic goods" according to Keown, is doubtless one of the pillars of Buddhist ethics and generally pervades the Lotus Sutra. It is a key to Buddhist health care ethics and will be discussed below. Knowledge (*prajñā*) as the second "basic good" or core principle of Buddhist ethics in Keown's analysis is also very generally acknowledged as central in Buddhist thought. *Prajñā* is both the supreme *pāramita* in the bodhisattva path and the culmination of cultivation of mind in Theravada traditions. It pervades the Lotus Sutra. *Prajñā* is often coupled with *karuṇā* (compassion) as summing up the Mahayana or bodhisattva path. Together, artfully supporting one another, they lead the practitioner to realise his or her Buddha nature. *Upāya* (skillful means), a fundamental theme which runs throughout the Lotus Sutra, can be understood as identical to *karuṇā*.

Keown, however, takes friendship rather than *karuṇā/upāya* as the third "basic good."[5] Friendship as a Buddhist ideal, he argues, is a complex bundle of rules, virtues, behaviours, and the like which guide us in our relations with all other living creatures. Friendship includes compassion (*karuṇā*) when appropriate, but much more as well. Identifying friendship as a basic Buddhist good is one of the innovations (a fruitful one in my view) in Keown's book. In the Lotus Sutra the qualities of friendship that Keown describes are found in the relationships between the various characters. For example, the parable of Devadatta in chapter 12 shows the efficacy of friendship, which goes beyond one particular lifetime into future incarnations to enable a very wicked man to realise his true nature, his Buddhahood.

Other attempts to develop Buddhist health care ethical theories are generally both less complete and more conventional than that of Keown. One approach has been to try to fit Buddhist and other traditions' ideas about health care into four principles: autonomy, beneficence, nonmaleficence, and justice.[6] These four principles have been very useful to many Western theorists, which is not surprising as they are drawn from Western philosophical, political, and medical sources. But do they apply well in the Buddhist context?[7]

Dr. Pinit Ratanakul of Mahidol University in Thailand is one of the leading Buddhist writers in the field of health care ethics. As would be expected, he is Theravādin, and his work is deeply rooted in his Thai Buddhist tradition. He also has his doctorate in philosophy from Yale and this too has influenced his thinking.

In Ratanakul's 1986 book *Bioethics: An Introduction to the Ethics of Medicine and Life Sciences*, he takes fidelity to the medical profession, autonomy, beneficence, nonmaleficence, and justice as the "prima facie duties" that underlie bioethics.[8] He does not develop them from Buddhist texts, traditions, or arguments. Rather they come from the Western philosophical and medical traditions.

Interestingly enough, in a later journal article, "Bioethics in Thailand," Ratanakul turns to his Thai Theravadin tradition as the source for fundamental bioethical principles and comes up with four. They are veracity, noninjury to life, justice, and compassion.[9] In the spirit of his comment, "There is much work to be done both in clarifying these and other principles and in applying them,"[10] let us turn our attention to his 1986 and 1988 formulations with especial attention to how these principles cohere with the teachings of the Lotus Sutra.

Autonomy

Ratanakul describes autonomy as the ability of an individual "to order, plan, and choose among the diverse human potentialities, the pattern of their own lives, as long as it is consistent with meeting the rightful claims of others upon them and the fulfilment of their responsibilities as moral agents."[11] In traditional Buddhist ethics, autonomy is not featured as a major category. The Buddhist emphasis on the responsibility of each person for his or her own karma or moral character implies something like this notion; however, there is something in the modern Western insistence on autonomy that goes against the Buddhist grain. While Ratanakul is careful not to fall into extremes, individualistic autonomy is contrary to the central Buddhist insight of coconditioned causality, which insists on the interdependence of all beings. It is particularly at odds with the bodhisattva ideal of sacrificing self for others that is at the heart of the Lotus Sutra. At any rate, we note that in his later formulation, autonomy has dropped from Ratanakul's list of fundamental principles.

Nonmaleficence or *Ahiṃsā*

Noninjury to living beings must, I think, be central to any Buddhist medical ethical system. As Ratanakul put it, "In a Buddhist society it is well known and accepted that a primary obligation is noninjury to others."[12] Noninjury to life (*ahiṃsā*) applies to all sentient life, but otherwise is the same as nonmaleficence, which in the Western world has usually referred only to human life, although this may be slowly changing. As mentioned earlier, Keown also identifies *ahiṃsā* as a basic concept at the foundation of Buddhist bioethics. Obviously, it is very powerful as a general principle in health care ethics and, as noted above, pervades the Lotus Sutra.

In his 1988 article Ratanakul identifies justice as a basic Buddhist teaching and singles it out as one of the fundamental principles on which to base a Buddhist bioethical system for Thailand. He explains his concept of justice to be understood in terms of impartiality and equal treatment, giving to each one what is his due. People may be different from us either by their economic condition or by their social status, but as moral potentialities they are equal to us and therefore deserve equal treatment.[13]

This concept of justice is a modern Western one; compare it to Gillon's formulation in *Principles of Health Care Ethics*, where justice is "often regarded as synonymous with fairness, and reasonably summarised as the moral obligation to act on the basis of fair adjudication between competing claims."[14] In practice, he continues, justice is based on the principle of equality for all persons and is discussed under three headings: "distributive justice" or fairness in the allocation of resources, "rights-based justice" or respect for individuals' rights, and "legal justice" or reliance on fair legal codes and procedures.

Traditional Buddhist sources have very little to say about justice. Buddhaghoṣa, for example, a Theravadin scholar of the fourth or fifth century C.E., who may be the greatest exegete that Buddhism has produced, does not seem to mention justice at all in his masterpiece, the *Viśuddhimagga*.[15] Shundō Tachibana, in his still valuable 1926 path-breaking book *The Ethics of Buddhism*, attempts to formulate a comprehensive ethical system from the texts of Theravada Buddhism. In the early parts of his book, he stays very close to the traditional terminology and formulations, and does not mention justice at all. Then he changes his tack and reformulates Buddhist ethics according to modern categories. "This is firstly to make the moral ideas of the Buddha clearer, and secondly to see how far a moral system designed twenty-four centuries ago can appeal to the modern mind."[16]

Justice appears as a major category in his modern reformulation, but he notes that it is not at all easy to find precise equivalents from the Buddha's time to our own twenty-first century for such basic terms as justice, righteousness, and impartiality.[17] In effect, he seems to admit that he was unable to show that justice is a fundamental ancient Buddhist principle of social ethics. Nonetheless, recognising that justice is a keystone for any ethical system which is to appeal to people shaped by modern Western thought, he goes ahead in a very appealing but not quite convincing way to use justice in his scheme of Buddhist ethics.

A review of current work in the field of Buddhist ethics generally confirms the impression that justice is not a fundamental category of understanding in Buddhist thought. First, in the 1991 book *Buddhist Ethics and Modern Society*, a compendium of papers from a major international conference of Buddhist scholars, justice is only mentioned in one passage, in the contribution of Sulak Sivaraksa, the noted Buddhist reformer from Thailand.[18] In his paper Sulak argues that there is indirect support in Buddhist thought for a "minimum distributive justice" (p. 163) from general Buddhist principles of the middle way. Sulak notes that there is nothing in the scriptures or in Theravada tradition that directly advocates radical social transformation.

Both Gunapala Dharmasiri's *Fundamentals of Buddhist Ethics*,[19] which appeared in 1989, and Damien Keown's *The Nature of Buddhist Ethics*,[20] a 1992 title, fail to discuss the issue of justice as such although there are indirect discussions of related issues. Two major books in the field appeared in 1995. The first, *Buddhism and Bioethics* by Damien Keown, is interesting for its complete lack of any discussion of justice.[21] The term itself, I believe, does not occur. Keown restricts his field of sources to the Pali texts and thus does not draw upon historical or ethnographical material. David Kalupahana, on the other hand, in *Ethics in Early Buddhism*, which mines the same sources as does Keown, devotes chapter 15 to "Law, Justice, and Morals."[22] There he argues that *dhamma* (Sanskrit: *dharma*), which is one of the most fruitfully pregnant terms in Buddhism, is the equivalent of "justice." At one level this is true, but I think the equation is ultimately misleading, since "justice" in the context of ancient India (the Pali and Sanskrit context) is quite different from justice in the contemporary English-speaking world. Kalupahana also recognises this implicitly, noting throughout the book that the Buddha's specific teachings on social order focus on two quite different models.

First is the more or less democratic order of monks, and second is lay society for which a universal king, following the ancient Indian model, whose job it is to turn the wheel of the Dharma for the world, is offered as the ideal ruler. Neither of these forms, in my opinion, has much to do with justice as understood in contemporary Western countries such as Canada. These forms, however, have worked well in the past in South and Southeast Asia as the foundations for a good society, and are still live options. In East Asia, the wheel-turning king as portrayed in the Lotus Sutra and other texts has also been a model for the ideal ruler.

Kalupahana argues that both the polity of the monks and the underlying basis for the universal wheel-turning monarch are consistent with John Rawls' view of the foundations for achieving a just society.[23] I would agree with both Sulak and Kalupahana that there is indirect support for ideas of social and individual justice in Pali–text Buddhist traditions. Or perhaps it would be better to say that there is no contradiction between Buddhist traditional teachings and the modern Western concepts of justice. Since Buddhism has been very successful in adapting itself to all sorts of social realities, and since we seem to be in an era in which Western social forms are increasingly dominant, perhaps it will be the work of Buddhists in the twenty-first century to synthesise *Buddhadharma* and justice.

Such a synthesis may well be different from the current egalitarianism in Western theories, if not practices, of justice. I have not found much evidence for egalitarian justice as a major theme in Buddhist tradition. Consider, for example, the way that Buddhaghosa interpreted the precept against taking life:

> "Taking life" is then the will to kill anything that one perceives as having life . . . insofar as the will finds expression in bodily action or in speech. . . . In the case of humans the killing is the more blameworthy the more virtuous they are. Apart from that the extent of the offence is proportionate to the intensity of the wish to kill.[24]

The severity of the offence is a function of the amount of virtue of the victim, hardly an egalitarian concept.

Dharmasiri notes that although the Buddha rejected the caste system and taught that all persons are equal in that they are subject to the same moral law and in that every person is a potentially enlightened being,[25] he also taught that class society is inevitable. Classes do not have equal rights and duties; rather they "should have reciprocal moral relationships with each other."[26] Indeed, this seems to be the major principle behind social relationships in traditional Buddhist countries and is quite consistent with the teaching of the Lotus Sutra. The basic model is paternalistic, as is very explicit in the case of the king, who, the Buddha taught, should rule according to the Dharma, "treating his subjects as parents treat their own children."[27] Some of the parables of the Lotus Sutra, such as the parable of the rich man and his sons in the burning house (chapter 3), the jewel in the gown (chapter 8), and the skilled physician (chapter 16) spring to mind as powerful teachings in favour of patriarchy.

These ancient, traditional social teachings do, however, strongly support the provision of adequate health care for all people, even all living creatures, in society. The higher individuals in the reciprocal relationships have a duty to be concerned for the welfare of those in their care, and this most definitely includes health matters. For example, masters are taught to give their servants help in times of sickness;[28] and at the highest level, the king's first duty to his subjects is to give them "help when and where it is needed, i.e., a material or verbal or manual help."[29]

In Buddhist political thought, the *Dharma-rāja* (the king who rules by righteousness or by Buddhist principles) or *cakravartin* (literally, the wheel-turner, or the king who turns the wheel of righteousness) is the ideal ruler.[30] The royal precepts and virtues enumerated above are drawn from that tradition. Aśoka, an emperor in India who reigned in the third century B.C.E., is the king revered today as the one who most nearly embodied the *Dharma-rāja* ideal, and he was very vigorous in promoting nonharming as a principle of governance and as a way of life for his subjects. As well, he took great interest in the physical welfare of his subjects and provided medical herbs to be distributed free of charge to the people of his kingdom and also to the animals.[31]

It seems that justice in the egalitarian sense does not have a firm base in Buddhist traditional thought. Perhaps a sounder Buddhist case for an equitable distribution of health services could be built on the foundations of *karuṇā* (compassion), a fundamental virtue for all Buddhists, friendship as a "basic good" (borrowing from Keown), and on the *noblesse oblige* expected of the ideal Buddhist monarch, all of which seem to be consistent with the teachings of the Lotus Sutra. All three of these entail helping the poor: *karuṇā* and friendship as primary virtues should motivate individuals, whether commoners or royalty, and the state should manifest the ideals of the *Dharma-rāja*, the king who rules according to the teachings of the Buddha.[32]

Compassion and Beneficence

Compassion is one of the most fundamental Buddhist categories, so fundamental that the entirety of the tradition can be described as compassion (*karuṇā*) and wisdom (*prajñā*) working together. It is important to keep in mind that the two are linked and one without the other is dangerous. For example, a person who is not wise may cause enormous problems by witlessly attempting to be compassionate, and a person who has penetrating insight without compassion is very dangerous indeed.

In order to help one attain this balance, to make sure that the practitioner develops skillful means (*upāya*), certain sublime states of mind are cultivated in Buddhism. Four of these are taught by all schools of Buddhists and recognised as necessary for living a moral life, generating *kusala karma*, or skillful deeds, rather than the opposite. The four are loving kindness for all sentient beings, compassion for the unhappiness of others, sympathetic joy for the happiness and good fortune of others, and equanimity.[33] On the level of practice, the Lotus Sutra could be interpreted as no less than an extended sermon on how to live the transcendental bodhisattva path by using skillful means compassionately, thus embodying the four sublime states just detailed. Were a nation to be governed according to these impulses, its health care system would be a most excellent manifestation of Buddhist beneficence.

Veracity

The fourth principle which Ratanakul sees as essential in Buddhist biomedical ethics is veracity, which he firmly bases on another of the five basic moral precepts: "I undertake to observe the rule to abstain from false speech." In applying this precept to medical ethics, he concludes that one must always tell the complete truth to the patient. Failure to disclose the truth is generally, he argues, due to denial and fear on the part of medical personnel. If the patient does not know all the facts of his or her condition, then his or her "strength, will-power, and endurance"[34] will be compromised. Buddhists know that life is hard and full of suffering and have always taught that these truths must be dealt with frankly and openly. Hiding from the unpleasant side of things is not part of the Buddhist way.

This insistence on veracity fits in very well with the current doctrine in Western medicine that the patient as an autonomous moral agent has a responsibility for his or her own health and care. However, in the Mahayana tradition, there is a rather different approach to the issue of veracity. In chapter 16 of the Lotus Sutra, there is a parable in which the Buddha compares himself to a skillful physician. All his sons have foolishly taken some powerful, poisonous medicine. Those who are most deranged by the poison refuse to take the antidote which he has quickly prepared. Therefore, he deceives them by feigning his own death, thereby shocking them back into their right minds so that they will take the remedy. Lord Buddha rhetorically asks the assembly, "Is there any man who can say that this good physician is guilty of the sin of wilfully false speech, or is there not?" And they reply: "There is not, O World-Honored One."[35] In his discussion of the Lotus Sutra in his recent book of readings, *Buddhism in Practice*, Donald Lopez demurs from the judgement of the assembly. He argues that "the claim to legitimacy of the earlier tradition is usurped by the Mahāyāna through the explanation that what the Buddha had taught before was in fact a lie,"[36] albeit a compassionately motivated lie. Too strong by far,[37] but it does point to an interesting question: is it not possible for the doctrine of skillful means, in less than skillful hands, to lead in a direction away from the Dharma? The parables of the Lotus Sutra are taught as examples of *upāya* or skillful means. It would seem that deception on the level of relative truth is quite justified as long as it advances the cause of absolute truth and, as in the story of the skillful physician, is beneficent. Of course, if a deception led to harm of sentient beings, it would be unskillful rather than skillful. Thus, in Mahayana thought at least, a case could be made for the health care team withholding the truth or even deceiving a patient if such withholding or deception was thought for good reason to be therapeutic.

This sort of paternalism is no longer favoured in the West and many current health care ethicists reject it, including Dr. Ratanakul, who writes, "The practice of paternalism in regard to truth-telling is therefore unacceptable to Buddhism."[38] Although his argument for veracity on medical, general ethical, and Buddhist grounds is strong, it nonetheless seems to me that his conclusion is overstated, especially in regard to the Mahayana. Medical paternalism may be justifiable in traditional Buddhist societies, which accept that society is to be governed by ancient hierarchical principles enshrined in the texts and traditions of Buddhism. It certainly has been the practice in Japan in regard to cancer diagnosis, where physicians practically never revealed the truth to their patients. While Mahayana teachings on skillful means provide a theoretical justification for this, Japanese cultural attitudes towards bodily disintegration are also important.[39]

References to Medicine in the Lotus Sutra

(1) Parable of the skillful physician

This parable, which occurs in chapter 16, is perhaps the most relevant and important passage in the Lotus Sutra in regard to the practice of medicine. It has been discussed above.

(2) Parable of the medicinal herbs

Chapter 5 consists of a lovely parable about how beneficent waters nourish all plants without discrimination, whether they are tiny medicinal herbs or awe-inspiring giant trees. In the Chinese version of the text, the one which is influential in East Asian Buddhist communities, there does not seem to be anything in this chapter that applies to medicine or medical ethics. The Sanskrit version (translated by Hurvitz and Kern) ends with a lengthy parable that is interesting in this regard. In this parable a man who has been blind from birth relies on his own experience to deny that there are any shapes at all in the world to be seen. A compassionate and supremely skillful physician takes pity on this man and collects and prepares four wondrous herbs which restore the man's sight. Seeing heavenly bodies for the first time, he now claims to be all-seeing and to have attained perfect extinction. Wise seers quickly correct him and point out how ignorant he actually remains.

This parable makes use of the classical metaphor of the Buddha as the supremely skilled physician. It could be taken as a practical example for all Buddhists, who should emulate his compassion by applying their efforts and skills to treating the ill. It is also making one of the primary points of the Lotus Sutra, that those who follow the lesser of the three vehicles need to be reminded that they are a long way indeed from the ultimate goal.

(3) Bodhisattva-*mahāsattva* Medicine King

The Bodhisattva Medicine King (*Bhaiṣajya-rāja*) occurs in several places in the Lotus Sutra. These passages seem to foreshadow the celestial Medicine Buddha (*Bhaiṣajya-guru*), who became very important in the Buddhist traditions of East Asia.[40] The Medicine Buddha is very explicitly charged with taking care of the physical and mental health of devotees and has taken vows to that effect. In the Lotus Sutra the medical aspects of the Bodhisattva Medicine King are not obvious.

Chapter 10 on the Teacher of the Law begins with the Lord Buddha addressing the assembly through the Bodhisattva Medicine King, but I find no medical references at all in the chapter. Similarly chapter 13 on Holding Firm begins by mentioning the Bodhisattva Medicine King as part of the audience, but has nothing in it about medicine. Some of the Buddha's previous existences are covered in chapter 23, a very interesting chapter in which the bodhisattva offers his entire body, his arms, and his fingers out of reverence as fire offerings, a practice which was frequently emulated up until recent times.[41] Near the end of chapter 23 there is a reference to the medical efficacy of the Lotus Sutra: anyone who hears it will be cured of sickness, old age, and death.

In the Dhāranī chapter, chapter 26, the Bodhisattva Medicine King offers a *dhāranī* for the protection of those who preach the Lotus Sutra. The spell has no medical references. However, in the same chapter, a horde of female demons offer a *dhāranī* that protects men, women, boys, and girls against all manner of demonic beings and against all manner of fevers. The final mention in passing of the Bodhisattva Medicine King, along with his brother Medicine Superior, is in chapter 27, dedicated to these two bodhisattvas' father. There are no medical references.

In summary, it appears that the passages about the Bodhisattva Medicine King, rather surprisingly, tell us little about the practice of medicine or of medical ethics.

(4) Medical benefits to those who revere the Lotus Sutra and medical penalties to those who do not respect it

Both chapter 14 on bodhisattva practices and chapter 18 on the benefits of joyous response to the Lotus Sutra detail the health benefits which accrue to those who have joy and faith in the sutra itself. As noted earlier, chapter 23 mentions similar wonderful effects.

On the other hand, those who slander or disparage the Lotus Sutra have much to lose. In chapter 3 there is a passage that says that anyone who speaks badly of the teachings shall be afflicted with all sorts of congenital deformities and illnesses. Furthermore, he or she will be unable to heal anyone else, and any medical attention he or she receives will exacerbate the condition treated. At the very end of the Lotus Sutra—perhaps the placement of this passage is a sign of its importance—terrible medical results are promised for those who disparage believers of the sutra. Blindness, deformity, or leprosy will be their fate for generation after generation.

(5) Bodhisattva practices

Chapter 14 details appropriate activities for one who is cultivating the bodhisattva path, and chapter 25 is a marvellous account of how a bodhisattva of great attainment, namely Avalokiteśvara, is able to help anyone who calls on him in a time of need. I find it interesting and somewhat surprising that medical matters are completely absent from both sets of practices. However, in the introductory chapter, bodhisattvas are commended for offering hundreds of different kinds of medicines to the Buddha and his disciples.

(6) Inquiries about the health of the Lord Buddha

The appearance of the jewelled stupa in the sky in chapter 11 and the emergence from the earth of an astounding number of bodhisattvas in chapter 15 are examples of the very exalted nature of buddhas in the Mahayana. It is a little jolting to find similar simple inquiries in both places about the health and vigour of the World-Honoured One:

> Is the World-Honoured One at ease,
> With few ailments and few troubles?
> In instructing all the living beings,
> Is he free from weariness?[42]

It is very strange that one so inconceivably splendid could possibly be ill or weary, and thus these well-meaning inquiries seem out of place.

Conclusion

In the study of ethics in the West there is widespread agreement, perhaps an emerging consensus, that certain principles—autonomy, beneficence, nonmalfeasance, and justice—apply *prima facie* to health care issues. Not all of these four principles fit into a Buddhist framework. Two of them, however, do fit well. Nonmalfeasance and the Buddhist principle of *ahiṃsā* (nonharming) appear to be practically identical. Furthermore, *karuṇā* (compassion), which perhaps is the central ethical principle of the Buddhist tradition, is very similar indeed to beneficence. Autonomy is also important in Buddhist practice, but, as argued above, is not central, and there are important differences both in theory and in application to health care from the way it is understood in the West.

Justice seems to be the sticking point. Egalitarian justice is not part of traditional Buddhism, although justice in health care can be approached using other Buddhist ideas and practices. As noted in the introduction, Buddhism has a wonderful flexibility, enabling it to adapt to and to learn from new situations. It is noteworthy, I think, that converts to Buddhism in the Western world, eastern Buddhists who have settled in the West, and those like Dr. Ratanakul who have been influenced by Western thought, are tending to make justice a central Buddhist value.[43]

"Cease to do evil, learn to do good, cleanse your own heart," the catch phrase which is popularly used to sum up the essence of Buddhism, suggests how important nonmalfeasance, beneficence, and self-reliance or moral autonomy are in Buddhist thought. All three are aspects of *karuṇā* (compassion) and *upāya* (skillful means), the qualities necessary to function well in the world as a Buddhist. These relative qualities must, of course, work in conjunction with *prajñā* (wisdom), insight into absolute truth. To be true to the Buddhist tradition, any theoretical system of health care ethics must be based on wisdom and compassion, and all applications should manifest skillful means. The underlying principles of the Lotus Sutra are consistent with these, and the parables and references to medical matters offer some specific guidance. At present, with great changes and challenges taking place in the heath care field, Buddhist thought, by applying wisdom, compassion, and skillful means to both theory and practice, can make a tremendous contribution to bioethics.

Notes

1. Raoul Birnbaum, *The Healing Buddha* (Boulder: Shambhala, 1979).
2. *The Journal of Buddhist Ethics,* vol. 3 (1996), has six papers from the 1995 American Academy of Religion panel "Revisioning Buddhist Ethics." These papers reflect some of the current excitement and flux in the field of Buddhist ethics. Their general comments are very apt as well for Buddhist health care ethics. One of their recurring themes is to suggest that there is very little commonality in theoretical approaches to ethical reasoning in Buddhist texts and traditions. It seems to me that there are many authentic ways or tools that Buddhists have used throughout the centuries to think about ethical issues, just as there are many paths in Christian and Western ethics. Today modern Buddhists, both Eastern and Western, are coming to grips with new problems and issues and are struggling to come up with practical solutions that are true to their religious heritage and their national traditions. No unified answers or approaches can be expected, and such really are not to be hoped for in the Buddhist tradition, which respects diversity.
3. Damien Keown, *Buddhism and Bioethics* (New York: St. Martin's Press, 1995).
4. Ibid., 43ff.
5. Ibid., 51ff.
6. Raanan Gillon, ed., *Principles of Health Care Ethics* (Chichester: Wiley, 1994). This very large book attempts to apply the four principles across the board around the world with varying success. For a good discussion of the four principles, see the editor's introductory essay, "Medical Ethics and the Four Principles."
7. What follows in the remainder of this section is based upon my paper "Buddhism and the Four Principles" in Gillon, *Principles,* 105–16.
8. P. Ratanakul, *Bioethics: An Introduction to the Ethics of Medicine and Life Sciences* (Bangkok: Mahidol University, 1986), 86.
9. P. Ratanakul, "Bioethics in Thailand: The Struggle for Buddhist Solutions," *The Journal of Medicine and Philosophy* (1988), 13: 301–12.
10. Ibid., 312.
11. Ratanakul, *Bioethics: An Introduction,* 83–84.
12. Ibid., 54.
13. Ratanakul, "Bioethics in Thailand," 311.
14. Gillon, "Medical Ethics," *Principles,* xxv.
15. Buddhaghosa, *The Path of Purification (Viśuddhimagga),* 2 vols. (Berkeley and London, 1976), Lamotte, *Histoire du Buddhisme Indien,* vol. 1, (Louvain: Université du Louvain, 1976), 25ff., and several other basic source books yielded nothing on justice as an early Buddhist concern. Similarly, S. Punyanubhab, "An Outline of Buddhist Tenets," in National Identity Board's *Buddhism in Thai Life* (Bangkok: Funny Publishing Limited Partnership, 1981), 19–28, and other contemporary popular treatments of Buddhism fail to include justice as a fundamental tenet.
16. Shundō Tachibana, *The Ethics of Buddhism* (1926; reprint, London: Curzon, 1975), 95.

17. Ibid., 264–65; see A. L. Basham, *The Wonder That Was India* (New York: Grove Press, 1959), 114–17 and *passim*, for an indication of how very different the ancient Indian concept of justice is from the current Western notion.
18. Sulak Sivaraksa, "Buddhist Ethics and Modern Politics: A Theravada Viewpoint," *Buddhist Ethics and Modern Society: An International Symposium*, ed. Charles Wei-hsun Fu and Sandra A. Wawrytko (New York: Greenwood Press, 1991), 163–64.
19. Gunapala Dharmasiri, *Fundamentals of Buddhist Ethics* (Antioch, California: Golden Leave, 1989).
20. Damien Keown, *The Nature of Buddhist Ethics* (New York: St. Martin's Press, 1992).
21. Damien Keown, *Buddhism and Bioethics*.
22. David J. Kalupahana, *Ethics in Early Buddhism* (Honolulu: University of Hawaii Press, 1995).
23. Ibid., 125.
24. E. Conze, trans. *Buddhist Scriptures* (Harmondsworth: Penguin, 1959), 70–71.
25. Dharmasiri, *Fundamentals*, 62.
26. Ibid., 61.
27. S. B. Indr, "The King in Buddhist Tradition," *Buddhism in Thai Life*, 61.
28. Phra Dhammadhajamuni, *Outline of Buddhism*, 2nd. ed. (Bangkok: Mahamakut Buddhist University, B.E. 2530). 43.
29. Ibid., 53.
30. S. J. Tambiah, *World Conqueror and World Renouncer: A Study of Buddhism and Polity in Thailand against a Historical Background* (Cambridge: Cambridge University Press, 1976).
31. Basham, *Wonder*, 53–57, 500.
32. It seems to me from my time in Thailand that the royal family there lives up to these Buddhist ideals very well indeed by sponsoring and financing many public health and other health-related projects. See, for example, T. Kraivixien, *His Majesty King Bhumibol Adulyadej: Compassionate Monarch of Thailand* (Bangkok: Kathavethin Foundation, 1982).
33. S. Taniguchi, *A Study of Biomedical Ethics from a Buddhist Perspective* (Berkeley: Graduate Theological Union and Institute of Buddhist Studies), 65–69 and E. Conze, *Buddhist Meditation* (London: Unwin, 1972), 118–32. Dr. Steven K. H. Aung in his "Loving Kindness: The Essential Buddhist Contribution to Primary Care," *Humane Health Care International* [formerly Humana], vol. 12.2 (April, 1996), 81–84, does an excellent job of explaining how *metta* can function in the day to day practice of medicine.
34. Ratanakul, "Bioethics in Thailand," 308.
35. L. Hurvitz, trans., *Scripture of the Lotus Blossom of the Fine Dharma* (New York: Columbia University Press, 1976), 240
36. Donald S. Lopez, *Buddhism in Practice* (Princeton, New Jersey: Princeton University Press, 1995), 29.
37. Nikkyō Niwano, *A Guide to the Threefold Lotus Sutra* (Tokyo: Kōsei Publishing Co., 1981), 110ff., provides a good corrective to Lopez's position.

38. P. Ratanakul, "Bioethics in Thailand," 308.
39. E. Ohnuki-Tierney, *Illness and Culture in Contemporary Japan: An Anthropological View* (Cambridge: Cambridge University Press, 1984), 62–65, 207–08.
40. Birnbaum, *The Healing Buddha* (Boston: Shambhala Publications, 1989), and Hajime Nakamura, "Buddhism, Schools of: Mahāyāna Buddhism," *The Encyclopedia of Religion*, vol. 2, Mircea Eliade, ed. (New York: Macmillan, 1987), 459.
41. Lopez, *Practice*, chapter 36; Paul Williams, *Mahayana Buddhism: The Doctrinal Foundations* (London and New York: Routledge, 1989), 154–55. In the introductory chapter to the Lotus Sutra it is noted with approval that bodhisattvas give their own flesh, hands, and feet as offerings.
42. Bunnō Katō, W. E. Soothill, et al., trans., *The Threefold Lotus Sutra* (Tokyo, New York: Kōsei Publishing Co., Weatherhill, 1975), 239.
43. F. Eppsteiner and D. Maloney, eds. *The Path of Compassion: Contemporary Writings on Engaged Buddhism* (Berkeley, California and Buffalo, New York: Buddhist Peace Fellowship and White Pine Press, 1985). This book is a good introduction to this phenomenon.

Social Responsibility, Sex Change, and Salvation: Gender Justice in the Lotus Sutra

Lucinda Joy Peach

I. Introduction

What does the Lotus Sutra have to teach us about social responsibility?[1] The immense influence and popularity of this Buddhist scripture throughout many parts of Asia[2] is reason itself to investigate its relationship to social responsibility. In addition, the text of the Lotus Sutra itself suggests a reason for examining its teachings on social responsibility by proclaiming itself to be the "one vehicle," the unifying law or truth, what Yoshirō Tamura describes as "the great unifying law of the universe that animates everyone and everything equally."[3] More specifically, if we think of social responsibility in the contemporary world as encompassing "gender justice"—that is, fairness and equitable treatment for all persons, regardless of their sex or gender—what is the Lotus Sutra's message?

Does the Lotus Sutra promote or deny gender justice, or is it simply indifferent on this issue? The continuing popularity and influence of the Lotus Sutra throughout many regions of Asia, including China, Korea, and Japan, during a period in which traditional understandings of patriarchal and male–dominated social relations are being challenged as unjust, provides a motivation for examining the Lotus's relationship to gender justice.[4] In particular, as Buddhism, in the words of George Tanabe, seeks "to justify itself as a religion suitable for modern Japan,"[5] a nation currently struggling with changing gender roles and relationships between men and women, what role does or could the Lotus Sutra's teachings about gender play in relation to gender justice?

Gender is an important category of analysis in the Lotus Sutra. It provides a means for differentiating and hierarchalizing the status of males and females, both human and nonhuman. It symbolizes differences in

437

temperament, capabilities, and virtues. Perhaps most importantly, it provides a basis for evaluating people's capacity for realizing the Mahayana ideal of full Buddhahood—*anuttara-samyak-saṃbodhi*—as opposed to the "lesser" Hinayana Buddhist goal of *arhatship*.

Before embarking on an analysis of the Lotus's teachings about gender, some qualifications are in order. First, although the Lotus Sutra has unquestionably had a significant influence in shaping attitudes about gender as Nancy Schuster reminds us,[6] the specific influence of the Lotus Sutra in shaping understandings of gender among its hearers and readers has varied significantly. The way the sutra's statements have been received, especially concerning normative gender roles, has undoubtedly varied in different places and times, given the multivocal and multivalent character of Buddhist scriptures, as well as the diverse social locations of the sutra's hearers and readers.

Second, the influence of gender images does not necessarily correlate in any direct way to the actual status of women in a particular social location.[7] For example, simply because negative images of females and views about women may abound in Buddhist texts widely disseminated in popular religious discourse does not necessarily mean that women will be subordinated in that society as a result. Conversely, positive textual images and valuations of females and the feminine do not necessitate that "real" women will be respected or esteemed. Indeed, the status of religious images of females and the feminine and the actual social status of women may even be negatively correlated. Thus, there is no one single or predictable way that gender images will influence those who encounter them.

In this paper, I will examine the gendered imagery in the Lotus Sutra in order to assess its messages regarding normative gender relations, and the implications of these messages for gender justice in the contemporary world. The first part of the paper explores gender imagery in the Lotus Sutra. The second part compares these images with those found elsewhere in the Buddhist tradition in order to provide a clearer assessment of how representative the Lotus's messages are regarding gender in Buddhism more generally.

II. Gender Imagery in the Lotus Sutra

General Observations

At the outset of this investigation, it should be noted that the Lotus Sutra contains a wide variety of gender images, not all of them consistent with one another. One of the most significant messages of the sutra as a whole is that because *all* persons possess the Buddha-nature, not only those of a certain birth, gender, aptitude, etc., the possibility of full enlightenment is available to all beings.[8] The specific passage providing perhaps the most egalitarian statement about gender relations in the text is the verse form of chapter 14, "Peaceful Practices." In an instruction to Mañjuśrī concerning appropriate bodhisattva conduct, the Buddha advises that "one should not make distinctions by saying, 'This is a man,' 'This is a woman.'" This admonition is closely followed by the statement that "All phenomena are empty, without being, without any constant abiding, without arising or extinction."[9] The universality of this message (although contradicted elsewhere in the text) suggests that women as well as men have the capacity to attain full, complete enlightenment. In fact, the translator Burton Watson claims that "the Lotus Sutra reveals that its revolutionary doctrines operate in a realm transcending all petty distinctions of sex or species."[10]

Within the Lotus Sutra's doctrine of the "two truths" of ultimate and conventional or relative reality, these passages describe the level of ultimate truth. Here, gender—as with all other distinctions—is irrelevant. At the level of conventional truth, however, gender distinctions are extremely relevant, as is obvious elsewhere in the Lotus. In contrast to the passage just cited, more often than not the gender of the beings populating the Lotus Sutra is specified. For example, in stating who is present at an assembly to hear the Buddha's teachings, a frequent description begins "monks, nuns, laymen, laywomen." When they are described at all, the Buddha's disciples are usually referred to as "good men and good women."[11] Gender is even used to make the argument of its own irrelevance, as when the *rākṣasa* demon's daughters tell the Buddha they will protect the followers of the Lotus Sutra against all manner of harm, regardless of the form it takes, "whether it be in man's form, in woman's form, in young boy's form, in young girl's form. . . ."[12]

The salience of gender is also suggested in chapter 19, "Benefits of the Teacher of the Law," which states that the benefits to "good men or good women" of accepting and upholding this Lotus Sutra include (in the verse form) knowing "the scent of living beings, the scent of men and women," including "wheel-turning kings of great authority, lesser wheel-turners and their sons," and "jeweled ladies of wheel-turning kings."[13] Gender is so important that the benefits of the heightened sense of smell include the ability to ascertain not only whether a pregnant woman's child "will lack normal faculties or be inhuman," but also whether it is male or female."[14]

Gender is often a significant characteristic of beings of the non-human realms as well, indicating that beings are gendered throughout the universe, regardless of which realm they inhabit.[15] Chapter 19 describes those who are moved by hearing the Lotus as including: "men and women of heaven, Shakra, Brahma and the other heavenly beings. . . . Dragons and dragon daughters, yakshas and yaksha daughters, gandharvas and gandharva daughters, asuras and asura daughters,[16] garudas and garuda daughters, kimnaras and kimnara daughters, mahoragas and mahoraga daughters. . . ." as well as "monks, nuns, laymen, laywomen" and others.[17] (Curiously, no explanation is given as to why the "sons" of these nonhuman beings are not also present.[18])

Similarly, chapter 26, "Dharani," relates that at the time of heavenly king Upholder of the Nation there were ten daughters of *rākṣasa* demons who, along with "the Mother of Devil Children," came to tell the Buddha of their vow to protect those who accept and uphold the Lotus Sutra.[19]

Gender is also specified with reference to the realms "above" the human. Chapter 19 refers to "heavenly women," who can be detected when "they whirl and circle in enjoyment," "adorned with lovely flowers and perfumes"[20] and chapter 27 predicts that those who copy the sutra will be reborn in the Trāyastriṃśa heaven where "eighty-four thousand heavenly women, performing all kinds of music, will come to greet them" and "ladies in waiting" will be available to amuse them. Those who also understand and practice the sutra will be reborn in the Tuṣita heaven where the Bodhisattva Maitreya has "hundreds, thousands, ten thousands, millions of heavenly women attendants."[21]

In contrast to the presence of women in these heavenly realms, in chapter 8, "Prophecy of Enlightenment for Five Hundred Disciples," the land of the future Buddha "Law Bright Thus Come One" is described as having "no evil paths of existence there, nor . . . any women."[22] This is one of a number of places in the Lotus where females are depicted as inferior, either explicitly or implicitly. The linking of women with "evil paths of existence" indicates that the two are integrally connected, and that the presence of one leads to the presence of the other. Similarly, chapter 23, "Former Affairs of the Bodhisattva Medicine King," portrays the Buddha Sun Moon Pure Bright Virtue Thus Come One's land as having "no women, hell dwellers, hungry spirits, beasts or asuras, and no kinds of tribulation."[23] The implications of this verse are that women are incapable of attaining the realization that would result in their inhabiting this Buddha-land and that they are akin to hell dwellers, etc.[24]

Similarly, in chapter 8, the Buddha's prophecy regarding Pūrṇa Maitrāyaṇīputra is that his Buddha worlds will be beautiful and purified: "There will be no evil paths of existence there, nor will there be any women." This is followed by the prophecy that "all living beings will be born through transformation and will be without lewd desires."[25]

Similarly, even women who follow the Lotus's teachings will be reborn in Amitāyus's Buddha land as males,[26] as will be discussed further later. Linking the absence of women to the absence of sex (both procreative and carnal) suggests that women are the cause of the problems resulting from sexuality. More specifically it indicates that human reproduction itself, which is here associated with women by proximity, is impure—perhaps because it is the immediate cause of rebirth into *samsaric* existence. Thus, the text's prescription for removing the problems of sexual desire and reproduction is to remove the women!

The absence of women from these Buddha-lands must be contrasted with the presence of women in the heavenly realms noted above. Although the "heavenly realms" are not nearly as advanced within the Lotus's cosmology as Buddha worlds, nonetheless, they are "higher" than the human realm. The presence of women in the heavenly realms may suggest that gender is not an obstacle to rising above the human realm, even if it may be a deterrent to attaining full Buddhahood. On the other hand, it may suggest that women are appropriately cast in heavenly realms only as sexual objects and pleasant playthings for men, not as a result of their own positive karma.

We thus find that the Lotus Sutra reflects a certain polyvocality of gender messages regarding women. Some of the specific images of females in the Lotus Sutra are inconsistent, even directly opposed. Females are portrayed as both laity and monastics, bodhisattvas and *śrāvakas*, human and nonhuman, wealthy and poor, beautiful and ugly, devotees and non-Buddhists, diligent practitioners and lazy slackers, virtuous and virtueless. They are also relatively invisible throughout most of the text.

Almost all of the significant individuals in the text are men, including all of the Buddhas, bodhisattvas, monarchs, etc. This makes the rare appearance of a woman—or even a female nonhuman being—notable by comparison. On several occasions, the Buddha refers to the gathered bodhisattvas and *mahāsattvas* as "good men,"[27] as "my sons" or "these sons,"[28] as "the countless sons of the Buddha"[29] or simply as "a son of the Buddha."[30] Chapter 3, "Simile and Parable," describes bodhisattvas as "great men"[31] and the Buddha as "the father of all living beings."[32] This description is repeated in chapter 14, where aspiring bodhisattvas are admonished to think of the Buddhas as "kindly fathers" and "unsurpassed fathers."[33] In the verse portion of chapter 7, "The Parable of the Phantom City," the Buddha describes himself as "the Dharma King."[34]

Such male-gendered and patriarchal language indicates either that all of those present before the Buddha are male or that any females who might be present are not significant enough for the Buddha to speak to directly. Such language also contributes to a presumption that the important participants in the Buddha's life are male. This presumption is some-times rebutted, however. In the introductory chapter, several of the women closest to Śākyamuni Buddha are specifically mentioned as being pre-sent. Among several categories of beings, women are mentioned in the category of "two thousand persons, some of whom were still learning and some who had completed their learning."[35] They include Śākyamuni's aunt and step-mother Mahāprajāpatī and her six thousand followers, and Yaśodharā, the wife Śākyamuni abandoned (along with their son Rāhula) when he left home to seek enlightenment. Both of these women have become Buddhist nuns, and are accompanied by their followers. Thus, the presence of women at the very beginning of the Lotus Sutra does convey the centrality of women as faithful followers of the Buddha. However, their placement after the *arhats* and before the bodhisattvas and *mahasattvas*[36] suggests that they are in neither category, but instead have some other status.

Indeed, sometimes a gender hierarchy which makes males superior to females (although relatively, and not absolutely) is explicit. For example, in chapter 20, "The Bodhisattva Never Disparaging," included in the as-sembly are "Bhadrapala and his group, five hundred bodhisattvas; Lion Moon and her group, five hundred nuns, and Thinking of Buddha and his group, five hundred laymen."[37] Were males absolutely privileged, they would presumably occupy all of the exclusively spiritual roles. Yet here females occupy an intermediate position between bodhisattvas and lay persons. This intermediate location signifies that although women are not at the apex of the spiritual hierarchy, neither are they at the bot-tom.

In other parts of the Lotus Sutra, women are the locus of non-virtue, as in chapter 14, "Peaceful Practices." Just before the verse quoted earlier regarding the irrelevance of gender distinctions, the Buddha is instruct-ing Mañjuśrī regarding the four rules that bodhisattvas and *mahāsattvas* should follow in preaching the Lotus Sutra in the evil age. Here, he advises that when preaching the law to women, they should not do so in a man-ner

> that could arouse thoughts of desire in them, nor should he delight in seeing them. If he enters the house of another person, he should not engage in talk with the young girls, unmarried women or wid-ows. Nor should he go near the five types of unmanly men or have any close dealings with them. . . . If he should preach the Law for a woman, he should not bare his teeth in laughter or let his chest be-come exposed.[38]

In the event that the purpose of this instruction is not obvious, it is clarified by the following statement that "he should not have any intimate dealings with her even for the sake of the Law, much less for any other purpose."[39]

In part, these admonitions seem designed simply, to use American legal terminology, to "avoid the appearance of impropriety" by removing bodhisattvas from sources of sexual temptation. The inclusion of "unmanly men" among the persons to avoid indicates that the problem is sex, not women. Nonetheless, the dominant references are to women, suggesting that it is the female sex that is problematic, not the males who risk experiencing sexual temptation. Such references thereby have the effect of symbolically linking women with sex, and thus with desire, and thus with attachment to samsara, a theme repeated in many other Buddhist texts. Consequently, the association of women with sexual temptation indicates that women are more closely linked to samsara than men are.

Overall, then, the specific gender images in the Lotus Sutra convey a somewhat inconsistent portrayal of women: they are apparently capable of full enlightenment, but are more closely tied to samsara than are men; they are present at the Buddha's teachings initially, yet are often absent, invisible, or ignored later. They are worthy of being instructed in the Dharma by bodhisattvas, but are at the same time dangerous sources of sexual temptation. This ambivalence or multivalent message about gender is also found in the Lotus Sutra's representations of gender in relation to enlightenment.

Gender and Enlightenment

There are two main narratives in the Lotus Sutra that address women's capacity for full, complete enlightenment, located in chapters 12 and 13, approximately the middle of the text. The famous story of the dragon king's daughter in chapter 12, "Devadatta," includes the most striking discourse in the entire text concerning women's capacity for enlightenment. Mañjuśrī describes the remarkable talents and wisdom of the eight-year-old daughter of the dragon king Sāgara as follows:

> She has mastered the dharanis, has been able to accept and embrace all the storehouse of profound secrets preached by the Buddhas, has entered deep into meditation, thoroughly grasped the doctrines, and in the space of an instant conceived the desire for bodhi and reached the level of no regression.[40]

Her final talent is that she is "capable of attaining bodhi."[41]

The Bodhisattva Wisdom Accumulated doubts the dragon girl's talents, skeptically saying, "I cannot believe that this girl in the space of an instant could actually achieve correct enlightenment." But even before he finishes speaking, the scripture relates that "the dragon king's daughter suddenly appeared before the Buddha" and recites verses of praise for him. She herself proclaims that having heard his teachings, she has attained *bodhi*, to which "the Buddha alone can bear witness." Now Śāriputra becomes the doubtful one, arguing that it is difficult to believe she has been able to attain so much in such a short time "Because a woman's body is soiled and defiled, not a vessel for the Law," because the path takes "immeasurable kalpas" in order to achieve success, and because "a woman is subject to the five obstacles," which means she cannot become a Buddha (or a universal monarch, a Śakra-god, Brahmā, or a Māra). Śāriputra's doubts are concluded with the question "How then could a woman like you be able to attain Buddhahood so quickly?"[42]

The dragon girl's response to the Bodhisattva Wisdom Accumulated and Śāriputra is to demonstrate how rapidly she can attain enlightenment. By comparing the speed with which she hands the Buddha a precious jewel (and he accepts it), she instructs those assembled, "Employ your supernatural powers and watch me attain Buddhahood. It will be even quicker than that!" She then changes into a man "in the space of an instant," carries out all the practices of a bodhisattva, attains "impartial and correct enlightenment," and expounds "the wonderful Law for all beings everywhere in the ten directions." In response, thousands of the assembled progress along the path to enlightenment, and "silently believed and accepted" the dragon girl's feats.[43]

In portraying enlightenment as an almost instantaneous process rather than a gradual one taking innumerable lifetimes, the dragon girl narrative differs from many other stories in the Lotus Sutra. In fact, Nancy Schuster argues that it "clearly and boldly" states that

> the old notion that a woman's body disqualifies her from Buddhahood is wrong, for here is a Buddha-to-be (the Dragon-princess) who was born female . . . Bodhisattvahood is not inconsistent with having a female body; in fact, one can be reborn as a woman, as the Dragon-princess was, after having progressed very far on the path to Buddhahood . . . .[44]

She contends that the Lotus Sutra's argument "is directed against the notion that some *bodies* (male) are fit for the highest destinies, and other *bodies* (female) are not. . . . It is the understanding of the disciples which is at fault; those who understand the *Lotus's* teaching—such as Mañjuśrī—see no problem in the sex or the age of the girl-Bodhisattva."[45]

Although Schuster is correct that this narrative disrupts conventional understandings that high levels of spiritual understanding and attainment are not possessed by females, her argument overlooks the necessity of a physical change from female to male before these females can attain complete enlightenment. The narrative in the Lotus Sutra thus affirms the very view Schuster claims it undermines, that is, that it is necessary to have a male body in order to become a Buddha. If Schuster was correct that this and analogous sutras established that "physical differences between male and female are irrelevant to the attainment of enlightenment" or that "the distinction of male and female is essentially a matter of incomplete misunderstanding,"[46] then there would be no need for the females in these narratives to transform themselves into males!

In supporting her view that these gender transformation stories collectively reflect a positive view of women as spiritually and intellectually equal, Schuster points out that the view we heard in Śāriputra's voice in the dragon girl narrative—that women are subject to the "five obstacles" or disqualifications—was a widespread belief in Mahayana Buddhism. Given this "problem" with the female body from the standpoint of Buddhist doctrine that makes male bodily characteristics critical "marks" of spiritual attainment in the conventional world, Schuster and others argue that the gender transformation narratives provide an effective way of resolving the difficulty while not precluding the possibility of females attaining complete Buddhahood in this very life.[47]

Similarly, Nikkyō Niwano argues that:

> Women of today may feel dissatisfied that the dragon's daughter was suddenly transformed into a male and then became a buddha. Such an expression was used merely because of the idea of women in ancient India. The sudden transformation of a woman into a male means nothing but the transcendence of the difference between male and female. . . . Observed with the Buddha's eyes, all living beings are equal. We must never misinterpret this.[48]

Along the same lines, Diana Paul explains the gender transformations as necessary, given the historical cultural context in which a woman's family responsibilities to marry and become the mother of sons would restrict her religious roles.[49]

Nonetheless, the dragon girl's gender transformation has dubious value for contradicting Śāriputra's assessment of the spiritual limitations of women. On the one hand, the dragon king's daughter demonstrates that there is nothing inherent about gender that prevents a woman from attaining enlightenment by becoming a man. On the other hand, her gender transformation into a male reinforces the belief that it is in fact necessary for females to take on a male form in order to become enlightened. The gender shift, although signifying the insubstantiality and ephemerality of sex, also reinforces the image that women are incapable of attaining enlightenment in female form. The sex change thus perpetuates a male-biased view that only men can achieve complete Buddhahood, and thereby limits the force of the Lotus Sutra for promoting gender justice.

In contrast to the dragon girl story in chapter 12, the "prediction" narrative in chapter 13 is the most affirmative statement of women's capacity for full Buddhahood in the entire Lotus Sutra. In this chapter, "Encouraging Devotion," the Buddha's stepmother Mahāprajāpatī and his former wife Yaśodharā, along with their entourages of followers, are gathered among an assembly, hundreds and thousands of which are being given prophecies of future enlightenment. The nuns are described by Watson as "some still learning" or "others with nothing more to learn,"[50] indicating that women *are* capable of high levels of spiritual achievement.

The Buddha asks Mahāprajāpatī why the nuns are all looking at him in a perplexed manner, suggesting that perhaps it is because their names are not among those prophesied to attain enlightenment. He then reminds her that he earlier made a general statement "saying that all the voice-hearers had received such a prophecy," implying that she has nothing to worry about. Then, seemingly to appease her insecurities, he continues by saying that

> in ages to come, amid the Law of sixty-eight thousands of millions of Buddhas, you will be a great teacher of the Law, and the six thousand nuns . . . will accompany you. . . . In this manner you will bit by bit fulfill the way of the bodhisattva until you are able to become a Buddha with the name Gladly Seen by All Living Beings Thus Come One.[51]

He then tells her that this Buddha will prophesy the future enlightenment of the six thousand bodhisattvas.

Next, Yaśodharā thinks she has been left out of the Buddha's prophecy, and the Buddha tells her that in future ages she too will become a bodhisattva, a great teacher of the Law, and will gradually fulfill the Buddha-way, becoming the Buddha Endowed with a Thousand Ten Thousand Glowing Marks Thus Come One. Mahāprajāpatī, Yaśodharā, and all the nuns together tell the Buddha that having heard the prophecies, their minds are peaceful and tranquil, and that they will be able to go to other lands to propagate the sutra.[52] Even though it will take "ages" to occur, these predictions are not accompanied by the qualification that women need to change their female bodies first, as is the dragon girl's narrative. Although these women are depicted as somewhat jealous and lacking in patience and faith, they are all deemed to be capable, worthy, and ultimately successful in attaining full, complete enlightenment.

These two narratives present an interesting juxtaposition. In the dragon girl story, enlightenment of the female is seemingly instantaneous, yet requires her to undergo a sex change operation. In the latter, enlightenment is predicted for women without any such prerequisite, yet it will take "ages to come." Despite the ambiguities and ambivalances, both narratives affirm women's capacity for enlightenment. They both thus generally support the principle of gender justice, albeit in a qualified way.

In addition to these two dominant narratives, other passages relate women's capacity for spiritual achievement, if not full, complete, enlightenment. For instance, in chapter 27, "Former Affairs of King Wonderful Adornment," after describing how two sons succeed in gaining their mother's permission to become renunciants, the text relates, "At that time the eighty-four thousand persons in the women's quarters of King Wonderful Adornment were all capable of accepting and upholding the Lotus Sutra" and the "king's consort had gained the samadhi of the Buddhas' assembly and was capable of understanding the secret storehouse of the Buddhas."[53]

But chapter 23 reinforces the message that only males can attain enlightenment in proclaiming, "If there is a woman who hears this chapter on the Former Affairs of the Bodhisattva Medicine King and is able to accept and uphold it, that will be her last appearance in a woman's body and she will never be born in that form again." This prediction continues:

> If in the last five hundred year period after the Thus Come One has entered extinction there is a woman who hears this sutra and carries out its practices as the sutra directs, when her life here on earth comes to an end she will immediately go to the world of Peace and Delight where the Buddha Amitayus dwells surrounded by the assembly of great bodhisattvas and there will be born seated on a jeweled seat in the center of a lotus blossom. He will no longer know the torments of greed, desire, anger, rage, stupidity or ignorance. . .[54]

The Buddha will join in praising this now-male woman with "Excellent, excellent, good man!" and the prediction "There will be none among the voice-hearers, prateyekabuddhas or bodhisattvas whose wisdom and ability in meditation can equal yours!"[55] This prediction reinforces the view of women as inferior to men, and serves to undermine the more positive gender messages in chapters 12 and 13.

As we can see, the gender imagery in the Lotus Sutra fails to provide any certain and clearly articulated teaching regarding women's status or capacity for enlightenment. Although the sutra states that gender distinctions are irrelevant, the gendering of most beings who appear in this sutra, and the frequent evaluation of their spiritual capabilities on the basis of gender, suggests that gender differences are significant, and that they are significant precisely for the purpose of hierarchalizing men as superior to women.

This negative assessment of the implications of the Lotus Sutra's teachings for gender justice is reinforced by a comparison with the gender imagery and narratives of gender transformation in other Buddhist texts.

III. COMPARISONS WITH OTHER BUDDHIST SCRIPTURES

Many other Buddhist scriptures contain gender imagery that might be used as a basis of comparison with the Lotus Sutra. The entire range of images we see in the Lotus appear in some other scripture, although perhaps there is no single scripture containing as wide a diversity of gender images. In general terms, earlier scriptures and Theravada texts tend to contain more negative female images, especially of the "women as sexual temptress" variety, while Mahayana texts reflect a broader array of feminine images, ranging from the most misogynistic to most elevated spiritual doctrines.

Scholars have suggested that the negative images of women in many early Buddhist texts, especially as sexual temptresses, indicate that monks considered women's sexuality as a threat, not only to their pursuit of the spiritual path, but also to the stability of the monastic order as a whole, and even to the cycles of birth and death within samsaric existence as a whole.[56] For example, in the *Udayana-vatsarāja-parivarta* Sutra, part of the *Ratnakūṭa* collection of sutras, the Buddha tells King Udayana that "when men have close relationships with women, they have close relationships with evil ways." The verse form continues:

> Fools
> Lust for women
> Like dogs in heat.
> They do not know abstinence.
>
> They are also like flies
> Who see vomited food.
> Like a herd of hogs,
> They greedily seek manure.
>
> Women can ruin
> The precepts of purity.
> They can also ignore
> Honor and virtue.

Causing one to go to hell
They prevent rebirth in heaven.
Why should the wise
Delight in them?

. . . .

Women can compound one's suffering.
By their perfume
One falls in love.

The fool,
Confused, yearns for her.
Being close and admiring
Insignificant things,
He turns away from wisdom.[57]

The use of the female body as a symbol of attachment to the world of sensuality is a common theme throughout the Buddhist world, beginning with the story of the Buddha's renunciation from lay life. Siddhārtha Gautama abandons not only his young wife and newborn son, but also a household of beautiful female musicians and dancing girls which his father had provided for his entertainment. The Buddha's struggle under the *bodhi* tree for enlightenment years later involves rejecting the sensual enticements of Māra's "daughters," who have been sent to seduce him away from his spiritual goal.

Even within the earliest stratum of Buddhist texts, however, positive images of women exist. For example, the *Therīgāthā*, "Songs of the Sisters," is a collection of the poems and narratives attributed to the first Buddhist nuns.[58] Many of these poems describe the female subjects and their enlightenment experiences very positively. Alan Sponberg suggests that "the most important point regarding the place of women in early Buddhism" is that "women could and did become arhats, fully liberated individuals." Nonetheless, he tells us that by the first century C.E., a vehement debate had emerged regarding whether a woman could become a Buddha. Evidence of that debate is apparent in the negative images of women and the emergence of the "five obstacles" included in the Lotus and a number of other Buddhist scriptures. For instance, the *Cullavagga* (chapter 10) includes "the eight special rules"—disciplinary rules only applicable to female renunciants which were designed to insure their subordination to the monks.[59]

Although, as we have seen, the Lotus Sutra contains some references to women as seductive "snares," these are not the dominant images. In addition, the Lotus does not emphasize the need to subjugate women to men in either monastic or lay life as early texts do. (Of course, the silence on this issue may simply reflect its institutionalization to the extent that it was no longer considered something needing to be remarked upon.)

Later, Mahayana, texts contain both negative and positive images of women. Diana Paul classifies Mahayana literature depicting women's role as bodhisattvas into three categories: (1) texts in which women are denied entrance to a Buddha land; (2) those in which women are accepted as lower-stage bodhisattvas; and (3) those in which women are accepted as advanced bodhisattvas and imminent Buddhas.[60] As Nancy Schuster points out, of the first type, the *Bodhisattvabhūmi* argues that women are inherently weak in intellect and virtue, traits which would certainly limit their capacity for Buddhahood.[61] In the Pure Land Sutra, a bodhisattva suggests that after his enlightenment, women who hear his name should despise their female nature and not be reborn as females.[62] Elements of this doctrine are also apparent in the Lotus, as we have seen.

According to Paul, sutras containing the second type are the most common. Women are depicted as having some spiritual capacity, but their authority remains secondary to men's. The device of gender transformation provides a means for extraordinary females to be recognized for their superior virtues and merits by changing their sex to become bodhisattvas or even Buddhas within this life.[63] I will further examine sutras in this second category shortly.

In the third category, gender is not an obstacle to complete Buddhahood or enlightenment. Sponberg suggests that some factions of the Mahayana—specifically Vajrayāna Buddhism—revived an earlier ideal of gender inclusiveness by positing "soteriological androgyny" in the sixth or seventh century C.E. The underlying assumption of this doctrine is that all beings possess the full range of both male and female characteristics. Sponberg claims that the earliest antecedents of this development are in the early Mahayana, in the *Prajñāpāramitā* (Perfection of Wisdom) sutras, in which the perfection of wisdom is portrayed as female, "the mother of all the Buddhas."[64]

The popularity and frequency of "enlightened female" images varies to some extent among Buddhist cultures, but they are readily available throughout Mahayana Buddhism. For example, the male Bodhisattva Avalokiteśvara in India underwent a gender transformation to become the female Bodhisattva Kuan Yin in China. Kuan Yin is tremendously popular in Taiwan, where almost every community has at least one temple devoted to her worship.[65] Similarly, Tibetan Vajrayāna texts contain a multitude of female images, many of them quite positive. These include symbolic representations of the perfection of wisdom as the Goddess Tārā, multitudes of Ḍākinīs (a kind of female spirit) who render spiritual

assistance to practititoners, and a number of female bodhisattvas and female "consorts" or partners of male Buddhas.[66]

Nonetheless, even in Mahayana Buddhist texts written a millennium
after the time of the Buddha, there remain quite negative images of
women, such as the "horrific figurations of the feminine" that Liz Wilson
describes, "grotesque" portrayals of disfigured and decaying females
who are characterized as vile, foul, disease-ridden, the cause of suffering
and death.[67] Such images are quite similar to those in popular Theravada
Buddhist texts, such as the Thai funeral sermon "Blessings of Disposing
of Corpses," in which the images of a beautiful young woman are contrasted with those of her rotting corpse in order to convey the principle
of impermanence, as noted by Charles Keyes.[68]

Paul's comparative analysis of gendered imagery in Buddhist texts
concludes that the sutras containing the most positive images of women
and the female or feminine are by far the smallest percentage. In addition, these positive female images—like the Bodhisattva Kuan Yin who
has a maternal role but is beyond sensuality, and Buddha Amitābha who
embodies a combination of masculine and feminine qualities—still tend to
associate women with passion and with physical and mental weakness.[69]
Even further (a point which Paul fails to note), the portrayal of females
as "advanced bodhisattvas" and "imminent Buddhas" is not synonymous
with a portrayal of women as Buddhas, and thus does not signify that being female is not an obstacle to full enlightenment.

Since a number of Buddhist texts in Paul's second category include
variants of the Lotus's two dominant gender narratives (the entry of the
Buddha's female kin Mahāprajāpatī and Yaśodharā into the monastic order, and the gender transformation of the dragon king's daughter), these
provide a useful basis for assessing how the Lotus Sutra's portrayal of
gender status and hierarchy compares to other parts of the Buddhist literary corpus. First, it is interesting to note that the Lotus Sutra excludes
certain negative aspects of the original renditions of the narrative in the
Pali canon relating to the entry of the Buddha's female relatives into the
Saṅgha. In the *Cullavagga*, the Buddha turns down Prajāpatī's request for
admission to the order on behalf of herself and her five hundred women
followers on three separate occasions, and only relents because his trusted
servant Ānanda intercedes on the women's behalf. And even then, although conceding that women are not lacking in capacity to pursue the
spiritual path, the Buddha proclaims that the entry of women into the
order will result in Buddhism lasting only five hundred years, rather
than the thousand years it otherwise would have endured.[70]

The absence of these aspects of the original narratives from the Lotus
suggests that they are irrelevant to its main purposes. As discussed earlier,

the Buddha's female relatives are presented in the Lotus in the context of the Buddha's predicting the future enlightenment of his followers. Thus, rather than highlighting the difficulties that women present to Buddhism, the Lotus's emphasis is on their capacity for full complete enlightenment (even if not in female bodies). This portrayal of women is consistent with the principles of gender justice.

Second, gender transformation narratives similar to those in the Lotus appear in several Mahayana sutras, especially in the *Mahā-ratnakūṭa*, a collection of forty-nine sutras. A brief description of these sutras reveals some interesting similarities and differences with the Lotus Sutra. Some of these follow the same gender transformation sequence that is evident in the Lotus. For example, the Sumatī Sutra also involves an eight-year-old female—here the daughter of a householder in Rājagrha—addressing the Buddha and his gathered assembly. Sumati asks the Buddha a series of questions. Conforming to gender role stereotypes, her first questions, as cited by Jan Nattier, concern appearance and wealth: "For what reason does one become beautiful? What causes someone to have great wealth, or an undivided retinue?"[71]

Then, as in the narrative of the dragon king's daughter in the Lotus Sutra, one of the Buddha's closest disciples—here, Mahāmaudgalyāyana, Śāriputra's counterpart—expresses skepticism regarding the girl's ability to fulfill the difficult teachings which the Buddha has just given. Sumati then performs two "acts of truth" which convince Mahāmaudgalyāyana of Sumati's capacities as a bodhisattva. In the first, she avers that if her future Buddhahood is true, and her Buddha-field "will be free from the faults of womankind," that the assembly may turn golden in color—which it immediately does![72]

The Bodhisattva Mañjuśrī challenges Sumati's understanding in a series of questions, which she answers to his satisfaction. He then asks her why she hasn't changed out of her female body. She tells him that the statements "'This is a woman, this is a man' are the [result of] objectivizing. You should become free of doubts about this."[73] Nonetheless, in a second act of truth, she says, "If it is true that I shall attain Tathagata-hood . . . may I now . . . change into a man,'" and then does.[74] "He" resolves that in his future Buddha-land, there will be no influence of Māra, no hells, and no "'women's demeanor'" and proclaims, "'If I shall accomplish this, let my body be like that to a 30-year-old monk.' This too, occurs."[75] The negative appraisal of women, coupled with Sumati's change of sex, makes this sutra's gender portrayal very similar to the Lotus Sutra's.

In the Pure Gift Sutra, the twelve-year-old daughter of King Prasenajit, called Pure Gift, with a company of five hundred women and five hundred brahmanas, encounters the Buddha accompanied by eight disciples and eight bodhisattvas. One by one, she questions them about the Dharma in ways that make them aware of the flaws in their own understandings, and leave them speechless. To the Bodhisattva Nondeluded Views, for example, she points out that the Buddha cannot be seen at all because his truth is formless, so those who see his material body do not see the Buddha. (This might be interpreted as a criticism of those who make distinctions based on bodily characteristics, such as sex.)

Pure Gift then asks the Buddha eighteen questions about the bodhisattva path. Among them are questions concerning how to obtain a transformation rebirth (question 8) and the thirty-two marks of a *mahā-puruṣa* ("great man") (question 13). Mahāmaudgalyāyana accuses her of not taking the bodhisattva career seriously or understanding it, since she cannot attain perfect enlightenment in a woman's body.[76] In response, Pure Gift makes an Act of Truth that if her words are true, a series of miracles will occur, including that her female form will change into that of a boy. These happens as she predicts, Mahāmaudgalyāyana is convinced, and the Buddha predicts her attainment of perfect Buddhahood.

Despite this evidence of her worthiness, Mahāmaudgalyāyana again challenges Pure Gift, asking her why, if she is so advanced in understanding, she hadn't changed her female body before this. She answers with a question of her own, asking him why, since he has been praised by the Buddha as best in the attainment of supernatural powers, he hadn't changed his male body! He is speechless, and she continues by telling him in Schuster's translation, "Neither with a female body nor with a male body is true enlightenment attained . . . for there is no achieving perfect enlightenment in any way."[77] At the conclusion of the sutra, both Mañjuśrī and the Buddha praise Pure Gift and the Buddha completes the prophecy of her Buddhahood. The Pure Gift Sutra also parallels the Lotus in both asserting the irrelevance of gender yet having the female bodhisatttva change into a male form. Despite these parallels, however, both the Sumati and Pure Gift sutras are more supportive of gender justice than the dragon girl's gender transformation in the Lotus because they include messages about the ultimate irrelevance of gender distinctions.

In Pure Faith's Question, King Prasenajit's young daughter Pure Faith goes with five hundred women companions to visit the Buddha in the Jeta grove at Śrāvastī, and questions him about bodhisattva practices. After the Buddha's twelve-part reply, which describes requirements of the bodhisattva to understand the sameness of all beings, all dharmas, and all ways of understanding, Pure Faith asks him what a woman must do to change her female body. The Buddha's answer as cited by Schuster lists sixteen things (two groups of eight each), to

> avoid envy, stinginess, flattery, anger, be truthful, slander no one, abandon desire, and all wrong views, revere Buddha and Dharma, make offerings to monks and to Brahmanas, give up attachment to home and family, accept the precepts, have no evil thoughts, become indifferent to her female body, abide in the thought of enlightenment and the dharmas of the Great Man, regard worldly life as like an illusion, like a dream.[78]

Pure Faith and her companions then scatter garlands and jewelry over the Buddha, and resolve to follow the bodhisattva path and to "abandon the corruptions of the female body." The Buddha predicts that at the end of their present lives, all of them will abandon their female bodies and be reborn in the Tuṣita Heaven to serve and make offerings to Maitreya and all the Tathāgatas of the present era. The Buddha predicts that after countless aeons, Pure Gift will become a Buddha with her own Buddha land, and the five hundred women will be the leaders of her retinue. The sutra ends with the promise that "if a woman hears this sutra, accepts it and recites it, when her female body dies, she will never again be reborn a woman and will quickly attain to perfect enlightenment."[79]

Schuster interprets Pure Faith's second question as indicating that she has not yet learned the truth of the Buddha's answer to her first question; that had Pure Faith truly comprehended the necessity of seeing the sameness of all beings, she wouldn't be distinguishing between male and female bodies. Unlike the pattern in other gender transformation sutras, here Pure Faith herself is asking how she can change her female body, rather than being pressured to do so by others. Nonetheless, the Buddha answers her question without hesitation or qualification. This, in combination with the conclusion of the sutra, reinforces the necessity that women change their female bodies in order to attain complete enlightenment. Under these circumstances, Pure Faith's second question to the Buddha does not seem at all to be the result of ignorance, but instead of awareness of the obstacles faced by a female striving to attain perfect enlightenment. In these respects, the Pure Faith Sutra expresses the same message as the Lotus.

Yet other gender transformation narratives can be viewed as more egalitarian than the Lotus. For example, the *Gangottara-sūtra* in the *Ratnakūṭa-sūtra* describes a dialogue between the Buddha and the lay disciple Gangottara in the Jeta Grove at Śrāvastī, as pointed out by Schuster. Gangottara is instructed to regard all dharmas, including herself, as being like magical creations, empty like space which is without any impediments. After their dialogue, she and the rest of the assembly become monastics, and the gods who had been listening note that "This *upāsikā* is truly extraordinary, for she is able to converse fearlessly with the Tathāgathas."[80]

The story called "Jewel Brocade Receives the Prediction" in the Sutra of Sāgara, the Nāga King, a sutra translated into Chinese in 285 C.E., bears marked similarities to—but also important differences from—the story of the dragon king's daughter in the Lotus Sutra. Here, as Paul notes, Mahākāśyapa tells Sāgara's daughter Jewel Brocade, "One cannot attain Buddhahood within a woman's body." She responds that if this is so, then it is also the case that one cannot attain Buddhahood within a man's body, since "the thought of enlightenment is neither male nor female," "the one who perceives through Emptiness is neither male nor female" and "the one who perceives through enlightenment has the Dharma which is neither male nor female."[81] At the end of the narrative, the Buddha predicts Jewel Brocade's future Buddhahood. Unlike the dragon girl's story in the Lotus Sutra, Jewel Brocade does not change her sex in deference to male monastic questioning, but rather refutes the entire mode of thinking which would make such a change necessary. Similarly, in the *Śrīmālā-devī-siṃhanāda-sūtra*, Queen Śrīmālā validates her spiritual attainments without being required to change her female form. As Schuster says, she is accepted as a true Dharma teacher in her female body.

Finally, in the *Vimalakīrti-nirdeśa-sūtra*, another early Mahayana sutra, a goddess suddenly appears after listening to Vimalakīrti (a householder bodhisattva) tell Mañjuśrī that all beings should be regarded as like creatures created by a magician or as a mirage. She sprinkles flowers on the assembly, and the petals roll off the bodhisattvas' bodies, but stick to those of the disciples, despite the latter's attempts to shake them off. The goddess asks Śāriputra why he wants to get rid of the flowers, and he says they are not proper for disciples. She accuses him of being obsessed by the false distinction between proper and improper, which is the very reason why the flowers are clinging to him while not troubling the bodhisattvas. Her explanation silences Śāriputra.[82]

Śāriputra then asks the goddess why she has not changed her female form. In Schuster's version she tells him she has looked for femaleness during the twelve years she has lived in Vimalakīrti's house, but has not found it, "for what one calls a woman is something created by magic—and can one ask something created by magic to change its femaleness?"[83] The goddess then exercises her powers to exchange bodies with Śāriputra, and she asks him: Why don't *you* change your female form?" He tells her he doesn't even know how he acquired a female body. She explains, as cited by Paul, that it is so with all women: "Just as you are not really a woman but appear to be female in form, all women also only appear to be female in form but are not really women. Therefore, the Buddha said all are not really men or women."[84] The goddess then switches their bodies back to their original forms.

Śāriputra asks her where she will be reborn next, and she says it will be where the Buddha's transformations are reborn. He retorts that these are *not* reborn, which is, the goddess notes, true for all beings. Śāriputra asks her when she will attain complete enlightenment, and she tells him that no one ever can, since enlightenment has nothing to rest upon and so cannot be grasped. At the conclusion of this narrative, Vimalakīrti informs Śāriputra that the goddess has already served many previous Buddhas and has attained the tolerance of the notion that dharmas do not arise. This gives her the resolve to attain Buddhahood that in Schuster's words "permits her to manifest wherever she wishes in order to teach and develop living beings."[85]

These last two sutras are more affirmative of women's spiritual capacities than many other gender transformation narratives, including that in the Lotus. The *Śrīmālā-devī-siṃhanāda-sūtra* and *Vimalakīrti-nirdeśa-sūtra* in particular promote gender justice by indicating that women are capable of highest spiritual achievement—Buddhahood—without having to change their female form. The Lotus Sutra lacks a corollary. Nevertheless, even these more positive representations still do not portray women as Buddhas, and thus fail to evoke a full-bodied principle of gender equality.[86]

IV. INTERPRETATION AND ANALYSIS

Measuring the gender imagery in the Lotus Sutra against that in comparable Buddhist texts reinforces the earlier assessment that this text reflects somewhat ambivalent and contradictory messages regarding women's capacity for enlightenment. Whereas the prediction story in chapter 13 is more positive than other scriptural accounts of the Buddha's interactions with his female relations because it omits their sexist underpinnings, the gender transformation narrative in chapter 12 is less affirmative of gender justice than counterparts in some other scriptures because it insists on the necessity that women change their sex in order to attain enlightenment.

Compared with the spectrum of gender imagery in Buddhist literature, the Lotus Sutra can be viewed as something of a microcosm: It includes representations of females as hindrances to (male) monastics' pursuit of enlightenment as well as depictions of females themselves—as nuns, laywomen, bodhisattvas, and even nonhuman beings—as sincere and dedicated practitioners of the Dharma. By comparison with the range of images of women in other Buddhist texts, those in the Lotus fall along the more positive than negative end of the scale. Negative images are fairly infrequent.

By the same token, the Lotus Sutra is not quite as egalitarian in its message as scriptures such as the Gangottara, the Nāga King, or the Sutra of Sāgara, where no gender transformation is necessary as a condition for women's enlightenment. Nor is the Lotus as positive as texts such as the *Vimalakīrti-nirdeśa-sūtra*, where proclamations of the irrelevance of gender are reinforced by playful gender-bending which changes males into females as well as the reverse. Even though the Lotus includes statements to the effect that gender is irrelevant to enlightenment, the dominant narratives in this text suggest that gender is indeed relevant: that being a woman is an impediment which must be eliminated before enlightenment can be achieved, or it will retard the achievement of this goal "for ages to come." By comparison with other Mahayana scriptures, then, the Lotus does not reflect the strongest possible message regarding gender equality and the irrelevance of gender distinctions.

Against such affirmative endorsements of the spiritual capacity of the female gender in other Buddhist texts, the dragon girl narrative is not as glowing a portrayal of women's spiritual capacity as some have claimed. Schuster actually seems somewhat equivocal in her assessment of the Lotus Sutra's positive message about the female's capacity for enlightenment, however, since she admits that this narrative's treatment of gender transformation is "less satisfactory" than in other texts because a "change of sex does seem to be necessary . . . if a woman is to take the final step to Buddhahood." She argues that in other gender transformation narratives, by contrast, change of body is like a magician's transformations, and so is *everything* which ordinary persons take to be real in this world. Femaleness, and the transformation into a male, are not ultimately real, but both can be used by the bodhisattva to reach and instruct benighted sentient beings.[87]

Schuster claims that the main difference between the Lotus Sutra and the other gender transformation narratives she discusses is that the latter all make magic a central element, whereas the former only includes "some mention of magic and supernormal powers," which may have been "added later under the influence of texts like the *Vimalakīrti* and the *Mahā-ratnakūṭa* sutras where magic is an essential component of the 'changing the female body' scenario."[88] Schuster's "magical" thesis ignores the extent to which the Lotus Sutra is filled with accounts of magic and supernormal powers, which any cursory perusal of the text reveals. Second, the gender narratives in most of these sutras are similar in ending, with the female becoming a male in order to achieve full enlightenment, however advanced her level of spiritual attainment in a female body. Thus, the Lotus cannot be distinguished from the other gender transformation narratives as Schuster contends.

Similarly, Schuster's contention that gender transformation in these stories "signifies the transcendence of ordinary worldly life and the sex distinctions that are part of it"[89] is also unsubstantiated, unless it is argued that all sex is signified by the female, so that when the transformation takes place, sex is eliminated by making the female into a nonsexual male.[90] But even in this case, it is still the female which is the problem. If the situation were otherwise, we would expect to find male beings engaging in gender transformations and becoming females, which occurs only—and unwillingly!—in the *Vimalakīrti-nirdeśa-sūtra*.

Schuster also tries to persuade us that gender transformation only takes place because of the imperfect understandings of the Buddha's disciples like Mañjuśrī, who just "doesn't get" the ultimate irrelevance of gender.[91] She argues that the women in these sutras change their bodies out of compassion—"to resolve a man's doubts."[92] Beyond being mere speculation, it is difficult to see how these acts of gender transformation can be interpreted as compassionate at all. Rather than resolving doubts, the gender transformations serve to perpetuate and reinforce these men's "ignorant" views that Buddhahood is accessible only to those in male form. Since this is inconsistent with the Mahayana teachings that gender is ultimately irrelevant, the gender transformations are actually the antithesis of compassion. To *truly* signify the irrelevance of gender, these narratives would conclude with females attaining Buddhahood in female form. By fulfilling the disciples' sexist expectations that a male body is a requirement for full Buddhahood, most of these narratives fail to demonstrate, as Schuster asserts they do, that females are truly the spiritual equals of males.

Further, if Schuster were correct that the purpose of these gender transformation narratives "is to assert that for those committed to the Bodhisattva career distinctions on the basis of sex no longer have any meaning" and that "when one consciously sets out on the Bodhisattva path, one abandons identification with the traditional roles of either sex,"[93] then the male bodhisattvas in these narratives would never have questioned the female characters about their gendered bodies. There would be no emphasis on the Buddha as a male bodied being possessing the thirty-two marks of a "great man." Instead, he would be depicted as a genderless or gender-neutral or androgynous being. In any event, the very requirement that females in these sutras become males indicates that "sex distinctions" continue to be quite important. The male continues to provide the normative standard by which the female is found to be deficient. This hardly represents the transcendence of gender distinctions that Schuster claims!

Schuster's conclusions about the irrelevance of gender are further undermined by comparing the Lotus Sutra with the gender transformation narratives in other Mahayana sutras. According to Paul, the Sutra on Changing the Female Sex,[94] for example, states that women can be freed of the female body and become sons by awakening to the thought of enlightenment, which will give them "the great and good person's state of mind, a man's state of mind, a sage's state of mind." This sutra also states that "the female's defects—greed, hate, and delusion and other defilements—are greater than the male's. . . . . 'Because I wish to be freed from the impurities of the woman's body, I will acquire the beautiful and fresh body of a man.'"[95]

In "The Goddess of the Ganges," an excerpt from the *Aṣṭasāhasrikā-prajñā-pāramitā-sutram*, the 8,000-line *Prajñāpāramitā-sūtra*, the Buddha predicts that after her death, the goddess will "change her sex from female to male and be born in the Buddha land called Delight."[96] Finally, in the later Mahayana Sutra of the Dialogue of the Girl Candrottarā,[97] the Bodhisattva Amogha-darśana says to the young woman Candrottarā: "Candrottarā, one cannot become a Buddha while being a female. Why don't you change your female sex now?" Although her reply seemingly suggests the irrelevance of sex—"the nature of Emptiness cannot be changed or altered. This is also true for all phenomena. [Consequently] how could I change my woman's body?"[98]—she then receives a prediction of Buddhahood and transforms into a young male.[99] Thus, these sutras further substantiate the significance rather than the irrelevance of gender distinctions; they reflect and reinforce the prevailing belief that women are incapable of Buddhahood in female form.

Paul interprets these gender transformation narratives in two ways: first, as involving a mental sexual power which controls physical sex changes; and second, as involving a change from the imperfection and immorality of human beings—symbolized by the female body—to the mental perfection of bodhisattvas and Buddhas—represented by the male body. In the latter, maleness symbolizes the perfection of the mind, and the sex change a mental change from sensual attachment to that perfection.[100] On the first interpretation, according to Paul, their female sex makes women incapable of fully pursuing the bodhisattva path, whereas in the second, it does not. The first interpretation is undermined by language in the Lotus regarding the irrelevance of gender distinctions at the level of ultimate truth, suggesting that the second, "symbolic," interpretation is more accurate. Nonetheless, even on this interpretation, the symbolic value of gender operates to denigrate females as more worldly, while

elevating males as more spiritual. These associations, even if only symbolic, can hardly be positive for "real women"!

What we find in these sutras is not the unequivocal message of the
transcendence of gender and the insignificance of gender distinctions,
as Schuster and Paul contend. Rather, at best, we can say that the texts
are polyvocal on the issue of the significance of gender and the character
of the female, especially in relation to *anuttara-samyak-saṃbodhi*. Such
polyvocality is to be expected, given that these sutras were translated
and (re)interpreted by many different persons from different cultural
and historical locations. Although the doctrinal assertions in these texts
may support the irrelevance of gender, the "acts" of gender transformation always follow the direction of female into male, never the reverse (at
least more than temporarily, as in the *Vimalakīrti-nirdeśa-sūtra*), thereby
reinforcing a privileging of male over female. Paul and Schuster are
overly optimistic in their interpretations of the type of gender transformation story that appears in the Lotus Sutra.

At the same time, against negative interpretations, the overall message
of the dragon girl's narrative is not a damning assessment of women either. Saichō (767–822), the founder of the Tendai sect of Japanese Buddhism, read this story as indicating the miraculous power of the Lotus
Sutra itself. Regarding Sāgara, Saichō says:

> She is an animal, (one of the lower levels of the) six destinies [realms],
> obviously the rest of bad karma. She is female and clearly has facul-
> ties which are not good. She is young and thus has not been practic-
> ing with religious masters for a long time. And yet, the wondrous
> power of the *Lotus Sutra* endows her with the two adornments of
> wisdom and merit.[101]

This interpretation accepts the premise that women generally lack the
capacity for full enlightenment. It is only the miraculous power of the
Lotus Sutra which makes the dragon girl's spiritual achievements possible, not the lack of impediment imposed by sex or gender.

A gender transformation narrative that was fully consistent with gender justice would affirm the capacity of both men and women for full
Buddhahood. This requires more than those passages in the Lotus Sutra
which assert the irrelevance of gender but continue to posit a sex change
as a prerequisite to enlightenment. The promotion of gender justice requires the dissemination of images of women as capable of becoming fully
enlightened beings as females, a characteristic not found in the Lotus
(aside from its attenuate affirmation in the prediction narrative of chapter 13), and rare in other Buddhist texts. The message in most of these
texts that a male form is a prerequisite for full, complete enlightenment

undermines gender justice. At best, then, we can say that other gender transformation narratives, including that in the Lotus, contain elements that point toward transcending the significance of gender differences and the denigration of women.

In sum, the Lotus communicates no one univocal message about the normative status of women, or the correct relationship between male and female genders. Women and females are in some passages depicted in affirmative and positive terms, but in others are disparaged and portrayed as lacking in capacities for full, complete enlightenment—at least as long as they remain in female form. The prediction narrative in chapter 13 remains silent on the issue of whether women can achieve this goal. The sutra thus leaves some ambiguity regarding whether it is possible for women to attain full complete enlightenment, at least while inhabiting a female form.

When compared with gender images in the entire corpus of Buddhist texts, however, those in the Lotus Sutra rank fairly positively in terms of promoting gender justice. As already noted, the most misogynistic references to women are absent. In addition, women's capacity for enlightenment is affirmed—even if with qualifications. The overall message of the Lotus Sutra that enlightenment is available to all beings, not only those of a certain birth, gender, aptitude, etc., presents a message that women are also capable of enlightenment; that this highest state is not reserved for beings of the male gender.

In addition, the two most dominant gender narratives in the text provide a positive message for women insofar as they suggest that all who are devoted to the Lotus, regardless of gender, will eventually attain enlightenment. This message may be interpreted as consistent with social responsibility by opposing the more sexist and misogynistic elements of other Buddhist teachings and practice. The Lotus's "streamlining" of the Path, making it possible to pursue the spiritual path without having to renounce householder life, also makes Buddhism more attractive to many women, who are committed to caring for others and do not have the ability or resources to become monastics.

However, the gender transformation narrative in the Lotus suggests that women, as females, have no possibility of attaining full buddhahood. The teachings that women will have to wait rebirth as males, or magically transform themselves, in order to be eligible for complete enlightenment, together with explicitly negative images of women and femaleness elsewhere in the Lotus Sutra, serve to denigrate the status of women, reinforce gender hierarchies of male domination, and obstruct social goals to end the oppression of women in both religious and secular spheres of life.

References

Campbell, June. *Traveller in Space: In Search of Female Identity in Tibetan Buddhism* (New York: George Braziller, 1996).

Falk, Nancy. "An Image of Woman In Old Buddhist Literature: The Daughters of Māra," in Judith Plaskow and Joan Arnold Romero, eds., *Women and Religion* (Missoula, MO: Scholars' Press, 1974), 105–12.

Groner, Paul. "The Lotus Sutra and Saicho's Interpretation of the Realization of Buddhahood with This Very Body," in George Tanabe and Willa Tanabe, eds., *The Lotus Sutra in Japanese Culture* (Honolulu: University of Hawaii Press, 1989), 53–74.

Gross, Rita. *Buddhism After Patriarchy: A Feminist History, Analysis, and Reconstruction of Buddhism* (Albany, NY: State University of New York Press, 1993).

Hardacre, Helen. "*The* Lotus Sutra in Modern Japan," in George Tanabe and Willa Tanabe, eds., *The Lotus Sutra in Japanese Culture* (Honolulu: University of Hawaii Press, 1989), 209–24.

Havnevik, Hanna. *Tibetan Buddhist Nuns* (Oslo: Norwegian University Press, 1991).

Hurvitz, Leon, trans. *Scripture of the Lotus Blossom of the Fine Dharma* (New York: Columbia University Press, 1976).

Katō, Bunnō, Yoshirō Tamura and Kōjirō Miyasaka, trans. *The Threefold Lotus Sutra: The Sutra of Innumerable Meanings; The Sutra of the Lotus Flower of the Wonderful Law; The Sutra of Meditation on the Bodhisattva Universal Virtue* (Tokyo: Kōsei Publishing Co., 1975).

Kajiyama, Yūichi. "Women in Buddhism," *Eastern Buddhist*, Vol. 15, no. 2 (new series), Autumn, 1982, 53–70.

Keyes, Charles. "Mother or Mistress But Never a Monk: Buddhist Notions of Female Gender in Rural Thailand," *American Ethnologist*, Vol. 11 (1984), 223–41.

Klein, Anne. *Meeting the Great Bliss Queen: Buddhists, Feminists, and the Art of the Self* (Boston: Beacon Press, 1995).

Lang, Karen. "Lord Death's Snare: Gender-Related Imagery in the Theragāthā and the Therīgāthā," *Journal of Feminist Studies in Religion*, Vol. 2, No. 1 (1986), 63–79.

Li, Jung-hsi. *Biographies of Buddhist Nuns, Pi-ch'iu-ni-ch'uan of Pao-chan* (Osaka: Tōhōkai, 1981).

Murcott, Susan. *The First Buddhist Women: Translations and Commentaries on the Therīgāthā* (Berkeley, CA: Parallax Press, 1991).

Nattier, Jan. "The Noble Sutra Entitled The Inquiry of the Young Girl Sumati," (unpublished draft translation from the Tibetan, 1994—on file with the author at American University).

Niwano, Nikkyō. *Buddhism for Today: A Modern Interpretation of the Threefold Lotus Sutra* (Tokyo: Kōsei Publishing Co., 1976).

Paul, Diana. *Women in Buddhism: Images of the Feminine in Mahayana Tradition* (Berkeley, CA: University of California Press, 1985, 2d ed.).

Rhys Davids, C. A. F., and K. R. Norman, trans. *Poems of Early Buddhist Nuns* (Oxford, Great Britain: Pali Text Society, 1989).

Ruether, Rosemary, ed. *Womanguides: Readings Toward a Feminist Theology* (Boston, MA: Beacon Press, 1985).

———. *Sexism and God-Talk* (Boston: Beacon Press, 1983).

Sangren, Steven P. "Female Gender in Chinese Religious Symbols: Kuan Yin, Ma Tsu, and the 'Eternal Mother'," *Signs*, Vol. 9, no. 1 (1983), 4–35.

Schussler Fiorenza, Elizabeth. *Bread Not Stone* (Boston, MA: Beacon Press, 2d ed., 1995).

Shaw, Miranda. *Passionate Enlightenment: Women in Tantric Buddhism* (Princeton, New Jersey: Princeton University Press, 1994).

Schuster, Nancy. "The *Bodhisattva* Figure in the *Ugraparipṛcchā*," in Anthony Warder, ed., *New Paths in Buddhist Research* (Durham, North Carolina: Acorn Press, 1985) (Schuster 1985a).

———. "Striking a Balance: Women and Images of Women in Early Chinese Buddhism," in Yvonne Yazbeck Haddad and Ellision Banks Findley, eds., *Women, Religion, and Social Change* (Albany: State University of New York Press, 1985), 87–112 (Schuster 1985b).

———. "Changing the Female Body: Wise Women and the Bodhisattva Career in Some *Mahāratnakūṭasūtras*," *Journal of the International Association of Buddhist Studies*, Vol. 4, No. 1 (1981), 24–69.

Sponberg, Alan. "Attitudes toward Women and the Feminine in Early Buddhism," in Jose Cabezon, ed., *Buddhism, Sexuality and Gender* (Albany, New York: State University of New York Press, 1992), 3–36.

Tamura, Yoshirō. "The Ideas of the Lotus Sutra," in George Tanabe and Willa Tanabe, eds., *The Lotus Sutra in Japanese Culture* (Honolulu: University of Hawaii Press, 1989), 37–51.

Tanabe, George. "Tanaka Chigaku: The Lotus Sutra and the Body Politic," in George Tanabe and Willa Tanabe, eds., *The Lotus Sutra in Japanese Culture* (Honolulu: University of Hawaii Press, 1989), 191–208.

Watson, Burton, trans. *The Lotus Sutra* (New York: Columbia University Press, 1993).

Welch, Sharon. *A Feminist Ethic of Risk* (Minneapolis, MN: Fortress Press, 1989).

Wilson, Liz. *Charming Cadavers: Horrific Figurations of the Feminine In Indian Buddhist Hagiographic Literature* (Chicago: University of Chicago Press, 1996).

Notes

1. This paper is based on English translations of the Lotus Sutra, principally that by Burton Watson, and supplemented by those of Leon Hurvitz (1975) and Bunnō Kato, Yoshirō Tamura, and Kōjirō Miyasaka (1975), all translating from Kumārajīva's fifth century C.E. (ca. 406) Chinese translation from the Sanskrit.
2. Cf. Watson 1995: ix
3. Tamura 1989: 41

4. Alan Sponberg contends that most contemporary Asian Buddhists "feel that women have equal access to the Dharma, but insist nonetheless that sexual differences are real and that the male sex is by nature superior to the female sex" (Sponberg, 1992: 12).

5. Tanabe 1989: 191

6. Schuster, 1985b: 91. In support, Schuster notes that eleven of the 56 biographies of fourth- through sixth-century Chinese Buddhist nuns, whose lives are recorded in the *Bi-qui-ni-chuan*, refer to practices involving the Lotus Sutra (Schuster, 1985b: 96). This text was translated into English by Li (1981).

7. Sangren, 1983: 4.

8. Watson 1995: xix; Niwano 1976: 153, 159, 161–62

9. Ibid.: 200; see also Hurvitz 1976: 14; Bunnō Katō 1997: 225

10. Ibid.: xix

11. Ibid.: 239–40, 251–52, 320

12. Ibid.: 310

13. Ibid.: 256

14. Ibid.: 257

15. Ibid.: 4, 249, 270

16. Another reference to "male and female asuras" is made earlier in the chapter (Watson, 1995: 257).

17. Watson 1995: 260

18. By contrast, in Chapter 27, the upholder of the Lotus Sutra is proclaimed to be protected from any "devil, devil's son, devil's daughter," etc. (Watson 1995: 320).

19. Watson 1995: 309–10. At other places in the Lotus Sutra where humans are referred to in gendered terms, however, beings from other realms are not. For instance, in Chapters Twenty-one, "Supernatural Powers of the Thus Come One," and Twenty-three, "Former Affairs of the Bodhisattva Medicine King," the assembly includes "monks, nuns, laymen, laywomen, heavenly beings, dragons, yakshas, gandharvas, asuras, garudas, kimnaras, mahoragas, human and nonhuman beings" (Watson 1995: 273, 280).

20. Ibid.: 258

21. Ibid.: 322

22. Ibid.: 145

23. Ibid.: 281

24. Nikkyō Niwano explains such linkages of women as evil as a product of Indian society at the time of the Buddha, in which "women were regarded as an obstacle to men's practicing religious disciplines, and it was thought that they could never be saved from suffering" (Niwano 1976: 154). He encourages us to focus instead on how revolutionary the Buddha's affirmation of women's capacity for enlightenment was, given the historical context in which women were considered to be intrinsically "sinful" (Niwano 1976: 154–55). Nonetheless, the negativity of such images promotes a view of women as intrinsically inferior to men.

25. Watson 1995: 145. The verse form of the text repeats the description of Pūrṇa's worlds as one where women, along with the "vile paths of existence," will be

absent (Watson 1995: 148), but it does not specify that desire and reproduction will also be absent.

26. Ibid.: 287
27. e.g. Watson 1995: 212, 219, 224
28. e.g. Watson 1995: 220
29. e.g. Watson 1995: 235
30. Watson 1995: 244
31. Ibid.: 53
32. Ibid.: 61
33. Ibid.: 204, 205
34. Ibid.: 72
35. Ibid.: 4
36. Ibid.: 4
37. Ibid.: 269
38. Ibid.: 197–98
39. Ibid.: 197–98
40. Ibid.: 187
41. Ibid.: 187
42. Ibid.: 188
43. Ibid.: 188–89
44. Schuster 1981: 43
45. Ibid.: 45
46. Ibid.: 44
47. Ibid.: 29; Kajiyama 1982: 66
48. Niwano 1976: 159
49. Paul 1985: 193
50. Watson 1995: 191
51. Ibid.: 191
52. Ibid.: 192
53. Ibid.: 315
54. Ibid.: 287
55. Ibid.: 288
56. Sponberg 1992: 20; Lang 1986: 64; Paul 1985: 303; Falk 1974: 108
57. Paul 1985: 30–32
58. Rhys Davids 1989; Murcott 1991
59. See Sponberg 1992: 6, 14–15, 24; Lang 1986: 65; Murcott 1991.
60. Paul 1985: 169
61. Schuster 1985b: 102
62. Paul 1985: 170
63. Ibid.: 170–71
64. Sponberg 1992: 24–25
65. Sangren 1983: 6–7
66. Campbell 1996; Gross 1995; Klein 1995; Shaw 1994; Havnevik 1990
67. Wilson 1996
68. Keyes 1984: 231
69. Paul 1985: 307–308

70. *Cullavagga*, Ch. 10. 1. 1–6, quoted in Murcott 1991: 13–19; Rhys Davids 1989: 71–73. The reasons for the abridgement are not given, however, leaving unresolved the issue of why women's acceptance into the Saṅgha would reduce the longevity of the Dharma. Is it because women are naturally "corrupting" or polluting forces? Because they will create discord and conflict with the monks? Because of the problems of sexual fraternization that could result—a rationale frequently given for excluding women from militaries, for example? All of these are plausible explanations, since they all appear in other places in the Canon.

71. Nattier 1994: 1

72. Ibid.: 5

73. Ibid.: 7

74. Schuster 1981: 30–31. Schuster's translation says: "'It cannot be apprehended, for dharmas are neither male nor female. But now I must remove your doubts . . . If it is true that I shall attain Tathagatahood . . . may I now . . . change into a man.'"

75. Ibid.: 31

76. Schuster points out that this version is found in T.12.338 and T.11.310 (33), but that a sixth century C.E. translation, T.12.339, has an alternative version which says that it is rare for a woman to cultivate this practice, not that it is impossible (Schuster 1981: 644, n. 46).

77. Schuster 1981: 35, citing T.12.338, p. 96.c25–27

78. Ibid.: 37

79. Ibid.: 37

80. Ibid.: 39

81. Paul 1985: 235–36

82. Schuster 1981: 41–42

83. Ibid.: 42

84. Paul 1985: 230

85. Schuster 1981: 42–43

86. I am indebted to Jan Nattier for this observation.

87. Schuster 1981: 44–45

88. Ibid.: 45

89. Ibid.: 55

90. There is actually some support for this position. As Paul observes, "the sexual change also encompasses mental attitudes. Being a male in mental attitude meant being unattached to sexuality and having responsibility over one's actions whereas being a female in Indian society did not entail such detachment and personal responsibility" (Paul 1985: 186–87).

91. Schuster 1985b: 91

92. Schuster 1981: 56

93. Ibid.: 55

94. *Fo shuo chuan nu shen ching*

95. Paul 1985: 176, 308

96. Ibid.: 183

97. Paul identifies this as a third- to fourth-century sequel to the *Vimalakīrti-nirdeśa-*

sūtra since Candrottarā is the daughter of Vimalakīrti, and is given his eloquent and insightful speech (Paul 1985: 191).
98. Paul 1985: 195
99. Ibid.: 179
100. Ibid.: 175, 306
101. Groner 1989: 61

Is the Lotus Sutra "Good News" for Women?

Miriam Levering

I. INTRODUCTION

There is ample reason for receiving the Lotus Sutra as "good news," not only for early Mahayanists, but also for people today. The central messages of the sutra have long been read in East Asia as the unity of diverse practices and teachings in one fundamental path and truth, and the good news that all beings are destined for ultimate Buddhahood. As Peter Gregory writes:

> In contrast to the understanding of the three vehicles as providing separate paths leading to different religious goals, the *Lotus Sutra* advances its central teaching of the one vehicle. The *Lotus* proclaims the universal message that all beings are ultimately destined to attain supreme Buddhahood. It was only because he was afraid that the exalted character of this goal would have daunted his followers that the Buddha expediently distinguished between the three vehicles. The *Lotus* declares that all Buddhas appear in the world for one great matter, to make clear the inconceivable insight and vision of the Buddhas.[1] All beings are destined for ultimate Buddhahood, even if they are unaware of it and follow a lesser vehicle, because such vehicles are nothing but expedients devised by the Buddha to lead them to the ultimate goal.[2]

Kotatsu Fujita calls this fundamental "good news" of the Lotus Sutra, its promise of unification of all spiritual striving in the highest spiritual fulfillment, namely the Buddha's level of insight into truth and awakened compassionate activity, "a practical demonstration of the Mahayana *Prajñāpāramitā* idea of Emptiness."[3] Fujita writes:

In what form, then, does, the *Lotus* actually preach 'Emptiness'? It is in the form of the 'One Vehicle'. As has already been demonstrated in various ways, one is entitled to say that the One Vehicle is nothing other than a practical demonstration of the abstract idea of Emptiness. What is meant by 'practical demonstration', or by 'demonstration in practical form'? It is the proposition that lets any person, equally and without distinction, be a Buddha. According to the *Lotus*, the Buddha's Sole Great Purpose in coming into the world lay in this and in nothing else.[4]

Many who know that they are not now great disciples of the Buddha have seen this "proposition that lets any person, equally and without distinction be a Buddha" as particularly good news. Those who feel that they might never be great bodhisattvas, or even great *śrāvakas* and *pratyeka-buddhas,* receive the good news in this sutra that ordinary people who undertake only the simplest of practices of devotion and faith will also give rise to the *bodhicitta,* the bodhisattva mind, and eventually become irreversible bodhisattvas and then Buddhas.[5] Not only is this true for good-hearted ordinary people, but it is also true, according to traditional interpretation, for evil people and weak and defiled women. For these the prediction of eventual Buddhahood is explicitly made in the sutra.

From the social location of an early twenty-first century American, white, middle-class woman who is concerned for the spiritual and social well-being of women, it is profoundly significant that in East Asia this sutra has been preached for a thousand years as a source of hope and affirmation for women, due to its good news that women also will be Buddhas. But there seems to be some ambiguity, or some reason for doubt. From the feminist perspective of Western students in our class-rooms, the sutra is not so obviously affirming. And historians of Buddhism are also not unanimous on this point. In his article "Women and Buddhism," Kajiyama suggests that "the philosophical liberation of women" culminated not in the Lotus Sutra, but rather in the second and third centuries of the Common Era, during which sutras such as the *Vimalakīrti-nirdeśa* and *Śrīmālā-devī-siṃhanāda* were written. These sutras represent the mature philosophy of emptiness and the Buddha-nature/*tathāgata-garbha* in all sentient beings, perspectives from which there cannot be any distinction or discrimination between men and women.[6]

Whether the sutra is good news for women clearly depends on how one reads relevant passages in the sutra and the sutra as a whole. I propose to discuss three passages in the sutra that are of great interest to women, followed by some comments of my own. The first two are the stories of the prediction of Buddhahood made by Śākyamuni to his aunt and stepmother

Mahāprajāpatī and his wife before his "great departure" Yaśodharā, both of whom are nuns (bhikṣunī) as the sutra opens. The third is the story of the nāga king Sāgara's daughter in chapter 12 of Kumārajīva's version.[7]

II. THE SUTRA PASSAGES

A. Mahāprajāpatī and Yaśodharā

1. Mahāprajāpati and Yaśodharā in chapter 1

In chapter 1, in the great assembly that is gathered to hear the Buddha preach the Lotus Sutra, Mahāprajāpatī and Yaśodharā are present. This certainly can be taken as a significant fact. Tsugunari Kubo writes: "The fact that they are described not only in the story in chapter 12–13 but also here in the assembly is a sign of a positive attitude toward women in the sutra."[8] The passage reads:

> Thus have I heard. At one time, the Buddha was dwelling in the city of Rājagṛha on Gṛdhrakūṭa mountain, together with twelve thousand [Skt., twelve hundred] great bhikṣus. All were arhants, their outflows already exhausted, never again to suffer anguish. . . . Their names were . . . [here twenty-one male names are given]. There were also another two thousand persons, including those who had more to learn and those who had not. There was Mahāprajāpatī, the bhikṣunī, together with six thousand followers. Yaśodharā, the bhikṣunī, was also there together with her followers. There were also eighty-thousand bodhisattva-mahāsattvas, all nonbacksliders in anuttara-samyak-saṃbodhi [the perfect enlightenment of a Buddha]. . . .[9]

What exactly the status of these famous women and their followers is is not made clear here: are they śrāvakas? Arhants? They are conspicuously not named among the arhants. We can assume from the structure that they are not bodhisattvas, since they are not numbered among the vast number of bodhisattva-mahāsattvas referred to next.

Kubo sees in the fact that they are the only named women in this passage reason to conclude that the preachers of the sutra have had to compromise between a supposed negative view of women in the contemporary culture and the Lotus Sutra group of Mahayanist's own desire to affirm women followers. He writes:

> Given the historical conditions, the sutra could only discuss the topic of women indirectly by using these two well-known women as symbols for women in general.[10]

This is a reading that testifies to Kubo's modern vision of the sutra as a whole as radically egalitarian and radically inclusive.

2. Mahāprajāpatī and Yaśodharā in chapter 13

In chapter 13, first Mahāprajāpatī and her followers and then Yaśodharā receive predictions for future attainment of Buddhahood. At the end of chapter 11, the Buddha had asked who would keep and teach the Lotus Sutra after his extinction.[11] In chapter 13, a vast group of bodhisattvas make such a promise. Then five hundred *arhants* receive a prophecy of eventual Buddhahood, and make such a promise. They were followed by eight thousand persons. Then Mahāprajāpatī and her six thousand nun followers rise and gaze up at the Buddha, their eyes not leaving him for an instant. The passage continues:

> At that time the World-Honored One said to Gautamī [another name for Mahāprajāpatī], "Why do you look at the Thus Come One in that perplexed manner? In your heart are you perhaps worrying that I have failed to mention your name among those who have received a prophecy of the attainment of anuttara-samyak-saṃbodhi? But Gautamī, I earlier made a general statement saying that all the śrāvakas had received such a prophecy.[12] Now if you would like to know the prophecy for you, I will say that in ages to come, amid the Dharmas of sixty-eight thousands of millions of Buddhas, you will be a great teacher of the Dharma, and the six thousand nuns, some still learning, some already sufficiently learned, will accompany you as teachers of the Dharma. In this manner you will bit by bit fulfill the way of a bodhisattva until you are able to become a Buddha with the name Gladly Seen by All Living Beings Thus Come One, worthy of offerings, of right and universal knowledge, perfect clarity and conduct, well gone, understanding the world, unexcelled worthy, trainer, teacher of heavenly and human beings, Buddha, World-Honored One.[13] Gautamī, this Gladly Seen by All Living Beings Buddha will confer a prophecy upon the six thousand bodhisattvas [presumably the nuns], to be passed from one to another, that they will attain anuttara-samyak-saṃbodhi."[14]

Roughly the same actions, thoughts and words are repeated for the mother of the Buddha's son Rāhula, the nun Yaśodharā. She too is worried that the Buddha has predicted Buddhahood for everyone but her. The Buddha promptly predicts Buddhahood for her after she practices the deeds of a bodhisattva for a very long time, becomes a great teacher of the Dharma, and gradually fulfills the Buddha way.[15] Nothing is said about her followers in this prediction, except that the next paragraph, in which the nuns respond, implies that she has nun followers who also respond with her and Mahāprajāpatī. In a pattern similar to that of the making of the promise by the five hundred *arhants* to preach this sutra broadly in other lands,[16] the nuns promise to "go to lands in other regions and broadly propagate this sutra."[17]

Here we learn that the Buddha considers them *śrāvakas*, a view consistent with pre-Mahayana literature. They receive a prediction of Buddhahood, but the fact that it is going to take many lifetimes of practice of the bodhisattva way before they attain the intermediate stage of becoming a *dharma-bhāṇaka*, a Dharma-preacher, and then further gradual attainment while carrying out the bodhisattva-activity of a Dharma-preacher, does tend to dilute the effect of the prediction as compared, say, to the prediction for fellow *śrāvakas* Ānanda and Rāhula in chapter 9.

Are there other places in the sutra where there is a prophecy of Buddhahood in which the gradualness of the approach to it and the various stages required to attain it are so fully spelled out? Or should we read this as a bit of a compromise between the affirmation of bodhisattvahood for women issuing in Buddhahood and the view that those born as women have a longer, harder path ahead of them than those born as men do?

Nikkyō Niwano, comparing this episode to the episode of the *nāga* king Sāgara's daughter in the previous chapter, says that we should not read this as meaning that Mahāprajāpatī and Yaśodharā are inferior to the *nāga* princess, but rather that people close to one, as these two have been to the Buddha, are sometimes harder to convert to the bodhisattva path than are strangers. Again, this reading not only makes a practical point about common experience but also reaffirms his intention to read the sutra as affirming the "different-but-equal" equality of men and women.[18]

B. The Nāga Princess

In the Devadatta chapter, as nowhere else in the sutra, the power of the preaching of the Lotus Sutra is demonstrated by having a nonhuman, female child make a tremendous leap to full understanding of its teaching and then perform a dramatic extinguishing of her female power and manifesting of her male power en route to a full demonstration of her Buddhahood. This is unusual in the text, for every other figure receives predictions of her or his future Buddhahood, but does not achieve Buddhahood before our eyes. The *nāga* princess is one of very few characters in Mahayana Buddhist sutras who can be interpreted as "realizing Buddhahood with this very body" or "attaining Buddhahood in this very body" in the present moment of the text, in front of the reader or hearer, as it were.

The story of the *nāga* king Sāgara's daughter goes as follows:

> The Bodhisattva Wisdom-Accumulation questioned Mañjuśrī [who had just been preaching the Lotus Sutra in the *nāga* kingdom under the sea], saying, "That scripture is very profound and subtle, a gem among the scriptures, a thing rarely to be found in the world. Are there any beings who, putting this scripture into practice by the strenuous application of vigor, speedily gain Buddhahood, or are there not?"
>
> Mañjuśrī said, "There is the daughter of the *nāga* king Sāgara, whose years are barely eight. Her wisdom is sharp-rooted, and well she knows the faculties and deeds of the beings. She has gained *dhāraṇī* [powerful verbal formulae]. The profound treasure house of secrets preached by the Buddhas she is able to accept and to keep in its entirety. She has profoundly entered into *dhyāna* concentration, and has arrived at an understanding of the dharmas. In the space of a moment she produced the aspiration to enlightenment, and has attained the point of nonbacksliding. Her eloquence has no obstructions, and she is compassionately mindful of the beings as if they were her babies. Her merits are perfect. What she recollects in her mind and recites with her mouth is subtle and broad. She is of good will and compassionate, humane and yielding. Her will and thought are harmonious and refined, and she is able to attain to enlightenment."
>
> The Bodhisattva Wisdom-Accumulation said, ". . . I do not believe that this girl in the space of a moment directly and immediately achieved right, enlightened intuition."
>
> Before he had finished speaking, at that very time the daughter of the dragon king suddenly appeared in front [of them], and, doing obeisance with head bowed, stood off to one side and spoke a hymn of praise, saying:
>
>> Having profoundly mastered the marks of sin and merit,
>> Universally illuminating all ten directions,
>> The subtle and pure Dharma-body
>> Has perfected the thirty-two marks,
>> Using the eighty beautiful features
>> As a means of adorning the Dharma-body.
>> The object of respectful obeisance for gods and men
>> It is reverently honored by all dragons and spirits.
>> Of all varieties of living beings,

None fails to bow to it as an object of worship.
I have also heard that, as for the achievement of *bodhi*,
Only the Buddha can know it by direct witness.
I, laying open the teachings of the Great Vehicle,
Convey to release the suffering beings.

At that time Śāriputra spoke to the *nāga* girl, saying, "You say that in no long time you shall attain the unexcelled Way. This is hard to believe. What is the reason? A woman's body is filthy, it is not a Dharma-receptacle. How can you attain unexcelled enlightenment? The Path of the Buddha is remote and cavernous. Throughout incalculable aeons, by tormenting oneself and accumulating good conduct, also by thoroughly cultivating the perfections, only by these means can one then be successful. Also, a woman's body even then has five hindrances. It cannot become first a Brahmā god king, second the god Śakra [Indra], third King Māra, fourth a universal monarch, fifth a Buddha-body. How can the body of a woman speedily achieve Buddhahood?"

At that time the dragon girl had a precious gem, whose value was the [whole] thousand-millionfold world, which she held up and gave to the Buddha. The Buddha straightway accepted it. The dragon girl said to the Bodhisattva Wisdom-Accumulation and to the venerable Śāriputra, "I offered a precious gem, and the World-Honored One accepted it. Was this quick or not?"

He answered, saying, "Very quick!"

The girl said, "With your supernatural power you shall see me achieve Buddhahood even more quickly than that!"

At that time, the assembled multitude all saw the dragon girl in the space of an instant turn into a man, perfect bodhisattva-conduct, straightway go southward to the world-sphere Spotless, sit on a jeweled lotus blossom, and achieve undifferentiating, right, enlightened intuition, with thirty-two marks and eighty beautiful features setting forth the Fine Dharma for all living beings in the ten directions. . . . The Bodhisattva Wisdom-Accumulation, as well as Śāriputra and all the assembled multitude, silently believed and accepted.[19]

1. Nāgas

Let us look at several remarkable features of this story that might bear on the question of whether this story is good news for women. The first has to do with the fact that the female in question in this story is a *nāga*, not a human. Does this mean that the good news is not for human women?

What exactly is a *nāga*? *Nāgas,* serpentlike beings with human faces having lower extremities resembling a snake, are unquestionably classified as animals in the sixfold classification system that became widespread in Buddhism: *devas* (gods), *asuras* (titans), humans, animals, hungry ghosts, denizens of the hells. Yet *nāgas* have extraordinary power that makes them resemble *devas,* and they have superior intelligence like humans. *Nāgas* were believed in parts of India, as reflected in Buddhist texts, to inhabit the depths of rivers, lakes and oceans, residing in luxurious aquatic palaces. *Nāgas* furthermore can take full human form; it was considered the highest compliment to say of a woman that she had the beauty of a *nāga* princess. Love stories between human heroes and *nāga* maidens are common folklore in India, and also included in Buddhist literature.[20]

While *nāgas* are guardians not only of the treasures of the sea and the sources of life but of the Dharma, one might not expect great progress on the Buddhist path from one, for a *nāga* is an animal. The Vinaya tells a story of a *nāga* who, taking human form, becomes ordained as a Buddhist monk. When asleep with a sense of security, he reverts unconsciously to his snake form, and is discovered. The Buddha tells him that as a *nāga* he cannot make progress in the Dharma and the Vinaya, and he is expelled, weeping, from the order. This story is given as the reason why the Saṅgha must make sure not to ordain animals, and why to this day in some parts of the Buddhist world a candidate for ordination is asked whether he is human.[21]

So the answer to our question may be that *nāga* females can fully resemble human females in appearance. They can be superior to human females in their power, and at the same time inferior in their karma from a Buddhist perspective in that they are born as animals, not humans. There is resemblance to human females in their possessing female gender, human form, power, beauty, fertility and auspicious wealth, and in their protecting and guarding the Dharma, as the many women lay and monastic donors do. At the same time there is resemblance to human females in their inferiority to other beings as social inhabitants of the cosmos and as students of the Dharma (as human women are inferior to men). Thus it seems from many texts that what *nāga* females can do can be at least substantially generalized to human females.

In south India *nāgas* are very popular deities, and many non-Buddhist groups worship the *nāga* as their principal deity. According to Mahayana tradition, the *nāgas* were entrusted with the Buddha's most precious teaching, the *Prajñāpāramitā.* The name of the greatest philosopher of early Mahayana Buddhism, Nāgārjuna, contains the element "*nāga.*" Diana Paul writes:

The Nāga princesses were especially renowned for their beauty, wit, and charm and were claimed to be the female ancestors of some South Indian dynasties. They were delicate water-sprite creatures similar to mermaids. It was considered the highest compliment to say that one had the beauty of a Nāga princess. Love stories between human heroes and Nāga maidens are common folklore and are also included in Buddhist literature.[22]

In Chinese the term "*nāga*" was translated as "dragon." There is also in Chinese elite and folk literature a considerable body of lore about dragon deities, particularly dragon maidens, who are also associated with lakes, water, and rain.[23]

A *nāga* princess, thus, has a lot in common with a woman as understood in Chinese and Indian traditional cultures. She is associated with water—we might say "nature"—and fertility, belonging to a race that are protectors of the source of life. She has beauty, charm, wit surpassing that of many human women. She is a protector and guardian of the Dharma, just as many women donors, particularly lay women, could be said to be. She has human speech and a human face. Furthermore, the discussion about the five hindrances assimilates her to the human female.

2. Five hindrances and change of body

A second issue which makes an appearance in this story is the sutra's use of the dictum of the five hindrances faced by those born in a woman's body. What is the force of Śāriputra's speech, and what is the significance of the *nāga* princess's answer to it?

(a) The "five hindrances" dictum is mentioned in a number of sutras and other texts. Kajiyama places the formation and widespread establishment of this dictum between the late third century and the first century B.C.E., but for various reasons prefers the first century B.C.E. date.[24] The dictum says that anyone born a woman in this lifetime cannot, by virtue of her woman's body, become in this lifetime any of the following five classes of beings: a Buddha, a universal monarch, a Śakra (or Indra) god, a Brahma god, or a Māra.[25]

The universal monarch (*cakravartin*) and the Buddha are recognized by possessing on their bodies thirty-two major and eighty minor marks: anyone born with these marks may become either a universal monarch or a Buddha. These marks include a sheathed penis. Śakra or Indra is the king of the gods, a warrior god; Brahma is the creator, and lord of the Brahma-worlds, in which there are no women. These gods were borrowed from the Brahmanic pantheon and made into adherents of the

Buddha. Māra is the god who tempts and destroys, lord of love and death. In the Mahayana Buddhist tradition, none of the gods is considered to be eternal, and the number of Śakras, Māras and other beings is unlimited, so it is possible for anyone eventually to become one of these gods.[26]

Kajiyama argues that the notion that, due to the "five hindrances," possessing a female body limited the forms of birth and, in the case of Buddhahood, the spiritual attainments that a woman could expect without "changing her body into that of a man" (normally, by being reborn as a man) was so established at the time of the composition of the Lotus Sutra and other early Mahayana texts that it had to be included in those texts (including the Lotus Sutra) despite the desire of the early Mahayanists to eliminate the discriminatory idea that women could not become Buddhas. But the Lotus Sutra and other early Mahayana sutras worked out a compromising device, the idea of women's sexual transformation.[27] This compromising device continued to be important in the literature of a number of Japanese Buddhist sects that were greatly influenced by the Lotus Sutra.[28]

Based on a survey of Mahayana sutras undertaken by a number of scholars who have worked on this topic, it could be argued that the five hindrances doctrine is never brought up in a Mahayana sutra without being immediately undercut, as it is here in this story. The concept of five hindrances, of the inadequacy of the female birth or the female body for attaining Buddhahood, does not ever, in a Mahayana sutra, prevent a woman from attaining Buddhahood or advanced bodhisattvahood, with change of body, on the spot. So in that way, while technically affirmed, it is undermined, because the outcome is always triumph for the woman. No woman ever says, "All right, I guess you are right, I'll go home and wait for the next birth."

In one sutra the reasons in woman's character and karma that result in each of the five hindrances are spelled out. But here again, the woman immediately changes her body and attains Buddhahood or high bodhisattvahood and a prediction for Buddhahood. In another sutra Māra uses the five hindrances to discourage a woman from attempting Buddhahood and to get her to settle for nirvana, *arhatship*, but the woman does not. She says: "I have heard that anyone who practices the bodhisattva path eventually attains Buddhahood."[29]

With respect to the Lotus Sutra, we should note first that no one speaking for the Buddha or for bodhisattvas brings up the dictum of the five hindrances. It is the former *śrāvaka* Śāriputra who brings up this objection; the long-time Bodhisattva Wisdom-Accumulation (Prajñākūṭa) is, rather, astonished at Mañjuśrī's tale because of the extreme shortness of the *nāga* princess's path to Buddhahood. The original question to which

Mañjuśrī responds is Wisdom-Accumulation's question: "Are there any beings who, putting this scripture into practice by the strenuous application of vigor, will speedily gain Buddhahood, or are there not?" Receiving an affirmative answer, Wisdom-Accumulation cannot believe it because the Buddha Śākyamuni's own path to Buddhahood, what we might call "the Jātaka path" involving many lifetimes of self-sacrifice, in which the Buddha-to-be torments himself by doing what is hard to do and casts away "body and life for the beings' sake," is apparently not required in the case of the *nāga* princess to whom the sutra has been preached. As some have also noted, the fact that it is not required reflects more on the power of the wisdom contained in the sutra than on any particular qualifications of the *nāga* princess. If the notion that a being who is first, nonhuman, second, female, and third, a child, through her profound understanding of the sutra attained with extreme rapidity a very advanced stage of bodhisattvahood (in the space of a moment directly and immediately achieved right, enlightened intuition) was potentially shocking to anyone in the world of the Lotus Sutra, Wisdom-Accumulation does not draw attention to those reasons for being shocked.

Śāriputra does, focusing on the female aspect. But the *nāga* princess appears in person to prove Mañjuśrī right and Śāriputra wrong. Mañjuśrī has said that she is very close to Buddhahood, and she shows that she is by attaining it in an instant before their eyes.

(b) Present-day Western feminists of course are not satisfied to see as good news for women a story in which a woman must change her form and extinguish her female nature prior to manifesting her complete Buddhahood. But the matter is perhaps not so simple. To the question, "Does she change her body?" there are reasons to give yes and no answers.

(1) On the "yes" side, it is unquestionable that large change takes place. It is important to note that it is not only physical appearance that must change. Diana Paul notes that in this literature not only is a woman challenged to change her physical appearance, she is also challenged to change her "woman's thoughts," her woman's nature, her mental attitude. She says that "being a male in mental attitude meant being unattached to sexuality and being responsible for one's actions, whereas being a female in Indian society did not entail such detachment and responsibility."[30] She also writes of how in some Indian Buddhist texts it is stated that female physiology and female sexual "power" result physiologically in weakness of will. Thus a woman who wants to advance on the spiritual path must seek rebirth in a male body and renounce and eradicate her woman's sexual "power," which, because it ties her to sexual desire, is seen as inferior and an obstacle. Once a woman's sexual "power" is eradicated, she can be reborn as a man, from which, if she can eradicate her

male sexual "power," she can become a Buddha.[31] As a Buddha, though, she retains her male form, for the male body was considered an image for the perfection of the mind. Transformation of sex represented a transition from the imperfection, impurity, and immorality of human beings (the female body) to the mental perfection of bodhisattvas and Buddhas (the male body).[32]

(2) The *nāga* princess changes her body, including the act of extinguishing her female power and manifesting a male one. But she does not do it in the manner that Śāriputra may have had in mind, by being reborn in a male body, becoming a monk, etc. She does it rather by an act of truth: if it is true that I am ready for Buddhahood, let it be shown to be true.

(3) On the "no" side, one possible reading might be that there has been no real change of body, but an act of magic. It is important to note that when the *nāga* princess appears before the assembly she is, according to Mañjuśrī's testimony, already a bodhisattva. Is it not the case that bodhisattvas possess and exercise remarkable powers to transform things at will? Let us look at this for a moment in general terms, not limited to the evidence in the Lotus Sutra, but rather from the perspective of the fully developed Mahayana.

In some Mahayana texts, at the higher stages of bodhisattvahood a person was understood to be beyond gender, and able to choose gender at will. She/he would acquire "skill-in-means," abilities to enlighten other beings, as well as certain supernormal powers (*rddhi*). These include transformation into various shapes, and projecting a mentally created body.[33] Luis Gomez writes:

> According to Asanga, in his description of the various supernormal powers that result from the Bodhisattva's *samādhi*, these powers (*rddhi-bala*) are divided into two types: powers of transformation and powers of creation. The first group includes, among others, the power to produce fire and emit rays of light of many colors, the sight of which allays all suffering; the power to produce light that pervades every corner of the universe; the power to make everything visible anywhere in an instant; the power to change the form of things; the power to introduce any object, however large, into his own body; and the power to appear and disappear anywhere.[34]

In the class of powers of creation, one of the most important subtypes is the capacity to create or project bodies. A Buddha or bodhisattva can create illusory bodies, similar or dissimilar to the creator. These bodies are illusory, or rather, "like magical creations, insofar as they exist for the sole purpose of being contemplated by living beings, yet they are real because they speak, drink, take food, etc."[35]

This interpretation of the powers of a bodhisattva is based on texts other than the Lotus Sutra. But it raises the interesting question of whether we might not read the story of the *nāga* princess as one of a female advanced bodhisattva simply exercising her *ṛddhi-bala* in creating a transformation in what she already knows to be insubstantial, as the goddess in the *Vimalakīrti-nirdeśa-sūtra* does.

(4) Again on the "no" side, perhaps one could read the story of the *nāga* princess as merely a case of a Mahayana bodhisattva teaching through transformations. Rolf Stein points out that there is a Mahayana theme of transformation through reversals. He cites the examples found in the Sutra of Indra's Net (*Fan-wang ching*): a bodhisattva using the great power of skillful means (*upāya*) can "turn a pure country into an evil country and an evil country into a land of wonder and happiness; turn good into evil and vice versa; form into nonform and vice versa; man into woman and vice versa; the six realms of rebirth into six realms of no rebirth and vice versa, and even turn the four great elements of earth, water, fire, and wind into no earth, water, fire and wind."[36] In all these cases a bodhisattva deconstructs the ordinary reality held by unenlightened people. By turning everything upside down the bodhisattva shocks them into a new vision.

(5) Returning to the main line of Lotus Sutra-inspired interpretations, we find support for the notion that the *nāga* princess's changing of her body is not best read as support for the idea that one cannot attain Buddhahood in a female body. The great Lotus Sutra commentator T'ien-t'ai Chih-i addresses the question of how to read the story of a female who transforms her body. He chooses to read the story as a demonstration of equality of all dharmas on the ultimate level, not as an occasion in which a female is able to leave a female body, or femaleness, behind. Paul Groner points out that the earliest use of the term *chi-shen ch'eng-fo* (Jpn. *sokushin jōbutsu*) in a T'ien-t'ai text is found in the *Fa-hui wen-chü chi* (T.34, no.1719, 314b), Chan-jan's subcommentary on Chih-i's line-by-line commentary on the Lotus Sutra, the *Fa-hua wen-chü* (T.34, no.1718). This occurs in a passage commenting on the realization by the *nāga* king's daughter. Both Chih-i and Chan-jan mention a text entitled [*P'u-sa ch'u*] *T'ai-ching*, a text in which the transformation of women into men and their subsequent realization of Buddhahood is described. According to Chih-i:

> The *T'ai-ching* states that "the women in the realms of Māra, Śakra and Brahmā all neither abandoned (their old) bodies nor received (new) bodies. They all realized Buddhahood with their current bodies (Ch. *hsien-shen*, Jpn. *genshin)*." Thus these verses state that the

dharma nature is like a great ocean. No right or wrong is preached (within it). Ordinary people and sages are equal, without superiority or inferiority."[37]

The point that Chih-i is making about the story of the *nāga* princess is that this is not a story about a female who abandons her old body and takes a new body. Her realization occurs within her current body. The dharma-nature which includes all beings, or indeed is the fundamental reality of all beings, is equal, without superiority for sages or men's bodies and inferiority for ordinary people and women's bodies. It is like a great ocean (the *nāga* king Sāgara's name means "ocean") in that it is one without distinctions and divisions and has one flavor.

(6) In Japan, Saichō took a somewhat different tack, but still seems to have held to the view of Chih-i that the *nāga* princess did not really need to change her body. Saichō employed the story of the *nāga* princess to prove that the Lotus Sutra applied to all sentient beings and would quickly bring them salvation:

> This passage (about the dragon king's daughter) concerns those beings who can realize buddhahood only with difficulty and reveals the power of the *Lotus Sutra* to help them. She is an animal, (one of lower levels of the) six destinies [realms], obviously the result of bad karma. She is female and clearly has faculties which are not good. She is young and thus has not been practicing religious austerities for a long time. And yet, the wondrous power of the *Lotus Sutra* endows her with the two adornments of wisdom and merit. Thus we know that the power of the *Lotus Sutra* reveals it to be the jewel among the scriptures and a rarity in the world.[38]

Saichō argued that the fact that those who observed her realization of Buddhahood also attained a significant advance shows that the power of the Lotus Sutra can be effective for virtually any sentient being. He wrote:

> The dragon king's daughter who converted others (to the ultimate teaching) had not undergone a long period of religious austerities; nor had the sentient beings who were converted [by her] undergone a long period of austerities. Through the wondrous power of the sutra, they all realized buddhahood with their bodies just as they are (*sokushin jōbutsu*). Those with the highest grade of superior faculties realize buddhahood in one lifetime; those with the medium grade of superior faculties require two lifetimes to realize buddhahood. And those with the lowest grade of superior faculties will realize buddhahood within three lifetimes. They will meet the bodhisattva

Samantabhadra, enter the ranks of the bodhisattvas, and acquire the *dhāraṇī* which will enable them to master nonsubstantiality.[39]

(7) In the twentieth century, another great *Saddharma-puṇḍarīka dharma-bhāṇaka*, Nikkyō Niwano, addressed the reader's probable response to her apparently changing her gender. He made an interesting point when he wrote that some today might object that in this story the dragon princess has to change into a male form; but for the Indian audience, the psychological impact of sitting there and watching her do all these things would really profoundly make the point of women's and men's "different but equal" natures. Niwano said that some have said that this is the earliest example of preaching the equality of men and women. Simply to predict Buddhahood for her would not have the same psychological impact, would not make the point of her capacity for Buddhahood as well.

(8) With respect to the question of whether the *nāga* princess's change of bodily form is good news for women, my own reading is thus that in the story, the princess defeats the notion of the five hindrances, but does not challenge the notion that advanced, irreversible bodhisattvas and Buddhas are characterized by male form, since, as her hymn of praise in the sutra passage avers, male form is the form in which perfect spiritual attainment represents itself and is worshiped in the world. The trope of the female changing her gender and becoming a Buddha by an act of truth is a stratagem, a rhetorical device, to overcome the notion that only males are *hōki* (Ch. *fa-ch'i*), receptacles or vessels of the Dharma. It almost succeeds in overcoming this notion, but is too easily reified into a doctrine, a new gender ideology, that says that women can, should, or must change their gender.

III. Females as Dharma-preachers in the Lotus Sutra

My own view is that, understood within the context of the sutra's messages as a whole, the *nāga* princess's rapid attainment of bodhisattvahood and *dharma-bhāṇaka* status is the chief good news for women.

I agree with Saichō that the chief point of the story within the larger text is to demonstrate the power of the Buddha's wondrous Dharma expounded by the Buddha in the Lotus Sutra. The story does make in dramatic form one of the chief points of the second half of the sutra, namely, that one who believes and understands the meaning of the Lotus Sutra—and the sutra does tell us that this is not easy to do—is very close to the full attainment of Buddhahood.

A. The *Dharma-bhāṇaka* in the Sutra

Here are two of the passages that bear this out: first, from chapter 10:

> But those who hear this *Dharmaparyāya* and thereupon accept, pene-
> trate, understand and comprehend it, are at the time near supreme,
> perfect enlightenment, so to say, immediately near it.[40]

And second, from chapter 21:

> What the Buddhas seated on the . . . *bodhimaṇḍa,*
> What secret, vital dharmas they attain,
> He who can hold to this scripture
> Shall in no long time also attain.
> He who can hold to this scripture
> Shall, with respect to the meanings of the dharmas,
> To names and words,
> And to joy in preaching (*pratibhānu*), be inexhaustible,
> As the wind in the midst of space
> Is unobstructed by anything.[41]

One way of reading the story of the *nāga* king's daughter in the context of the sutra is to see it as a dramatic illustration of these points about the nearness of the one who has understood the sutra to *anuttara-samyak-saṃbodhi,* to Buddhahood. In that way, it fits well into the sutra. And in making that point, the sutra is good news for women.

To state this in a more general form, the rapid leap of the *nāga* king's daughter to advanced bodhisattvahood and then to Buddhahood is an excellent illustration for the general "suddenism" and denial of the ne-cessity of a long path that particularly characterizes the second half of the sutra. Not only does believing in and/or understanding the sutra re-sult in rapid progress, the requirement of practice of the six-*pāramitā* path for attaining Buddhahood is sometimes undermined. One passage in chapter 16 says that the merits of those who are just open-minded and trust the teaching are beyond those who practice the five *pāramitās* (that is, the six except for *prajñā-pāramitā*) for an astronomical length of time in order to obtain ultimate *bodhi.* The verse recapitulation of the same pas-sage in prose says: "Now, the merits which will be attained by a woman or man who believes in the length of the Buddha's life for even a single moment will be infinite." Where merits are infinite, the path tends to be-come telescoped or disappear. Under such circumstances, women and men are more readily seen as more nearly equal.

B. The *Nāga* Princess as Dharma Preacher

To my mind, the most important good news that women receive in the story of the *nāga* princess's attainment of Buddhahood, if one reads the story in the context of the whole sutra, is that a female through hearing the sutra with her sharp roots attains very advanced bodhisattvahood and becomes a fully accomplished *dharma-bhāṇaka*, a preacher and teacher of the highest Dharma of the Buddha. While Buddhahood is the goal that is promised to everyone in the sutra, the practical goals that are in fact placed in the foreground are to give rise to the *bodhicitta*, to attain irreversibility as a bodhisattva, and to become an effective *dharma-bhāṇaka* devoted to the salvation of others through the preaching of the sutra. Mañjuśrī tells his audience that the *nāga* princess, in her female form, has attained all three, and is effectively preaching the sutra.

One of the things that is very clear in this depiction of the *nāga* princess as bodhisattva, as well as in the *Śrīmālā-devī-siṃhanāda-sūtra* and in the depiction of the nun teacher in the *Gaṇḍavyūha* whom Sudhana encounters in his travels is that exceptional powers of verbal expression and speech are marks of the advanced bodhisattva, and that women can experience and deploy them as well as men. Extraordinary powers of verbal expression are a mark of sanctity in this tradition, since being able to lead others to enlightenment to the nature of the Dharma is one of the chief aspirations, goals, and marks of Buddhas and of those on the bodhisattva path. This particular mark of sanctity occurs in women as well as men.

A principal message of this sutra is that becoming a bodhisattva is to take part in the glorious task of the Buddha and all other Buddhas, namely to enable others to reach Buddhahood by preaching and teaching. A strong emphasis on the importance of the *dharma-bhāṇaka*, who fulfills the Tathāgata's role and, in doing so is assimilated to the Tathāgata, is a striking characteristic of this sutra's teaching about the bodhisattva path.[42] Chapter 10, called "The Dharma Teacher" or "The Dharma Preacher," and chapter 19, "Merits of the Dharma Teacher," are particularly eloquent testimonies to the way in which this sutra emphasizes teaching the sutra as the principal activity of the bodhisattva. Gene Reeves, in a summary of the Lotus Sutra, offers the following summary of sections of chapter 10:

> Any good man or woman who privately explains even a phrase of the sutra to a single person is a messenger of the Buddha, one who does the Buddha's work. How much more so, anyone who explains the

whole sutra to a lot of people. When anyone hears such a person teaching the sutra, they will immediately become fully enlightened. . . .

Anyone who copies, keeps, reads and recites, make offerings to, or preaches this sutra will be covered by the Buddha's robe and be protected by Buddhas of the other worlds; he will have the powers of faith, of will and of virtue. He will live with the Buddha and have his head patted or caressed by the Buddha. . . .

After the Buddha has passed away, those who would explain this sutra should enter the room of the Tathāgata, which means having great compassion, wear the robe of the Tathāgata, which means being gentle and patient, and sit on the seat of the Tathāgata, which means seeing the emptiness or interdependence of all things. Though the Buddha will be in another land after passing away, he will conjure up and dispatch various people and other creatures to hear the Lotus Sutra taught, enable the teacher to see the Buddha from time to time, and help the teacher if he forgets a phrase of the sutra. Those who follow such a teacher will be able to see many Buddhas.

Graeme MacQueen provides a summary of what the Lotus Sutra teaches about the *dharma-bhāṇaka*. He writes:

Within the [theistic framework of the Lotus Sutra] the inspired speaker, the *Dharma-bhāṇaka*, is primarily one who achieves communion with divine persons, for whom he then acts as a channel and a messenger. He attempts to live open to the sacred realm; the Buddha appears before him in visions and dreams, comforting him and assuring him that he acts correctly, and he intermingles with *devas* and other supernatural beings, receiving their help and protection. He hears the Buddha expound the Dharma and he catches its true meaning. When he preaches, his accuracy and fluency are assured by Buddhas and *devas*. His exegesis of the text is given authority by the Buddha, who guarantees the validity of his interpretation. Thus supported he may answer all public challenges and questions confidently and without hesitation. He is the messenger or deputy of the Buddha. More, *qua* bearer of the holy word, he is the Buddha incarnate. He is to be treated with great respect, and those who spurn him and his message are doomed.[43]

In the context of the whole sutra it is of great significance for women that the Buddha in chapter 13 predicts for his aunt and foster mother, Mahāprajāpati, and for his erstwhile wife, Yaśodharā, who are now nuns, that they will eventually become great teachers of the Dharma. In joyful gratitude they vow to go out to foreign lands immediately to broadly propagate the Lotus Sutra.[44] In other words, they put the sutra into practice in the way that the sutra most recommends.

One might conclude that in the sutra women are encouraged to become *dharma-bhāṇakas*, not only as evidenced by this prediction but also as evidenced by the fact that in the beginning of chapter 10 sons and daughters of good family (*kula-putras* and *kula-duhitṛs*) are both encouraged to become *dharma-bhāṇakas*. But these instances are not anywhere near as reassuring and encouraging to women as the description that Mañjuśrī offers of the *nāga* king's daughter as a bodhisattva who teaches:

> Her wisdom is sharp-rooted, and well she knows the faculties and deeds of the beings. She has gained dhāraṇī [powerful verbal formulas]. The profound treasure house of secrets preached by the Buddhas she is able to accept and to keep in its entirety. She has profoundly entered into dhyāna concentration, and has arrived at an understanding of the dharmas. In the space of a moment she produced the aspiration to enlightenment, and has attained the point of nonbacksliding. Her eloquence [*pratibhāna*] has no obstructions, and she is compassionately mindful of the beings as if they were her babies. Her merits are perfect. What she recollects in her mind and recites with her mouth is subtle and broad. She is of good will and compassionate, humane and yielding. Her will and thought are harmonious and refined. . . .[45]

This description assimilates the *nāga* princess before her transformation in form to standard descriptions of bodhisattvas that include preaching and teaching with eloquence, clear-minded mastery of the Dharma, and inspired speech.[46]

Unfortunately, we do not get to see in this passage or in this sutra a fully elaborated image of a female *dharma-bhāṇaka* at work. That would perhaps do the most to make the sutra fully good news for women. Mahāprajāpatī and Yaśodharā promise to go off to spread the teaching, but their status as *dharma-bhāṇaka* is still in the future. The *nāga* king's daughter becomes a *dharma-bhāṇaka*, but we have only brief descriptions of her activities in that role. She so very soon becomes a Buddha.

IV. Conclusions

Seen in the light of the encouragement given to women and to females of other species that they can become bodhisattvas and *dharma*-teachers, can share in the great work of the Buddhas, that they can attain irreversibility (as the *nāga* princess does before her appearance in the assembly), and that as bodhisattvas who have faith in, understand and preach the sutra they are very near to Buddhahood, the *nāga* princess's transformation into a full Buddha serves chiefly as a concrete, vivid illustration of the power of the sutra's teaching and of principles that apply to women now. Thus, from the standpoint of that faith, it is good news for women.

Notes

1. T.9.7a21-28; Hurvitz, *Scripture of the Lotus Blossom of the Fine Dharma*, New York: Columbia University Press, 1976, 30. I quote from a number of different translations in this essay.
2. P. Gregory, "Expedient Means and the Hermeneutical Problem in Buddhism," an abridgment of the first section of chapter 3 of Peter N. Gregory, *Tsung-mi and the Sinification of Buddhism*, Princeton: Princeton University Press, 1991.
3. Perhaps this is a somewhat ahistorical view? See Yūichi Kajiyama, "Women in Buddhism," *The Eastern Buddhist*, vol. 15, no. 2 (new series), Autumn, 1982. See also notes 5, 6, and 7 on 322–23 in Tsugunari Kubo, *Hokekyō bosatsu-shisō no kiso* (The Fundamental Philosophy of the Lotus Sutra with Respect to the Practices of the Bodhisattva), Tokyo: Shunjū-sha, 1987, for information on Japanese studies of the equality of women in the Mahayana, and on the origins of the Devadatta chapter.
4. Kōtatsu Fujita, "One Vehicle or Three." The original version of this article was published in 1969 in a festschrift for Enichi Ōchō, *Hokke shisō*. This selection has been abridged and adapted from the translation by Leon Hurvitz published in *The Journal of Indian Philosophy*, vol. 3, nos. 1–2 (1975), 79–166.
5. I got this idea from Nikkyō Niwano, who points out in the second of two English-language books on the Lotus Sutra: "The message of the sutra is that not just greatly enlightened elite bodhisattvas, with whom it is hard for us to identify, can be Dharma teachers, even we can if we give ourselves to it." Cf. Niwano, *A Guide to the Threefold Lotus Sutra*, Tokyo: Kōsei Publishing Co., 1981.
6. Yūichi Kajiyama, "Women in Buddhism," *Eastern Buddhist*, vol. 15, no. 2 (new series), Autumn 1982, 69–70.
7. The more detailed version of this essay focuses on the historical context for these passages provided by other early Mahayana literature and offers some additional arguments.
8. Kubo, op. cit., 16–17.
9. Hurvitz, op. cit., 1, with slight changes.
10. Kubo, 17.
11. *The Lotus Sutra*, Burton Watson, trans., New York: Columbia University Press, 1993, 176.
12. In chapter 8.
13. Hurvitz translates these epithets "worthy of offerings, of right and universal

knowledge, his clarity and conduct perfect, well gone, understanding the world, an unexcelled Worthy, a Regulator of men of stature, a Teacher of gods and men, a Buddha, a World-Honored One." Hurvitz, *Scripture of the Lotus Blossom of the Fine Dharma*, 203. Watson translates them: "worthy of offerings, of right and universal knowledge, perfect clarity and conduct, well gone, understanding the world, unexcelled worthy, trainer of people, teacher of heavenly and human beings, Buddha, World-Honored One." Cf. Burton Watson, trans., *The Lotus Sutra*, 191–92. The way Watson and Hurvitz translate these does make them sound more gender-neutral than the Chinese or Japanese reader would perceive them to be, and than the Sanskrit original no doubt was. For example, "unexcelled Worthy" in Chinese is "peerless *shih*, knight." The epithet which Hurvitz translates "Regulator of men of stature" and Watson translates "trainer of people" is literally "the man who tames and controls" the passions of humans, as a trainer or master does a wild elephant or horse. Hurvitz and Watson miss the meaning of the original Indian phrase in taking *jang-fu* (Jpn. *jōbu*) to be the object of the verb. Graeme MacQueen translates this epithet of the Buddha: trainer of the human steer *(purisa-damma-sārathi)*.

14. *The Lotus Sutra*, B. Watson, trans., 191–92, with slight changes.

15. Ibid., 192.

16. Ibid., 191.

17. Ibid., 192.

18. Niwano, *A Guide to the Threefold Lotus Sutra*, 95–96.

19. Hurvitz, op. cit., 199–201, with some word substitutions, especially *"nāga"* for "dragon."

20. Diana Paul, *Women in Buddhism*, Berkeley: Asian Humanities Press, 1979, 185. In this pioneering work Paul gives a very good description of a *nāga*, from which much of this paragraph is taken.

21. Strong, John S. *The Experience of Buddhism.* Belmont, CA: Wadsworth, Inc, 1995, 61–63. Strong's own translation from the Vinaya pitikam, ed. Hermann Oldenberg (London: Williams and Norgate, 1879), 1: 86–87.

22. Paul, 185. We should remember, though, that the Lotus Sutra was most likely not written in the south of India. So perhaps not all features of the *nāga* lore from south India on which Paul draws may have been relevant in north India.

23. See Edward H. Schafer, *The Divine Woman: Dragon Ladies and Rain Maidens in T'ang Literature*, Berkeley: University of California Press, 1973.

24. Kajiyama, op. cit., 58.

25. There are other variations on this list. See Kajiyama, 55–58.

26. Nancy Schuster, "Changing the Female Body: Wise Women and the Bodhisattva Career in Some *Mahāratnakūṭasūtras*," *Journal of the International Association of Buddhist Studies*, IV:1 (1981), 59.

27. Kajiyama, 66.

28. In a longer version of this paper I have argued that Kajiyama's view that early Mahayanists desired to eliminate the discriminatory idea that women could not become Buddhas is called into question by Paul Harrison's findings published in his "Who Gets to Ride in the Great Vehicle," *Journal of the*

International Association of Buddhist Studies, 10:1 (1987), 67–89. Harrison shows that a group of very early Mahayana sutras seems to reflect a lack of interest in seeing women as bodhisattvas, much less Buddhas.

29. Hae-ju Sunim (Ho-Ryeon Jeon), "Can Women Achieve Enlightenment? A Critique of Sexual Transformation for Enlightenment," in *Buddhist Women Across Cultures,* edited by Karma Lekshe Tsomo, Albany: State University of New York Press, 1999, 123–41.

30. Paul, 186–87.

31. Ibid., 171–73.

32. Ibid., 175.

33. Schuster, 1981, points out that there is an assumption common to Indian thought that the attainment of extraordinary levels of understanding of reality naturally entail the attainment of extraordinary powers. On these powers as discussed in the *Visuddhi-magga,* see the discussion in Schuster, 1981; in Luis Gomez, "The Bodhisattva as Wonder-worker," in *Prajñāpāramitā and Related Systems,* edited by Lewis R. Lancaster, Berkeley: University of California Press, 1977, 221–61; and in *The Path of Purification,* by Bhadantacariya Buddhaghosa, Seattle: Vipassana Research Publications of America, 1999, 414–20.

34. Gomez, op. cit., 230; I have deleted some Sanskrit terms.

35. Ibid., 230; I have deleted some Sanskrit terms.

36. Rolf A. Stein, "Avalokiteśvara/Kouan-yin, un exemple de transformation d'un dieu en déesse," *Cahiers d'Extrême Asie,* vol. 2 [1986], 29–30.

37. Chih-i, *Fa-hua wen-chü,* T.34.117a. translation by Paul Groner, "The *Lotus Sutra* and Saichō's Interpretation of the Realization of Buddhahood with This Very Body," W. Tanabe and G. Tanabe, eds., *The Lotus Sutra in Japanese Culture,* University of Hawaii Press, 1989, 58. The passage in the *T'ai-ching* to which Chih-i referred is found in T.12.1034a–35c. "*Hsien-shen ch'eng-fo* (Jpn. *Genshin jōbutsu)*" is mentioned on T.12.1034c. See Groner, note 22, 71. The same idea appears in Chan-jan's *Fa-hua wen-chü chi,* cf. Groner, n. 35, 72.

38. Saichō, *Hokke-shūku,* in *Dengyō Daishi zenshū,* Tokyo: Nihon Bussho Kankōkai, 1975, 3:261. Translated and discussed in Groner, 61.

39. Ibid., 3: 266–67. Groner also writes that Saichō developed the idea that *sokushin jōbutsu* is a partial realization, a major one with very important physical and karmic changes, equivalent to the fifth identity, but still is not supreme enlightenment, or the ultimate of the six identities Chih-i developed as a map of the stages of attainment.

40. Kern, H. *The Saddharma-puṇḍarīka, or The Lotus of the True Law,* Sacred Books of the East, vol. 21, first published by Oxford University Press in 1884; reprinted by Motilal Banarsidass, 1965, 220–21, chapter 10; cf. Hurvitz, 179.

41. Hurvitz, 289–90.

42. Kubo tells us that the *dharma-bhāṇaka* is the Dharma-preacher, teacher. In the "merits of the Dharma teacher" section, the statement is made that the *dharma-bhāṇaka* is said to be one who must be recognized as a Tathāgata and the one who will do the Buddha's task. The *dharma-bhāṇaka* does not belong to the Sangha-treasure among the three treasures, but the *dharma-bhāṇaka* is part of the Buddha-treasure. "The sentient beings who approach a *dharma-bhāṇaka*

will soon become Bodhisattvas." The sutra, rather than treating people as mere followers of the Buddha, teaches them that, as representatives of the Buddha, they should lead others to enlightenment. the one who leads others to enlightenment is the Buddha. (Kubo, 9) For references in Japanese scholarship on the *dharma-bhāṇaka* (*hōshi*, Ch. *fa-shih*), see Kubo, 233–34, note 3.

43. Graeme MacQueen, "Inspired Speech in Early Mahāyāna Buddhism" (part II), *Religion*, vol. 12, no. 1 (1982), 56–57.
44. Watson, 192.
45. Hurvitz, 199–200, with some minor changes.
46. See Graeme MacQueen, "Inspired Speech," parts I (in *Religion*, vol. 11, no. 4, Oct. 1981, 303–19) and II.

Bibliography of Works in English
Related to the Lotus Sutra

This bibliography is not inclusive, though it leans in that direction. Sōka Gakkai, which is clearly within the Nichiren tradition, alone has produced and elicited a large volume of literature in English. Some is included here because it is clearly related either to the Lotus Sutra or to the Nichiren tradition, but much is not, simply because, while it is from within that tradition, it is not about that tradition. On the other hand, I have not tried to separate the "scholarly" from the nonscholarly in any systematic way. That is a distinction which does not work very well in this case. Some nonscholars produce quite scholarly works, while some scholars produce decidedly nonscholarly works. In constructing this bibliography I have leaned toward being inclusive. When in doubt about an item, I have included it.

The bibliography is divided into five sections. The first is the Lotus Sutra itself in English translation and transliteration. The second section includes books written about the Lotus Sutra, which is followed by articles about the Lotus Sutra in magazines and books. The last two sections include works about the T'ien-t'ai/Tendai and Nichiren traditions respectively. Naturally, some works could easily be included in at least two of these lists. One cannot write much about Nichiren, for example, without also writing about the Lotus Sutra. I've made choices, sometimes arbitrary I suppose, to have works appear on only one of these lists, including them in the list which seemed most appropriate.

Like all such bibliographies, this one is dependent on prior bibliographies, but the final, Nichiren, section is especially indebted to the Nichiren tradition bibliography which appeared in the Fall 1999 "Revisiting Nichiren" issue of the *Japanese Journal of Religious Studies,* edited by Ruben Habito and Jacqueline Stone.

The Lotus Sutra in English Translation and Transliteration

Saddharmapuṇḍarīkasūtra: Central Asian manuscripts. Romanized text. Edited by Hirofumi Toda. Tokushima, Japan: Kyōiku Shuppan Center, 1981.

Saddharma-Puṇḍarīka or *The Lotus of the True Law*. Translated by H. Kern (from Sanskrit). Oxford: Clarendon Press, 1884 (The Sacred Books of the East, vol. XXI); New York: Dover Publications, 1963.

The Lotus of the Wonderful Law, or The Lotus Gospel: Saddharma Puṇḍarīka Sūtra, Miao-fa Lien Hua Ching. Translated by W. E. Soothill. Oxford: Clarendon Press, 1930; New Jersey: Humanities Press, 1987.

The Threefold Lotus Sutra: Innumerable Meanings, The Lotus Flower of the Wonderful Law, and Meditation on the Bodhisattva Universal Virtue. Translated by Bunnō Katō, et al., Tokyo: Kōsei Publishing Company, 1975.

Scripture of the Lotus Blossom of the Fine Dharma. Translated by Leon Hurvitz. New York: Columbia University Press, 1976.

The Wonderful Dharma Lotus Flower Sutra, vols. 1–10. Translated by The Buddhist Text Translation Society, with commentary by Tripitaka Master Hua. San Francisco: Sino-American Buddhist Association, 1976–82.

The Lotus Sutra: The Sutra of the Lotus Flower of the Wonderful Dharma. Translated by Senchū Murano. Tokyo: Nichiren Shu Headquarters and Nichiren Shu Shimbun Co., 1974 (First edition), 1991 (Second revised edition).

The Lotus Sutra. Translated by Tsugunari Kubo and Akira Yuyama. BDK English Tripiṭaka 13-I. Berkeley: Numata Center for Buddhist Translation and Research, 1993.

The Lotus Sutra. Translated by Burton Watson. New York: Columbia University Press, 1993.

Books Primarily on the Lotus Sutra

Davidson, J. Leroy. *The Lotus Sutra in Chinese Art*. New Haven: Yale University Press, 1954.

Dykstra, Yoshiko K. *Miraculous Tales of the Lotus Sutra from Ancient Japan: The Dainihonkoku Hokekyōkenki of Priest Chingen*. Honolulu: University of Hawaii Press, 1983.

Fuss, Michael. *Buddhavacana & Dei Verbum: A Phenomenological & Theological Comparison of Scriptural Inspiration in the Saddharmapuṇḍarīka Sūtra & in the Christian Tradition*. Leiden: E. J. Brill, 1991.

Ikeda, Daisaku. *The Flower of Chinese Buddhism*. New York: Weatherhill, 1986.

Kim, Young-Ho. *Tao-sheng's Commentary on the Lotus Sūtra: A Study and Translation*. Albany: State University of New York Press, 1990.

Montgomery, Daniel B. *Fire in the Lotus: The Dynamic Buddhism of Nichiren*. London: Mandala, 1991.

Niwano, Nikkyō. *Buddhism for Today: A Modern Interpretation of the Threefold Lotus Sutra*. Tokyo: Kōsei Publishing Company, 1976.

———. *A Guide to the Threefold Lotus Sutra*. Tokyo: Kōsei Publishing Company, 1981.

Pye, Michael. *Skilful Means: A Concept in Mahayana Buddhism*. London: Duckworth, 1978.

Tamura, Yoshirō and Bunsaku Kurata, eds. *Art of the Lotus Sutra*. Tokyo: Kōsei Publishing Company, 1987.

Tanabe, Jr., George J. and Willa Jane Tanabe. *The Lotus Sutra in Japanese Culture.* Honolulu: University of Hawaii Press, 1989.

Tanabe, Willa Jane. *Paintings of the Lotus Sutra.* Tokyo: Weatherhill, 1988.

Yuyama, Akira. *A Bibliography of the Sanskrit Texts of the Saddharmapuṇḍarīkasūtra.* Canberra: Australian National University Press, 1970.

Selected Articles (on the Lotus Sutra or related to the Lotus Sutra) in Journals and Books

Berthrong, John. "Considering the Lotus Sutra." *Dharma World* 23 (July/Aug. 1996), 37–42.

Bloom, Alfred. "The Humanism of the Lotus Sutra." *Dharma World* 3:10 (Oct. 1976), 18–20.

Chandra, Lokesh. "The Lotus Sutra and the Present Age: The Philosophy of SGI President Daisaku Ikeda." *The Journal of Oriental Studies* 6 (1996), 20–27.

Chappell, David W. "Organic Truth: Personal Reflections on the Lotus Sutra." *Dharma World* 23 (Mar./Apr. 1996), 9–13; (May/June 1996), 19–22.

————. "Global Significance of the Lotus Sutra." *The Journal of Oriental Studies* 6 (1996), 1–10.

Ch'en, Kenneth K. S. "The Lotus Sutra." In chapter 13 of *Buddhism in China: A Historical Survey*, 378–82. Princeton: Princeton University Press, 1964.

Deal, William E. "The Lotus Sutra and the Rhetoric of Legitimization in Eleventh-Century Japanese Buddhism." *Japanese Journal of Religious Studies* 20:4 (Dec. 1993), 261–95.

de Jong, J. W. "Review article of Bunnō Katō, trans., *The Threefold Lotus Sutra* and Senchū Murano, trans., *The Sutra of the Lotus Flower of the Wonderful Law.*" *The Eastern Buddhist* 8:2 (Oct. 1975), 154–59.

Eckel, Malcolm David. "By the Power of the Buddha." *Dharma World* 22 (Sept./Oct. 1995), 9–15; (Nov./Dec. 1995), 14–18.

Education Section of Rissho Kosei-kai. "A Guide to the Lotus Sutra." *Dharma World* 13 (Jan. 1986), 20–26; (Feb. 1986), 36–43; (Mar. 1986), 36–43; (Apr. 1986), 24–31; (May 1986), 22–29; (June 1986), 32–36; (July 1986), 30–36; (Aug. 1986), 20–25; (Sept./Oct. 1986), 29–31; (Nov./Dec. 1986), 22–24. *Dharma World* 14 (Jan./Feb. 1987), 36–39; (Mar./Apr. 1987), 29–33; (May/June 1987), 40–42; (July/Aug. 1987), 40–42; (Sept./Oct. 1987), 34–37; (Nov./Dec. 1987), 40–42. *Dharma World* 15 (Jan./Feb. 1988), 40–43.

Endo, Takanori, "The Lotus Sutra and the Philosophy of Soka Gakkai." *The Journal of Oriental Studies* 6 (1996), 41–57.

Florida, Robert E. "The Lotus Sutra and Health Care Ethics." *Journal of Buddhist Ethics* 5, (1998).

Fujita, Kōtatsu. "One Vehicle or Three?" Translated by Leon Hurvitz. *Journal of Indian Philosophy* 3 (1975), 79–166.

Fuss, Michael A. "*Upāya* and *Missio Dei.*" *Dharma World* 23 (Sept./Oct. 1996), 36–41.

Grapard, Allan G. "Lotus in the Mountain, Mountain in the Lotus." *Monumenta Nipponica* 41:1 (1986), 21–50.

———. "The Textualized Mountain—Enmountained Text: The *Lotus Sutra* in Kunisaki." In *The Lotus Sutra in Japanese Culture*, edited by George J. Tanabe, Jr. and Willa Jane Tanabe, 159–89. Honolulu: University of Hawaii Press, 1989.

Griffiths, Paul J. "The Lotus Sūtra as Good News: A Christian Reading." *Buddhist-Christian Studies* 19 (1999), 3–17.

Habito, Ruben L. F. "Buddha-body Theory and the Lotus Sutra: Implications for Praxis." *Dharma World* 23 (Nov./Dec. 1996), 47–53.

Hardacre, Helen. "The *Lotus Sutra* in Modern Japan." In *The Lotus Sutra in Japanese Culture*, edited by George J. Tanabe, Jr. and Willa Jane Tanabe, 209–24. Honolulu: University of Hawaii Press, 1989.

Hirakawa, Akira. *"The Lotus Sūtra."* In *A History of Indian Buddhism from Śākyamuni to Early Mahayana* by Hirakawa, translated by Paul Groner, 282–86. Honolulu: University of Hawaii Press, 1990.

Hubbard, Jamie. "Buddhist-Buddhist Dialogue? The Lotus Sutra and the Polemic of Accommodation." *Buddhist-Christian Studies* 15 (1995), 119–36.

Hunter, Doris. "The Nature of the True Self: A Comparison of Parables." *Dharma World* 15 (May/June 1988), 30–33.

Hurvitz, Leon. "The Lotus Sutra in East Asia: a Review of *Hokke Shisō*." *Monumenta Serica* 29 (1970–71), 697–792.

Ignatovich, Alexander. Interview with author. "The Lotus Sutra into Russian." *Dharma World* 23 (Sept./Oct. 1996), 30–32.

———. "Echoes of the Lotus Sutra in Tolstoy's Philosophy." *Dharma World* 25 (Sept./Oct. 1998), 20–22.

Kajiyama, Yūichi. "Buddhist Eschatology, Supernatural Events and the *Lotus Sūtra*." *The Journal of Oriental Studies* 8 (1998), 15–37.

Kalupahana, David J. "The *Saddharmapuṇḍarīka-sūtra* and Conceptual Absolutism." In *A History of Buddhist Philosophy* by Kalupahana, 170–75. Honolulu: University of Hawaii Press, 1992.

Kasimow, Harold. "A Buddhist Path to Mending the World." *Dharma World* 26 (May/June 1999), 6–10.

Kawada, Yōichi. "The Lotus Sutra as a Doctrine of Inner Reformation." *The Journal of Oriental Studies* 6 (1996), 28–40.

Keown, Damien. "Paternalism in the Lotus Sutra." *Journal of Buddhist Ethics* 5 (1998).

Kubo, Tsugunari. "The Fundamental Philosophy of the Lotus Sutra with Respect to the Practices of the Bodhisattva." In *Hokkekyō bosatsu-shisō no kiso* by Kubo. Tokyo: Shunjūsha, 1987.

Kuno, Takeshi. "The Precious Stupa of the Lotus Sutra." *Dharma World* 22 (May/June 1995), 25–27.

LaFleur, William R. "Symbol and Yūgen: Shunzei's Use of Tendai Buddhism." In *The Karma of Words: Buddhism and the Literary Arts in Medieval Japan* by LaFleur, 80–106. Berkeley: University of California Press, 1983.

Lai, Whalen. "The Predocetic 'Finite Buddhakāya' in the *Lotus Sutra*: In Search of the Illusive Dharmakāya Therein." *Journal of the American Academy of Religion* 49 (Spring 1981), 447–69.

————. "The Humanity of the Buddha: Is Mahāyāna Docetic?" *Ching Feng* 14:2 (June 1981), 97–107.

————. "Seno'o Girō and the Dilemma of Modern Buddhism: Leftist Prophet of the Lotus Sutra." *Japanese Journal of Religious Studies* 11 (March 1984), 7–42.

————. "Why the Lotus Sutra?—On the Historic Significance of Tendai." *Japanese Journal of Religious Studies* 14:2-3 (June-Sept. 1987), 83–100.

————. "Tao-sheng's Theory of Sudden Enlightenment Re-examined." In *Sudden and Gradual Enlightenment: Approaches to Enlightenment in Chinese Thought*, edited by Peter N. Gregory, 169–200. Honolulu: University of Hawaii Press, 1989.

Lopez, Jr., Donald S. "Introduction." In *Buddhism in Practice*, edited by Donald S. Lopez, Jr., esp. 28–31. Princeton: Princeton University Press, 1995.

Matsumoto, Shirō. "The *Lotus Sutra* and Japanese Culture." In *Pruning the Bodhi Tree: The Storm over Critical Buddhism*, edited by Jamie Hubbard and Paul L. Swanson. Honolulu: University of Hawaii Press, 1997.

Mattis, Susan. "Chih-i and the Subtle Dharma of the Lotus Sutra: Emptiness or Buddha-nature?" *Dharma World* 27 (Mar./Apr. 2000), 28–32.

Mayer, John R. A. "Reflections on the Threefold Lotus Sutra." *Journal of Buddhist Ethics* 5 (1998).

Miya, Tsugio. "Pictorial Art of the *Lotus Sutra* in Japan." In *The Lotus Sutra in Japanese Culture*, edited by George J. Tanabe, Jr. and Willa Jane Tanabe, 75–94. Honolulu: University of Hawaii Press, 1989.

Mochizuki, Kaishaku and Nikkyō Niwano. "The Lotus Sutra and Modern Society." *Dharma World* 11 (May 1984), 10–14.

Morgan, Peggy. "Ethics and the Lotus Sutra." *Journal of Buddhist Ethics* 5 (1998).

Murase, Miyeko. "Kuan Yin as Savior of Men: Illustrations of the Twenty-fifth Chapter of the *Lotus Sutra*." *Artibus Asiae* 33:1 & 2 (1971), 39–74.

Nakamura, Hajime. "The Lotus Sutra and Others." In *Indian Buddhism: A Survey with Bibliographical Notes*, by Nakamura, 183–93. Delhi: Motilal Banarsidass, 1987.

Nattier, Jan. "The Lotus Sutra through American Eyes." *Dharma World* 25 (Sept./Oct. 1998), 23–26.

Niwano, Nikkyō. "Can the Lotus Sutra Rescue a World in Crisis?" *Dharma World* 2:3 (March 1975), 2–7.

————. "How to Read the Lotus Sutra." *Dharma World* 4:12 (Dec. 1977), 2–6.

————. "How Do We Read the Lotus Sutra?" *Dharma World* 7:12 (Dec. 1980), 2–6.

————. "The Perfection of the Lotus Sutra: Action." *Dharma World* 8:6 (June 1981), 2–6.

————. "The Seven Parables of the Lotus Sutra: Many Teachings, but One Meaning." *Dharma World* (Special Issue 1991), 56–63.

————. "The Threefold Lotus Sutra: A Modern Commentary." Translated by Gaynor Sekimori, et al., from the 10-volume *Shinshaku Hokke Sambukyō* by Nikkyō Niwano. *Dharma World* 18 (Mar./Apr. 1991–ongoing).

Ōchō, Enichi. "From the *Lotus Sutra* to the Sutra of Eternal Life: Reflections on the Process of Deliverance in Shinran." *The Eastern Buddhist* 11:1 (May 1978).

Odin, Steve. "The Lotus Sutra in the Writing of Kenji Miyazawa." *Dharma World* 26 (Nov./Dec. 1999), 13–19.

Ogden, Schubert M. "The Lotus Sutra and Interreligious Dialogue." *Dharma World* 22 (July/Aug. 1995), 14–18.

Ohnuma, Reiko. "Teaching the Lotus Sutra." *Dharma World* 25 (Nov./Dec. 1998), 33–39.

Pye, Michael. "Hoben & Shinjitsu." *Dharma World* 1:4 (Aug. 1974), 10–12.

———. "The Lotus Sutra and the Essence of Mahāyāna." In *Buddhist Spirituality*, edited by Takeuchi Yoshinori, 171–87. New York: Crossroad, 1997.

———. "The Length of Life of the Tathāgata." *Dharma World* 25 (July/Aug 1998), 43–50.

Reeves, Gene. "A Buddhist Practice for the Modern World: Risshō Kōsei-kai and the Lotus Sutra." In *1990 Anthology of Fo Kuang Shan International Buddhist Conference*. Kaosing, Taiwan: Fo Kuang Shan, 1990.

———. "The Lotus Sutra and Process Thought." *Process Studies* 23 (Summer, 1994), 98–118.

———. "Appropriate Means as the Ethics of the Lotus Sutra." *Journal of Buddhist Ethics* 5 (1998).

Saitō, Eizaburō. "The Lotus Sutra in My Political Life." *Dharma World* 14 (May/June 1987), 34–36.

Shioiri, Ryōdō. "The Meaning of the Formation and Structure of the *Lotus Sutra*." In *The Lotus Sutra in Japanese Culture*, edited by George J. Tanabe, Jr. and Willa Jane Tanabe, 15–36. Honolulu: University of Hawaii Press, 1989.

Stevenson, Daniel B. "Tales of the Lotus Sutra." In *Buddhism in Practice*, edited by Donald S. Lopez, Jr, 427–51. Princeton: Princeton University Press, 1995.

Stone, Jacqueline I. "Inclusive and Exclusive Perspectives on the One Vehicle." *Dharma World* 26 (Sept./Oct. 1999), 20–25.

———. "Lotus Sutra millenialism in Japan: From militant nationalism to postwar peace movements." In *Millenialism, Persecution and Violence: Historical Cases*, edited by Catherine Wessinger, 536–72. Syracuse, New York: Syracuse University Press, 2000.

Swanson, Paul L. "The Innumerable Meanings of the Lotus Sutra." *Dharma World* 19 (May/June 1992), 42–43.

Tamura, Yoshirō. "The Lotus Sutra." In *Art of the Lotus Sutra*, edited by Tamura and Bunsaku Kurata, 17–29 . Tokyo: Kōsei Publishing Company, 1987.

———. "The Ideas of the Lotus Sutra." In *The Lotus Sutra in Japanese Culture*, edited by George J. Tanabe, Jr. and Willa Jane Tanabe, 37–51. Honolulu: University of Hawaii Press, 1989.

Tanabe, Willa Jane. "The Lotus Lectures: *Hokke Hakkō* in the Heian Period." *Monumenta Nipponica* 39:4 (Winter 1984), 393–407.

Unno, Taitetsu. "The Somatic in Religious Life." *Dharma World* 23 (Jan./Feb. 1996), 13–17.

Venturini, Riccardo. "The Lotus Sutra and Human Needs." *Dharma World* 19 (May/June 1992), 43–64.

Watson, Burton. "The Lotus Sutra and the Twenty-first Century." *The Journal of Oriental Studies* 6 (1996), 11–19.

Williams, Paul. "The *Saddharmapuṇḍarīka (Lotus) Sūtra* and its influences." In *Mahā-*

yāna Buddhism: The Doctrinal Foundations, by Williams, 141–66. London: Routledge, 1989.

Wiseman, James. "Buddhist-Christian Dialogue on the Lotus Sutra." *Dharma World* 22 (May/June 1995), 46–47.

Wolf, Douglas. "The Lotus Sutra and the Dimension of Time." *Dharma World* 22 (Jan./Feb. 1995), 53–54.

———. "Models for Interfaith Dialogue from the Lotus Sutra." *Dharma World* 27 (Mar./Apr. 2000), 13–15.

Yamada, Shōzen. "Poetry and Meaning: Medieval Poets and the Lotus Sutra." In *The Lotus Sutra in Japanese Culture,* edited by George J. Tanabe, Jr. and Willa Jane Tanabe, 95–117. Honolulu: University of Hawaii Press, 1989.

Yuyama, Akira. "Why Kumārajīva Omitted the Latter Half of Chapter V in Translating the Lotus Sutra." In *Festschrift: Dieter Schlingloff,* edited by Friedrich Wilhelm, 325–30. Reinbek: Verlag für Orientalistische Fachpublikationen, 1996.

Selected Works on the T'ien-t'ai/Tendai Tradition

Abé, Ryūichi. "Saichō and Kūkai: A Conflict of Interpretations." *Japanese Journal of Religious Studies* 22:1-2 (Spring 1995), 103–37.

Chappell, David W., ed. *T'ien-t'ai Buddhism: An Outline of the Fourfold Teachings.* Tokyo: Daiichi-Shobō (Distributed by University of Hawaii Press), 1983.

———. "Is Tendai Buddhism Relevant to the Modern World?" *Japanese Journal of Religious Studies* 14:2-3 (June-Sept. 1987), 247–66.

Ch'en, Kenneth K. S. "The T'ien-t'ai School." In *Buddhism in China: A Historical Survey* by Ch'en, 303–13. Princeton: Princeton University Press, 1964.

Donner, Neal A. "Chih-i's Meditation on Evil." In *Buddhist and Taoist Practice in Medieval Chinese Society,* edited by David W. Chappell, 49–64. Honolulu: University of Hawaii Press, 1987.

———. "Chih-i." In *The Encyclopedia of Religion* 3. New York: Macmillan and Free Press, 1989.

———. "Sudden and Gradual Intimately Conjoined: Chih-i's T'ien-t'ai View." In *Sudden and Gradual Enlightenment: Approaches to Enlightenment in Chinese Thought,* edited by Peter N. Gregory, 201–26. Honolulu: University of Hawaii Press, 1989.

———. and Daniel B. Stevenson. *The Great Calming and Contemplation: A Study and Annotated Translation of the First Chapter of Chih-i's Mo-ho chih-kuan.* Honolulu: University of Hawaii Press, 1993.

Gishin. *The Collected Teachings of the Tendai School.* Translated by Paul L. Swanson. Berkeley: Numata Center for Buddhist Translation and Research, 1995.

Goddard, Dwight. "Self-cultivation according to the T'ien-t'ai (Tendai) school." In *A Buddhist Bible,* edited by Goddard. Boston: Beacon Press, 1938.

Grapard, Allan. "Linguistic Cubism—A Singularity of Pluralism in the Sannō Cult." *Japanese Journal of Religious Studies* 14:2-3 (June-Sept. 1987), 211–34.

———. "Enchin." In *The Encyclopedia of Religion* 5, 105–06. New York: Macmillan and Free Press, 1987.

———. "Honjisuijaku." In *The Encyclopedia of Religion* 6, 455–57. New York: Macmillan and Free Press, 1987.

Groner, Paul. *Saichō: The Establishment of the Japanese Tendai School.* Berkeley Buddhist Studies Series 7, Seoul: Po Chin Chai Ltd., 1984.

———. "Saichō." In *The Encyclopedia of Religion* 6, 455–57. New York: Macmillan and Free Press, 1987.

———. "Annen, Tankei, Henjō, and Monastic Discipline in the Tendai School: The Background of the *Futsū jubosatsukai kōshaku.*" *Japanese Journal of Religious Studies* 14:2-3 (June-Sept. 1987), 129–59.

———. "The *Lotus Sutra* and Saichō's Interpretation of the Realization of Buddhahood with This Very Body." In *The Lotus Sutra in Japanese Culture,* edited by George J. Tanabe, Jr. and Willa Jane Tanabe,53–74. Honolulu: University of Hawaii Press, 1989.

———. "Shortening the Path: The Interpretation of the Realization of Buddhahood in This Very Existence in the Early Tendai School." In *Paths to Liberation: The Mārga and Its Transformations in Buddhist Thought,* edited by Robert Buswell and Robert Gimello. Honolulu: University of Hawaii Press, 1992.

———. "A Medieval Japanese Reading of the *Mo-ho chih-kuan*: Placing the *Kankō ruijū* in Historical Context." *Japanese Journal of Religious Studies* 22:1-2 (Spring 1995), 49–81.

Habito, Ruben L. F. "Buddha-body Views in Tendai *Hongaku* Writings." *Journal of Indian and Buddhist Studies* 34:2 (1991), 54–60.

———. "The Self as Buddha—in Tendai Hongaku Writings—Orthodoxy and Orthopraxis in Japanese Buddhism." In *Ātmajñāna—Professor Sengaku Mayeda Felicitation Volume.* Tokyo: Shunjūsha, 1991.

———. "The New Buddhism of Kamakura and the Doctrine of Innate Enlightenment." *The Pacific World* 7 (Fall 1991), 26–35.

———. "The Logic of Nonduality and Absolute Affirmation: Deconstructing Tendai *Hongaku* Writings." *Japanese Journal of Religious Studies* 22:1-2 (Spring 1995), 83–101.

———. *Original Enlightenment: Tendai Hongaku Doctrine and Japanese Buddhism.* Studia Philologica Buddhica. Occasional Paper Series XI. Tokyo: The International Institute of Buddhist Studies of ICABS, 1996

Hazama, Jikō. "The Characteristics of Japanese Tendai." *Japanese Journal of Religious Studies* 14:2-3 (June-Sept. 1987), 101–12.

Hurvitz, Leon. Chih-i (538–97): *An Introduction to the Life and Ideas of a Chinese Buddhist Monk.* Mélanges Chinois et Bouddhiques 12. Brussel: Institut Belge des Hautes Ètudes Chinoises, 1961–62.

———. "The First Systematizations of Buddhist Thought in China." *Journal of Chinese Philosophy* 2 (1975), 361–88.

Kuroda, Toshio. "Historical Consciousness and *Hon-jaku* Philosophy in the Medieval Period on Mount Hiei." In *The Lotus Sutra in Japanese Culture,* edited by George J. Tanabe, Jr. and Willa Jane Tanabe, 143–58. Honolulu: University of Hawaii Press, 1989.

Lai, Whalen. "Faith and wisdom in the T'ien-t'ai Buddhist tradition: A letter by Ssu-ming Chih-li." *Journal of DHARMA* 6 (1981), 283–98.

———. "A different religious language: The T'ien-t'ai idea of the triple truth." *Ching Feng* 25:2 (1982), 67–78.

Lu, K'uan-yü [Charles Luk]. "Self-cultivation according to the T'ien-t'ai (Tendai) school: Samath-vipasyana for Beginners." In *The Secrets of Chinese Meditation,* 109–62. New York: Samuel Weiser, 1964.

Matsunaga, Daigan and Alicia Matsunaga. Chapter-4A: "Tendai." In *Foundation of Japanese Buddhism,* vol. 1, 139–71. Los Angeles: Buddhist Books International, 1974.

McMullin, Neil. "The Sanmon-Jimon Schism in the Tendai School of Buddhism: A Preliminary Analysis." *Journal of the International Association of Buddhist Studies* 7 (1984), 83–105.

———. "The Enryaku-ji and the Gion Shrine-Temple Complex in the Mid-Heian Period." *Japanese Journal of Religious Studies* 14:2-3 (June-Sept. 1987), 161–84.

———. "The *Lotus Sutra* and Politics in the Mid-Heian Period." In *The Lotus Sutra in Japanese Culture,* edited by George J. Tanabe, Jr. and Willa Jane Tanabe, 119–41. Honolulu: University of Hawaii Press, 1989,

Ng Yu-Kwan. *T'ien-t'ai Buddhism and Early Madhyamika.* Honolulu: University of Hawaii Press, 1993.

Ozaki, Makoto. "Saichō's Role and Significance in the Expectation of the Mappō Era." *Studies in Interreligious Dialogue* 1 (1991), 116–et seq.

Petzold, Bruno. *Tendai Buddhism.* Yokohama: International Buddhist Exchange Center, 1979.

Pruden, Leo M. "T'ien-t'ai." In *The Encyclopedia of Religion* 14, 510–19. New York: Macmillan and Free Press, 1987.

Reischauer, Edwin O. *Ennin's Diary: The Record of a Pilgrimage to China in Search of the Law.* New York: Ronald Press, 1955.

———. *Ennin's Travels in T'ang China.* New York: Ronald Press, 1955.

Rhodes, Robert F. "Saichō's Mappō Tōmyōki: The Candle of the Latter Dharma." *The Eastern Buddhist* 13:1 (1980), 79–103.

———. "The Four Extensive Vows and Four Noble Truths in T'ien-t'ai Buddhism." *Annual Memoirs of the Otani University Shin Buddhists Comprehensive Research Institute* 2 (1984), 53–91.

———. "Annotated Translation of the *Ssu-chiao-i* (On the Four Teachings), *chüan 1.*" *Annual Memoirs of the Otani University Shin Buddhists Comprehensive Research Institute* 3 (1985), 27–101; 4 (1986), 93–141.

———. "The *Kaihōgyō* Practice of Mt. Hiei." *Japanese Journal of Religious Studies* 14:2-3 (June-Sept. 1987), 185–202.

Saichō. *The Candle of the Latter Dharma.* Translated by Robert Rhodes. Berkeley: Numata Center for Buddhist Translation and Research, 1994.

Saso, Michael. "The Oral Hermeneutics of Tendai Tantric Buddhism." *Japanese Journal of Religious Studies* 14:2-3 (June-Sept. 1987), 235–46.

Shinohara, Kōichi and Phyllis Granoff. "Quanding's Biography of Zhiyi, the Fourth Chinese Patriarch of the Tiantai Tradition." In *Speaking of Monks: Religious Biography in India and China,* 97–232. New York: Mosaic Press, 1992.

Shirato, Waka. "Inherent Enlightenment and Saichō's Acceptance of the Bodhisattva Precepts." *Japanese Journal of Religious Studies* 14:2-3 (June-Sept. 1987), 113–27.

Sonoda, Kōyū. "Saichō." In *Shapers of Japanese Buddhism*, edited by Yūsen Kashi-wahara and Kōyū Sonoda, 26–38. Tokyo: Kōsei Publishing Company, 1994.

Stevenson, Daniel B. "The Four Kinds of Samadi in Early T'ien-t'ai Buddhism." In *Traditions of Meditation in Chinese Meditation*, edited by Peter N. Gregory, 45–98. Honolulu: University of Hawaii Press, 1986.

———. *The T'ien-t'ai Four Forms of Samadhi and Late North-South Dynasties, Sui, and Early T'ang Buddhist Devotionalism.* Ann Arbor: University of Michigan Press, 1987.

Stone, Jacqueline I. "Medieval Tendai Hongaku Thought and the New Kamakura Buddhism: A Reconsideration." *Japanese Journal of Religious Studies* 22:1-2 (Spring 1995), 17–48.

Sueki, Fumihiko. "Two Seemingly Contradictory Aspects of the Teaching of In-nate Enlightenment (*hongaku*) in Medieval Japan." *Japanese Journal of Religious Studies* 22:1-2 (Spring 1995), 3–16.

Swanson, Paul L. "Chih-i's Interpretation of Jñeyāvaraṇa: An Application of the Threefold Truth Concept." *Annual Memoirs of the Otani University Shin Buddhists Comprehensive Research Institute* 1 (1983), 51–72.

———. "Chih-i's Interpretation of the Four Noble Truths in the *Fa hua hsüan i.*" *Annual Memoirs of the Otani University Shin Buddhist Comprehensive Research Institute* 1 (1985), 103, 131

———. "T'ien-t'ai Studies in Japan." *Cahiers d'Extrême-Asie* 2 (1986), 219–32.

———. *Foundations of T'ien-t'ai Philosophy: The Flowering of the Two Truths Theory in Chinese Buddhism.* Berkeley: Asian Humanities Press, 1989.

———. "T'ien-t'ai Chih-i's Concept of Threefold Buddha Nature—A Synergy of Reality, Wisdom, and Practice." In *Buddha Nature.* Reno: Buddhist Books International, 1990.

Swanson, Paul L., ed. "Tendai Buddhism in Japan" issue of the *Japanese Journal of Religious Studies* 14: 2-3 (1987).

Takagi, Yutaka. "The Origins and Development of the Tendai Sect." Edited by Kazuo Kasahara. *Dharma World* 11 (April 1984), 35–38; (May 1984), 40–45; (June 1984), 41–44; (July 1984), 39–42; (Aug. 1984), 40–43; (Sept. 1984), 40–43.

Takakusu, Junjirō. "The Tendai School (Phenomenology, Lotus, Saddharma-puṇḍarīka, T'ten-t'ai)." In *The Essentials of Buddhist Philosophy*, 131–47. Bombay: Asia Publishing House, 1956.

Tamura, Yoshirō. "Japanese Culture and the Tendai Concept of Original Enlight-enment." *Japanese Journal of Religious Studies* 14:2-3 (June-Sept. 1987), 203–10.

———. "Tendaishū." In *The Encyclopedia of Religion* 14, 396–401. New York: Macmillan and Free Press, 1987.

———. "Japan's Experience of Buddhism: Saicho and Kukai." *Dharma World* 16 (Sept./Oct. 1989), 32–37.

———. "Japan's Experience of Buddhism: Original Enlightenment and Rebirth in the Pure Land." *Dharma World* 16 (Nov./Dec. 1989), 30–36.

Unno, Taitetsu. "San-lun, T'ien-t'ai, and Hua-yen." In *Buddhist Spirituality*, edited by Takeuchi Yoshinori, 343–65. New York: Crossroad, 1997,

Weinstein, Stanley. "The Beginnings of Esoteric Buddhism in Japan: The Neg-lected Tendai Tradition." *Journal of Asian Studies* 34 (1974), 177–91.

Ziporyn, Brook. *Evil and/or/as the Good: Omnicentrism, Intersubjectivity, and Value Paradox in Tiantai Buddhist Thought*. Cambridge: Harvard University Press, 2000.

Selected Works on the Nichiren Tradition

Allam, Cheryl M. "The Nichiren and Catholic confrontation with Japanese nationalism." *Buddhist-Christian Studies* 10 (1990), 35–84.

Anesaki, Masaharu. *Nichiren, the Buddhist Prophet*. Cambridge: Harvard University Press, 1916.

Asai, Endō. "Nichiren Shōnin's View of Humanity: The Final Dharma Age and the Three Thousand Realms in One Thought-Moment." *Japanese Journal of Religious Studies* 26:3-4 (Fall 1999), 239–59.

Bloom, Alfred. "Observations in the study of contemporary Nichiren Buddhism." *Contemporary Religions in Japan* 6:1 (1965), 58–74.

Brinkman, John T. "The Simplicity of Nichiren." *The Eastern Buddhist* (new series) 28:2 (1995), 248–64.

Causton, Richard. *Nichiren Shoshu Buddhism*. London: Rider, 1988.

Christensen, J. A. *St. Nichiren*. Tokyo: Nichiren-shū, 1981.

Deal, William E. "Nichiren's *Risshō ankoku ron* and Canon Formation." *Japanese Journal of Religious Studies* 26:3-4 (Fall 1999), 325–48.

del Campana, Pier P. "*Sandaihihō-shō*: An essay on the three great mysteries by Nichiren." *Monumenta Nipponica* 26:1-2 (1971), 205–24.

———. "Innovators of Kamakura Buddhism: Shinran and Nichiren." In *Great Historical Figures of Japan*, edited by Hyōe Murakami and Thomas J. Harper, 102–13. Tokyo: Japan Cultural Institute, 1978.

Dolce, Lucia. "Awareness of *mappō*: Soteriological interpretations of time in Nichiren." *The Transactions of the Asiatic Society of Japan* 7 (fourth series 1992), 81–106.

———. "Esoteric patterns in Nichiren's thought." *The Japan Foundation Newsletter* 23:5 (1996), 13–16.

———. "Buddhist hermeneutics in medieval Japan: Canonical texts, scholastic tradition and sectarian polemics." In *Canonization and Decanonization*, edited by A van der Kooij and K. van der Toorn, 229–43. Leiden: Brill, 1998.

———. *Nichiren and the Lotus Sutra: Esoteric Patterns in a Japanese Medieval Interpretation of the Lotus* (working title). Leiden: Brill, forthcoming.

———. "Criticism and Appropriation: Nichiren's Attitude toward Esoteric Buddhism." *Japanese Journal of Religious Studies* 26:3-4 (Fall 1999), 349–82.

Dollarhide, Kenneth. "History and time in Nichiren's *Senji-shō*." *Religion* 12 (1982), 233–45.

———. *Nichiren's Senji-shō: An Essay on the Selection of the Proper Time*. New York: Edwin Mellen Press, 1982.

Fujii, Manabu. "Nichiren." In *Shapers of Japanese Buddhism*, edited by Yūsen Kashiwahara and Kōyū Sonoda, 123–34. Tokyo: Kōsei Publishing Company, 1994.

Gosho Translation Committee, ed. and trans. *The Major Writings of Nichiren Daishonin*. 7 vols. Tokyo: Nichiren Shōshū International Center, 1979–94.

———. *The Writings of Nichiren Daishonin*. Tokyo: Sōka Gakkai, 1999.

Habito, Ruben. "Lotus Buddhism and its liberational thrust: A re-reading of the *Lotus Sūtra* by way of Nichiren." *Ching Feng* 35:2 (1992), 85–112.

———. "The mystico-prophetic Buddhism of Nichiren: An exploration in comparative theology." In *The Papers of the Henry Luce III Fellows in Theology*, vol. 2, edited by Johnathan Strom, 433–62. Atlanta, GA: Scholars' Press, 1997.

———. "Bodily Reading of the *Lotus Sūtra:* Understanding Nichiren's Buddhism." *Japanese Journal of Religious Studies* 26:3-4 (Fall 1999), 281–306.

———. "The Uses of Nichiren in Modern Japan." *Japanese Journal of Religious Studies* 26:3-4 (Fall 1999), 424–39.

Habito, Ruben and Jacqueline I. Stone. "Revisiting Nichiren," *Japanese Journal of Religious Studies* 26:3-4 (Fall 1999), 223–36.

Hammond, Phillip and David Machacek. *Soka Gakkai in America.* Oxford: Oxford University Press, 1999.

Hori, Kyōtsū, trans. and ed. *Kaimoku-shō.* Tokyo: Nichiren Shu Overseas Propagation Promotion Association, 1987.

———. *Kanjin Honzon-shō, Nyosetsu Shugyō, and Kembutsu Mirai-ki.* Tokyo: Nichiren Shu Overseas Propagation Promotion Association, 1991.

———. *Risshō Ankoku-ron and Letters and Tracts Concerning It.* Tokyo: Nichiren Shu Overseas Propagation Promotion Association, 1992.

Hubbard, Jamie. "A Tale of Two Times: Preaching in the Latter Age of the Dharma." *Numen* 46:2 (1999), 186–210.

Hunter, Jeffrey. "The *fuju fuse* controversy in Nichiren Buddhism: The debate between Busshō-in Nichiō and Jakushō-in Nichiken." Ph.D. dissertation. University of Wisconsin at Madison, 1989.

Iida, Shōtarō. "'A Lotus in the Sun'—An Aspect of the Soka Gakkai in Japan." In *Facets of Buddhism,* by Iida, 133–43. Delhi: Motilal Banarsidass Publishers, 1991.

Ingram, Paul O. "Nichirin's (*sic*) three secrets." *Numen* 24:3 (1977), 207–22.

Itohisa, Hōken. "Development of the Nichiren sect in Kyoto: Formation of 'monryū' or sub-sects and their organizational structure." *Ōsaki gakuhō* 140 (1985), 1–8.

Jaffe, Paul D. "Rising from the Lotus: Two bodhisattvas from the Lotus Sutra as a psychodynamic paradigm for Nichiren." *Japanese Journal of Religious Studies* 13:1 (1986), 81–105.

———. "On Nichiren's appropriation of the truth." *Ōsaki gakuhō* 141 (1986), 1–10.

Kadowaki, Kakichi. "Nichiren and the Christian Way." *Dharma World* 26 (Mar./Apr. 1999), 14–18.

———. "What Christians Can Learn from Nichiren." *Dharma World* 26 (May/June 1999), 19–23.

———. "The Future of Humanity as Viewed by Nichiren and Christianity." *Dharma World* 26 (July/Aug. 1999), 22–25.

Kim, Ha Poong. "Fujii Nichidatsu's *tangyō raihai:* Bodhisattva practice for the nuclear age." *Cross Currents* (1986), 193–202.

Kitagawa, Zenchō. "Characteristics of Nichiren's interpretation of the Lotus Sutra." *Ōsaki gakuhō* 138 (1983), 21–28.

———. "The path for realization of a pure land on earth pursued by Nichiren."

In *The "Earthly" Pure Land and Contemporary Society: The Proceedings of the Third Chung-Hwa International Conference on Buddhism,* edited by Sandra Wawrytko. Greenwood Press, forthcoming.

Kodera, Takashi James. "Nichiren and his nationalistic eschatology." *Religious Studies* 15 (1979), 41–53.

Lamont, H. G. "Nichiren (1222–82)." In *Kōdansha Encyclopedia of Japan* 5. Tokyo and New York: Kōdansha, 1983, 375–76.

———. "Nichiren sect" in *Kōdansha Encyclopedia of Japan* 5. Tokyo and New York: Kōdansha, 1983, 376–77.

Large, Stephen S. "Buddhism, socialism and protest in prewar Japan: The career of Seno'o Girō." *Modern Asian Studies* 21:1 (1987), 153–71.

Lee, Edwin B. "Nichiren and nationalism: The religious patriotism of Tanaka Chigaku." *Monumenta Nipponica* 30 (1975), 19–35.

Lloyd, A. "Nichiren" [poem]. *Transactions of the Asiatic Society of Japan* 22 (1984), 482–506.

Métraux, Daniel A. *The History and Theology of the Sōka Gakkai.* Lewiston, New York: Edwin Mellen Press, 1988.

———. "The Dispute Between the Sōka Gakkai and the Nichiren Shōshū Priesthood." *Japanese Journal of Religious Studies* 19:4 (Dec. 1992), 325–36.

———. *The Sōka Gakkai Revolution.* Lanham, MD, New York and London: University Press of America, 1994.

———. "The Soka Gakkai: Buddhism and the Creation of a Harmonious and Peaceful Society." In *Engaged Buddhism: Buddhist Liberation Movements in Asia,* edited by Christopher S. Queen and Sallie B. King, 365–400. Albany: State University of New York Press, 1996.

Murano, Senchū, trans. Nyorai metsugo go gohyakusai shi kanjin honzon shō *or The true object of worship revealed for the first time in the fifth of five-century periods after the great decease of the Tathāgata.* Tokyo: Young East Association, 1954.

———. "Nichirenshū." In *The Encyclopedia of Religion* 10, 427–31. New York: Macmillan, 1987.

———. *Manual of Nichiren Buddhism.* Tokyo: Nichiren Shu Headquarters, 1995.

Naylor, Christina. "Nichiren, imperialism, and the peace movement." *Japanese Journal of Religious Studies* 18:1 (1991), 51–78.

Petzold, Bruno. *Buddhist Prophet Nichiren: A Lotus in the Sun.* Edited by Shōtarō Iida and Wendy Simmonds. Tokyo: Hokke Jānaru, 1978.

———. In collaboration with Shinshō Hanayama. "The Nichiren system." Chapter 27 in *The Classification of Buddhism (Bukkyō Kyōhan),* edited by Shōhei Ichimura, 607–90. Wiesbadan: Harrassowitz, 1995.

Rodd, Laurel Rasplica. "Nichiren and *setsuwa.*" *Japanese Journal of Religious Studies* 5:2-3 (1978), 159–85.

———. *Nichiren: A Biography.* Occasional paper, no. 11. Tempe, Arizona: Arizona State University, 1978.

———. *Nichiren: Selected Writings.* Asian Studies at Hawaii, no. 26. Honolulu: University of Hawaii Press, 1980.

———. "Nichiren." In *Great Thinkers of the Eastern World,* edited by Ian P. McGreal, 327–29. New York: HarperCollins, 1995.

————. *Nichiren's teachings to women.* Selected papers in Asian studies, new series, no. 5. Western Conference of the Association for Asian Studies, n.d.

Satō, Hiroo. "Nichiren's View of Nation and Religion." *Japanese Journal of Religious Studies* 26:3-4 (Fall 1999), 307–23.

Shinohara, Kōichi. "Religion and Political Order in Nichiren's Buddhism." *Japanese Journal of Religious Studies* 8:3-4 (1981), 225–35.

Stone, Jacqueline I. "How Nichiren saw Chishō Daishi Enchin." In *Chishō Daishi kenkyū,* edited by Chishō Daishi Kenkyū Henshū Iinaki, 55–65. Ōtsu: Tendai Jimonshū, 1989.

————. "Some disputed writings in the Nichiren corpus: Textual, hermeneutical and historical problems." Ph.D. dissertation. University of California at Los Angeles, 1990.

————. "Rebuking the enemies of the *Lotus*: Nichirenist exclusivism in historical perspective." *Japanese Journal of Religious Studies* 21:2-3 (1994), 231–59.

————. "Original enlightenment thought in the Nichiren tradition." In *Buddhism in Practice,* edited by Donald S. Lopez, Jr., 228–40. Princeton: Princeton University Press, 1995.

————. "Chanting the august title of the *Lotus Sutra: Daimoku* practices in classical and medieval Japan." In *Re-visioning "Kamakura" Buddhism,* edited by Richard K. Payne, 116–66. Honolulu: University of Hawaii Press, 1998.

————. "Priest Nisshin's ordeals." In *Religions of Japan in Practice,* edited by George J. Tanabe, Jr., 384–97. Princeton: Princeton University Press, 1999.

————. "Nichiren and his successors." Part 3 in *Original Enlightenment and the Transformation of Medieval Japanese Buddhism,* 237–355. Honolulu: University of Hawaii Press, 1999.

————. "Placing Nichiren in the 'Big Picture'—Some Ongoing Issues in Scholarship." *Japanese Journal of Religious Studies* 26:3-4 (Fall 1999), 383–421.

————. "Biographical Studies of Nichiren." *Japanese Journal of Religious Studies* 26:3-4 (Fall 1999), 442–58.

————. "The ideal of *risshō ankoku* in the Nichiren Buddhist Movements of postwar Japan." In *The "Earthly" Pure Land and Contemporary Society: The Proceedings of the Third Chung-Hwa International Conference on Buddhism,* edited by Sandra Wawrytko. Greenwood Press, forthcoming.

Sueki, Fumihiko. "Nichiren's Problematic Works." *Japanese Journal of Religious Studies* 26:3-4 (Fall 1999), 261–80.

Takagi, Yutaka. "The Development of the *Daimoku.*" Edited by Kazuo Kasahara. *Dharma World* 14 (July/Aug. 1987), 43–48; (Sept./Oct. 1987), 44–48; (Nov./Dec. 1987), 43–47.

Takakusu, Junjirō. "The Nichiren School (Lotus-pietism, New Lotus)." In *The Essentials of Buddhist Philosophy,* 186–94. Bombay: Asia Publishing House, 1956.

Tanabe, George J., Jr. "Tanaka Chigaku: The *Lotus Sutra* and the Body Politic." In *The Lotus Sutra and Japanese Culture,* edited by George J. Tanabe, Jr. and Willa Jane Tanabe, 191–208. Honolulu: University of Hawaii Press, 1989.

————. "The Matsumoto debate." In *Buddhism in Practice,* edited by Donald S. Lopez, Jr., 241–48. Princeton: Princeton University Press, 1995.

Tanaka, Chigaku. *What is Nippon Kokutai?* Translated by Satomi Kishio. Tokyo: Shishi-ō Bunko, 1937.

Uchimura, Kanzō. "Saint Nichiren—A Buddhist priest." In *Uchimura Kanzō zenshū*, vol. 15, 288–314. Tokyo: Iwanami Shoten, 1933.

Watanabe, Hōyō. "Nichiren's thought appearing in the *Risshō ankoku ron* and its acceptance in the modern age." *Ōsaki gakuhō* 138 (1985), 11–20.

———. "Nichiren." In *The Encyclopedia of Religion* 10, 425–27. New York: Macmillan, 1987.

Woodard, William P. "The wartime persecution of Nichiren Buddhism." *The Transactions of the Asiatic Society of Japan* 7 (third series 1959), 99–122.

Yampolsky, Philip B., with Burton Watson, et al., trans. *Selected Writings of Nichiren*. New York: Columbia University Press, 1990.

———. *Letters of Nichiren*. New York: Columbia University Press, 1996.

Contributors

John H. Berthrong has been the associate dean for academic and administrative affairs, director of the Institute for Dialogue Among Religious Traditions, and assistant professor of comparative theology at the Boston University School of Theology since 1989. He has published numerous articles in the areas of interfaith dialogue, Chinese religions, religion and ecology, and comparative theology. His more recent books are *Transformations of the Confucian Way* (1998, Westview), *Concerning Creativity: A Comparison of Chu Hsi, Whitehead, and Neville* (1998, State University of New York), and *The Divine Deli* (1999, Orbis)."

David W. Chappell, professor of Chinese religion and Buddhism at the University of Hawaii, is the director of the East-West Religions Project and former president of the Society for Buddhist-Christian Studies.

Lucia Dolce is lecturer in Japanese Religions in the Departments of East Asia and of the Study of Religions at SOAS, University of London. She graduated from the University of Venice (Italy) and is completing her Ph.D. at the University of Leiden (The Netherlands), with a dissertation on the influence of esoteric Buddhism on Nichiren.

Malcolm David Eckel is associate professor of religion and associate director of the Division of Religious and Theological Studies at Boston University. His book, *To See the Buddha: A Philosopher's Quest for the Meaning of Emptiness*, was published by Princeton University Press.

Robert E. Florida recently retired from Brandon University in Manitoba, Canada, where he was professor of Religious Studies and Dean of Arts. He is an Emeritus Fellow at the Centre for the Study of Religion and Society at the University of Victoria, British Colombia, where he is working on a book on human rights and the Buddhist religious tradition, to appear in the Greenwood Press series, Human Rights and the World's Main Religions. His chapter on abortion is in press in *Contemporary Buddhist Ethics*, edited by D. Keown, in the Curzon Series on Critical Buddhism, and his "Response to Damien Keown's 'Suicide, Assisted Suicide and Euthanasia: A Buddhist Perspective" will appear in Vol. XIII-2 of the *Journal of Law and Religion.*

Michael A. Fuss is professor of Comparative Religions at the Pontifical Gregorian University, Rome. After ordination as a Catholic priest, he specialized in Buddhist studies and today is engaged in Buddhist-Christian dialogue. Among his publications is *Buddhavacana and Dei Verbum,* a comparative study on scriptural inspiration in the Lotus Sutra and the New Testament (Brill, 1991), *Le grandi figure del Buddhismo,* a Buddhist history through biographies (Assisi: Cittadella, 1995), and *Rethinking New Religious Movements* (Rome: PUG, 1998).

Ruben L. F. Habito is professor of World Religions and Spirituality, Perkins School of Theology, Southern Methodist University, Dallas, Texas. He is the author of numerous scholarly articles and a dozen books in Japanese and English, including *Original Enlightenment: Tendai Hongaku Doctrine and Japanese Buddhism* (Tokyo: International Institute for Buddhist Studies of ICABS, 1996). He is the co-editor with Jacqueline Stone of "Revisiting Nichiren," a special issue of the *Japanese Journal of Religious Studies,* Vol. 26.

Jamie Hubbard is the Yehan Numata Lecturer in Buddhist Studies at Smith College, Northampton, Massachusetts. With Paul Swanson, he is co-editor, contributor to, and translator of *Pruning the Bodhi Tree: The Storm Over Critical Buddhism* (University of Hawaii Press, 1997).

Alexander Ignatovich died in 2001 after a long illness. He was an associate professor in the Department of East and Southeast Asian History at the Institute of Asian and African Studies affiliated with Moscow State University. The author of many works on Buddhism and the history of religion and culture in Japan and China, he recently completed a translation of the Threefold Lotus Sutra into Russian, published by Ladomir in Mos-cow, 1998.

Harold Kasimow is George Drake Professor of Religious Studies at Grinnell College, Grinnell, Iowa, where he teaches courses in Judaism, Islam, and Buddhism. In 1988–89 he was visiting professor in the International Division at Waseda University in Tokyo. His recent publications include *John Paul II and Interreligious Dialogue* (Orbis, 1999), containing the pope's core writings on Buddhism, Islam, and Judaism and responses to him by prominent Buddhist, Muslim, and Jewish scholars. Kasimow is also the editor of a special issue of *Shofar: An Interdisciplinary Journal of Jewish Studies on Judaism and Asian Religions.*

Damien Keown is reader in Buddhism at Goldsmiths' College, the University of London, and author of several articles and books on Buddhist ethics, including *The Nature of Buddhist Ethics* (Macmillan, 1992) and *Buddhism and Bioethics* (St. Martin's, 1995). He is co-editor of the *Journal of Buddhist Ethics.*

Miriam Levering, who has a Ph.D. from Harvard in comparative history of religion, with specialties in Buddhism and Chinese religion, is now an associate professor of religious studies at the University of Tennessee and has taught as the

Numata lecturer in Buddhist Studies at SOAS, London University. She is the author of *Rehinking Scripture* (State University of New York Press), on scripture and sacred text, and has published a number of articles on women in Chan and Zen Buddhism and on Chan in China in the eleventh and twelfth centuries.

Susan Mattis received her Ph.D in philosophy at Boston College in 1994, with a dissertation on "Chih-i and Madhyamaka: Changing Conceptions of Truth and the Buddha's Relation to the Phenomenal World." She is currently doing research on the relation of phenomenology and postmodern thought to the Buddhist tradition. She is a lecturer in the humanities in the Boston College Arts and Sciences Honors Program.

John R. A. Mayer recently retired as professor of Philosophy and dean at Brock University, St. Catharines, Ontario, Canada. A collection of essays in his honor, *Varieties of Universalism* edited by Marko Zlomislic, David Goicoechea and Zdenko Zeman, has been published by Global Publications, IGCS, Binghamton University, State University of New York.

Peggy Morgan lectures at Mansfield and Westminster Colleges, Oxford, is president-elect of the British Association for the Study of Religions, and the director of the Religious Experience Research Centre. She has written widely on Buddhism and co-edited *Testing the Global Ethic* (WCR and Co-nexus), *Ethical Issues in Six Religious Traditions* (Edinburgh University Press) and *Six Religions in The Twenty-First Century* (Stanley Thornes).

The late Nikkyō Niwano (1906–99) was the founder and for many years president of Risshō Kōsei-kai. The recipient in 1979 of the Templeton Prize for Progress in Religion, he was dedicated to interreligious cooperation in the quest for peace and played a leading role in the establishment of the World Conference on Religion and Peace (WCRP). Many of his books on Buddhism have been translated into English.

Steve Odin is professor of Philosophy at the University of Hawaii, where he has been teaching Japanese, American and East-West comparative philosophy since 1982. He is the author of many articles and several books, including *Process Metaphysics and Hua-yen Buddhism* (State University of New York, 1982) and *The Social Self in Zen and American Pragmatism* (State University of New York, 1996).

Schubert M. Ogden is University Distinguished Professor Emeritus at Southern Methodist University. A former president of the American Academy of Religion, he is the author of numerous scholarly articles and seven books, including the latest, *Is There Only One True Religion or Are There Many?* (Southern Methodist Univesity, 1992) and *Doing Theology Today* (Trinity, 1996). He has been a participant in the International Buddhist-Christian Theological Encounter Group since 1984.

Lucinda Joy Peach is an assistant professor in the Department of Philosophy and Religion at American University. She received a Ph.D. in ethics from Indiana University and has a J.D. from New York University School of Law. She conducts research in and teaches moral philosophy, applied ethics, religion and politics, and gender and religion. She is editor of *Women in Culture: An Anthology* (Blackwell, 1998), and is working on a textbook entitled *Women and World Religions* for Prentice-Hall.

Michael Pye is professor of religious studies at Marburg University, Germany. Apart from a specialist knowledge of East Asian Buddhism and contemporary Japanese religions, he has broad interests in religion and society in the modern world. He is currently president of the International Association for the History of Religions (1995–2000). His writings include *Skilful Means: A Concept in Mahayana Buddhism* (Duckworth, 1978).

Gene Reeves recently retired from teaching at the University of Tsukuba, where he taught Buddhism and American Studies. He is currently doing research, teaching, and writing on the Lotus Sutra at Risshō Kōsei-kai in Tokyo.

Masahiro Shimoda is an associate professor in Indian Philosophy and Buddhist Studies at the University of Tokyo. He is the author of *A Study of the Mahaparinirvanasutra: with a focus on the methodology of the study of mahayanasutras* (Tokyo: Shunju-sha, 1997).

Michio T. Shinozaki is director of the Planning Division of Risshō Kōsei-kai after serving as dean of Risshō Kōsei-kai's Gakurin seminary since receiving a Ph.D. in Religious Studies from Vanderbilt University in 1988. He has contributed a number of articles on Buddhist ethics to various journals and is co-author which Gene Reeves of the forthcoming publication of a translation of Yoshirō Tamura's introduction to the Lotus Sutra.

Jacqueline I. Stone is associate professor in the Department of Religion at Princeton University. She is the author of *Original Enlightenment and the Transformation of Medieval Japanese Buddhism* (University of Hawaii Press, 1999) and is working on a new biography of Nichiren. She is the co-editor with Ruben Habito of "Revisiting Nichiren," a special issue of the *Japanese Journal of Religious Studies,* Vol. 26.

Paul L. Swanson is a permanent fellow of the Nanzan Institute for Religion and Culture and a professor of Nanzan University. He is the editor of the *Japanese Journal of Religious Studies,* author of *Foundations of T'ien-t'ai Philosophy* (Asian Humanities Press, 1989), and co-editor, contributor to, and translator of *Pruning the Bodhi Tree: The Storm Over Critical Buddhism* (University of Hawaii Press, 1997).

Willa Jane Tanabe is dean of the School of Hawaiian, Asian and Pacific Studies, at the University of Hawaii and professor of Art History. She is the author of *Paintings of the Lotus Sutra* (Weatherhill, 1988), and co-editor of and contributor to *The Lotus Sutra in Japanese Culture* (University of Hawaii Press, 1989). Recently she has published "The Persistence of Self as Body and Personality in Japanese Art" in *Self as Image in Asian Theory and Practice,* ed. by Roger Ames (State University of New York, 1998).

Taitetsu Unno, recently retired as the Jill Ker Conway Professor of Religion at Smith College in Northampton, Massachusetts. He is the editor of *The Religious*

Philosophy of Nishitani Keiji (Albany: SUNY Press, 1990), co-editor of *The Religious Philosophy of Tanabe Hajime* (Albany: SUNY Press, 1990), and author of *River of Fire, River of Water: An Introduction to the Pure Land Tradition of Shin Buddhism* (Doubleday, 1998).

Riccardo Venturini is professor of clinical psychophysiology at the Università degli studi di Roma "La Sapienza," and a member of the Board of Directors of the Maitreya Foundation—Institute of Buddhist Studies (an affiliate of the Italian Buddhist Union).

J. Douglas Wolfe is a computer trainer and musician living in Sacramento, California, and co-president of Valley Sidewalk Astronomers. He is a member of the Risshō Kōsei-kai Church of San Francisco.

Publication History

1. INTRODUCTORY

"The Threefold Lotus Sutra: An Introduction" by Nikkyō Niwano was translated from the first four sections of vol. 1 of the 1989 second-edition ten-volume publication in Japanese, *Shinshaku Hokke Sambu-kyō* (New Commentary on the Three-fold Lotus Sutra), first published by Kōsei Publishing Co. in 1964. The English translation is being serialized in *Dharma World*.

"The Innumerable Meanings of the Lotus Sutra" by Paul L. Swanson previously appeared in *Dharma World*, vol. 19, May/June 1992 issue.

"Organic Truth: Personal Reflections on the Lotus Sutra" by David W. Chappell appeared in *Dharma World*, vol. 23, Mar./Apr. and May/June 1996 issues.

"Somatic Realization of the Lotus Sutra" by Taitetsu Unno is a revised version of an article which appeared in *Dharma World*, vol. 23, Jan./Feb. 1996 issue.

2. THEOLOGICAL REFLECTION AND DIALOGUE

"Considering the Lotus Sutra" by John H. Berthrong is a slightly revised version of a paper which appeared in *Dharma World*, vol. 23, July/Aug. 1996 issue.

"The Lotus Sutra and Interreligious Dialogue" by Schubert M. Ogden previously appeared in *Dharma World*, vol. 22, July/Aug. 1995 issue.

"*Upāya* and *Missio Dei:* Toward a Common Missiology" by Michael A. Fuss previously appeared in *Dharma World*, vol. 23, Sept./Oct. 1996 issue.

"By the Power of the Buddha" by Malcolm David Eckel previously appeared in *Dharma World*, vol. 22, Sept./Oct. and Nov./Dec. 1995 issues.

3. Philosophical Reflection

"Reflections on the Threefold Lotus Sutra" by John R. A. Mayer was previously published in the *Journal of Buddhist Ethics,* vol. 5, 1998.

"The Lotus Sutra and the Dimension of Time" by J. Douglas Wolfe previously appeared in *Dharma World,* vol. 22, Jan./Feb. 1995 issue.

"The Length of Life of the Tathāgata" by Michael Pye previously appeared in *Dharma World,* vol. 25, July/Aug. 1998 issue.

"A Tale of Two Times: Preaching in the Latter Age of the Dharma" by Jamie Hubbard, which has also appeared in *Numen* 46: 2, 1999, was originally presented at the Third International Conference on the Lotus Sutra (Tokyo, 1997) and the author is grateful to Gene Reeves and Jan Nattier, associate professor of Buddhist studies at Indiana University, for their comments; portions are also drawn from his forthcoming work on the decline of the dharma and developments in Chinese Buddhism.

"Chih-i and the Subtle Dharma of the Lotus Sutra: Emptiness or Buddha-nature?" by Susan Mattis: A version of this paper appeared in *Dharma World,* vol. 27, Mar./Apr. and May/June 2000 issues.

"The Lotus Sutra in the Writings of Kenji Miyazawa" by Steve Odin: A version of this essay appeared in *Dharma World,* vol. 26, November/December 1999 issue.

"Echoes of the Lotus Sutra in Tolstoy's Philosophy" by Alexander Ignatovich previously appeared in *Dharma World,* vol. 25, Sept./Oct. 1998 issue.

4. Buddhism and Society

"Buddha-body Theory and the Lotus Sutra: Implications for Praxis" by Ruben L. F. Habito previously appeared in *Dharma World,* vol. 23, Nov./Dec. 1996 issue.

"A Buddha Teaches Only Bodhisattvas" by Riccardo Venturini previously appeared in *Dharma World,* vol. 19, May/June 1992 issue.

"A Buddhist Path to Mending the World" by Harold Kasimow is a slightly revised version of a paper which appeared in *Dharma World,* vol. 26, May/June 1999 issue.

5. The Lotus Sutra and Buddhist Ethics

"Ethics and the Lotus Sutra" by Peggy Morgan was previously published in the *Journal of Buddhist Ethics,* vol. 5, 1998.

"Paternalism in the Lotus Sutra" by Damien Keown was previously published in the *Journal of Buddhist Ethics*, vol. 5, 1998.

"Appropriate Means as the Ethics of the Lotus Sutra" by Gene Reeves: An earlier version of this paper was published in the *Journal of Buddhist Ethics*, vol. 5, 1998.

6. PARTICULAR ISSUES

"The Lotus Sutra and Health Care Ethics" by Robert E. Florida was previously published in the *Journal of Buddhist Ethics*, vol. 5, 1998.

"Social Responsibility, Sex Change, and Salvation: Gender Justice in the Lotus Sutra" by Lucinda Joy Peach was immeasurably improved by the careful review, comments and suggestions of Jan Nattier on an earlier draft.

"Is the Lotus Sutra 'Good News' for Women?" by Miriam Levering: A different version of this essay will appear in *Buddhist-Christian Studies*.

Index

different questions, it has been suggested to employ the random effects model as a way of performing a sensitivity analysis to check the robustness of conclusions derived from the fixed effects model whenever the estimate of between study heterogeneity is positive. [15,23,24]

STUDY HETEROGENEITY

Investigation of heterogeneity remains a key issue in the conduct of meta-analysis. Heterogeneity, in general, can be broadly categorized into three types: clinical, methodological and statistical. [25] Clinical heterogeneity reflects differences between studies in patient populations or in the context in which care was provided. Methodological heterogeneity reflects differences between studies in design, conduct or analysis (e.g. high versus low quality studies) that may be associated with results. Statistical heterogeneity relates to variation in effects and reflects the probability that differences observed between studies are consistent with chance variation. Statistical heterogeneity can be a consequence of clinical or methodological heterogeneity, or can be due to chance alone. Numerous factors could cause heterogeneity, including differences in inclusion and exclusion criteria, patients' baseline risk profile, outcome measures (e.g. definition, follow-up time), intervention (e.g. dose, timing, brand), or variability in methodological quality (e.g. analysis to handle withdrawals, blinding of assessment of outcomes). [26-29] A variety of approaches have been introduced to explore heterogeneity in meta-analyses.

The simplest and most frequently used approach to test for heterogeneity is the Cochrane Chi-square heterogeneity test (the Q statistic). [30] Heterogeneity can be quantified using the index of heterogeneity-I^2, which describes the percentage of total variation across the studies due to heterogeneity rather than random variation (I^2=100% *(Q-df)/Q (df=degrees of freedom), with I^2 ranging between 0% and 100%). The I^2 values of 25%, 50%, and 75% suggest low, moderate and high degree of heterogeneity. [31] It should be noted that the Q statistic can yield falsely negative results for heterogeneity, particularly when the number of patients in the meta analysis is small or the variance of the outcome varies significantly across studies. [32,33] Setting the critical-alpha at the 10% level has been suggested as a conservative method to compensate for this problem. [34,35] Other statistical tests have been developed to investigate the heterogeneity within and between studies, including the test proposed by Breslow and Day, [36] likelihood ratio tests based on the marginal likelihood of individual trial, [15] an exact test proposed by Zelen, [37] or the interaction test of study and treatment if linear or logistic regression are used to combine studies. [38] Compared with the Q statistic, these analytical methods are infrequently used in investigating heterogeneity. For the evaluation the presence of heterogeneity, the principle should be to explore or investigate potential influences of the specific clinical differences between studies rather than to merely rely on an overall statistical test of heterogeneity.

Other than standard statistical tests for heterogeneity, several graphical methods have been introduced as adjuncts for the investigation of heterogeneity in meta-analyses. Visual inspection of data using these plots can assist in the decision as to how to proceed with data synthesis, even in the absence of a statistically significant test for heterogeneity. Forest plots are the most frequently used graphic method to present the summary results of meta-analyses.

For each study, the effect estimate and respective confidence interval, as well as the pooled effect estimates with their confidence intervals are plotted on a single dimension. The variability between estimates on the plot highlights the heterogeneity of trials. One example of such plots is given: Figure 1 displays the results of the meta analysis of calcium in the prevention of preeclampsia. [39] The variability between estimates can be seen on the plot, indicating the presence of heterogeneity. However, the Forest plot is not very informative in identifying the trials that contribute most to the measured heterogeneity.

Galbraith proposed an alternative diagram for detecting heterogeneity, on which the z statistic (the ratio of the log RR-relative risk or log OR-odds ratio to its standard error) is plotted against the reciprocal of the standard error. [40] Hence, the least precise results from small trials appear near the origin of the plot, whereas the results of the larger trials appear towards the right. The pooled effect estimate is represented by the slope of the line that through the origin. The 95% confidence limits are positioned 2 units above and below of the line of original line (line of pooled effect estimate). In the absence of significant heterogeneity, the points representing studies will scatter with constant variance along the original line. Points outside of those two 95% limit lines indicate the studies that contribute most to heterogeneity. (Figure 2)

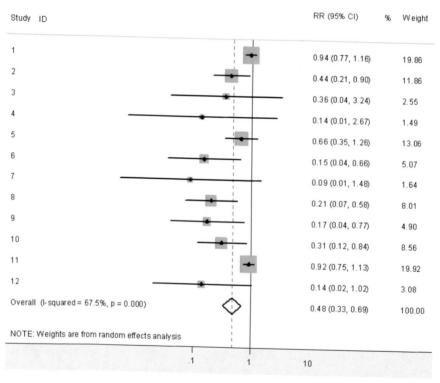

Figure 1. Forest plot for relative effect of calcium supplementation during pregnancy on the risk of preeclampsia.

L'Abbé and colleagues suggested a graphical means for exploring variation across studies by plotting the event rate in the treatment group (vertical axis) versus that of the control group (horizontal axis). [41] If the trials are fairly homogeneous, the points would lie around a line and the gradient of which corresponds to the pooled treatment effect. Large deviations from the line indicate possible heterogeneity. [41] A line of equal rates between groups, and hence of no treatment effect, can be added to the graph. Points below the line indicate that the experimental treatment is superior to that received by controls. Conversely, points above the line signify that the results are in favour of the control or placebo group. It has been suggested that the L'Abbé plot should be standardized before making comparisons for exploring clinical and methodological heterogeneity. [42] A further feature of L'Abbé's method is that it can address the question "Is the treatment effect size related to the baseline risk levels?" A non-consistent band of data points on the scatter-plot indicates a differential treatment effect related to baseline risk factors.

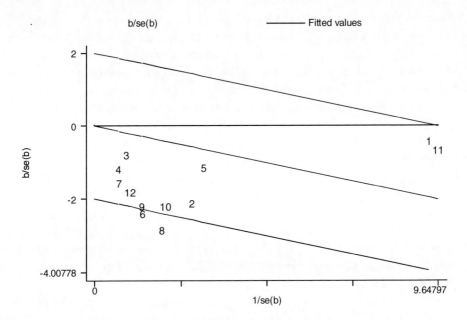

Source: Reprint with permission of Paediatr Perinat Epidemiol. 2008, Suppl 1:18-28.

Figure 2. Galbraith plots for the rates of preeclamsia in the calcium and placebo groups.

Some researchers would simply exclude the identified "outliers" to reduce the heterogeneity. However, the simple exclusion of outlying studies does not always improve the credibility of the meta-analysis. Furthermore, such exclusions further reduce the power of statistical tests for heterogeneity. Such a practice has been proven to be dangerous in some cases. [43] It is often the case that different methods may identify different "outliers" and therefore the conclusions of meta analysis may change considerably. [44] Thus, it may be practical to consider the exclusion of "outliers" as a part of sensitivity analysis.

META-REGRESSION

Meta-regression remains an important means to explore sources of heterogeneity in meta-analysis and allows simultaneous examination of multiple characteristics. As with non-regression meta-analysis, fixed and random effects regression models are available. A fixed effect regression model assumes that the considered covariates completely account for variations across studies, while random effects regression assumes that covariates capture only a part of the heterogeneity and therefore includes a random term to explain the residual heterogeneity. The simple meta-regression model can be written as $y_i \sim N(\alpha + \beta\chi_i, v_i)$, where y_i is the observed log-odds ratio of study i (θ_i), v_i is the variance of log-odds ratio for study i, χ_i-covariate (e.g. baseline calcium intake). The model that incorporates the residual heterogeneity is then $y_i \sim N(\alpha + \beta x_i, v_i + \tau^2)$, where τ^2 reflects the additive between-study variance. Regression modelling is not a trivial task and it is beyond the scope of this chapter to give a comprehensive introduction of regression techniques.

The issues related to the methodology of meta regression along with its strengths and limitations have been extensively discussed in the literature. [32,44-47] Meta-regression remains an essential approach to investigate whether particular covariates explain the heterogeneity of treatment effects between studies. For instance, it can be used to investigate the relationship between the baseline risk (i.e. the observed risk of events in the control group, or the average risk in the control and treatment group) and treatment effect, which could be clinically important. It should be noted that, in the presence of misclassification of baseline risk, more complex models addressing measurement errors are required to obtain valid results for the relationship between the baseline risk and treatment effect. [26,47,48] It is appropriate to use meta-regression to explore the sources of heterogeneity even if the overall statistical test for heterogeneity (e.g. Q test) is not significant.

Meta regression faces similar challenges related to bias as do observational studies in general (e.g. confounding) and a causal interpretation is therefore difficult to derive from the results of meta regression models. [26,48] Similar to the situation in subgroup analysis, pre-specification of potential covariates is essential to reduce the likelihood of the false positive conclusions when conducting a meta-regression. Furthermore, one requires the effect estimate of treatment, its variance, and covariate values for each study in the systematic review to conduct a meta regression. Such data are not always available and reported in all included studies. Thus, analysis may be only based on the subgroup studies that provide such information, which introduce the potential bias. It has been reported that analyses based on individual patient data would be less prone to bias compared with the analyses based on study level characteristics, although such data is difficult to obtain for the conduct of meta analysis. [45,49] It worth pointing out that the potential for robust conclusions from meta –regression models is very limited and such analysis is most useful when the number of studies is large. [50]

STRATIFICATION (SUBGROUP) ANALYSIS

Subgroup analysis is frequently used by researchers as a means of explaining or reducing heterogeneity that is often observed in the overall analysis. One can stratify either by study or patient characteristics. For instance, studies can be stratified with respect to many factors such as treatment assignment, control group, patient inclusion criteria, quality control, study conduct, and follow-up maturity. It is important that subgroups used for analysis should be specified before the analysis is commenced. The number of candidates for effect modifiers should be "kept to a minimum" as the likelihood of false positive (spurious) findings increases with the number of effect modifiers. Inappropriate conduct of subgroup analysis could be very misleading and therefore could change the conclusion of a systematic review. [51,52] Nevertheless, appropriate conduct of subgroup analysis, with increased sample size, can help to understand whether treatment effects differ systematically across patients, settings, and treatment variations (e.g. dose), which is difficult to address with a single trial.

PUBLICATION BIAS

The results of meta-analysis may be seriously distorted if the included studies are biased samples. The classic form of this problem is publication bias: an editorial pre-selection for publishing particular findings, e.g., positive results, which could lead to the failure of authors to submit negative findings for publication. [53] If such bias is present, a meta analysis that includes only published reports will yield results biased away from the null effect. Meta analytic approaches for correction of such bias may not be sufficient for bias removal. Nevertheless, various methods have been developed and useful for detecting such biases. A simple informal visual way to detect publication bias is the funnel plot. A plot of sample size versus treatment effect from individual studies should be shaped like a funnel in the absence of publication bias. It has been suggested that the shape of funnel plot is largely determined by the arbitrary choice of the method to construct the plot. When a different definition of precision and/ or effect measure is used, the conclusion about the shape of the plot can be altered. [55] Therefore, asymmetrical funnel plots should be interpreted cautiously in the absence of a consensus on how the plot should be constructed. [54] Other statistical methods, including the rank correlation test, [55] Egger's method, [56] Begg's method, [57] maximum likelihood approach [58] , and Rosenthal's "fail-safe N" [59] have also been developed.

Some investigators have also attempted to exclude studies under a certain size in order to minimize the problem of publication bias, as small studies tend to display more publication bias. However, the choice of the exact size is rather arbitrary, which may in fact aggravate the bias. The optimum way to eliminate publication bias may be to prevent it from occurring in the first place, either by prospective registration of every trial undertaken, or by publishing all studies, regardless of their outcome. However, these solutions will be difficult to achieve in the near future. Thus, researchers should always be aware of the potential for publication bias and make efforts to assess to what extent publication bias may affect their results.

SENSITIVITY ANALYSIS

A sensitivity analysis remains an important approach for reviewers to test how robust the results of the review are, relative to key decisions and assumptions that were made in the process of conducting a review. [60] Several approaches to sensitivity analysis have been proposed in the Cochrane Collaboration handbook, including 1) changing the inclusion criteria, 2) including or excluding studies where there is some ambiguity as to whether they meet the inclusion criteria, 3) including or excluding unpublished studies, 4) including or excluding studies with low methodological quality, 5) re-analysing the data where uncertainties concerning values extracted exist, 6) re-analysing the data where missing values exist, and 7) simulation of extra trials. In addition, as mentioned earlier, it has been recommended to analyze data using different statistical approaches, namely fixed and random effects models, which serves a means of conducting a sensitivity analysis to check the robustness of results. The importance of sensitivity analysis should be emphasized and such analysis should be routinely done when conducting a meta-analysis.

META ANALYSIS OF SURVIVAL DATA

There is a tendency in the literature to use survival curves for the outcome analysis, especially when the time to the event is of interest. Performing a meta-analysis on this kind of data requires special statistical techniques and has been extensively discussed in literature. The simplest way to carry out such as a meta analysis would be to extract data as the (log) hazard ratio and its variance from each study and then combine them using standard methods of meta analysis as fixed or random effects models. However, published reports seldom provide such data. Fortunately, the log hazard ratio and its variance can be estimated either directly from the observed number of events and the logrank expected number of events or indirectly from the p-value for the logrank, Mantel-Haenszel, or chi-square test. In addition, if none of these is possible, the statistics can be estimated from survival curves. Given the fact that there is often censoring in survival data, the ideal way to perform a meta-analysis of survival data may be to use individual patient data.

BAYESIAN METHODS IN META ANALYSIS

A Bayesian model describes the structural relationship between data and unknown parameters, whereby both data and parameters are considered random variables with uncertainty. Bayesian modeling can efficiently incorporate all sources of variability and relevant quantifiable external information and it provides a more informative summary of the likely value of parameters than non-Bayesian approaches. The model can be simply written as $y_i \sim N(\xi_i, \psi_i)$, $\xi_i = \alpha + \beta x_i$, and $\psi_i = v_i + \tau^2$. Previous evidence is expressed through prior distributions about quantity of interest (e.g. log OR). Current data are expressed through the likelihood, on the basis of the appropriate model. Posterior distribution for the quantity of interest then can be obtained. The derived posterior distributions, in particular full posterior distribution, borrow strength from all studies and enable direct inference regarding probabilities about expectations, and give substantially more information than single point estimates.

ROLE AND LIMITATION OF META ANALYSIS

The role of systematic review and meta-analysis has been increasingly endorsed in evidence-based decision making. Clinicians and researchers should consider the results of meta-analysis before recommending a clinical practice. They can be used to ascertain whether scientific findings are consistent and generalizable across populations, settings, and treatment variations or whether findings vary significantly by particular subgroup. Nevertheless, meta-analyses have inherent limitations because of their retrospective nature. For instance, pooling results does not overcome the epidemiological biases present in the original studies. New biases could even be introduced into meta-analyses by inappropriately pooling heterogeneous studies. For those reasons, the clinical interpretation of meta-analysis must be performed with appropriate caution. Variables that can account for the heterogeneity and which are candidates for stratified or 'influence' analysis should always be identified in the protocols of systematic reviews. Strong recommendation should not be solely based on a meta-analysis. Findings derived from meta-analysis must be primarily considered as hypothesis generating rather than hypothesis testing. On the other hand, data from large trials are not necessarily definitive for patients. A large trial may still be underpowered if the event studied is rare or the treatment effect is small, but clinically meaningful to detect. Expected power in a large trial may be still compromised by missing data, loss to follow up, and null bias. We should view evidence from small and large trials and meta-analyses as offering a complementary, evolving continuum of information. Comparison of large trials and meta-analysis may reach different conclusions depending on how trials and meta-analyses are selected and how end points and agreement are defined. Scrutiny of these two research methods and critical evaluation of evidence derived from both are essential for guiding medical practice.

REFERENCES

[1]   Pearson K. Report on certain enteric fever inoculation statistics. *Br Med J* 1904; 3:1243-6.

[2]   Glass GV. Primary, secondary, and meta-analysis of research. *Educ Res* 1976; 5:3-8.

[3]   Chalmers I, editor. Oxford Database of Perinatal Trials. Oxford*: Oxford University Press.* 1988 – 1992.

[4]   Chalmers I, Hetherington J, Newdick M, Mutch L, Grant A, Enkin M, Enkin E, Dickersin K. The Oxford Database of Perinatal Trials: developing a register of published reports of controlled trials. *Control Clin Trials.* 1986;7: 306-24.

[5]   Chalmers I. The Cochrane Collaboration: preparing, maintaining, and disseminating systematic reviews of the effects of health care. *Ann N Y Acad Sci.* 1993; 703:156-65.

[6]   Bero L, Rennie D. The Cochrane Collaboration. Preparing, maintaining, and disseminating systematic reviews of the effects of health care. *JAMA* 1995; 274: 1935-8.

[7]   Cook TD, Campbell DT. 1979. Quasi-experimentation: *Design & Analysis Issue for Field Settings.* Boston: Houghton Mifflin.

[8]   Moher D, Jadad AR, Nichol G, Penman M, Tugwell P, Walsh S. Assessing the quality of randomized controlled trials:an annotated bibliography of scales and checklists. *Control Clin Trials* 1995; 16: 62-73.

[9]   Deeks J, Glanville J, Sheldon T. Undertaking systematic reviews of research on effectiveness: CRD guidelines for those carrying out or commissioning reviews CRD Report *Number 4, 2nd edn. In: Khan K., Riet G.,* Glanville J.*, Sowden A. & Kleijnen,* J.,

eds CRDCentres for Reviews and Dissemination. York: York Publishing Services Ltd; 2001.

[10] Jüni P, Witschi A, Bloch R, Egger M. The hazards of scoring the quality of clinical trials for meta-analysis. *JAMA.* 1999;282 :1054-60.

[11] Greenland S, O'Rourke K. On the bias produced by quality scores in meta-analysis, and a hierarchical view of proposed solutions. *Biostatistics.* 2001;2:463-71.

[12] Mantel N, Haenszel W. Statistical aspects of the analysis of data from retrospective studies of disease. *J Natl Cancer Inst.* 1959; 22: 719-48.

[13] Peto R, Pike MC, Armitage P, Breslow NE, Cox DR, Howard SV, Mantel N, McPherson K, Peto J, Smith PG. Design and analysis of randomized clinical trials requiring prolonged observation of each patient. II: analysis and examples. *Br J Cancer* 1977; 35: 1-39.

[14] Hasselblad V, McCrory DC. Meta-analytic tools for medical decision making: a practical guide. *Med Decis Making* 1995; 15: 81-96.

[15] Hardy RJ, Thompson SG. A likelihood approach to meta-analysis with random effects. *Stat Med.*1996; 15: 619-29.

[16] DerSimonian R, Laird N. Meta analysis in clinical trials. *Control Clin Trials.* 1986;7: 177-88.

[17] Dempster AP, Laird NM, Rubin DB. Maximum likelihood from incomplete via the EM algorithm. *Journal of the Royal Statistical Society* 1977; B39: 1-38.

[18] Berlin JA, Laird NM, Sacks HS, Chalmers TC. A comparison of statistical methods for combining event rates from clinical trials. *Stat Med* 1989; 8: 141-51.

[19] Mengersen KL, Tweedie RL, Biggerstaff BJ. The impact of method choice in meta-analysis. *Austral J Statist* 1995; 37: 19-44.

[20] Villar J, Mackey ME, Carroli G, Donner A. Meta-analyses in systematic reviews of randomized controlled trials in perinatal medicine: comparison of fixed and random effects models. *Stat Med.* 2001; 20: 3635-47.

[21] Greenland S. Quantitative methods in the review of epidemiologic literature. *Epidemiol Rev.* 1987; 9:1-30.

[22] Peto R. Why do we need systematic overviews of randomized trials? *Stat Med.*1987; 6: 233-244.

[23] Thompson SG, Pocock SJ. Can meta-analyses be trusted? *Lancet* 1991; 338: 1127-30.

[24] Spector TD, Thompson SG. The potential and limitations of meta analysis. *J Epidemiol Community Health.*1991; 45: 89-92.

[25] Thompson SG. Why sources of heterogeneity in meta-analysis should be investigated. *BMJ* 1994; 309: 1351-5.

[26] Thompson SG, Smith TC, Sharp SJ. Investigating underlying risk as a source of heterogeneity in meta-analysis. *Stat Med.*1997; 16: 2741-58.

[27] Brand R, Kragt H. Importance of trends in the interpretation of an overall odds ratio in the meta-analysis of clinical trials. *Stat Med* 1992; 11: 2077-82.

[28] Davey Smith G, Egger M. Commentary on the cholesterol papers: statistical problems. *BMJ.* 1994; 308: 1025-7.

[29] Gelber R D, Goldhirsch A. Interpretation of results from subset analyses within overviews of randomized clinical trials. *Stat Med* 1987;6:371-8.

[30] Cochran WG. The combination of estimates from different experiments. *Biometrics* 1954; 10: 101-29.

[31] Higgins JP, Thompson SG, Deeks JJ, Altman DG. Measuring inconsistency in meta-analysis. *BMJ*. 2003; 327: 557-60.

[32] Hardy RJ, Thompson SG. Detecting and describing heterogeneity in meta-analysis. *Stat Med*. 1998; 17: 841-56.

[33] Jones MP, O'Gorman TW, Lemke JH, Woolson RF. A Monte Carlo investigation of homogeneity tests of the odds ratio under various sample size configurations. *Biometrics* 1989; 45: 171-81.

[34] Fleiss JL. Analysis of data from multiclinic trials. *Control Clin Trials*. 1986; 7: 267-75.

[35] Jackson D. The power of the standard test for the presence of heterogeneity in meta analysis. *Stat Med*. 2006; 25: 2688-99.

[36] Breslow, N.E. and Day, N.E. The analysis of case-control studies. *In: Davis W. Lyon, eds. Statistical Methods in Cancer Research, Volume1*. IARC Scientific Publications,1980: pp 142-3.

[37] Zelen M. The analysis of several 2×2 contingency tables. *Biometrika* 1971; 58: 129-37.

[38] Rosenthal R. Parametric measures of effect size. In: Copper H, Hedges LV, eds. *The handbook of Research Synthesis*. New York: Russell Sage Foundation; 1994; pp.231-44.

[39] Hofmeyr GJ, Atallah AN, Duley L. Calcium supplementation during pregnancy for preventing hypertensive disorders and related problems. *Cochrane Database Syst Rev* 2006; 3:CD001059.

[40] Galbraith RF. A note on graphical presentation of estimated odds ratios from several clinical trials. *Stat Med*. 1988; 7: 889-94.

[41] L'Abbé KA, Detsky AS, O'Rourke K. Meta-analysis in clinical research. *Ann Intern Med*. 1987; 107:224-33.

[42] Song F. Exploring heterogeneity in meta-analysis: is L'Abbé plot useful? *J Clin Epidemiol*. 1999; 52: 725-30.

[43] Berlin JA, Antman EM. Advantages and limitations of meta-analytic regressions of clinical trial data. *Online Journal of Clinical Trials* 1994; 3: Doc. No. 134.

[44] Sharp SJ, Thompson SG, Altman DG. The relation between treatment benefit and underlying risk in meta-analysis. *BMJ* 1996; 313:735-8.

[45] Arends LR, Hoes AW, Lubsen J, Grobbee DE, Stijnen T. Baseline risk as predictor of treatment benefit: three clinical meta-re-analyses. *Stat Med*. 2000;19:3497-518.

[46] Schmid CH. Exploring heterogeneity in randomised trials via meta-analysis. *Drug Information Journal* 1999; 33: 211-24.

[47] Greenwood CM, Midgley JP, Matthew AG, Logan AG. Statistical issues in a metaregression analysis of randomized trials: impact on the dietary sodium intake and blood pressure relationship. *Biometrics* 1999; 55: 630-6.

[48] Thompson SG, Higgins JP. How should meta-regression analyses be undertaken and interpreted? *Stat Med*. 2002; 21: 1559-73.

[49] Begg CB, Pilote L. A model for incorporating historical controls into a meta analysis. *Biometrics* 1991; 47: 899-906.

[50] Smith TC, Spiegelhalter DJ, Thomas A. Bayesian approaches to meta analysis: a comparative study. *Stat Med*. 1995; 14: 2685-99.

[51] Higgins J, Thompson S, Deeks J, Altman D. Statistical heterogeneity in systematic reviews of clinical trials: a critical appraisal of guidelines and practice. *J Health Serv Res Policy*. 2002; 7:51-61.

[52] Oxman AD, Guyatt GH. A consumer's guide to subgroup analysis. *Ann Intern Med.*1992;116: 78-84.

[53] Last JM, editor. A Dictionary of Epidemiology. Oxford: *Oxford University Press,1983.*p.12.

[54] Tang JL, Liu JL. Misleading funnel plot for detection of bias in meta-analysis. *J Clin Epidemiol.* 2000; 53: 477-84.

[55] Begg CB. Publication bias. *In: Cooper H, Hedges LV, eds. The handbook of Research Synthesis.* New York: Russell Sage Foundation, 1994. pp. 399-409.

[56] Egger M, Davey Smith G, Schneider M, Minder C. Bias in meta-analysis detected by a simple, graphical test. *BMJ* 1997; 315:629-34.

[57] Begg CB. A measure to aid in the interpretation of published clinical trial. *Stat Med.*1985;4:1-9.

[58] Rust RT, Lehmann DR, Farley JU. Estimating publication bias in meta-analysis. *J Market Res.* 1990; XXVII:220-6.

[59] Rosenthal R. The 'file drawer problem' and tolerance for null results. *Psychol Bull* 1979; 86:638-41.

[60] Oxman AD, editor. The Cochrane Collaboration handbook: preparing and maintaining systematic reviews. Second ed. *Oxford: Cochrane Collaboration.* 1996;p83.

In: Handbook of Methodological Concepts in Perinatal Medicine   ISBN: 978-1-62081-252-5
Editor: Eyal Sheiner   © 2013 Nova Science Publishers, Inc.

Chapter 10

DECISION ANALYSIS IN PERINATAL MEDICINE

William A. Grobman[*]

Department of Obstetrics and Gynecology, Feinberg School of Medicine,
Northwestern University, Chicago, Illinois, US

DEFINITIONS

- Decision analysis: A quantitative analysis that combines information, using a formal stepwise process, in an attempt to aid decision making.
- Decision tree: A model that illustrates the choices and probabilistic events that are relevant for a given decision analysis, and which also can be used to calculate outcomes of interest for the decision analysis.
- Markov model: A methodology that is used in decision analysis to allow for the inclusion of recursive processes, such as the moving back and forth between events, and complex changing of the values of input variables during the analytical timeframe.
- Quality-adjusted life year: Health effectiveness measure which represents the quality of health achieved during a year of life.
- Sensitivity analysis: A process whereby the stability of results and corresponding conclusions are assessed through alterations in the input variables.

DECISION ANALYSIS: ADVANTAGES AND LIMITATIONS

Physicians increasingly depend upon evidence-based medicine to aid in their decision making. Randomized controlled trials, which often provide the basis for the identification of a treatment's beneficial effect or adverse consequences, are considered to provide the "gold

---

[*] Corresponding author: William A. Grobman, MD, MBA, 250 East Superior Street, Suite 05-2175, Chicago, IL 60611, 312-472-4685, 312-472-4687 fax, w-grobman@northwestern.edu.

standard" of medical evidence. Yet, although the information provided by these trials is quite powerful, not all questions are amenable to being answered by this type of study design.

In some cases, for example, an outcome of interest may be relatively uncommon. For example, a permanent brachial plexus injury occurs in approximately 0.01% of cases, making it difficult to randomize women to different regimens (such as with regard to estimated fetal weight assessment by ultrasound) to assess if this outcome can be significantly reduced. Alternatively, an outcome can take so long to develop that a randomized trial focusing on that outcome is not feasible. Such a circumstance may exist with regard to the screening for and the development of cervical cancer. Although women with no cervical dysplasia could be randomized to different screening strategies (e.g. routine Pap smear vs. Pap smear with the addition of HPV testing), the length of time until cervical cancer develops, and the corresponding follow-up that would be necessary, would be so long that a trial may be too difficult and expensive to perform.

Observational studies, such as those with a cohort or case control design, may provide helpful information in such cases, as they can be accomplished with less use of time and resources. However, even these types of studies cannot provide answers for all types of outcome assessments. For example, two treatments may have similar benefits but different types of undesirable consequences. In this circumstance, a randomized trial may not be able to define which treatment is "better". Also, even if an interventional or observational trial can be performed to answer a given clinical question, the results may not give insight into public health ramifications, such as the cost effectiveness of a medical intervention. In such settings, another type of study design may be necessary to inform the decision making of both caregivers and patients.

Decision analysis is one type of study design that can provide useful insights, and is particularly helpful in circumstances when an interventional or observational study design cannot provide the required information that is needed to differentiate between different tests or therapies. Some examples of decision analyses from the obstetrical and gynecological literature can help to illustrate this point. The best management strategy after identification of ASCUS on a Pap smear has been debated. The different screening intervals (e.g. 1 or 3 years) and many types of testing (e.g. liquid-based Pap smear, HPV DNA testing) that can be utilized result in many different potential strategies that need to be assessed. Moreover, as noted earlier in the chapter, the primary outcome of interest, namely cervical cancer, occurs relatively infrequently and may take years to develop. Theoretically, many different strategies could be compared in a randomized trial over many years, but the logistics of such a trial are overwhelming and the results may not allow a comprehensive assessment of all costs and benefits of different strategies. Using decision analysis, on the other hand, Kim et al were able to assess the outcomes of multiple different ASCUS triage strategies and make recommendations regarding the best strategy. [1] Thus, decision analysis provided a methodology to explicitly compare a multitude of treatment approaches and suggest the optimal one.

Another medical intervention that has been controversial is the need for routine thromboembolic prophylaxis at the time of cesarean delivery. Although a randomized trial of different treatment strategies is theoretically possible, many thousands of women would need to be randomized to discern a difference between treatments. Investigators who have attempted such a trial have had difficulty randomizing even several hundred women. [2] Observational studies also have not been able to provide an adequate answer, as ascertainment of women who have received prophylaxis, of women who have had a complication of prophylaxis, and of women who have had a thromboembolic event has been problematic. [3] Using decision analysis, however, Quinones et al were able to account for both the benefits and risks of different thromboprophylactic strategies and illustrate that intermittent pneumatic compression, compared to other thromboprophylactic treatments, would result in the fewest adverse events. [4] Other investigators also demonstrated that under certain circumstances, the use of intermittent pneumatic compression is cost-effective compared to no prophylaxis at all. [5]

Even though there are many circumstances in which decision analysis may be helpful, it is not a tool that can be used to answer all clinical questions. For example, it is best utilized when individual components of a larger decision are known and can be explicitly organized into an analytical model. Conversely, if the pieces of data needed to construct a reasonable analysis are not known, a decision model will be of little help in determining an optimal strategy. For example, Rouse et al undertook an analysis to better understand whether the use of ultrasound to diagnose macrosomia, and thereby indicate the need for cesarean, was a cost-effective strategy. For this question, the investigators were able to discern and use the relevant data they needed to obtain outcome measures. [6] Conversely, if the sensitivity of ultrasound for macrosomia or the probability of shoulder dystocia at different birth weights were unknown, a decision analysis could not have been used to arrive at a reliable outcome assessment, as these individual pieces of data are seminal in calculating the frequency of the primary health outcome of interest, namely, permanent brachial plexus palsy. Also, despite the contribution a decision analysis can make to an evidence-based assessment, it is important that the analysis be considered in the context of other available data and study outcomes. Caution should be applied in using a decision analytical model alone to define the most preferred test or treatment strategy; instead, a decision analysis is best used as one component in a body of evidence that can provide additional perspective to the question at hand.

THE ANALYTIC STRUCTURES UNDERLYING DECISION ANALYSES

Decision Trees

Decision models are often represented using a decision "tree". This "tree" is an explicit and graphical depiction of the decisions under consideration, and the chance events that can occur after different decisions are made. For example, several investigators have studied the extent to which the introduction into a labor and delivery unit of a rapid HIV test for parturients with unknown HIV status at their admission for delivery reduces the number of perinatal HIV infections. [7,8] A partial and simplified tree for this analysis is shown in Figure 1. The initial choice in this analysis would be whether or not to use a rapid HIV test for the population under consideration. Typically, the point at which different decisions are made is represented in a decision tree as a square. Subsequent to that initial decision, there are several events that may or may not occur in the "HIV test available arm" – these probabilistic events are commonly represented by a circle. In the illustrated scenario, a woman may accept (probability "A") or decline ("1-probability A") the rapid HIV test. If she declines the test then her HIV status remains unknown, whereas if she accepts the test then she may have a positive ("probability B") or negative ("1-probability B") result. In contrast, if the test is not available, all women will have unknown status and be treated accordingly.

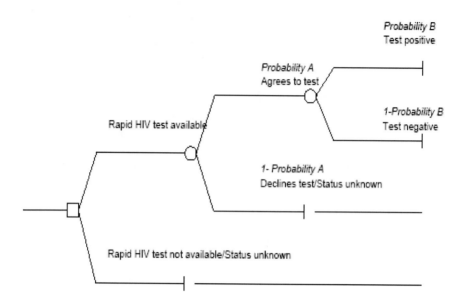

Figure 1. Simplified decision tree for an investigation to discern whether rapid HIV testing in labor and delivery for women with unknown HIV serostatus is a cost-effective strategy.

Markov Models

For many analyses, a simple decision tree will be sufficient to calculate the outcomes of interest. In some cases, however, a tree may not easily allow events that have changing probabilities of occurring during the course of the analysis to be depicted or incorporated into the calculations. In such a case, other analytic approaches are needed. Markov analysis is one type of methodology that is frequently used in the circumstance when a single event may occur with different probabilities, often contingent on other probabilistic events and when these events occur, during the timeframe of the analysis. [9-11] One analysis that demonstrates the usefulness of Markov analysis is that performed by Plunkett et al, who studied perinatal transmission of hepatitis C. [12] Once a person is chronically infected by hepatitis C, several different health states, including remission, cirrhoses, carcinoma, and death may arise. Moving from one health state to another does not always occur after a single length of time or via a single path of health states. In such a circumstance, a simple decision tree without Markov modeling could not have efficiently or accurately represented the dynamically complex life events experienced by a woman with hepatitis C. The use of Markov modeling, however, enabled these complex health state transitions to be incorporated into the analysis. Rather than being represented by a linear tree-like schematic, the complex relationships of variables in a Markov model are often represented by the use of a figure with arrows, depicting the different transitions that can be made between health states. Such a schematic is presented in Figure 2.

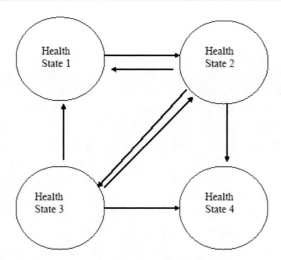

Figure 2. Schematic of the events incorporated in a Markov analysis. The arrows indicate which health states can transition to one another. For example, an individual may move from health state 1 to 2 or from 3 to 2; alternatively, after being in health state 2, the individual may move to health state 1 or 3 or 4.

APPROACH TO A DECISION ANALYSIS

Type of Analysis

Before undertaking a decision analysis, investigators need to decide several important approaches to that analysis. First, investigators need to determine the outcomes of interest. In some cases, investigators may choose to compare strategies only on the basis of clinical outcomes, and not incorporate any other outcomes, such as economic ones. One example of this approach is provided by Quinones et al, who compared 4 strategies of thrombo-prophylaxis at the time of cesarean. [4] Outcomes assessed in this study included heparin-induced thrombocytopenia (HIT), HIT-related thrombosis, major maternal bleeding, and venous thromboembolism. They concluded that intermittent pneumatic compression was preferred to anticoagulation for prevention of thromboembolism because the former was associated with the lowest number of adverse events. Similarly, in trying to arrive at a recommendation with regard to the use of recurrent antenatal corticosteroids, Caughey and Parer compared different dosing regimens on the basis of neonatal morbidity and mortality events. [13] Analyses limited to only health states can help to answer specific clinical questions, such as "Which type of thromboprophylaxis leads to the fewest complications?" Yet, unless costs among the different strategies are essentially equivalent, analyses that examine only health outcomes cannot provide guidance as to the most preferred strategy from a cost-effectiveness perspective. In essence, even though one strategy may improve the health outcome, it is important to understand at what cost that improved outcome is obtained.

Analyses that incorporate costs may be of several different types. In a cost-minimization analysis, the investigators assess only cost as an outcome, and the decision of choice is the one that leads to the lowest costs incurred. One example of this type of analysis is that of Lavin et al, who compared one-tiered and two-tiered screening protocols for gestational diabetes mellitus and concluded that the 2-tiered approach was associated with lower costs.

[14] If this type of analysis is going to identify a preferred strategy, the underlying assumption is that health outcomes are essentially equivalent. If not, even if one strategy is cheaper, it is not clear that it would be preferred, as the impact of that cost savings on health outcomes would remain unknown.

Since most alternate strategies have neither equivalent health nor cost outcomes, many investigators choose to incorporate both health and economic measures into the assessed outcome of their decision analyses. In the obstetric and gynecologic literature, the most common analysis of this type is the cost-effectiveness analysis. In this type of analysis, the outcome is a ratio that is composed of a numerator of a cost measure and a denominator of a health-effectiveness measure. For example, in evaluating whether cesarean delivery without labor for women infected with HIV was a desirable strategy, Chen et al performed a cost-effectiveness analysis in which they utilized "United States dollars" as their cost measure and "cases of perinatal HIV" as their health-effectiveness measure. [15] Each strategy, (i.e. labor vs. cesarean without labor), therefore, was associated with a certain number of dollars spent and neonates who had perinatally-acquired HIV. The cost-effectiveness of the cesarean delivery strategy was represented by the marginal expense required to prevent an HIV-infected neonate. Although the type of effectiveness measure used in this analysis is "case of illness averted", there are many other types of effectiveness measures, including number of lives saved, years of life saved, and quality-adjusted life years saved. These will be further discussed below.

Choice of Perspective

Another important consideration is the perspective that informs the analysis. Analyses may be from the perspective of the individual, the hospital, the third-party payer, or society as a whole. The perspective of the analysis is crucial to consider so that the proper costs and health outcomes can be included in the decision model. In the previously noted article by Quinones et al, for example, the perspective is that of the individual. [4] Thus, the health outcomes that are included are only those that occur in the context of thromboprophylaxis, and the chosen strategy is the one that results in an individual having the least chance of an adverse outcome. If an analysis from the perspective of the individual assesses costs, only those costs borne by the individual should be considered. Yet, in a health system that involves many economic stakeholders, an economic analysis from the perspective of an individual will give little guidance as to the best allocation of resources among members. A better understanding of resource allocation can be obtained by examining higher-order perspectives. The analysis by Chen et al, for example, utilized the perspective of a third-party payer, given that the entity responsible for paying for additional cesareans and benefitting from savings due to fewer cases of perinatal HIV infection can be a health care organization. [15] As illustrated by these examples, there is not one perspective that is unequivocally best, but different perspectives that enable investigators to achieve different objectives. It should be noted, though, that if an investigator wishes to choose a strategy based upon its ability to optimally allocate resources among members of a society, then a societal perspective need be chosen. [16]

Choice of Inputs

Costs

In order to determine a preferred strategy, several different types of information need to be known for an analysis to be possible. From a qualitative perspective, all the different strategies and the probabilistic events that can occur as a consequence of each strategy need to be determined. From a quantitative perspective, the probability that each event occurs needs to be established. Furthermore, if costs and measures of health effectiveness (such as quality-adjusted life years) are being assessed, the value of these measures associated with each event and health state need to be ascertained.

The quantitative information can be obtained in several ways. First, a thorough review of the literature should be performed to identify pre-existing estimates of the relevant probabilities, costs, and measures of health effectiveness. This review, moreover, should not just accumulate estimates, but choose the best estimates based on a critical review of the available studies. In their analysis on thromboprophylaxis, Quinones et al not only list their chosen estimates and the references from which these estimates were derived, but also provide a level of evidence designation to indicate the strength of the methodology in the investigation from which the estimate is based. [4]

Several other types of resources may be particularly helpful for cost assessment. Visco et al, in their study of universal cystoscopy to identify ureteral injury at hysterectomy, have illustrated the use of government reimbursement databases to derive cost estimates. [17] Other investigators have turned to local institutional data to obtain estimates of cost for particular medical procedures. [18, 19]

Regardless of the source, estimates of economic variables should adhere to several standards. One should strive to ensure that the estimate is of costs and not of charges. The latter are not representative of the actual economic consequences of an event and any estimates that are obtained as charges should be converted to costs. [20] Most simply, this can be done with a single cost:charge ratio (e.g. 0.6). In actuality, however, charges are related to costs by different proportions in different settings (e.g. laboratory, pharmacy), and all attempts should be made to obtain the most relevant and specific cost:charge ratios for a given analysis. [21] Also, all costs should be expressed in equivalent units, such as the same type of currency, and be valued at equivalent times. If, for example, one estimate was available as "2004 US dollars" and one as "2007 US dollars", the "2004 US dollars" should be updated to "2007 US dollars" using the medical care component of the US Consumer Price Index (www.bls.gov). Lastly, costs that will accrue into the future should be discounted, as a given amount of money in the future has less value than that same amount in the present. Essentially, it is better to have $10 today than to be given $10 in five years. The Panel on Cost-Effectiveness has recommended that a discount rate of 3% be used as a baseline in cost-effectiveness analyses, although changes in the economic environment could lead to changes in this recommendation. [20]

Health-Effectiveness Measures

Health effectiveness may be expressed by several different measures. When Randolph et al attempted to determine whether acyclovir prophylaxis in late pregnancy was a cost-effective strategy to prevent neonatal herpes infection, they chose the number of infants with either neurodevelopmental disability or death as a measure of effectiveness. [22] The choice of an explicit health state as a measure of effectiveness often can simplify the analysis, as the health state can be easily defined and its probability of occurrence in each strategy can be derived from the basic probabilities that are embedded within the decision tree. Nevertheless, this type of effectiveness measure has some drawbacks. The final cost-effectiveness ratio will not account for the ramifications of other potentially relevant health outcomes on the overall health effectiveness of a given strategy. Indeed, the focus upon a single health outcome is a particular problem if the strategies that are being compared could result in differences in other types of health outcomes. Moreover, even if there were to be no other important health outcomes to consider, the final cost-effectiveness result from the analysis is difficult to compare within the context of a more general resource allocation. What is the benchmark, for example, to decide the number of dollars it would be reasonable to spend to avoid one case of neurodevelopmental disability or death due to perinatal HSV infection?

Other types of measures of health effectiveness can avoid these potential drawbacks. Kulasingham et al, who attempted to determine the most cost-effective screening interval for pap smears among low-risk women, used the number of life-years saved as their measure of health effectiveness. [23] A measure such as this allows the contribution of multiple different health states to be incorporated into the health-effectiveness measure of the analysis. Additionally, it allows the straightforward comparison of the results of this analysis with the results of other analyses that use the same health-effectiveness measure, even if those analyses examine very different health states and strategies. The study by Tengs et al demonstrates the many different medical (e.g. beta-blocker use for myocardial infarction) and non-medical (e.g. seat belt use) interventions that can be compared once the type of outcome measure is the same. [24]

Because some medical interventions may not result in a change in life expectancy, but may alter the quality of life, other measures of effectiveness, such as quality-adjusted life years (QALY), allow both survival and quality of survival to be incorporated into a single outcome measure. [25] Indeed, because of these advantages, QALY's are frequently used as a measure of health effectiveness in cost-effectiveness analyses. [26] QALY's can be calculated as a product of the number of years spent at a given "quality of life". This "quality of life" is typically represented by a "utility" value, which is a number between 0 and 1. Most commonly, a utility value of 1 represents full health while a utility value of 0 represents death. Thus, if a health state was considered to have a utility of 0.5, and an individual spent three years in that health state, he or she would have accumulated 1.5 (i.e. 3 * 0.5) QALY's.

Nevertheless, a measure such as a QALY adds some complexity to the analysis, as all health states within the analysis need to be converted to their QALY equivalent. In some cases, the reduction in quality of life associated with particular health states can be found in other cost-effectiveness analyses or in compilations of effectiveness measures. [26] If this estimate is not readily available in the literature, however, investigators need to determine it. De novo determination of a QALY for a given health state may involve the input of an expert panel, as was demonstrated in a study of the cost-effectiveness of routine hepatitis C screening in pregnancy. [27] Alternatively, investigators may use one of several methodologies to determine these effectiveness measures from a population of patients. Methodologies that have been used to obtain utilities include the time tradeoff and standard gamble techniques. [25] In the obstetrics literature, both Kuppermann et al and Grobman et al have used these types of methodologies to determine the utilities for the health states associated with the decision to proceed with prenatal diagnosis for the detection of Down Syndrome. [28,29]

DETERMINING THE DIFFERENCE IN COST-EFFECTIVENESS BETWEEN STRATEGIES

The comparison of the cost-effective outcomes between two different strategies is best, and typically, represented by the marginal difference of the two ratios. For example, consider 2 strategies. Strategy 1 costs $700 to implement, and yields a gain of 10 QALY's for a given patient, while strategy 2 costs $1200 to implement but results in 12 QALY's for a given patient. One method to calculate the difference in the two strategies would be 1200/12 − 700/10, yielding a result of $30/QALY. This result, however, is not the marginal difference, which instead, would be calculated as (1200 − 700) / (12-10), or a cost-effectiveness of $250/QALY. It should be noted that if one strategy is both less costly and more effective than another strategy, the former strategy is said to "dominate" the latter.

SENSITIVITY ANALYSIS

The process whereby inputs are changed and the outcomes are re-assessed is commonly called "sensitivity analysis". Given that the results of a decision analytical model are based on inputs that have been chosen by the investigators, it is extremely important to assess the extent to which the results may be altered by changes in those inputs. For example, if small alterations in the inputs cause a strategy to change from being considered "cost effective" to "not cost effective", there should be less confidence that the model can clearly provide guidance as to the preferred strategy. Conversely, if the results of the model remain unchanged despite changes in the input variables (in which case the results of the model are called "stable" or "robust"), an investigator will have more confidence in the conclusions. Examining the effects engendered by changing the inputs can be further useful to the investigator, as the process can help to determine which particular circumstances are necessary in order for a strategy to be preferred. One particular use of sensitivity analysis is to alter the input variable (or variables) in such a way as to discern the value (or values) at which a given strategy changes from "cost effective" to "not cost effective". Such an analysis is called a "threshold analysis."

The range over which the variable is changed in a sensitivity analysis is determined by the investigator, who may use different methods to determine this range. In some cases, the investigator may base the range upon the range of different estimates for a given variable that is present in the literature. When less data is available, the investigator may choose to derive a range using other methods, such as the 95% confidence interval of a single proportion. In still other cases, for data such as costs or utilities, investigators may choose to use reasonable estimates, such as multiples of the baseline estimate, that are derived from their own judgment. The basis of the range that is chosen should be specified.

In one - way sensitivity analysis, the investigator changes one variable at a time, and assesses the resulting change in the outcome for each variable alteration. The results of this analysis may be presented in tabular format, in which the respective results for each "high" and "low" input are presented. Alternatively, graphical depictions may sometimes help a reader to more easily conceive which variable changes are associated with the greatest magnitude of outcome changes. One such depiction, presented in figure 3, is called a "tornado" diagram, for reasons obviously related to its shape.

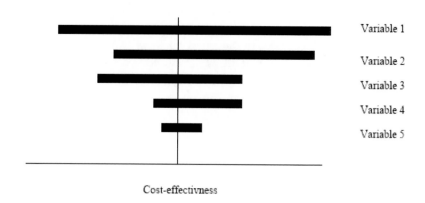

Cost-effectivness

Figure 3. Tornado diagram. Each bar represents the range of results for cost effectiveness that are obtained when each respective variable is varied over its own range of inputs. The vertical line represents the cost-effectiveness value which is obtained when the baseline estimates are placed into the model.

A one-way sensitivity analysis is relatively easy to perform, but because only one variable at a time is changed, the one-way analysis cannot allow an investigator to understand to what extent the model's results are altered under more varied circumstances. One method to overcome this limitation is to perform a "best case" and "worst case" scenario, in which all variables are simultaneously changed to the values that favor or do not favor, respectively, a certain strategy. Certainly, if these changes in all the variables do not alter the basic conclusion of the analysis (e.g. that a given strategy is cost-effective), the model is very robust. Yet, many models will not be so robust, and a more nuanced assessment of the exact circumstances under which a strategy is cost effective will be desired. For example, an investigator may want to examine whether a strategy is cost-effective at different prevalences of illness and at different costs of treatment. In order to assess these circumstances, a two-way sensitivity analysis, in which multiple combinations of two variables are entered into the model and used to calculate the respective outcomes, can be performed. Often presented graphically, this analysis can demonstrate the combinations that are required to result in a cost-effective strategy. An example of the graphic of a two-way sensitivity analysis is presented in Figure 4. If more than two variables are altered at one time, then the sensitivity analysis continues to be characterized by the number of variables that are being simultaneously altered – thus, if three variables are being changed, the appellation for the process would be a "three-way" sensitivity analysis.

In the sensitivity analyses described so far, one or several inputs simultaneously may be altered along their chosen ranges. One type of sensitivity analysis that is less restrictive and adds a further level of complexity is called a "Monte Carlo" analysis. In this analysis, not only the ranges for each variable, but also the distribution patterns within these ranges (e.g. Gaussian, logarithmic) are specified. Subsequently, all variables that are being assessed have a value simultaneously and probabilistically (according to the specified distribution) chosen from within the range, and placed into the model. This process is subsequently repeated many times (e.g. 10,000), and the distribution of consequent results assessed. In this way, an investigator may discern the distribution of possible results, which provides further information, such as the percent of simulated runs that lead to a strategy being cost-effective. One example of Monte Carlo simulation is provided by Cahill et al, who used decision analysis to assess whether magnesium sulfate should be used for seizure prophylaxis in women with mild preeclampsia. [30]

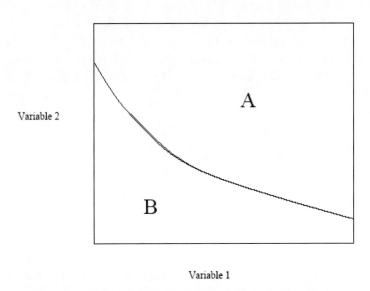

Figure 4. Graphical depiction of two-way sensitivity analysis for a model with two possible strategies. At all combinations of variables in sector "A", one strategy is preferred, while all combinations of variables in sector "B" will result in the other strategy being preferred.

FURTHER CONSIDERATIONS

When is a Strategy Cost-Effective?

A strategy need not save both money and health to be considered cost-effective. In fact, most strategies that are used as well as accepted as reasonable allocations of resources improve health but at a cost. [24] Accordingly, it is important to consider the amount of expenditure that is acceptable, from a societal perspective, to obtain improved health. Those strategies that are less costly than this threshold are considered "cost effective".

For many years, a cost-effectiveness ratio less than $50,000 (United States dollars) per QALY saved has been used as a benchmark to indicate that a strategy is cost effective. Recently, however, the reasonableness of this benchmark has been questioned. [31] First, the benchmark is essentially arbitrary, as it is based upon the cost effectiveness of a US governmental entitlement, namely renal dialysis. Correspondingly, others have suggested replacement benchmarks. Laupacis et al, for example, have recommended a system whereby results of the analysis are not merely dichotomized (i.e. cost-effective or not cost-effective) but categorized into several grades: a grade A intervention is cost saving, a grade B intervention costs less than \$20,000/QALY, a grade C intervention costs \$20,000 to \$100,000/QALY, a grade D intervention costs more than \$100,000/QALY, and a grade E intervention is both no more effective and more costly. [32] Also, the \$50,000/QALY benchmark, despite being established approximately one-quarter of a century ago, has not been adjusted for inflation. Ubel has argued that whatever cost-effective threshold is used needs to be adjusted regularly to account for inflation as well as other changing circumstances in the economic and medical realms. [31] Others have contended that cost-effectiveness thresholds, rather than being based on governmental benchmarks, should be more directly based upon patients' actual willingness to pay for additional QALY's. [33] Attempting to discern the exact value of this willingness to pay, however, has proven difficult. [34] Thus, at this point, many authors continue to use \$50,000/QALY as a cost-effective threshold, although thresholds ranging up to \$100,000/QALY, given the adjustment for inflation, are utilized as well.

SUMMARY

Decision analysis is a type of study design that can help to explicitly compare different medical strategies and provide additional perspective to information provided by observational and interventional studies. Depending on the metrics that are used, decision analysis allows comparison of medical strategies according to health outcomes alone, costs alone, or a combined cost-effectiveness measure. Moreover, depending on the input data that are used, individuals, third-party payers, and society as a whole can better understand the most desirable choices from each of their perspectives. In an effort to achieve proper and consistent methodology, investigators should adhere to the consensus guidelines promulgated by the Panel on Cost-Effectiveness in Health and Medicine. [15,19]

REFERENCES

[1]   Kim JJ, Wright TC, Goldie SJ. Cost-effectiveness of alternative triage strategies for atypical squamous cells of undetermined significance. *JAMA* 2002;287:2382-90.

[2]   Gates S, Brocklehurst P, Ayers S, Bowler U. Thromboprophylaxis in Pregnancy Advisory Group. Thromboprophylaxis and pregnancy: two randomized controlled pilot trials that used low-molecular-weight heparin. *Am J Obstet Gynecol* 2004 191:1296-303.

[3]   Drife J. *Brit Med Bulletin* 2003;67:177-90.

[4]   Quinones JN, James DN, Stamilio DM, Cleary KL, Macones GA. Thromboprophylaxis after cesarean delivery: a decision analysis. *Obstet Gynecol* 2005;106:733-40.

[5]   Casele H, Grobman WA. Cost effectiveness of thromboprophylaxis with intermittent pneumatic compression at cesarean delivery. *Obstet Gynecol* 2006;108:535-40.

[6]   Rouse DJ, Owen J, Goldenberg RL, Cliver SP. The effectiveness and costs of elective cesarean delivery for fetal macrosomia diagnosed by ultrasound. *JAMA* 1996;276:1480-6.

[7]   Stringer JS, Rouse DJ. Rapid testing and zidovudine treatment to prevent vertical transmission of human immunodeficiency virus in unregistered parturients: a cost-effectiveness analysis. *Obstet Gynecol* 1999;94:34-40.

[8]   Grobman WA, Garcia PM. The cost-effectiveness of voluntary intrapartum rapid human immunodeficiency virus testing for women without adequate prenatal care. *Am J Obstet Gynecol* 1999;181:1062-71.

[9]   Detsky AS, Naglie G, Krahn MD, Redelmeier DA, Naimark D. Primer on medical decision analysis: Part 2 – building a tree. *Med Decis Making* 1997;17:126-35.

[10] Krahn MD, Naglie G, Naimark D, Redelmeier DA, Detsky AS. Primer on medical decision analysis: Part 4 – analyzing the model and interpreting the results. *Med Decis Making* 1997;17:142-51.

[11] Sonnenberg FA, Beck JR. Markov models in medical decision making: a practical guide. *Med Decis Making* 1993;13:322-38.

[12] Plunkett BA, Grobman WA. Elective cesarean delivery to prevent perinatal transmission of hepatitis C virus: a cost-effectiveness analysis. Am J Obstet Gynecol 2004;191:998-1003.

[13] Caughey AB, Parer JT. Recommendations for repeat courses of antenatal corticosteroids: a decision analysis. *Am J Obstet Gynecol* 2002;186:1221-9.

[14] Lavin JP, Lavin B, O'Donnell N. A comparison of costs associated with screening for gestational diabetes with two-tiered and one-tiered testing protocols. *Am J Obstet Gynecol* 2001;184:363-7.

[15] Chen KT, Sell RL, Tuomala RE. Cost-effectiveness of elective cesarean delivery in human immunodeficiency virus-infected women. *Obstet Gynecol* 2001;97:161-8.

[16] Weinstein MC, Siegel JE, Gold MR, Siegel JE, Daniels N, Weinstein MC,et al. Recommendations of the panel on cost-effectiveness in health and medicine. *JAMA* 1996;276:1172-7.

[17] Visco AG, Taber KH, Weidner AC, Barber MD, Myers ER. Cost-effectiveness of universal cystoscopy to identify ureteral injury at hysterectomy. *Obstet Gynecol* 2001;97:685-92.

[18] Cowett AA, Golub RM, Grobman WA. Cost-effectiveness of dilation and evacuation versus the induction of labor for second-trimester pregnancy termination. *Am J Obstet Gynecol* 2006;194:768-73.

[19] Grable IA. Cost-effectiveness of induction after preterm premature rupture of the membranes. *Am J Obstet Gynecol* 2002;187:1153-8 .

[20] Gold MR, Siegel JE, Russel LB, et al, eds. *Cost-effectiveness in health and medicine.* New York:Oxford University Press, 1996.

[21] Rogowski J. Measuring the cost of neonatal and perinatal care. *Pediatrics* 1999;103:329-35.

[22] Randolph AG, Hartshorn RM, Washington AE, Acyclovir prophylaxis in late pregnancy to prevent neonatal herpes: a cost-effectiveness analysis. *Obstet Gynecol* 1996;88:603-10.

[23] Kulasingham SL, Myers ER, Lawson HW, McConnell KJ, Kerlikowske K, Washington AE, et al. Cost-effectiveness of extending cervical cancer screening intervals among women with prior normal pap tests. *Obstet Gynecol* 2006;107:321-8.

[24] Tengs TO, Adams ME, Pliskin JS, Safran DG, Siegel JE, Weinstein MC, et al. Five-hundred life-saving interventions and their cost-effectiveness. *Risk Analysis.* 1995;15:369-90.

[25] Giesler RB, Ashton CM, Brody B, Byrne MM, Cook K, Geraci JM, et al. Assessing the performance of utility techniques in the absence of a gold standard. *Med Care* 1999;37:580-88.

[26] Tengs TO, Wallace A. One thousand health-related quality-of-life estimates. *Med Care* 2000;38:583-637.

[27] Plunkett BA, Grobman WA. Routine hepatitis C virus screening in pregnancy: a cost-effectiveness analysis. *Am J Obstet Gynecol* 2005;192:1153-61 .

[28] Kuppermann M, Nease RF, Learman LA, Gates E, Blumberg B, Washington AE. Procedure-related miscarriages and Down syndrome-affected births: implications for prenatal testing based on women's preferences. *Obstet Gynecol* 2000;96:511-6.

[29] Grobman WA, Dooley SL, Welshman EE, Pergament E, Calhoun EA. Preference assessment of prenatal diagnosis for Down syndrome: is 35 years a rational cutoff? *Prenatal Diagnosis* 2002;22:1195-200.

[30] Cahill AG, Macones GA, Odibo AO, Stamilio DM. Magnesium for seizure prophylaxis in patients with mild preeclampsia. Obstet Gynecol 2007;110:601-7.

[31] Ubel PA. What is the price of life and why doesn't it increase at the rate of inflation? *Arch Intern Med* 2003;163:1637-41.

[32] Laupacis A, Feeny D, Detsky AS, Tugwell PX. How attractive does a new technology have to be to warrant adoption and utilization? Tentative guidelines for using clinical and economic evaluations. *Can Med Assoc J* 1992;146:473-81.

[33] Johannesson M, Meltzer D. Some reflections on cost-effectiveness analysis. *Health Econ* 1998;7:1-7.

[34] Hirth RA, Chernew ME, Miller E, Fendrick M, Weissert WG. Willingness to pay for a quality-adjusted life year: in search of a standard. *Med Decis Making* 2000;20:332-42.

In: Handbook of Methodological Concepts in Perinatal Medicine   ISBN: 978-1-62081-252-5
Editor: Eyal Sheiner   © 2013 Nova Science Publishers, Inc.

Chapter 11

ETHICS OF RESEARCH ON PERINATAL MEDICINE

Frank A. Chervenak[1,] and Laurence B. McCullough[2]*

[1]Department of Obstetrics and Gynecology, Weill Medical College of Cornell University,
New York, New York, US
[2]Center for Medical Ethics and Health Policy, Baylor College of Medicine,
Houston, Texas, US

INTRODUCTION

Less than optimal treatment of pregnant and fetal patients can have serious clinical sequelae. These include ill effects on the pregnant woman's health. A fetal patient's and future child's health-related interests may also be injured by inadequate treatment or non-treatment. These clinical concerns lend urgency to the need to conduct well designed clinical investigations of interventions with pregnant women and fetuses to improve the outcomes of perinatal medicine.

Ethics is an essential component of research in perinatal medicine.[1] This is because investigators in perinatal research must address and responsibly manage ethical challenges related to the protection of both the pregnant patient's and fetal patient's health-related interests. The purposes of this chapter are to identify the international consensus that has formed on research ethics and to the ethics of perinatal research, focusing on research of fetal interventions and obstetric ultrasound. First, we provide key definitions. We then explicate the ethical concept of the fetus as a patient. Third, we identify three components of research ethics. Fourth, we consider the examples of fetal research and of innovation and research in obstetric ultrasound.

---

* Correspondence: Frank A. Chervenak, M.D., Weill Cornell Medical Center, 525 East 68th Street - J130, New York, N.Y. 10065, Telephone: (212) 746-3045, FAX: (212) 746-8727, fac2001@med.cornell.edu.

KEY DEFINITIONS

The international consensus on research ethics presumes familiarity with a limited number of key definitions and concepts. We provide definitions of medical ethical and the two major ethical principles of beneficence and respect for autonomy.

Medical Ethics

Ethics is the disciplined study of morality. Medical ethics is the disciplined study of morality in medicine and concerns the obligations of physicians and health care organizations to patients as well as the obligations of patients.[2] It is important not to confuse medical ethics with the many sources of morality in a pluralistic society. These include, but are not limited to, law, our political heritage as a free people, the world's religions (most of which now exist in our country), ethnic and cultural traditions, families, the traditions and practices of medicine (including medical education and training), and personal experience. Medical ethics since the eighteenth century European and American Enlightenments has been secular.[3] It makes no reference to God or revealed tradition, but to what rational discourse requires and produces. At the same time, secular medical ethics is not intrinsically hostile to religious beliefs. Therefore, ethical principles and virtues should be understood to apply to all physicians, regardless of their personal religious and spiritual beliefs.[1]

The traditions and practices of medicine constitute an obvious source of morality for physicians. They provide an important reference point for medical ethics because they are based on the obligation to protect and promote the health-related interests of the patient. This obligation tells physicians what morality in medicine ought to be, but in very general, abstract terms. Providing a more concrete, clinically applicable account of that obligation is the central task of medical ethics, using ethical principles.[1,2]

THE PRINCIPLE OF BENEFICENCE

The principle of beneficence in its general meaning and application requires one to act in a way that is expected reliably to produce the greater balance of benefits over harms in the lives of others.[2] To put this principle into clinical practice requires a reliable account of the benefits and harms relevant to the care of the patient, and of how those goods and harms should be reasonably balanced against each other when not all of them can be achieved in a particular clinical situation, such as a request for an elective cesarean delivery.[4] In medicine, the principle of beneficence requires the physician to act in a way that is reliably expected to produce the greater balance of clinical benefits clinical over harms for the patient.[1]

Beneficence-based clinical judgment has an ancient pedigree, with its first expression found in the Hippocratic Oath and accompanying texts.[5] It makes an important claim: to interpret reliably the health related interests of the patient from medicine's perspective. This perspective is provided by accumulated scientific research, clinical experience, and reasoned responses to uncertainty. As rigorously evidence-based, beneficence-based judgment is thus not the function of the individual clinical perspective of any particular physician and therefore should not be based merely on the clinical impression or intuition of an individual physician. On the basis of this rigorous clinical perspective, focused on the best available evidence, beneficence-based clinical judgment identifies the benefits that can be achieved for the patient in clinical practice based on the competencies of medicine. The benefits that medicine is competent to seek for patients are the prevention and management of disease, injury, disability, and unnecessary pain and suffering, and the prevention of premature or unnecessary death. Pain and suffering become unnecessary when they do not result in achieving the other goods of medical care, e.g., allowing a woman to labor without effective analgesia.[6]

Nonmaleficence means that the physician should prevent causing harm and is best understood as expressing the limits of beneficence. This is also known as *"Primum non nocere"* or "first do no harm." This commonly invoked dogma is really a Latinized misinterpretation of the Hippocratic texts, which emphasized beneficence while avoiding harm when approaching the limits of medicine.[1,2] Non-maleficence should be incorporated into beneficence-based clinical judgment: when the physician approaches the limits of beneficence-based clinical judgment, i.e., when the evidence for expected benefit diminishes and the risks of clinical harm increase, then the physician should proceed with great caution. The physician should be especially concerned to prevent serious, far-reaching, and irreversible clinical harm to the patient. It is important to note that there is an inherent risk of paternalism in beneficence-based clinical judgment. By this we mean that beneficencebased clinical judgment, if it is *mistakenly* considered to be the sole source of moral responsibility and therefore moral authority in medical care, invites the unwary physician to conclude that beneficence-based judgments can be imposed on the patient in violation of her autonomy. Paternalism is a dehumanizing response to the patient and, therefore, should be avoided in the practice of obstetrics and gynecology.

In clinical practice the preventive ethics response to this inherent paternalism is for the physician to explain the diagnostic, therapeutic, and prognostic reasoning that leads to his or her clinical judgment about what is in the interest of the patient so that the patient can assess that judgment for herself. This general rule can be put into clinical practice in the following way: The physician should disclose and explain to the patient the major factors of this reasoning process, including matters of uncertainty. In neither medical law nor medical ethics does this require that the patient be provided with a complete medical education.[7] The physician should then explain how and why other clinicians might reasonably differ from his or her clinical judgment. The physician should then present a well-reasoned response to this critique. The outcome of this process is that beneficence-based clinical judgments take on a rigor that they sometimes lack, and the process of their formulation includes explaining them to the patient. It should be apparent that beneficence-based clinical judgment will frequently result in the identification of a continuum of clinical strategies that protect and promote the patient's health-related interests, such as the choice of preventing and managing the complications of menopause. Awareness of this feature of beneficence-based clinical judgment provides an important preventive ethics antidote to paternalism by increasing the likelihood that one or more of these medically reasonable, evidence-based alternatives will be acceptable to the patient. This feature of beneficence-based clinical judgment also provides a preventive ethics antidote to "gag" rules that restrict physician's communications with the managed care patient.[8] All beneficence-based alternatives must be identified and explained to all patients, regardless of how the physician is paid, especially those that are well established in evidence-based perinatal medicine.

THE PRINCIPLE OF RESPECT FOR AUTONOMY

In contrast to the principle of beneficence, there has been increasing emphasis in the literature of medical ethics on the principle of respect for autonomy.[1,2] This principle requires one always to acknowledge and carry out the value-based preferences of the adult, competent patient, unless there is compelling ethical justification for not doing so, e.g., prescribing antibiotics for viral respiratory infections. The female or pregnant patient increasingly brings to her medical care her own perspective on what is in her interest. The principle of respect for autonomy translates this fact into autonomy-based clinical judgment. Because each patient's perspective on her interests is a function of her values and beliefs, it is impossible to specify the benefits and harms of autonomy-based clinical judgment in advance. Indeed, it would be inappropriate for the physician to do so, because the definition of her benefits and harms and their balancing are the prerogative of the patient. Not surprisingly, autonomy-based clinical judgment is strongly antipaternalistic in nature.[1,2]

To understand the moral demands of this principle in clinical practice, we need an operationalized concept of autonomy to make it relevant to clinical practice. To do this, we identify three sequential autonomy-based behaviors on the part of the patient: 1) absorbing and retaining information about her condition and alternative diagnostic and therapeutic responses to it; 2) understanding that information (i.e., evaluating and rank-ordering those responses and appreciating that she could experience the risks of treatment; and 3) expressing a value-based preference. The physician has a role to play in each of these. They are, respectively, 1) to recognize the capacity of each patient to deal with medical information (and not to underestimate that capacity), provide information (ie, disclose and explain all medically reasonable alternatives, ie, supported in beneficence-based clinical judgment), and recognize the validity of the values and beliefs of the patient; 2) not to interfere with but, when necessary, to assist the patient in her evaluation and ranking of diagnostic and therapeutic alternatives for managing her condition; and 3) to elicit and implement the patient's value-based preference.[1]

THE ETHICAL CONCEPT OF THE FETUS AS A PATIENT

We now invoke these two principles in explaining the ethical concept of the fetus as a patient, which is a core ethical concept for the ethics of research in perinatal medicine.[1] This is because perinatal investigators have an ethical obligation to protect the health-related interests of both the pregnant woman and the fetus. To say that the fetus has health-related interests invokes the ethical concept of the fetus as a patient.

We have argued that the ethical concept of the fetus as a patient involves dependent moral status.[1] Dependent moral status is conferred on an entity by others freely, not out of an obligation to do so. This contrasts with independent moral status, which others must recognize as a matter of obligation, usually to respect the rights of an entity. The dependent moral status of the fetus as a patient is a function of whether the fetus should be reliably expected later to achieve the moral status of becoming a child (itself a form of dependent moral status) and a person (a form of independent moral status, i.e., a rights-bearer). The previable fetus is a patient when the pregnant woman confers this dependent moral status on it, which she is free to do or not do as she decides. Once she does confer this status, she and her physicians have beneficence-based obligations to protect the fetus' health-related interests. The previable fetus is a patient solely as a function of the pregnant woman's autonomy. The viable fetus is a patient in virtue of both its ability to survive ex utero and access to medical technology that makes this possible, as well as being presented to the physician.

The ethical concept of the fetus as a patient, in sharp contrast to the legal concept of the fetus, does not invoke the divisive discourse of fetal rights. In this discourse some claim that the fetus has moral and therefore legal status as an unborn child. Such claims involve at least two serious, disabling errors. First, such claims, often implicitly and less often explicitly, assert that the fetus, as an unborn child, has the same moral and legal status as a child. This claim ignores the ethical analysis that the moral status of a child involves dependent, not independent, moral status. Thus, the claim that the fetus is an unborn child does not in fact establish that the fetus has independent moral status. Such claims also assert that the fetus has the legal status of a person, which a child surely does. The U.S. Supreme Court, in Roe v. Wade, considered in detail whether the constitutional concept of a person applies to the fetus and showed that it did not. Re-asserting a claim to such legal status without refuting the Court's extensive analysis of the issue is intellectually irresponsible. Second, such claims implicitly assert that the previable fetus has independent moral status, an assertion that requires for its success an indisputable account of why everyone should accept this. In more than 2,000 years of global debate on this subject, no universally agreed-upon method for resolving these deep differences has emerged. Proponents of the claim that the previable fetus is an unborn child ignore this long and contentious history, which is also intellectually irresponsible.

When the fetus is a patient, both the pregnant woman and her physician have beneficence-based obligations to it. As the moral fiduciaries of the fetal patient, the woman and her physician should protect and promote the fetus' health-related interests. The physician's beneficence-based obligations to the fetal patient must in all cases be balanced against the physician's autonomy-based and beneficence-based obligations to the pregnant woman.

The concept of the fetus as a patient has immediate ethical implications for research undertaken for the purpose of meeting the pregnant woman's health needs, because it allows us to identify a central ethical challenge of such research: balancing maternal and fetal interests. Brody is correct to point out that federal regulations in the United States do not require investigators to balance maternal and fetal health-related interests in the design and conduct of such research.[9] Section 36.204 of the U.S. research regulations requires the identification and assessment of risk to the pregnant woman and fetus but does not provide an ethical framework to guide these.[10]

The ethical concept of the fetus as a patient provides the basis for the needed ethical framework. In research designed to determine whether an intervention benefits the fetus, e.g., surgical management of spina bifida, the concept of the fetus as a patient requires a study design in which pregnant subjects take only reasonable risks to their own health.[1,11] In research designed to benefit the pregnant patient, the ethical concept of the fetus as a patient requires a different balancing, namely of her obligation to protect and promote the health-related interests of her fetal patient against her own legitimate interest in participating in research. The physician faces parallel ethical challenges: how to balance these competing beneficence-based obligations in the design and conduct of clinical trials and how to assist the pregnant woman to address her balancing considerations during the informed consent process.

There is an additional ethical consideration pertaining to the investigator's, funder's, and sponsoring organization's legal liability, especially for wrongful injury to a future child. Preventing unnecessary liability of these parties surely counts as legitimate self-interest for all of them. In our judgment, the best way to protect and promote this quite legitimate self-interest is to undertake a thoroughgoing balancing of both maternal and fetal interests, with an emphasis on eliminating major risks to the fetal patient, as required by beneficence-based obligations to the fetal patient. In other words, ethically responsible study design and management can help to manage risks of liability to a minimum. The thorough consent process that we describe below may add additional protection, to the extent that informed consent confers immunity in such cases.

RESEARCH ETHICS

We next provide a definition of research and describe the three components of research ethics that have emerged from the history of research with human subjects.

Definition of Research

The definition of research in the federal regulations in the United States is the following: "an activity designed to test an hypothesis, permit conclusions to be drawn, and thereby to develop or contribute to generalizable knowledge."[10]

Three Components of Research Ethics

The history of human experimentation appears to be coincident with the history of medicine. Concern about the scientific and ethical quality of research with human subjects begins to emerge in eighteenth-century medical ethics. One of major figures of that period, Dr. John Gregory (1724-1773) of Scotland, wrote the first modern medical ethics in the English language.[12] He developed a research ethics to address the potential abuse of patients in the Royal Infirmary of Edinburgh by younger physicians anxious to establish their reputations. These physicians would pronounce infirmary patients incurable, not to abandon them (which was the common practice), but to justify introducing experimental medicines into patient care.

Gregory condemned this practice, on two grounds. His first concern was that such experimentation was premature: standard remedies had not yet been attempted and shown to be ineffective in a patient's care. His second concern was that experimentation was often poorly designed. For example, compound drugs would be used without attention to the question of which elements of the compound might cause observed clinical effects. His third concern was that such physicians used the sick poor to advance their own reputational interests, subjecting them to unnecessary risk of clinical harm (a violation of the ethical principle of beneficence) out of personal self-interest. Gregory called this "sporting" with the sick poor; we now call it exploitation.

Gregory's research ethics introduced one of the key components of any adequate research ethics: the protection of research subjects. Such protection was gained by ensuring that there is a clinical justification for research and that the research is scientifically well designed. A second key component of any adequate research ethics, the consent of research subjects, was introduced in the nineteenth century.

Making a reasonable effort to prevent what is known as the *therapeutic misconception* is one of the major responsibilities of clinical investigators in the informed consent process. The therapeutic misconception occurs when potential subjects fail to appreciate that some aspects of what they will experience in a study are not justified by a clinical judgment of what in the patient's health-related interest but by scientific considerations. Subjects, instead, confuse these scientific study design issues with regular medical care.[13] For example, in a randomized study of ultrasound potential subjects would need to understand that whether they would receive an ultrasound examination will be based on a random selection process and not on their physician's clinical judgment.

The need for both scientific and ethical integrity as components of research ethics was reinforced by the scientific and ethical catastrophe of the Nazi medical war crimes. A major result of the trials of the Nazi physicians was the promulgation of the Nuremberg Code. This is regarded as the founding document of contemporary research ethics and insists on sound scientific method and consent, which have become two of the three main components of research ethics globally.[9]

The third and final key component of research ethics was introduced by the Declaration of Helsinki. It requires independent overview of clinical investigation, for both its scientific and its ethical integrity.[9]

As a result of this centuries-long history of medical ethics, there has emerged an international consensus that there are three key components of research ethics:[14]

1) Clinical research with human subjects must be clinically justified and scientifically sound. The clinical need for research should be well established, on the basis of a critical, evidence-based evaluation of current clinical practice. Clinical research should be well designed scientifically, with clearly stated research questions and testable hypotheses and a method adequate to test the hypotheses and this answer the research questions.

2) Informed consent is required. The Nuremberg Code did not allow any exceptions to this requirement, a position that is no longer part of the international consensus. It has been recognized in recent decades that there are populations of patients for whom we need to improve the quality of medical care but who cannot consent to becoming research subjects. This may be a result of the clinical circumstances of research (e.g., in emergencies for which there is no time for the consent process) or the inability of the potential subject to engage in the informed consent process (e.g., fetuses).

3) Oversight of research is required. Investigators are not obligated to prepare research protocols that establish clinical need, meet standards of scientific integrity, and describe the informed consent process (or justify its waiver) and submit protocols for prospective review by independent committees established for this purpose (known in the United States as Institutional Review Board and in most of the rest of the world as Research Ethics Committees.

FETAL RESEARCH

Ethical Criteria for Innovation

Innovation in fetal research begins with the design of an intervention and its implementation in animal models, followed by a single case and then case series. This rigorous approach is required to determine the feasibility, safety, and efficacy of innovations in fetal research. It is a basic tenet of research ethics that potential subjects should be protected from potentially harmful innovation. Three criteria must be satisfied in order to conduct such preliminary investigations in fetal research in an ethically responsible fashion, by taking into account beneficence-based obligations to the fetal patient and beneficence-based obligations to the pregnant woman. The pre-viable fetus is a patient in these cases because, as explained above, the woman has made a decision to continue her pregnancy, in order to have the opportunity to gain the potential benefits of the innovation. She remains free to withdraw that status before viability.

1) The proposed fetal intervention is reliably expected on the basis of previous animal studies either to be life-saving or to prevent serious and irreversible disease, injury, or disability for the fetus;
2) Among possible alternative designs, the intervention is designed in such a way as to involve the least risk of mortality and morbidity to the fetal patient (which is required by beneficence and will satisfy the U.S. research requirement of minimizing risk to the fetus[10]); and
3) On the basis of animal studies and analysis of theoretical risks both for the current and future pregnancies, the mortality risk of the fetal intervention to the pregnant woman is reliably expected to be low and the risk of disease, injury, or disability to the pregnant woman is reliably expected to be low or manageable. [11]

The first two criteria are based on beneficence-based obligations to the fetal patient. Research on animal models should suggest that there would be therapeutic benefit without disproportionate iatrogenic fetal morbidity or mortality. If animal studies result in high rates of mortality or morbidity for the animal fetal subject, then innovation should not be introduced to human subjects until these rates improve in subsequent animal studies.

The third criterion reflects the fact that fetal intervention in the form of fetal surgery is necessarily also maternal surgery. This criterion reminds investigators that the willingness of a subject, in this case, the pregnant woman, to consent to risk does not by itself establish whether the risk/benefit ratio is favorable. Judgments about an acceptable risk/benefit ratio should not be autonomy-based, but beneficence-based. This is because investigators have an independent beneficence-based obligation to protect human subjects from unreasonably risky research and should use beneficence-based, not autonomy-based, risk-benefit analyses. Phrases such as "maternal-fetal surgery" are useful if they remind investigators of the need for such comprehensive analysis. If they are used systematically to subordinate fetal interests to maternal interest and rights, and therefore to undermine the concept of the fetus as a patient in favor of the concept that the fetus is merely a part of the pregnant woman, such phrases lack ethical utility.

ETHICAL CRITERIA IN RANDOMIZED TRIALS

Preliminary innovation should end and randomized clinical trials begin when there is clinical equipoise. Clinical equipoise means that there is "a remaining disagreement in the expert clinical community, despite the available evidence, about the merits of the intervention to be tested."[9] Brody notes that one challenge here is identifying how much disagreement can remain for there still to be equipoise.[9] Lilford has suggested that when 2/3 of the expert community, measured reliably, no longer disagrees, equipoise is not satisfied.[15] When the experimental intervention is more harmful than non-intervention, equipoise cannot be achieved.

The satisfaction of the previous three criteria, with slight modifications, should count as equipoise in the expert community.

1) The initial case series indicates that the proposed fetal intervention is reliably expected either to be life saving or to prevent serious and irreversible disease, injury, or disability;

2) Among possible alternative designs, the intervention continues to involve the least risk of morbidity and mortality to the fetus; and

3) The case series indicates that the mortality risk to the pregnant woman is reliably expected to be low and the risk of disease, injury, or disability to the pregnant woman, including for future pregnancies, is reliably expected to be low or manageable.[11]

One useful good test for the satisfaction of the first and third criteria is significant trends in the data from the case series. When equipoise has been achieved on the basis of these three criteria, randomized clinical trials should commence. They must have relevant and clearly defined primary and secondary endpoints and a design and sample size adequate to measure these endpoints.

The above three criteria can be used in a straightforward manner to define stopping rules for such a clinical trial. When the data support a rigorous clinical judgement that the first or third criterion is not satisfied, the trial should be stopped.

CRITERIA FOR DEFINING A STANDARD OF CARE

When a clinical trial of a fetal intervention is completed, its outcome can be assessed to determine whether the innovative fetal intervention should be regarded as standard of care. Trial results should meet the following three criteria in order to establish the innovation as a standard of care:

1) The fetal intervention has a significant probability of being life saving or preventing serious or irreversible disease, injury, or disability for the fetus.
2) The fetal intervention involves low mortality and low or manageable risk of serious and irreversible disease, injury, or disability to the fetus, and
3) The mortality risk to the pregnant woman is low and the risk of disease, injury or disability is low or manageable, including for future pregnancies.[11]

Brody has underscored the value of data safety and monitoring boards to prevent investigator bias and to protect subjects.[9] Such boards should be used in fetal research, especially to ensure adherence of the above-mentioned ethical criteria as a basis for monitoring such research.

RESEARCH IN OBSTETRIC ULTRASOUND

An important goal of research in obstetric and gynecologic ultrasound is to improve the technique of examination and its interpretation.[16] This process begins with innovation. Innovation or pre-research takes the form of a case report to determine whether an improvement in imaging or interpretation is feasible. This does not involve the production of generalizable knowledge. Reporting feasibility does warrant subsequent investigation of the improvement to determine whether it is promising innovation, i.e., results in trends in findings that support a hypothesis of efficacy. Testing of such hypotheses requires systematic data collection, retrospectively or prospectively, with the explicit purpose of producing generalizable knowledge, i.e., research.

There is no doubt that this last stage in a process of improvement meets the definition of research and should be brought under the legally applicable human subjects protection review process. Innovation is best considered pre-research.

Ultrasound end-users in obstetrics and gynecology should not take this as license to undertake innovation or pre-research without consideration of scientific and ethical rigor. The risk of taking such license is twofold. First, innovation undertaken in a scientifically informal or, worse, haphazard fashion, creates a weak foundation for subsequent research and clinical practice. Moreover, such undisciplined innovation could result in widespread adoption of new "standards" of care in a scientifically premature fashion. Second, innovation can be carried out over a prolonged period of time, to determine whether it is practical and valuable, a form of innovation that can drift into research, e.g., creating a prospective case series without study design or consent and therefore without the transition from innovation to research being managed in a scientifically and ethically responsible fashion.

The key to addressing these two related concerns prospectively is to manage the transition from innovation to research in a scientifically and ethically appropriate fashion. Consider the following recent examples that are in various stages of the progression from innovation, to research, to clinical care. Initially, one might seek to determine, making small modifications of accepted transducer technique, whether a part of fetal anatomy could be measured consistently and thus become a marker for Down syndrome. Another example would be to determine whether aspects of fetal behavior could be assessed in utero. A third example would be to determine whether it is possible to detect coronary artery blood flow in the fetus. Finally, one might attempt to determine whether 4-D ultrasound can improve imaging of fetal anatomy. In none of these examples of innovation would a physician be initially seeking generalizable knowledge, because doing so would be premature. In addition, because there is no departure from accepted practice, there is no increment of harm to the pregnant woman or fetus. These examples did not initially involve research but they did, in our judgment, involve innovation or pre-research to determine the feasibility of an improvement in obstetric ultrasound.

On the basis of innovation, retrospective or prospective case series should be designed and undertaken to obtain results and assess whether they support a hypothesis of efficacy. It is therefore crucial to establish feasibility as the first stage of innovation, so that resources are not wasted on subsequent investigation with little likelihood of generating testable hypotheses and therefore producing generalizable knowledge.

It is very important to encourage innovation, because it is the seedbed of scientific and clinical progress in obstetric and gynecologic ultrasound. If innovation or pre-research with patients were to be treated as human subjects research with its strict requirements, innovation might be discouraged. The central challenge becomes how to manage innovation in a scientifically and ethically disciplined fashion that does not create such a burdensome oversight mechanism that physicians will be discouraged from undertaking improvement in obstetric and gynecologic ultrasound and that protects patients.

The key to managing this challenge is to apply scientific and ethical rigor to innovation or pre-research. Analogous to recent proposals about responsible management of surgical innovation,[11] we propose that academic departments but not institutional review boards or research ethics committees establish oversight mechanisms in which case reports are analyzed for scientific merit and ethical appropriateness before submission for publication. The main scientific concern is whether feasibility has been demonstrated. The goal is to minimize the bias in reaching this judgment by the investigator and in the formulation of hypotheses. The main ethical concern is the level of risk involved in innovation. Ethical review should examine whether the innovation is consistent with accepted principles and practices of obstetric and gynecologic ultrasound, in which case there is no increment of risk. Consent therefore is not required. Of course, if there is any incremental risk, the investigation should immediately come under legally applicable research regulations.

The transition from innovation or pre-research, i.e., case reports, to research, i.e., case series, should always be subject to prospective oversight. This is because initiating a case series to produce results for the purpose of generating or testing hypotheses is always a planned, not serendipitous, decision. As required by human subjects research regulations, oversight should be both scientific and ethical. The scientific review should determine whether the proposed study design for a case series is adequate to generate or test hypotheses. The ethical review centers not just on risk but on the fact the investigator intends now to use patients as subjects, i.e., as sources of generalizable knowledge. Whenever a patient is used prospectively as a scientific subject, consent is required, even when there is no increment of risk. In the technical language of ethics, respect for autonomy is classified as a *deontological* ethical principle, an ethical principle the meaning of which is independent of consequences: patients who will be used prospectively for non-clinical purposes should be respected as persons and autonomous decision makers independently of whether they are at clinical risk.[9] This prospective oversight should be managed at the IRB/IEC level.

CONCLUSION

Ethics is an essential dimension of research in perinatal medicine. The ethical concept of the fetus as a patient should guide investigators, granting agencies, institutional review board, and clinicians in reaching ethically justified balancing of autonomy-based and beneficence-based obligations to the pregnant patient and beneficence-based obligations to the fetal patient. For research on fetal interventions, ethically justified criteria for the design, conduct, and evaluation of clinical investigation can be identified on the basis of obligations to both the pregnant and fetal patients. For research in obstetric ultrasound ethical criteria for innovation and for the transition from innovation for research can be identified on the basis of obligations to both the pregnant and fetal patients.

REFERENCES

[1]   McCullough LB, Chervenak FA. *Ethics in Obstetrics and Gynecology*. New York: Oxford University Press, 1994.

[2]   Beauchamp TL, Childress JF. *Principles of Biomedical Ethics, 6th ed*. New York: Oxford University Press, 2009.

[3]   McCullough LB. The discourses of practitioners in eighteenth-century Britain. In Baker RB, McCullough LB, eds. *The Cambridge World History of Medical Ethics*. Cambridge: Cambridge University Press, 2009: 403-413.

[4]   Chervenak FA, McCullough LB. An ethically justified algorithm for offering, recommending, and performing cesarean delivery and its application in managed care practice. *Obstet Gynecol* 1996; 87: 302–305.

[5]   Hippocrates. Oath of Hippocrates.In: Temkin O, Temkin CL, eds. Ancient Medicine: *Selected Papers of Ludwig Edelstein*.Baltimore, Md: Johns Hopkins University Press; 1976: 6.

[6]   Chervenak FA, McCullough LB, Birnbach DJ. Ethics: an essential dimension of clinical obstetric anesthesia. *Anesth Analg* 2003; 96: 1480-1485.

[7]   Faden RR, Beauchamp TL. A History and Theory of Informed Consent.New York, NY: *Oxford University Press*; 1986.

[8]   Brody H, Bonham VL Jr. Gag rules and trade secrets in managed care contracts: ethical and legal concerns. *Arch Intern Med* 1997; 157: 2037-2043.

[9]   Brody BA. *The Ethics of Biomedical Research: An International Perspective*. New York: Oxford University Press, 1998.

[10]   Department of Health and Human Services. Regulations for the Protection of Human Subjects. 45 CFR 46. Available at *http://www.hhs.gov/ohrp/,* accessed December 8, 2008.

[11]   Chervenak FA, McCullough LB: A comprehensive ethical framework for fetal research and its application to fetal surgery for spina bifida. *Am J Obstet Gynecol* 2002; 187: 10-14.

[12]   McCullough LB. *John Gregory and the Invention of Professional Medical Ethics and the Profession of Medicine.* Dordrecht, The Netherlands: Kuwer Academic Publishers, 1998.

[13]   Lidz CW, Appelbaum PS, Grisso T, Renaud M. Therapeutic misconception and the appreciation of risks in clinical trials. *Soc Sci Med* 2004; 58: 1689-1697.

[14]   Brody BA, McCullough LB, Sharp R. Consensus and controversy in research ethics. *JAMA* 2005: 294: 1411-1414.

[15]   Lilford RJ. The substantive ethics of clinical trials. *Clin Obstet Gynecol* 1992; 35: 837-845.

[16]   Chervenak FA, McCullough LB. Scientifically and ethically responsible innovation and research in ultrasound in obstetrics and gynecology. *Ultrasound Obstet Gynecol* 2006; 28: 1-4.

INDEX

Q

R

S

T

U

V

W

Y